Michael Faraday

Michael Faraday as a young man

MICHAEL FARADAY

A BIOGRAPHY BY

L. Pearce Williams

LONDON
CHAPMAN AND HALL
1965

First published in 1965
by Chapman & Hall Limited
11 New Fetter Lane, London EC4
© *1965 Chapman & Hall Limited*
Printed in Great Britain
by The Camelot Press Ltd., Southampton
Catalogue No. 4/0773/16

Contents

List of Plates   *page* vii

Preface   xi

A Note on Sources   xv

Prologue   1
    1. The Early Faradays. 2. The Sandemanian Church. 3. Clapham Wood Hall. 4. Faraday's Early Years. References.

1. *The Education of a Chemist*   10
    1. The Apprentice Years. 2. The City Philosophical Society. 3. The Fledgeling. 4. The University of Europe. 5. Journeyman Chemist. References.

2. *The Education of a Philosopher*   53
    1. The Imponderable Fluids. 2. The Forces of Matter. 3. The Theory of Point Atoms. 4. Michael Faraday as Philosopher. References.

3. *The Fallow Years*   95
    1. Marriage. 2. Faraday, the Sandemanian. 3. The Practising Chemist. 4. Pure Chemistry. References.

4. *The Discovery of Electromagnetic Induction*   137
    1. The Theories of Electromagnetism. 2. The Discovery of Electromagnetic Rotations. 3. The Discovery of Electromagnetic Induction. References.

5. *The Nature of Electricity (1)*   191
    1. The Conditions of the Induction of Electrical Currents. 2. The Birth of the Field Concept. 3. The Identity of Electricities. References.

6. *The Nature of Electricity (2)*   227
    1. Electrochemistry before 1833. 2. Faraday's Theory of Electrochemical Action. 3. The New Electrochemical Nomenclature. References.

7. *The Nature of Electricity (3)*   274
    1. Intermolecular Forces. 2. The Nature of Electrostatic Force. 3. The Unity of Electrical Action. References.

8. *Faraday in the World*   320

  1. The Royal Institution. 2. Faraday, the Educator. 3. Faraday and British Science. 4. Faraday and Politics. References.

9. *The Correlation of Forces*   364

  1. The Theory of the Voltaic Pile. 2. Force and Matter. 3. The Discovery of Diamagnetism. 4. The Magnetic Properties of Gases and Terrestrial Magnetism. References.

10. *The Origins of Field Theory*   408

  1. The Magnecrystallic Force. 2. The Search for Polarity. 3. The Physical Reality of the Lines of Force. 4. The Field and the Transmission of Force. References.

11. *The Last Years*   465

  1. Last Researches. 2. Withdrawal from Practical Affairs. 3. Retirement and Death. References.

Epilogue   506

Index   515

Plates

Frontispiece
   Michael Faraday as a young man

between pages 100 and 101
   1a. Notes for Tatum's Lecture on Galvanism at the R.I.   b. Drawing from Lecture on Mechanics – Tatum, R.I.
   2a. Edward Magrath   b. Faraday's notes on Davy's Lectures
   3. Davy's laboratory notebook
   4. Pencil sketch of Sarah Barnard

between pages 132 and 133
   5a. Sir Joseph Banks, P.R.S.   b. Sir Humphry Davy
   6a. J. J. Berzelius   b. William Thomas Brande
   7a. Thomas Thomson   b. Joseph Gay-Lussac
   8a. John Dalton   b. Sir William Herschel
   9a. Claude-Louis Berthollet   b. James Clerk Maxwell
   10a. Hans Christian Oersted   b. André-Marie Ampère
   11a. William Hyde Wollaston   b. Peter Barlow
   12a. Dr J. A. Paris   b. François Arago

between pages 164 and 165
   13. The Laboratory of the Royal Institution
   14a. Faraday as a young man   b. Charles Wheatstone
   15a. Thomas Young   b. Joseph Henry
   16a. The page in Faraday's Diary describing the Induction Ring Experiment
   b. The Induction Ring

between pages 212 and 213
   17. Page from Faraday's Diary showing sketch of the first dynamo
   18a. R.I. electromagnetic induction apparatus   b. Faraday's electromagnetic induction apparatus
   19a. Faraday's electrostatic apparatus   b. Faraday's electrochemical apparatus
   20. J. F. Daniell and Faraday (1841)
   21a. J. Hachette   b. William Whewell
   22. The Royal Institution

23. Charles Augustin Coulomb
24. Georg Simon Ohm

between pages 228 and 229

25. Faraday lecturing before the Prince Consort and the Prince of Wales
26a. Davies Gilbert, P.R.S.   b. Charles Babbage   c. Sir William Rowan Hamilton
27a. Justus von Liebig   b. Carlo Matteucci   c. Gerritt Moll   d. J. B. Dumas
28. The Royal Institution's great electromagnet

between pages 324 and 325

29a. Edward Sabine   b. Wilhelm Weber   c. Sir John F. W. Herschel   d. John Tyndall
30a. Lord Kelvin   b. Sir George B. Airy   c. Heinrich D. Ruhmkorff   d. Henry Bence Jones
31. a, b, c, d. Faraday in later life
32. a, b, c, d. Faraday in later life
33. a, b. Faraday in later life
34. Michael and Sarah Faraday
35a. Faraday at the Royal Institution   b. Faraday in later life   c. Faraday in later life
36. The library of the Royal Institution

Acknowledgements

Burndy Library: 5b, 6a, 6b, 7a, 7b, 8a, 8b, 9a, 9b, 10a, 10b, 11a, 12b, 15b, 23, 24, 26c, 29b, 29c, 30a, 30b, 30c

Miss Lucy Boyd Faraday: 4

R. E. W. Maddison: 35c

Old Ashmolean Museum, Oxford: 35a

Royal Institution: 2b, 3, 13, 14a, 16a, 16b, 17, 18a, 18b, 19a, 19b, 22, 25, 28, 29d, 34, 35b, 36

R.I. Faraday's Portrait and Autograph Collection—Photograph by Miss Jean Mason: 2a, 11b, 12a, 15a, 21a, 21b, 27a, 27b, 27c, 27d, 29a, 30d

A. C. Wild: 20

To
Geoffrey Parr (1899–1961)

Preface

When I first began to collect the manuscript evidence for a life of Faraday, I was fortunate enough to make the acquaintance of one of his relations. She was an elderly lady who very kindly invited me to tea, sat me down in a comfortable chair, and fixing me with a stern look, asked: 'Young man, do you really think another biography of Uncle Michael is necessary?' At that time, I could only stammer out a rather weak 'yes'; my considered answer lies in the pages that follow. I have there tried to give a full picture of Faraday the man and Faraday the scientist. This is not to denigrate those biographers of Faraday who have preceded me; my debt to them is great. But, I think it can be said that the manuscript and printed sources for a life of Faraday have never been fully exploited and this I have attempted to do. Furthermore, the perspective of Faraday's achievement has changed with each generation. In his own lifetime he was regarded as a heretic; in the next generation, he was transformed into the arch-empiricist; in our own time, he has been viewed as a kindly experimentalist who laid the foundations on which the true physicists – those who control the tool of higher mathematics – would build classical and modern field theory. He was all these things, and more. My hope has been to reveal the full dimensions of his genius and to place him more accurately in the mainstream of the history of science.

This work could not have been undertaken without the generous financial support of a number of institutions. The University of Delaware permitted me to begin my research by awarding me a liberal grant for summer research in 1958. The National Science Foundation allowed me to follow up the rich manuscript vein I then uncovered by naming me a Post-doctoral Fellow for the year 1959–60. The Committee on Faculty Research of Cornell University and the American Philosophical Society have come to my rescue more than once with funds for the micro-filming or transcription of materials.

The necessary preliminary groundwork for any biography was made infinitely easier for me by the publication of two important bibliographical guides. Mme Lukomskaya of the Soviet Union, some years ago compiled

a bibliography of Faradayiana which was appended to the Russian edition
of Faraday's *Experimental Researches in Electricity*. Those interested in
other biographies of Faraday will find the most complete list of them there.
Mr Alan Jeffreys more recently has completed a bibliography of Faraday's
writings and this has proved invaluable to me. (Alan Jeffreys, *Michael
Faraday, A List of his Lectures and Published Writings*, London, Chapman
and Hall, 1960). I was fortunate to meet Mr Jeffreys and to profit from his
deep knowledge of Faraday's works and it is a pleasure here to acknowledge my debt to him.

I wish here also to record my gratitude to the large number of libraries
and archives which responded to my pleas for information and sent me
microfilms of their Faraday manuscripts. I should also like to single out
the following institutions and individuals and thank them for their personal attention. The staff of the Manuscript Room of the British Museum
was of inestimable help in my search. Mme Pierre Gauja of the *Académie
des Sciences* in Paris placed her unequalled knowledge of the Academy's
archives at my disposal and laid before me a number of hitherto unknown
documents by and about Faraday. Mr I. Kaye, Librarian, and his colleague, Mr N. Robinson, Assistant Librarian, of the Royal Society
patiently endured my constant requests for microfilms and permitted me
to explore the riches of the Royal Society's collection of Faraday manuscripts. Mr J. E. Wright, Librarian, and Mr K. Lansley, then Assistant
Librarian of the Institution of Electrical Engineers, took many hours
of their precious time from service to the electrical industry to help me
in my work on the Faraday materials which the I.E.E. contains. Mr W. P.
Preston, Librarian of the Royal Observatory, permitted me to explore
the Airy papers preserved in the Observatory's archives. My guide
through this mass of material was Mr P. L. Laurie who gave most
generously of his time and to whom I am greatly indebted. Mrs Dorothea
Williams of the Edgar Fahs Smith Collection at the University of Pennsylvania gave me the benefit of her knowledge of the history of chemistry
and helped me to avoid many a pitfall. Mr. Bern Dibner, President of
the Burndy Library, Norwalk, Conn., called my attention to many Faraday
items in his possession and took time from his many responsibilities to
give me the opportunity to study and copy them. It is a pleasure to thank
him here for his help. Finally, the staff of the Cornell University Library,
particularly the Reference Librarians, have spared no efforts to procure
essential works for me which were not in the Cornell Library.

I have saved a special paragraph for Mr Kenneth D. C. Vernon,
Librarian of the Royal Institution. It would be impossible to indicate the

full extent of my debt to him. I can only thank him for the interest he took in this volume and in me and the care with which he made sure that I did not miss a single piece of Faraday material at the R.I. Without his constant help this book would have been unthinkable.

I know that the more than sixty relatives of Faraday who responded so generously to my appeals for letters and other manuscript remains will understand my inability here to name them individually. I do hope that they will accept a collective 'thank you'. I cannot, however, pass by Mr F. W. Parrott of Kirkby Stephen who, though not a member of the Faraday family, has collected the lore of the early Faradays and who generously placed himself at my disposal when I visited the north of England to see where Faraday's ancestors lived. I should also like to thank the collectors of Faraday manuscripts who permitted me to see their treasures and use them in the biography. In the References, I have mentioned the names of the owners of those manuscripts actually cited, but I should like to add here, as well, the statement of my gratitude.

In the writing of this book, I have profited greatly from the wide knowledge of my colleague, Professor Henry E. Guerlac. My debt to him goes back some sixteen years now, and its enumeration would fill pages. My thanks here, I hope, will in some small measure repay his constant kindness to me.

To Professor Donald Kagan of Cornell University and Professor Giorgio de Santillana of the Massachusetts Institute of Technology I owe invaluable linguistic help. All errors, needless to say, are mine alone.

To Miss G. J. Peat of Forest Hills, Oxford, and Mrs Paul Ludgate of Ithaca, New York, I owe the gratitude of one whose handwriting borders on the cryptic. They both patiently deciphered my copy and presented me with a legible draft for revision.

Manuscripts are cited with permission from the following institutions.

La Bibliothèque publique et universitaire de Génève; Staatsbibliothek, Marburg/Lahn (Stiftung Preussischer Kulturbesitz); Deutches Museum, Munich; Institut de France, Archives de l'Académie des Sciences; the Wellcome Historical Medical Library (manuscripts are quoted by permission of the Wellcome Trustees); the Royal Institution of Great Britain; County Record Office, County of Glamorgan, Cardiff; the Science Museum, South Kensington; Trinity College Library, Cambridge, (through the courtesy of the Master and Fellows of Trinity College); the British Museum (by courtesy of the Trustees of the British Museum); the Public Record Office, London (unpublished Crown copyright material in the Public Record Office, London, has been reproduced by permission of the Controller of H.M. Stationery Office); the Patent Office, London; the Royal Greenwich Observatory, Herstmonceux, Hailsham, Sussex; the Royal Society, London (copyright of the material used remains in the hands of the Royal Society); the National Research Council of Canada, Ottawa; the Burndy Library, Norwalk, Connecticut.

The illustrations were drawn largely from two sources and I should like to acknowledge them here. Mrs Adele Matthysse of the Burndy Library took her valuable time to aid me in the selection of many. Miss Jean Mason of the Royal Institution photographed those portraits which Faraday himself had collected and which he left to the Royal Institution after his death. I am deeply grateful to both Mrs Matthysse and Miss Mason for their help.

The figures were drawn by Mr Edward Korba of Vestal, New York, who was able to translate my amateur efforts into drawings that will permit the reader to follow the text with greater ease.

The graduate students in the History of Science at Cornell have, over the years, provided many critical insights and substantive points which I have shamelessly appropriated. I would hope that my thanks to Robert Kargon, David Kubrin, Thomas Hankins, Ruth Ann Gienapp, Joan Winters, Roman Jackiw, Jerry Gough, John Goodman, Thomas Moss, Thomas Settle and Henry Steffens will repay them, in some small measure, for their assistance.

Finally, I wish to thank my wife and children who patiently endured the years during which this volume gradually took shape.

ITHACA, N. Y.
July, 1964

A Note on Sources

A large amount of hitherto unpublished manuscript material has been included in this work. Because of the obscurity of much of what Faraday wrote, both for publication and privately, I have quoted his words extensively rather than attempting to summarize what I thought a passage signified. What has been lost in art has, hopefully, been gained in accuracy. Furthermore, where questions of interpretation are involved (and there are many such) the reader will be able to form his own opinion by reference to the original document and not to my interpretation of it.

The transcription of Faraday's manuscripts has presented a few minor difficulties of which the reader should be made aware. Punctuation was, at best, haphazard and spelling was never Faraday's *forte*. I have supplied the bare minimum of punctuation necessary to bring comprehensibility and relative ease of reading to a passage. In general, I have avoided the profusion of [*sic*]'s that would have been required if every fault were to be pointed out. Only in those cases where confusion is possible have such indications been made. The printed text has been carefully checked against the sources; where errors occur, therefore, they may be assumed to be Faraday's and not the author's or the printer's. I have consistently rendered Faraday's & as *and*; I have also omitted the period after Mr. and Dr., otherwise, except as noted the text is as Faraday wrote it.

The two most important sources for the study of Faraday's scientific work are his published papers and his laboratory *Diary*. When Faraday began his *Experimental Researches in Electricity*, he also started the practice of numbering the paragraphs in both his papers and the *Diary*. I have followed his practice of referring to the paragraphs in the published papers by placing the number in parentheses, thus ( ) and the paragraphs in the *Diary* by placing the respective numbers in brackets, [ ]. Faraday unfortunately started his numbering of the *Diary* paragraphs twice. One series of numbers, [1–441], referring to his early work on electromagnetic induction comes at the end of the first volume of the published *Diary* (pp. 367–430). These paragraphs will be referred to specifically by placing a Roman numeral, I, before the paragraph number, thus [I-]. The second volume of the published *Diary* starts once again with [1] and, henceforth, continues consecutively until the end of Faraday's active scientific life. Reference to the papers in the *Experimental Researches* and to the *Diary* will be made immediately following the passage cited and will, therefore, be included in the text itself.

Prologue

---

1. The Early Faradays

There is a family legend that the first Faraday fled to England from Ireland when the forces of Queen Elizabeth put down the rebellion of the O'Neill in 1567. Although there is no evidence to support this rather dashing tale, the family does seem to have derived from Ireland. The name, Faraday, probably comes from Gaelic and these early Faradays were most likely Irish farmers who had been swept up in the great burst of nationalism and rebellion touched off by the finest and last of the O'Neills.

Legend yields to history at the end of the seventeenth century. The parish register of Bolton-le-Sands (Lancashire) reveals that on 11 August 1683 William Faraday and Elizabeth Gardner were wed.[1] On the 17th of July 1684, "Richard, son of William Faraday" made his appearance in the register, to be followed by a sister, Frances, on 9 October 1692.

From Bolton-le-Sands, a small village near Carnforth on the west coast of England, Richard Faraday moved to Clapham in Yorkshire. In terms of distance, the move was insignificant, comprising some fifteen miles. Yet, in a sense, one world was left behind and a new one was entered. Bolton-le-Sands or Nether Kellet, where the Faradays lived, have never been bustling towns. But they were near the sea which always has stimulated the imagination by its ceaseless activity, with Lancaster, the county seat, within easy walking distance. Clapham is and was a small village near the border of Westmorland where the fells and dales begin to slide toward the great Yorkshire plain. It is a land of many beauties and great loneliness, whose silence is broken only by the shrill call of the peewit and the occasional bleat of a lamb. It is a land of taciturn, friendly, matter-of-fact people whose geographical horizons are limited by the bounding mountains, but whose inner selves have been tempered by the generations of struggle with a harsh nature which only grudgingly permits even sheep to find sustenance. Into this land moved Richard Faraday, describing himself as 'stonemason and tiler' but who, no doubt, also kept a flock of sheep, for there is a Faraday Ghyll still to be found on the Ordnance map.

In 1708 the Clapham parish register recorded the birth of Richard Faraday's first child. From then until 1730 ten children were born among whom was Robert (1724–86), Michael's grandfather.

It was during Robert Faraday's lifetime that the great evangelical religious wave, associated primarily with the name of John Wesley, swept over England and reached even to the New World. There was something in the air of eighteenth-century England that seemed fairly to generate sects and schisms. The Church of England could loftily ignore most of these little splashes of dissent, but many a parish was severely torn with doctrinal strife. Thus it was in the north where the evangelical tradition was strong and dissent an honourable tradition. The itinerant preacher, sustained by a deep conviction of his mission and the truth of his message, was a familiar sight. Covering great distances on foot or on horseback, he not only lifted up the souls of those who came to listen but also was one of the few links with the outside world. In the 1750's and 60's three such men came together in the West Riding of Yorkshire. Out of Scotland came John Glas and Robert Sandeman. From Yorkshire, by way of Queen's College, Oxford, came Benjamin Ingham. The resulting clash brought forth what Michael Faraday later called 'a small and despised set of Christians known, if known at all, as Sandemanians.' Robert Faraday was a convert to this sect and his grandson was raised within its discipline. It was one of the first and foremost influences upon his development.

2. The Sandemanian Church[2]

John Glas, like so many other dissenting ministers of the eighteenth century, preached himself into heresy. Born in 1695 at Auchtermuchty in Fife and educated at Edinburgh and St Andrews, he was licensed by the Presbytery of Dunkeld in 1721. As he composed his sermons and followed the Word, it gradually dawned upon him that there was no scriptural sanction for the existence of his own Church! Where in the New Testament were there foundations upon which a National Church could rest? Where did the New Testament give warrant for the alliance of Church and State? If God's kingdom is not of this world, by what right did the worldly State intrude upon His Church? The Church Elders became more and more perturbed as Glas convinced himself that the proper answers to these questions must lead to the separation of the Church from the State. In 1728 he was summoned before the Presbytery and in 1730 deposed from his position. But, though the Elders condemned his heresy, enough of his congregation followed him to create a new Church. The first Glasite chapel was founded in 1730 at Dundee. In 1863, Faraday was to preach there.

The creed of the new sect was simple. The letter of the New Testament guided all Church observances and its spirit permeated the congregation. The Agape or love-feast was reinstituted as the central ritual. The congregation gathered around a common table in the spirit of the Last Supper. The spiritual nutriment of communion was supplemented by a bowl of broth, leading non-believers to refer contemptuously to the sect as the 'kail Kirk'. The simplicity and sincerity of the Glasites, however, appealed to many in Scotland and the movement gradually grew until by the 1760's it was well established.

John Glas was not unique. Many another clergyman exercised his reason to read himself out of the established Church both in Scotland and England. Benjamin Ingham (1712–72) also felt that later accretions served to obscure and distort the real Word of God. As a fellow member with John and Charles Wesley of the 'Holy Club' at Queen's College, Oxford, he was early convinced of the necessity of a new reformation of the Church. After a brief period spent in preaching to the Indians of Georgia, he returned to Yorkshire and began his life's work of bringing the gospel to the dales. In 1739 he was officially prohibited from preaching in any church within the diocese of York, but his zeal could not be so easily thwarted; he preached in fields, in barns, anywhere and everywhere that people would listen to him. By 1743, no fewer than sixty congregations in Yorkshire and on the boundaries of Lancashire awaited his arrival eagerly. At this point, the Glasite movement in Scotland and the Inghamite fervour in Yorkshire were completely separate, each with its own rationale and united only by the same devotion to the undiluted Word of God. But as the fame of Glas and Ingham spread, as they each read what the other wrote, there was a mutual desire for contact. The districts through which they rode bordered on one another and, as their aims seemed to coincide, nothing could be more natural than that some form of union be devised. In 1760, Ingham took the initiative and brought his flock within the pale of the Glasite communion.

The very success of Glas and Ingham created new problems. No man, regardless of his zeal, fervour and devotion, can serve sixty congregations and as the followers of Ingham and Glas multiplied, the need for more preachers became intense. As the number of circuit riders increased, there was an even greater need to define orthodoxy, for the problem of Protestant individualism has always been how to create authority on the basis of a fallible human judgement. In short, the movement which had begun by insisting upon adherence only to the Word of God soon found itself, because of disagreements over what the Word of God meant, in need of a theology. This was supplied by Glas's son-in-law, Robert Sandeman.[3]

Sandeman, like Glas, was a son of Scotland and of the University of Edinburgh. For a while after his graduation he engaged in the linen trade and then took to the roads as an itinerant preacher. Early in his career he met Glas, found his teachings good, married his daughter, and devoted his life to the furtherance of his father-in-law's Church. His fervour carried him to America where he met with little success in the rather stuffy atmosphere of Puritan New England. He died at Danbury, Connecticut, on 2 April 1771, and is buried there.

Sandeman, unlike Glas or Ingham, was aware that his position needed intellectual justification. It was not enough simply to insist on the Word of God or to *feel* the presence of Christ within one. How do we know the words of Christ are true? and if true, what shall we, as sinners, do about it? What does Christ's sacrifice on the cross really mean? Sandeman's arguments were directed towards these points.

That God exists, said Sandeman, is evident from the intricate contrivances of nature. Let him who doubts cast up his eyes at the heavens and all doubt must vanish.[4] This is by no means a new idea but it should be kept firmly in mind. Faraday always insisted that he kept his science and his religion separate, yet his deepest intuitions about the physical world sprang from this religious faith in the Divine origin of nature. We shall see later how his 'proof' of the conservation of force (as he called it) derived essentially from the nature of God and of God's world.

That God exists is of little consolation to the man conscious of his own sin and unworthiness. What is important is God's intentions towards him. How are these to be determined? This was the message of the crucifixion and resurrection:

> As Jesus came into the world not to suffer for any sin of his own, being without sin, but, as he declares himself, to give his life a ransom for many; so God, in raising him from the dead, gave the highest demonstration of his being well pleased with the ransom which he gave; And as Jesus put the truth of all that he said, upon the issue of his being raised again from the dead, which you see his enemies also were apprised of; his resurrection, by this means turn out to be the highest proof of the divine assent to everything he spoke.[5]

From this it followed that God, having accepted Christ's sacrifice, as proven so dramatically by the resurrection, had thereby provided for the salvation of all men. Christ had died not for the few but for all mankind. This knowledge led to the Sandemanian ritual and ethic. To keep in memory Christ's ransom of mankind, the love-feast and the washing of one another's feet were instituted. To emphasize that Christ's kingdom was not of this world, members of the Church were cautioned against the accumulation of wealth and the neglect of the poor.

The true Christian was guided in his actions by the deep conviction that he had been saved by the crucifixion.

> This is the influencing principle, the leading line of his life. This leads him to love God and keep his commandments. His motives to his deeds of greatest self-denial arise directly from *this*. His persuasion, that the character of Jesus was so amiable in the eyes of God, as to procure his favour to the guilty, draws him to imitate that character; for 'tis plain, he that says he believes *this,* and does not make conscience of imitating Jesus, tells a lie.[6]

Finally, the knowledge that they were saved, and the urge to live in imitation of Christ, led the Sandemanians to seek out one another, for only in the communion of the saved and the godly could the bonds of real friendship be found. Friendship, indeed, is too weak a word; here, and only here, was that love of which the New Testament spoke.

Those whose hearts had been opened to God's truth were no longer as other men. They were the members of the one true Church. Only in them did grace reside and only upon them did the full force of God's love fall. From this followed the spirit of exclusiveness that characterized the Sandemanians. Husbands and wives were to be chosen from the congregation for otherwise association with the impure on such a fundamental level might lead one from the path of righteousness. In this deep-felt knowledge of God's grace was also to be discovered the source of the Sandemanian discipline. To be expelled from the congregation was to be cast out of Eden and to fall from God's favour.

No man's character can be deduced from the precepts of the religion or philosophy he follows, but there are so many striking coincidences here between Sandemanian preaching and Michael Faraday's attitudes that they deserve, at least, to be mentioned.

Sandemanianism was a serene faith, for the communicant was never tortured by the sense of guilt, or fear of the hereafter which so troubled the adherents of other sects. He was saved, for this was the (personal) message of the resurrection. Kindness, too, flowed naturally from gratitude to Christ for His sacrifice. The *imitatio Christi* meant a literal adherence to the Golden Rule with thankfulness that one could give and the knowledge that one could never give enough. Asceticism, too, was characteristic of the group. Yet, a peculiar aura of good nature surrounded it. The Sandemanian denied himself worldly goods and many worldly pleasures with cheer and gladness knowing that it was pleasing in the eyes of the Lord. There was, finally, a streak of anti-sociability. One's everyday acquaintances were not of the Sandemanian community, and hence, could not share in the full blessings of the Church. Only at meeting on the Lord's day could the full measure of human love be experienced. For the denial of ordinary social intercourse throughout the week, one was rewarded by the extraordinary companionships of the Church. Much later Tyndall noted this effect on Faraday in his diary.

> I think that a good deal of Faraday's week-day strength and persistency might be referred to his Sunday Exercises. He drinks from a fount on Sunday which refreshes his soul for the week.[7]

Serene, kind, ascetic and anti-social: these Faraday certainly was. How many of these characteristics he owed to his religion it is impossible to say, but certainly any natural tendencies towards them were stimulated by his religious training.

There is one thing we can say with certainty he received from the Sandemanian Church: his parents.

3. Clapham Wood Hall[8]

In 1756 Robert Faraday married Elizabeth Dean and moved into the Dean household, Clapham Wood Hall. The property had been left by John Dean to his wife and, thereafter, as 'tenants in common to those of his family (and their heirs) as should be alive at the time of his death'.[9] When he died in March 1756, Elizabeth, his second daughter, was engaged to be married and arrangements were made to have the newlyweds manage the property.

It was not a large holding, never exceeding forty-six acres, and the wonder is that it ever supported the growing Faraday family. Even with the addition of a bobbin mill operated by the little stream that ran through the property and the additional income that came from selling the products of the loom, there must have been many times when the family only scraped through. By 1775 there were ten children of whom James, the third, was to become Michael's father. As seven of the children were sons, it was clear that trades must be found for them; only one could hope to work the land for a living. One son became an innkeeper and grocer, another a weaver, still another a tailor. James was apprenticed to a blacksmith.

Shortly after 1774 Robert Faraday's eldest son, Richard, left Clapham

Wood Hall for Kirkby Stephen where he became a prosperous business-man. There, in the little Sandemanian chapel, he met and later married Mary Hastwell. As his affairs prospered, he suggested to James that he set up shop in Outhgill, near Kirkby Stephen, where there was a thriving inn and the prospects of considerable work for a blacksmith. Nearby was Deep Gill Farm where Margaret Hastwell, Mary's sister, worked as a maidservant.

No great effort of the imagination is needed to fill in those pages of the historical record that are blank here. James Faraday and Margaret Hast-well met at the Sandemanian Church and at their respective brother's and sister's home in Kirkby Stephen. The Faradays are a handsome family and Margaret Hastwell has been described as a neat, dark-haired girl who must, even as a lass, have shown that good sense which her son later praised. The walk from Outhgill to Kirkby Stephen is a long one and the two young people no doubt trod it together often enough. Miss Hastwell was pious, industrious and all that a man could desire in a wife. On 11 June 1786 they were married.

At first all went well. The smithy prospered and there was enough work for James Faraday to provide adequately for his growing family. In 1787 a daughter, Elizabeth, was born, to be followed in 1788 by a son, Robert. But times were beginning to change. With the outbreak of the French Revolution in 1789, a gradual depression settled over England. Prices rose, trade was disorganized and prospects for the future were dim. James Faraday's health began to fail and the cares and physical labour of running his own smithy became increasingly burdensome. From travellers who stopped at the inn he no doubt heard of the bustle of London and felt he could do better there. In 1791, the family moved into rooms in Newington in Surrey. There, Michael Faraday was born on 22 September 1791.

4. Faraday's Early Years

Faraday's early years were hard ones. The family lived in cramped quarters over a coachhouse in Jacob's Well Mews, Charles Street, Man-chester Square. Michael's father's health steadily deteriorated and he could work only sporadically, bringing in only enough money to keep the family together. In 1801, when prices were very high, Michael was allotted one loaf of bread which had to last him a week.

Faraday's elementary education was almost nil. Bence Jones quotes him as remarking: 'my education was of the most ordinary description, con-sisting of little more than the rudiments of reading, writing, and arithmetic at a common day-school. My hours out of school were passed at home and in the streets.'[10]

His family life must, however, have been pleasant. His mother was a kind, neat woman of whose love he was assured. He and his brother, Robert, were on friendly terms. Later, when Faraday and Benjamin Abbott became close friends, the older brothers of both were almost constantly with them when they set off on excursions. He fairly worshipped his younger sister, Margaret. Although poor, his poverty seems to have left little mark on him for there is never a mention of it in his later correspondence. Again, perhaps, the Sandemanian faith led him to view it as a blessing rather than a curse.

In 1804 Faraday began to work as an errand boy for Mr G. Riebau of 2 Blandford Street, bookseller and bookbinder. His duties consisted of carrying round newspapers loaned out by Mr Riebau and then calling back to pick them up again. Between times we may assume he rested in Mr Riebau's shop where the wonder of the world of books was first revealed to him. Mr Riebau was a kind man, Faraday must learn a trade and the handling of books was as fine a one as any other. On 7 October 1805 he was bound apprentice to Mr Riebau and a new era in his life had begun. No simple journeyman bookbinder was to emerge from this apprenticeship, but an ardent and devoted chemist.

Prologue References

1. I am indebted to Mr Joseph E. Faraday of Woking, Surrey, who referred me to the parish register of Bolton-le-Sands.

2. For the background of the Faraday family and its connexion with the Sandemanian Church I have drawn heavily upon the excellent study by Dr James F. Riley, *The Hammer and the Anvil, a background to Michael Faraday* (Clapham, Yorkshire, 1954).

3. The main ideas upon which Sandeman based his teaching were most clearly expressed in his *Letters on Theron and Aspasia. Addressed to the Author* (Edinburgh, 1757), and *Some Thoughts on Christianity in a Letter to a Friend* (Boston, 1764).

4. *Some Thoughts . . .* , 9.

5. Ibid., 5.

6. Ibid., 6.

7. R.I., Tyndall's Journals (MS., vol. 5, 163), Sunday, 24 October 1852.

8. Riley, op. cit.

9. Ibid., 24.

10. H. Bence Jones, *Life and Letters of Faraday* (2 vols., London, 1870), cited henceforth as B.J., *1* or *2*. There were two editions published in 1870 and they differ in pagination. All references here are to the first edition.

Although this work is indispensable to any study of Faraday's life, it should be noted that Bence Jones often 'edited' the documents he reproduced. Where possible, therefore, reference will be made to the original manuscripts, but the appropriate reference in B.J. will also be given. When the citation differs from B.J. it is because Bence Jones either erred in his reading of the document or changed the language of the original to conform to proper grammatical usage.

B.J., *1*, 7 ff. gives the only detailed account of Faraday's early years.

CHAPTER ONE

The Education of a Chemist

1. The Apprentice Years

At the age of fourteen, Michael Faraday began his term of apprenticeship at Mr Riebau's shop. Mr Riebau must have been a most kind and generous master, for Faraday dedicated the bound volumes of notes he had taken at the City Philosophical Society to him in the following terms:

Sir

When first I evinced a predeliction for the sciences but more particularly for that one denominated electricity you kindly interested yourself in the progress I made in the knowledge of facts relating to the different theories in existance readily permitting me to examine those books in your possession that were any way related to the subjects then occupying my attention. To you, therefore, is to be attributed the rise and existence of that small portion of knowledge relating to the sciences which I possess and accordingly to you are due my acknowledgements.[1]

It might be noted parenthetically that Mr Riebau seemed singularly unsuccessful in persuading his apprentices to follow the trade of bookbinder. Of Faraday's two fellow workers, one became a well-known comedian and the other a professional singer. The company must have been a congenial one. All his life Faraday had a marvellous sense of fun, and music and singing were dear to him. 2 Blandford Street was no Dickensian industrial inferno with cruel master, miserly mistress and brutish louts trampling upon the sensitivity of our hero, but rather a closely-knit, happy group in which there were ample opportunities for genius to bud.

Nothing whatsoever is known about Faraday's activities in the first four years of his apprenticeship. We may assume that he was busily occupied in learning his new trade and the operations that were necessary to it – sewing pages, pounding them tightly together with a wooden mallet, selecting and cutting the leather, printing the titles on the spine, and putting all together. His ability is testified to by the volumes still in existence at the Royal Institution and elsewhere which he bound for his own purposes. In the performance of his tasks, there was probably a good bit of friendly competition between the apprentices for in later life Faraday mentioned, with some pride, that he could strike 1,000 blows with the mallet in succession without resting.[2] Part of his scientific training can be traced to these early years. Faraday was certainly one of the most able members of the 'bees' wax and string' school of English experimental physics. His extraordinary skill in laboratory manipulation and his ability to construct the instruments and apparatus required in his researches contributed greatly to his success as a scientist. The ability to work rapidly and accurately with his hands was developed in Mr Riebau's workshop.

All was not work at Riebau's. There were spare moments and evenings when a young apprentice could follow his own bent. For Faraday, the choice of sparetime occupation was easy. 'There were plenty of books there, and I read them.'[3] To a certain extent, his reading tended to be determined by the books that came in to be bound. Thus it was that he made the acquaintance of Miss Burney's *Evelina*, was transported in imagination to the East of the *Arabian Nights* and felt the first stirrings of scientific enthusiasm as a result of reading about electricity in the *Encyclopaedia Britannica*. And, as his interests were aroused, he strove to satisfy his curiosity by field trips, by more extensive reading (now being given permission to draw upon Mr Riebau's library for books) and by any means at all. Mr Riebau has left a vivid description (in somewhat idiosyncratic English) of the intellectual hunger of his extraordinary apprentice:

> . . . after the regular hours of Buisiness, he was chiefly employed in Drawing and Copying from the Artists Repository a work published in Numbers which he took in weekly – also Electrical Machines from the Dicty. of Arts and Sciences and other works which came in to bind . . . he went an early walk in the Morning Visiting always some Works of Art or searching for some Mineral or Vegitable curiosity – Holloway water Works Highgate Archway, W Middlesex Water Works – Strand Bridge – Junction Water Works etc. etc. . . . his mind ever engaged, besides attending to Bookbinding which he executed in a proper manner. . . .
>
> If I had any curious book from my Customers to bind, with Plates, he would copy such as he thought Singular or Clever, which I advised him to Keep by him. Irelands Hogarth, and other Graphic Works, he much admired [Thomson's] Chemistry in 4 vols. he bought and interleaved great part of it, Occationally adding Notes with Drawings and Observations.[4]

There is a note of frenzy about this activity. Copying, drawing, noting, exploring but to what end? Where was the unifying thread that could

bind these isolated and insulated facts together? Faraday was too intelligent not to realize that while his industry was laudable, the results of
his intellectual labours were meagre. What he required was system,
method, and a point of view which would allow him to organize his search
for truth. It was with these needs that Faraday first met with the writings
of Dr Isaac Watts. Dr Watts was a clergyman of the eighteenth century,
perhaps most famous today for his hymns, still sung in many churches.
He was also a philosopher whose *Logic* carried on the tradition of Lockean
empiricism and whose *The Improvement of the Mind* was to serve as a guide
to many a young man in Faraday's position. In 1809, a new edition of this
latter work was published and it is probable that Mr Riebau stocked it for
sale in his shop. Here Faraday discovered it. To the young apprentice
struggling with the immense world of knowledge it was like a gift from
the gods. His enthusiasm was boundless as he plunged into it. Riebau
mentioned: 'Dr Watts improvement of the mind, was then read and
frequent took in his Pocket. . . .'[5]

What was it in this treatise that so attracted Faraday? It was simply that
Dr Watts offered precisely the advice on method and system that Faraday
was so desperately seeking. In the preface, he addressed himself to 'persons
in younger years' who needed a guide through the maze of learning.
Common-sense suggestions were made on improving and enlarging the
mind. The relative merits of lectures, reading, conversation, and direct
observation as means for the acquisition of knowledge were discussed in
exhaustive detail and advice was given on the best methods to be adopted
for drawing maximum profit from these activities. Faraday faithfully
followed each and every one of these suggestions. Dr Watts advised that
a commonplace book be kept, so that ideas, interesting facts and other
jottings could be preserved for future reference. In 1809, Faraday began
to keep such a book. Its title and purpose, as given by the author himself,
were: ' "The Philosophical Miscellany" being a collection of notices,
occurrences, events, &c., relating to the arts and sciences, collected from
the public papers, reviews, magazines, and other miscellaneous works;
intended to promote both amusement and instruction, and also to
corroborate or invalidate those theories which are continually starting
into the world of science. Collected by M. Faraday, 1809–10.'[6] Attendance
at lectures was suggested by Dr Watts; in 1810, Faraday began to frequent
Mr Tatum's lectures at the City Philosophical Society. Dr Watts recommended the exchange of letters with a person of similar interests and
attainments as a means of improving the understanding; in 1812, Faraday
began his lengthy correspondence with Benjamin Abbott. Dr Watts

It's that simple:

Buy Books.
Do Good.

- **$34 million**
  raised for literacy
- **35 million**
  books donated
- **100 million**
  books sold
- **450 million**
  books reused or recycled

SCAN ME

emphasized the worth of a small discussion group devoted to an exchange of ideas on various topics; in 1818, Faraday helped to organize such a group.[7]

There was more in *The Improvement of the Mind*, however, than the mechanics of the acquisition of knowledge. It also contained and preached a philosophical point of view which strongly influenced Faraday. Dr Watts, as a disciple of John Locke, constantly drew attention to the importance of the observed fact and the dangers of imprecise language. In particular the student was cautioned to distinguish carefully between words and things lest he 'feed upon husks instead of kernels'.[8] To this important distinction was added the even more fundamental injunction to 'be not too hasty to erect general theories from a few particular observations, appearances, or experiments'.[9] Confusion in language and over-hasty generalization were the two traps laid by human nature for the unwary.

Such a philosophical viewpoint was commonplace at the beginning of the nineteenth century. Dr Watts's impact on Faraday, however, must not be judged by his originality but rather by the fact that his position provided Faraday with the necessary critical apparatus without which the accumulation of bits and pieces of information, no matter how enthusiastically obtained, becomes a magpie-like activity having no ultimate purpose or meaning. It is here that Faraday's lack of schooling must be taken into account. Formal education has one great advantage over self-education in that it places the student within a long and critical tradition. The foundations of his knowledge rest, not just upon personal conviction, but upon the intellectual experience of generations. The self-educated man has no such assurance. He may read omnivorously, as Faraday did, but by what criteria shall he judge what he reads? All has the uniform authority of the printed page and the result may as easily be a swamp of contradictions as a firm road to truth. Dr Watts's emphasis upon the carefully observed and precisely described fact equipped Faraday with a seemingly infallible guide. When he read Sir Francis Bacon and found the same emphases, he must have experienced a feeling of intellectual security of considerable strength.[10] His extreme semantic caution and experimental temper were, no doubt, reinforced by his later scientific training but their origins are to be found in Dr Watts's warnings and exhortations.

With Dr Watts's advice and counsel, Faraday was prepared to investigate subjects of his own choosing confident that he had grasped the thread which could lead him from the labyrinth of error to the clear day of truth. Dr Watts had given no prescription for selecting a branch of knowledge to study and Faraday stumbled upon one that interested him quite by chance. One day while binding a volume of the *Encyclopaedia Britannica* he paused to glance at the article on electricity and was fascinated by what he read.[11] This article of 127 double column pages of small print was written by one James Tytler who contributed a number of articles to the *Encyclopaedia*. His talents were recognized in a rather odd way by the editors. 'Aerology, Aerostation, Chemistry, Electricity, Gunnery, Hydrostatics, Mechanics, Meteorology, with most of the separate articles in the various branches of natural history, we have reason to believe were compiled by Mr James Tytler chemist; a man who, though his conduct has been marked by almost perpetual imprudence, possesses no common share of Science and genius'.[12]

Tytler first sketched in the history of electricity, relying heavily on Joseph Priestley's, *The History and Present State of Electricity*.[13] This section was copiously illustrated with drawings of electrical apparatus and gave careful descriptions of the experiments upon which the science had been erected in the eighteenth century. Faraday was immediately stimulated to construct his first scientific instruments. Too poor to buy the various parts, he saw two bottles in an old rag shop in nearby Little Chesterfield Street, but the price was too high. Daily he watched them until he was able to purchase the one for sixpence and the other for a penny. The larger bottle became the cylinder of an electrostatic generator and the smaller was turned into a Leyden jar. With this primitive apparatus, Faraday made his first experiments and entered the exciting realm of science.[14]

Tytler did not content himself with recounting the history of electricity. He was also bent upon destroying the theories of electricity then current. He began with a detailed and generally fair examination of the various schemes brought forth in the eighteenth century to explain electrical effects.[15] His criticisms were first levelled at the two-fluid theory still held by the French. This theory, he demonstrated, was too cumbrous, inconsistent, and insufficient to be true. The one-fluid theory suggested by Benjamin Franklin was then subjected to his scrutiny and demolished.[16] Having thus cleared the way, Tytler proceeded to introduce his theory of electricity. Light, heat, and electricity, he claimed, were identical in substance, differing only in their modes of action. A single fluid underlay them all, but this fluid could move in different ways. When it streamed forth in a simple laminar flow the result was light; when the fluid converged to a focus, heat was produced. Electricity differed from light and heat in that it was not a current or flow, but a vibration likened by Tytler to the waves produced by a stone being cast into a pool of still water. This theory, Tytler was confident, was far superior to either the one-fluid or two-fluid theory. Both the latter theories had had to assume that some substances, such as glass (i.e. modern insulators) although filled with the electric fluid(s) were also impermeable to it. When it was motion, rather than a material fluid that passed through these bodies, this difficulty disappeared. 'We may easily suppose it possible', he wrote, 'that glass should obstruct one kind of motion and not another: In which case, the glass would seem to be permeable by the fluid when manifesting itself by the first kind of motion [flow] and not so when it manifests itself by the other [vibration]'.[17] Although Faraday could not accept Tytler's ideas at this time, they remained with him and became increasingly seductive as the years went by.[18]

With the reading of Tytler's article, Faraday plunged into the science of electricity. His curiosity had been aroused and he began to read extensively on the subject and to perform whatever experiments his primitive equipment permitted. Also, at this time, he began to attend lectures on science given by Mr John Tatum at his home at 53 Dorset Street. The shilling fee was given him by his brother. With these lectures a whole new world opened for Faraday and the course of his thoughts turned increasingly to the science he now loved so well.

2. The City Philosophical Society

In 1808 a group of young men interested in improving themselves met together and formed the City Philosophical Society. The guiding spirit was Mr John Tatum who contributed his house, his library, his scientific apparatus, and his talents as a lecturer to the success of the enterprise. Meetings were held every Wednesday evening. Every two weeks Mr Tatum delivered a lecture on some branch of science and on the Wednesdays in between one of the members of the Society would hold forth on whatever subject interested him. Some of the members were later to gain some measure of fame, even of notoriety. Among these were Edward Magrath, later secretary of the Athenaeum Club, Richard Phillips, chemist and editor of the *Philosophical Magazine* and Horn, notorious for his parodies and for being thrice tried for blasphemy and acquitted.

Faraday was introduced into this company in February, 1810, when he attended his first lecture. The care and attention he gave to this and subsequent meetings is testified to by the method he adopted for insuring maximum profit from these evenings.

My method [he noted at the end of one lecture] was to take with me a sheet or two of paper stitched or pinned up the middle so as to form something like a book. I usually got a front seat and there placing my hat on my knees and my paper on the hat I as Mr Tatum proceeded on in his lecture set down the most prominent words, short but important sentences, titles of the experiments names of what substances came under consideration and many other hints that would tend to bring what had passed to my mind. . . .

On leaving the lecture room I proceeded immediately homewards and in that and the next night had generally drawn up a second set of notes from the first. These second notes were more copious, more connected and more legible than the first. . . .

These second set of notes were my guide whilst writing out the lecture in a rough manner. They gave me the order in which the different parts came under consideration and in which the experiments were performed and they called to mind the most important subjects that were discussed. I then referred to memory for the matter belonging to each subject and I believe I have not let much of the meaning and sense of Mr Tatum's lectures slip (I allude to the latter ones).

As I ultimately referred to memory for the whole of the lecture it is not to be supposed that I could write it out in Mr Tatum's own words. I was obliged to compose it myself but in the composing of it I was aided by the ideas raised in my mind at the lecture and I believe I have (from following my pattern as closely as I could) adopted Mr Tatum's style of delivery to a considerable degree (perhaps no great acquisition).[19]

Tatum may not have been the most exciting lecturer in London, but he was thorough and covered a wide range of subjects quite adequately. His method of presentation was to give the general theory of the subject first and then illustrate this with particular experiments. From Faraday's descriptions of the experiments, Tatum would seem to have been a clever and ingenious demonstrator, able to illustrate well the main points of his discourse. Tatum served as Faraday's secondary school master and in the years 1810–11 he managed to lay a firm foundation for his gifted pupil's later scientific career. In these years, Faraday attended, carefully noted, and digested lectures on electricity, galvanism, hydrostatics, optics, geology, theoretical mechanics, experimental mechanics, chemistry, aerology (pneumatic chemistry), astronomy, and meteorology. The basic principles of each subject were clearly set forth and Faraday had the opportunity to examine a whole host of experimental apparatus. It was at Tatum's, for example, that he first observed the workings of the voltaic pile.

Faraday was no passive recorder who simply absorbed what he was told. In some cases, as in the lecture on astronomy, he took notes which were meaningless to him at the time. Thus, throughout he wrote of the *recession* of the equinox.[20] At the end, however, is a diagram taken from

'Ferguson'[21] and the term is corrected to read 'precession'. Similarly, in the lecture on geology, Faraday noted:

> The science of Geology or more properly this lecture on the science of Geology admitted of but few experiments. In fact Mr Tatum performed only one (i.e. the solution of silex by an alkali) as nearly the whole of it consisted in exhibiting various minerals and explaining their component parts and formation. To make this sketch of the lecture as complete as I could I have given in the ensuing pages a description of above fifty minerals exhibited during the evening. But having not the slightest knowledge of the science before I attended this lecture, the descriptions of the minerals must be very imperfect and perhaps full of errors.
>
> I did in order to render the matter as correct as I could refer to the only book on this subject that I was in possession of, namely Thomson's Chemistry 4 vols. 8⁰, the third and fourth volumes of which contain a short but correct system of geology.[22]

Sometimes Faraday's emendations came from disagreement with either Tatum's method of presentation or his actual views. In the lecture on Mechanics, Faraday wrote:

> Note: I am now going to enter upon a description of the mechanic power: but I think it necessary to remark that I have here proceeded in a different order to that which Mr Tatum pursued when speaking of them. He first explained the pulley, then the wheel and axle, and lastly the lever; but as both the pulley and the wheel and axle are much easier explained when considered as levers, I thought it proper to enter upon the consideration of a simple lever before we proceeded to the more compound states of it.[23]

It was on the subject of electricity, however, that he and Mr Tatum were most widely separated. Tatum was an advocate of Franklin's one-fluid theory whereas Faraday had accepted Tytler's criticism as valid. Scattered throughout the notes he took, therefore, are challenges and arguments refuting Tatum. There is no doubt that he made his objections known and he was, therefore, invited to present his views to the members of the City Philosophical Society. Sometime in the spring of 1810 Michael Faraday delivered his first lecture.[24] His nervousness is indicated by the fact that the entire talk is carefully written out even to the salutation, 'Ladies and Gentlemen'. Faraday, like Tytler, began by giving a brief history of electricity taken verbatim from Tytler's article. He then repeated Tytler's criticisms of the one-fluid theory but here his reliance on the *Encyclopaedia Britannica* ceased. Instead of adopting Tytler's undulatory theory of electricity, he presented a two-fluid theory which he had found expounded in the works of Major Henry Eeles and his disciples.[25] His adherence to this theory was enthusiastic and unconditional.

We shall now beg leave to introduce Mr Eeles' hypothesis, as delivered by Mr Atwood at Trinity College, Cambridge, and if we carefully compare this theory with the experiments that we shall make – there can be no doubt that it is – as Mr Adams asserts – more simple than Dr Franklin's, speaks more strictly the language of experience, and is much less embarrassed with hypothetical *suppositions*. It pointed out to the Author many phenomena, which have not only been considered as wonderful, but which have also much embarrassed the partizan of Dr Franklin's opinion. There are no *known* Phenomena but which are *more readily accounted for* on this system, than any other at present known. First. The Electric substance is not a simple, but a compound body capable of being divided by Friction or Excitation into 2 Portions or Powers, one of which (when separated) always attracts itself to the rubber; the other to the excited Electric, which for distinction's sake are called the Vitreous and the Resinous powers – for the one can be produced at pleasure by the friction of Glass, the other of Resin – not but what both powers exist *united* in each substance, for we produce by a different process, either power from both. Thus by friction we are enabled to exhibit them in a divided state and being forcibly separated, they have a tendency equally strong to *Unite*.

Secondly. As they condense each other *when United*, they can be rendered evident to the senses only by their separation. Thirdly. The two Powers are separated in Non Electrics (as the cushion, etc.) either by the *excitation* of *Electrics*, or by the application of excited Electrics. Fourthly. The two Powers attract each other strongly through the substance of Electrics. Fifthly. Either Power when applied to an unelectrified body repels the Power of the same sort, and attracts the contrary.[26]

One cannot help but admire the courage and daring of the young Faraday. To his mind, the one-fluid theory made no sense whereas the assumption of two fluids permitted all phenomena to be explained. Unfortunately, the scientific community in England did not agree. In the preface to his work, Major Eeles had stated that he was publishing his book because the Royal Society had refused even to answer the letters he had sent there. Priestley, too, ignored Eeles's ideas as seemingly beneath notice. Yet here was Michael Faraday, nineteen-year-old bookbinder's apprentice stating that 'there can be no doubt' of the superiority of the hypothesis he was presenting!

We know Faraday the man too well to believe that Faraday the lad was arrogant or filled with self-importance. In this lecture, he was presenting a point of view in which he firmly believed and for whose correctness he was willing to vouch. But, inside, he must have wondered if he were not in error; if the simplicity and consonance of his theory with observed phenomena were not merely an illusion buttressed by his own ignorance. It was in this state that he made the acquaintance of a work which he lauded throughout his life, Mrs Jane Marcet's *Conversations on Chemistry*.

Just when Faraday read these little volumes can be dated with considerable precision. In his 'Lecture on Electricity', his reasonings were based entirely upon the phenomena of static electricity. Nowhere was there the slightest hint that he was aware of the existence of galvanic electricity or that the new field of electrochemistry had forced a serious revision of the commonly held theories of the nature of electricity. Assuming, as seems only reasonable, that his lecture was given in response to Tatum's, then his discovery of Mrs Marcet probably came between 19 February, when Tatum delivered his first lecture on electricity, and 2 April 1810, when he discoursed upon galvanism. Faraday's enthusiasm for Mrs Marcet's volumes arose from the fact that in it he was introduced to electrochemistry and, according to Mrs Marcet, electrochemical effects seemed to require two electrical fluids.

Mrs Marcet wrote for an audience newly created by Humphry Davy. Probably the handsomest man in the history of science and a brilliant lecturer, Davy captivated the young ladies of the higher ranks of English society who flocked to the Royal Institution. So successful was he, indeed, that he served to subvert the original purpose for which the Royal Institution had been founded in 1799. Benjamin Thomson, Count Rumford, had originally envisioned it as a centre for the dissemination of practical knowledge to the artisan class, but financial difficulties and Davy's genius soon turned it into a centre for chemical research and popular scientific lectures. The young ladies who came to the lecture hall to hear Davy were drawn there more by his charm and the vivacity of his person than by any passion for chemistry. His popularity was such that when he lay ill in 1807 the press of carriages was so great in Albemarle Street and inquiries about the state of his health so numerous that it was necessary to post a slate at the entrance to the Royal Institution with a graph showing the hourly state of his temperature so that his progress could be perceived at a glance. As one of his fair listeners put it, 'those eyes were made for something besides poring over crucibles'.[27]

It was to this audience that Mrs Marcet addressed her *Conversations*, so that Davy's followers could understand as well as admire him. She began by insisting, with Davy, that chemistry was not and should not be confined to the activities of the apothecary or refiner of metals. Rather, 'the most wonderful and the most interesting phenomena of nature are almost all of them produced by chemical powers'.[28] It was within this cosmic framework that the conversations took place. Instead of a dry recital of the properties of substances and of a host of chemical reactions, the attempt was made to penetrate to the first principles of the science. Here were singled out those 'imponderable' fluids – light, heat, and most importantly, electricity – upon which the whole of chemical dynamics depended. This new view of the importance of electricity in chemistry was taken from Davy.

> Mr Davy . . . whose important discoveries have opened such improved views on chemistry, has suggested an hypothesis which may throw great light upon that science. He supposes that there are two kinds of electricity with one or other of which all bodies are united. These we distinguish by the names of *positive* and *negative* electricity; those bodies are disposed to combine which possess opposite electricities, as they are brought together by the attraction which these electricities have for each other. But whether this hypothesis be altogether founded on truth or not, it is impossible to question the great influence of electricity in chemical combinations.[29]

The electrical states of bodies provided a basic clue to the mechanics of chemical combination. Up to this time, the only way of determining whether two substances would react with one another to form a new compound was to mix them together and see what happened. Now, it was hoped, reactions could be predicted from a knowledge of the fundamental electric charges of the reagents.

We can easily imagine the effect of Mrs Marcet's volumes on Faraday. Hitherto, he had been fascinated by electrical effects but there was about this fascination a certain aimlessness. Static electrical phenomena were interesting but appeared to be unrelated to anything else. Now Faraday realized that the forces he had so passionately studied and experimented with were of fundamental importance in the universe for they appeared to regulate all chemical change. Before 1810, in short, he had been an ardent student of electricity; after April 1810 he became a student chemist. All the lectures at Mr Tatum's and all his readings served to broaden his outlook, but his passion now centred upon chemistry.

3. The Fledgeling

At the City Philosophical Society, Faraday met a number of young men who had similar tastes and desires for self-improvement. Of them all, Faraday was the least prepared to advance himself. Thus it was that he called upon his companions for help. His first concern was to improve his language, for he was painfully aware of his own shortcomings. His spelling was poor, grammar left much to be desired, and punctuation was non-existent.[30] To remedy these faults, he induced Edward Magrath to devote two hours every week to his instruction. This instruction lasted some seven years during which time Faraday's ability to express himself constantly improved.[31] At the same time, he took drawing lessons from a French *émigré*, M. Masquerier. His major helper, however, was Benjamin Abbott, a young clerk in the City whose piety and good education fitted him uniquely to be Faraday's friend. The two met frequently, usually at Abbott's father's house in Long Lane, Bermondsey, where they discussed the various chemical problems that interested them both so much.

Faraday recognized the deficiencies in his self-education and turned to his friend to aid him in overcoming them. The main instrument of instruction was to be the mutual exchange of letters. Faraday initiated the correspondence with a touch of pomposity which revealed his diffidence.

I was lately engagedi n conversation with a gentleman who appeared to have a very extensive correspondence: for within the space of half an hour he drew observations from two letters that he had received not a fortnight before; one was from Sicily and the other from France. After a while I adverted to his correspondence, and observed that it must be very interesting and a source of great pleasure to himself. He immediately affirmed with great enthusiasm that it was one of the purest enjoyments of his life (observe, he like you and your humble servant, is a Bachelor). Much more passed on the subject, but I will not waste your time in recapitulating it; however, let me notice, before I cease from praising and recommending epistolary correspondence, that the great Dr Isaac Watts (great in all the methods respecting the attainment of learning) recommends it as a very effectual method of improving the mind of the person who writes and the person who receives. Not to forget, too, another strong instance in favour of the practice. I will merely call to your mind the correspondence that passed between Lord Chesterfield and his son. In general, I do not approve of the moral tendency of Lord Chesterfield's letters, but I heartily agree with him respecting the utility of a written correspondence. It, like many other good things, can be made to suffer an abuse, but that is no effectual argument against its good effects.[32]

The tone soon became less formal and Faraday spelled out his reasons for wishing to write to his friend even though they saw each other often.

I speak not of the abuse but the use of epistolation (if you will allow me to coin a new word to express myself) and that use, I have no doubt, produces other good effects. Now I do not profess myself perfect in those points, and my deficiency in others connected with the subject you well know, as grammar, &c.; therefore it follows that I want improving on these points; and what so natural in a disease as to revert to the remedy that will perform a cure? and more so when the physic is so pleasant; or, to express it in a more logical manner and consequently more philosophically, M. F. is deficient in certain points that he wants to make up, epistolary writing is one cure for those deficiencies, therefore, I should practice epistolary writing.[33]

Although a major purpose was to be the improvement of Faraday's English, the exchange of scientific ideas and experiences was no less important. In the back of Mr Riebau's shop a small 'laboratory' was created. The fireplace for warming the room and heating the tools used in gilding was, at night, with the aid of some milled boards, converted to a furnace. The mantelpiece served as a laboratory bench and there Faraday observed the results of his various experiments.[34] The apparatus, though crude, worked and stimulated his imagination. His excitement with the success of his first galvanic pile was matched only by his confusion over what precisely was happening.

I, Sir [he wrote to Abbott], I my own self, cut out seven discs [of zinc] of the size of half-pennies each! I, Sir, covered them with seven halfpence and I interposed between seven, or rather six pieces of paper soaked in a solution of muriate of soda!!!! But laugh no longer, dear A., rather wonder at the effects this trivial power produced. It was sufficient to produce the decomposition of the sulphate of magnesia – an effect which extremely surprised me for I did not, could not have any idea that the agent was competent to the purpose. A thought here struck me: I will tell you. I made the communication between the top and bottom of the pile and the solution with copper wire. Do you conceive that it was the copper that decomposed the earthy sulphate – that part, I mean, immersed in the solution?[35]

Seeing what a small pile could do, Faraday promptly built a larger one and subjected water from the cistern to it. The resultant action, complicated by the possible presence of iron from the pipes and lead from the cistern, totally confused him and he pleaded with his friend and mentor to explain the theory of what he had observed. At the same time, however, another fact did not escape his keen sight, and he immediately pounced upon it as significant for the theory of electrochemistry.

Another phenomenon [he wrote] I observed was this: on separating the discs from each other, I found that some of the zinc discs had got a coating – a very superficial one in some parts – of metallic copper, and that some of the copper discs had a coating of oxide of zinc. In this case the metals must both have passed through the flannel disc holding the solution of muriate of soda, and they must have passed by each other. I think this circumstance well worth notice, for remember, no effect takes place without a cause. The deposition, too, of the oxide of zinc in the flannel was curious, and will tend to illustrate the passage of the metals from one side to the other.[36]

This was, indeed, a curious thing! According to the current theory of electrochemistry, the substances that were decomposed in the circuit of the voltaic pile were torn apart by the oppositely charged poles of the pile. Each fragment, with its electric charge, was then attracted to the appropriate pole. How, then, could such particles have *passed* one another? Should not the positively and negatively charged particles have coalesced into a neutral molecule? No wonder that Faraday asked of Abbott, 'Think of these things and let me, if you please, Sir, if you please, let me know your opinion.'[37] This problem was to remain in Faraday's mind for years. The solution of it was to provide him with the basic concept which led to all his famous discoveries.[38]

Not all the letters from Faraday to his friend were on such important matters. Nowhere do we get a better picture of Faraday's sense of fun in these years than in a description of his walk home from Long Lane during a July rainstorm.

Were you to see me instead of hearing from me I conceive that one question would be how did you get home on Sunday evening. I suppose this question because I wish you to know how much I congratulate myself upon the very pleasant walk or rather succession of walks, runs, and hops I had home that evening and the truly Philosophical reflections they gave rise to.

I set off from you at a run and did not stop untill I found myself in the midst of a puddle and a quandary of thoughts respecting the heat generated in animal bodies by exercise. The puddle however gave a turn to the affair and I proceeded from thence deeply immersed in thoughts respecting the resistance of fluids to bodies precipitated into them. I did not at that time forget the instances you and your Brother had noticed in the afternoon to that purpose.

My mind was deeply engaged on this subject and was proceeding to place itself as fast as possible in the midst of confusion when it was suddenly called to take care of the body by a very cordial affectionate and also effectual salute from a spout. This of course gave a new turn to my ideas and from thence to Black Friars Bridge it was busily bothered amongst Projectiles and Parabolas. At the Bridge the wind came in my face and directed my attention as well and as earnestly as it could to the inclination of the pavement. Inclined Planes were then all the go and a further illustration of this point took place on the other side of the Bridge where I happened to proceed in a very smooth, soft and equable manner for the space of three or four feet. This movement which is vulgarly called slipping introduced the subject of friction and the best method of lessening it and in this frame of mind I went on with little or no interruption for some time except occasional and actual experiments connected with the subject in hand or rather in head.

The Velocity and Momentum of falling bodies next struck not only my mind but my head, my ears, my hands, my back and various other parts of my body and tho I had at hand no apparatus by which I could ascertain those points exactly I knew it must be considerable by the quickness with which it penetrated my coat and other parts of my dress. This happened in

Holborn and from thence I went home, sky-gazing and earnestly looking out for every Cirrus, Cumulus, Stratus, Cirro-Cumuli, Cirro-Strata and Nimbus that came above the horizon.[39]

Whenever anything attracted his attention, he would write to Abbott and ask his opinion. The subjects ranged from the strange and, to Faraday, inexplicable, motions of a piece of camphor on water to a kind of glass he had heard about which was transparent only when viewed from one side. In these matters he freely confessed his ignorance and turned to his friend for explanations. On one subject, however, Faraday considered himself sufficiently well versed to instruct his companion. Faraday held definite views upon the controversy over the composition of muriatic acid that was then disturbing the calm of the chemical world.

Chemistry had only recently emerged from relative chaos with the epoch-making achievement of Antoine Laurent Lavoisier. Lavoisier had banished the strange element, phlogiston, which could never be captured alone by the chemist but always had to be inferred from its effects. In its place, as the active agent in combustion, he substituted oxygen which had the great advantage of being a ponderable substance which the chemist could measure and weigh like any other reagent. Lavoisier, however, did not stop with the revolutionizing of the theory of combustion. Oxygen was seen as a substance of fundamental importance. Combustion was a unique reaction occurring only in the presence of oxygen; life, itself, was clearly possible only when oxygen was available; and, since oxygen was present, by analysis, in all acids, Lavoisier saw this substance as the principle of acidity. When another element had become saturated to a certain degree with oxygen, the compound was an acid.

> It is seen [Lavoisier wrote in his *Elementary Treatise on Chemistry*] that oxygen is a principle common to all [acids], and that this is what constitutes their acidity; that they are distinguished from one another by the nature of the substance which is acidified. In every acid, therefore, the Acidifiable base, to which M. de Morveau has given the name of radical, should be distinguished from the acidifying principle, that is, oxygen.[40]

Almost immediately, chemists pointed out certain difficulties in this theory. Lavoisier's countryman, Claude-Louis Berthollet, showed that hydrocyanic acid (HCN) contained no oxygen, nor could any be found in muriatic acid (HCl). Hydrocyanic acid, being a very weak acid, was rather cavalierly dismissed as a borderline case which should not be considered as decisive. Muriatic acid, however, was a powerful substance of undoubted acidity. At the time, it was felt that Lavoisier's reform of chemistry was all of a piece and that to reject one part meant the rejection of all. The revelation of the role of oxygen in combustion had so clarified chemical processes that few chemists were willing to return to the fuzziness and confusion of the days of phlogiston. Hence, the 'phenomena were saved' by making muriatic acid an oxide of some unknown base (murium). The oxide was supposedly so stable that ordinary attempts to break it down were doomed to failure.

In the first decade of the nineteenth century a new analytical tool of enormous power was placed in the hands of the chemist. In 1800 Alessandro Volta invented the voltaic pile which produced a steady electric current. Within months of the announcement of this discovery, it was found that the pile could decompose water and various neutral salts. Using a pile of great power, Humphry Davy produced metallic sodium and potassium from their compounds for the first time. Surely, if muriatic acid were ever to yield its secret, it would surrender under the torture of the electric current. Davy's efforts were unavailing. The green gas obtained from the decomposition of muriatic acid, supposedly a higher oxide of murium named oxymuriatic acid, stubbornly refused to yield up its oxygen. After years of effort, Davy finally concluded that the gas was not an oxide but an element to which he gave the name chlorine. His conclusion was based on Lavoisier's own criterion for the identification of elementary substances. 'If', Lavoisier had written, '. . . we associate the name of elements or principles of bodies with the idea of the last product of analysis, all the substances that we have not yet decomposed by any means are elements to us.'[41] If any substance deserved to be called an element, chlorine did. Most chemists, however, remained unconvinced and Davy fought a lonely battle for many years.

Faraday became an ardent champion of Davy's views, for Davy not only persuaded him by his arguments but was also, in a sense, Faraday's hero long before the two met. It was Davy (through Mrs Marcet) who had supported Faraday in his speculation about the nature of electricity and after hearing Davy explain his theory of chlorine in person, Faraday was convinced. How Michael Faraday, apprentice bookbinder, gained entry to Davy's lectures at the Royal Institution is a story known to all, but as this was to change the whole course of Faraday's life and of modern science, it bears retelling. Since Mr Riebau was indirectly responsible, it is fitting that he recount the circumstances.

At Mr Tatum's he fell in Company with some Other Young Men and Occationaly coresponded with them on Subjects of Chemistry several Letters too and fro he shewed me, he had now written. Four Quarto vols. of Lectures with Drawings, etc. on different Subjects these I occationaly shewed to my

Friends and Customers. I hapned One Evening to shew them to Mr Dance Junr. of Manchester St., who thought them very clever – and who in a Short time returned and requested to let him shew them to his Father, I did so, and the next day Mr Dance very kindly gave him an Admission ticket to the Royal Institution Albemarle St. He Attended and took down Sir Humphry Davy's Lecture which he Afterwards Wrote out and drew making drawing, of the Different Apparatus Used – this he took also to the Above Gent. who was well pleased.[42]

In all, Faraday attended four lectures by Davy at the Royal Institution on 29 February, 14 March, 8 April and 10 April 1812. There he heard Davy defend his point and immediately became a convert to Davy's views. Like a good disciple, he set out to convert his friend who clung to Lavoisier's theory. Abbott was informed of the experiments which Davy had used to support his views.

That Oxymuriatic Acid gas is obtained by heating a mixture of the Per-oxide of Manganese, Muriate of soda and sulphuric acid is I conceive no objection to Sir H. D. theory. I have not heard the particular fact explained but conceive it to be thus. Sulphuric acid we will consider as a simple substance. The Per-oxide of Manganese as a lesser oxide and oxygen and the Muriate of Soda as a compound of Chlorine and the metal Sodium. This perhaps you are not fully convinced of but the experiments of Davy prove it. In the process of dis-engaging chlorine the Sulphuric Acid decomposes both the oxide and the Muriate. It combines with the Manganese when united to a lesser portion of oxygen and of course oxygen is liberated. The Muriate being composed of but two parts chlorine and Sodium can only be resolved into those principles. The Chlorine is given out as a gas and is received in jars. The Sodium combines with the Oxygen liberated from the oxide and Soda is formed which is dissolved by the Sulphuric Acid.[43]

This answer to a single objection did not satisfy Abbott and Faraday set out now in earnest to force his friend to capitulate.

I shall therefore enter immediately upon such experiments as I am acquainted with that tend to prove it a simple body, that is, an undecomposed one. You well know that when a taper is immersed burning in Chlorine gas the combustion becomes very dim, the flame appears of a dull red and a great quantity of smoke is emitted. This smoke is the carbonaceous part of the taper. Now on the supposition that Chlorine or Oxymuriatic Acid is a compound of the Muriatic Acid and Oxygen how happens it that [the] hydrogen of the combustible burns and not the carbon. Carbon is considered as having the strongest affinity [for] oxygen of any combustible yet here Hydrogen will burn and Carbon will not; Carbon which has the strongest affinity cannot do what Hydrogen does. Several of the Metals will burn spontaneously in this gas, a proof that the supporter of combustion is not held by so strong an affinity from them and tho' the Carbon will decompose the oxides of those

Metals it cannot combine with the Oxygen of the gas. The fact is no oxygen is present. Nothing but Chlorine, a simple substance, and with Chlorine charcoal has no apparent affinity. Hydrogen possesses a strong attraction for it and therefore we see why that part of the combustible burns and not the Carbon. As a still more simple and decisive experiment I will relate the following of Davy's. He had a glass globe filled with dry chlorine gas and by means of a Voltaic Battery he ignited in this gas two points of charcoal but no change took place, both the combustible and the gas remained unaltered. Carbon at a white heat could abstract no oxygen from chlorine gas whereas at the same time he made Gold, a metal which has the least affinity for oxygen burn in the same portion of gas and by the same power. It combined with the chlorine.

When Chlorine gas is mixed with Hydrogen gas, equal parts of each being put together and are submitted to the action of the Sun's rays or electric sparks are passed through them it is affirmed that the Hydrogen combines with the Oxygen and both Muriatic Acid gas and Water are formed but this affirmation is false. It is not so if the gasses are both perfectly dry. No condensation takes place; no water is formed; nothing but Muriatic Acid remains. This is a very decisive experiment and therefore particular attention has been paid to it. It has been performed with every possible care both by the French Chemists and by Davy and the result has been as I have stated it – no water was obtained; nothing but pure Muriatic Acid gas and as Chlorine and Hydrogen were present it follows that Muriatic Acid is composed of these two bodies.[44]

In still another letter he returned to the charge and fairly overwhelmed his friend. If only he could show Abbott the experiments, let him *see* with his own eyes the results of these experiments. It was all right to describe them, but only when one was actually present could their full force be felt. This, unfortunately, was precisely what Faraday could not do. At the very moment he was led to recognize the fundamental importance of analytical techniques in the evaluation of chemical hypotheses, he also was made aware of his own inadequacies in this area. He could retell other peoples' experiments but this never satisfied him. Just as he had repeated the demonstrations used by Tytler, Major Eeles, and others in electricity, he must, if possible, do the same in chemistry. At the end of his scientific career, he made it clear how important seeing things for himself had been to him.

I was never able to make a fact my own without seeing it [he wrote to a friend], and the descriptions of the best works altogether failed to convey to my mind, such a knowledge of things as to allow myself to form a judgment upon them. It was so with *new* things. If Grove, or Wheatstone, or Gassiot, or any other told me a new fact and wanted my opinion, either of its value, or the cause, or the evidence it could give in any subject, I never could say any thing until I had seen the fact.[45]

The practice of analytical chemistry requires more than a few pieces of sheet metal, a fireplace and a kitchen sink; recourse to a well equipped laboratory is essential, for only from accurate balances and standard reagents can scientific results come.

By the autumn of 1812 Faraday had seemingly reached a dead end in his pursuit of science. His apprenticeship was nearly over and life as a journeyman would offer neither the leisure nor the encouragement that he had found in Mr Riebau's shop. He could still play at science but he knew that without the proper facilities, he must remain forever outside the magic and wondrous realm of scientific discovery. If possible, he must learn to reconcile himself to the role of an interested but passive witness of the drama of science. In a letter to his friend, Huxtable, he cried out his misery.

> I have to beg your pardon for such delay and scarce know how satisfactorily to account for it. I have indeed acted unadvisedly on that point, for conceiving that it would be better to delay my answer until my time was expired, I did so. That took place on October 7, and since then I have had far less time and liberty than before. With respect to a certain place I was disappointed,[46] and am now working at my old trade, the which I wish to leave at the first convenient opportunity. I hope (though fear not) that you will be satisfied with this cause of my silence; and if it appears insufficient to you, I must trust to your goodness. With respect to the progress of the sciences I know but little, and am now likely to know still less; indeed, as long as I stop in my present situation (and I see no chance of getting out of it just yet), I must resign philosophy entirely to those who are more fortunate in the possession of time and means. . . .
>
> I am at present in very low spirits and scarce know how to continue on in a strain that will be anyway agreeable to you. . . .[47]

It was out of this despair that Faraday drew the courage to apply to Sir Joseph Banks, President of the Royal Society, to place him in any scientific situation, however menial. He left a letter pleading for help and called back in a few days. After repeatedly finding no reply he was at last told that Sir Joseph had said 'the letter required no answer'.[48]

Fortune, however, was on Faraday's side. Late in October, Sir Humphry Davy, while working on the explosive substance, chloride of nitrogen, was injured in his eye and could not read or write. Probably upon the recommendation of Mr Dance who had seen examples of his penmanship, Faraday was recommended to Sir Humphry and served for a few days as his amanuensis. In late December, Faraday wrote to Sir Humphry begging for a position in science and sending along the bound volume of notes which he had taken at Davy's lectures. Davy was naturally flattered but could do nothing at the time. Again, however, fortune smiled.

William Payne, who had served (without distinction) as 'fag and scrub' in the laboratory of the Royal Institution, became involved in a brawl and was summarily discharged. That evening, as Faraday was undressing in his bedroom in his home on Weymouth Street he was startled by a thundering knock at the door. On the street below he saw a carriage from which a footman had alighted and left a note for him in which Sir Humphry requested him to call the next morning at the Royal Institution. We may imagine the eagerness and trepidation with which Faraday approached Albemarle Street. At the Royal Institution, Davy asked him if he were still eager to accept any position in science, and when assured that nothing had changed, offered him the place of Assistant in the laboratory. The salary was to be a guinea a week with two rooms at the top of the Institution and fuel and candles. Stipulating only that the Institution should provide him with aprons and that he should be at liberty to use the apparatus, Faraday accepted.[49] The minutes of the meeting of the Managers of the Royal Institution for 1 March 1813, read: 'Resolved – That Michael Faraday be engaged to fill the situation lately occupied by Mr Payne on the same terms'.[50] Faraday had finally entered the Temple!

At the Royal Institution, Faraday plunged happily into his new duties. A mere week after his engagement he was actively at work on chemical problems. His first assignment was the extraction of sugar from beetroot and the making of carbon disulphide, routine tasks but offering the opportunity to improve his skill in chemical manipulation. His extraordinary ability in this area was almost immediately noticed. By the beginning of April he was entrusted with the responsibility of preparing the samples of chloride of nitrogen on which Sir Humphry Davy persisted in working.[51] This compound is very unstable and must be handled with great care. Even the dangers of the laboratory, however, could not dampen his enthusiasm. There is an almost child-like excitement in his tone as he recounted to Abbott the various ways in which things may be blown to smithereens. 'With respect to its detonating power', he wrote, 'it exhibits them with many bodies when a small portion of it is placed in a bason and covered with water and oil or Phosphorus is then brought in contact with it it explodes violently. The bason is shattered to pieces and the water is thrown in all directions. . . .'[52] Faraday did not always escape unscathed. On 9 April he wrote his friend that he had escaped 'not quite unhurt' from some explosions.

> Of these the most terrible was when I was holding between my thumb and finger a small tube containing about $7\frac{1}{2}$ grains of it. My face was within twelve

inches of the tube but I fortunately had on a glass mask. It exploded by the slight heat of a small piece of cement that touched the glass above half an inch from the substance and on the outside. The expansion was so rapid as to blow my hand open, tear off a part of one nail and has made my fingers so sore that I cannot yet use them easily.[53]

Faraday's duties at the Royal Institution were not confined to the laboratory. As other people became aware of his dexterity, he was used more and more as a helper in the lectures which were an integral part of the Institution's functions. No experience was ever lost on Faraday, and he took the opportunity of observing lecturers to refine his own views upon the subject and lay down certain principles which amount almost to a 'Manual for the Lecturer'.[54] No detail escaped his attention. He took up, in order, the best form for a lecture room, modes of lighting and of ventilation, proper subjects for lectures, pointing out why science is the best subject to be presented in this way, the nature of the audience and how and why the lecturer should adjust his discourse to the level of his hearers; the use of diagrams and experiments and, finally, the manner of the lecturer himself. His judgements were shrewd and penetrating and most of his advice will bear listening to today. After reading these remarks no one need wonder that Faraday became the prince of lecturers in Victorian England.

The spring and summer of 1813 passed rapidly as Faraday threw himself into his work. He continued, when possible, to frequent the meetings of the City Philosophical Society although the series of carefully kept notebooks ceased in 1812. With Edward Magrath, he established a 'mutual-improvement plan' consisting of a half-dozen friends from the City Philosophical Society who met periodically 'to read together, and to criticise, correct, and improve each other's pronunciation and construction of language. The discipline was very sturdy, the remarks very plain and open, and the results most valuable.'[55] Other than improving himself and refining and extending his knowledge of chemistry, Faraday had no plans for the future.

Sir Humphry Davy did. In 1812 he had married a rich, handsome widow, Mrs Apreece, and he now felt it time to see more of the world than London. The very idea of a journey outside the British Isles must have seemed silly in 1813 as the Continent was convulsed by the death throes of Napoleon's empire. To believe that an Englishman, representative of that country which with dogged persistence had refused to grant Napoleon his conquests, would be allowed to set foot on French soil without immediate arrest and imprisonment appeared incredible. Yet Davy had certain grounds for hope. In the midst of hostilities, in 1807, the French Institute had awarded him the prize created by Napoleon for outstanding work in galvanic electricity. Napoleon knew full well the power of good public relations, especially when science was involved, for much of his appeal lay in his claim to represent the progressive forces of the Enlightenment in their battle against the darkness of the *Ancien Régime*. Hence, when Davy applied for passports for himself, Lady Davy and their retinue, they were immediately forthcoming. Davy offered Faraday the opportunity of going along and the promise of retrieving his position upon his return. To Faraday, who had never been more than a few miles from London, this was a unique chance to see the world. He accepted and on 13 October 1813, the great adventure began.

4. The University of Europe

In the seventeenth century the English aristocracy developed a unique method of education. After a number of years spent in the study of Latin and Greek and a short stay at Oxford or Cambridge where the necessary polish of a gentleman was obtained, the young aristocrat set out for the Continent accompanied by his tutor. There, amidst the art, architecture, and strange manners of the French, Italians, and Germans, he acquired all the attributes required for his station. Exposed on all sides to strange and new experiences, with a learned companion who could explain all that was mysterious, the young man educated his judgement. To be a man of the world was the goal of this education and, in its pure sense, this worldliness prescribed wide horizons, a sense of tolerance, and the sharpening of one's discrimination and perceptions.

It was on such a Grand Tour that Faraday embarked in 1813. True, he was neither wealthy nor an aristocrat, but Sir Humphry Davy could help him overleap both these obstacles. And, as tutor, he had Sir Humphry himself. Davy was at the height of his fame, could gain entrée to any society which might be expected to interest Faraday, and was ever eager to explain the phenomena met with on the road and in the cities through which they passed. It was this unique educational opportunity which Faraday grasped so eagerly. With high excitement and eagerness he set out on the great adventure.

> This morning [he wrote in his Journal started especially for this trip] formed a new epoch in my life. I have never before within my recollection left London at a greater distance than twelve miles and now I leave it perhaps for many years and to visit spots between which and home whole realms will

intervene. 'Tis indeed a strange venture at this time to trust ourselves in a foreign and hostile country where also so little regard is had to protestations and honour that the slightest suspicion would be sufficient to separate us for ever from England and perhaps from life. But curiosity has frequently encurred dangers as great as these and therefore why should I wonder at it in the present instance. If we return safe the pleasures of recollection will be highly enhanced by the dangers encountered and a never failing consolation is that whatever be the fate of our party variety a great source of amusement and pleasure must occur.[56]

From the very first he was made aware of how limited his horizons had been. On the trip to Plymouth his naïve concepts of geology suffered a rude shock by the revelations provided by the 'mountainous' (!) terrain through which the coach passed.

I was more taken by the scenery today than by any thing else I have ever seen. It came upon me unexpectedly and caused a kind of revolution in my ideas respecting the nature of the earth's surface. That such a revolution was necessary is I confess not much to my credit and yet I can assign to myself a very satisfactory reason in the habit of ideas induced by an acquaintance with no other green surface than that within 3 miles of London. Devonshire however presented scenery very different to this. The mountainous nature of the country continually put forward new forms and objects and the landscape changed before the eye more rapidly than the organ could observe it. This day gave me some ideas of the pleasures of travelling and have raised my expectations of future enjoyments to a very high point.[57]

These expectations were very rapidly dashed, however, as France hove into view. The port and town of Morlaix at which the company disembarked was a dismal place with only the most primitive accommodation. Faraday could not believe his eyes when he was preceded through the 'hotel' door by a local horse! His impressions of France were not improved by the next morning's ritual of going through Customs. Anyone who has ever been kept waiting while eager to pass beyond the forbidding office of the Douane will sympathize with Faraday.

. . . The Douane was not yet open and we had to wait patiently or otherwise for some time looking on our things but not daring to touch them. At last business commenced. The officers having arranged themselves on the edge of the quay some thirty or forty inhabitants of the town ran and tumbled down the steps and leaping into the barge seized some one thing and some another and conveyed them to the landing place above. This sight alone was a curious one for they being totally destitute of all method and regularity it seemed as if a parcel of thieves were scampering away with what was not their own.[58]

After some delay all was cleared, passports had been checked, the carriage reassembled, baggage loaded, horses and a postillion obtained and

Morlaix left behind. In his Journal Faraday now noted aspects of the scenery and the odd (because different) customs of the natives. How many other travellers have echoed his words!

On French cuisine:

On the right hand of the passage . . . is the kitchen. Here a fire of wood is generally surrounded by idlers, beggars or nondescripts of the town who meet to warm themselves and chatter to the mistress and they hold their stations most tenaciously though the processes of cooking are in progress. I think it is impossible for an English person to eat the things that come out of this place except through ignorance or actual and oppressive hunger and yet perhaps appearances may be worse than the reality for in some cases their dishes are to the taste excellent and inviting but then they require whilst on the table a dismissal of all thoughts respecting the cooking or kitchen.[59]

On French living quarters:

In the internal decoration of apartments the French apply glass and marble two beautiful materials in much greater abundance than the English do. In Brass working also they have risen to great perfection and their application of this material to the construction of ornamented time pieces is exceedingly ingenious and beautiful. In most of the good rooms that I have seen glass has appeared in profusion either as large framed mirrors or as plates of considerable magnitude let into the wall and in some of the coffee houses where decoration has been carried to its utmost bounds the number is so great and the positions are so judicious that they produce on every side an appearance of infinity.

. . . To conclude, French apartments are magnificent, English apartments are comfortable; French apartments are highly ornamented, English apartments are clean; French apartments are to be seen, English apartments enjoyed; and the style of each kind best suits the people of the respective countries.[60]

On buying souvenirs in Paris:

I am quite out of patience with the infamous exhorbitance of these Parisians. They seem to have neither sense of honesty nor shame in their dealings. They will ask you twice the value of a thing with as much coolness as if they were going to give it you and when you have offered them half their demand and on their accepting it you reproach them with unfair dealings they tell you 'you can afford to pay'. It would seem that every tradesman here is a rogue unless they have different meanings for words to what we have.[61]

Although France at times tried his patience, it also fascinated him. From French pigs, which he likened to greyhounds in build, to the glowworm which intrigued him, France seemed to breed wonders. In Paris, when Sir Humphry Davy did not need him, he visited all the tourist attractions. Armed with a special passport which allowed him to enter all public property such as museums and libraries on any day, he spent many a happy hour.[62] Indeed, much of his Journal during his stay both at Paris and later at Rome reads like an ordinary guide-book. Every important building was described in detail, with dimensions where possible, and it is more than probable that Faraday did simply copy out descriptions in order better to call to his memory the sights he had seen.

Some towns and activities, however, were quite off the beaten track. Sir Humphry had embarked upon the journey not only to see the world but to meet the men of science whom he had hitherto known only in their writings. As a practical chemist, he was also interested in laboratories, courses in chemistry and chemical manufactures. After the first confusion of settling in Paris, Davy set out to see the Parisian world of science and Faraday accompanied him.

On 13 November they visited a sugar factory. Faraday's first task at the Royal Institution had been the extraction of sugar from beetroot and he was anxious to observe the industrial process in action. On the 18th, Faraday was off to the laboratory of Nicolas-Louis Vauquelin who combined the career of analytical chemist with that of manufacturer of chemical products. There Faraday observed the French method of chlorine manufacture (used in the preparation of commercial bleach) and noted the differences between the English and French processes. The real excitement began, however, on Tuesday, 23 November. André-Marie Ampère, later to achieve eternal renown from his theory of electrodynamics, together with the chemists, Nicolas Clément and Charles Bernard Desormes, called on Davy to show him a peculiar substance. In 1811, Bernard Courtois, a former student at the *École polytechnique* and then a manufacturer of commercial soda, was purifying a solution obtained from burned sea algae by adding sulphuric acid to the liquor. To his great surprise, a beautiful purple vapour with an odour similar to that of chlorine arose and condensed on cold objects into dark crystals with a metallic lustre. Courtois noted some of the reactions of this substance with oxygen and carbon and suspected a close similarity between it and chlorine. His means were too limited and he felt his training insufficient for him to investigate the material with the necessary rigour. Hence, he asked his friends Clément and Desormes to work upon it. Both men were competent chemists but they were hindered by their adherence to the prevailing chemical theory of the day. Like Courtois they rapidly discovered the similarity between their unknown substance and chlorine. But, the question was, what was chlorine? Davy was almost alone in insisting that it was an element. Clément and Desormes were not prepared to challenge their peers and so were content to describe the properties of the substance and leave the question of its ultimate chemical nature untouched.

When Davy was presented with a sample, he immediately went to work on it. When he travelled, he always took a small, portable chest of chemical apparatus with him and he now proceeded to apply such simple tests as he could make. 'From them', Faraday noted, 'he is inclined to consider it as a compound of chlorine and an unknown body.'[63] By the afternoon of the same day, after more tests and time for reflection, Davy changed his mind and Faraday reported, 'Sir Humphry Davy now thinks it contains no chlorine'.[64] With that rapidity of thought which so often dazzled his contemporaries, Davy had leaped from similarity to analogy. The new substance did not have similar properties to chlorine because it contained chlorine but because it was *like* chlorine. And, if chlorine were an element, as Davy so firmly believed, then so must this new substance be one. With this idea, and master of the method by which he had proven the elementary nature of chlorine, Davy, with Faraday at his side, launched his attack. The compounds and reactions of the substance were carefully studied.[65] By 11 December Davy was prepared to apply the force of electricity and, as he suspected, could not effect a decomposition.

Sir Humphry Davy had occasion today for a voltaic pile to make experiments on the new substance now called iodine and I obtained one from M. Chevreul. This pile consisted of circular plates about four inches in diameter. They were united in pairs, a zinc and copper plate being soldered together by the whole of one of the surfaces. They were made dishing or concave by which means a greater quantity of the solution used could be retained between them. Twenty four of these double plates with a solution of muriate of ammonia to which a little nitric acid had been added produced a good ignition with a little charcoal and platina wire. This ignition had no effect on the violet coloured gas and as yet it must be considered as a simple body.[66]

Davy did not hesitate a moment in sending his results to the Royal Society. In a paper dated Paris, Dec. 10, 1813, Davy described the series of experiments he had performed and suggested the name *iodine* for the new substance. He also insisted 'from all the facts that have been stated, there is every reason to consider this new substance as *an undecompounded body*'.[67] We may imagine Faraday's excitement in all this. Recall the enthusiasm with which he had regaled Abbott with the proofs of the elementary nature of chlorine. Now he was actually on the scene of discovery, aiding, in however minor a way, at the birth of a new element.

There was more in this for Faraday than the discovery of iodine. In later life he was always aware of the trap of mental complacency and over-confidence in human knowledge. Behind his discoveries lay the ever-present attitude that what was known was infinitesimal in proportion to what remained to be discovered. He was, therefore, constantly alert to the small anomaly, the minor quiver of a needle which ought not to move, but, heedless of theory, did. The lesson was often taught in the nine-teenth century and Faraday was an apt pupil. The discovery of iodine served him as a valuable lesson in humility in the face of nature's complexity and mysteries. As Faraday wrote at the time in his Journal:

> The discovery of this substance in matters so common and supposed so well known must be a stimulus of no small force to the enquiring minds of modern chemists. It is a proof of the imperfect state of the science even in those parts considered as completely understood. It is an earnest of the plentiful reward that awaits the industrious cultivator of this the most extensive branch of experimental knowledge. It adds in an eminent degree to the beautiful facts that abound in it and presents another wide field for the exercise of the mind.[68]

On 29 December the party left Paris on its way south. The day was clear, the scenery beautiful and Faraday still eager to travel and see new places. At Lyon they rested for a short while, then took the road to Montpellier, by way of Avignon and Nîmes. In his Journal Faraday noted the major points of interest – the Pont du Gard, the Arena, and beautiful Greek-style temple (La Maison carrée) at Nîmes. On 8 January Mont-pellier was reached and everyone settled down again for a more or less extended stay. Not much was done here in the way of science, but Faraday thoroughly enjoyed himself. The scenery surrounding Montpellier pleased him and he spent many happy hours walking and viewing the sights. Behind the peace, serenity, and bucolic tone of Faraday's Journal lies a most incongruous situation. While Faraday was roaming the countryside at will, the inhabitants of Montpellier were bracing them-selves for an invasion by the forces of the Duke of Wellington. It is almost impossible for an inhabitant of the twentieth century to believe that a party of English citizens could go about their ordinary affairs in the middle of an empire locked in a struggle to the death with England without the slightest inconvenience. Only occasionally was there even a hint of suspicion and this came about on quite suspicious occasions. In his walks Faraday noted the fort above the town and, realizing that the view from there would be magnificent, casually entered it.

> On that side of the Esplanade furthest from the town stands the fort, a place of considerable sise, great strength and having the town completely in its

power. I entered it and after winding along some dark passages came out into the open space within. The stroll round the ramparts was pleasant but I imagine that at times whilst enjoying myself I was transgressing for the sentinels regarded me sharply and more particularly, at least I thought so, as I stood looking at one corner where from some cause or other the fortifications were injured. I finished my walk however without personal interruption and was not sorry for it as I had opportunities of seeing the distant country from higher points and better situations than from the esplanade itself.[69]

On 7 February, in an effort to find some warmth, for the season had been very cold, Davy and his companions left Montpellier on the road to Italy. The party retraced its steps to Nîmes, where Faraday again explored the architectural ruins, and then on to Nice. On the road, Sir Humphry gave extemporaneous lectures on geology, meteorology, and the zodiacal light which were received with interest. All was noted in Faraday's Journal.

From Nice, the voyage became more difficult. A passage over the *Alpes maritimes* in the middle of an unusually severe winter must not have been the most comfortable trip imaginable. Faraday made no mention of Lady Davy and her maid, who were probably carried over the pass in chaises, but he and Sir Humphry walked. The way led through deep snow in bitter cold weather, but again Faraday chose to record the scenery and the geological formations rather than the hardships. On 21 February the travellers were at Turin where Faraday enjoyed the spectacle of the *carnivale*. Turin was soon left behind in favour of Genoa. There Davy procured some electric fishes to try and determine whether the electric shock they gave would decompose water. They were too small and weak, however, to produce a perceptible result.[70] The sought-for effect was an important one for there was some doubt as to whether 'animal electricity' was the same as that obtained from other sources. In 1832 Faraday was to return to the problem and prove this identity.[71]

At Genoa, the party embarked for Tuscany and proceeded to Florence, where they were to stay from 10 March to 3 April. Davy was particularly eager to borrow the use of the laboratory and equipment of the *Accademia del Cimento*. Faraday was excited by a glimpse of Galileo's telescope and impressed by the richness of the equipment.

Almost immediately upon arrival in Florence Davy went to work. The first matter at hand was to check his earlier results of experiments on iodine with the more accurate equipment now available. This occupied three days after which Davy turned his attention to another problem. The Grand Duke owned a superb and large lens which could be used for igniting diamonds. The question of the nature of the diamond had intrigued chemists for half a century and the results were still in doubt. The problem arose from the fact that the only detectable product of combustion was carbon dioxide, indicating that the diamond was composed of pure carbon. But if this were so, what was ordinary carbon black composed of? It was impossible to believe that substances as different in physical and chemical properties as diamond and charcoal could be the same in substance.

Davy had for years been sharpening his analytical powers and he now felt confident that the elusive difference would not escape him. With the great lens of the Grand Duke he ignited a number of diamonds and collected the combustion product. It was pure carbon dioxide. When graphite was burned in a similar fashion after care had been taken to exclude water, water vapour as well as carbon dioxide was produced. 'From these experiments,' Faraday wrote, 'according to Sir H. Davy it is probable that diamond is pure carbon and the black compounds such as plumbago, carbon etc. combinations of carbon and hydrogen.'[72] Davy's results were erroneous but understandable for it is very difficult to dry finely divided carbon completely. Hence, the water vapour observed was not the product of the combustion of a supposed combined hydrogen, but the release of water as the carbon burned. When the amount of hydrogen 'present' was calculated from the quantity of water 'formed' it turned out to be very small. In his published paper based on the experiments at Florence and others at Rome, Davy abandoned his supposition that graphite was a compound of diamond and hydrogen and supported the view that the diamond, graphite, charcoal, and carbon black were all carbon but in different crystalline forms.[73]

Florence was the high spot, both scientifically and personally, for Faraday. He remarked in his Journal as he took the road for Rome, 'Left Florence this morning with regret for in no place since I left England have I been so comfortable and happy.'[74]

In Rome, the only science done was to accompany Davy to the laboratory of Signor Morichini who claimed to be able to magnetize a needle by drawing the violet rays of the solar spectrum along it. This connexion of light and magnetism had long been sought but the experiment did not succeed and neither Davy nor Faraday was convinced of the truth of the phenomenon. For the rest, it was one sight-seeing tour after another. With his usual energy, Faraday threw himself into the exploration of the Holy City, covering an amazing amount of territory and seeing everything he could. There was a side trip to Naples and an ascent of Mount Vesuvius with Davy there to explain the geology and chemistry of volcanoes. The Queen of Naples presented Sir Humphry with some pots of colours unearthed at Pompeii and Davy undertook their analysis. Except for being the first application of analytical chemistry to the problems of archaeology this diversion was of little importance.[75]

From Rome, the road led to Geneva, then back to Rome where the first hint of personal difficulties between Faraday and Lady Davy is to be found. The Journal is strangely silent about the day-to-day relations of Faraday, Sir Humphry, and Lady Davy, but in a great emotional rush, Faraday's complaints now poured out in a letter to his friend, Benjamin Abbott. After a year away from home and after suffering constant humiliation at Lady Davy's hands, Faraday questioned the wisdom of the whole journey.

Alas! how foolish perhaps was I to leave home, to leave those whom I loved and who loved me for a time uncertain in its length, but certainly long and which perhaps may stretch out into eternity! And what are the boasted advantages to be gained? Knowledge. Yes, knowledge but what knowledge? Knowledge of the world, of men, of manners, of books, and of languages – things in themselves valuable above all price but which every day shews me prostituted to the basest purposes. Alas! how degrading it is to be learned when it places us on a level with rogues and scoundrels! How disgusting when it serves but to shew us the artifices and deceit of all around! How can it be compared with the virtue and integrity of those who, taught by nature alone, pass through life contented, happy, their honour unsullied, their minds uncontaminated, their thoughts virtuous – ever striving to do good, shunning evil and doing to others as they would be done by? Were I by this long probation to acquire some of this vaunted knowledge in what should I be wiser? Knowledge of the world opens the eyes to the deceit and corruption of mankind; of men, serves but to shew the human mind debased by the vilest passions; of manners, points out the exterior corruptions which naturally result from the interior; of books, the most innocent, occasions disgust when it is considered that even that has been debased by the corruptions of many; and of languages serves but to shew in a still wider view what the knowledge of men and of manners teaches us. What a result is obtained from knowledge and how much must the virtuous human mind be humiliated in considering its own powers, when at the same time they give him such a despicable view of his fellow creatures! Ah, Ben, I am not sure that I have acted wisely in leaving a pure and certain enjoyment for such a pursuit.[76]

We may imagine Abbott's surprise upon receiving this *cri de cœur* and, although his letters to Faraday have not survived, there can be little doubt that he wrote his friend to ask what had caused this deep despair. By the time he received this request and was able to write again, Faraday's mood had improved somewhat and he was able to discuss his problem with fair objectivity.

The origins of his unhappiness lay in the fact that Sir Humphry Davy's valet's wife had been fearful that her husband (a native of Flanders) would never return alive if he accompanied Sir Humphry to the Continent. Her tears were stronger than Sir Humphry's arguments and Sir Humphry had been forced to leave England without a manservant. Davy then had asked Faraday if he would perform a few extra services until the party reached Paris, at which time, a proper valet would be engaged. Faraday reluctantly agreed and was trapped. At Paris, Davy could find no one who suited him, nor was anyone who seemed qualified met with at the other cities they visited. As often happens, a temporary arrangement turned into a permanent responsibility. Faraday did not resent his relationship with Davy for 'Sir Humphry has at all times endeavoured to keep me from the performance of those things which did not form a part of my duty and which might be disagreeable.'[77] The real problem was Lady Davy. Abbott, many, many years later recounted a tale told him by Faraday that illustrated one of her faults.

> When in a boat in the Gulf of Genoa a sudden storm of wind (not unusual there) placed them for a time in some danger, and she (Lady D.) was so alarmed that she became almost faint and in consequence ceased from talking. This, [Faraday] told me, was so great a relief to him that he quite enjoyed the quiet and did not at all regret the cause that produced it, though the situation was for some time critical.[78]

Besides being a chatterbox, Lady Davy was a towering snob.

> She is haughty and proud to an excessive degree and delights in making her inferiors feel her power. She wishes to roll in the full tide of pleasures such as she is capable of enjoying but when she can with impunity, that is when her equals do not notice it and Sir H. is ignorant of it, she will exert herself very considerably to deprive her family of enjoyments. When I first left England, unused as I was to high life and to politeness, unversed as I was in the art of expressing sentiments I did not feel I was little suited to come within the observation and under the power in some degree of one whose whole life consists of forms, etiquette and manners. I believed at that time that she hated me and her evil disposition made her endeavour to thwart me in all my views and to debase me in my occupations. This at first was a source of great uneasiness to me and often times made me very dull and discontented and if I could have come home again at that time you should have seen me before I had left England six months. As I became more acquainted with the manners of the world and those things necessary in my station and understood better her true character I learned to despise her taunts and resist her power and this kind of determined conduct added to a little polishing which the friction of the world had naturally produced in your friend made her restrain her spleen from its full course to a more moderate degree. At present I laugh at her

whims which now seldom extend to me but at times a greater degree of ill humour than ordinary involves me in a fray which on occasion creates a coolness between us all for two or three days, for on these occasions, Sir H. can scarcely keep neuter and from different reasons he can scarcely choose his side.[79]

This unpleasantness, which would seem to have been getting worse as Faraday refused to suffer insults silently, together with the fact that Napoleon had made his escape from Elba and again threatened Europe, probably determined Davy to end the tour. On 16 April 1815 Faraday wrote his mother from Brussels to inform her that he hoped to be home within three days.[80] The great adventure was over, and Faraday returned to the London he loved.

The young man who landed on English soil in the spring of 1815 was quite different from the youth who had left it in 1813. He had seen a good part of the world, realized its complexity and diversity, and gained a good deal of insight into the ways of men. He had met some of the foremost scientists of the day and had both impressed and been impressed by them. With Davy he had gained entrée to society and many an entry in his Journal testifies to his low opinion of the worth of society's acceptance. Unlike Davy he was never to be seduced away from the pursuit of truth by the glitter of the salon.

On the practical level, he had learned French and Italian well enough to speak the former adequately and to read both with facility. The brief visits the party had made to the German states had not been long enough to permit him to gain any familiarity with that tongue. Throughout his life he remained dependent upon translations for knowledge of the achievements of the German scientists. In the realm of chemistry, he had continued to sharpen his analytical skill. Davy's portable chemical kit required extreme care if results were to be meaningful and although much work was done in fully equipped laboratories, quite a bit was also successfully carried out with the bare minimum of apparatus.

In one area, it is astonishing to realize that Faraday learned little and cared even less. One would suppose that the political convulsions through which Europe was passing under his very eyes would have had some interest for him. All his life, England and France had been locked in battle but the issues, their causes, their possible effects on Europe and the world simply did not engage his attention. When news of Napoleon's escape from Elba reached his ears, he noted in his Journal: 'I heard for news that Bonaparte was again at liberty. Being no politician, I did not trouble myself much about it, though I suppose it will have a strong influence on the affairs of Europe.'[81] This total lack of political interest remained with him throughout his life. When other scientists like Charles Babbage or Sir John Herschel were exercising themselves with the task of reforming Parliament or reforming the Royal Society, Faraday could spare the time only for a casual glance away from his research.

Of all the advantages of his journey, however, none was more important than his constant and close association with Sir Humphry Davy. With all his faults, and they were many, Davy was still one of the most brilliant scientists of his time. Furthermore, Davy's trip coincided with a profound alteration in his theoretical ideas. As Davy strove to reweave the fabric of chemical theory which his own researches on chlorine had rent, he was forced to recast his ideas in new moulds. Faraday not only witnessed but learned from this theoretical reorientation. As we shall see in the next chapter, it was at this time that Faraday's basic theoretical views were formulated and it was from Davy that Faraday received a way of looking at the activities of matter which was to lead him to his great discoveries. By 1815, then, the fledgeling was ready to try his wings. He was master of chemical technique and armed with a vision of the structure of matter. It was time to begin to give, rather than take, and to launch himself upon the broad stream of scientific advance.

5. Journeyman Chemist

Almost immediately upon his return to England, Faraday was engaged again at the Royal Institution. His new position, whose duties he took up on 7 May 1815, reflected his advance in knowledge. He was now an Assistant and Superintendent of the Apparatus of the Laboratory and Mineralogical Collection! His salary was raised to thirty shillings a week and, after a short battle with the occupant who refused to relinquish them, he moved into the rooms at the top of the Institution to which his new responsibilities entitled him.

The pattern of his occupations was now significantly different from what it had been before his European tour. Sir Humphry Davy was often absent from the Royal Institution and from London, and Faraday's services were often required for the preparation of lectures by the staff of the Institution and guest speakers. In particular, his duties threw him into almost constant contact with William T. Brande, the Professor of Chemistry who offered a yearly course in chemistry for medical students. Faraday aided Brande in setting up the experiments used to demonstrate the principles of chemistry and also worked with him on the commercial analyses which Brande undertook. His skill as an analytical chemist soon made him indispensable.

His duties, his interests, and his burning desire for self-improvement combined to drive him onward. By the middle of July he wrote to Abbott that 'Friday is my only spare evening this week',[82] and in September he pointed out to his friend that 'had you come last night you must have been content with the laboratory for I did not leave it (and could not) 'till 9^h 30^m.'[83] The same theme runs through most of his letters to his friend and the letters themselves became hasty notes where before they had been lengthy and carefully composed communications.

All his time, however, was not spent in the laboratory. Faraday utilized the library facilities of the Royal Institution to their fullest extent. To keep his theoretical knowledge at the same level as his laboratory skill, he set out systematically to investigate the progress of chemistry since the end of the eighteenth century. The record of this herculean task is, fortunately, preserved. In the Wellcome Medical Historical Library are three volumes bound by Faraday. They consist of William Thomas Brande's *A Manual of Chemistry* (8vo, London, 1819) which Faraday tore apart and then rebound with blank quarto pages interleaved. Opposite each topic treated by Brande, Faraday jotted bibliographical references and other notes. The sheer volume of this work, together with the demands of his other duties, indicates that this was a labour of many years. Since the systematic notations generally end in 1821, it is probable that he began the project soon after he returned from the Continent, and, because of his already failing memory, kept a file of his readings. These were then later transferred to their proper place opposite Brande's text. The list of journals searched is a silent testimony to Faraday's energy, determination, and thoroughness. It is here reproduced as it appears on the last page of volume I.

Quarterly Journal of Science to Vol. 13
Edinburgh Phil. Jour. to Vol. 7
Annals of Philosophy Old Series to Vol. 15. All that were published
Annals of Philosophy N.[ew] S.[eries] to Vol. 6
Philosophical Transactions xci to cxi 1821
Nicholson's 4to Philosophical Journal. Vols. i, ii, iii, iv, v (the whole)
Philosophical Magazine
Annales de Chimie
Bibliothèque Brittanique [*sic*]
Bibliothèque Universelle
Journal de Physique
Manchester Memoires

Cambridge Phil. Trans.
Edin. Phil. Trans.
Nicholson 8vo Philosophical Journal. 36 volumes (the whole)
Lewis' Commerce of the Arts 4th 1763
Quar. Jour. of Sci. N.S. 6 and 7 not 1.2.3.4. & 5 as yet

In 1816, Faraday published his first scientific paper, 'Analysis of Native Caustic Lime of Tuscany'.[84] The distance from his original employment and views of his future was steadily becoming greater. It was now even possible to dream of a creative career in science, although his first paper was a slight effort. Nevertheless, it was an important step for Faraday. His account of the circumstances attending its appearance reveals what it meant to him. Writing at the end of his scientific career, in 1859, he appended a note to the reprinted paper in his *Experimental Researches in Chemistry and Physics.*

> I reprint this paper at full length. It was the beginning of my communications to the public, and in its results very important to me. Sir Humphry Davy gave me the analysis to make as a first attempt in chemistry at a time when my fear was greater than my confidence, and both far greater than my knowledge; at a time also when I had no thought of ever writing an original paper on science. The addition of his own comments and the publication of the paper encouraged me to go on making, from time to time, other slight communications....[85]

The papers that followed in the next three years have obvious origins and may be put into three categories. They are on topics suggested by Sir Humphry Davy's work or by that of Brande or analyses requested by friends of the Royal Institution and entrusted to Faraday. Papers such as 'Notice of some experiments on flame made by Sir H. Davy'[86] and 'On the wire-gauze safe-lamps'[87] were the results of working with Davy on the invention of the safety lamp. The articles on benzoic acid and the benzoates of mercury, iron, and zinc[88] followed work done by Brande earlier.[89] The analyses of palm wine[90] and of the strength of Aetna wines[91] were done as favours and printed only because of their curiosity value.

The analyses, in general, are terse and impersonal, reporting only the necessary details. One example will suffice to illustrate this aspect of Faraday's style.

Benzoates – Benzoates of Mercury

Benzoic acid combined with both oxides of mercury, forming salts which are perfectly distinct one from the other. The black oxide with benzoic acid forms a salt of a dull white colour, insoluble in water or in alcohol, and yielding black oxide to alkalies. Heated, it melted and was decomposed; part of the acid flew off whilst another part was decomposed.

The red oxide heated with benzoic acid in water, gave a yellowish white salt, insoluble in water or alcohol, fusible when heated, and yielding red oxide to alkalies.[92]

The human element was not always so rigorously excluded. The frankness and willingness to acknowledge mistakes which were to mark his mature papers were foreshadowed by the remark at the end of his analysis of palm wine that, 'An accident prevented any experiments on the quantity of salts contained in this portion of wine.'[93]

His analytical skill was not always confined to such trivial topics. In 1818 a Dr von Vest (or West) from Vienna reported the discovery of a new metal which he christened Sirium. Some of this new metal was sent to Sir Humphry Davy, who sent it to the chemist Hatchett, who, in turn, gave some to Faraday to analyse. After careful examination, Faraday concluded, 'It is evident that it has no claim to the character of a peculiar metal, but is a very impure mixed regulus. It contains sulphur, iron, nickel and arsenic; and these made up very nearly, if not quite, its whole mass.'[94]

Davy was delighted with his pupil's work and wrote warmly from Rome:

> . . . by a letter from Mr Hatchett I find that you have found the parallax of Mr West's Sirium, and that, as I expected, he is mistaken. . . . Mr Hatchett's letter contained praises of you which were very gratifying to me; and pray believe me there is no one more interested in your success and welfare than your sincere well-wisher and friend,
>
>   H. Davy.[95]

These modest little articles served to create some respect for Faraday as an analyst of skill and a competent chemist. His reputation was enhanced by Sir Humphry Davy who acknowledged his indebtedness to Faraday's laboratory ability. In the preface to the paper 'On the Safety Lamp for Preventing Explosions in Mines, Houses Lighted by Gas, Spirit Warehouses or Magazines in Ships, etc., with some Researches on Flame'[96] Davy wrote, 'I am myself indebted to Mr Michael Faraday for much able assistance in the prosecution of my experiments.'[97] In his work on the compounds of phosphorus, Davy went even further. 'In these experiments,' he wrote, 'and in all the others detailed in this paper, I received much useful assistance from Mr Faraday, of the Royal Institution; and much of their value, if they shall be found to possess any, will be owing to his accuracy and steadiness of manipulation.'[98]

Such praise must have done much to encourage Faraday and help him overcome the diffidence he felt in assuming the mantle of chemist. Fame, however, had its drawbacks. The analysis of the salts of benzoic acid, or of palm wine added miniscule facts to the corpus of chemistry, and could not be expected to arouse any spirit of controversy. Davy in his work on phosphorus, however, was challenging a man of equal stature – Jöns Jacob Berzelius of Stockholm. Berzelius, the steady, thorough analyst, had always been suspicious of Davy's seemingly slipshod methods. To have his results questioned, not even by Davy, but by Davy's unknown assistant was too much. A thunderbolt was hurled in the most prestigious chemical journal of the time – the *Annales de chimie et de physique*. After pointing out the manifold sources of error in the various analyses made, Berzelius concluded with a chilling paragraph directed at Faraday and Davy alike.

> If M. Davy would be so kind as to take the pains of repeating these experiments himself he should be convinced of the fact that when it comes to exact analyses, one should never entrust them into the care of another person; and this is above all a necessary rule to observe when it comes to refuting the works of other chemists who have not shown themselves ignorant of the art of making exact experiments.[99]

Faraday never mentioned this incident but its effect upon him can readily be imagined. He knew he was but a beginner and was ever conscious of his shortcomings. We have already noted the emphasis which Dr Watts had placed upon the accurate determination of facts. His errors in the analysis of the compounds of phosphorus now drove that lesson home. Henceforth, his determinations were to be repeated time and time again until no doubt of their accuracy could be entertained. His laboratory Journal bears eloquent witness in page after page devoted to the torturing of his evidence to the lesson so painfully learned. There were to be further challenges to the interpretations of the facts Faraday presented, but never again was the charge of factual inaccuracy to be maintained against him.

From 1815 to 1819 Faraday not only contributed to chemistry through the pages of the *Quarterly Journal of Science*. He also spread his knowledge of chemical science through the medium of lectures. On 17 January 1816 he addressed the members of the City Philosophical Society on the subject of the general properties of matter. Throughout 1816, 1817, and 1818 this was followed at more or less equal intervals by a total of sixteen further lectures treating the whole of inorganic chemistry. A detailed analysis of these lectures must be deferred until the next chapter, but it is appropriate to notice the maturity and breadth of Faraday's thought here. Most of the lectures were carefully written out and even more carefully organized.[100] The organization of the series is admirable. Faraday began with a discussion of the general properties of matter. In the next lecture he introduced and illustrated the phenomenon of attraction, particularly as it was manifested in cohesion. This was then contrasted in the third lecture with the force of chemical affinity and instances were cited to illustrate the differences between these two attractive forces. The fourth lecture dealt with that form of matter that appeared to be exempt from the ordinary natural laws – namely radiant matter. Having thus presented the general properties of all substances, Faraday then began a detailed examination of specific chemicals. He followed Davy in dividing the elements into those which are electronegative and those which are electropositive. Oxygen, chlorine, iodine, and fluorine were then examined as the only (then) known members of the former class. Hydrogen and the electropositive elements formed the subject of the sixth lecture. Because of their peculiar properties, separate lectures were devoted to nitrogen, sulphur and phosphorus, and carbon. The importance of combustion and its mechanism was then outlined. The lectures finished with a series on the metals (treated generally and then individually) and the alkalis and earths. As a whole, these lectures provided a well-balanced and well-thought-out introduction to inorganic chemistry. The exposition was clear, the ideas orderly and the experiments both apt and striking. There is not here that brilliance and spontaneity for which Faraday was later to be renowned, but his competence is unquestionable. By 1818 Faraday had become a professional.

Faraday was not, however, narrowly professional. Although he was aware of his ability in chemistry, he did not, for that, give up his efforts for self-improvement in other areas. In his commonplace book there are the notes he took, almost verbatim, of lectures on oratory by a Mr B. H. Smart.[101] In July 1818 he also joined enthusiastically in the formation of another smaller group devoted to self-improvement in which both subject and method of presentation would be subjected to close critical scrutiny. Together with four members of the City Philosophical Society, a class book was instituted. Each member was to serve as secretary for two months. The secretary's duty was to inscribe the essays written by the members in the book and to pass the book around amongst the membership. Periodic meetings were held in which the essays were discussed. These essays will be considered more fully in Chapter Two but their range should be noted. A few titles will give some idea of the subjects treated.[102] They include, 'On Study', 'On Argument', 'The Charms of Sleep', 'A Mathematical Love Letter', 'On the early introduction of Females to Society', 'Reflections on Death', 'Effeminacy and Luxury'.

Ben Abbott still retained his primary place in Faraday's affections as friend and was still appealed to for help in the development of good English usage,[103] but time for purely social pleasures was becoming increasingly rare. In 1817, Faraday had taken on a pupil recommended to him by Sir Humphry Davy; he had his lectures at the City Philosophical Society; periodic meetings with his class-book society; laboratory preparations to make and so on. By the spring of 1819, his weekly schedule ran thus:

> On Monday evening there is a scientific meeting of Members here and every other Monday a dinner, to both of which my company is requested. On Tuesday evening I have a Pupil who comes at 6 o'clk and stops till 9, engaged in private lessons. On Wednesday the [City Philosophical] Society requires my aid. Thursday is my only evening for accidental engagements. Friday, my pupil returns and stops his three hours; and on Saturday I have to arrange my little private business.[104]

His daytime hours were occupied by his duties at the Royal Institution and growing clientele who desired his professional services. In 1818, for example, he was engaged by a Mr Cocks to give technical advice on a patent suit in which Cocks was engaged,[105] and in 1820 he was retained as a scientific expert in a suit involving the question of the inflammability of hot oil used in the refining of sugar.[106] On top of all this, he had, in 1818, begun his first important original research with James Stodart on the nature of steel and its alloys. By 1819, therefore, he could no longer be considered as anything but a professional and practising chemist. He had finished his course of studies and was prepared to launch forth upon a career of discovery.

Faraday, himself, rarely referred to himself as a chemist. He preferred the title of natural philosopher. We have, so far, focussed attention solely upon his technical development. Before scrutinizing the decade of intense chemical activity from 1820 to 1830 we must retrace our steps somewhat. Having followed the education of a chemist, let us now trace out the stages in the education of a philosopher.

References

1. R.I., Faraday MSS., 'Three Lectures on Electricity illustrated with Experiments and Observations delivered by Mr Tatum at No. 53 Dorset St., Salisbury Square, Fleet Street and copied by M.F. 1810.'

2. R. Warner, Burford, Oxon., England, owns the original letters of Faraday and Benjamin Abbott and two essays by Abbott on Faraday written after the latter's death. Mention of Faraday's skill with the mallet is made in 'Jottings

from Memory in reference to my dear and deceased Friend M. Faraday', p. 2. These letters and essays will be cited henceforth as 'Warner MSS'.

3. Quoted in Sir F. Pollock, *Personal Remembrances of Sir Frederick Pollock* (2 vols., London, 1887), *1*, 247.

4. R.I., Faraday MSS., G. Riebau to ——, n.p. n.d. The letter may be dated some time between late 1813 and early 1815. Internal evidence also shows that it was addressed to the editor of some publication. Riebau was holding Michael Faraday up as an example worth emulating by 'your younger readers'.

5. Ibid.

6. B.J., *1*, 12.

7. For Dr Watts' suggestions, see I. Watts, *The Improvement of the Mind* (London, 1809), Chapters 2, 4, 6, 9.

8. Ibid., 118.

9. Ibid., 44.

10. M. Faraday, *Some Observations on the Means of Obtaining Knowledge and on the Facilities Afforded by the Constitution of the City Philosophical Society* (London, 1817). Here Faraday wrote, 'My store of learning respecting knowledge abstractedly considered, has been gathered some time since from the writings of Lord Bacon, and from a work by Dr Watts. . . .' It is quite clear from his own early letters and the account of his life by Riebau that Dr Watts was first both in time and in effect.

11. B.M.Add.MS. 40419, f. 81, 'Faraday, Memoir of his Life'.

12. *Encyclopaedia Britannica*, 3rd ed. (18 vols., Edinburgh, 1797), *1*, XV.

13. 1st ed. (2 vols., London, 1767).

14. 'Faraday, Memoir of his Life'.

15. Article 'Electricity', *Ency. Brit.*, *6*, 440 ff.

16. For a more detailed treatment of Tytler's criticisms, see L. Pearce Williams, 'Michael Faraday's Education in Science', *Isis*, *51* (1960), 515 ff. Also see below, p. 18.

17. Tytler, loc. cit., 450 ff. The quotation is to be found on 452.

18. T. Martin, ed., *Faraday's Diary* (8 vols., London, 1932–6), [3467], [3567], [3570].

19. R.I., Faraday MSS., *Tatum's Lectures*, 'A Lecture on Geology, Feb. 17, 1811'.

20. R.I., Faraday MSS., *Tatum's Lectures*, 'Astronomy', n.d. but *ca.* 1811.

21. See James Ferguson, *Astronomy Explained upon Sir Isaac Newton's principles and made easy to those who have not studied mathematics* (London, 1756, and many other editions).

22. R.I., Faraday MSS., *Tatum's Lectures*, 'Lecture on Geology, Feb. 17, 1811'. The work by Thomson is Thomas Thomson, *A System of Chemistry* (1st ed., London, 1802, 2nd ed., 1804). In the third edition, Dalton's atomic theory is mentioned for the first time.

23. R.I., Faraday MSS., *Tatum's Lectures*, 'Mechanics, 16 September, 1811'.

24. The lecture is undated, but as Tatum's lectures on electricity were delivered on 19 February, 5 March, and 19 March 1810, it is probable that Faraday's rebuttal was delivered soon after.

25. Major Henry Eeles, *Philosophical Essays in several letters to the Royal Society*

(London, 1771); George Atwood, *An analysis of a course of lectures on the Principles of Natural Philosophy, Read in the University of Cambridge* (London, 1784); George Adams, *An Essay on Electricity: in which the theory and practice of that useful science are illustrated by a variety of experiments, arranged in a methodical manner. To which is added, an Essay on Magnetism* (London, 1784).

26. R.I., Faraday MSS., 'Lecture on Electricity'. Compare with Atwood, op. cit., 116, and Adams, op. cit., 137.

27. T. E. Thorpe, *Humphry Davy: Poet and Philosopher* (London, 1896), 75.

28. Jane Marcet, *Conversations on Chemistry* (2 vols., London, 1809), *1*, 2.

29. Ibid., *1*, 23.

30. The notes of Tatum's lectures clearly reveal all these defects.

31. B.M.Add.MS. 40419, f. 81, 'Faraday, Memoir of his Life, 1835'.

32. Warner MSS., Faraday to Benjamin Abbott, 12 July 1812. See also, B.J., *1*, 16 ff.

33. Ibid.

34. Warner MSS., B. Abbott, 'Jottings from Memory in reference to my dear and deceased Friend M. Faraday'.

35. Warner MSS., Faraday to B. Abbott, 12 July 1812, B.J., *1*, 19.

36. Ibid., B.J., *1*, 21.

37. Ibid., B.J., *1*, 22.

38. See below, Chapter Five.

39. Warner MSS., Faraday to B. Abbott, 20 July 1812. This part of the letter has been omitted in B.J.

40. Antoine Laurent Lavoisier, *Traité élémentaire de chimie*, in *Œuvres de Lavoisier* (6 vols., Paris, 1862–93), *1*, 57. The original edition of this work appeared in 1789.

41. Ibid., 7.

42. R.I., Faraday MSS., Riebau's letter, cited above.

43. Warner MSS., Faraday to Abbott, 11 August 1812. This section is omitted in B.J., *1*, 27 ff.

44. Warner MSS., Faraday to Abbott, 19 August 1812. This section is omitted in B.J., *1*, 30 ff.

45. R.I., Faraday MSS., Faraday to Dr Becker, 25 October 1860, B.J., *2*, 439.

46. In his letter of 12 July he had written to Abbott, 'I am just now involved in a fit of vexation. I have an excellent prospect before me,' and cannot take it up for want of ability: had I perhaps known as much of mechanics, mathematics, mensuration, and drawing, as I do perhaps of some other sciences – that is to say, had I happened to employ my mind with these instead of other sciences – I could have obtained a place – an easy place, too, and that in London – at 5, 6, 7, 800 £ per annum. Alas! Alas! Inability. I must ask your advice on the subject. . . .' B.J., *1*, 23.

47. Faraday to Huxtable, 18 October 1812, B.J., *1*, 51.

48. 'Faraday, Memoir of his Life, 1835', f. 81.

49. B. Abbott, 'Jottings . . .', Warner MSS.

50. B.J., *1*, 56.

51. Warner MSS., Faraday to Abbott, 5 April 1813.

52. Ibid.

53. Warner MSS., Faraday to Abbott, 9 April 1813, B.J., *1*, 60.

54. For a more detailed examination of Faraday's ideas on lecturing, see Chapter Eight.

55. Faraday quoted in B.J., *1*, 58.

56. Faraday's foreign Journal, entry for Wednesday, 13 October 1813. This Journal has been reproduced in part in B.J., *1*, 83 ff. There is an odd circumstance which deserves notice. The Institution of Electrical Engineers has a manuscript volume entitled *Common Place Book, Volume 2* in which the Journal is kept. But, from the watermark of 1815 and 1816 of the paper, and the fact that the Journal ends abruptly at the bottom of a recto sheet, it is clear that this is a fair copy made from the original. It ends on Wednesday 20 April 1814. I shall cite this Journal (giving the appropriate reference in B.J.) until that date. After 20 April 1814, reference will be made to the printed excerpts in B.J.

57. *Journal*, Friday, 15 October 1813, B.J., *1*, 84.

58. Ibid., Wednesday, 20 October 1813, B.J., *1*, 86.

59. Ibid., Thursday, 21 October 1813, B.J., *1*, 88.

60. Ibid., Wednesday, 24 November 1813, B.J. (with elisions), *1*, 96.

61. Ibid., Tuesday, 21 December 1813, B.J., *1*, 101.

62. Faraday's description on his passport read, 'a round chin, a brown beard, a large mouth, a great nose, etc. etc.' *Journal*, 9 November 1813, B.J., *1*, 94.

63. *Journal*, Tuesday 23 November 1813, B.J., *1*, 95.

64. Ibid.

65. *Journal*, Wednesday, 1 December 1813, B.J., *1*, 97, and Friday, 3 December 1813, B.J., *1*, 98.

66. Ibid., 11 December 1813, B.J., *1*, 100.

67. 'Some Experiments and Observations on a New Substance which becomes a violet-coloured Gas by Heat', in *The Collected Works of Sir Humphry Davy, edited by his Brother, John Davy* (9 vols., London, 1839–40), *5*, 453, cited henceforth as Davy, *Works*. The date of this paper is odd, for according to Faraday's Journal, the experiments described with the voltaic pile did not take place until 11 December.

68. *Journal*, Wednesday, 7 December 1813, B.J., *1*, 98.

69. *Journal*, 17 January 1814.

70. *Journal*, 4 March 1814, B.J., *1*, 115. The date in B.J. is wrongly given as 4 February.

71. See below, Chapter Four.

72. *Journal*, Saturday, 2 April.

73. 'Some Experiments on the Combustion of the Diamond and other Carbonaceous Substances', Davy, *Works*, *5*, 478 ff. See below, Chapter Two. Davy's work on the diamond was of great importance in the development of his and Faraday's theories of the nature of matter and of the origins of chemical and physical qualities.

74. *Journal*, Sunday, 3 April 1814.

75. 'Some experiments and observations on the Colours used by the Ancients', Davy, *Works*, 6, 131.

76. Warner MSS., Faraday to B. Abbott, Rome, 26 November 1814, B.J., *1*, 170.

77. Warner MSS., Faraday to Abbott, Rome, 25 January 1815, B.J., *1*, 180 ff. The letter is not published in its entirety in B.J.

78. Warner MSS., B. Abbott, 'Jottings from Memory in reference to my dear and deceased Friend, M. Faraday'.

79. Faraday to Abbott, Rome, 25 January 1815, B.J., *1*, 180 ff. The passage cited is omitted in B.J.

80. Faraday to his Mother, Bruxelles, 16 April 1815, B.J., *1*, 206.

81. B.J., *1*, 198.

82. Warner MSS., Faraday to Abbott, n.p. n.d. but *ca.* July 1815.

83. Warner MSS., Faraday to Abbott, R. I., Wednesday, 13 September, 1815.

84. *The Journal of Science and the Arts*, *1* (1816), 261. This journal was edited by Brande at the Royal Institution but was not an official journal of the R.I. In 1820, it became *The Quarterly Journal of Science, Literature and the Arts* and will be cited henceforth as *Q.J.S.*

85. M. Faraday, *Experimental Researches in Chemistry and Physics* (London, 1859), *1*, note.

86. *Q.J.S.*, *2* (1817), 463.

87. Ibid., 464.

88. *Q.J.S.*, *6* (1818), 152, 159, 160.

89. See, William Nicholson, *A Dictionary of Practical and Theoretical Chemistry* (London, 1808), article, Benzoin.

90. *Q.J.S.*, *7* (1819), 387.

91. *Q.J.S.*, *8* (1820), 168.

92. *Q.J.S.*, *6* (1818), 159.

93. *Q.J.S.*, *7* (1819), 388.

94. M. Faraday, 'On Sirium', *Q.J.S.*, *6* (1819), 114.

95. Quoted in J. H. Gladstone, *Michael Faraday* (London, 1873), 18. The phrase 'parallax of Mr West's Sirium' refers presumably to a jocular analogy with the discovery of the asteroid Ceres by Piazzi in 1801 which stimulated Gauss to work out his well-known method of orbit computation.

96. Published as a separate pamphlet in 1818, revised by Davy in 1825, and most easily consulted in Davy, *Works*, *6*, 3 ff.

97. Ibid., 4.

98. H. Davy, 'New Experiments on some of the Combinations of Phosphorus', *Works*, *5*, 373.

99. J. J. Berzelius, 'Note. Sur la composition de l'acide phosphorique et de l'acide phosphoreux', *Ann. de chim. et de phys.*, *10* (1819), 202.

100. These lectures are at the Institution of Electrical Engineers, Faraday collection, cited henceforth as I.E.E., Chem. Lect.

101. I.E.E., Common Place Book, vol. 1.

102. R.I., Faraday MSS., 'A Class Book for the Reception of Mental Exercises instituted July 1818'.

103. Warner MSS., Faraday to Abbott, R.I., Sunday Evening, 15 January 1816, B.J., *1*, 229.

104. Warner MSS., Faraday to Abbott, R.I., 27 April 1819, B.J., *1*, 312.

105. Wellcome Medical Historical Library, Faraday to S. Cocks, R.I., August 1818.

106. See below, Chapter Three.

CHAPTER TWO

The Education of a Philosopher

1. The Imponderable Fluids

The years during which Faraday was attempting to educate himself and profit from his close association with Davy were ones of considerable turmoil in science. The series of discoveries that flowed from the invention of the voltaic pile threatened to overturn the very basis of Newtonian science. Some natural philosophers eagerly embraced this alternative; others fought desperately to preserve what appeared to them to be nothing less than Truth. From this clash of opposing theories and philosophies, Faraday was to devise his own point of view which was to be of fundamental importance throughout his creative scientific life.

The magnitude of the battle was directly proportional to the success of Newtonian science in the eighteenth century.

The publication of the *Principia* in 1687 brought order into the universe of ponderable matter. From falling apples in the orchard at Newton's home to the stars and planets in their courses, all bodies were found to obey Newton's three laws of motion and to act in accordance with the inverse square law of gravitational attraction. What remained for future generations to do was to carry the insights of Newton's genius to their logical conclusions and extend the mantle of Newtonian mechanics over the totality of natural phenomena.

Even in Newton's time certain effects seemed difficult to account for on purely Newtonian grounds. Sir Isaac himself had wrestled with the problem of light and many of its actions had puzzled, if not mystified, him. Heat, too, caused some anxiety. It was all well and good to speak of it, as Bacon had done, as the intestine motion of the particles of bodies, but since such motions remained undetectable, this hypothesis could not resist the first serious attack upon it. Most curious, however, were the strange phenomena of electrical and magnetic attraction and repulsion. The eighteenth century was a period of great activity in the investigation of electricity and magnetism but the early explanations for electrical and magnetic behaviour were not very satisfying.[1]

One of the striking scientific achievements of the eighteenth century was the reduction of the phenomena of electricity, magnetism, light, and heat to the action of 'imponderable' fluids which, except for their imponderability, obeyed the rules of Newtonian mechanics. The history of this achievement is a complicated one, for the various imponderable fluids appeared separately and were not seen as analogous to one another until the end of the century.[2]

The theory of light prevalent at the end of the eighteenth century owed its origin to Newton. The corpuscles of which light was composed were of differing magnitudes, the size determining the colour. These corpuscles were attracted by ordinary matter so that they could be pulled out of their rectilinear paths (or refracted) when approaching a dense, transparent medium. The particles of light appeared to repel one another for when released from their connexion with ponderable matter, they flew off in all directions.

The mechanical theory of heat was discarded when Joseph Black of Glasgow discovered latent heat in 1857. Black had been struck by the slowness with which snow melted in the warmth of the spring sun, and this led him to investigate the heat absorbed or liberated when a change of state took place. He discovered that when a body, such as ice, passed from the solid to the liquid state, a considerable amount of heat was absorbed without there being any corresponding change in temperature. When the process was reversed, this heat was released indicating that it had always been present, but in a latent form. To Black, a chemist, the easiest way to account for such strange behaviour was to deal with it in strictly chemical terms. If heat were a fluid instead of the motion of the constituent particles of bodies, a straightforward chemical reaction could be assumed. Water could be viewed as a compound of ice and the fluid of heat and steam as composed of water plus more of the heat fluid. That heat was intimately connected with matter without manifesting itself as temperature also became obtrusively clear when the work of Lavoisier focused attention on combustion. Independently of Black, Lavoisier also devised a material theory of heat, christening this fluid caloric.[3] Caloric could not be detected by the balance and was, therefore, simply made imponderable. It could associate itself with ponderable matter in chemical combination, in which case it manifested itself in ways other than in temperature. Or it could exist, like water in a sponge, within the material interstices of a body, and temperature would then indicate its state of 'compression'. Caloric particles were mutually repulsive so that increase in temperature meant expansion, and change of state with absorption of heat always increased the distance (and the mobility) between the particles of a caloric–matter compound.

The development of reasonably coherent theories of electricity and magnetism was beset with far more difficulties than was the case with light and heat. Electricity and magnetism exhibited a duality which made it extraordinarily difficult to explain their actions in any simple way. Opposite poles of a magnet and oppositely charged bodies attracted whereas similar poles and charges repelled one another. The attempt was made to apply cartesian vortices of electrical and magnetic 'effluvia' to this problem but it was not successful. When 'effluvia' had to be circulating in different directions at the same time in order to explain both attraction and repulsion, the model became too clumsy and another was sought.[4]

By the end of the eighteenth century it was generally agreed that electrical and magnetic phenomena could be adequately explained only by the assumption of imponderable fluids acting upon one another at a distance. Benjamin Franklin had tried to simplify matters by accounting for the opposition of charges in terms of the deficiency or superfluity of a single fluid, but most workers felt more at home with separate positive and negative, and austral and boreal fluids. The particles of each fluid were mutually repulsive, while particles of the opposite kind (+ and −, or N and S) attracted one another. It was not clear what relation these fluids had with ponderable matter. Generally, it was felt that if there were any attraction between ponderable matter and these fluids, it was not of any great or fundamental importance. Ponderable matter merely served as the container of the electrical or magnetic fluids and was not affected by their presence. The interaction was always between the particles of the fluids, and did not involve the ponderable matter at all.[5] Only occasionally was a voice raised to suggest that the relation was both more intimate and more important than this. Joseph Priestley insisted upon the importance of the study of electricity for chemistry since 'chymistry and electricity are both conversant about the latent and less obvious properties of bodies'. Unfortunately, as Priestley noted, 'few of our modern electricians having been either speculative or practical chymists',[6] the true role of electricity in chemical reactions remained to be discovered. What this role might be was suggested by Charles Coulomb. 'Perhaps', he wrote, '. . . all chemical affinities depend upon two actions, the one repulsive, the other attractive, analogous to those which we find in electricity and magnetism.'[7] Such hints fell on deaf ears and the study of the imponderable fluids remained more or less divorced from other areas of science.

In 1791 a new imponderable made its appearance when Luigi Galvani announced the discovery of animal electricity produced by living tissue. This fluid, secreted by the nerves, was completely analogous to all the other imponderables except for its connexion with life. The wave of excitement over this epoch-making discovery was accompanied by a ripple of scepticism from those who had recently seen the existence of

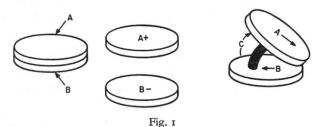

Fig. 1

Anton Mesmer's animal magnetism denied by the Paris Academy of Sciences. Among the sceptics was Alessandro Volta of the University of Pavia who, as a physicist, was convinced that the undoubted signs of electricity could be explained in purely physical terms with no need to call upon vital or other mysterious forces. From 1791 to 1800, Volta carefully scrutinized and criticized the conditions under which animal electricity was produced. In 1794 he showed that the mere contact of two dissimilar metals could produce an electrostatic charge; when the metallic contact was supplemented by the intervention of a fluid conductor, a continuous circulation of the electrical fluid resulted (see Figure 1).

> What do you think of the so-called animal electricity? As for me, I have been convinced for a long time that the whole action comes from metallic contact with any damp body or water itself; as a result of this contact, the excess of the electric fluid passes through the damp body from the metal which has more [fluid] to the one that has less (most of all from zinc, almost the least of all from silver); from this non-interrupted contact with the various conductors, there arises a continuous circulation of [the electric] fluid.[8]

Volta's views on the mechanism by which the electric current was set in motion were purely mechanical. All substances, including metals, contained the electric fluid, but the metals permitted it to flow through them with little or no resistance. Not all bodies contained the same quantity of electricity, however. Hence when two dissimilar metals were placed in contact, the metal which contained more of the fluid 'overflowed' into the other leading to the creation of a charge on each metal when the two were separated. If, however, a humid conductor is used to create a real circuit, then the electric fluid kept moving around the circuit.

The effect with two metals and a humid connecter was a very small one and Volta set out to multiply it. What was needed was a great reservoir of electric fluid and an increase in the electric 'pressure' between the metals. Volta reasoned that this could be achieved by increasing the number of metallic contacts and the total quantity of the metals. If dissimilar metal discs were piled on top of one another with interposed humid conductors between the pairs of metals, a greater amount of electricity should be put in motion and the effects enhanced. This device was the voltaic pile whose invention was announced to the scientific world in a letter to Sir Joseph Banks, President of the Royal Society[9] (see Figure 2). Volta again made it perfectly clear that the effect was a purely mechanical one leading to a *mouvement perpetuel* (Volta's italics) of the electric fluid.[10] There were no immediate objections to the idea of a perpetual motion for such motion was held to be impossible only when ponderable matter was involved. The peculiar properties of the imponderables did not seem to rule out a perpetual circulation. Nor did anyone, at this time, question the use of the word *current* to describe the action of the electric fluid in the circuit of the pile. Given the concept of the imponderable fluids, it was only natural to think in terms of a flow of something through the wires. It was not to be long, however, before both Volta's fundamental views were to be subjected to intense criticism.

Fig. 2

It became immediately evident that there was more to the activity of the voltaic pile than the mere circulation of the electric fluid. Before Volta's letter was made public, Sir Joseph Banks had informed William Nicholson and Anthony Carlisle of Volta's discovery. These two set out, in April 1800, to reproduce the effects Volta had described and to repeat his experiments. Much to their surprise, they found that when the current was passed through water by means of copper wires dipped into a tumbler, a gas was evolved at one wire. Upon examination this proved to be hydrogen. In order to account for this, Nicholson and Carlisle were led to a rather startling conclusion.

We had been led by our reasoning on the first appearance of hydrogen to expect a decomposition of the water; but it was with no little surprise that we found the hydrogen extricated at the contact with one wire, while the oxigin fixed itself in combination with the other wire at the distance of almost two inches. This new fact still remains to be explained, and seems to point at some general law of the agency of electricity in chemical operations. As the distance between the wires formed a striking feature in this result, it became desirable to ascertain whether it would take place to greater distances. When a tube three quarters of an inch in diameter, and thirty-six inches long was made use of, the effect failed, though the very same wires inserted into a shorter tube, operated very briskly. The solicitation of other objects of enquiry prevented trial being made of all the various intermediate distances; but from the general tenor of experiments, it appears to be established, that this decomposition is more effectual the less the distance between the wires, but that it ceases altogether when the wires come into contact.[11]

No light or heat accompanied the decomposition of water so the active agent had to be electricity. Here, for the first time, was positive proof that electricity was intimately associated with ponderable matter and even influenced its combinations. What was not clear, however, was the exact nature of this association. Presumably, the molecule of water contained the electric fluids and when water was placed in the voltaic circuit, the ordinary forces of electrical attraction and repulsion tore the water molecules into two parts – oxygen and hydrogen. But this did not explain how it was possible for the oxygen and hydrogen to migrate through the solution to the charged wires. Why did they not simply bubble up in the middle? The electrical decomposition of water thus posed the first serious threat to the fluid theory of electricity. As we shall see, by some it was used to attack Lavoisier's theories in which the compound nature of water was essential; by others, it became the starting-point for the construction of a new theory of the action of electrical forces. Old theories die hard, however, and the fluid theory was no exception. In an attempt to 'save the phenomena' a number of chemists of respectable attainments put forth rather fantastic schemes which would permit the retention of the concept of fluids and still account for the newly discovered facts. Typical of such attempts was that made by Luigi Brugnatelli, editor of the *Annali di chimica*. Electricity, said Brugnatelli, was simply an acid. Like other acids it turned the tincture of sunflowers pink and attacked metals. There was no problem of ionic transfer since the gases observed in electrochemical reactions were formed at the wires by the action of the electric acid there. The compounds electricity formed with the metals Brugnatelli christened electrates and he proceeded to isolate and describe them. Gold electrate was 'brilliant and transparent'; silver electrate formed 'prismatic crystals . . . which reflect light strongly and of a transparent white colour'; copper electrate was a 'beautiful transparent green'.[12] Even so could commitment to a particular hypothesis lead a competent chemist astray.

The revelation of the chemical activity of electricity was accompanied immediately by the discovery of strange new properties of another imponderable. In the same volume of the *Philosophical Transactions* which carried Volta's announcement of the discovery of the pile, Sir William Herschel described his experiments on the heating power of the different parts of the spectrum. To his surprise, the point of maximum heating fell beyond the red end of the spectrum.[13] Excited by this discovery, Johann Ritter of Jena turned his attention to the chemical effects of various parts of the spectrum. Exposing 'muriate of silver' (silver chloride) to the action of the sun's rays, he found that the rate of decomposition of this salt increased towards the violet end of the spectrum. The maximum rate was found to exist outside the visible spectrum in the ultra-violet, and so another species of 'invisible rays' was announced. When the blackened silver chloride was exposed to infra-red radiation, Ritter reported, the original salt was reconstituted. From these phenomena, he concluded that 'the solar spectrum is thus accompanied by two invisible rays, one on the red side which favours oxygenation, the other on the violet side, which favours deoxygenation'.[14] Light, like electricity, was now shown to play an active chemical role. Chemical composition and decomposition were clearly associated somehow with the electric fluids, caloric, and light. All acted in analogous fashion. The analogy, indeed, between all the imponderables was becoming obtrusive. Could it really be that all these similar effects were due to distinct and separate fluids which had no connexion with one another? And, if this were so, how did these various fluids associate with one another in or around the particles of ponderable matter? If one accepted John Dalton's chemical atoms, the imponderables surrounded them like the layers of an onion. In short, the model was beginning to get clumsy and unmanageable. The yearning for simplicity that plays such an important role in scientific advance led some investigators to ask if the whole problem should not be re-examined. Might there not be some single basis of which electricity, magnetism, light, and heat were simply different manifestations? And, if this were the case, might not these phenomena be convertible into one another? The foundations for such speculations had been laid by Immanuel Kant in the eighteenth century. His system of dynamic physics provided the framework within which forces, not fluids, could be viewed as the active principles of matter.

2. The Forces of Matter

Kant's primary concern was not with the specific concepts of contemporary science. He aimed, rather, at the far more ambitious goal of providing a firm foundation for the study of the human understanding and, in this way, creating the necessary conditions for a clear apprehension of God. One of the main obstacles to the achievement of this programme was the duality of matter and spirit which seemed to divide the universe into two isolated systems. On the one hand, there existed the world of matter, sufficient unto itself with its inherent properties and laws; on the other, was the world of Spirit and Mind in which matter was negligible. The success of physics in the seventeenth and eighteenth centuries had served to emphasize the material world at the expense of the spiritual, in spite of the efforts of men like Newton and Boyle to balance them. Atheism appeared to be a direct result of scientific progress and served to worry a good number of the pious. Only two alternatives seemed possible if religion (and its social consequence, order) were to be preserved. Either the sciences were to be condemned and suppressed, or some new approach must be tried in which the gulf between matter and Spirit was bridged. For a man of Kant's intellect and interests, only the latter was possible. He had, in his earlier years, dabbled in science and had even suggested a process of cosmological evolution of more than passing interest.[16] The task Kant set himself was to find some system of principles by which the laws of the starry firmament above him and the moral law within him could be shown to be harmonious.

The foundation of this system was the *Critique of Pure Reason* which was first published in Riga in 1781. In this work, Kant set out to examine the limits of the human reason and to determine, with all possible precision, what the human mind could know. Were space and time, for example, empirically knowable – i.e. the result of experience or were they, rather, the *a priori* conditions of such knowledge? Kant, as is well known, insisted that space and time were purely mental intuitions which made the perception of external reality possible. The point is not without importance for the science of Kant's day. Much of the success of the scientific revolution of the seventeenth century was the result of the geometrization of space by Galileo, Descartes, and Newton. The proponents of the Mechanical Philosophy dreamed of reducing all phenomena to the motion of atoms through Euclidean space. Such a space, Kant pointed out, was the result of mental confusion, not empirical observation. Empty space could not be perceived for space, being the mode in which the mind *related* its perceptions, could not be empty. 'By this argument', Kant wrote, 'I do not mean to deny the existence of empty space: it may exist where perceptions cannot reach and thus no empirical knowledge of it can be gained; such a space is no possible object of our experience.'

If empty space were, literally, inconceivable then what was the space with which natural science dealt? It must be a plenum but this merely raised the further problem of determining what space was filled with. Clearly, the accepted atomic doctrine of the day could no longer suffice for in this concept empty space was as essential as the material particles in it. To resolve this difficulty, Kant once again turned to the nature of the human mind. The concept of substance, he suggested, was the consequence of still another intuition. Just as the intuition of space permits perception, so does the intuition of time give rise to the idea of causality. 'This [idea of] causality leads to the concept of action, this to the concept of force, and thereby to the concept of substance.'[17] Substance, therefore, rather than being an immediate perceptual datum, was really the end result of a long chain of suppositions. Furthermore, substance, as such, could never really be known. The famous Kantian *Ding an sich* or thing in itself was forever hidden from the human reason. Substance or the *Ding an sich* appeared to be necessary only as a metaphysical substratum which gave rise to the perceptible qualities of force and action. In this sense, Kant was close to the position taken by Bishop Berkeley although he was specifically attacking Berkeley's concept that human perceptions were ideas in the mind of God. For both Berkeley and Kant, however, reality was to be found in the perceptions and both, more or less, denied the independent existence of matter.

If matter does not exist (or if it is unknowable – both propositions being equivalent for the practical task of unravelling the laws of the perceptual universe), then what is the basis of perception of the external world? Kant insisted that physical reality could be reduced to two basic qualities. 'We know substance in space', Kant wrote, 'only through the forces which work in this space, either by drawing others to it (attraction) or by preventing penetration (repulsion and impenetrability); we know no other quality pertaining to the concept of substance existing in space which we call matter.'[18] Having banished matter, Kant had removed the duality of matter and spirit. But, he had also destroyed the concept of the material world upon which the science of the eighteenth century was based. It remained to be seen whether a new science, dealing with forces, could be erected.

Kant was fully aware of the problem he had created by his criticism of atomism. In 1786 he published a treatise on the *Metaphysical Foundations of Natural Science* in which he tried to show how a new dynamic physics, based only upon the fundamental forces of attraction and repulsion could be created.[19] Kant's exposition laid out Propositions, Proofs, and Corollaries in logical order. Proposition 1 stated: 'Matter fills space, not by its pure existence, but by its special active force.'[20]

The universe, then, was a plenum, but filled with forces rather than matter. This concept is a bit difficult to digest, for if all is filled with forces, then how can the observed expansions and contractions of everyday 'matter' be explained? The answer was simple; forces, like what used to be called matter, could be condensed or rarefied. Such condensation or rarefaction merely intensified or relaxed the conflict of attraction and repulsion.

Every point in space was, therefore, associated with attractive and repulsive forces whose 'conflict' produced all the phenomena of the observable world. Forces gave Kant the plenum required by his epistemological conclusions; they also provided a continuity in nature which the older atomic theory violated so flagrantly by its insistence upon the dichotomy between matter and space. The problem of continuity should be insisted upon for it was a driving force in Kant's own thought, and was to have important scientific consequences when applied by his disciples. The reduction of all physical phenomena to attractive and repulsive forces acting upon one another was seductively simple. The different *kinds* of attraction and repulsion – electrical, magnetic, etc. – were the results of different conditions under which the two basic forces manifested themselves. Behind these differences lay the essential *unity* of all forces. From this it followed logically that all the forces of nature were convertible into one another; one need only find the proper conditions for accomplishing the conversion. This fundamental insight was to serve as the stimulus for two generations of scientists amongst whom may be numbered Ritter, Davy, Oersted, and Michael Faraday.

The first application of Kant's ideas to a specific scientific problem was made by Johann Ritter. In 1798, two years before the invention of the voltaic pile, Ritter attempted to create an electrochemical theory in which the forces of electricity and chemical affinity were treated as identical.[21] Kant's influence, however, was not restricted to Germany. A few of Kant's early essays were translated into English before the end of the eighteenth century,[22] and in 1801 a French analysis of the Kantian philosophy was published.[23] The most important channel for the spread of transcendental idealism in the British Isles was not the printed word; it was, rather, the glowing enthusiasm of Samuel Taylor Coleridge.

In 1798 Coleridge set out for Germany on a *Wanderjahre* whose influence upon English science was to be incalculable.[24] While there he made the acquaintance of the Kantian philosophy and immediately embraced it with all the passion of which his extraordinarily passionate being was capable. To Coleridge, Kant's resolution of the matter-spirit problem came almost as a revelation and it was this which particularly appealed to him. By reducing the essence of matter – impenetrability – to the action of force in space Kant had, in Coleridge's eyes, removed the last obstacle to the creation of a truly universal science embracing both the material universe and God. 'For since impenetrability is intelligible only as a mode of resistance,' Coleridge wrote in his *Biographia Literaria*, 'its admission places the essence of *matter* in an act or power, which it possesses in common with *spirit*; and body and spirit are therefore no longer absolutely heterogeneous, but *may* without any *absurdity* be supposed to be different modes, or degrees in perfection, of a common substratum.'[25]

This position had an enormous appeal in England in the nineteenth century. To many, the threat posed by the traditional British philosophy of Locke, Hume, and Hartley was a serious one and to be combatted. Materialism was a mighty foe to be fought wherever and whenever it appeared. Materialism also seemed to be losing its effectiveness as a philosophical basis for scientific research. The sense of the interconnectedness of phenomena which followed upon the discovery of galvanism and of the electric current served to revive an organic concept of nature which was in direct opposition to the mechanical ideas of the orthodox. Men like Humphry Davy and Faraday were deeply religious. Unlike the pure mechanist, Laplace, they did have need of God, even as the basis of scientific hypotheses. Their God was an active one who, like the vital force in man, provided the spiritual *élan vital* upon which the universe and its laws depended. The argument was put with telling force by Coleridge.

Again: in the world we see everywhere evidences of a unity which the component parts are so far from explaining, that they necessarily pre-suppose it as the cause and condition of their existing as those parts; or even of their existing at all. This antecedent unity, or cause and principle of each union, it has since the time of Bacon and Kepler been customary to call a law. This crocus, for instance, or any other flower, the reader have in sight, or choose to bring before his fancy. That the root, stem, leaves, petals, etc., cohere to one plant, is owing to an antecedent power or principle in the seed, which existed before a single particle of the matters that constitute the size and visibility of the crocus, had been attracted from the surrounding soil, air and moisture. Shall we turn to the seed? Here too the same necessity meets us.

An antecedent unity – (I speak not of the parent plant, but of an agency antecedent in the order of operance, yet remaining present as the conservative and reproductive power) – must here too be supposed. Analyze the seed with the finest tools, and let the solar microscope come in aid of your senses – what do you find? Means and instruments, a wondrous fairy tale of nature, magazines of food, stores of various sorts, pipes, spiracles, defences – a house of many chambers, and the owner and inhabitant invisible! Reflect further on the countless millions of seeds of the same name, each more than numerically differenced from every other: and further yet, reflect on the requisite harmony of all surrounding things, each of which necessitates the same process of thought, and the coherence of all of which to a system, a world, demands its own adequate antecedent unity, which must therefore of necessity be present to all and in all, yet in no wise excluding or suspending the individual law or principle of union in each. Now, will reason, will common sense, endure the assumption that it is highly reasonable to believe a universal power as the cause and pre-condition of the harmony of all particular wholes, each of which involves the working principle of its own union – that it is reasonable, I say, to believe this respecting the aggregate of objects, which, without a subject (that is, a sentient and intelligent existence), would be purposeless; and yet unreasonable and even superstitious or enthusiastic to entertain a similar belief in relation to the system of intelligent and self-conscious beings, to the moral and personal world?[26]

The universe was a cosmic web, woven by God, and held together by the crossed strands of attractive and repulsive forces. As the fundamental phenomenal evidence of His universal activity they were almost like neo-platonic divine emanations.

The phenomena of the visible universe were but different manifestations of the underlying forces of attraction and repulsion. This basic identity should lead to the convertibility of the forces of nature into one another. 'Things identical must be convertible', Coleridge remarked in the *Biographia Literaria*.[27] It was this vision which guided Hans Christian Oersted in his twenty-year search for the effect of electricity upon magnetism. It was the conviction that forces were inherently identical and convertible that inspired Michael Faraday during the major portion of his scientific career.

Forces were not only identical and convertible, but indestructible. Nor should one wonder at this. They were the basic fabric of existence and could not, therefore, fade from being. Long before anything even resembling the Principle of the Conservation of Energy had been enunciated, Coleridge could write to his friend Thomas Poole:

Death in a doting old age falls upon my feelings ever as a more hopeless phenomenon than death in infancy; but *nothing* is hopeless. What if the vital force which I sent from my arm into the stone as I flung it in the air and skimmed it upon the water – what if even that did not perish! It was *life*! it was a particle of *being*! it was power! and how could it perish? *Life, Power, Being!* Organization may and probably is their *effect* – their *cause* it *cannot* be! I have indulged very curious fancies concerning that force, that swarm of motive powers which I sent out of my body into that stone, and which, one by one, left the untractable or already possessed mass, and – but the German ocean lies between us. It is all too far to send you such fancies as these.[28]

The idea that force could not be annihilated, but could only change its guise, was to be a leading thread in the science of the early nineteenth century. It was the mainstay of the argument of those who opposed Volta's contact theory of the pile; it was used by James Prescott Joule in his great researches on the conversion of forces, and it was the fundamental concept out of which the kinetic theory of gases was born.

Forces had still another quality of great scientific importance. Unlike atoms, they are continuous. No jumps or discontinuities are to be found in nature. Hence, for example, the good Kantian almost instinctively rejected the new chemistry of Lavoisier. It was inconceivable that oxygen should occupy the unique position assigned to it. The voltaic pile revealed what the Kantian had already guessed – that the chemical elements formed a series, rather than two permanently separated groups. When Davy discovered that chlorine supported combustion, and later that a series consisting of iodine, chlorine, oxygen, and fluorine could be discerned, this seemed to corroborate the law of continuity.

Finally, the fundamental reality of attractive and repulsive forces implied a basic polarity in the universe.

Every power in nature and in spirit must evolve an opposite as the sole means and condition of its manifestation: and all opposition is a tendency to re-union. . . . The principle may be thus expressed. The identity of *thesis* and *antithesis* is the substance of all being; their opposition the condition of all existence or being manifested; and every thing or *phenomenon* is the exponent of a synthesis as long as the opposite energies are retained in that *synthesis*. Thus water is neither oxygen nor hydrogen, nor yet is it a commixture of both; but the *synthesis* or indifference of the two: and as long as the *copula* endures by which it becomes water, or rather which alone is water, it is not less a simple body than either of the imaginary elements, improperly called its ingredients or components. It is the object of the mechanical atomistic philosophy to confound *synthesis* with *synartesis*, or rather with mere juxta-position of corpuscles separated by invisible interspaces. I find it difficult to determine, whether this theory contradicts the reason or the senses most: for it is alike inconceivable and unimaginable.[29]

From these properties of forces, Coleridge went on to fashion a complete (and somewhat fantastic) physics and physiology[30] but his detailed system created only a minor eddy in the mainstream of scientific development. His main influence lay in the transmission of Kantian ideas on forces to England. The primary channel by which the dynamic philosophy flowed into English science was Humphry Davy.

The precise moment of Davy's conversion to Kant's views is impossible to determine. Conversion, indeed, may even be too strong a word; for all his life Davy played with various hypotheses concerning the nature of matter and sometimes used one and sometimes another in his private speculative jottings. It is clear, however, that from an early age he was interested in the very problems that had led Coleridge to wax enthusiastic over the Transcendental philosophy. In one of his early notebooks, he examined the mind–body problem and concluded 'that which thinks is not matter'.[31] His brother, John, later reported that in the 1790's, Humphry devoured all the works on philosophy he could lay his hands on. This list included Locke, Hartley, Berkeley, Hume, Helvetius, Condorcet, and Reid. At this time, too, his brother and biographer states that 'he appears to have had some acquaintance with the doctrines of Kant and the Transcendalists'.[32]

His scientific ideas, however, were still in the process of being formed. He was perfectly orthodox in his view of imponderable fluids and their importance to science. 'We cannot account well for the phenomena of electricity', he wrote in an early notebook, 'without supposing the existence of a peculiar fluid. Is this fluid the same as heat, i.e. are electricity and galvanism currents of a fluid which when expanding in right lines constitutes light.'[33]

Davy, only a little later, was one of the first to doubt the doctrine of the materiality of heat. In his earliest publication, *An Essay on Heat, Light and the Combinations of Light* (1799), he attacked the doctrine of caloric with some severity.

> Now since caloric is supposed compressible [he pointed out] that is, capable of having its volume diminished by pressure, its particles cannot be in actual contact; there must consequently act on them some power which prevents their actual contact, that is, the repulsive motion. So that to admit the existence of an imaginary fluid in conformity to the absurd axiom, *bodies cannot act where they are not,* is in fact the solution of a small difficulty by the creation of a great one. After all, a principle must be admitted, (that is, repulsion); to do away the necessity of which, caloric has been invented.[34]

This essay, however, did not attack the concept of imponderable fluids in general. It was Davy's purpose, rather, to suggest the importance of the imponderable fluid of light and reduce heat to mere molecular motion. Yet the germ of the rejection of all imponderables was there. If it were absurd to invent a fluid of heat to account for repulsion, might it not be equally absurd to think in terms of electric and magnetic fluids when only forces were involved? Davy's writings give us no clue as to why he finally rejected all fluids. The reason, however, does not appear too difficult to ascertain. The answers to many of the questions Davy was asking in 1799 were to be found in Kant's *Metaphysiche Anfangsgründe der Naturwissenschaft*; no English translation of this work was available in 1799 and Davy did not read German. Knowledge of Kant's ideas, therefore, came through another person and it is obvious that this person was Samuel Taylor Coleridge. The two met at the Pneumatic Institution near Bristol, where Davy was engaged by Dr Thomas Beddoes, a man of extensive if somewhat eccentric ideas, to investigate the therapeutic values of gases. It was here that Davy performed those classic experiments on nitrous oxide that were to bring him fame. Coleridge and Davy became fast friends. Coleridge was sincerely interested in chemistry, for he felt that this science somehow held the key to the mysteries of matter.[35] Davy was a more than competent poet.[36] Both were ardent amateur metaphysicians.

Even before the two met, Davy was toying with ideas which were similar to those Coleridge embraced so ardently. On 10 April 1799, while Coleridge was still in Germany, Davy wrote his dear friend and patron, Davies Gilbert: 'The supposition of active powers common to all matter, from the different modifications of which all the phenomena of its changes result, appear to me more reasonable than the assumption of certain imaginary fluids alone endowed with active powers, and bearing the same relation to common matter, as the vulgar philosophy supposes spirit to bear to matter.'[37]

Such a position could only serve to endear Davy to Coleridge. There is, unfortunately, very little recorded in their letters about the topics which they discussed but it does not seem to strain historical probability too much to believe that a good part of their time was spent on metaphysics and its relationship to chemistry.

> Davy will be here in the first week of September at the farthest; [Coleridge wrote to James Tobin in the summer of 1800] and then, my dear fellow, for physiopathy and phileleutherism – sympathy lemonaded with a little argument – punning and green peas with bacon, or *very ham*; rowing and sailing on the lake (there is a nice boat obsequious to my purposes). Then, as to chemistry, there will be Davy with us. We shall be as rich with reflected light as yon cloud which the sun has taken to his very bosom![38]

Of one thing we can be certain and that is that Davy received as much as he gave.

Those who remember him in his more vigorous days [the author of Coleridge's obituary in the *Gentleman's Magazine* remarked] can bear witness to the peculiarity and transcendant power of his conversational eloquence. It was unlike anything that could be heard elsewhere; the kind was different, the degree was different, the manner was different. The boundless range of scientific knowledge, the brilliancy and exquisite nicety of illustration, the deep and ready reasoning, the strangeness and immensity of bookish lore . . . all went to make up the image and to constitute the living presence of the man.[39]

This was the man with whom Davy walked and conversed. This, too, was the philosopher bursting with enthusiasm for his new-found truths of the transcendental philosophy to whom any listener was a potential convert. Davy was more than that; he was a chemist for whom Kantian ideas, Coleridge was convinced, could work wonders in providing insights into the *true* nature of chemical phenomena.

The most obvious result of his association with Coleridge was the reinforcement of his earlier distrust of the use of imponderable fluids to explain events. By 1809 there was no longer any doubt in his mind on the subject.

Vulgar idea [he wrote in notes for a lecture] like that of the peasant, every thing done by a spring; so every thing must be done by a fluid. The ether was the ancient fluid, then there was a phlogistic fluid; we have had the magnetic fluid, the vitreous fluid, the resinous fluid: and within the last few years there has been a fluid of sounds; and, in a book which I lately received from France, published by M. Azais, all the phenomena of nature are explained by a gravic fluid.[40]

In a lecture on radiant matter, attended by Michael Faraday, Davy reiterated his doubts on the value of accepting imponderable fluids too facilely. Faraday reported his views on heat:

In our considerations on this subject, it will be essentially necessary that we distinguish between knowledge and speculation. These terms in their meaning are palpably different but yet have been intermixed and combined together in a very singular manner. The French chemists in particular speak of the materiality of heat and the nature of the compounds it forms with other material bodies as confidently and as fluently as if they had undeniably proved it to be a body. They have blended their knowledge with speculation and formed a theory that is very possibly untrue.[41]

Davy's position here was of considerable interest. His metaphysical investigations had led him to a position of strict empiricism. It was only after the epistemological foundations of thought had been thoroughly investigated that the human reason could know its own limitations. Thus, according to Kant and Coleridge, matter in its essence and reality could never be an object of human perception. Only the forces of matter are part of the phenomenal world. The imponderable fluids were, therefore, unnecessary. They were used by the philosophically naïve who insisted upon a material basis for force. Empirical reality consisted of forces; a theory which dealt only with forces contained fewer speculations and assumptions than one which postulated imaginary fluids as carriers of forces. In the 1840's, when Faraday's revolutionary ideas were the topic of considerable discussion, he was to insist upon this very point. Thus, paradoxical as it may seem at first glance, a position which depended upon the most abstruse philosophical arguments could be legitimately defended as more in accord with everyday experience than one that seemed the epitome of common sense.

In 1800, Davy began the series of electrochemical investigations which was to culminate in the discovery of potassium and sodium. The first great result of these studies was the Bakerian Lecture for 1806, 'On some chemical Agencies of Electricity', which won for him the prize in Galvanism established by Napoleon. In this lecture, Davy evaded mention of the fluids of electricity but did not introduce his own concept of forces. He still smarted, no doubt, from the critical volleys which had been directed at his essay on light and was unwilling to incur another such condemnation of speculation. His only remarks on the nature of electricity were to suggest that no one knew what it was. Nevertheless, he went on, may it not be identical with chemical affinity and, therefore, an essential property of matter?[42] It was with this idea in mind that he proceeded to construct a theory of electrochemical action. Chemical dynamics was to be the science of the interaction of the attractive and repulsive forces associated with chemical entities. In this scheme, there was no place for fluids.

As his fame grew and his confidence increased, Davy became less reticent. He dropped his pretence of agnosticism regarding the nature of electricity and openly adopted the theory of forces. Thus, from 1807 on, Davy referred constantly to 'electric powers' and 'electric energies'. These powers or energies were inseparable from matter and constituted the main forces by which chemical combinations and decompositions occurred.

Davy's radical approach did not escape censure. The fluid theory appealed to the majority of the scientists of the day and its rejection was met with hostility. In 1815, for example, Davy was criticized in the *Annals of Philosophy*. After discussing the standard theories, the anonymous author went on:

... Several writers have substituted a phraseology that gives a more specious illustration to certain results, but at the same time involves the whole subject in greater obscurity; for the attempt has been made to explain some of the most interesting effects in galvanism, by what are termed 'electrical energies,' without supposing the existence or action of any distinct galvanic or electric matter.

This vague and general notion may give a plausible solution to the transfer of small bodies through a fluid medium, by supposing that the electrical character of the wires from the battery influences and gives a similar character to the particles of the fluid medium that come in contact with them, and that these portions of the medium influence or give a corresponding electrical character to their adjoining particles. That this communicating principle of the electrical energies may extend itself through the whole of the medium, and produce the transfer in question, does not appear very improbable: but this principle will not readily explain the heating and melting of steel wire when placed in the circuit of the battery; for we can scarcely imagine that the particles of a steel wire ten or twelve inches long, which are evidently held together by a stronger cohesive force than the particles of any other body in nature, can be heated red-hot and torn asunder merely by the wires from the battery being in contrary electrical states, without imparting an active matter to the wire, which must be the case if we do not admit the existence and circulation of the galvanic fluid or fluids.[43]

To an advocate of the kinetic theory of heat, such an objection was far from convincing. Moreover, Davy's views had been strengthened and broadened by his own researches. During the decade 1800–10, he gradually extended the doctrine of forces to include ponderable as well as imponderable matter. There is little doubt that this extension satisfied his deepest philosophical yearning, but the evolution of his ideas was directed by strictly scientific considerations.

Davy astonished the scientific world in 1807 by his announcement of the decomposition of the oxides of sodium and potassium and the isolation of the pure metals. The discovery of a new element is always an exciting event, but in this case, the consequences appeared even more dramatic than the discovery. This was a severe blow to Lavoisier's theory of acids. Oxygen, according to Lavoisier, was the principle of acidity. Yet here its combination with two metals produced the two strongest alkalis known. The reaction of the French chemists was immediate; potassium and sodium could not be elements! They must be compounds in order for the new chemistry to be saved. Gay-Lussac and Thenard even threatened one of Davy's partisans with police action if he dared publish Davy's views![44] Davy, however, refused to be moved, and gradually forced the admission of this seemingly anomalous behaviour of oxygen. Worse, however, was to come. His researches on the nature of muriatic acid led to a frontal assault upon the theory of acidification. By 1810 Davy was convinced of the elementary nature of chlorine and the consequent falsity of the oxygen theory of acids. If acidity were not a property carried by some material entity, what then could it be? This question occupied his mind for years and its resolution was made possible only by a considerable alteration in his theoretical views.

Before 1810 Davy was quite orthodox in his ideas of the origin of chemical qualities. The observable properties of bodies were the result of the presence of specific elements in the compound which carried these properties with them. The effect of combination might dilute the intensity of the various properties, but the presence of an element ought to ensure the presence of its associated quality. His work on sodium and potassium and the discovery of chlorine created serious doubts in Davy's mind. These doubts were further reinforced by his analysis of the diamond. In 1808, he was still of the opinion that carbon and the diamond must have different chemical compositions in order to account for their enormous physical and chemical differences.[45] By 1812 his opinion had shifted considerably. Somewhat hesitantly he suggested that chemical qualities, rather than being associated with particular chemical bodies, might be the result of molecular form. The diffidence felt by Davy in suggesting this concept is revealed by his appeal to the antiquity and respectability of the idea.

> That the forms of natural bodies may depend upon different arrangements of the same particles of matter [he noted] has been a favourite hypothesis advanced in the earliest era of physical research, and often supported by the reasonings of the ablest philosophers. This sublime chemical speculation sanctioned by the authority of Hooke, Newton and Boscovich must not be confounded with the ideas advanced by the alchemists concerning the convertibility of the elements into each other.[46]

He might have added that Coleridge had felt the key to chemistry lay in this concept. 'That which most discourages me', Coleridge had written him in 1801, '. . . is that I find all *power* & vital attributes to depend on modes of *arrangement*.'[47] Certainly, the idea was not a new one to Davy by 1812 and, while it discouraged Coleridge, his researches on the diamond with Faraday seemed to require its adoption.

> The only chemical difference perceptible between diamond and the purest charcoal, is that the last contains a minute proportion of hydrogen; but can a quantity of an element, less in some cases than $\frac{1}{50000}$ part of the weight of the substance, occasion so great a difference in physical and chemical characters? This is possible, yet it is contrary to analogy, and I am more inclined to adopt

the opinion of Mr Tennant, that the difference depends upon crystallization. Transparent solid bodies are in general non-conductors of electricity, and it is probable that the same corpuscular arrangements which give to matter the power of transmitting and polarizing light, are likewise connected with its relations to electricity; . . .[48]

By 1816 Davy had repudiated his earlier position, and even suggested that the whole concept of chemical qualities adhering to the elements was thoroughly unscientific. In a passage often (and erroneously) cited as evidence for Davy's dim apprehension of the hydrogen theory of acids, he criticized his French rival Gay-Lussac in harsh terms:

> I cannot admit M. Gay-Lussac's views on the classification of the undecompounded substances, nor can I adopt his ideas respecting their properties as chemical agents. He considers hydrogen as an *alkalizing* principle, and azote as an *acidifying* principle. This is an attempt to introduce into chemistry a doctrine of occult qualities, and to refer to some mysterious and inexplicable energy what must depend upon a peculiar corpuscular arrangement. If hydrogen be an alkalizing principle, it is strange that it should form some of the strongest acids by uniting to bodies not in themselves acid; and if azote be an acidifying principle, it is equally strange that it should form nearly nine-tenths of the weight of the volatile alkali. It is impossible to infer what will be the qualities of a compound from the qualities of its constituents. . . .[49]

The idea of molecular form as the cause of chemical and physical properties was not new, as Davy indicated. Before the early nineteenth century, however, it had been a purely metaphysical concept incapable of experimental test. By 1815 it appeared to Davy to be the only way to explain such observations as the identity of substance in the diamond and carbon and their widely differing properties. But to suggest molecular arrangement as a solution raised another question of almost equal importance with the one that had been answered. How and why did the particles of matter arrange themselves in the specific forms from which the observed qualities arose? In 1808 John Dalton had suggested that the chemical elements were composed of atoms endowed with the power of universal attraction. Could not molecular form be envisioned merely as the spatial arrangement of these atoms under the influence of the attractive force? To many, perhaps most, of the chemists who ultimately accepted the atomic theory, the piling up of 'billiard-ball' atoms in space in regular forms seemed both possible and plausible. Davy, however, could not accept this view. His metaphysical training had made him extremely cautious in regard to the existence of a material sub-stratum of observed reality. Daltonian atoms were in the same category as imponderable fluids; hypothetical entities invented to account for observed phenomena.

Furthermore, Davy recognized that the simple picture of little hard spheres arranged in regular forms could not be a true one. In the first place, atoms could not be in contact with one another since cooling a body caused it to contract. There must, therefore, be space between atoms to permit contraction to take place. Daltonian atoms must repel as well as attract one another. More importantly, the mere force of universal attraction could never give rise to regular forms. Atoms would form amorphous clumps, not geometrical solids, if left solely to the influence of attraction acting uniformly on all atoms in all directions with an intensity that varied only inversely with the square of the distance. Finally, Dalton's atomic theory violated the law of continuity for there were jumps of weight which distinguished the elements from one another. This, Davy would not accept.

In order to account for molecular form without having recourse to solid atoms, Davy turned to an atomic theory which had first been suggested in the eighteenth century. With this theory all difficulties disappeared.

3. The Theory of Point Atoms

In 1763 a remarkable book was published in Venice by a Jesuit priest, Roger Joseph Boscovich.[50] Its title, *Theoria naturalis philosophiae* (A Theory of Natural Philosophy) was modest enough but its aim was nothing less than a universal scientific theory by which all natural phenomena could be explained. It contained an atomic theory which was to influence the course of science throughout the nineteenth century.

Boscovich had been led to his atomic theory by the consideration of what appeared, at first sight, to be a very simple problem – the exact mechanism of atomic impact. Like most Newtonians, Boscovich had accepted the mechanical philosophy for the explanation of natural events. In this system, observable reality was the result of the motion, impact, and form of atoms. Atoms were like little billiard balls, only perfectly hard, elastic, and impenetrable. To most natural philosophers of the eighteenth century, the collision of two atoms was exactly analogous to the collision of two billiard balls. Boscovich realized that the situation was more complicated. When two billiard balls collide, the result is elastic deformation and recovery; the deformation is made possible by the fact that the molecules of the billiard balls can move relative to one another. It is the displacement of these molecules and their subsequent return to normal position that leads to elastic rebound. With atoms, such a process is clearly impossible. Since atoms have no parts and are perfectly hard, deformation is impossible. What happens, then, when two moving atoms meet? If they are little billiard balls, Boscovich argued, and if deformation is impossible, no time can elapse between contact and rebound. Thus, at the moment of impact, the atoms will have two velocities at the same time. They will have their original velocity and the velocity of rebound. To Boscovich this was logically and physically absurd yet it was a necessary consequence of the theory of material atoms. Boscovich's solution was a radical one; he eliminated matter completely as a separate entity and replaced it with attractive and repulsive forces. An atom was to be considered as a dimensionless mathematical point. Surrounding this point were forces which were alternately attractive and repulsive. Thus

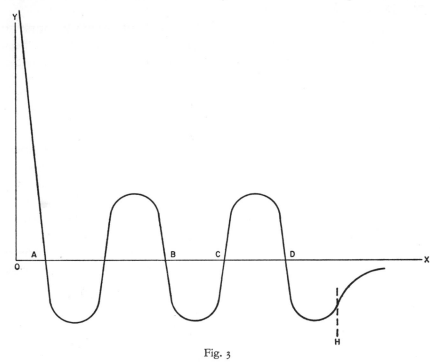

Fig. 3

in Figure 3, if another point were to approach an atomic point at O, it would pass along the series of curves which cut the x-axis. From infinity to H, this curve represents the inverse square law of universal gravitation. At H, the dividing line between the macroscopic and the atomic world, the attractive force intensifies until it reaches a maximum and then decreases, ultimately becoming repulsive as one passed D. The repulsive force, in turn, increases to a maximum and then decreases to zero. At A, still another change takes place. As we move closer to O, the repulsive force constantly increases so that at O, it is infinite.

With this model, Boscovich was able to account for atomic impact with no difficulty. Since the curve of atomic forces was continuous, the repulsion between two colliding atoms increased continuously with time and the absurdity of the Newtonian case was avoided. Moreover, Boscovich's atoms preserved all the essential qualities of Newtonian atomism. By postulating an infinite repulsive force at O, impenetrability could be retained as an essential property of matter. Extension, too (although now it was force that was extended) remained as a basic attribute of 'matter'.

Point atoms not only could explain phenomena as well as their Newtonian rivals, but in some instances, were notably more convenient. One of these was the problem of change of state. Here, again, was a seeming discontinuity in nature that the concept of billiard balls did little to explain. Why, when heat was added to a substance, did it suddenly change its physical form at a specific temperature? If, as Joseph Black, the discoverer of latent heat, suggested, the change from ice to water, or water to steam was a simple chemical reaction between a ponderable base and caloric, then this reaction was unique for only the physical properties of the base were altered. If change of state was to be explained upon the purely mechanical principles of the repulsion of caloric, it was difficult to see why the change was so sudden and dramatic. With point atoms, however, no difficulties appeared. There were certain stable points on the curve (i.e. B); when heat (in the form of atomic or molecular motion) was added to a body composed of these atoms, their oscillations would eventually push them over the 'hump' of repulsion to a new stable position at a great distance from one another. Thus, the specificity of melting- and boiling-points of substances followed directly from a consideration of the curve of forces.

The problem of crystalline form also was more easily solved within the framework of point atoms. Boscovich insisted upon, and his later disciples emphasized, the fact that the elements of the chemist were *not* these simple point atoms. Chemical elements were, rather, complex combinations of atoms. The association of a number of atoms gave rise to a very complex pattern of forces surrounding the molecule. Attractive and repulsive forces would cancel one another out at certain points; at others, forces would add together so that the 'shell' of force would be the resultant of these complex interactions. The association of molecules with one another will depend upon the compatibility of the forms of their force shells. If attractive forces can mesh, they will do so and always in the

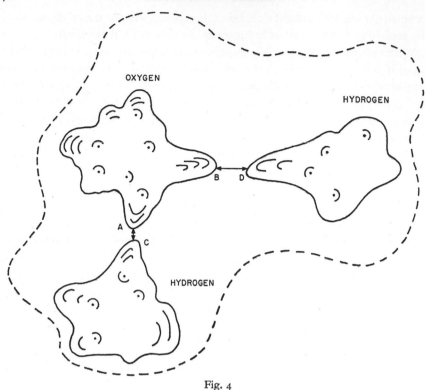

Fig. 4

same pattern. The regularity of crystalline form, therefore, can be deduced (qualitatively) from the molecular forces although it was impossible to deduce specific forms for specific crystals until the pattern of force for individual molecules could be determined.

The complex pattern of molecular forces also made it possible to visualize the mechanism of chemical combination. The problem of elective affinity had long occupied chemists; at the beginning of the nineteenth century it was further complicated by the enunciation of the laws of definite and multiple proportions. Very simply stated, the problem was this. Given billiard ball atoms attracting one another according to the law of universal attraction, why did not the mixture of any two reagents result in combination? Why, in short, did not all reactions 'go'? The answer, in terms of point atoms, was simple. Only those reactions could take place in which the constituent molecules had force patterns that permitted them to interlock. The 'lock and key' concept also explained why only certain combinations occur in specific proportions of the constituents. Instead of amorphous clumps, the result was regularly formed compounds in which the molecules were associated with one another in definite proportions and with definite configurations.

Figure 4 may serve to illustrate what a water molecule might look like in the Boscovichean system. The association of the point atoms together gives rise to a resultant pattern of forces – in the figure, the outline represents the strength of the attractive force at different distances from the centre of gravity of the elementary particle. Oxygen has two places of intense attractive force at *A* and *B*. The hydrogen particle has but one such 'peak' of force at *C* in the one and *D* in the other. The most stable arrangement will occur when these areas of intense attraction come together and this will then form a molecule of water. This molecule, in turn, will have a resultant pattern of force surrounding it (dotted line) that will give it the properties of water. *All* water molecules will, then, have the same form and, therefore, the same properties. The same general argument is applicable to crystalline bodies.

The only disadvantage of this theory was its rejection of matter. This was the hurdle that most practising chemists could not vault. Typical of the reasons for rejecting the whole concept of point atoms were those given by Alexander Tilloch, the editor of the *Philosophical Magazine* which, next to the *Philosophical Transactions* of the Royal Society, was the most prestigious general scientific journal in England in the nineteenth century. After describing Boscovich's ideas, Tilloch concluded:

> On this theory we shall only observe, that whatever conviction it may carry to minds habituated to profound mathematical investigations, it can convey but little information to a man who merely aims at a knowledge of the properties of matter, as consisting, not of *inextended* atoms, but of such moleculae as occupy sensible space. What the wiser is such a man for being told that certain forces exist, and that some idea may be formed of their mode of operating by conceiving them to act in the directions of certain curves, and with powers varying according to circumstances? He may assent to this; but as his weak mind can conceive nothing of matter inextended, either in itself or in its atoms, he cannot consider his difficulties as solved by merely having them stated to him in a new form; for to him the whole of this system appears to be no more at best but a regular mathematical statement of those operations of matter, the causes of which he still wishes to explore.[51]

A similar judgement was passed by Thomas Thomson, editor of the *Annals of Philosophy* and author of one of the most widely-read textbooks of chemistry.[52]

The opposition to Boscovich's theory is of importance for the understanding of both Davy's and Faraday's work. Although he did not publicly announce his commitment to the theory of point atoms until 1844,

Faraday worked within this framework from his earliest productive years. The fact that both Davy and Faraday knew that their atomic theories would be dismissed as metaphysics at best or meaningless at worst led them both to keep them in the background. In both men's papers, the reader was informed, almost casually, of the theoretical framework within which new results were being reported. Only rarely, however, was this framework insisted upon. The result has been that Davy and Faraday are characterized in the history of science as empiricists without any general theoretical foundation of any importance. This, it will be shown, is both false and misleading.

Exactly when Humphry Davy accepted the Boscovichean theory can only be guessed at. His biographer, Dr Paris, mentions that he had occupied himself in his youth with a study of impact and elasticity.[53] It is possible that his studies here brought him into touch with Boscovich's solution of the problem of atomic collisions. If so, the theory played no active role in his own original investigations. As his mind wrestled with the problem of the cause of acidity after he had convinced himself of the elementary nature of chlorine, the doctrine of molecular form became increasingly seductive. In 1812 in his *Elements of Chemical Philosophy*, he cautiously introduced the idea of point atoms, but only as one possible way of conceiving the basis of observed phenomena. Thus he wrote, 'Whether matter consists of indivisible corpuscles, or physical points endowed with attraction and repulsion, still the same conclusions may be formed concerning the powers by which they act, and the quantities in which they combine; and the powers seem capable of being measured by their electrical relations, and the quantities on which they act of being expressed by numbers.'[54] And again, later on: 'If the particles of matter be supposed to be globular, or to act in spheres of attraction and repulsion, it would be easy to account for their forms, by supposing a few independent primary arrangements. Thus, four particles may compose a tetrahedron, give a tetrahedral pyramid, six an octahedron, or a triedral prism, and eight a cube or a rhomboid.'[55]

During his travels on the Continent while he was occupied with the problem of the diamond, Boscovich's theory appeared to offer the only solution. It was sometime in 1815 that Davy began to use this hypothesis as a general concept by which all phenomena could be explained.

By assuming certain molecules endowed with poles in points of attraction and repulsion as Boscovich has done [he noted in his *Common Place* book] and giving them gravitation and form, i.e. weight and measure, all the phenomena of chemistry may be accounted for. They will form spherical masses when their attractions balance the repulsions ... and chemical combination will depend upon particles meeting so as to be in polar relations – so that their spheres of attraction may coincide; but we may suppose inherent powers (thus we suppose iron naturally polar with respect to the magnet) – Heat may assist chemical action by enlarging the sphere of action and by expanding bodies – electrical attractions and repulsions, an increase of corpuscular attractions – conductors, polar ... nonconductors, primary multipolar, imperfect (bipolar) conductors, panapolar – Transparent bodies nonconductors, particles further removed, and they are polar with respect to light – certain liquids imperfect conductors, when solid, nonconductors. This owing ... to crystalline arrangements which interferes with the communication of polarity.[56]

From 1815 until the end of his life, Davy thought of matter in terms of point atoms surrounded by attractive and repulsive forces. It was not until his scientific career was at an end, however, that he publicly stated his position. Lest there be any who still feel that Davy's adoption of Boscovich's ideas was but momentary and of no great importance, a final citation may perhaps be permitted. In 1829, he published his philosophical Last Testament. In *Consolations in Travel: or, The Last Days of a Philosopher* he gave utterance to all those speculative ideas which lay behind his researches. This was no careful experimentalist, marshalling his evidence in detail; instead there was Davy the poet and dreamer who wished to pass on his vision of the universe to coming generations. Speaking through the medium of a character so clothed in romantic mystery as to be identified only as 'The Unknown' Davy presented his last argument for his atomic beliefs.

The Unknown: You mistake me if you suppose I have adopted a system like the *Homooia* of Anaxagoras, and that I suppose the elements to be physical molecules endowed with the properties of the bodies we believe to be indecomposable. On the contrary, I neither suppose in them figure nor colour, – both would imply a power of reflecting light: I consider them, with Boscovitch, merely as points possessing weight and attractive and repulsive powers; and composing according to the circumstances of their arrangements either spherules or regular solids, and capable of assuming either one form or the other. All that is necessary for the doctrines of the corpuscular philosophy is to suppose the molecules which we are not able to decompose, spherical molecules; and that by the arrangement of spherical molecules regular solids are formed; and that the molecules have certain attractive and repulsive powers which correspond to negative and positive electricity. This is not mere supposition unsupported by experiments; there are various facts which give probability to the idea, which I shall now state to you. The *first fact* is, that all bodies are capable of being rendered fluid by a certain degree of heat, which supposes a freedom of motion in their particles that cannot be well explained except by supposing them spherical in the fluid state. The *second fact* is, that all bodies in becoming solid are capable of assuming regular poly-hedral forms. The *third fact* is that all crystalline bodies present regular electrical poles. And the *fourth* is, that the elements of bodies are capable of being separated from each other by certain electrical attractions and repulsions.[57]

With these words, Davy concluded the last work he was ever to publish. He fell victim to a stroke and died on 29 May 1829.

4. Michael Faraday as Philosopher

Faraday's interest in the fundamental problems of philosophy was aroused in his very early years. He appears to have puzzled over the question of man's relation to an external reality even as a boy for he later wrote to his friend Abbott:

> Six or seven years ago whilst standing at the door of a gentleman's house and waiting until my knock should be answered, I thrust my head through some iron railing that separated the doorway from another and then I began to consider on which side of the rail I was. In my mind I affirmed that the side possessing my head was my station for there was my perception, my senses. I had just sufficient time to ascertain this when the door opened and my nose began bleeding by the contact of the rail and such matter as that quickly put flight to my rude metaphysics. Simple as is this instance, it did more in illu-strating this case to me than all the arguments I have heard since on the sub-ject or all the affirmations that have been made.[58]

Faraday, unfortunately, did not go on to spell out the conclusions he drew from this experience but they seem to be rather obvious.[59] If we assume, as appears to have been the case, that Faraday had somehow come in contact with the philosophy of Bishop Berkeley, the iron railing provided the opportunity for an interesting internal dialogue. Having effected the separation of Mind and Body, the young philosopher could indulge in his metaphysical fancies until the real world of matter intruded itself suddenly and unpleasantly upon his musings. From that time on, he never seriously doubted the reality of the external world.

Time, too, appears to have attracted his attention and again Berkeley appears to have influenced him. There was nothing very profound in his concept of time, but it is of some interest to notice that the problem even occurred to him. Time, according to the common-sense definition, is a separate entity which one measures by clocks in the same way that linear dimensions are measured by rulers. Time is, therefore, an absolute entity, a position taken by Sir Isaac Newton himself.

Opposition to such a view of time was quick to arise. Leibnitz and Berkeley both attacked it but on totally different grounds. Berkeley's definition is worth citing for Faraday repeated it almost verbatim. 'Time', Berkeley wrote, 'is the train of ideas succeeding each other.'[60] In a similar fashion Faraday wrote to his friend Abbott: 'For as time is measured merely by the events that succeed each other the more of these that are put together the greater will appear the space over which they are expanded and the more distant will be two objects that bound them.'[61]

The difference between this way of looking at time and that of New-tonian physics may appear trivial at first glance. In reality, it was of considerable importance in the development of Faraday's mature thought. In his view, time was equated with a succession of physical events hence any phenomenon which endured in time necessarily implied a physical process. His efforts to detect the propagation of electric, magnetic, and gravitational fields in time were inspired by this concept for if such a time relation could be found, it would provide strong evidence for his view of the progressive transmission of force through space.

In his years as a fledgeling philosopher, however, the deeper questions of physical reality served primarily as the background against which he could project his fervour for mental improvement. In a series of essays written in the Class Book of the little study group he organized in 1818, he urged his friends on to greater efforts.

In two essays, 'On Imagination and Judgement' and 'On the Pleasures and Uses of the Imagination' he explored these two faculties. Imagination, in its pure state, Faraday described as akin to idle wool-gathering yielding pleasure but little else. Judgement, on the other hand, was what forced the mind to attend to its business and unravel the twisted skein of events. But, Faraday insisted, there is really no opposition between these two faculties. It was from their combined powers only that important results come.

> Judgement [he wrote] is united to learning; its employment is the finding differences and truth is its offspring while imagination is busy in tracing like-nesses and wit is the result. It would be too much perhaps to say which pro-duces the greatest satisfaction but certainly that resulting from judgement is the noblest and that of imagination the most enticing but where a union of the two takes place in a strong degree there will always be a great cause for our admiration. The fairest fruits are the highest hung and few there are who can reach them.[62]

An imagination which could soar to heights far beyond those of his contemporaries held in check by a judgement which subjected the vision provided by the imagination to the most careful and critical scrutiny marked Faraday's mature mind. His juvenile essays are more than mere didactic pieces; they are autobiographical fragments reflecting the facets of his genius.

In his second essay, Faraday turned his attention more particularly to the imagination and the sources from which it springs. The sense of sight was singled out as the most important element because of its immediacy and its seeming independence of matter. The other senses, as they are more closely tied to material causes, are grosser and, therefore, less fit to feed a faculty of the mind. Through the sight, however, the soul itself is stirred. The romantic love of nature struck a responsive chord in Faraday, and he used natural beauty to illustrate his point.

> A sensitive mind will always acknowledge the pleasures it receives from a luxuriant prospect of nature; the beautiful mingling and gradations of colour, the delicate perspective, the ravishing effect of light and shade, and the fascinating variety and grace of the outline, must be seen to be felt; for expressions can never convey the extatic joy they give to the imagination, or the benevolent feeling they create in the mind. There is no boundary, there is no restraint 'til reason draws the rein, and then imagination retires into its recesses, and delivers herself up to the guidance of that superior power.[63]

Faraday's treatment of the imagination was light and graceful as befits the subject. When he turned to the Mind, however, the tone changed. The colour deepened, the language became solemn and the subject was wrapped in a gravity which Faraday reserved only for subjects of the greatest importance to him. The opening paragraph of his essay 'On Mind and the Duty of improving it' set forth his views with force and clarity.[64]

> Associated together in Man by the strongest ties, still no two things are more distinct from each other than Mind and Matter. We can not in any way assimilate them, or make them identical, or can we confound their relations, or trace them to one common origin. Every effect, or motion, or change dependant on the one part, or the other, carries with it that mark of its source which it is impossible for an *indifferent* mind to mistake; and even Materialists are spited by their very reasonings proving in each step of their progress the opposite of the conclusion which *is* to come.[65]

The main message was the duty of the rational man to assert the supremacy of mind over matter in himself. The body, to be sure, must be satisfied but it must not be indulged. Bodily pleasures should not be denied but in the hierarchy of pleasure they must rank below those of the mind. Only when the mind has been developed through exercise and use, can it truly be appreciated.

Of more interest and importance was the subtlety which Faraday introduced into his argument. He did not, like Coleridge, draw a sharp line of demarcation between mind and matter; nor did he, like Berkeley, enclose matter in mind. Instead, he recognized the extraordinarily complex relations that exist between mind and matter in the individual human being.

> The two parts of which man is formed [he remarked] are not associated in any of their proper habits, pleasures, or perceptions; but have distinct objects, distinct modes of action, and distinct gratifications. They *are*, however, associated together in one being; and may be said to a certain extent, to have a common existence, in consequence of the relations and connections, which in that being are found necessary between them. The line, therefore, which may be supposed to divide the two sets of relations and habitudes belonging to Mind and Matter, has no existence; for wherever we presume to draw it, it trespasses either on the one set or the other. In enumerating and associating together, the modes, affection, and dependencies of the mind, we should at once claim the Judgement, Memory, and Imagination, with their Progeny, and we should reject Solidity and Extension, with the qualities Opacity, Hardness, Mobility, etc., dependant on them: But in gathering up the strings which tie Mind and Matter together, doubts would arise respecting their place, and consideration would only render us more undecided. Sensation, for instance, would at first be given to the corporeal system: but, surely, *all* sensation is not corporeal; or if you affirm that it is; inform me where sensation terminates, and how, and when it is, that mind aids and at last makes the pleasure.[66]

This realization of an area in which mind and matter were inextricably combined strongly influenced Faraday's approach to the material world. On the one hand, it revealed itself in his extraordinary sensitivity to sources of error. Where others made a rigid distinction between fact and theory, analogous to the distinction between matter and mind, Faraday recognized that the edges between these two areas were often blurred and indistinguishable. His reliance on fact was made possible by the constant vigilance he exercised to prevent a mental concept from being taken prematurely for a physical effect.

His theoretical daring also owed much to his idea of mind and matter. Laws of nature were the result of Mind; the mental constructs of his mind, therefore, might reasonably be supposed to reflect the order imposed upon brute matter by Mind. When a harmony between rigorously determined physical facts and a logically coherent theory was reached, then philosophic and scientific truth were in sight. It was the recognition of this harmony which gave Faraday the strength and patience to ignore his critics, secure in the knowledge that future generations would judge his theories aright.

It was one thing to state broad metaphysical principles concerning the roles of mind and matter in the universe; it was another to find a satisfactory solution to the specific problems in chemistry to which his association with Davy and the Royal Institution exposed him after 1812. In the years from 1812 to 1819 his views on the more detailed aspects of the material world shifted back and forth between a number of different positions. We can best follow these shifts by tracing his ideas on two questions of basic importance in his whole scientific career. What was the nature of the imponderable fluids? and what was the fundamental nature of matter?

We have already witnessed the early development of Faraday's ideas on electricity. In 1812, when he first made Davy's acquaintance, he was a confessed and ardent believer in the real existence of imponderable fluids. Davy, in the first lecture Faraday attended, soon shook this belief. Having warned his audience of the dangers of creating new material entities without sufficient evidence, as the French had done with caloric, Davy went on to consider the general properties of radiant matter. Each species was carefully analysed and described. What intrigued Davy, however, were the analogies between various actions of ponderable and radiant matter. 'There is a very singular analogy', he noted, 'that exists between the Rays at the Violet end of the spectrum, Hydrogen gas, and the Negative Pole of the Voltaic Battery and opposed to it stands the analogy of the rays at the Red end of the Spectrum to Positive . . . Electricity.'[67]

The analogy between such disparate 'substances' seemed to militate against a theory of individual fluids all endowed with the same qualities. On this point, Davy was both explicit and eloquent. 'If we suppose that each radiant body is a peculiar and separate substance then we shall have one for heat, one for electricity, one for Violet rays, another for Blue rays, a third for Red rays, others for the other coloured rays of the spectrum and by that means we should soon have an infinite variety of substance that we know little or nothing about.'[68]

The hypothesis of imponderable fluids was still further undermined by Faraday's study of Davy's *Elements of Chemical Philosophy*. Faraday's guide through this work was Davy himself for when the two were in Paris in 1814, Davy set about revising the text for a new edition. The copy of the original edition in which the revisions were made is now in the Royal Institution. All the revisions are in Faraday's hand. Although neither Davy nor Faraday mention the work of revision, it is not impossible to reconstruct what must have been the course of events. Davy showed every sign of being quite fond of his young amanuensis and, considering the inconveniences to which his lack of a valet put Faraday, was no doubt willing to go out of his way to be cordial to him. Faraday's critical faculties were never dormant and we can imagine the two men going over the text together. Davy, the brilliant lecturer and natural teacher, would explain why such a change here, or use of a different phrase there improved upon the original. Faraday, copying down these changes, would ask for clarifications of points he did not understand, would point out seeming inconsistencies, would ask for the empirical evidence for this or that theoretical statement.

The result was that Faraday found himself in an intellectual muddle. The fluid theory had the great virtue of simplicity and was not to be discarded lightly. Nor could Davy's arguments be ignored. The result was a combination of agnosticism and confusion as far as the imponderable agents were concerned. This can be seen most clearly in the series of lectures that Faraday delivered to the members of the City Philosophical Society between 1816 and 1819.

In his notes for the introductory lecture he summed up his knowledge of the nature of electricity thus: 'Electricity – instances of it – no definition can be given of it – a proof that its first principles are unknown.'[69]

The fact that electricity could be varied in bodies led him to hazard a guess on its nature in spite of his confession of ignorance. 'Electric powers of matter . . . – powers of matter increased or diminished by circumstances – lead to a supposition that it was truly a power and not a variety of matter.'[70]

The influence of Davy can be clearly discerned for the fluid theory can as easily account for the increase and decrease in electrification as can a theory of powers of matter.

In the lecture on the general properties of matter, however, Faraday slipped back into the terminology of the fluid theory.[71] He also spoke approvingly of another theory of electric action which deserves mention. In 1814 George John Singer had published his *Elements of Electricity and Electrochemistry* in which, while retaining the fluid theory, he rejected the concept of repulsive action at a distance. All cases of so-called repulsion Singer reduced to the differential attractions between the medium in which two electrified bodies are immersed and the bodies themselves.

Faraday's account of this new theory revealed his reaction to still another theory of electrical action. Having described the phenomenon of static electric induction, he wrote:

This induced Electricity is very well accounted for by Mr Singer, who refuses repulsive powers to the electric fluid; and he shews that attraction alone is

D

sufficient to produce the effect. My plan, however, does not permit me to be diffuse in the theoretical parts of the science. It is my endeavour at present is [*sic*] to point out to you what is certain; not what is hypothetical, and to lay before you the principal effects produced by this important agent, that we may form some idea of such a singular power or variety of matter.[72]

Faraday's treatment of magnetism was similar to that of electricity except that he was able to compress all the theoretical confusion into one short paragraph.

It is difficult to form any satisfactory ideas respecting the nature of magnetism; it may be a modification of gravitation, or the power producing it, in certain bodies. It may be a modification of electricity, or the causes which produce it. Or it may be dissimilar from all other powers, or forms of matter and perfectly distinct. And again it may be a peculiar kind of attraction or a peculiar and subtil fluid.[73]

This was in 1816. By 1819, after three years of constant attendance to the theory and practice of chemistry, Faraday's ideas had become clearer and his position more firm. In a lecture on the forms of matter, delivered 26 May 1819, he presented his thoughts again on the question of the nature of the imponderables.

The nature of heat electricity, &c., are unsettled points. . . . Some boldly assert them to be matter. Others more cautious, and not willing to admit the existence of matter without that evidence of the senses which applies to it, rank them as qualities. It is almost necessary that in a lecture on Matter and its states, I should give you my opinion on this point, and it inclines to the immaterial nature of these agencies. One thing however is fortunate which is, that whatever our opinions, they do not alter or derange the laws of nature. We may think of heat as a property, or as matter, it will still be of the utmost benefit and importance to us. We may differ with respect to the way in which it acts, it will still act effectually and for our good; and after all, our differences are merely squabbles about words, since nature our object is one and the same.[74]

In 1819 Faraday was nearing the end of his apprenticeship as a chemist. He had, as yet, made no new discovery. Theory, therefore, was useful to him only as a kind of shorthand by which empirical facts could be conveniently classed and generalized. It was not until 1821 that he was to realize the importance of theory as an instrument of discovery. Mere squabbles over words were then to take on a new light and become of central concern to him.

The development of his ideas on the fundamental nature of matter followed much the same course as the evolution of his concepts of the imponderables. Before he met Davy, his most important source of theoretical ideas on the nature of matter had been Thomas Thomson's *A System of Chemistry*. In these early days of his scientific career, he had been quite pleased with Thomson's approach. In one of his first letters to Benjamin Abbott, Faraday cited Thomson's definition of chemistry:

> Definitions, dear A., are valuable things; I like them very much, and will be glad, when you meet with clever ones, if you will transcribe them. I am exceedingly well pleased with Dr Thomson's definition of chemistry; he calls it the science of insensible motions; 'Chemistry is that science which treats of those events or changes in natural bodies which consist of insensible motions,' in contradistinction to mechanics, which treats of sensible motions.[75]

In his third edition of 1807, Thomson introduced Dalton's atomic theory and the definition made perfect sense within this framework. Atoms bump into one another, stick together, or are torn apart, thus giving rise to the chemical changes observable in the ordinary world. The definition had only one major fault; it was totally worthless as a practical theory of chemical action. By definition the motions of atoms were insensible and hence, unlike mechanics, they could not be subjected directly to analysis. They could, of course, be inferred from other phenomena but this involved a long chain of hypotheses which, as Faraday became more scientifically sophisticated, he was ever less willing to accept.

Thomson did not confine himself to a discussion of Daltonian atomism; he also included a long section on the ideas of Boscovich. He rejected the notion of point atoms, but gave a fair summary of the theory as a whole. There is no indication that Faraday's first contact with Boscovich's ideas had any effect whatsoever on him. In his discussion with Abbott of the reactions of chlorine, he spoke of atoms in an orthodox Daltonian sense. It was not until he associated closely with Davy that his ideas began to change. It was Davy's work on the diamond that appears to have been the crucial factor. In 1812 Faraday had heard Davy insist that the difference between carbon and the diamond must consist in the presence of some material difference in the two substances.[76] Faraday was at Davy's side throughout the investigations at Florence when Davy changed his mind and attributed the difference in quality to difference in molecular configuration. The lesson was not lost on him. In a lecture on the attraction of cohesion given before the City Philosophical Society on 10 April 1816, he pointed out why the Daltonian concept was unable to account for the difference in crystalline forms. 'We still however remain ignorant', he pointed out, 'after all that has been stated of that power of matter which causes it to assume regular forms. A *knowledge* of the attractive power which all the particles of matter possess one on *another* is not sufficient to account for them for this power would cause them to combine indiscriminately and without any tendency to certain particular situations.'[77]

What was surprising was that instead of going on to describe the Boscovichean system which provided a most eloquent solution to this problem, Faraday preferred a kind of hybrid theory which retained a core of matter but limited the ways in which molecules could associate with one another.

> Haüy [he informed his listeners] has made it probable not only that the particles of matter are of certain definite and similar forms but that these particles when left at liberty combine or unite only in particular positions, certain sides of the particles always coming into contact. This however can only be explained by supposing a polarity to exist in the particles and that certain points attract whilst others repel and there are many other phenomena which seem to indicate a polarity of this kind in many of the varieties of matter.[78]

In spite of his inability to take the jump from billiard ball atoms to points surrounded by forces, a subtle change in his attitude is apparent. The little material *something* at the centre of a Daltonian or Haüyian atom or molecule had gradually faded in importance. What was central were the powers associated with these molecules; and, even here, there was a fundamental distinction. It was not the force of attraction or repulsion that claimed the attention of the chemist, but the *pattern* of such forces. Thomson's definition of chemistry was modified by this awareness of the effect of complex actions of force. 'Chemistry, then,' Faraday pointed out to his audience, 'is that science which treats of those events or changes in natural bodies, which are *not* accompanied by *sensible* motions.'[79] Where Thomson had seen chemistry as a kind of micro-mechanics, Faraday now told his listeners that it was *not* macro-mechanics. What chemistry *is* was quite another matter. 'It is a knowledge of the powers and properties of matter and of the effects produced by these powers.'[80] The transition from this definition to the acceptance of point atoms was not a large one but it was more than Faraday felt was justifiable at this time. His only reference in these lectures to this theory was very guarded and noncommittal. Discussing solidity as a quality of material bodies, he wrote:

> This idea of solidity has been opposed, and it is still contested by some whether such solidity exists. It implies a plenum or fullness of matter; but a theory has been started, which supposes matter to be merely a collection of mathematical points of attraction, and repulsion; and these points having no parts, it is said that they have neither extension or solidity; and, that if it were possible to overcome the repulsive and attractive forces, two portions of matter might co-exist in the same place.[81]

It was not until the 1820's when he began to wrestle more closely with theoretical questions that the hypothesis of point atoms finally was accepted.

Faraday's suspension of judgement on the nature of electricity, magnetism, and matter itself well illustrates a distinguishing characteristic of his mind. He was always willing to refrain from leaping to a conclusion until the evidence appeared to justify it. More importantly, he was constantly aware of the possibility, nay the inevitability, of error in any general statement. He did not, for this, refuse to make such statements. Rather, he was one of those rare philosophers who recognized the enormous utility of error; Bacon's phrase 'Truth is more likely to arise from error than from confusion' was constantly quoted by him. In the career which, in 1819, was just opening before him he was to strive for truth, but always welcome correction of his errors. At the end of his last lecture to the City Philosophical Society, he enunciated the philosophical credo which was to guide him all his life.

> Nothing is more difficult and requires more care than philosophical deduction, nor is there any thing more adverse to its accuracy than fixidity of opinion. The man who is certain he is right is almost sure to be wrong; and he has the additional misfortune of inevitably remaining so. All our theories are fixed upon uncertain data, and all of them want alteration and support. Ever since the world began opinion has changed with the progress of things, and it is something more than absurd to suppose that we have a certain claim to perfection; or that we are in possession of the acme of intellectuality which has, or can result from human thought. Why our successors should not displace us in our opinions, as well as in our persons, it is difficult to say; it ever has been so, and from an analogy would be supposed to continue so. And yet with all the practical evidence of the fallibility of our opinions, all and none more than philosophers, are ready to assert the real truth of their opinions.
>
> The history of the opinions on the general nature of matter would afford remarkable illustrations in support of what I have said but it does not belong to my subject to *extend upon it*. All I wish to point out is by a reference to Light, Heat, Electricity, &c., and the opinions formed on them the necessity of cautious and slow decision on philosophical points, the care with which evidence ought to be admitted, and the continual guard against philosophical prejudices which should be preserved in the mind. The man who wishes to advance in knowledge should never of himself fix obstacles in the way.[82]

With these words, Faraday's philosophical apprenticeship ended. By 1819 he had the breadth of vision, the necessary critical apparatus, and the technical training to enter the ranks of the creative scientist. An unparalleled career in scientific discovery was about to begin.

References

1. For a detailed analysis of electrical and magnetic investigations and theories in the eighteenth century, see I. Bernard Cohen's magistral *Franklin and Newton* (Philadelphia, 1956).

2. For some of the questions that remain to be answered, see L. Pearce Williams, 'The Physical Sciences in the First Half of the Nineteenth Century: Problems and Sources', *History of Science, 1* (1962), 1 ff.

3. Henry E. Guerlac, 'A Lost Memoir of Lavoisier', *Isis, 50* (1959), 125 ff.

4. The failure of the Abbé Nollet's model with separate pores for the incoming and outgoing effluvia marks an important point in the development of electrical and magnetic theory. Newton, as Faraday later was to insist upon time and time again, had never accepted action at a distance as a *physical* cause. From a close reading of the *Opticks*, and from his famous *Third Letter to Bentley* it appears certain that Newton felt he had to account for attraction and repulsion by means of direct impact of some kind. After the failure of Nollet's model, primarily because of its *physical* clumsiness, such impact explanations were quietly abandoned and action at a distance introduced. The *mechanism* of such action was simply ignored.

5. For the generally accepted views of the relation between the electrical and magnetic fluids and ponderable matter, see L. Pearce Williams, 'Ampère's Electrodynamic Molecular Model', *Cont. Phys., 4* (1962), 113 ff.; also below, Chapter Four.

6. Joseph Priestley, *The History and Present State of Electricity* (3rd ed., 2 vols., London, 1775), 79.

7. C. Coulomb, 'Deuxième Mémoire où l'on détermine quelles lois le fluide magnétique ainsi que le fluide électrique agissent soit par repulsion, soit par attraction', in *Collection de Mémoires relatifs à la physique, publiés par la Société française de physique, 1, Mémoires de Coulomb* (Paris, 1884), 126.

8. A. Volta, 'Nuova memoria sull-elettricità animale divisa in tre lettere dirette al Signor Abate Anton Maria Vassalli, Professore di Fisica nella R. Universita di Torino', *Giorn. Fisico Medico del Sig. Brugnatelli, 2* (1794), 248 ff. Most easily consulted in *Collezione dell'Opere del Cavaliere Conte Alessandro Volta* (3 vols., Firenze, 1816), *2*, 197.

9. 'On the Electricity excited by the mere Contact of conducting Substances of different kinds. In a Letter from Mr. Alexander Volta, F.R.S., Professor Natural Philosophy in the University of Pavia, to the Rt. Hon. Sir Joseph Banks, Bart., K.B., P.R.S., Read June 26, 1800'. *Phil. Trans.*, 1800, Part II, 403 ff.

10. Ibid., 421.

11. W. Nicholson, 'Account of the new Electrical or Galvanic Apparatus of Sig. Alex. Volta, and Experiments performed with the same', *Nich. Jour.*, 4to, *4* (1800), 183.

12. J. C. Delamétherie, 'Discours Préliminaire', *J. de Phys., 54* (1802), 14. See also Brugnatelli's account in the *Annali di chimica, 18* (1800), 136 ff., or a German report in Gilbert's *Annalen der physik, 8* (1801), 284 ff. Brugnatelli's work was summarized in England in the *Phil. Mag., 9* (1801), 181.

13. W. Herschel, 'Investigation of the Powers of the prismatic Colours to heat and illuminate Objects; with Remarks, that prove the different Refrangibility of radiant Heat. To which is added, an Inquiry into the Method of viewing the Sun advantageously, with Telescopes of large Apertures and high magnifying Powers', *Phil. Trans.*, 1800, Part II, 255 ff. 'Experiments on the Refrangibility of the invisible Rays of the Sun', ibid., 284 ff. 'Experiments on the solar, and on the terrestrial Rays that occasion Heat; with a comparative View of the Laws to which Light and Heat, or rather the Rays which occasion them, are subject in order to determine whether they are the same or different', ibid., 293 ff., Part III, 437 ff.

14. J. Ritter, 'Expériences sur la lumière, communiquées par J. C. Oersted', *J. de Phys.*, 57 (1803), 409 ff.

15. Mary Hesse, *Forces and Fields* (London, 1961), gives an excellent account of Kant's ideas on force and matter.

16. For Kant's scientific ideas, see the somewhat enthusiastic account by Erich Adickes, *Kant als Naturforscher* (2 vols., Berlin, 1924).

17. I. Kant, *Critik der reinen Vernunft* (Riga, 1781), 214 and 204. I have used the Insel-Verlag edition of Kant, edited by Wilhelm Weischedel. The pagination refers to the original edition.

18. Ibid., 265.

19. I. Kant, *Metaphysische Anfangsgründe der Naturwissenschaft* (Riga, 1786).

20. Ibid., 33.

21. Johann Wilhelm Ritter, *Beweis dass ein beständiger Galvanismus den Lebensprocess in dem Thierreich begleitet; Nebst neuen Versuchen und Bemerkungen über den Galvanismus* (Weimar, 1798).

22. George M. Duncan, 'English Translations of Kant's Writings', *Kantstudien*, 2 (1898), 253 ff.

23. Charles Villiers, *Philosophie de Kant* (Metz, 1801).

24. For a brief summary of the importance of this year in Coleridge's life, see L. A. Willoughby, 'Coleridge und Deutschland', *Germanisch-Romanisch Monatsschrift*, 24 (1936), 112 ff.

25. S. T. Coleridge, *Biographia Literaria*, ed. by J. Shawcross (2 vols., Oxford, 1958), *1*, 88.

26. T. E. Shedd, ed., *The Complete Works of Samuel Taylor Coleridge* (7 vols., New York, 1884), *1*, 150. Cited henceforth as Coleridge, *Works*.

27. *Biog. Lit.*, *2*, 49.

28. E. H. Coleridge, ed., *Letters of Samuel Taylor Coleridge* (2 vols., Boston, 1895), *1*, 283. This letter, dated 6 April 1799, was written from Germany at the time when Coleridge was first delving into Kant.

29. Coleridge, *Works*, *2*, 91, note. Coleridge's philosophy, particularly the part that dealt with the essential polarity of the universe, is extraordinarily similar to the system put forward by the German *Naturphilosoph*, Friedrich Wilhelm Joseph Schelling. It is well known that Coleridge eagerly read Schelling's works but he insisted all his life that he had devised his philosophy independently of Schelling. 'As my opinions were formed before I was acquainted with the Schools of Fichte and Schelling,' he wrote to his friend J. H. Green in 1817, 'so do they remain independent of them.' [E. L. Griggs, ed.,

Collected Letters of Samuel Taylor Coleridge (4 vols., Oxford, 1956–9), *4*, 792.]
There seems no reason to doubt Coleridge here and it was certainly through
him, and not Schelling, that *Naturphilosophie* reached England.

30. See his *Aids to Reflection*, Appendix C, in *Works, 1*.

31. Davy, *Works, 1*, 17.

32. Ibid., 28. This seems doubtful and is probably a reflection of Davy's philosophical interests after Coleridge's return from Germany.

33. R.I., Davy MSS., Journal 22b.

34. Davy, *Works, 2*, 20.

35. For Coleridge's chemical views, see *Aids to Reflection*, Appendix C. Also,
letters to John Thelwall and H. Davy in E. H. Coleridge, op. cit., *1*, 181 and *1*,
346.

36. J. Z. Fullmer, 'The Poetry of Sir Humphry Davy', *Chymia, 6* (1960), 102 ff.

37. John Ayrton Paris, M.D., *The Life of Sir Humphry Davy* (London, 1831),
54. There is also a two-volume edition of this biography. All references here are
to the one-volume edition.

38. Coleridge to James Webbe Tobin, Friday, 25 July 1800, in Grigg, op. cit.,
1, 613.

39. *Gent. Mag.*, N.S., *2* (1834), 548.

40. Davy, *Works, 8*, 348.

41. R.I., Faraday MSS., 'Four lectures being part of a course on the Elements
of Chemical Philosophy delivered by Sir H. Davy at the Royal Institution and
taken off from notes by M. Faraday, 1812'. On Radiant Matter – 29 February
1812. Cited henceforth as Davy, *Four Lects*.

42. Davy, *Works, 5*, 40.

43. 'Remarks on the Phenomena of Galvanism', *Ann. of Phil., 5* (1815), 432.

44. For a good summary of the opposition to Davy's views, see H. Davy,
'The Bakerian Lecture for 1809. On some new electrochemical researches, on
various objects, particularly the metallic bodies, from the alkalies, and earths,
and on some combinations of hydrogen', in *Works, 5*, 225 ff. For the threat of
police action, see Joseph Agassi, 'An Unpublished Paper of the Young Faraday',
Isis, 52 (1961), 88.

45. 'An Account of some new Analytical Researches on the Nature of certain
Bodies, Particularly the Alkalies, Phosphorus, Sulphur, Carbonaceous Matter,
and the Acids hitherto undecomposed; with some general observations on
Chemical Theory', *Works, 5*, 171 and 175.

46. H. Davy, *Elements of Chemical Philosophy* (first published in 1812), *Works, 4*,
364.

47. Grigg, op. cit., *2*, 727.

48. 'Some Experiments on the Combustion of the Diamond and other Carbonaceous Substances', *Works, 5*, 489.

49. 'On the Analogies between the undecompounded substances, and on the
Constitution of Acids', *Works, 5*, 513.

50. For an account of Boscovich's life and achievements, see L. L. Whyte, ed.,
Roger Joseph Boscovich, S.J. (London, 1961). The *Theoria Naturalis* exists in an
English edition, *A Theory of Natural Philosophy put forward and explained by Roger
Joseph Boscovich* (Chicago and London, 1922).

51. A. Tilloch, 'On Elasticity. An Essay read before the Askesian Society in the Session 1802–3', *Phil. Mag.*, 22 (1805), 141.

52. For Thomson's discussion of Boscovich, see Thomas Thomson, *A System of Chemistry* (4 vols., Edinburgh, 1802), *3*, 154 ff. See also the second edition (4 vols., Edinburgh, 1804), *3*, 278 ff.

53. John A. Paris, op. cit., 16.

54. *Works, 4,* 39.

55. Ibid., 90.

56. R.I., Davy MSS., *Common Place Book,* 1814–15.

57. *Works, 9,* 388.

58. Warner MSS., Faraday to Abbott, 2 August 1812.

59. In a Royal Institution Discourse delivered on 4 May 1960, I suggested that this passage should be interpreted as evidence for Faraday's knowledge and acceptance of Bishop Berkeley's philosophy. The essays in the *Class Book* which now appear to me to be by Faraday militate against this view and I now believe that the influence of Berkeley was much less than I had previously thought. For these views see my 'Michael Faraday and the Evolution of the Concept of the Electric and Magnetic Field', *Proc. R.I., 38* (1960), 235.

60. A. C. Fraser, ed., *The Works of George Berkeley* (4 vols., Oxford, 1901), *1*, 58.

61. Warner MSS., Faraday to Abbott, R.I., 15 April 1817. This was not just a casual definition. He had obviously discussed his view of time with Abbott who disagreed with it. See Faraday to Abbott, R.I., 9 February 1816.

62. R.I., Faraday MSS., *A Class Book, for the Reception of Mental Exercises Instituted July, 1818,* 'On Imagination and Judgement', 24–25.

63. 'On the Pleasures and Uses of the Imagination', ibid., 41.

64. The assignment of this essay to Faraday rests upon the following points:

1. The content is completely consonant with what we know of Faraday's views from other sources.

2. The subject was one dear to Faraday's heart. In the years 1816–18, he preached the gospel of mental improvement to all and sundry who would listen.

3. The author's remarks on religion are exactly those Faraday would have made.

   'I have first to remind you of what with me is a principle, the separation of morality from Religion' (p. 111), and,

   'I think too highly of Religion to regulate it by mere moral duties, or to subject it to the weak powers of reason which I or any can exert.'

4. On page 115 the author refers, in a tone which implies personal knowledge, to French cuisine and it is probable that he alone of all the company had visited France in such circumstances as to experience its products.

65. 'On Mind and the Duty of improving it', ibid., 105.

66. Ibid., 106.

67. R.I., Faraday MSS., Davy, *Four Lects.*, 46.

68. Ibid., 57.

69. I.E.E., Chem. Lect., May 26, 1819 – 'Forms of Matter', 2.

70. Ibid.

71. Ibid., 16.

72. Ibid.

73. Ibid., 30.

74. Ibid. The pages are not numbered after 339. The passage occurs on the 506th leaf of the book. Unnumbered pages will be indicated by a bracket.

75. Warner MSS., Faraday to Abbott, 11 August 1812, B.J., *1*, 29.

76. R.I., Faraday MSS., Davy, *Four Lects.*, 249.

77. I.E.E., Chem. Lect., 70.

78. Ibid., 71.

79. Ibid., 18.

80. Ibid., [1].

81. Ibid., 4.

82. Ibid., [506].

CHAPTER THREE

The Fallow Years

---

1. Marriage

During the years during which Faraday had applied himself unrelentingly to the acquisition of knowledge and polish, he had travelled in an exclusively masculine society. With his friend Benjamin Abbott he had explored both chemistry and London; his acquaintances at the City Philosophical Society had served as the audience for the reception and criticism of his gradually expanding views; Sir Humphry Davy had showered him with kindness and had stimulated his intellectual progress. In all these situations Faraday stood in a curious relation to those surrounding him. He was either the teacher or the pupil. With Abbott he was both; when their friendship began, Faraday confessed his ignorance and expressed the hope that Abbott would exert himself to improve Faraday. As the years passed, it was Faraday who gradually took on the task of educating Abbott. The same development occurred at the City Philosophical Society. Faraday went to learn and stayed to teach. The teacher-pupil relationship is a close one, but it always contains some element of strain. Only rarely can there be a total relaxation of both parties and the recognition of this is, in itself, a strain.

The opportunities for social relaxation during Faraday's years as an apprentice chemist were also few and far between. Days were occupied with the affairs of the Royal Institution and evenings were devoted to self-improvement or the instruction of others. Only occasionally was this rigid self-discipline relaxed. Fifty years after the events, Benjamin Abbott could still recall the occasions when teaching or learning were temporarily forgotten.

> In these early days of his residence at the R[oyal] Institution our intercourse and enjoyment of each other's society was very frequent. Besides the interchange of letters we frequently spent our evenings together, either at the Institution or at my Father's where I then resided. At that time my Brother was living and I was a clerk in a Merchant's Office in the City, whence I could usually escape early and readily reach Albemarle St. with my Brother who

was similarly engaged. There we had the pleasure of seeing many experiments and making some ourselves, as well as of assisting in others of importance. . . . There too we several times tried the effect of Nitrous Oxide gas and produced upon each of us some of its curious effects. On one occasion when under its influence he with great emphasis declared that 'now he could get tipsy for three pence' – which I am certain he never did at any price. . . . Our conversations at these times were chiefly on scientific subjects but not exclusively so. Not infrequently other of his friends would look in with whom he would join in singing whilst we were content to listen and did so with great pleasure. . . . Amongst other ideas we had an antipathy to stiff hats, and on one occasion he accompanied us as far as Temple Bar without one, attracting of course some notice. On another occasion when there was a general illumination for some victory we prepared some detonating mixture and making our way into some of the densest crowd produced smart explosions without the surrounding persons perceiving whence they came or how they were produced. Such little frolics were however of very rare occurrence.[1]

Their rarity was not caused by Faraday being a prig but by his high sense of purpose and humility. He knew his education had been defective and that he must run longer and faster than more fortunate colleagues if he were ever to reach the front ranks of science. But even the dedicated runner must sometimes relax. The obvious and most usual resting place is the domestic hearth where the skeins of thought can be untangled by the tender fingers of love. Such a prospect had little appeal for Faraday in his early twenties. His single-minded pursuit of truth left no room for the fair sex and love appeared to him only as a bother and a nuisance. His Common Place Book contains a most unflattering picture of his concept of matrimonial entanglements.

What is the pest and plague of human life?
And what the curse that often brings a wife?
'tis Love.
What is the power that ruins man['s] firmest mind?
What that deceives its host when alas too kind?
What is it that comes in false deceitful guise
Making dull fools of those that before were wise?
'tis Love.
What is it that oft to an enemy turns a friend?
What is it that promising never attains its end?
What that the wisest head can never scan?
Which seems to have come on the earth to humble man?
'tis Love.
What is it directs the madman's hot intent?
For which a dunce is fully competent?

What that the wise man always strives to shun?
Though still that ever o'er the world has run?
       'tis Love.
Then shew me love howe'er you find it
      'tis still a curse
A thing which throws good sense behind it
    sometimes much worse
'Tis always roving rambling seeking
      t'unsettle minds.
And makes them careless, idle, weeping
    changeful as winds.
Then come to me we'll curse the boy
The cyprian goddess brought on earth
He's but an idle senseless toy
and has no claim on manly worth.
The noble heart will ne'er resign
Reason the light of mental day
Or idly let its force decline
  Before the passions boisterous sway
  We've honor friendship all the powers
That still with virtue do reside.
They've sweetly strew'd our lives with flowers
  Nor do we wish for aught beside
    Love, then thou 'ast nothing here to do.
    Depart, Depart to *yonder* crew.[2]

The 'idle, senseless toy' paid no heed to Faraday's command, but skilfully fashioned the net in which the misogynist was to be caught.

One of the little group who contributed to the *Class Book, for the Reception of Mental Exercises* was Edward Barnard, the son of an elder of the Sandemanian Church which Faraday attended. To his sister, Sarah, he related the passages against love which Faraday had shown him and no doubt jestingly referred to Faraday's invulnerability to female wiles. Few things are so calculated to summon up all a woman's resources as a claim of total disinterest by a man. We know nothing of the courtship of Sarah Barnard, but there is a set to the young lady's chin which reveals a certain determination. Michael Faraday was a fine looking man of high standards of conduct with a respectable place in the world. That Miss Barnard set her cap at him is not to be wondered at and Faraday, like so many before and after him, surrendered absolutely. Instead of cursing the plague that often brings a wife, he threw himself on the tender mercies of his conqueror. 'You know me', he wrote her, 'as well or better than I do myself. You know my former prejudices, and my present thoughts – you know my weaknesses, my vanity, my whole mind; you have converted me from one erroneous way, let me hope you will attempt to correct what others are wrong.'[3]

With an energy hitherto reserved for the pursuit of chemical truth, Faraday laid siege to Sarah's heart. Somewhat frightened by the passions she had aroused, Miss Barnard showed the letter to her father who agreed with Faraday's former position that love made philosophers into fools.[4] Mrs Barnard recognized that a separation of the two lovers would be wise and Sarah left with her sister for a short stay at Ramsgate. Faraday was miserable. For a few days he endured the separation and then took action. 'I made up my mind yesterday afternoon to run all risks of a kind reception at Ramsgate, and force myself into favourable circumstances if possible.'[5] His reception was kind but reserved and the atmosphere a bit forbidding. Faraday was clearly upset and acted in a manner calculated to annoy everyone.

> I was in strange spirits [he later wrote] and had very little command over myself, though I managed to preserve appearances. I expressed strong disappointment at the look of the town and of the cliffs, I criticized all around me with a malicious tone, and, in fact, was just getting into a humour which would have offended the best-natured person, when I perceived that, unwittingly, I had, for the purpose of disguising the hopes which had been raised in me so suddenly, and might have been considered presumptuous, assumed an appearance of general contempt and dislike. The moment I perceived the danger of the path on which I was running, I stopped, and talked of home and friends.[6]

This strange behaviour seemed to have reassured Sarah and her sister that Faraday was merely love-sick. There was no further attempt to elude him and for some days he basked in the warmth of his loved-one's presence. He was soon forced to return to London but continued his suit by letter. Miss Barnard must gradually have begun to return his affection for his letters, though ardent, gradually lost their rather frenzied note and took on the tone of one who knows that his love is returned. On 12 June 1821 Sarah Barnard became his wife.

Sarah Barnard was the perfect mate for Faraday. From his accounts of her and from the accounts of others, she emerges as a warm and charming person. She was filled with maternal feelings which, in the absence of children of her own, she lavished upon her nieces and upon Faraday himself. This was precisely what Faraday needed. Oftentimes he would become so absorbed in his work in the laboratory that he would forget his meals. Quietly Mrs Faraday would serve him and see that his health did not suffer.

Sarah was not an intellectual. She never pretended to understand what her husband was doing. Once when she was asked why she did not study chemistry, she replied, 'Already it is so absorbing, and exciting to him that it often deprives him of his sleep and I am quite content to be the pillow of his mind.'[7] Nor did Faraday really need someone to whom he could talk. In 1857 when Christian Hansteen, the Danish student of terrestrial magnetism, inquired about the possibility of one of his young acquaintances working with Faraday, the latter replied:

> ... I have never had any student or pupil under me to aid me with assistance; but have always prepared and made my experiments with my own hands, working and thinking at the same time. I do not think I could work in company, or think aloud, or explain my thoughts at the time. Sometimes I and my assistant have been in the Laboratory for hours and days together, he preparing some lecture apparatus or cleaning up, and scarcely a word has passed between us.[8]

Faraday's dialogue was with nature. In his experiments he conversed with her and reported the conversations in his papers. He never really *discussed* his views with anyone. He presented them knowing that if they had value they would be incorporated into the body of science; if not, they would be discarded.

Although each went his own way, Michael and Sarah were united by a deep and enduring love. And life was not always gripped in the silence of concentration. At times the Royal Institution fairly burst with relatives come to celebrate some family occasion. In 1826, when Faraday's younger (and favourite) sister Margaret was married, the Faradays and Barnards gathered at the Royal Institution to toast the bride. The occasion, as recorded by Mrs Faraday's sister Charlotte, allows us a rare glimpse of Faraday at leisure in the midst of his family.

> My dear Sister [Charlotte wrote]
> I am now going to give you a circumstantial account of the wedding and as laconically as possible. I daresay you thought of us on Tuesday which was the day it took place. We had some delightful weather previous so *I* never anticipated a wet day; however when we got up it had every appearance of being a soaking day. Michael and Sally slept here Monday night, in the morning, the former went accompanied by the principal bridesmaid (Jane) to Mr Gray's to take the bride to church. I escorted (with George's assistance) the bridegroom. It had just left off raining and I spied out a little bit of blue to my great joy and the day was extremely fine. The company at Church (which by

the by was in Watling Street) consisted of bride and bridegroom, Michael, Sally, father, William, George, Mr and Mrs Robert Faraday, Mr and Mrs Livermore, Mr Gray, Mary and Eliza, Jane and self all in regular winter dresses excepting Margaret and Mrs Livermore in silk bonnets. We all except father breakfasted at Smithfield and very merry we were. Numerous droll sayings and witticisms were given out after breakfast. Jane and I went home to dress in our new frocks. About ten or eleven of us set off in two coaches to Dulwich to the gallery of pictures. We were very much gratified and returned about ½ pt. 3 to dinner at the Institution. Besides the party at church there was Mrs Faraday, Mrs Edward Barnard, Mrs Reid and Mary. We had a very good plain dinner, three boiled fowls (top), Roast beef bottom, ham middle, pigeon pie, greens and potatoes, apple pie, ground rice pudding, lemon cheese cakes, blanc mange. I believe that was all. Mrs Livermore helped Sally the day before which was a great comfort. . . . ½ past 8, the bride, bridegroom, Sally and Michael went off to Hampstead, Martha had gone in the stage. All the gentlemen went to hear a lecture on astronomy and afterwards came up to supper.[9]

Even when there was not a special occasion such as a wedding, the general tone of the Faraday household was one of considerable gaiety. In spite of the long periods of intense concentration, Faraday was always able to relax and enjoy himself. In 1826 he built himself a velocipede and illustrated its performance to awed onlookers by dashing around the corridor surrounding the Lecture Theatre of the Royal Institution. Even the laboratory had its social usages. After Faraday's death, his niece Constance Reid could still recall the joys of visiting her uncle while he worked

What a treat [she wrote in her diary] a visit to the Laboratory used to be! After the busy time of the day was over and when there were no strangers about we sometimes went down to see what my uncle was about. Perhaps my aunt had an appointment with him to manufacture soda or lavender lozenges for home consumption, then how busy they were and how appropriate to the place were all the implements, the pestles and mortars, the glass slabs on which the paste was rolled with a small glass rod for a roller. All those lozenges were made square, and they could thus never be mistaken for shop lozenges, nor would they otherwise for they were not half so nice to the taste and I never voluntarily put one in my mouth though I was fully convinced they possessed virtues unknown to any other composition.[10]

The laboratory not only served as the mixing place for home remedies, but as the manufactory of a totally different kind of medicine.

Then once a year was the grand brewing of ginger wine, that was a very interesting process to watch. It used to be all conducted under the master's own superintendence but the fermentating went on up in the kitchen in a great red pan.

66 are each about one foot long and five or six inches wide

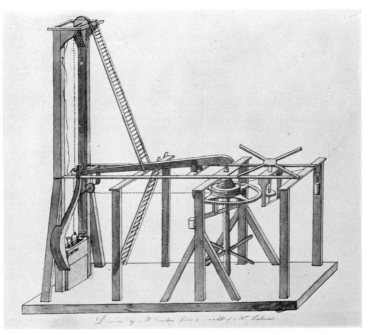

The partition of the cells are made at the same time as the trough and of the same material so that the whole was one compact piece of ware the cells are made very wide and the trough being but short there is but few perhaps ten or twelve in each the plates are soldered together at the top by a slip of the metal and all the pairs belonging to one trough

1a Notes for Tatum's Lecture on Galvanism at the R.I.

1b Drawing from Lecture on Mechanics – Tatum, R.I.

2a *Edward Magrath*

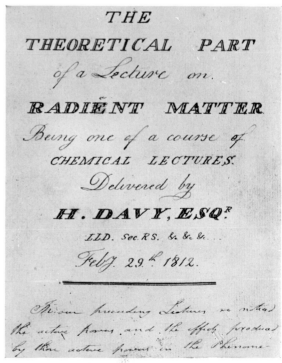

2b *Faraday's notes on Davy's Lectures*

Sep.r 13.th

— Objects much wanted in the
Laboratory of the Royal Institution,

Cleanliness.

Neatness

Regularity. —

— The laboratory must be cleaned
every morning & no operations are
going on before ☐ o Clock. —
— It is the business of Wm
Payne to do this & It is
the duty of Mr Davy to
see that it is done & to take
care of & keep in order ☐ apparatus.

— There must be in the laboratory.
Pen, Ink & paper. & wafers &
these must not be kept in the
slovenly manner in which they usually
are kept. I am now writing with
a pen & ink such as was never used
in any other place. —

They are nothing at all

3 Davy's laboratory notebook

4 Pencil sketch of Sarah Barnard

I remember well the taste of those great swollen raisins one of which we used sometimes to have for a treat out of the pan.

By and bye the wine was turned into a large Carboy and was placed in one of the offshoots of the laboratory. . . . I don't remember much about the bottling, perhaps Anderson did that, but my uncle used to bottle off the contents of a graybeard of gin sometimes.[11]

Even when no domestic products were being made, the laboratory was a friendly place, at least for children. When Constance Reid or Jane Barnard, the two nieces who lived off and on with the Faraday's from the 1820's until Michael's death, came to visit him at his work, he could always spare a moment. If they brought some friends, he would introduce himself by tossing some potassium into water and joining in the excitement that followed upon its ignition.[12] Then he would take a bit of glass and seal up some mercury in it to produce a 'treasure' for children.

Similar exciting phenomena were exhibited even in his own rooms. Every now and then Faraday brought in some kind of living creatures whose actions or development both he and his nieces watched with great interest. On one occasion it was a mass of frog spawn which was closely observed until, as Miss Reid observed, 'at last one morning on counting them [the mature frogs] as usual the number 23 I think, could no longer be found, 21 was all, next day there were but 19'.[13] The remaining frogs were immediately taken to a nearby park and let go!

On another occasion, the attention of everyone was directed towards a number of glass jars filled with planaria. The attraction of these little animals was their amazing powers of regeneration. 'Cut them in two, each part became perfect, cut them down half through the head a fresh half was developed to each side; divide them any way, they seemed able to supply all wants. Some which were only joined by part of the tail developed a will each of their own till they fought and separated themselves.'[14]

Faraday's domestic life was completely satisfactory to him. His work absorbed him; his wife provided a calm and warmth that allowed him to relax and stretch his mental legs in comfort and tranquillity. His nieces brought the necessary excitement of childhood into his life and, as the natural teacher he was, he enjoyed his demonstrations and lessons as much as they did. During the years before his marriage Faraday had enjoyed a certain amount of social concourse. As he settled into his new role of husband and loving uncle, the need for such outside diversion gradually left him. He became more and more selective about the invitations he would accept. By the mid-1830's the rejection of invitations had become almost complete. He would attend only the Anniversary dinners of the

Royal Society and a *very* few other events. His apartment in the Royal Institution and the laboratory in the basement provided everything he needed for his personal happiness. The serenity and calm which marked both Faraday's countenance and his work were the results of this domestic harmony.

Only one flaw in this picture of personal happiness could be discerned in the 1820's. Since his early manhood, Faraday had suffered from a poor memory. His Common Place Book begun in 1816 contained a system (fantastically complex!) for improving his memory. As he learned more and as it became more and more necessary for him to keep large amounts of data in his mind, this failing became increasingly serious to him. His poor memory also became associated with real physical symptoms that were to grow worse with age.[15] In 1828 he wrote his friend Richard Phillips: 'Sarah and I have been rambling about for nearly two months. I have not been at home many days. I am very much better for the country etc. and think I begin to feel as usual: all I am annoyed about are the nervous headaches and weakness. They unsettle me and make me indisposed to do anything but they are much better than they were.'[16]

The headaches were to increase in severity and the loss of memory was to become more serious as the years went by. The forced vacation in 1828 was to be repeated many times. The pattern of his life was formed by the alternation of work and rest. He would attack a problem with almost total concentration, following out every lead with enormous patience and skill. After some six or seven years of such intense application, his head would be capable of no more and he would have to cease all work for some months or even years. Then, refreshed, he would return to his laboratory and the papers would begin to flow out again. Throughout even the periods of mental idleness he retained the robust physical health with which he had been blessed. A thirty-mile hike was a common thing; in 1845 (when he was 54 years old) his wife became worried only when he had marched forty-five miles one day with her brother!

2. Faraday, the Sandemanian

Faraday's religious feelings were deep and permanent. We know nothing of his early religious instruction but can safely assume that he was exposed to the London community of Sandemanians as a child. His father was a very devout man and, although his mother never formally declared her adherence to the Church, there can be no doubt of her deep piety. Under these influences, a vigorous and unshakeable religious faith was planted in Faraday's heart. To it he owed some of his most charming attributes. No man in the history of science has been referred to as humble more often than Faraday. But it was a very definite kind of humility that shone from his eyes. When he and science were ill-used by Melbourne, England's Prime Minister, Faraday showed no trace of conventional humility – he broke off the interview and turned a deaf ear to all explanations until Melbourne apologized. Similarly, he was ever conscious of his honour; one trespassed upon this only at great risk. His true humility lay in a profound consciousness of his debt to his Creator. That Michael Faraday, poor, uneducated son of a journeyman blacksmith and a country maid was permitted to glimpse the beauty of the eternal laws of nature was a never-ending source of wonder to him. God's beneficence was to be seen in these laws and in the intricacy of a universe devised for the ultimate Good of all His creatures. In a lecture on Ozone, delivered in 1859, he made this point with feeling and eloquence:

> These are the glimmerings we have of what we are pleased to call the *second causes* by which the *one Great Cause* works his wonders and governs this earth. We flattered ourselves we knew what air was composed of, and now we discover a *new* property which is imponderable, and invisible, except through its *effects* which I shewed you in the last experiment; but while it fades the ribbon, it gives the glow of health to the cheek, and is just as necessary for the good of mankind, as the other parts of which air is composed.[17]

The interesting thing about this position, by no means uncommon in Faraday's day, was that Faraday insisted upon the primacy of faith. The world was intelligible, beautiful, and adapted to the needs of mankind because God was rational and good. One could not legitimately argue th other way around, according to Faraday, to prove the existence of God. In a talk in a series of lectures on education delivered by himself and others at the Royal Institution he made this point perfectly clear.

> Let no one suppose for a moment that the self-education I am about to commend in respect of the things of this life, extends to any considerations of the hope set before us, as if man by reasoning could find out God. It would be improper here to enter upon this subject further than to claim an absolute distinction between religious and ordinary belief. I shall be reproached with the weakness of refusing to apply those mental operations which I think good in respect of high things to the very highest. I am content to bear the reproach.[18]

In a very real sense, Faraday's science was firmly rooted in his faith. All scientific investigators must believe in the intelligibility of the universe; its beauty and symmetry is grasped by fewer. The reasons for pursuing science are as various as the pursuers, but in Faraday's case, the motives seem clear. What higher goal could a man seek than the knowledge of God's creation? In this way, he could participate, however infinitesimally, in the Divinity.

While knowledge of the physical universe was something to be gained slowly and painfully by the use of man's finite intelligence, knowledge of God was something else again. This was a faith which only God could grant. The Sandemanian congregation was composed of those people to whom God had revealed His presence and consciousness of this priceless boon was what held the Church together. One month after his marriage, Faraday made his profession of faith before the Sandemanian Church. The intensity of his feeling and his recognition of the essential privacy of his faith were revealed by the fact that even his bride was told nothing. When she asked him why he had not discussed it with her he simply answered, 'That is between me and my God.'[19] Even the most intense mundane love could not hope to rival the celestial!

From 1821 to the end of his life Faraday was a faithful member of the Sandemanian Church. He served as an Elder, preached both in London and in Dundee, and gratefully followed the way his faith led him. As his work became more and more controversial, the church and his faith became increasingly important to him. There are few creative persons who are truly content to permit posterity, rather than contemporaries, to judge the worth of a lifetime of work. Faraday was. He would not enter into controversy but was convinced that truth would ultimately prevail. If some parts of this truth were to be found to have been due to him, then he would have partially repaid his Maker for the gift of life. If he were wrong, he had at least done the best of which he was capable. It was rather unimportant whether the evaluation of his achievement was made today, tomorrow, or in a hundred years. When one basks every week in the glow of eternity, years, decades, even centuries seem trivial.

Faraday's faith also strongly moulded his scientific method and philosophy. Ever since the time of Galileo natural philosophers had, when pushed, admitted the fallibility and limits of human intelligence. The results of scientific investigation were, therefore, mere approximations to be tested, refined, or even rejected as science advanced. Such was science in theory. In practice, however, these grand views faded and were replaced by bitter enmities and struggles to establish personal views as accepted doctrine. The threat to use police force to suppress the publication of Davy's views in France was only the most extreme of a fairly prevalent (and only human) attitude.[20] There can be no doubt that

Faraday felt such displays were inimical to the progress of science. But he went far beyond this. He sincerely felt that the essence of humanity was its fallibility. The spectacle of man, this petty, forked radish, confronting the immensity of the universe was constantly before his eyes. His Bible[21] bears testimony to this realization of man's place. 'If I justify myself mine own mouth shall condemn me: if I say, I am perfect, it shall also prove me perverse,' cried Job and Faraday marked the passage vigorously.[22] In 1826 Faraday expressed his credo in all its fullness of humility and faith.

I have been watching the clouds on these hills for many evenings back [he wrote his brother-in-law, Edward Barnard]: they gather when I do not expect them; they dissolve when, to the best of my judgment, they ought to remain; they throw down rain to my mere inconvenience, but doing good to all around; and they break up and present me with delightful and refreshing views when I expect only a dull walk. However strong and certain the appearances are to me, if I venture an internal judgment, I am always wrong in something; and the only conclusion that I can come to is, that the end is as beneficial as the means of its attainment are beautiful. So it is in life; and though I pretend not to have been much involved in the fogs, mists, and clouds of misfortune, yet I have seen enough to know that many things usually designated as troubles are merely so from our own particular view of them, or else ultimately resolve themselves into blessings. Do not imagine that I cannot feel for the distresses of others, or that I am entirely ignorant of those which seem to threaten friends for whom both you and I are much concerned. I do feel for those who are oppressed either by real or imaginary evils, and I know the one to be as heavy as the other. But I think I derive a certain degree of steadiness and placidity amongst such feelings by a point of mental conviction, for which I take no credit as a piece of knowledge or philosophy, and which has often been blamed as mere apathy. Whether apathy or not, it leaves the mind ready and willing to do all that can be useful, whilst it relieves it a little from the distress dependent upon viewing things in their worst state. The point is this: in all kinds of knowledge I perceive that my views are insufficient, and my judgment imperfect. In experiments I come to conclusions which, if partly right, are sure to be in part wrong; if I correct by other experiments, I advance a step, my old error is in part diminished, but is always left with a tinge of humanity, evidenced by its imperfection. The same happens in judging of the motives of others; though in favourable cases I may see a good deal, I never see the whole. In affairs of life 'tis the same thing; my views of a thing at a distance and close at hand never correspond, and the way out of a trouble which I desire is never that which really opens before me. Now, when in all these, and in all kinds of knowledge and experience, the course is still the same, ever imperfect to us, but terminating in good, and when all events are evidently at the disposal of a Power which is conferring benefits continually upon us, which, though given by means and in ways we do not comprehend, may always well claim our acknowledgment at last, may we not be induced to suspend our dull spirits and thoughts when things look cloudy, and, providing as well as we can against the shower, actually cheer our spirits by thoughts of the good things our past lives convince us that in doing this we are far more likely to be right than wrong.

. . . you quote Shakespeare: the quotation may be answered a thousand times over from a book just as full of poetry, which you may find on your shelf. The uses of the world can never be unprofitable to a reflecting mind, even without the book I refer to; and I am sure can only appear so to you for a few hours together.[23]

It was this attitude that earned for Faraday his reputation for saintliness. He never stooped to petty quarrels or sought revenge for any real or imagined slight. His consciousness of his own fallibility stimulated him to cultivate his critical faculties to the utmost and his remarks on other's work were never more severe than those he directed at his own. When Faraday spoke of the work of others he was attended to for everyone knew that he was guided only by the love of truth. Secure in his faith and beloved by his wife and relatives he was able to devote his entire energy for forty years to the task of uncovering one corner of it.

3. The Practising Chemist

During the months in which he had been courting Sarah Barnard, Faraday had also been 'improving his prospects' in proper nineteenth-century fashion. Analytical chemists were in extremely short supply in England after the fall of Napoleon. Neither of the two great universities felt any strong urge to train such technicians, and those who desired the services of an analyst had to seek out the very few men like Faraday who had been fortunate enough to receive a good chemical education in a well-equipped laboratory. Faraday soon built up a large practice. In the *Note Book and Scrap Book of Things Examined in the Laboratory*, whole pages are devoted to the analysis of water samples from places as diverse as Russell Square and Windsor.[24] Faraday also was called upon by the East India Company and other dealers in sodium nitrate (used in the manufacture of gunpowder) to carry out rough analyses of the proportion of water contained in various samples.[25] Some of his analyses were presumably for the Admiralty and dealt with the victualling of ships. In October 1820, for example, he investigated the results of drying various meats such as beef, veal, pork, codfish, and chicken. In June of the same year he had run a series of tests on the gases evolved by chicken eggs kept over periods of time. From this work, Faraday made a tiny income more than sufficient to keep his new bride.

By 1820, Faraday's work as an analytical chemist was well enough known to qualify him as an expert in the trial of Messrs. Severn, King and Company versus some insurance companies. The case is of more than casual interest for two reasons. Faraday was the primary witness for the insurance companies and thereby found himself on the opposite side from both Davy and Brande who were called by the plaintiffs. This, no doubt, contributed to the growing coolness between Davy and Faraday which was to have such unpleasant consequences when Faraday was proposed as a Fellow of the Royal Society. More importantly, work for the insurance companies began Faraday's acquaintance with the oil used by the plaintiffs in their manufacturing process. The ultimate result was the discovery of benzene.

The question at issue was the characteristics of the oil used by Messrs. Severn, King and Company in the refining of sugar. A fire had broken out in one of the company's plants and the insurance companies which had written the policies protecting the company against fire claimed that the oil was at fault and that failure to inform them of this added hazard constituted fraud vitiating the policy. The company insisted that it was the sugar which had caught fire and that, therefore, the oil was irrelevant to the outbreak of the fire. The scientific problems to be resolved were the ignition points of the oil and the sugar and the likelihood, under factory conditions, of fire breaking out in the oil and the sugar. Faraday was asked by the insurance companies to determine these points.

The chemists retained by the plaintiffs claimed that under 580°F. any vapour produced from the oil was not flammable and that the fire had, therefore, been due to the heating of the sugar. This claim was based upon small-scale experiments and arguments by analogy. Faraday worked on a larger scale and tested the vapour at various temperatures. At 382° he noted 'apparently inflammable vapour in very small quantity' and at 435° 'Plenty of vapour combustible.'[26] By all scientific standards, the case appeared open and shut but the case was decided on other grounds when the plaintiff's lawyers proved that no fraud had been intended.

Although the case was finished for Faraday after he had presented his testimony, his interest had been aroused by the various decomposition products of the heated oil.[27] This interest was further stimulated by the fact that his older brother, Robert, had begun to work with the oil-gas illuminating systems which were being introduced into London. The process of manufacture was a very simple one; whale or codfish oil was dropped into a furnace maintained at a red heat. From this destructive distillation arose various vapours which were bottled under a pressure of about thirty atmospheres (441 pounds per square inch). The containers were then carried around to private or public buildings and attached to the gas line to provide the fuel for illumination. In the bottling operations, it had long been noticed that a fluid separated from the gas and collected in the bottom of one of the intermediate receivers. One of the officials of the Portable Gas Company, a Mr Gordon, sent some of this liquid to Faraday in April 1825, and Faraday immediately began its analysis.

The fluid was a mixture of various components which Faraday first separated roughly by collecting fractions which came over in ten-degree intervals of temperature. These fractions were again distilled until rather distinct substances were procured. During these operations, he noticed that a large quantity of liquid distilled over between 176° and 190° at a relatively constant temperature. This led him to suspect that a definite chemical substance was present and he ultimately succeeded in isolating a new compound of carbon and hydrogen to which he gave the name of bicarburet of hydrogen. This was benzene. With characteristic thoroughness, he then determined its various physical qualities with great accuracy. By exploding the vapour with oxygen and absorbing the carbon dioxide produced in a caustic potash solution, he was able to find the ratio of carbon to hydrogen.[28]

Because of the fundamental importance of benzene in both the theory of organic chemistry and in industrial processes, it is easy to over-estimate the importance of Faraday's work. This is one of the few discoveries he made about which it can be confidently stated that it would have been made by another sooner or later. In 1825 it was little more than a chemical curiosity. It was not until 1834 that the German chemist Mitscherlich showed its relationship to other chemical compounds and, incidentally, suggested the name of *benzin* for it. When, in 1856, W. H. Perkin discovered the first aniline dye, benzene moved closer to the centre of interest of the chemical world. Its fundamental importance in the development of organic chemistry did not become clear until 1860 when August Kekulé first suggested a ring structure for it and thereby laid the theoretical foundations for the prodigious growth of organic chemistry which marked the last part of the nineteenth century.

The discovery of benzene was, even to Faraday, a worth-while result of his activities as an analytical chemist. His growing reputation in the early 1820's, however, did not always lead to such important results. Instead they served merely to divert his attention from other problems of greater interest to him. Thus from about 1825 on, he was called upon frequently by the Admiralty to conduct standard tests of various substances of interest to the Royal Navy. Faraday was a man of deep patriotic feeling and was always willing to assist the Government when asked to do so. There were times, however, when the Admiralty's requests were singularly ill-timed. In 1832, for example, when he was feverishly tracking down the theoretical consequences of his discovery of electromagnetic induction, he had to lay aside his researches to test some thirty-two samples of oatmeal suspected of containing adulterants![29] During the 1820's Faraday began to despair of ever getting any really important work done. As he wrote to Ampère in 1825: 'Every letter you write me states how busily you are engaged and I cannot wish it otherwise knowing how well your time is spent. Much of mine is unfortunately occupied in very common place employment and this I may offer as an excuse (for want of a better) for the little I do in original research.'[30]

Even the work to which he devoted enormous amounts of time during the period from 1818 to 1830 grew out of his skill as an analytical chemist. Although he could complain to Ampère that his employment was 'common place', his researches on the alloys of steel and on optical glass strained his manipulative skill and experimental ability to the utmost. To be sure, nothing world-shaking emerged from this work. The years devoted to these investigations, however, were not wasted; it was in the course of them that Faraday's hand, eye, and mind learned to work together in the close harmony that made him the foremost experimentalist of the nineteenth century. And, as he worked with the extraordinarily complex substances of glass and steel, his mind was forced to wrestle with questions of molecular structure of basic importance to the whole of chemical science.

As the son of a blacksmith, Faraday had an early interest in iron, the methods of working it, and the properties which those who used it found desirable. This interest was not transformed into scientific curiosity until 1818 when James Stodart requested help from the Royal Institution with his researches into the alloys of steel.

James Stodart was a cutler whose shop at 401 Strand advertised 'Surgeon's Instruments, Razors and other Cutlery made from . . . (wootz) a Steel from India, preferred by Mr S. to the best steel in Europe after years of comparative trial.'[31] Stodart's interest in wootz can be traced back to the closing years of the eighteenth century. At that time Dr Helenus Scott of Bombay sent some specimens of wootz to Sir Joseph Banks, President of the Royal Society, who turned over a sample for analysis to Dr George Pearson, F.R.S. Dr Pearson performed the chemical part of the examination while Stodart forged a piece into a penknife to test its value in tools. As early as 1795, Stodart had concluded that 'wootz is superior for many purposes to any steel used in this country'.[32] From 1795 until his death in 1823 Stodart devoted himself to the improvement of steel using wootz as the standard of comparison. Until his collaboration with Faraday, however, this devotion produced very little of any worth. There are articles in *Nicholson's Journal* on attempts to imitate the Damascus sword blade, on the protection of steel with platinum and on a method of gilding steel.[33] In 1812 he was able to correct Sir Humphry Davy's statement that the changes of colour produced by heat on the surface of polished steel did not depend upon oxidation. This was Stodart's introduction to the laboratory of the Royal Institution, for there he demonstrated to Davy that when oxygen was excluded, no colour changes took place. Although there is no record of Stodart's meeting with Faraday, it requires little imagination to picture it. Stodart was a member of the Royal Institution and had undoubtedly made his interests known to everyone there. Davy was far too occupied with other matters, including the pursuit of trout and salmon, to wish to enter into any long investigation of iron and steel. William Brande was charged with all the duties of the Professor of Chemistry and could not spare the time. The Chemical Assistant was the perfect choice in the research Stodart envisioned. He had more than a passing acquaintance with iron working and understood in general, if not in detail, those properties of iron and steel that were desirable; his growing reputation as an analytical chemist insured the accuracy with which this part of the investigation would be treated; most importantly, his ability in the laboratory was already well known and this was of basic importance in operations which promised to be of great difficulty. In the late autumn or winter of 1818-19, Stodart and Faraday began their attack on the problem of creating new and improved alloys of steel.[34]

The immediate objective was the seemingly simple one of duplicating wootz. To do this, it was first necessary to determine its chemical composition and to this task Faraday directed his efforts. For some reason, his analytical skill deserted him here. He found significant amounts of silex and alumine present and immediately seized upon these as the cause of the superior quality of the wootz. In fact, modern analysis of wootz shows a much smaller amount of silicon than that indicated by Faraday and no alumine at all.[35] That something must have been wrong with his analysis soon became evident to Faraday. Having determined what appeared to him to be the alloying substances upon which the quality of wootz depended, he tried to make wootz by introducing these substances into the melt. The results were disappointing:

I have obtained specimens of iron, giving abundance of silex and alumine on analysis [he wrote] and such alloys or combinations have been obtained by others; but they never present the appearance of wootz during the action of acids upon them, even though the metal used in making the alloy be in the state of steel; and if wootz owes its excellence to any portion of the bases of the earths, silex or allumine, combined with it, those substances must, I think, be either in a more perfect, or in a different state of combination, to what they are in alloys obtained by fusing iron for three or four hours, in contact with wood and the earths.[36]

Here the investigation stalled for some months for the simple reason that there was no hint as to what procedure might ultimately prove worth trying. As the authors pointed out later, 'Almost an infinity of different metallic combinations may be made, according to the nature and relative proportions of the metals capable of being alloyed.'[37] The path of analysis having led nowhere there was nothing to do but cast about for some other avenue to follow.

During the same months in which Faraday was working with Stodart, he was also employed by Mr J. J. Guest, an iron manufacturer of Dowlais (Glamorgan) near Merthyr. Mr Guest sent some samples of iron ore and of his finished product to Faraday to be analysed. Mr Guest also invited Faraday to visit his works and Faraday accepted eagerly.[38] Faraday had always enjoyed visiting factories and workshops. When his science failed to show him a profitable avenue to explore in the search for new alloys, such a visit could be regarded as possibly providing the clue which would permit his work to go forward. Although he could, by 1819, consider himself a trained chemist, Faraday did not scorn the knowledge that the intelligent but uneducated artisan commanded. He was conscious enough of this to enter a memorandum to himself in his *Common Place Book*.

Whilst passing through Manufactories [he wrote] and engaged in the observance of the various operations in civilized life we are constantly hearing observations made by those who find employment in those places and are accustomed to a minute observation of what passes before them which are new or frequently discordant with received opinions. These are generally the results of facts and though some are founded in error, some on prejudice yet many are true and of high importance to the practical man. Such as come in my way I shall set down here without waiting for the principle on which they depend and though three fourths of them ultimately prove to be erroneous yet if but one new fact is gathered in a multitude it will be sufficient to justify this mode of occupying time.[39]

It was in quest of this elusive single fact that Faraday set off to Wales in July 1819, on a walking tour whose first important stop was Mr Guest's iron manufactory.

The contrast between the working of steel on a small scale in the peace and quiet of the laboratory and the manufacture of iron on a large scale in the din of a factory struck him forcibly.

> I was much amused [he wrote] by observing the effect the immensity of the works had on me. The operations were all simple enough, but from their extensive nature, the noise which accompanied them, the heat, the vibration, the hum of men, the hiss of engines, the clatter of shears, the fall of masses, I was so puzzled, I could not comprehend them, except very imperfectly. The mind was drawn to observe effects, rather for their novelty than their importance; and it was only when by going round two or three times, I could neglect to listen to sounds at first strange, or to look at rapid motions, that I could readily trace the process through its essential parts, and compare, easily and quickly, one part with another.[40]

For three days, Faraday carefully studied the industrial processes involved in the commercial manufacture of iron but there is no hint in his Journal that he learned anything of real importance. When he left Dowlais to continue his walk through Wales, the problem of where to start in improving the alloys of steel remained unsolved.

From Dowlais, Faraday and his friend Edward Magrath, proceeded through Wales. Faraday's Journal is filled with descriptions of the strange sights, sounds, and scenery they experienced but we cannot pause to sample them. Our goal must be Faraday's: the copper works of Mr Vivian some little distance out of Swansea. There Faraday was initiated into the mysteries of the metallurgy of copper. The whole process from the roasting of the sulphide ore to the final casting was detailed with loving care in his Journal. Here, too, lies the probable source of the clue which permitted him to return to London and recommence his work on iron and steel with some hope of success. In the French report on experiments undertaken in France to confirm and continue Faraday's work, the remark is made, 'it is a natural idea to harden steel as one hardens copper'.[41] It is, of course, only natural if one knows how copper is hardened and this vital piece of information was not given to Faraday until the summer of 1819. Copper is hardened by alloying it with silver, gold, and the other 'noble' metals. When Faraday and Stodart returned to their work, it was to investigate the effects of the noble metals upon the quality of steel produced.

Alloys of iron and the noble metals must be made in a molten state so that a proper mixture can take place. To accomplish this, very high heats were required and Faraday was forced to devise his own furnaces and crucibles. They are characteristic of his inventiveness. The furnace was simplicity itself, consisting of two 'blue pots' made of clay and graphite mixed together, and placed one inside the other. A place was left for the introduction of a blast of air and a grate was provided for the crucibles. As Faraday remarked in his *Chemical Manipulation*, 'it is sufficiently powerful to melt pure iron in a crucible, in twelve or fifteen minutes. . . . All kinds of crucibles, including the Cornish and the Hessian, soften, fuse, and become frothy in it.'[42] To prevent the crucibles from collapsing, two of the most refractory kind (Hessian or Cornish) were placed inside one another and separated by a paste of Stourbridge clay and water which, after drying, effectively bound the two together into a single thick crucible. With these crucibles in his blast furnace, Faraday was able to begin an intensive attack on the alloys of steel.

The procedure was a simple one. Those metals which form alloys with copper (platinum, rhodium, silver, nickel, and tin) were chosen as the ones most likely to have an improving effect upon steel. These metals were then melted together with iron and the results examined. The homogeneity of the alloy was detected by the etching of the surface with dilute acid and microscopic examination. When silver, for example, was mixed in relatively large proportions with iron, the result was a mechanical mixture immediately detectable by etching. 'If an alloy of this kind be forged into a bar, and then dissected by the action of dilute sulphuric acid, the silver appears, not in combination with the steel, but in threads throughout the mass; so that the whole has the appearance of a bundle of fibres of silver and steel, as if they had been united by welding.'[43] Etching was not resorted to simply because it provided a fast and simple comparison between the test alloy and wootz; Faraday also realized, albeit dimly, that there was some relationship between the damask produced by etching and the crystalline state of the steel and that the state of crystallization provided a valuable clue to the quality of the steel. His discussion of the etching of wootz is worth citing.

We have ascertained, by direct experiment, that the wootz, although repeatedly fused, retains the peculiar property of presenting a damask surface, when forged, polished, and acted upon by dilute acid. This appearance is apparently produced by a dissection of the crystals by the acid; for though by the hammering the crystals have been bent about, yet their forms may be readily traced through the curves which the twisting and hammering have produced. From this uniform appearance on the surface of wootz, it is highly probable that the much admired sabres of Damascus are made from this steel; and if this be admitted, there can be little reason to doubt that the damask itself is merely an exhibition of crystallization. That on wootz it cannot be the effect of the mechanical mixture of two substances, as iron and steel, unequally acted upon by acid, is shown by the circumstance of its admitting re-fusion without losing this property. It is certainly true that a damasked surface may be produced by welding together wires of iron and steel; but if these welded specimens are fused, the damask does not again appear. Supposing that the damasked surface is dependent on the development of a crystalline structure, then the superiority of wootz in showing the effect, may fairly be considered as dependent on its power of crystallizing, when solidifying, in a more marked manner, and in more decided forms than the common steel.[44]

This passage reveals the theoretical basis for Faraday's seemingly pure empirical investigation of alloys. As one might expect from someone who had witnessed Davy's work on the diamond and who had been exposed to the theory of point atoms, Faraday singled out crystal structure as the fundamental factor determining the quality of steel. Just as carbon could exist as graphite and diamond by a simple rearrangement in its crystalline form, so the physical properties of steel ought to depend upon this factor. The alloying elements, 'it is reasonable to infer . . . combined with the iron and carbon render the mass more crystallizable'.[45] Since the noble metals performed this function for copper, it was equally reasonable to infer that they would do the same for steel, a conjecture upheld by experiment.

The experiments themselves were perfectly straightforward. Various proportions of iron or steel were mixed with the alloying element, fused, forged, and tested. The properties were carefully reported and the correlation between physical properties and crystalline structure noted.

Stodart and Faraday had begun their work not only for the purpose of discovering new alloys of steel, but also to introduce such new alloys into commerce. Their success in producing improved steels in the laboratory was, therefore, only part of the task they had set themselves. The next step was to see if results in the laboratory could be duplicated in the factory. Operations were accordingly moved to Sheffield where 'The superintendence of the work was . . . entrusted to an intelligent and confidential agent.'[46] As they had hoped, the experiments on a large scale also produced superior steels. The problem now was no longer scientific but commercial. Could steels alloyed with such expensive metals as platinum, iridium, and silver be manufactured at a cost which would not be prohibitive? Only one company – Green, Pickslay and Company – makers of high-class cutlery attempted to introduce the new alloys into commercial use,[47] but does not seem to have made a success of it. In any case, Stodart and Faraday had done all they could have done. After Stodart died on 11 September 1823, Faraday gradually lost interest and abandoned his metallurgical researches. His contribution to iron and steel metallurgy was a modest one. His belief in its basic importance was to be justified in the work of Henry Sorby and his followers later in the century, but his influence on these later developments was almost nil.[48] In terms of his own development, these researches sharpened his experimental skill and made him extremely sensitive to the difficulties encountered by the experimentalist in a long, drawn-out, investigation. They probably added little to his theoretical concepts although the correlation of structure and physical properties may have reinforced his growing confidence in the theory of point atoms.

By 1823 Faraday had shown himself to be a laboratory worker without peer, able to plan and carry out extensive and tedious operations requiring delicacy of touch, manipulative ability, precision and, above all, patience. It was these qualities which led him to be chosen by the Royal Society to perform the experimental part of the researches on optical glass which that Society initiated in 1824. For Faraday the transition from the alloys of steel to the composition of optical glass was a fairly easy one; he was an expert on the management of furnaces, and on the treatment of molten materials. The new task must have appeared to him simply as a variation of the metallurgical researches upon which he had been engaged since 1818. In this he was to be mistaken, for the difficulties he was to encounter were to absorb ever-increasing amounts of his time and turn the work on glass into a real chore and burden.

Why did Faraday undertake this task especially when, in 1827, it became obvious that it would demand time which he wished to devote to other work? The answer does him credit and deserves mention. In 1827 the University of London was being organized and Faraday was sounded out about accepting the chair of chemistry there. At the same time, the Royal Institution was passing through one of its periodic crises and Faraday's concern was reflected in his reply to the offer of the chemistry chair.

> You will remember [he wrote to Dr Dionysius Lardner] from the conversation which we have had together, that I think it a matter of duty and gratitude on my part to do what I can for the good of the Royal Institution in the present attempt to establish it firmly. The Institution has been a source of knowledge and pleasure to me for the last fourteen years, and though it does not pay me in salary for what I *now* strive to do for it, yet I possess the kind feelings and good-will of its authorities and members, and all the privileges it can grant or I require; and, moreover, I remember the protection it has afforded me during the past years of my scientific life. These circumstances, with the thorough conviction that it is a useful and valuable establishment, and the strong hopes that exertions will be followed with success, have decided me in giving at least two more years to it, in the belief that after that

time it will proceed well, into whatever hands it may pass. . . . I have already (and to a great extent for the sake of Institution) pledged myself to a very laborious and expensive series of experiments on glass, which will probably require that time, if not more, for their completion; and other views are faintly opening before us. Thus you will see, that I cannot with propriety accede to your kind suggestion.[49]

Together with John (later Sir John) F. W. Herschel and George Dollond, a practising optician, Faraday began the investigation.

From 1825 until 1827, little of any real importance was accomplished. Two glassmakers, Messrs. Pellatt and Green permitted the men to use their facilities and Faraday took advantage of this offer to familiarize himself with the processes involved in the manufacture of glass. Except for a few analyses of various glass samples, however, he seems to have done very little else until 1827.[50] In September of this year, a special room and furnace were constructed at the Royal Institution and Faraday could settle down to some intensive research.

The early trials were disappointing and showed how difficult the road ahead would be. On 26 December 1827 the first results were examined.

> This morning opened the furnace which we found nearly at common temperatures. The pots were all undisturbed as to position – but with the exception of V all of them adhered to the hearth of the furnace and the latter was found covered with a slag. . . . The pots were now examined in order.
>
> I *Frit* (2) the cover of this pot had disappeared during the high heat – found it inside – it had softened and turning up all round the edge had sunk into the pot and come in contact with the melted glass in one place. . . .
>
> On breaking up the crucible and cover the latter was found full of air bubbles and very frothy – it was quite black inside – red where air had had access it had much injured the glass where in contact with it.
>
> Crucible II frit (3). . . . The top was rather green, full of small bubbles and short upright striae as in I but they were more abundant and had not cleared off from the lower part of the glass as much as in the former case.[51]

And so on, through the other samples.

For six months Faraday wrestled with the problems that this first trial revealed: pots, bubbles, and striae. The pots remained an insuperable difficulty. Even when they did not crack, fuse, or decompose under the intense heat of the furnace, it was found that the glass they contained was imperfect because of the bubbles and striae. The bubbles and striae might be got rid of if the molten glass could be stirred, but this was impossible for the pots would shatter if touched in the furnace. In April, Faraday noted a possible solution to the problem. 'Find that in small quantities i.e. in platina foil a clear glass may be made containing as much as 70 litharge to 10 of silica. . . .'[52]

This glass could be stirred but the use of the platinum foil created new difficulties. One of the basic ingredients of the heavy glass Faraday was trying to make was lead oxide. If any of the lead oxide in the molten glass escaped from the platinum dish, it came in contact with the red-hot iron plate upon which the dish rested and was immediately reduced to lead. The lead then formed an easily fusible alloy with the platinum, resulting in the perforation of the foil. Time after time the glass notebook recorded 'the entire bottom of the platina vessel disappeared . . . and the experiment was suddenly put an end to.'[53] Nevertheless the process did appear to offer advantages and Faraday was determined to perfect it.

For another six months, each aspect of the new method was carefully studied and refined. A silicated borate of lead was substituted for the lead oxide with good results, producing a clear glass which proved less susceptible to reduction. By careful regulation of the furnace, frothing and splattering could be prevented so that no metallic lead came in contact with the platinum. Even the method of folding the corners of the platinum foil to produce the dish was carefully examined for it was found that the glass, when molten, could climb up the fold by capillary action and spill over on to the iron. To minimize the possibility of reduction of the lead leading to the destruction of the platinum dish, another piece of platinum was placed between the dish and the iron plate. The discovery of the cause and cure of each of these sources of failure took weeks. Every new process was tried over and over again until there was no doubt of its efficacy and until Faraday had gained perfect mastery of the manipulations required. His faithful assistant, Sergeant Anderson, who had been hired specifically to help in the glass researches, was never allowed to do more than determine the specific gravities of the finished product, and prepare the ingredients. All other steps were taken by Faraday.

At last, in January 1829, all was deemed ready for a large-scale run to produce a glass which could actually be turned into a telescope's objective lens. A large platinum dish was filled with the necessary ingredients, the furnace was fired and the results eagerly awaited.

This morning [Friday, January 16] opened the furnace; it was still warm. Took out the glass and to my great disappointment found it bad. The fault altogether of a new kind. . . . The plate of glass is full of dark clouds in some places nearly black and the whole of the glass has a greenish black tint which the rough glass had not. The clouds are in most parts twisted, an effect which is partly due to a slight stirring which it received just before the commencement of cooling and partly as I judge from the way in which they have gradually spread into the glass. Each particular cloud is often made up of several part[s] arrange[d] parrallel to each other something resembling a mackerel

E

sky and I do not think this the effect of stirring but due to successive and intermitted formations or else propulsions of coloured glass.[54]

Faraday's discovery of the cause of this new difficulty provides a
beautiful example of a kind of 'experimental thinking' that is not often
discussed. The criticism of a theory by a well-designed *experimentum
crucis* is of fundamental importance in experimental science for it provides
one side of the dialectic between experience and theory by which science
advances. The results of an experiment, however, must also be subjected
to the most severe criticism before they can be used theoretically. The
experimentalist, therefore, must always be wary of his results and must
constantly dissect his experiments in his search for error. This ability to
take an experiment apart, isolate its elements in thought, and discover
weaknesses is essential. Without it, the experimentalist may make important discoveries but he is also liable to commit major blunders.
That Faraday possessed this talent in an eminent degree can be well
illustrated by this case of the darkened glass. The situation is beautifully
simple; there was no theoretical point to be made. The 'experiment'
actually was an exercise in precision cooking yet something went
wrong. How does a master experimenter go about discovering its cause
and cure?

Calling upon his experience with glass, he listed a series of hypotheses:

> I am strongly inclined to suspect that colour is due to platina and that there
> has been action on the metal by the glass. The colour is not that which would
> be communicated by iron but *is* that given to some enamels by finely divided
> platina. I am doubtful whether to suppose that all platina will be acted upon
> by this kind of glass at a very high temperature; or only impure platina.
>
> But the platina tray was alloyed in two places with gold and the stain may
> be from gold – though from the disposition I think that is not likely. The
> platina itself also seemed decidedly acted upon and stained. It has been used
> once before for the piece in the large telescope.
>
> I sometimes think that the effect may have taken place from a want of
> oxygen. The pan was well closed and no doubt the iron plate used would soon
> abstract much of the oxygen within but whether this circumstance together
> with attraction of the platina could in any way reduce a minute portion of the
> lead and so cause action upon and disintegration of the platina we must
> ascertain by experiment.[55]

By experiment the first two possibilities were eliminated and Faraday
now turned to an intensive examination of the third. It was one thing to
suspect that the colour was caused by the reduction of lead and another
to prove it and provide an explanation for it. Two possibilities presented
themselves; one was that the reduction was caused by the platinum and

the other that it depended upon the iron plate. To examine the maximum effect of the platinum, both finely divided and spongy platinum were added to the molten glass. Nothing happened. The iron, then, must be at fault. Slowly the actual steps by which the colour was produced were coaxed forth. In the Bakerian Lecture weeks of effort were summed up in a paragraph.

> At last the cause was discovered. To understand it, it must be known that the platinum tray, with the glass in it, was either placed directly upon the bottom of the iron pan, or, for greater security, with only a plate of platinum inter-vening; and that the whole was covered by an evaporating basin turned upside down, forming a sort of inner chamber within the large one. In this confined state the oxygen of the portion of air present was soon abstracted by the heated metal, an oxide of iron being formed in consequence, and at the same time also a portion of carbonic oxide [carbon monoxide] from the carbon in the cast iron. At the high temperature to which the experiment was raised, this carbonic oxide was competent to reduce a portion of the oxide of lead in the glass to the metallic state, itself becoming carbonic acid; but as soon as the carbonic acid so produced came in contact with the heated iron, it was again converted, according to the well-known condition of the chemical affinities at these temperatures, into carbonic oxide, and went back to the glass to repeat its evil operation and produce more metallic lead. In this way it was that the glass became sullied by smoky clouds consisting of metallic lead.[56]

Thus, in characteristic fashion, the cause of the error was laid bare by Faraday. Throughout his life, he followed the same pattern. The unlooked for result was never ignored or avoided. It must be investigated and analysed until its cause was revealed. In the case of the researches on glass, this merely enabled him to remove a practical difficulty in the way to the production of improved lenses; in other researches, these aberrations were to serve as starting-points for investigations of great theoretical importance.

The discovery of the role of the iron plate in spoiling glass was the last hurdle to be passed. When this was removed and refractory stone sub-stituted, all went well. In April 1829, a full eighteen months after intensive work had begun, Faraday could write in the glass notebook: 'Today sent for the large piece of glass . . . which Mr Dollond has had to polish on the bottom and edges. It proves to be very good as to bubbles containing very few indeed and not in the slightest degree cloudy. I trust that now we know how to avoid or conquer these two difficulties.'[57]

Removal of the striae was still difficult, but involved only the mech-anical problem of proper stirring. When he reported his results to the Royal Society in November 1829, Faraday could state with some pride that considerable obstacles had been overcome to produce new specimens of optical glass of some value.

Although the work continued into 1830 and 1831, Faraday lost interest in it and devoted less and less time to it. On 4 July 1831, he wrote to Dr Roget, Secretary of the Royal Society:

> With reference to the request which the Council of the Royal Society have done me the honour of making – namely that I should continue the investigation – I should, under circumstances of perfect freedom, assent to it at once; but obliged as I have been to devote the whole of my spare time to the experiments already described, and consequently to resign the pursuit of such philosophical inquiries as suggested themselves to my own mind, I would wish, under present circumstances, to lay the glass aside for a while, that I may enjoy the pleasure of working out my own thoughts on other subjects.[58]

The Royal Institution had weathered its storm, helped by the funds with which the glass research had been supported. Faraday had done his job well and could see that future results would be dearly won in terms of time and effort. Other areas were beginning to require his full attention and so it was time to close this investigation. Except for the feeling of a job well done, the only direct benefit Faraday received from this work (and he could not know it at the time) was the heavy borate of lead glass which was to aid him greatly in his researches on diamagnetism in the 1840's.

4. Pure Chemistry

In the little time that was left him from his duties at the Royal Institution and his work in applied chemistry, Faraday devoted himself to chemical and electrical questions of a fundamental nature. The electrical researches will be discussed in the next chapter, but his work in pure chemistry belongs here, for the decade of the 1820's was the period of his most intense activity in this area. Two problems particularly engaged his attention; one was the seemingly anomalous behaviour of chlorine and the other was the more general problem of molecular forces and the states of matter.

Ever since 1812 when Davy's lectures had fired him with enthusiasm for science, chlorine had intrigued him. As he later wrote to his friend Phillips, 'chlorine was with me a favourite object'[59] and it was with its odd behaviour that he was concerned. Specifically, it was the failure of chlorine to combine with carbon that appeared strange. Faraday was early convinced of Davy's proposition that chlorine, like oxygen, was a supporter of combustion. The experimental evidence for this was overwhelming and undeniable. Only when this fact was interpreted within a general theory of combustion did difficulties arise. According to Sir Humphry Davy, the difference between supporters of combustion and combustibles must be attributed to the difference in the electrical states of their constituent molecules. Thus carbon burned with great vigour in oxygen because the carbon and the oxygen were in opposite electrical states. Why, then, did not carbon burn in chlorine which, as a supporter of combustion, must be in the same electrical state as oxygen? This anomaly was a disturbing one and the electrochemical theory of combustion demanded its resolution.

Although chlorine and carbon resolutely refused to combine when thrust into one another's presence, there was some chemical evidence which did suggest that such a combination was possible.

> That the difficulty met with in forming a compound of chlorine and carbon was probably not owing to any want or weakness of affinity between the two bodies, was pointed out by Sir H. Davy; who, reasoning on the triple compound of chlorine, carbon and hydrogen, concluded that the attraction of the two bodies for each other was by no means feeble; and the discovery of phosgene gas by Dr Davy, in which chlorine and carbon are combined with oxygen, was another circumstance strongly in favour of this opinion.[60]

This passage is of considerable interest for it reveals the theoretical background of Faraday's work. Given the generally prevalent theory of chemical combination of the day it made little sense. The mere appearance of three substances in a single compound implied very little about the strength of the affinity between any two of them. When two of the three will not combine into a binary compound, it would appear inescapable that the ternary compound was a result of the overcoming of an antagonism, not evidence for affinity. To put it another way and in terms of the specific case cited, orthodox theory would explain the case in this way: carbon forms a compound with oxygen; chlorine also forms a compound with oxygen. Phosgene, then, is a ternary compound in which the oxygen serves as the mediating influence by which the chlorine and carbon are bound together in a single molecule. The *lack* of affinity of carbon for chlorine is *overcome* by the oxygen, thus permitting a stable ternary compound to be formed. This was not Faraday's interpretation; the presence of carbon and chlorine in the same compound led him to state that there was no 'want or weakness of affinity between the two bodies'. When looked at from the standpoint of the theory of point atoms this conclusion can be shown to make good sense. We must remember that the chemical elements in this theory were compounded of a number of point atoms and each molecule was, therefore, surrounded by a complex pattern of attractive and repulsive forces. It was entirely possible that the force patterns of carbon and chlorine molecules did not fit together so that a binary compound could be formed merely by exposing one to the other. Another molecule, however, might so modify the pattern of forces surrounding one of these elements that the other might enter into combination with it and remain attached to it after the third substance was removed. Thus the ternary compound of oxygen, carbon, and chlorine would indicate a strong affinity between chlorine and carbon and permit Faraday to make the statement he does.[61]

His attack on the problem confirms this interpretation of his train of thought. He did not try to effect the combination of carbon and chlorine by subjecting them to extremes of heat or pressure in the hopes of forcing them into combination. He worked, rather, with chlorine, and with olefiant gas (C_2H_4 – ethylene), a compound of hydrogen and carbon. By gentle means he attempted to coax the carbon and the chlorine into forming a permanent relationship. The two gases were placed together in a retort and exposed to the sun.[62] The power of sunlight to influence chemical reactions had been known since the beginning of the century and had always intrigued Faraday. Sunlight seemed to have a unique ability to foster combinations or decompositions which had little relationship to the gentleness of its appearance. In 1822 Faraday noticed that some plate glass in houses in Bridge Street, Blackfriars, had become coloured by the action of the sun. Experiment confirmed the action of the light and he concluded 'that the sun's rays can exert chemical powers even on such a compact body and permanent compound, as glass'.[63]

His attempts to bring about the combination of chlorine and carbon were successful. He first produced a solid crystalline material which he called the perchloride of carbon and is our modern hexachlorethane (C_2Cl_6). This compound was carefully studied in order to determine its physical properties and also to estimate its stability. Faraday carefully noted that it 'is not precipitated by Nitrate of silver'[64] thus showing that the chlorine was bound strongly to the carbon. The failure of strong sulphuric acid to affect it also appeared to confirm his suspicions that the affinities between the carbon and chlorine were powerful. To test his hypothesis that an antagonism between the two could be overcome only by the presence of a mediating substance, he filled a retort with pure powdered carbon and chlorine and left it on the roof of the Royal Institution to be exposed to the 'solar influence'. Two years later, no reaction had taken place.[65]

While testing his perchloride of carbon, he observed the formation of another chloride. The protochloride of carbon, as he named it, was tetrachlorethylene (C_2Cl_4) and he immediately began to determine its properties. Faraday's keenness as a chemist was once more obvious, for he immediately detected the gap between C_2Cl_4 and C_2Cl_6 and tried unsuccessfully to fill it.[66]

The two chlorides of carbon that he had produced were sufficient to his purpose. An anomaly had been removed from chemical theory and chlorine, a supporter of combustion, had been shown to combine with carbon, a combustible. The revision of Lavoisier's theory of combustion which had so upset the chemical world when Davy had first suggested it could now be considered complete. The last brick had been neatly laid in place by Davy's disciple.

This investigation had also served to direct Faraday's attention ever more closely to the forces surrounding molecules and their roles in chemical processes. The conjecture that a strong affinity existed between carbon and chlorine in spite of the impossibility of combining them directly had been proved true. That the play of affinities was far more complex than the Daltonian atomic theory suspected also seemed to be proven.

The increasing focus on the forces surrounding atoms or molecules, rather than the qualities of these supposed entities themselves, led Faraday (and Davy) to another important discovery. In 1817, he discovered an effect which tended to weaken whatever faith he may have had in the generally accepted atomic theory. The investigation began as a simple exploration of the logical consequence of the concept of atoms of different sizes and weights moving through empty space.

As the mobility of a body, [he wrote in a brief paper] or the ease with which its particles move among themselves, depends entirely upon its physical properties, little delay would arise in the mind, on a consideration of the probable comparative mobilities of the different gases. These bodies being nearly similar in all the physical properties, except specific gravity, which can interfere with internal motions generated in them, would be supposed to have those motions retarded in proportion as this latter character increased; but as this supposition has not been distinctly verified, the following experiments, though possessed of no peculiar claim to attention, may deserve to be recorded.[67]

At ordinary pressures, the expected correlation between specific gravity and rate of gas flow was found. When the conditions were varied, however, the simplicity vanished.

These experiments [Faraday noted] have been carried much further, in consequence of some peculiar results obtained at low pressures; but as I have not been able to satisfy myself respecting the causes, and have probably taken a wrong view of the phenomena, I shall refrain from detailing them, and merely observe, that there is no apparent connexion between the passage of gases through small tubes and their densities at low pressures. Olefiant gas then passes as readily as hydrogen, and twice as rapidly as either carbonic oxide or common air, and carbonic acid escapes far more rapidly than much lighter gases. Similar results are also obtained by diminishing the bore of the tube, and then even at considerable pressures, the effect produced by mobility alone is interfered with by other causes, and different times are obtained. These anomalies depend, probably, upon some peculiar loss or compensation of forces in the tube, and offer interesting matter of discussion to mathematicians.[68]

There the matter rested for a year. Faraday's time and mind were occupied with other matters and the mathematicians showed a great lack of interest in investigating the anomalies. It was probably his work on illuminating gas that led Faraday back to the problem.[69] In 1818 he set out to discover, as quickly as possible, what the causes of the peculiar properties of the gases at low pressure could be. He was unsuccessful in so far as he could not solve the problem. He was able, however, to give a more accurate account of the conditions under which the anomaly appeared.

It was not sufficient, he found, merely to have the gases flow through small apertures or slits; they had to pass through tubes for the effect to occur. Moreover, the effect was not caused by simple obstruction, for when ground glass was used to hinder the passage of the gases, they still passed at a rate inversely proportional to their densities. Variation in gas pressure merely pointed up the anomaly: 'that the velocity of gases in passing through tubes should be in some proportion to the pressure on them is nothing particular; but the singularity is, that the ratio for the same gas varies with the pressure, and that this variation differs in different gases; thus the one which passes with the greatest facility at low pressure, passes with the least at high pressure'.[70]

After excluding all external factors, Faraday concluded by saying that 'perhaps these effects may be accounted for by the supposition of some power of expansion peculiar to each gas'.[71] Once again Faraday attributed an effect to a power peculiarly and intimately associated with individual species of matter. Just how this power worked, Faraday could not say, but that he did have some ideas and intended to keep his eyes open for further clues was shown by the concluding sentence of the article. 'I will therefore refrain', he wrote, 'from mixing up crude notions with facts, and at some more convenient opportunity endeavour to supply what is wanting in this paper.'[72]

Increased knowledge of the powers associated with matter in the gaseous state was to come from two areas. His work on the alloys of steel had led him to observe some interesting effects of very high temperatures, and his own private interest in chlorine was to lead to some very unexpected and important observations on the behaviour of gases under high pressures.

In 1820, writing to Professor G. de la Rive at Geneva about his work on the alloys of steel with Stodart, Faraday mentioned a fact which he found surprising. 'The positive effect', he told de la Rive, 'is the volatilization of silver. We often have it in our experiments sublimed into the upper part of the crucible and forming a fine dew on the sides and cover so that I have no doubt at present on the volatility of silver though I had before.'[73] If silver were volatile, how many other 'solid' substances also had atmospheres of their own vapours surrounding them and to what distance did this atmosphere extend? These were questions that could be answered by experiment and the answers could then be applied to test a hypothesis of the nature of the physical states of matter which Faraday had first encountered in 1812.[74] At the first lecture he attended at the Royal Institution, he had heard Davy state:

> In solids the matter exerts its attractive powers and remains fixed. In fluids there is an equilibrium between the attractive and repulsive powers. In Gasses the repulsive power preponderates over the Attractive but is not sufficiently strong to overcome the specific nature of the body and in Radient matter the repulsion is free and unconfined and projects the body in right lines.[75]

The physical states of matter, then, were merely functions of the two powers of attraction and repulsion with which the 'matter' was associated. By 'exalting' these powers through the agencies of heat and electricity, their effects under different conditions could be studied. If it were shown, as Faraday now suspected, that every body could be made to exist in a solid, liquid, and gaseous form, it would provide unassailable experimental proof for the philosophical principle of continuity upon which both Kant and Boscovich had so insisted. There was, as well, a purely physical consequence of some importance; the phrase, permanent fixed body, or, permanent gas, would no longer have any significance.

To Faraday, to conceive an idea was tantamount to conceiving an experiment to test it. His first essay was a simple one; he suspended a piece of gold over some mercury in a bottle and put the whole thing away in a dark place for a while to see what would happen.[76] The results were encouraging; the gold was whitened by the mercury vapour that condensed upon it, and Faraday was able to report: 'at common temperatures, and even when the air is present, mercury is always surrounded by an atmosphere of the same substance'.[77] From the example of the silver and the mercury, it was possible to conclude that *all* bodies, under suitable circumstances, could pass into the state of vapour. The next question to be resolved was the distance to which this atmosphere of vapour extended. The problem was of considerable theoretical importance for the existence of such vapours under *all* conditions had long been assumed, and this assumption could not be experimentally justified.

> It is well known [he wrote] that within the limits recognized by experiment, the constitution of vapour in contact with the body from which it rises, is such, that its tension increases with increased temperature, and diminishes with diminished temperature; and though in the latter case we can, with many substances, so far attenuate the vapour as soon to make its presence inappreciable to our tests, yet an opinion is very prevalent, and I believe general, that still small portions are produced; the tension being correspondent to the comparatively low temperature of the substance. Upon this view it has been supposed that every substance *in vacuo* or surrounded by vapour or gas, having no chemical action upon it, has an atmosphere of its own around it; and that our atmosphere must contain, diffused through it, minute portions of the vapours of all those substances with which it is in contact, even down to the earths and metals. I believe that a theory of meteorites has been formed upon this opinion.[78]

One might well ask here if this was not precisely Faraday's position? Had he not just finished establishing that every body is surrounded by a gaseous atmosphere of its own molecules? And would not the proof of a limit to this process of vaporization destroy the very principle of continuity which Faraday was supposedly so eager to uphold? The apparent contradiction vanishes if we appeal again to the theory of point atoms and recall Faraday's contention that all bodies will vaporize *under certain conditions*. In the theory of point atoms it was possible to have the discontinuity implied by suggesting a limit to vaporization without sacrificing the principle of continuity itself. If the gaseous state were defined in terms of intermolecular distance, then reference to the Boscovichean curve will immediately reveal a limit to vaporization although the curve is itself continuous. Until two particles can leap over the hump of repulsion and pass from one stable point to another, change of state will not take place. The volatilization of silver would occur when, by heat, the repulsive power of the silver molecules was 'exalted' to permit the required separation.

Upon cooling, as the repulsive force lost its 'exaltation' a critical point would be reached where the attractive and repulsive forces just balance. Any further diminution of repulsion would push the particle into the attractive arch and the intermolecular distance would become that of solid silver. Faraday did not present the argument in these terms. Rather, he wrote:

> The metal, silver for instance, when violently heated, as on charcoal urged by a jet of oxygen, or by the oxy-hydrogen or oxy-alcohol flame, is converted into vapour; lower the temperature, and before the metal falls beneath a white heat, the tension of the vapour is so far diminished, that its existence becomes inappreciable by the most delicate tests. Suppose, however, that portions are formed, and that vapour of a certain tension is produced at that temperature; it must be astonishingly diminished by the time the metal has sunk to a mere red heat; and we can hardly conceive it possible, I think, that the silver should have descended to common temperatures, before its accompanying vapour will, by its gradual diminution in tension, if uninfluenced by other circumstances, have had an elastic force far inferior to the force of gravity; in which case, that moment at which the two forces had become equal, would be the last moment in which vapour could exist around it; the metal at every lower temperature being perfectly fixed.[79]

Again, it is impossible to *prove* that Faraday was thinking in terms of point atoms. But, the passage can be interpreted intelligently in these terms. That Faraday, by the time this article was written (1826), was more or less committed to this theory will be shown when his work on the liquefaction of gases is considered. All Faraday did here was to end on a tantalizing note. 'I refrain', he wrote, 'from extending these views, as might easily be done, to the atomic theory, being rather desirous that they should first obtain the sanction or correction of scientific men.'[80] Would the extension of these views to the atomic theory have introduced atomic 'limits' of powers? Would these not, then, have had to follow the essential shape of Boscovich's curve? We can, unfortunately, only cry *ignorabimus* and pass on to other matters.

The problem of the existence of an atmosphere of vapour surrounding solid bodies had its converse. If all bodies could be vaporized should not all gaseous bodies be capable of liquefaction or solidification? The essential symmetry of these two questions was so obvious that it seems impossible that Faraday should not have seen it. Yet, the record is quite clear. Although he did, indeed, liquefy a number of the so-called permanent gases, this was something he stumbled upon, rather than looked for consciously. It was, nevertheless, an important investigation both for the history of chemistry and for Faraday's own development.

Faraday is his own best historian on the discovery of the liquefaction of gases. In 1836, Dr John Davy, Sir Humphry's brother, accused Faraday of failing to do justice to his late brother in giving him the proper credit for suggesting the operation which led to the discovery of liquid chlorine.[81] Faraday requested his friend Richard Phillips, then editor of the *Philosophical Magazine*, to print his account of the discovery.

> The facts of the case, [he wrote] as far as I know them, are these: – In the spring of 1823, Mr Brande was Professor of Chemistry, Sir Humphry Davy Honorary Professor of Chemistry, and I Chemical Assistant, in the Royal Institution. Having to give personal attendance on both the morning and afternoon chemical lectures, my time was very fully occupied. Whenever any circumstance relieved me in part from the duties of my situation, I used to select a subject of research, and try my skill upon it. Chlorine was with me a favourite object, and having before succeeded in discovering new compounds of that element with carbon, I had considered that body more deeply, and resolved to resume its consideration at the first opportunity: accordingly, the absence of Sir Humphry Davy from town having relieved me from a part of the laboratory duty, I took advantage of the leisure and the cold weather and worked upon frozen chlorine, obtaining the results which are published in my paper in the 'Quarterly Journal of Science' for the 1st of April, 1823.[82] On Sir Humphry Davy's return to town, which I think must have been about the end of February or the beginning of March, he inquired what I had been doing, and I communicated the results to him as far as I had proceeded, and said I intended to publish them in the 'Quarterly Journal of Science.' It was then that he suggested to me the heating of the crystals in a closed tube, and I proceeded to make the experiment which Dr Paris witnessed, and has from his own knowledge described.[83]

The experiment was a simple one clearly described (along with his debt to Davy) in the paper 'On Fluid Chlorine' which appeared in both the *Phil. Trans.* and *Phil. Mag.* in 1823. After having briefly explained why he was working on the hydrate of chlorine, he went on:

> The President of the Royal Society [Davy] having honoured me by looking at these conclusions, suggested, that an exposure of the substance to heat under pressure would probably lead to interesting results; the following experiments were commenced at his request. Some hydrate of chlorine was prepared, and, being dried as well as could be by pressure in bibulous paper, was introduced into a sealed glass tube, the upper end of which was then hermetically closed. Being placed in water at 60°, it underwent no change; but when put into water at 100°, the substance fused, the tube became filled with a bright yellow atmosphere, and on examination was found to contain two fluid substances: the one, about three fourths of the whole, was of a faint yellow colour, having very much the appearance of water; the remaining fourth was a heavy bright yellow fluid, lying at the bottom of the former, without any apparent tendency to mix with it.[84]

The heavy fluid, although Faraday did not yet realize it, was liquid chlorine. Dr Paris, who was present, chided Faraday at the time for using dirty tubes which produced the oily substance observed.

It was only after determining that the two fluids were not more common (and to be expected) compounds of chlorine that Faraday realized what he had done. In jubilation he wrote to Dr Paris:

Dear Sir,
    The *oil* you noticed yesterday turns out to be liquid chlorine.
                                        Yours faithfully,
                                                        M. Faraday.[85]

At the end of the short paper announcing the discovery and a few of the properties of liquid chlorine, Faraday appended a note by Sir Humphry Davy in which Davy gave his reasons for suggesting that Faraday heat the crystals: 'In desiring Mr Faraday to expose the hydrate of chlorine to heat in a closed glass tube, it occurred to me that one of three things would happen: that it would become fluid as a hydrate; or that a decomposition of water would occur, and euchlorine and muriatic acid be formed; or that the chlorine would separate in a condensed state.'[86]

This is a crucial point in the argument for dating Faraday's acceptance of the theory of point atoms. Up to now, we have seen how the theory of point atoms *might* have been used to explain effects and guide research. Given Faraday's early exposure to the theory and his philosophical bent, it has appeared most probable that he did use the theory at least to help him visualize some processes. With Davy's statement, we are at last face to face with a direct test case. If Davy was telling the truth[87] and actually did visualize the possibility of fluid chlorine being condensed, the experiment Faraday performed was actually an *experimentum crucis* which could decide between the Daltonian and Boscovichean theories.

According to the Daltonian theory, gases consisted of atoms attracting one another by the force of universal gravitation, but held apart by the repulsive force of the caloric surrounding each atom. What would happen in such an enclosed system if more caloric (heat) were added? The pressure of the caloric might conceivably effect a chemical decomposition if the gas particles were compound, and it would certainly ultimately cause an explosion as the repulsive force increased. But no one would have predicted that the addition of caloric, the very essence of the gaseous state, would destroy this state.

The situation was quite otherwise as concerned the theory of point atoms. Davy had long considered heat to be the result of the motion of the constituent molecules of bodies. The various states of matter, in the Boscovichean theory, depended upon the distances between molecules and these distances were determined by the attractive and repulsive forces which surrounded each molecule. Imagine now two molecules at such a distance from one another that each resists displacement. Confine these molecules and add heat in the form of motion. Each molecule will now vibrate about the stable point; the pressure will prevent the further separation of the two, so as the motion becomes more violent (as the temperature rises) the only direction in which they can move to a permanent state is towards one another. When the combination of temperature and pressure is powerful enough to overcome the repulsive hump in the Boscovichean curve, condensation will take place. The molecules will now be closer to one another, hence change of state will have taken place. Davy explicitly stated this as the result of heating gases under pressure.

'I cannot conclude this note without observing,' he wrote in the same appended note, 'that the generation of elastic substances in close vessels, either with or without heat, offers much more powerful means of approximating their molecules than those dependent upon the application of cold, whether natural or artificial.'[88]

Here was dramatic proof, if any were needed by Faraday, of the power of the theory of point atoms to lead to new phenomena and new ideas. It must be emphasized again that it was not until 1844, when some of his published ideas were relatively meaningless unless interpreted according to the theory of point atoms, that Faraday explicitly stated his adherence to this theory. Even at this late date he explicitly stated that he 'had no intention of publishing the matter further'[89] except that this might help people to grasp his views. The theory of point atoms was utilized in his electrical researches from 1831 on,[90] so that he must have become a convert sometime between his last lecture to the City Philosophical Society in 1819 and 1831. It is entirely possible that the theory simply grew on him as he delved more deeply into the complexities of nature. If, however, a precise date can be suggested, the spring of 1823 would appear to have much to recommend it. The liquefaction of chlorine, therefore, may be viewed as a crucial point in the development of his thought.

Having liquefied one gas, Faraday immediately turned to others, many of which succumbed to the new technique. The quiet of the Royal Institution was punctured regularly with the sound of exploding apparatus. The sang-froid with which Faraday accepted these accidents inspires both awe and wonder. In March 1823, he wrote to his friend Huxtable:

'I met with another explosion on Saturday evening, which has again laid up my eyes. It was from one of my tubes, and was so powerful as to drive the pieces of glass like pistol-shot through a window. However, I am getting better, and expect to see as well as ever in a few days. My eyes were filled with glass at first.'[91]

The liquefaction of the 'permanent' gases destroyed a discontinuity which had been introduced into chemistry by Lavoisier. Matter could exist in all three states given the proper conditions, and the problem of accounting for these states was enormously simplified. In spite of the fact that Faraday himself showed that he was not the first to liquefy the 'permanent' gases[92] he was certainly the first to drive this point home.

With the liquefaction of gases, Faraday's sustained research (and even this was done in snatches) ceased for years. To increase the popularity (and the income) of the Royal Institution he instituted the Friday Evening Discourses which did much to popularize science in Great Britain. The Juvenile Lectures, given at Christmas time, were to become a cherished tradition and a real source of enjoyment to Faraday himself. In the 1820's, too, Faraday began to lecture at the Royal Military Academy at Woolwich. With his lectures at the Royal Institution and Woolwich, his work on glass, his great demand as an analytical chemist, his position as a consultant to the Admiralty, his life was full and his income assured. By 1830 he stood as a respected man of science with a comfortable income and an enviable situation. Had anyone then been so rash as to rank the European scientists, Faraday would have been found near the very top of the second rank. The discovery which was to occupy him for thirty years and lead to immortality in the history of science was to be made in 1831. He had been thinking of it for years. The discovery of electromagnetic induction was no accident and its consequences were to revolutionize our concepts of the physical world.

References

1. Warner MSS., B. Abbott, 'Jottings from Memory . . .', 4.

2. I.E.E., *Common Place Book, Volume 1*, 73. This volume was begun in 1816, and the poem probably dates from 1817. Faraday was in the habit of jotting down quotations and short poems which he encountered in his reading. The poem on Love has all the earmarks of an original creation and bears eloquent witness to his inferiority in this department to his teacher, Sir Humphry Davy.

3. B.J., *1*, 317. Faraday to Miss Sarah Barnard, 5 July 1820.

4. Ibid.

5. Ibid.

6. Ibid., 318.

7. R.I., Faraday MSS., Constance Reid, *Diary*, 43.

8. Faraday to Christian Hansteen, R.I., 16 December 1857. Copy (only) in Institutt for Teoretisk Astrofysikk, Oslo, Norway.

9. Charlotte Barnard to her sister, Elizabeth Barnard (Mrs Davy Reid) in Newcastle, Saturday Morning, 18 March 1826. This letter is owned by Miss M. F. Blaikley, with whose kind permission it is quoted.

Most of the people mentioned in the letter were either Faradays or Barnards or married to them. As was often the case within the Sandemanian Church, more than one member of a family tended to marry into another family. Margaret Faraday married Michael's brother-in-law.

10. Reid, *Diary*, 152.

11. Ibid., 154.

12. Ibid.

13. Ibid., 158.

14. Ibid., 159.

15. It has been suggested that Faraday's loss of memory and other symptoms were the result of mercury poisoning brought about by his constant contact with this element in his electrical and chemical researches. The fact that his memory was failing in 1816 before such exposure became at all important seems to rule out this interpretation. Faraday's acute sensitivity to smells, especially of guttering candles and snuffed oil lamps, has also led to the suggestion of an allergy which produced the giddiness of which he complained. I have been unable to discover any medical basis for this supposition. There is, finally, the psychoanalytical point of view which attributes his headaches, giddiness, and loss of memory to a neurosis. As we know almost nothing about those areas of Faraday's life upon which the psychologist would base his diagnosis of a contemporary patient, I find this of little help in understanding the workings of Faraday's mind. I must, therefore, be content to state that Faraday suffered from giddiness, loss of memory, and headaches throughout most of his adult life and ask the reader to provide his own causes for this condition.

16. Preussische Staatsbibliothek, Marburg, acc. Darmstaedter 1926. 10. Faraday to R. Phillips, R.I., 29 August 1828.

17. Reid, *Diary*, 45. For an account of this lecture, see *Proc. R.I.*, *3* (1858–62), 70 ff.

18. M. Faraday, 'Observations on Mental Education', *Exp. Res. in Phys. and Chem.* (London, 1859), 464. The lecture is reprinted as 'On the Education of the Judgment' in E. L. Youmans, *The Culture Demanded by Modern Life* (New York, 1867).

19. B.J., *1*, 337.

20. See above, p. 30.

21. Now in the possession of Mr E. Duckworth of Cheltenham who very kindly permitted me to make notes from it. Another, similarly annotated Bible is in the Southwark Public Library.

22. Job ix. 20.

23. B.J., *1*, 411, Faraday to E. Barnard, Niton, 23 July 1826.

24. R.I., *Note Book and Scrap Book of Things Examined in the Laboratory, Sept.*

5a Sir Joseph Banks,
   P.R.S.

5b Sir Humphry Davy

6a J. J. Berzelius

6b William Thomas
Brande

7a Thomas Thomson

7b Joseph Gay-Lussac

8a John Dalton

8b Sir William
Herschel

9a Claude-Louis Berthollet

9b James Clerk Maxwell

*10a Hans Christian
Oersted*

*10b André-Marie
Ampère*

11a William Hyde Wollaston

11b Peter Barlow

12a Dr J. A. Paris

12b François Arago

1820 to Dec. 1823. This manuscript volume is indispensable for following Faraday's activities in the years 1820–31. It contains much of the daily work which he later copied out into the *Diary*, published in 1931 by Thomas Martin. Faraday was not the only one to enter things in this volume. There are also passages there by Davy and W. T. Brande.

25. See, for example, the entries for June and July 1820 in the *Note Book*.

26. Burndy Library, Faraday to Richard Phillips, postmarked 26 Ju. 1820. For a summary of the evidence produced at the trial, see *Phil. Mag.*, *55* (1820), 252 ff. and *Q.J.S.*, *10* (1821), 316 ff.

27. M. Faraday, 'On new Compounds of Carbon and Hydrogen, and on certain other Products obtained during the Decomposition of Oil by Heat', *Phil. Trans.*, 1825, 440 ff. Henceforth Faraday's papers will be cited as they exist in the volumes of his collected researches. For this paper, see *Exp. Res. in Chem. and Phys.*, 154 ff.

28. See *Note Book*, 26 April 1825 ff.; *Faraday's Diary*, *1*, 197 ff. and the article cited above for the details of these operations. Sir William J. Pope discussed Faraday's work on benzene in a discourse delivered at the Royal Institution on Friday, 12 June 1925, as part of the Benzene Centenary. This discourse was published as part of a supplement to *Nature*, *115* (1925), 1002, under the title, 'Faraday as a Chemist'.

29. Public Record Office, Adm. 1, 4610.

30. Burndy Library, Faraday to Ampère, R.I., 17 November 1825.

31. Quoted in Sir Robert A. Hadfield, Bt., *Faraday and His Metallurgical Researches* (London, 1931), 39. This volume, already rare, is a mine of information on the history of metallurgy in the nineteenth century and I have relied upon it heavily for the more technical aspects of Faraday's work on steel.

32. George Pearson, M.D., F.R.S., 'Experiments and Observations to investigate the Nature of a kind of Steel, manufactured at Bombay, and there called Wootz: with Remarks on the Properties and Composition of the Different States of Iron', *Phil. Trans.*, 1795, 322 ff. Very little is known of Stodart. Hadfield, op. cit., has some interesting information which can be supplemented by the biographical article in *The English Cyclopaedia, Cyclopaedia of Biography* (6 vols., London, 1858), *5*, 734.

33. *Nich. Jour.*, 7 (1804), 120; *11* (1805), 215 and 282.

34. Hadfield, op. cit., 123, states that Faraday started to work with Stodart on the alloys of steel in the summer of 1818. He bases this upon a sentence from a letter of Faraday to G. de la Rive dated 26 June 1820, which he quotes thus: 'You can easily understand that during the two years that we have worked upon this subject. . . .' In manuscript, however, the passage runs: 'You will readily suppose that during nearly 2 years that we have been at work on this subject. . . .' Given the dating of the published results and this passage, I feel it necessary to date the commencement of the work on iron as late 1818 or early 1819.

35. Hadfield, op. cit., 81.

36. M. Faraday, 'An Analysis of Wootz, or Indian Steel', *Q.J.S.*, 7 (1819), 288.

37. J. Stodart and M. Faraday, 'Experiments on the Alloys of Steel, made with a View to its Improvement', [1820] in *Exp. Res. in Chem. and Phys.*, 58.

38. Glamorgan County Record Office, Cardiff. Faraday to J. J. Guest, R.I., 6 June 1819.

39. I.E.E., *Common Place Book*, *1*, 326.

40. I.E.E., *Common Place Book*, *2*, 'Walking Tour in Wales', 60.

41. *Bull. de la Soc. d'Enc. pour l'Ind. Nat.*, July 1821, 'Note sur les expériences faites par la Commission de la Société d'Encouragement pour l'amélioration de l'acier par son alliage avec différentes substances', cited in Hadfield, op. cit., 256. See page 87 for the quotation. Hadfield did not know of Faraday's visit to the copper works so did not connect the two.

42. M. Faraday, *Chemical Manipulation, being Instructions to Students in Chemistry on the Methods of Performing Experiments of Demonstration or of Research with Accuracy and Success* (2nd ed., London, 1830), 95. This was the only book Faraday ever wrote. It was an excellent guide to laboratory practice.

43. 'On the Alloys of Steel', *Exp. Res. in Chem. and Phys.*, 64.

44. Ibid., 59.

45. Ibid., 60. Faraday's focus upon the structure of the materials with which he was working also led him to announce the artificial production of plumbago or graphite. Ordinary carbon, after long heating, was discovered to have undergone molecular rearrangement to produce graphite.

46. J. Stodart and M. Faraday, 'On the Alloys of Steel', *Exp. Res. in Chem. and Phys.*, 68. The quotation is on page 69.

47. See the letters of Charles Pickslay to Faraday in Hadfield, op. cit., 133. The originals are at the R.I. bound in a volume containing Faraday's chemical papers, opposite the article on alloys of steel.

48. For the later fate of the idea of structure, see Cyril Stanley Smith, *A History of Metallography* (Chicago, 1960).

49. B.J., *1*, 405, Faraday to Dr Lardner, R.I., 6 October 1827.

50. M. Faraday, *The Bakerian Lecture*, 'On the Manufacture of Glass for Optical Purposes', read to the Royal Society on 19 November, 3 and 10 December 1829, reprinted in *Exp. Res. in Chem. and Phys.*, 231 ff. See also R.S., Faraday MSS., Faraday to J. F. W. Herschel, R.I., 14 November, Monday [1825], in which Faraday remarked, 'I am afraid we shall not do much by the present desultory mode of discussing the matter (i.e. by notes and at a distance from each other) and think that the sooner we can meet at the works to examine the annealing furnace and turn it or other parts of the place to account as fritting furnaces, the better.' The 'works' however were three miles from the Royal Institution and it was very difficult to get anything done.

51. R.S., Faraday MSS., *Glass Furnace Notebook*, *1*, 35 ff.

52. Ibid., 142.

53. Ibid., 234, 8 October 1828.

54. Ibid., 286, 16 January 1829.

55. Ibid., 288.

56. *Exp. Res. in Chem. and Phys.*, 256.

57. *Glass Furnace Notebook*, 352.

58. B.J., *1*, 402, Faraday to Dr Roget, R.I., 4 July 1831.

59. B.J., *1*, 375, Faraday to R. Phillips, R.I., 10 May 1836.

60. M. Faraday, 'On two new Compounds of Chlorine and Carbon, and on a

new Compound of Iodine, Carbon, and Hydrogen' (read to the Royal Society, 21 December 1820), in *Exp. Res. in Chem. and Phys.*, 34.

61. The reader should be warned that this conclusion rests on no direct documentary evidence. Faraday's extant laboratory diaries begin in September 1820, and in his paper he tells us that he began to work on the subject during the summer of 1820. I have been unable to locate any record of these first efforts.

In spite of this lack of documentary evidence, I feel confident of the essential accuracy of the argument. We know Faraday's interest in the theory of point atoms; his statement makes little sense in terms of other theories of chemical combination, whereas it follows from the theory of point atoms. Furthermore, his other chemical researches during the 1820's involve the concept of molecular forces and I feel the idea of Boscovichean atoms was never long out of his mind.

62. *Diary*, *1*, 2–45, records his experiments on the chlorides of carbon.

63. M. Faraday, 'Purple Tint of Plate-glass affected by Light', in *Exp. Res. in Chem. and Phys.*, 142.

64. *Diary*, *1*, 4.

65. Ibid., 44 and 64.

66. Ibid., 31.

67. M. Faraday, 'On the Escape of Gases through Capillary Tubes', in *Exp. Res. in Chem. and Phys.*, 5.

68. Ibid., 6.

69. All Faraday says is, 'I have lately had my attention again called to the subject' ('Experimental Observations on the Passage of Gases through Tubes', *Exp. Res. in Chem. and Phys.*, 7).

70. Ibid., 9.

71. Ibid., 10.

72. Ibid.

73. Bib. pub. et univ. de Génève, MS. 2311 28 A4, f. 57, Faraday to G. de la Rive, R.I., 26 June 1820. The manuscript differs in small details from the version published by B.J., *1*, 330.

74. Sir Humphry Davy would insist on a fourth state: radiant matter.

75. Davy, *Four Lects.*, 56.

76. *Diary*, *1*, 28. 21 October 1820.

77. M. Faraday, 'On the Vapour of Mercury at common Temperatures', *Exp. Res. in Chem. and Phys.*, 57.

78. M. Faraday, 'On the existence of a Limit to Vaporization', *Exp. Res. in Chem. and Phys.*, 199.

The theory of terrestrial 'exhalations' has a long and honourable history, extending back to classical antiquity. It is a beautiful example of the difficulty of getting rid of an idea once it has become an accepted part of science.

79. Ibid., 201.

80. Ibid., 205.

81. See John Davy, *Memoirs of the Life of Sir Humphry Davy* (2 vols., London, 1836), *2*, 160–4. Dr Davy wrote: 'I am surprised that Mr Faraday has not come forward to do him [Sir Humphry Davy] justice.'

82. M. Faraday, 'On Hydrate of Chlorine', *Exp. Res. in Chem. and Phys.*,

81 ff. By 'frozen chlorine', Faraday was referring to the hydrate and not to solid chlorine.

83. M. Faraday, 'On the History of the Condensation of the Gases, in reply to Dr Davy, introduced by some Remarks on that of Electromagnetic rotation', *Exp. Res. in Chem. and Phys.*, 136.

84. M. Faraday, 'On Fluid Chlorine', *Exp. Res. in Chem. and Phys.*, 85.

85. Dr Paris, *The Life of Sir Humphry Davy*, 391.

86. H. Davy, 'Note on the Condensation of Muriatic Acid Gas into the liquid Form', *Exp. Res. in Chem. and Phys.*, 88.

87. This point, of course, can never be decided, but, although important it is not essential to the argument. It is possible that Davy actually only suspected that the first two products would be formed and added chlorine when he was presented with a *fait accompli*. Whether one accepts Davy's story depends on one's estimate of his character. Though vain and a bit jealous of Faraday, it is my feeling that he would not have made up the account to fit the discovery. The fact that the theory of point atoms to which Davy adhered permitted the prediction of such an effect lends credence to Davy's statement.

88. H. Davy, 'Note . . .', *Exp. Res. in Chem. and Phys.*, 88.

89. M. Faraday, 'A speculation touching Electric Conduction and the Nature of Matter', *Exp. Res. in Elect.*, 2, 284. His ideas were presented in a Friday evening discourse at the Royal Institution and were not, therefore, even then intended as a general statement of his theoretical views.

90. See below, Chapter Four.

91. B.J., *1*, 373, Faraday to Huxtable, R.I., 25 March 1823.

92. M. Faraday, 'Historical Statement respecting the Liquefaction of Gases', *Exp. Res. in Chem. and Phys.*, 124.

The Discovery of Electromagnetic Induction

1. The Theories of Electromagnetism

The possibility that electricity and magnetism were but different modes of action of the underlying and fundamental forces of attraction and repulsion was a primary tenet of the Kantian dynamic philosophy. One of Kant's most ardent disciples, the young Dane Hans Christian Oersted, devoted twenty years of his life to making this possibility manifest.

As the son of the village apothecary of Rudkoebing on the island of Langeland, Oersted was exposed at an early age to the charms of chemistry. At the University of Copenhagen, from which he received the degree of Doctor of Philosophy in 1799, Oersted first came into contact with *Naturphilosophie* and immediately became an ardent adherent. Some years later he explained its attraction for him by contrasting the two basic attitudes upon which the progress of science, in his view, depended.

> One class of natural philosophers [he wrote] have always a tendency to combine the phenomena and to discover their analogies; another class, on the contrary, employ all their efforts in showing the disparities of things. Both tendencies are necessary for the perfection of science, the one for its progress, the other for its correctness. The philosophers of the first of these classes are guided by the sense of unity throughout nature; the philosophers of the second have their minds more directed towards the certainty of our knowledge. The one are absorbed in search of principles, and neglect often the peculiarities, and not seldom the strictness of demonstrations; the other considers the science only as the investigation of facts, but in their laudable zeal they often lose sight of the harmony of the whole, which is the character of truth. Those who look for the stamp of divinity on every thing around them, consider the opposite pursuits as ignoble and even as irreligious; while those who are engaged in the search after truth, look upon the other as unphilosophical enthusiasts, and perhaps as phantastical contemners of truth. . . . This conflict of opinions keeps science alive, and promotes it by an oscillatory progress. . . .[1]

Throughout his life Oersted threw in his lot with those to whom the universe was a Divine work of art held together by a few simple forces.

That 'all phenomena are produced by the same power'[2] was a basic principle in his personal philosophy which he reiterated time and time again. In 1806 he suggested that this power 'appears in different forms as, for example, Light, Heat, Electricity Magnetism, etc.',[3] but gave no ideas as to how one basic force could produce these different effects. In a work published in 1813, he gave some hints concerning the nature of the forces involved. There is a vagueness and looseness in the language characteristic of the worst aspects of *Naturphilosophie* but also enough of legitimate physics to enable one to picture the way in which Oersted envisioned the process of the transmission of forces and their transformations into electricity, light, and heat.

> There are two opposing forces which exist in all bodies and which can never be completely removed from them. Each of these forces has an expansive and repulsive action in the volume which it dominates; but each attracts [the other] and produces a contraction when it acts on the other. When these forces act most freely they produce electrical phenomena. These forces can be condensed, retained in a limited volume, or even rendered completely latent by the attraction of one for the other.
> . . . when these forces are too latent to produce electrical phenomena, they constitute the chemical properties of bodies.
> . . . every time that the forces unite in circumstances of imperfect conduction, heat is produced. . . .[4]

The concept of the electric current which Oersted first expounded in this work is also of considerable interest. 'We know that the force being transmitted attracts its opposite,' he wrote, 'whereas it repels the force of the same kind. When the attracted force has reached a certain intensity, it combines with a portion of the attracting force, leaving the repelled force in an even more perfect state of liberty. This force produces a new distribution by its attractive and repulsive faculty and, a moment later, a new equilibrium is achieved like the first and so on.'[5] The result is 'a kind of dynamic oscillation'[6] or wave motion of forces down the wire. The ease of conduction determined whether these forces manifested themselves as heat or light.

It was this rather vague concept that led Oersted to the discovery of electromagnetism. The exact description of the circumstances under which the discovery was made was given by Oersted himself (writing in the third person) in the article on thermo-electricity which he wrote for David Brewster's *Edinburgh Encyclopaedia*.

> In the winter of 1819–20, he delivered a course of lectures upon electricity, galvanism, and magnetism, before an audience that had been previously acquainted with the principles of natural philosophy. In composing the

lecture, in which he was to treat of the analogy between magnetism and electricity, he conjectured that if it were possible to produce any magnetical effect by electricity, this could not be in the direction of the current, since this had been so often tried in vain, but that it must be produced by a lateral action. This was strictly connected with his other ideas; for he did not consider the transmission of electricity through a conductor as an uniform stream, but as a succession of interruptions and re-establishments of equilibrium, in such a manner that the electrical powers in the current were not in quiet equilibrium but in a state of continual conflict. As the luminous and heating effect of the electrical current goes out in all directions from a conductor, which transmits a great quantity of electricity; so he thought it possible that the magnetical effect could likewise eradiate. . . . He was nevertheless far from expecting a great magnetical effect of the galvanic pile; and still he supposed that a power, sufficient to make the conducting wire glowing might be required. The plan of the first experiment was, to make the current of a little galvanic trough apparatus, commonly used in his lectures, pass through a very thin platina wire, which was placed over a compass covered with glass. The preparations for the experiment were made, but some accident having hindered him from trying it before the lecture, he intended to defer it to another opportunity; yet during the lecture the probability of its success appeared stronger, so that he made the first experiment in the presence of the audience. The magnetical needle, though included in a box, was disturbed; but as the effect was very feeble, and must, before its law was discovered, seem very irregular, the experiment made no strong impression on the audience.[7]

Like Davy, the young Oersted had been severely burned by rushing prematurely into print, and he wanted to be absolutely certain that his enthusiasm and belief in the effect had not misled him. It seems almost incredible that Oersted did absolutely nothing further for three months. The discovery which was to give him immortality in the history of science was put to one side while he concerned himself with other matters. Finally, in July 1820, he resumed the investigation. There could now be no doubt of the effect and late in July he sent a four-page, 4to announcement of his discovery in Latin to all the learned bodies and most distinguished scientists of Europe. The faith of those who believed in the essential unity of all natural forces had finally been justified!

In his account of the discovery, Oersted pointed out the one really peculiar feature of the electromagnetic effect. Although he had anticipated some magnetic action from the electric current he was not prepared for the fact that the magnetic force was *circular*, surrounding the wire like a magnetic sheath. His puzzlement was obvious in the concluding paragraphs in which he summed up the results of his investigation.

We may now make a few observations towards explaining these phenomena.

The electric conflict acts only on the magnetic particles of matter. All non-magnetic bodies appear penetrable by the electric conflict, while magnetic bodies, or rather their magnetic particles, resist the passage of this conflict. Hence they can be moved by the impetus of the contending powers.

It is sufficiently evident from the preceding facts that the electrical conflict is not confined to the conductor, but dispersed pretty widely in the circumjacent space.

From the preceding facts we may likewise collect that this conflict performs circles; for without this condition, it seems impossible that the one part of the uniting wire, when placed below the magnetic pole, should drive it towards the east, and when placed above it towards the west; for it is the nature of a circle that the motions in opposite parts should have an opposite direction. Besides, a motion in circles, joined with a progressive motion, according to the length of the conductor ought to form a conchoidal or spiral line; but this, unless I am mistaken, contributes nothing to explain the phenomena hitherto observed.[8]

This short paper caused a sensation. In every laboratory throughout Europe and America, men rushed to repeat Oersted's experiment and see this amazing effect for themselves. The fact that an electric current produced magnetic effects, although startling, had nevertheless been anticipated by some. What was really new was the nature of the magnetic force produced. Hitherto, only central forces (i.e. forces acting in straight lines between points) had been known. A *circular* force was both unanticipated and inexplicable. The first 'skew' force in the history of mechanics threatened to upset the whole structure of Newtonian science. Any theory of electromagnetism would somehow have to come to grips with this peculiar phenomenon and either reduce it to the resultant action of central forces or create a new mechanics in which circular forces would be allowed a role. Oersted's theory was of little help here. His 'electric conflict' created a longitudinal wave which passed along the wire. Although the effects of the conflict extended into the space surrounding the wire, Oersted could give no satisfactory reason for the conflict to move in circles. His statement that it did was only a presentation of the fact of the existence of the circular force, not an explanation of it.

Almost immediately after the publication of Oersted's paper, two theories of electromagnetism were forthcoming. One emanated from Austria and the other from France. Both attempted to reduce electromagnetism to previously known facts and both tried to eliminate one of the pair – electricity or magnetism – from consideration. The explanation put forward by J. J. Prechtl is now almost unknown; the rival theory of André-Marie Ampère won almost universal acceptance.[9] Were this a history of electricity, Prechtl could perhaps be ignored and immediate attention paid to the epoch-making achievements of Ampère. Faraday, however, never fully accepted Ampère's concepts and did feel strongly enough about Prechtl's views to note the fact that he had read them.[10] In the third paper in the series of *Experimental Researches in Electricity*, he also felt it necessary to state publicly his disagreement with Prechtl's views.[11] Prechtl's ideas are, therefore, of more than casual interest and deserve mention.

J. J. Prechtl, in 1820, was Director of the Vienna Polytechnic Institute and, like Oersted, a *Naturphilosoph*.[12] He was firmly opposed to any theory of electromagnetism which made use of imponderable fluids and insisted upon speaking only of forces. His problem, therefore, was so to arrange the rectilinear forces of attraction and repulsion that the resultant was a circular sheath of force surrounding a current-carrying wire. It was the solution to this problem that Prechtl reported in a paper entitled 'On the true condition of the Magnetic State in the Connecting Wire of the Voltaic Cell,' published in *Gilbert's Annalen* in 1821.[13] All the appearances of electromagnetism could be reproduced if the cross-section of the wire was thought to be composed of a vast number of tiny magnets, arranged in such a way that in each magnet one pole lay in the centre of the wire and the other on the periphery. If, then, the surface of the wire consisted of opposite poles as one passed around the wire, the result would be a circular sheath of magnetic force (Figure 1). Prechtl was not content merely to argue verbally about the *possibility* of transversal magnetism as he christened it; he immediately constructed a model.

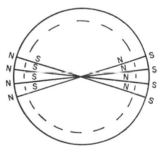

Fig. 1

Among the many curious papers on *Electro-magnetism* with which Gilbert's Annalen have been lately enriched [wrote W. T. Brande, the editor of the *Quarterly Journal of Science*] we have been particularly pleased with that of M. J. J. Prechtl, of Vienna. . . . He coils round a glass tube or wooden cylinder, steel-wire covering the surface as with a continuous sheath. To one end of this cylindric spiral, he applies the south or north pole of a magnet, and draws it along the cylinder in a straight line, parallel to the axis. In this way a magnet is formed, which possesses the following properties:

(*a*) Along its whole length, it has on one side the north, and on the opposite side the south pole.

(*b*) These transversal magnetisms are in every point of the length of the wire-cylinder, equally strong.

(*c*) Both of its ends exhibit on the contrary no particular polarity, and they have no other magnetism than that which belongs to every individual point of the whole length. Thus the transversal magnet is in the same condition as the conjunctive wire of the voltaic column.

(*d*) If we hold this transversal magnet over a magnetic needle, in the declination-plane, it repels exactly like the conjunctive wire, the north pole of the needle to the right or to the left, according as the effective north-pole of its transversal magnetism lies to the left or to the right hand; and with greater or less force, according to the strength of its magnetism, even to 90 degrees.

(*e*) If we draw the one pole of a magnet along this transversal-magnet, in a spiral direction, the wire becomes magnetized longitudinally; the transversal magnetism disappears, the two poles are found at the two extremities, and it now resembles an ordinary magnetized steel wire. The longitudinal and transversal magnetisms are not compatible with each other, in their full exhibition.[14]

Electromagnetism was simply transverse magnetism and the seeming interaction between electricity and magnetism could be reduced to a new kind of magnetic action affecting the compass needle.

The idea that electromagnetism could be explained satisfactorily by recourse to magnetic effects alone received powerful support from the pen of Jöns Jakob Berzelius. Independently of Prechtl he had been led to consider the electromagnetic effect as merely the result of the arrangement of magnetic poles.[15] Neither Prechtl nor Berzelius were very specific on the precise mechanism by which the transversal magnetic state was created. Presumably, the closing of the voltaic circuit threw the particles of the connecting wire into an arrangement whereby their inherent magnetic powers could come into play. This arrangement was similar to that described by Prechtl and the result was a circular shell of force surrounding the wire.

The opposite tack was taken by André-Marie Ampère. Where Prechtl and Berzelius reduced electromagnetism to magnetic action, Ampère eliminated magnetism and showed how all the phenomena could be accounted for by the action of the two electric fluids.

The news of Oersted's discovery astonished Ampère. According to Coulomb, interaction between electricity and magnetism was impossible. In a letter, Ampère revealed just how powerful Coulomb's influence had been in France.

You are quite right [he wrote to his friend Roux-Bordier] to say that it is inconceivable that for twenty years no one tried the action of the voltaic pile on a magnet. I believe, however, that I can assign a cause for this; it lies in Coulomb's hypothesis on the nature of magnetic action; this hypothesis was believed as though it were a fact [and] it rejected any idea of action between electricity and the so-called magnetic wires. This prohibition was such that when M. Arago spoke of these new phenomena at the Institute, they were rejected. . . . Every one decided that they were impossible.[16]

Ampère, himself, had been an ardent adherent to Coulomb's ideas for years. In 1802 the syllabus of his course in experimental physics announced that he would 'DEMONSTRATE that the electrical and magnetic phenomena are due to *two different fluids* which act independently of each other.'[17] When Oersted revealed that the impossibility of interaction was an illusion Ampère's mind was in a turmoil. 'Since I have heard of the beautiful discovery of M. Oersted . . .', he wrote to his son, 'I have thought of it constantly. . . .'[18] In his thoughts he remained faithful to the spirit, if not the letter, of Coulomb's theory. Coulomb had rejected electric and magnetic interaction because these fluids were essentially dissimilar and like acted only upon like.[19] Ampère apparently retained this view for his thoughts seem to have run something along these lines:[20] Since like acts only upon like, electricity and magnetism cannot be *essentially* unalike as Coulomb had said. As an amateur chemist, Ampère had played with electrochemistry and the reality of the electrical fluids was probably stronger in his mind than that of the magnetic fluids. Electricity, then, must be the cause of magnetism and the action of an electric current upon a magnetic needle was, therefore, *not* an interaction between two dissimilar entities but rather the action of electricity upon itself. If this were the case, then *two* currents of electricity ought to act upon one another in a way different from the interaction of electrostatic charges. It was this experiment which Ampère reported on in his first memoir on electromagnetism. Two current-carrying wires did affect one another and Ampère's insight was justified![21] The science of electrodynamics was born.

From this fundamental fact, Ampère proceeded in two essentially different directions. In a series of classic memoirs, he investigated mathematically the mutual relations of electric currents. This line of research culminated in the great 'Memoir on the Mathematical Theory of electrodynamic phenomena deduced solely from experiment'[22] in which the laws of electrical action were expressed with elegance, economy and severe mathematical beauty. It was this work which deservedly won for him the title of the 'Newton of electricity'. This part of Ampère's achievement was totally beyond Faraday's grasp. As he wrote to Ampère in 1825, 'With regard to your theory, it so soon becomes mathematical that it quickly gets beyond my reach. . . .'[23]

The other line of investigation pursued by Ampère was a purely physical one. At the end of his first memoir on electrodynamics, Ampère listed his preliminary findings.

1. Two electric currents attract one another when they move parallel to one another in the same direction; they repel one another when they move parallel but in opposite directions.

2. It follows that when the metallic wires through which they pass can turn only in parallel planes, each of the two currents tends to swing the other into a position parallel to it and pointing in the same direction.

3. These attractions and repulsions are absolutely different from the attractions and repulsions of ordinary [static] electricity.

4. All the phenomena presented by the mutual action of an electric current and a magnet discovered by M. Oersted . . . are covered by the law of attraction and of repulsion of two electric currents that has just been enunciated, if one admits that a magnet is only a collection of electric currents produced by the action of the particles of steel upon one another analogous to that of the elements of a voltaic pile, and which exist in planes perpendicular to the line which joins the two poles of the magnet.

5. When a magnet is in the position that it tends to take by the action of the terrestrial globe, these currents move in a sense opposite to the apparent motion of the sun; when one places the magnet in the opposite position so that the poles directed toward the poles of the earth are the same [S to S and N to N, not south-seeking to S, etc.] the same currents are found in the same direction as the apparent motion of the sun.

6. The known observed effects of the action of two magnets on one another obey the same law.

7. The same is true of the force that the terrestrial globe exerts on a magnet, if one admits electric currents in planes perpendicular to the direction of the declination needle, moving from east to west, above this direction.

8. There is nothing more in one pole of a magnet than in the other; the sole difference between them is that one is to the left and the other to the right of the electric currents which give the magnetic properties to the steel.

9. Although Volta had proven that the two electricities, positive and negative, of the two ends of the pile attract and repel one another according to the same laws as the two electricities produced by means known before him, he has not by that demonstrated completely the identity of the fluids made manifest by the pile and by friction; this identity was proven, as much as a physical truth can be proven, when he showed that two bodies, one electrified by the contact of [two] metals, and the other by friction, acted upon each other in all circumstances as though both had been electrified by the pile or by the common electric machine. The same kind of proof is applicable here to the identity of attractions and repulsions of electric currents and magnets.[24]

In these nine paragraphs Ampère summed up his electrodynamic theory. Magnetic forces were the result of the motion of the two electric fluids; permanent magnets contained these currents running in circles concentric to the axis of the magnet and in a plane perpendicular to this axis. Similarly, by implication, the earth contained currents which gave it its magnetic properties.

The weaknesses of this theory are immediately obvious. Where did the electric current come from in permanent magnets and why was it not detectable by ordinary means? What does the sentence which suggests that the current is produced by the particles of steel in a way 'analogous to that of the elements of a voltaic pile' mean when subjected to critical scrutiny? Volta, after all, had spoken of dissimilar metals as the source of the current. Why should the mere contiguity of two steel molecules create an electromotive force? If one were not an adherent of the contact theory of the pile (as Faraday was not) then the question of the origin of the electric current became even more obtrusive. This was a problem which Ampère would have to solve before he could expect acceptance of his theory by those who concentrated more upon his physics than his mathematics.

Almost immediately after Ampère's announcement of the identity of electricity and magnetism his friend, Augustin Fresnel, whose work on the undulatory theory of light heavily influenced Ampère's theoretical concepts, tried to detect the intermolecular currents of a permanent magnet.

> Since [he wrote] one finds a steel cylinder made magnetic by an electric current passing through a metallic helix enveloping it, it is natural to see if a bar magnet will not produce a voltaic current in the enveloping helix; not that this appears, at first sight, a necessary consequence of the facts for, if the magnetic state of the steel is only, for example, a new arrangement of its molecules or a particular distribution of a fluid, one can see that this new state need not reproduce the motion which established it.[25]

Fresnel, accordingly wrapped a permanent magnet with insulated iron wire and plunged the ends of the wire into acidulated water. On 6 November 1820, he announced to the Academy of Sciences in Paris that the experiment was a success.[26] The water was decomposed and the bar magnet produced a current similar in every way to that of a voltaic pile. The symmetry of the situation was perfect; an electric current produced magnetism in a steel bar and a magnetized steel bar produced an electric current. But, as Fresnel admitted, 'I have since observed a number of anomalies whose cause I could not discover and which now make very doubtful that which seemed to me at first so certain.'[27] As so often happens in such a case, doubt of the certainty of the results obtained by testing a hypothesis extended to the hypothesis itself. Although Fresnel had never committed himself completely to Ampère's idea of currents concentric to the axis of a permanent magnet, he had certainly regarded it with favour. Now, however, he subjected it to intense scrutiny. Instead of relying upon arguments drawn from the hoped-for symmetry of effects, Fresnel directed his attention solely to these currents. What, he asked, should be the observed effects of these currents other than magnetism? Or, to put it another way, was it enough for Ampère to show that electric currents produced magnetic effects? Was it not also necessary to accept the other known effects of electric currents and rest the acceptance of the reality of the intermolecular currents upon *all* these effects?

In a private note to Ampère, not published until 1885, Fresnel communicated his thoughts to his friend and convinced him of the impossibility of his co-axial currents. The document is fascinating for Fresnel came within a hair's breadth of discovering electromagnetic induction. Assuming that electric currents did circulate around the axis of a magnet, Fresnel argued:

> 1. that the current of a conjunctive wire should produce another current in a steel wire parallel to the first, and whose ends are connected by a conductor; [!]
> 2. that by means of a sort of polarization produced in the particles of the steel wire by the action of the conjunctive wire the current should continue in the first [wire] after the conjunctive wire has ceased to act upon it in the same way that currents continue in a cylinder after it is removed from the helix; [i.e., the magnetization of a steel cylinder in a current-carrying helix]
> 3. that if one removes the connexion between the two extremities of the steel wire, the polarization of its particles, being no longer able to produce a current ought to manifest itself by the tension of opposite charges at its two extremities, and I conceived the idea of a voltaic apparatus composed of a bundle of similar wires.[28]

When these experiments were tried 'they gave no result'. Fresnel, of course, could not predict that the current produced by (1) in the steel wire would be momentary and not continuous. Faraday was to try the same experiment in 1825 and also report a negative result.

From these experiments Fresnel was led to suggest that the electric currents circulated around each *molecule*, rather than around the axis of the magnet. If this were the case, then the experiments enumerated above should yield negative results. In a second note to Ampère, Fresnel raised an even more serious objection to co-axial currents: such currents, being completely analogous to ordinary currents in a wire, should have the same heating effects. A permanent magnet, then, would always be a few degrees warmer than its environment. The failure of this prediction to be confirmed by the facts provided the *coup de grâce* to Ampère's first hypothesis.

It did not, however, provide any real support to Fresnel's concept of intra-molecular currents. This did not seem to bother him.

> I will add [he wrote to his friend] that the fact that a magnet is not hot, although it ought to be according to the hypothesis of currents around its axis, is not a difficulty in the hypothesis of currents around the molecules. Although a current, in traversing a mass of molecules of a conducting body, heats it there is no necessity to believe that currents around the molecules of a similar mass should also heat it: the circumstances are no longer the same. We know little about the heat developed by an electric current and our ideas on the constitution of bodies are too incomplete for us to know whether electricity ought to produce heat in this case.[29]

These arguments were enough for Ampère. In a memoir read before the Academy of Sciences on 15 January 1821, he tentatively introduced the concept of molecular currents.[30] From this time forward, these currents were an integral part of his physical theory of electrodynamics.

The use of the concept of molecular currents created a new problem for Ampère. Hitherto he had been able to explain electromagnetic effects without bringing in any fundamentally new processes. The co-axial currents were just like ordinary electric currents; their production could be explained by slightly modifying Volta's explanation of the production of electricity by the pile. Molecular currents could not be so easily fitted within the realm of the known. They called for a whole new theory of matter in which they would be an integral part of all molecular processes, not just magnetism. This is a fact that must be insisted upon for it is often neglected. The mathematical physicist might accept Ampère's theory because of its elegance and the accuracy with which it described observed facts. The chemist had to be more careful; he was being asked to accept a comprehensive theory which pretended to explain all the actions of molecules. Faraday's coolness towards Ampère's idea was not due, therefore, to narrowmindedness or lack of appreciation of Ampère's positive achievements. Rather it was a legitimate caution stimulated by the feeling that intra- and intermolecular actions were more complicated than Ampère seemed to realize.

Ampère, himself, had no such reservations. Although it was his own idea of co-axial currents that had to be rejected, he seemed to take the step calmly, even eagerly. The necessity of having to create a comprehensive theory of matter did not appear to disturb him unduly. Indeed, his thoughts had long been occupied with the structure of matter and Fresnel's remarks now forced him to concentrate the full power of his mind upon the problem. The result was a theory of considerable ingenuity but based upon a system of interlocking hypotheses which were certainly open to criticism.

As early as 1814, Ampère had turned his attention to the nature of the constituent molecules of bodies and their mutual relations.[31] At that time he had described the basic properties of atoms and molecules without reference to electricity or the luminiferous ether. Having read Kant (but apparently not Boscovich)[32] Ampère rejected the conventional concept of atoms as little impenetrable spheres of matter. Ampère's atoms were mere mathematical points associated with attractive and repulsive forces. These points, being dimensionless, could not be the particles of palpable matter; four, at least, must be associated together in order to occupy volume and thereby exhibit the property of extension.[33] The forms of the resultant molecules determined both the chemical and physical properties of the substance composed of these molecules. Ampère ingeniously explained chemical dynamics by referring to the geometrical relationships of molecules.

> If one tries, for example [he wrote], to combine tetrahedra and octahedra in such a way that the number of the first is half that of the second, one only finds bizarre forms which exhibit no regularity or proportion between the relative sizes of their different faces. One is forced to conclude that a body, A, whose particles have the representative form of the tetrahedron, and a body, B, whose particles form octahedra, will not combine in such a way that there are two proportions of B to one of A; this combination is a simple one to accomplish, however, with two proportions of A and one of B, since two tetrahedra and one octahedron together form a dodecahedron.[34]

In his earliest publication on electrodynamics none of this theory of matter figures. There Ampère spoke only of currents of electricity acting at a distance upon one another. All the phenomena of electrodynamics were treated independently of the particles of matter around or through which the electric current flowed. Fresnel's criticism changed all this. By making the currents circulate around the molecules of matter, Ampère was forced to devise a mechanism for their production which included the material particles.

The agent which brought matter and electricity together into a single scheme was the luminiferous ether. Ampère had carefully followed the work of Fresnel on the undulatory theory of light and had become one of its earliest supporters. The ether appeared to be a necessary consequence of Fresnel's theory for if light waves were assumed to exist they had to exist in something and this something was the ether. The wave theory of light only required that the ether have certain physical properties: it must be ubiquitous, perfectly elastic, and offer no resistance to ponderable bodies passing through it.[35] To these properties, Ampère added an essentially chemical one. The ether was not a simple substance but a compound one which 'can only be considered, in the generally adopted theory of two electric fluids, as the combination of these two fluids in that proportion in which they mutually saturate one another'.[36] The ability to transmit vibrations and to decompose and recombine were sufficient for Ampère to account for electrodynamic effects.

The vibrations of the ether permitted Ampère to explain the attractive or repulsive forces between two current-carrying wires. When a voltaic pile was put into action, the contact of the dissimilar metals of which the pile was composed disturbed the equilibrium of the ether and caused its decomposition into positive and negative electricity. The two electricities then were pushed in opposite directions by the electromotive force of the pile. This led to a recomposition of the ether as the portion of negative electricity moving in one direction met the positive electricity coming the other way. Since all the original conditions remained, a second decomposition occurred, followed by a second recomposition. In this way, there was both a movement of the electrical fluids from one point to another, and a series of 'chemical' vibrations set up in the wire.[37] These vibrations, transmitted to the encompassing ether, produced the attractions or repulsions observed between two currents.

> . . . it is difficult not to conclude that attraction and repulsion can be produced by the rapid motion of the two electric fluids passing in opposite directions in the conductor by a series of almost instantaneous decompositions and recompositions. . . . In attributing the attractions and repulsions of the conducting wires to this cause, it is impossible not to admit that the motion of the two electricities in these wires is propagated in the neutral fluid which is formed by their union, and which fills all space. . . . When the movements produced in the surrounding fluid by two small portions of electric currents are mutually in phase [se favorisent mutuellement], there is a resulting tendency for them to approach one another; and when the same motions are opposed to one another, the two small portions of the currents tend to move away from one another, as experiments show.[38]

The ether was not only decomposed by the contact of dissimilar metals; the very presence of the particles of matter had a disturbing effect upon it, tending to its decomposition.

> One can consider each particle [Ampère wrote] as a little voltaic pile in which the currents, entering by one extremity of the molecule and leaving by the opposite end, come together across the space around the first of these two extremities, thus forming a closed solenoid which, according to what we have

said before, cannot exert any action since all these currents are of the same intensity and equidistant before the molecule is magnetized.[39]

Magnetization took place when all the electrodynamic molecules were aligned by the action of other electric currents. 'The electric currents . . . around each particle of magnets exist around these particles before magnetization in iron, nickel, and cobalt but, being turned in all directions, no external action can result since some tend to attract what others repel, as happens with light in which various rays, being polarized in all directions, present no sign of polarization.'[40] Theoretically, there should be no essential difference between bodies that could be magnetized and those that could not. All molecules were accompanied by currents of positive and negative electricity circulating around and through them. The only difference between bodies that could be turned into magnets and those that could not 'consists in the property possessed by the particles of the former to allow the displacement of the electric currents which circulate around them while in other bodies the currents created around each particle cannot change direction, or can only do so by the action of a force superior up to now to any which have been applied'.[41] It should be noted that, in Ampère's view, magnetization consisted in the alignment of the molecular *currents*, and not of the molecules, themselves.

The physical theory of electrodynamics was now complete. Given the concepts of the ether and the electromotive force of matter as Ampère had formulated them, all the observed effects could be explained; not only explained, but subjected to mathematical analysis. The combination was a potent one and the accuracy of Ampère's calculations and the depths of his insight led many to embrace his theory. Ampère, however, was not satisfied with merely creating a model of electrodynamic action. By 1821 he was intoxicated by his vision and convinced that his electrodynamic molecules really existed. They must, then, also explain other areas of physics and chemistry.

In his 'Answer to the Letter of M. van Beek' published in October 1821, Ampère turned his attention once again to the problem of chemical combination. Gone were the geometrical symmetries which had been used in the 'Letter to Berthollet . . .' of 1814. It was now totally irrelevant whether molecules were tetrahedra, cubes, or octahedra. What determined whether a reaction would take place and if so, with what violence, was the electrical condition of the participating molecules. To explain the mechanism of chemical combination, Ampère had recourse to another analogy; molecules were not only like voltaic piles, but also like Leyden jars. The facts of electrochemistry proved 'that the particles of . . . substances are essentially in two opposed electrical states'.[42] In order to preserve its electrical neutrality, each molecule, therefore, decomposed the ambient ether to attract the electricity of the opposite sign. Ampère did not say if this was why each molecule was surrounded by electric currents but his use of the Leyden jar analogy would appear to rule out this possibility. The molecule, presumably, had both an inherent electrical charge and electric currents associated with it. It was the inherent *static* charge that caused chemical combination; the resultant combination of the two electricities gave rise to heat and light and both the material and energy relations of reactions could be understood in terms of the same mechanism.[43] In 1832 Ampère further generalized this scheme and considered some of the finer details of chemical thermodynamics.[44] There can be no doubt that he took his own theory seriously as a general theory of matter. Nor was he alone in this. During the 1820's Becquerel in Paris and Auguste de la Rive in Geneva used the electrodynamic model in their researches in electrochemistry. Faraday's scepticism must be seen in this light. Acceptance of Ampère's explanation of magnetism meant acceptance of a comprehensive theory of matter and this Faraday was too cautious to do. There were, after all, a number of hypothetical elements which Faraday found difficult to swallow. Was there really an ether? Did it consist of a combination of positive and negative electricity? Fluids did not appeal to Faraday and the whole new area of imponderable fluid chemistry must have seemed particularly clumsy. The electrodynamic molecule, too, could not command his belief. Molecular currents were purely hypothetical and since they were deduced from the contact theory of the pile which Faraday suspected, their real existence was, to say the least, doubtful. And yet, and yet – the striking success of Ampère's theory could not help but impress Faraday to whom experimental evidence was so important. His reaction was characteristic. He would check each step by his own experiments; he would take Ampère seriously enough to try to subject his ideas, again and again, to experimental test. Out of these tests and the criticisms of Ampère's theory was to emerge his own theory of electromagnetic action.

2. The Discovery of Electromagnetic Rotations

News of Oersted's discovery was slow in arriving in England. It was not until 1 October 1820, some six weeks after Arago had announced it to the Academy of Sciences in Paris, that Sir Humphry Davy dashed into the laboratory of the Royal Institution to tell Faraday of electromagnetic interaction. The two immediately set to work and repeated the experiments reported by Oersted.[45] Davy in his eagerness and enthusiasm, however, misinterpreted his results and confused the situation. Oersted had clearly stated the circular nature of the force surrounding the current-carrying wire and had been puzzled by this fact. Davy, on the other hand, noted 'that the south pole of a common magnetic needle (suspended in the usual way) placed under the communicating wire of platinum (the positive end of the apparatus being on the right hand) was strongly attracted by the wire, and remained in contact with it. . . .' The fact that iron filings also clung to the wire while a current was passing through it convinced Davy that 'the wire itself became magnetic during the passage of the electricity. . . .'[46] Faraday also was misled. As late as August 1821 he thought the forces acting between the magnetic needle and the wire were simple attractions and repulsions.[47]

Others in England saw more clearly. William Hyde Wollaston, whose keen eye was matched by his extraordinary experimental skill, realized almost immediately that the simplicity of central forces could not be preserved. Wollaston, like Ampère, assumed circular currents to explain electromagnetic action. Unlike Ampère, these currents were not in the magnets, but in the wires.[48] When the circuit was closed, the electricity followed a spiral path within the wire from one terminal of the circuit to the other (in much the same fashion as Oersted's electric conflict). If, in two wires, the currents were moving in the same direction, Wollaston showed how this would lead to attraction and, in the same way, he illustrated the repulsive action of currents moving in opposite directions (see Figure 2). From the concept of 'vertiginous electricity', Wollaston was led to an idea that ultimately was to affect Faraday's life seriously. Wollaston reasoned that the existence of a helical current ought to make a current-carrying wire revolve around its own axis when a permanent magnet was brought close to it. In April 1821, he and Davy tried the experiment in the laboratory of the Royal

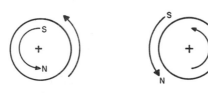

SIMILAR CURRENTS = ATTRACTION

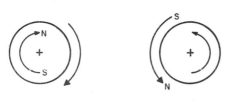

DISSIMILAR CURRENTS = REPULSION

Fig. 2

Institution. No matter how the apparatus was arranged the expected rotation did not occur. Faraday was not present during the actual experiments, but when he did arrive Davy and Wollaston were discussing the problem. There is no evidence that this incident made any great impression on him. Indeed, there is considerable evidence to indicate that his mind was occupied with other matters than electromagnetism. Although he had assisted Davy in all his experiments and later admitted that he 'thus had my mind prepared for the subject'[49] his laboratory diary is almost bare of allusions to electromagnetism.[50] During this period (November 1820 to June 1821) he was engaged with Stodart in the time-consuming and laborious experiments on the alloys of steel; he was also pursuing his 'hobby' of chlorine and attempting to discover its compounds with carbon. This was also the period of his courtship of Sarah Barnard, and it seems fair to conclude that while he found Oersted's discovery an exciting one, he had not the time to pursue its consequences for himself.

The occasion for his serious interest in electromagnetism was a letter from his good friend R. Phillips requesting that Faraday write an historical account of this new branch of science for the *Annals of Philosophy*. To do this, Faraday had to repeat the major experiments performed by Oersted, Arago, Ampère, and others and also examine their theoretical views closely. When he began in the summer of 1821, he was still under the impression that electromagnetic forces were rectilinear and analogous to other known forces. Only as he carefully followed the experimental trail blazed by others did he realize his error. The outcome of his work was two papers: the 'Historical Sketch of Electromagnetism' which appeared in volumes 2 and 3 (new series) of the *Annals of Philosophy* and an article 'On some new Electro-Magnetical Motions, and on the Theory of Magnetism' which was published in volume 12 of the *Quarterly Journal of Science*. In these papers Faraday came to grips, for the first time, with the theory of electric and magnetic action; the result of his own experimental investigations and theoretical reasonings was a startling new phenomenon – electromagnetic rotation – which threatened to destroy all previous theoretical structures.

Faraday began the 'Historical Sketch' with a statement of his motive for undertaking it. 'Having been engaged latterly in looking over the various papers that have been written on the subject of electro-magnetism', he wrote, 'I found much difficulty in gaining a clear idea of what had been done, and by whom, in consequence of their great variety, the number of theories advanced in them, their confused dates, and other circumstances.'[51] Faraday's confusion was not entirely dissipated by his researches for he still found it difficult to grasp many of the theoretical suppositions put forward by others.

The early sections of the paper were devoted almost entirely to a clear and simple account of the experiments upon which the science of electromagnetism rested. Even when considering the experimental part, however, Faraday could not resist cautioning his readers about the danger of hidden hypotheses concerning the nature of electricity and magnetism. In particular, he warned against the facile assumption of a material current flowing through the wire. 'There are many arguments in favour of the materiality of electricity,' he pointed out, 'and but few against it; but still it is only a supposition; and it will be as well to remember, while pursuing the subject of electro-magnetism, that we have no proof of the materiality of electricity, or of the existence of any current through the wire.'[52] The alternative to a current Faraday suggested only in passing. 'Whatever be the cause which is active within the connecting wire, whether it be the passage of matter through it, or the *induction of a particular state of its parts*, it produces certain very extraordinary effects.'[53] Although he was still suspending judgement, it is of considerable interest to note this first appearance, in embryo form, of an intermolecular 'state' which was to play a central role in the development of his mature concepts.

In the part of the 'Historical Sketch' which dealt with electromagnetic theories, Faraday returned again to the concept of the electric current. Oersted's 'electric conflict' he dismissed by admitting that 'I do not quite understand it.'[54] What he did comprehend led him to attribute things to Oersted with which Oersted would certainly not have agreed.

> The theory of M. Oersted, [as Faraday interpreted it] therefore, seems to require that there be two electric fluids; that they be not either combined or separate, but in the act of combining so as to produce an electric conflict; that they move nevertheless separate from each other, and in opposite spiral directions, through and round the wire; and that they have entirely distinct and different magnetical powers; the one electricity (negative) propelling the north pole of a magnet, but having no action at all on the south pole; the other electricity (positive) propelling the south pole, but having no power over the north pole.[55]

In spite of protestations that he did not fully understand the theory, his exposition of it revealed his attitude towards it. Anything so complicated and requiring so many forces and gyrating fluids could not be true.

It was Ampère's theory which really interested Faraday. Precisely because of the extent of Ampère's theoretical views, their seeming congruence with experiment, and their elegance and simplicity, Faraday felt it necessary to subject it to the most severe criticism of which he was capable. Ampère's views, as Faraday freely admitted, were 'alone among all those that have been given to the public, which deserve, if any do, the title of *A Theory*'.[56] Unerringly, Faraday went directly to what he considered the heart of the matter.

M. Ampère [he stated] commences by assuming the existence of two electric fluids, according to the theory which is now general, I believe, in France. There appears to be no doubt about his meaning on this point, for though he uses the term electricity very frequently, and in a way which might be under-stood, perhaps, as applying equally either to a particular state of a body, or to a particular fluid existing among its particles, yet by the use of the term *electric fluids* in one place, and by the mention of electric currents as currents of matter, it is nearly certain that M. Ampère means to speak of electricity as consisting of two distinct fluids, which, though the one is called positive, and the other negative electricity, are to be considered as equally positive in their existence, and possessed of equal powers.[57]

This assumption was not only gratuitous but the source of much con-fusion since Ampère never (in Faraday's opinion) really revealed what a current was. Faraday's failure to understand Ampère is instructive for it indicates the power of his own concepts over his mind. The passage of a 'current', Faraday insisted, creates a 'state' in the wire.

Now as it is in this state [he wrote] that the wire is capable of affecting the magnetic needle, it is very important for the exact comprehension of the theory that a clear and precise idea of its state, or of what is assumed to be its state, should be gained, for on it in fact the whole of the theory is founded. Portions of matter in the same state as this wire, may be said to constitute the materials from which M. Ampère forms, theoretically, not only bar magnets, but even the great magnet of the earth; and we may, therefore, be allowed to expect that a very clear description will first be offered of it. This, however, is not the case, and is, I think very much to be regretted, since it renders the rest of the theory considerably obscure, for though certainly the highly interesting facts discovered by M. Ampère could have been described, and the general laws and arrangements both in conductors and magnets stated with equal force and effect without any reference to the internal state of the wire, but only to the powers which experiment proves it to be endowed with, yet as M. Ampère has chosen always to refer to the currents in the wire, and in fact founds his theory upon their existence, it becomes necessary that *a current* should be described.[58]

Was Ampère's current like Oersted's 'electrical conflict'? or was it a continual circulation in one direction? Faraday could not make out which. His difficulty was compounded by the suggestion of molecular currents which, considering the obscurity he found in the definition of an ordinary current, were even more difficult for him to visualize. That Ampère's theory was ingenious he had no doubt. With scrupulous fairness he cited effects deduced by Ampère from his theory and confirmed by experiment. Had these experiments failed, he remarked, their failure 'would have been fairly urged against the theory'.[59] Their success must, therefore, count in its favour. He remained unconvinced. 'I must again say', he wrote at the conclusion of the paper, 'that having assumed the existence of two distinct electric fluids, and the identity of electricity with magnetism, I think the first part of the theory by no means sufficiently developed.'[60]

Just as he was putting the finishing touches to his discussion of the history of electromagnetism, his attention was diverted from hypothetical currents to real effects. On September 3rd, 1821, he recorded certain odd facts in his laboratory diary. The 'attractions' and 'repulsions' between the magnetic needle and the current-carrying wire were not as simple as he had assumed. The progress of his discovery is charted admirably by the series of sketches he made of the electric and magnetic interaction. The first merely showed the positions of attraction and repulsion; the second and third gave a deeper insight for the attractions and repulsions were here discovered not to be simple push-pulls between points in the wire and in the needle. In the fourth and fifth, the true nature of the forces was revealed; the points of attraction and repulsion indicated that the force would tend to create motion in circles around each pole of the magnetic needle[61] (see Figure 3).

Faraday immediately saw what this meant. Whereas Wollaston had suspected that his helical currents should make a wire rotate around its own axis, Faraday realized the effect was different. 'Magnets of different power', he wrote, 'brought perpendicularly to this wire did not make it revolve as Dr Wollaston expected, but thrust it from side to side.' Hence, he concluded, 'The effort of the wire is always to pass off at a right angle from the pole, indeed to go in a circle round it.'[62]

To translate this 'effort' into an actual rotation, Faraday devised a most ingenious and simple apparatus. A magnet was stuck upright in a piece of wax at the bottom of a deep basin, and then the basin was filled with mercury until only the pole of the magnet was above its surface. A wire, free to revolve around the magnetic pole, was connected to a galvanic circuit. When the current was turned on, the wire rotated around the magnet. In a similar fashion, Faraday arranged things so that the magnet would rotate around the wire.[63] The first electric motor had been invented; the rotatory power of the magnetic force surrounding a current-carrying wire was made obtrusively manifest; the conversion of electricity into mechanical work had been achieved, lending still further weight to the belief in the convertibility of all natural forces.

The announcement of his discovery was made in the October 1821 issue of the *Quarterly Journal of Science* and it was this paper 'On some new Electro-Magnetical Motions, and on the Theory of Magnetism' which thrust Faraday into the first rank of European scientists. It was translated almost immediately into French by Anatole Riffault, accompanied by notes by Ampère and Savary in which these two savants tried to answer Faraday's objections to Ampère's theory.[64] In every laboratory throughout Europe copies of Faraday's rotation apparatus were made and the strange nature of the motive force contemplated.

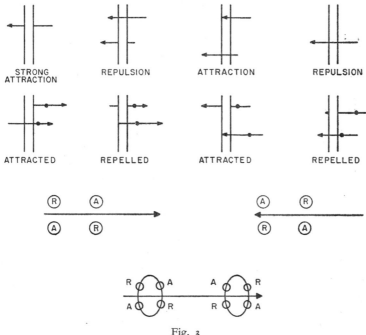

Fig. 3

Faraday knew full well the importance of his discovery. Electromagnetic rotation threw down a serious challenge to every theory of electromagnetism which had been proposed and Faraday felt that the nature of the electric and magnetic interaction had not been truly understood previously. It was this sense of the fundamental importance of his discovery which led him to rush his results into print and thereby create the most unpleasant incident in his whole life.

It was well known in English scientific circles that Wollaston had expected a wire to rotate on its own axis when subjected to magnetic influence. Faraday referred to it in the account in his *Diary* cited above, and casually dismissed it for what he had discovered was something quite different. His results, he knew, would interest Wollaston and, as he later wrote,

> upon obtaining the results . . . which I showed very readily to all my friends, I went to Dr Wollaston's house to communicate them also to him, and to ask permission to refer to his views and experiments. Dr Wollaston was not in town, nor did he return whilst I remained in town; and, as I did not think I had any right to refer to views not published, and as far as I knew not pursued, my paper was printed and appeared without that reference whilst I remained in the country.[65]

For the first and only time Faraday's motto, 'Work, Finish, Publish', betrayed him and his realization of his blunder was poignantly declared when he stated, 'I have regretted ever since I did not delay the publication, that I might have shown it first to Dr Wollaston.'[66]

Almost immediately upon the appearance of Faraday's paper, there were subterranean rumblings throughout the intellectual world of London. Wollaston was a highly respected member of this community and that most sensitive of all English qualities, his honour, appeared to be threatened. The distinction between the rotation of a current-carrying wire about its own axis and about a magnetic pole appeared to be too fine to be discerned by the casual observer.[67] Wollaston had talked of rotations and the newly-announced discovery seemed to be nothing else than what Wollaston had been looking for. The Chemical Assistant at the Royal Institution appeared to have stolen an idea without acknowledgement and this in 1821, as now, was a cardinal sin.

On 8 October, less than one week after the publication of his first really important paper, Faraday wrote to James Stodart, his collaborator in the work on the alloys of steel. His anguish leaps from the page.

> I hear every day [he wrote] more and more of those sounds, which, though only whispers to me, are I suspect spoken aloud amongst scientific men, and which, as they in part affect my honour and honesty, I am anxious to do away with, or at least to prove erroneous in those parts which are dishonourable to me. You know perfectly well what distress the very unexpected reception of my paper on magnetism in public has caused me, and you will not therefore be surprised at my anxiety to get out of it, though I give trouble to you and other of my friends in doing so.[68]

To Stodart he categorically denied that he had received any clues from Wollaston's supposition, that he had in any way sought to conceal Wollaston's views or influence upon him, that he had knowingly invaded an area upon which Wollaston was working. 'My love for scientific reputation', he pointed out, 'is not yet so high as to induce me to obtain it at the expense of honour, and my anxiety to clear away this stigma is such that I do not hesitate to trouble you even beyond what you may be willing to do for me.'[69] Faraday then appealed to Stodart to arrange an interview with Dr Wollaston so that he could plead his case. Knowing in his own heart that he was innocent of the charges being made against him, his only fear was that Dr Wollaston who 'is so very far above me that even if he does feel himself wronged, . . . may not permit himself to think it is of any importance, and may therefore think it unnecessary to allow anything to pass on the subject'.[70] Faraday intended to make his appeal, if such were the case, to Wollaston's very prominence in the world of science. It is impossible today to suppress a slight smile upon reading the following lines for only a few specialists know of Wollaston's work while Faraday's changed the world. 'I am but a young man, and without a name,' he continued to Stodart, 'and it probably does not matter much to science what becomes of me; but if by any circumstances I am subjected to unjust suspicions, it becomes no one more than him who may be said to preside over the equity of science, to assist in liberating me from them.'[71]

Stodart was unable or unwilling to arrange an interview with Wollaston. At the end of October, Faraday wrote to Wollaston begging for an opportunity to explain his actions with regard to his discovery of electromagnetic rotation. Wollaston's reply was chillingly cold: 'Sir,' he wrote, 'you seem to me to labour under some misapprehension of the strength of my feelings upon the subject to which you allude.

'As to the opinions which others may have of your conduct, that is your concern, not mine; and if you fully acquit yourself of making any incorrect use of the suggestions of others, it seems to me that you have no occasion to concern yourself much about the matter.'[72]

Although Wollaston offered to meet with Faraday if he were still desirous of an interview, nothing came of it at this time. It was not until December that Faraday's discovery of the rotatory action of the earth's magnetic field led Wollaston to the laboratory of the Royal Institution where Faraday again asked him for help. Of this visit, Faraday wrote:

My object was then to ask him permission to refer to his views and experiments in the paper which I should immediately publish, in correction of the error of judgment of not having done so before. The impression that has remained on my mind ever since (one and twenty months) and which I have constantly expressed to every one when talking on the subject, is, that he wished me not to do so. Dr Wollaston has lately told me that he cannot recollect the words he used at that time; that, as regarded himself, his feelings were it should not be done, as regarded me, that it should; but that he did not tell me so. I can only say that my memory at this time holds most tenaciously the following words: 'I would rather you should not;' but I must, of course, have been mistaken.[73]

The net result of all this was to permit the affair to die of its own accord. Unfortunately, this it refused to do. Davy, for one, seems to have been offended by the action of his assistant and to have done little to squelch the persistent rumours of plagiarism. In fact, he appears to have lent his support to the charge. In March 1823, he read a paper on the new phenomenon of electromagnetism to the Royal Society in which he was reported as implying that Faraday had, indeed, stolen Wollaston's ideas.[74] Although he denied that he had spoken as the reporter said he had (and, fifteen years later still insisted he had) the damage had been done and the issue reopened. It could not have happened at a more inopportune time for Faraday. He had just been proposed as a candidate for the Fellowship of the Royal Society and the knowledge that Davy, his protector for so long and President of the Royal Society, still harboured doubts about the integrity of his protégé could not help but affect his cause. There is little doubt that Davy was beginning to feel jealous of Faraday. The discovery of electromagnetic rotations in 1821 had raised Faraday's reputation to the point of international renown. Davy's research activities were sporadic at best and he saw his pre-eminence in English science gradually fading before the achievements of his former laboratory helper. Davy was not a vicious man, but he was vain and the rise of Faraday's reputation could not be accepted by him with good grace. He no doubt felt that Faraday had unconsciously stolen Wollaston's ideas; Wollaston was his good friend and must, therefore, be given credit that was due him. And, behind it all was probably the feeling that it was impossible for Faraday, still a neophyte, to conceive a kind of electromagnetic action that had escaped both his and Wollaston's minds. Whatever the motives, it remains true that Davy actively opposed Faraday's election to the Royal Society. Some years after the affair ended, Faraday described an interview with Davy on his candidacy for election to the Royal Society:

Sir H. Davy told me I must take down my certificate. I replied that I had not put it up; that I could not take it down, as it was put up by my proposers. He then said I must get my proposers to take it down. I answered that I knew they would not do so. Then he said, I as President will take it down. I replied that I was sure Sir H. Davy would do what he thought was for the good of the Royal Society.[75]

In January 1824, Michael Faraday was elected a Fellow of the Royal Society. There was one blackball.

The contretemps with Wollaston had one permanent effect. By focusing attention upon the *fact* of rotation, it helped to feed the nascent myth of Faraday as a clever manipulator and served to obscure the important theoretical consequences of this effect. In the historical survey of electro-magnetism, Faraday had already expressed (anonymously) his doubts on the adequacy of Ampère's electrodynamic molecular model. The dis-covery of electromagnetic rotations now convinced him that his doubts had been justified. In the face of the almost universal acceptance of Ampère's ideas, this was a hardy step to take but Faraday felt himself justified by the facts. He, himself, was still unclear in his own mind as to *how* electromagnetic effects were produced, but he felt new confidence in criticizing Ampère's ideas. For the next ten years, there was to be a true and fertile dialogue between these two men. As Faraday tested the con-sequences of his own ideas and those of Ampère – still holding an open but sceptical mind – his concepts became clearer and clearer until he was led by them to the discovery of electromagnetic induction.

Faraday's fundamental point of disagreement with Ampère was over the nature of the interaction between electricity and magnetism. Ampère had insisted that the fundamental interaction was a straightforward attraction or repulsion between moving currents of electricity; Faraday maintained that this was not a simple action at all, but the result of the combination of other forces. To Faraday, the primitive force was the circular force which pushed a magnet around the current-carrying wire, or vice versa. The apparent polarity exhibited by Ampère's two wires was merely the result of this force having different directions on different sides of the wire. Or, as Faraday put it, 'it is, indeed, an ascertained fact, that the connecting wire has different powers at its opposite sides; or rather, each power continues all round the wire, the direction being the same, and hence it is evident that the attractions and repulsions of M. Ampère's wires are not simple, but complicated results'.[76] The conse-quences of this point of view were quite extraordinary although they only came dimly to Faraday's mind at this point.

Perhaps because of his lack of academic scientific training, the idea of a circular force did not particularly perturb Faraday. Whereas Ampère felt forced to reduce all action to that of central forces in order to preserve the Newtonian view of physical action, Faraday could and did simply rely upon his experimental results which clearly revealed that the force emanat-ing from a magnetic pole or a current-carrying wire was circular. Out of this came what Faraday was later to call the magnetic or electric line of force. He first illustrated how attraction and repulsion could result from a circular force of uniform strength surrounding a straight wire. Figure 4 shows such a wire; one need only note that the force on the right side is directed in the opposite way from the force on the left side. If the wire is now bent into a circle, as shown by the dotted lines, the net effect will be to intensify the forces within the loop as the various 'circular' forces

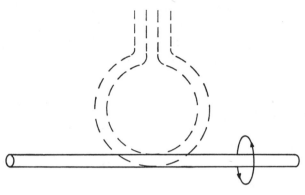

Fig. 4

converge there. The wire loop will now appear to have poles, and will act like a magnet.[77] To illustrate further how the forces on opposite sides of the wire could be separated, Faraday wound an insulated wire into a spiral as shown in Figure 5. Upon this he then sprinkled iron filings which assumed the form of a cone with its apex over the centre of the spiral where the force was at a maximum.[78] When the wires were coiled into a helix, the results were of even greater interest.

Fig. 5

If in place of putting ring within ring, they be placed side by side, so as to form a cylinder, or if a helix be made, then the same kind of neutralization takes place in the intermediate wires, and accumulated effect in the extreme ones, as before. The line which the pole would now travel, supposing the inner end of the radius to move over the inner and outer surface of the cylinder, would be through the axis of the cylinder round the edge to one side, back up that side, and round to the axis, down which it would go, as before. In this case the force would probably be greatest at the two extremes of the axis of the cylinder, and least at the middle distance on the outside.

Now consider the internal space of the cylinder filled up by rings or spirals, all having the currents in the same direction; the direction and kind of force would be the same, but very much strengthened: it would exist in the strongest degree down the axis of the mass, because of the circular form, and it would have the two sides of the point in the centre of the simple ring, which *seemed* to possess attractive and repulsive powers on the pole, removed to the ends of the cylinder; giving rise to two points, apparently distinct in their action, one being attractive, and the other repulsive, of the poles of a magnet. Now conceive that the pole is not confined to a motion about the sides of the ring, or the flat spiral, or cylinder; it is evident that if placed in the axis of any of them at a proper distance for action, it, being impelled by two or more powers in equal circles, would move in a right line in the intersection of those circles, and approach directly to or recede from, the points before spoken of, giving the appearance of a direct attraction and repulsion; and if placed out of that axis, it would move towards or from the same spot in a curve line, its direction and force being determined by the curve lines representing the active forces from the portions of wire forming the ends of the cylinder, spiral, or ring, and the strength of those forces.[79]

The vectorial addition of all the circular forces surrounding the wire wound into a helix would, thus, yield the pattern of forces observed when iron filings were sprinkled over a magnet. These were 'lines of force' and represented the *path* a single magnetic pole (if such were possible) would follow. Such lines were closed curves and Faraday realized that if a single magnetic pole could be isolated, it would circulate *through* the magnet and around the magnetic curves. Again, to drive home the primacy of the circular force, Faraday illustrated his concept by experiment.

A helix of silked copper wire was made round a glass tube, the tube being about an inch in diameter; the helix was about three inches long. A magnetic needle nearly as long was floated with cork, so as to move about in water with the slightest impulse. The helix being connected with the apparatus and put into the water in which the needle lay, its ends appeared to attract and repel the poles of the needle according to the laws before mentioned. But, if that end which attracted one of the poles of the needle was brought near that pole, it entered the glass tube, but did not stop just within side in the neighbourhood of this pole (as we may call it for the moment) of the helix, but passed up the tube, drawing the whole needle in, and went to the opposite pole of the helix, or the one which on the outside would have repelled it; on trying the other pole of the magnet with its corresponding end or pole of the helix the same effect took place; the needle pole entered the tube and passed to the other end, taking the whole needle into the same position it was in before.

Thus each end of the helix seemed to attract and repel both poles of the needle; but this is only a natural consequence of the circulating motion before experimentally demonstrated, and each pole would have gone through the helix and round on the outside, but for the counteraction of the opposite pole.[80]

The reduction of both electric and magnetic phenomena to the actions of the circular force surrounding a current-carrying wire led Faraday here, at least, to agree with Ampère. Again, however, the agreement was couched in Faraday's most cautious terms. 'Thus', he wrote, 'the phenomena of a helix, or a solid cylinder of spiral silked wire, are reduced to the simple revolution of the magnetic pole round the connecting wire of the battery, and its resemblance to a magnet is so great, that the strongest presumption arises in the mind, that they both owe their powers, as M. Ampère has stated, to the same cause.'[81] So far, and only so far would Faraday go. The whole theoretical edifice which Ampère had constructed upon this presumption was still suspect and could not be admitted without much more experimentation. In fact, Faraday immediately went on to point out that the 'resemblance' was not an identity, for a current-carrying helix did differ from a permanent magnet. The most important of these differences was in the location of the poles in the two.

> . . . The poles, or those spots to which the needle points when perpendicular to the ends or sides of a magnet or helix, and where the motive power may be considered perhaps as most concentrated, are in the helix at the extremity of its axis, and not any distance in from the end; whilst in the most regular magnets they are almost always situate in the axis at some distance in from the end; a needle pointing perpendicularly towards the end of a magnet is in a line with its axis, but perpendicularly to the side it points to a spot some distance from the end, whilst in the helix or cylinder, it still points to the end. This variation is, probably, to be attributed to the distribution of the exciting cause of magnetism in the magnet and helix. In the latter, it is necessarily uniform everywhere, inasmuch as the current of electricity is uniform. In the magnet it is probably more active in the middle than elsewhere; for as the north pole of a magnet brought near a south one increases its activity, and that the more as it is nearer, it is fair to infer that the similar parts which are actually united in the inner part of the bar, have the same power.[82]

The account of the experiments on which Faraday based his inference is tantalizing for it was written in haste and did not spell out his ideas. It is, nevertheless, of sufficient importance to warrant citation.

> Expts. on position of pole in Magnet.
> Pole of needle floated, bar magnet brought over. Needle rested under the true pole. Piece of soft iron put to the magnet end, pole immediately moved towards the end.
> One pole of horse shoe magnet brought over the needle: position of pole ascertained. Piece of iron put on, pole approached the end instantly. The iron made to connect both poles the needle, i.e. the poles, then moved the other way and became weaker.

13 The Laboratory of the Royal Institution

14a Faraday as a young man

14b Charles Wheatstone

15a Thomas Young

15b Joseph Henry

Aug 29th 1831.

Expts on the production of Electricity from Magnetism &c

Have had an iron ring made (soft iron), iron round and ⅞ inches thick and ring 6 inches in external diameter – Wound many coils of copper wire round one half the coils being separated by twine & calico – there were 3 lengths of wire each about 24 feet long and they could be connected as one length or used as separate lengths by twine with a trough each was insulated from the other. Will call this side of the Ring A. on the other side but separated by an interval was wound wire in two pieces together amounting to about 60 feet in length the direction being as with the former coils this side call B.

Charged a battery of 10 pr plates 4 inches square. Made the coil on B side one coil and connected its extremities by a copper wire passing to a distance and just over a magnetic needle (3 feet from wire ring) then connected the ends of one of the pieces on A side with battery: immediately a sensible effect on needle. It oscillated & settled at last in original position. On breaking connection of A side with Battery again a disturbance of the needle

16a The page in Faraday's Diary describing the Induction Ring Experiment

16b The Induction Ring

On making the contacts better the effects all stronger, and if they had been perfect with the horse shoe magnet the polarity would probably have ceased altogether. Contact by other metals produces no effects of this kind; [though] of course it is not the position in which it should be expected.[83]

The movement of the poles as soft iron was applied indicated that the magnetic 'power', whatever it was, must be intermolecular in nature. By introducing more matter into the magnetic 'circuit' the centres of the 'power' were shifted. If the contacts could be made perfect (presumably, if the soft iron became an integral part of the magnet in a closed curve), the magnetic power would disappear since the intermolecular relationships would cancel one another out around the curve. The use of 'other metals, provides a beautiful opportunity for speculation. Was Faraday testing out Ampère's ideas? If magnetism were merely the result of electric currents, should not these currents spill over into other conducting substances and thereby influence the original magnetic state? Faraday's failure to detect any such influence he dismissed by saying that 'it is not the position in which it should be expected' although this position, whatever it might be, was never explained.

The value of these experiments and Faraday's musings upon them lies in the light they shed on his thought at this time. Electric currents did reproduce many of the effects of magnets, but Faraday was not yet willing to admit their identity. The difference lay in the matter that appeared to be associated with the permanent magnet, and the immaterial cause of electromagnetism. In his *Diary* he had noted that he could not make a magnet or a wire turn around its own axis. This he had explained by remarking that 'if the revolution depends on the motions of the currents essentially and not on the conductors except as the media, then perhaps those currents in the axis may turn without the media while those in the circumference cannot'.[84] This idea was made more explicit in the published paper where, after announcing the failure to achieve rotation about a magnetic or wire axis, he went on:

The motions evidently belong to the current, or whatever else it be, that is passing through the wire, and not to the wire itself, except as the vehicle of the current. When that current is made a curve by the form of the wire, it is easy to conceive how, in revolving, it should take the wire with it; but when the wire is straight, the current may revolve without any motion being communicated to the wire through which it passes.[85]

Except for that phrase, 'or whatever else it may be', the statement was that of one who accepted the fluid theory of electricity and this was, indeed, as close as Faraday ever came to accepting it. The important point was that his view of electricity in 1821 was that it could act independently of matter. Magnetism could not, for it seemed always to be tied, not only to material bodies, but to a very restricted number of particular chemical entities. As a chemist, Faraday could not ignore this fact. Electricity 'whatever it might be' might produce certain effects of magnetism but until the identity between the two could be firmly and experimentally established, Faraday would not accept the assumed identity as truth.

Writing to Gaspard de la Rive at the same time that he was putting the paper on electromagnetic rotations together, he again revealed his unwillingness to view magnetism *solely* as the result of electricity in motion.

> I am by no means decided [he remarked] that there are currents of electricity in the common magnet. I have no doubt that electricity puts the circles of the helices into the same state as those circles are in that may be conceived in the bar magnet but I am not certain that this state is directly dependant on the electricity, or that it cannot be produced by other agencies and therefore until the presence of Electrical currents be proved in the magnet by other than magnetical effects, I shall remain in doubt about Ampère's theory.[86]

His experiments on electromagnetic rotations had clarified the area of disagreement considerably. Magnetism, according to Faraday, was some kind of intermolecular power, permeating the magnet, and concentrated at the poles. How such a power could be produced by electricity he did not know. Ampère's theory, on the other hand, depended only upon the existence of electric currents. But, until the molecular currents that Ampère's theory required could be made manifest, Faraday could not accept them. Although he appeared *almost* a partisan of Ampère's theory in his paper on electromagnetic rotations, he was too conscious of the conflict in his own mind to go all the way. When Gaspard de la Rive reproached him (and the English) for not appreciating Ampère, he replied that he had lately written a paper 'which will appear in a week or two and that will as it contains experiment be immediately applied by M. Ampère in support of his theory much more decidedly than it is by myself'.[87]

Faraday was only partially correct, for although Ampère felt that the new rotations did, indeed, support his theory, he was also aware that Faraday's interpretation of the cause of these motions differed from his own. Specifically, Faraday had challenged his statement of the primacy of the action of two currents upon one another and this, in turn, had contributed to Faraday's scepticism regarding Ampère's electrodynamic molecules. Since Ampère's system rested upon the reduction of magnetism to the push-pull of electric forces and the circulation of the electric fluids around the particles of matter, it was necessary for him to answer Faraday's objections.

Ampère's reply was forthcoming in the notes he added to the French translation of Faraday's paper.[88] He was not always successful in refuting Faraday but his views are of interest for they reveal the fundamental difference between Ampère, the mathematical physicist to whom models served as the starting-points for mathematical analysis, and Faraday, the experimentalist, to whom the observed fact was of primary importance. Faraday's suggestion that the true interaction between a current-carrying wire and a magnet involved the rotation of one around the other was rejected by Ampère for reasons that Faraday could not accept. 'The revolving action of the conducting wire and of a magnet around each other which M. Faraday considers as the primary fact throughout this memoir', Ampère wrote, 'will not permit the phenomena to be reduced to mathematical analysis.'[89] The circular motion of either the wire or the magnet must be 'the resultant of a multitude of elementary actions'. Ampère did not stop here; he went on to point out that Faraday had misunderstood him:

> The attractions and repulsions of two conducting wires of finite length, discovered by M. Ampère, are also not simple facts; it seems to us that this designation cannot be given except to laws of mutual action between two points, but not between two groups of an infinity of these points, as is presented to us in this phenomenon. This being so, the simple facts cannot be immediately observed, but only deduced from observations with the aid of mathematics.[90]

Such a position could have little effect on Faraday. 'Simple facts' were for him the observed facts and to *deduce* these facts from observations was not a legitimate procedure. Although he was mathematically illiterate, Faraday had a keen sense of the fallibility of mathematicians and he was not prepared to abandon the experimental way merely because Ampère could not fit his results into an equation. As he wrote to Gaspard de la Rive, 'when I confess my want of mathematical knowledge and see mathematicians themselves differing about the validity of the arguments used it will serve as my apology for waiting for experiment'.[91] Ampère's calculations, however, had led him irresistibly to the deduction of molecular currents and if experiment could not follow him into the intimate recesses of matter, so much the worse for experiment.

Ampère's criticism of Faraday's views and exposition of his own did not stop at words. Almost immediately upon receiving news of Faraday's work, Ampère realized that the rotation of a magnet about its own axis, for which Faraday had sought in vain, ought to occur if his theory were correct. In December 1821, he announced the production of this rotation to the Academy of Sciences in Paris.[92] The news of this discovery was also dispatched to Faraday in London where Faraday repeated the experiments. Although again paying tribute to Ampère's skill and ingenuity, Faraday still begged to differ with his illustrious co-worker.

> You mention your opinion [he wrote to Ampère] that this experiment will be competent to decide the question whether the currents of electricity assumed by your theory exist round the axis of the magnet or round each particle from which I gather that the view you take of it differs from the one I at present have, since to me it seems a modification of the revolution of a wire round a pole. . . .
>
> The rotation of the magnet seems to me to take place in consequence of the different particles of which it is composed being put into the same state by the passing current of electricity as the wire of communication between the voltaic poles, and the relative position of the magnetic pole to them. Thus the little arrows [see Figure 6] may represent the progress of the electricity; then any line of particles parallel to them except that line which passes as an axis through the pole (represented by a dot) will be in the situation of the revolving wire and will endeavour to revolve round the pole and as all the lines act in the same direction or tend to go one way round the pole the whole magnet revolves. . . .
>
> . . . I am naturally sceptical in the matter of theories and therefore you must not be angry with me for not admitting the one you have advanced immediately. Its ingenuity and applications are astonishing and exact but I cannot comprehend how the currents are produced and particularly if they be supposed to exist round each atom or particle and I wait for further proofs of their existence before I finally admit them.[93]

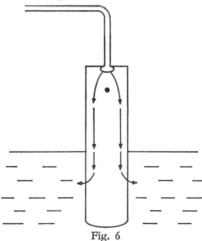

Fig. 6

Here, for all practical purposes was where the matter rested between Ampère and Faraday. Ampère became more and more convinced of the reality of his molecular currents, of the existence of the ether, and of the two electric fluids of which the ether was composed. Faraday remained sceptical.

3. The Discovery of Electromagnetic Induction

After 1821 Faraday's mind was occupied by a host of other problems and his time was too filled with other duties to permit him to bring his full attention to bear on electromagnetism. During the ten years that passed between the discovery of electromagnetic rotation and that of electromagnetic induction, there are only a dozen short entries in his *Diary* on electromagnetic matters. Even his letters during this period give no hint as to the full evolution of his ideas. We are, therefore, faced with a serious problem. If we are to understand Faraday's mental evolution, both before and after 1831, the development of his ideas on the nature of electricity and the reasons behind his famous ring experiment must be seen as clearly as possible. The sources, however, are extremely meagre. What follows is an attempt to reconstruct Faraday's thoughts from the hints thrown out in the laboratory diary and follow him as he struggled towards success. The reader, therefore, is warned that this account contains a good deal more conjecture than is desirable. The result is a coherent tale, but perhaps not the only nor the correct one; unfortunately, it seems unlikely that new evidence will be uncovered and we must make do with what we have.

There are three separate phases in the development of Faraday's ideas that led him in 1831 to the discovery of electromagnetic induction. The first was a continuation of his examination of Ampère's theory. He was sceptical, but, for some time, was not prepared to reject the theory without further experimental examination. From Ampère's ideas he deduced certain consequences which, as we shall see, almost led him to the discovery of electromagnetic induction in 1825. The failure of these experiments seems to have convinced him that Ampère was wrong.

The second line of thought that led to the induction ring experiment of 1831 was that devoted to the development of his own ideas on the nature of electricity and its mode of propagation through conductors.

The third aspect was that involving the construction of powerful electromagnets by Joseph Henry of Albany, New York, and the almost instantaneous reversal of polarity noticed by G. Moll of Utrecht when the leads to the electromagnet were rapidly interchanged.

These phases followed one another, more or less chronologically, and do appear to reflect the actual course of Faraday's thought between 1821 and 1831. We shall, therefore, deal with them separately and show how, in

1831, they were put together to form the necessary conditions for the production of electromagnetic induction.

For some years after 1821 no new opportunities arose for Faraday to test Ampère's theory experimentally. The two had, more or less, agreed to disagree and left it at that. In 1824 and 1825, however, a new electromagnetic effect was announced which offered the possibility of trying anew Ampère's ideas on the anvil of experience. François Arago in France and Peter Barlow and S. H. Christie in England found that the rotation of a copper disc (Arago) or of a mass of iron (Barlow and Christie) made these substances magnetic.[94] Arago's apparatus was the more impressive for by utilizing copper, a non-magnetic substance, it seemed to show that mere motion could induce magnetism in a metal. It consisted of a magnetic needle freely suspended over a copper disc. When the disc was rotated around its axis, the magnetic needle began to rotate as well. Arago's wheel was an immediate scientific sensation. Why motion should make a body magnetic was a mystery that intrigued all those who had worked on electromagnetism. Opinions differed widely on its explanation. In France, Jean-Baptiste Biot privately but triumphantly viewed the new phenomenon as a refutation of Ampère and a verification of Coulomb's ideas on the magnetic fluids. To him, it was a simple separation of the magnetic fluids by centrifugal force.[95]

Ampère, strangely enough, did not seem to feel that Arago's wheel presented any challenge. His discussion of it centred around the fact that a current-carrying helix could be substituted for the magnetic needle, thus reinforcing his idea of the identity of electricity and magnetism.[96] The only serious attempt to deal with the new effect in terms of the electrodynamic molecule was made by two Englishmen, John Herschel and Charles Babbage. Both were mathematical physicists who found Ampère's theory especially appealing because of its mathematical elegance. In a paper read before the Royal Society on 16 June 1825, Herschel and Babbage set out to describe the effect minutely and explain it in terms of Ampère's physical model.[97]

They first verified the effect itself and then proceeded to vary the conditions in order better to reveal the mechanism of rotational magnetism. To make their apparatus more sensitive, they suspended a copper disc over a large horseshoe magnet placed vertically and capable of being rotated rapidly around its axis of symmetry. Various non-ferrous discs were then interposed between the magnet and the copper disc. No effect on the rotation of the copper disc was noticed. When soft iron was interposed, the copper would not move. Such an effect was to be anticipated for the iron, being capable of absorbing the magnetic force, effectively screened the disc. From these and other experiments, Babbage and Herschel felt that they could satisfactorily account for the 'magnetic virtue exhibited by the copper and other bodies in these experiments. It is obviously *induced* by the action of the magnetic bar, compass needle, etc., on their molecules.'[98] It was, however, a peculiar kind of induction for it took place only when either the magnet or the disc was in motion. Leaving this problem aside for the moment, Babbage and Herschel determined the degree to which the magnetic virtue could be induced in various bodies. They reported, without comment, that only the metals and carbon could receive the magnetic virtue. The metals were then ranked in order of inductive susceptibility with silver at the top and bismuth at the bottom.

The experiments were then varied to investigate the effect of continuity of the disc upon its magnetic susceptibility. Slits were cut radially in the copper disc; the magnetic effect was almost totally destroyed. When the slits were soldered up with tin, the magnetic susceptibility was strengthened. 'The magnetic action was now found to be so far restored as to enable it to perform its six revolutions . . . very nearly in the same time as when entire. This is the more remarkable, since tin, as we have seen, is not above half so energetic as copper when acting directly.'[99] When the slits were filled with powdered metals, the magnetic susceptibility of the disc was greatly reduced.

To the modern reader, the principle lying behind the above-cited facts is so obvious that it seems impossible that men of the calibre of Babbage and Herschel could have missed it. The degrees of 'magnetic susceptibility' followed exactly the ability of the metals to conduct electricity; of the non-metallic substances, only carbon (which conducts electricity) exhibited magnetic susceptibility. When the disc was slit so that electric currents in the disc were made impossible, the effect was destroyed; when electric conduction was again made possible by solder, the effect was restored; when the resistance was made large, as with the powdered metal, the effect was greatly diminished. Clearly, the 'magnetic susceptibility' depended upon the ability of electric currents to circulate in the discs. In short, what Babbage and Herschel were dealing with was the induction of electricity, not magnetism, by a moving magnet. Yet, hindsight is of no value to the researcher and Babbage and Herschel found an explanation which satisfied them in Ampère's theory.

When we come to reason on the above facts [they wrote] much caution is doubtless necessary to avoid over-hasty generalization. Whoever has considered the progress of our knowledge respecting the magnetic virtue, which, first supposed to belong only to iron and its compounds, was at length reluctantly conceded to nickel and cobalt, though in a much weaker degree – then suspected to belong to titanium, and now extended, apparently with an extraordinary range of degrees of intensity to all the metals – will hardly be inclined to stop short here, but will readily admit, at least the probability, of all bodies in nature participating in it more or less. Yet if the electro-dynamical theory of magnetism be well founded, it is difficult to conceive how that internal circulation of electricity, which has been regarded as necessary for the production of magnetism, can be excited or maintained in non-conducting bodies. Without pretending to draw a line, however, in what is perhaps at last only a question of degree, one thing is certain, that all the unequivocal cases of magnetic action observed by us, lie among the best conductors of electricity.[100]

To explain Arago's wheel, utilizing the electrodynamical theory, was no easy thing, but Herschel and Babbage made a gallant attempt. The effect must be dependent upon induced magnetism, i.e. the molecules of the disc must align themselves in directions determined by the permanent magnet. Mere alignment, however, was not enough, for this would produce only attractions and repulsions, not rotation. The alignment of the particles must, therefore, be delayed or, to put it another way, the point of maximum induced magnetism must always be behind the moving magnet. 'There will thus arise an oblique action between the pole of the magnet and the opposite pole of the plate so lagging behind it' and this oblique action will cause the plate to rotate.[101] The delay was presumably caused by the fact that it took time for the electrodynamic molecules to turn into position. That this was a considerable amount of time could be shown by the fact that even slow rotations of the magnet caused the disc to revolve.

What this paper left unexplained, was why the induced magnetism occurred *only* when either the disc or the magnet was in motion. According to Ampère's model, which the authors accepted, motion should be irrelevant. The electric currents surrounding the molecules of the copper disc should be affected by the currents surrounding the molecules of the magnet without the intervention of relative motion.

Faraday saw this point. He had followed Babbage's and Herschel's analysis carefully and undoubtedly found their account somewhat unsatisfactory. Again molecular currents, magnetic inductions (which could not be detected when the magnet and disc did not move) and the whole shaky structure of hypotheses which Babbage and Herschel had had to erect strained his credulity. To Faraday, Arago's wheel provided an excellent new opportunity to test Ampère's fundamental hypothesis of magnetic action.

If magnetic action [he noted] be simply electrical action as M. Ampère considers it then magnetic induction must be electrical induction and M. Arago's
experiments must depend upon induced electrical action. Hence electrical
poles or surfaces ought to produce similar effects for though the electricity
will not be in such quantity and not in motion still it has sufficient attractive
and repulsive powers and it appears to me that the mere difference of motion
or rest as respects the electricity in the inducing body will not explain such
retention of the induced state in one case (magnetism) and such resignation
of it in the other (the expt. proposed) as to account for dragging attraction in
the former and not in the latter state of things.[102]

A dry pile (De Luc's column) was suspended horizontally over a copper
disc. The pile played the part of the magnet, but when the disc was rotated,
the pile remained stationary. A Leyden jar was then charged and suspended over the plate in such a way that the positive and negative surfaces
were separated in imitation of the magnetic poles (see Figure 7). Again,
the disc was revolved but the jar remained unaffected.[103]

Babbage and Herschel's paper also
appears to have stimulated Faraday to
try some experiments quite unrelated
to Arago's wheel. If, as Faraday had
suggested, magnetic action were
merely electrical action, should not
one be able to produce an *electrical*
reaction from the magnetic force
associated with an electrical current?
And, since magnetism was simply
induced electricity in a peculiar form,
should not one current actually induce
another in a neighbouring wire? In
November 1825, applying this reasoning to experiment, Faraday came within
a whisker of discovering electromagnetic induction.

Fig. 7

Two copper wires were tied close together, a thickness of paper only
intervening for a length of five feet.
One of them was made the connecting
wire of a battery 40 pr. of plates 4 inch square in rather weak action and the
ends of the other wire connected with a galvanometer. No effects however
upon its needle could be observed consequently no visible proofs of induction
by the wire through which the current was passing upon its neighbour could
this way be perceived.

In reference to certain views with respect to the axis of action the connecting wire of the battery passed through the centre of a helix but no results. Again a helix being in connection with the poles of the pile a straight wire occupying its axis was connected with the galvanometer, but no apparent effects. The galvanometer was not a very delicate one.[104]

The rationale of these experiments was clearly given by Ampère's theory. To Ampère, the electric current consisted of the flow of positive and negative electricity in opposite directions through a wire. At any given instant of time, three entities existed in the wire: positive electricity, negative electricity, and the neutral ether which was the result of their combination. The length of time during which the two electricities existed in separate states was very small, but finite. During this time, the two charges should act exactly like static electrical charges and induce charges of the opposite sign in neighbouring matter. In a wire brought near the current-carrying wire, a pattern of charges should be induced which, except for change of sign, reproduced the pattern in the inducing wire. Such a pattern of charges would then move along the secondary wire exactly as they did in the primary. In short, a current would be induced (Figure 8).

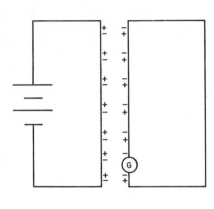

Fig. 8

When the primary circuit was closed to produce the current in the first wire, the galvanometer in the secondary circuit should move. Faraday didn't see it move for the simple reason that he did not do the experiment in this way. The primary circuit was already closed when the secondary circuit, containing the galvanometer, was closed. What Faraday was looking for was a steady effect caused by the constant reappearance of charges in the primary. He had no reason to suppose that the deflection of the galvanometer would take place only when the primary circuit was made and broken. Nor would he have had any reason to suspect that a more sensitive galvanometer was required. The effect in the secondary should parallel that in the primary. If the galvanometer were sufficiently sensitive to detect the electric current in the one, it should do the same for the other.

The experiments with the helix also followed from Ampère's theory. If Ampère were correct, permanent magnetism was merely the result of the alignment of electrodynamic molecules, or, what amounted to the same thing, the resultant of the action of electric currents concentric to the magnet's axis. The full power of the electric current in a helix, therefore, should be concentrated in the axis of the helix. Such a concentration of power should be expected to disturb the etherial equilibrium in a wire placed in this axis. No effect, however, was produced and once again Ampère's theory appeared unable to meet the test of experiment.

Faraday's failure to produce results which he felt could legitimately be deduced from Ampère's theory convinced him that he had been right to view this theory with scepticism. This failure did not, however, bring him any closer to an understanding of the mechanism of electromagnetic action. In fact, his own experiments seemed to indicate that his vague hypothesis concerning this mechanism was untenable. As has been shown, he leaned strongly to the view that electromagnetism was the result of a peculiar *state* into which the particles of a conductor were thrown, and not merely the action of the two electrical fluids upon one another. In 1822 he tried to detect this state, but was unsuccessful.

> Polarized a ray of lamp light by reflection and endeavoured to ascertain whether any depolarizing action exerted on it by water placed between the poles of a voltaic battery in a glass cistern – one Wollaston's trough used – the fluids decomposed were pure water – weak solution of sulphate of soda and strong sulphuric acid. None of them had any effect on the polarized light either when out of or in the voltaic circuit, so that no particular arrangement of particles could be ascertained in this way.[105]

His own discovery of electromagnetic rotation forced a modification in his idea of what the *state* of a current-carrying wire must be. It clearly had to be something more complicated than a mere arrangement of particles, for it was difficult to see how a static arrangement could cause a dynamic rotation. To the arrangement, something dynamic had to be added (282–3). Faraday was now in a real predicament. He had rejected fluids which provided a simple, dynamic agent. Forces, inherent in matter, could account for arrangement but how could these forces be transmitted through wires as electromagnetic rotation appeared to require? What he had to find if his ideas were to lead him anywhere, was some way in which force could be transmitted without the transmission of matter, either ponderable or imponderable. Fortunately, the way had been prepared for him and he was able to seize upon a new theory, apparently unrelated to electrical or magnetic phenomena, and bend it to his own uses.

Before 1800, force generally was considered to be transmitted in only two ways. It could be transferred from one body to another by direct

impact (as in colliding billiard balls) or by action at a distance. By the
1820's a new and exciting physical theory which also postulated the
transmission of force without the transfer of matter was gaining widespread support. The idea that light, one of the 'imponderable fluids', was
actually a wave motion had been suggested by Dr Thomas Young in 1801.
The theory was violently attacked and Young had dropped the subject.
It was again put forward by an engineer in the *Corps des Ponts et Chaussées*
of the French Empire. While he languished in provincial isolation,
Augustin Fresnel sought some intellectual stimulation and turned to the
study of the nature of light. Independently of Young, and in ignorance
of Young's work, he wrestled with some of the difficulties presented by
the corpuscular theory of light. Soon it became apparent to Fresnel that
this theory simply would not do. Some form of undulatory nature had to
be attributed to light if the indubitable optical facts were to be explained.
In a series of highly mathematical papers, Fresnel presented his theory to
the *Académie des Sciences* and the undulatory theory of light gradually
gained support.[106]

The original memoirs were of little use to Faraday. Fresnel's experiments
were beautiful but the mathematical reasoning which had led him to them
was far more than Faraday could understand. Furthermore, Faraday was
not particularly interested in optics at the time when these papers first
appeared. There is only one reference to Fresnel in the annotated copy of
Brande's *Manual of Chemistry*. Physical optics, before 1824, seemed
remote from his interests and from chemistry.

After 1824 this changed. The task of improving optical glass necessarily
led him to ponder the nature of light. More importantly, the problem of
the transmission of electrical force was beginning to preoccupy him. He
had already discovered the use of light as a molecular probe when he
attempted to detect some kind of arrangement in an electrolytic solution.
Could not a deeper understanding of what light itself was help to clarify
his ideas on the other imponderables? Luckily, just as these interests were
becoming paramount, Fresnel's theory was put in a form which the experimentalist could grasp.

On 8 February 1827, the Council of the Royal Society voted the
Rumford Medal to Fresnel for his work on the theory of the polarization
of light. W. T. Brande, editor of the *Quarterly Journal of Science*, recognized
the importance of this award and immediately asked Dr Thomas Young to
translate Fresnel's own description of his work which had appeared as
the supplement to the French translation of Thomas Thomson's *System
of Chemistry*. From 1827 to 1829 Fresnel's 'Elementary view of the

Undulatory Theory of Light' appeared in a series of articles in the *Q.J.S.* The mathematics was kept to a bare and elementary minimum. Fresnel's ideas emerged clearly and Faraday was provided with a solution to the problem of the transmission of force without the transfer of matter.

Faraday read this account with great interest and had no difficulty in assimilating the concepts. When he was soliciting articles for the new *Journal of the Royal Institution* in 1830, the kind of paper he suggested to others was one 'not too profound and mathematical but yet clear and good and fit to be an authority; something indeed like Fresnel's account of the undulatory [theory] of light'.[107]

Physical optics was not the only subject which dealt with wave motion. At the same time that Fresnel's theory was being published in the *Quarterly Journal*, Faraday was dabbling in the science of sound. Dabble appears to be the proper word, for there is not a mention of any serious experimental attack upon sound before 1831. In the years 1828 to 1830, however, Faraday served as the spokesman for Charles Wheatstone in some Friday Evening Discourses at the Royal Institution. Faraday loved music and was intrigued by Wheatstone's researches into the nature of musical sound and instruments. The account of the first such discourse conveys some of the flavour of the meeting.

February 15 [1828]

The subject this evening, in the Lecture Room, was on Resonance, or the Reciprocation of Sound. It was delivered by Mr Faraday, who, however, gave all the credit belonging to the illustration, and the new information communicated, to Mr C. Wheatstone. It was illustrated by some striking experiments, by many curious instruments of music from Java, for the loan of which the Institution was indebted to Lady Raffles; and by some very novel and curious musical performances on the Jew's-harp, by Mr Eulenstein.[108]

Later discourses moved onwards from the Jew's-harp to sirens, organs, and stringed instruments. Even whistlers were not neglected. The report of the meeting on 3 April 1829, records with awe the peculiar talent of a Mr Mannin who could whistle two notes at the same time![109] There was more behind these discourses, however, than a desire to amuse. Wheatstone's researches had led him to the invention of a new instrument which he christened the kaleidophone, by which the actual vibrations of strings and rods could be analysed and directly viewed.[110] The waves which Fresnel could see only in mathematical equations and his mind's eye could now be projected upon a screen. Wheatstone was also fascinated by the figures produced when sand was strewn upon a glass or steel plate and the plate put into vibration by drawing a violin bow across one edge.

These figures had been discovered by Chladni in 1785 and attracted attention only because of their beauty and symmetry. In a discourse, Faraday showed how they could be produced, but no conclusions were drawn from these appearances. One section of the report of the meeting, however, dealt with a variation of the method of producing these figures, and is worth recounting. 'An account was then given of the production of figures, not upon surfaces directly thrown into a vibratory state, but such as were made to vibrate by reciprocation. These are due to Savart, and by making use of thin extended membranes, he had shewn various new facts in addition to those of Chladni, and especially the possible transformation of figures.'[111]

Although Faraday or Wheatstone did not remark the fact at this time, they were dealing with what might be called acoustical induction. An arrangement of particles on one plate could be effected by another plate thrown into a vibratory state. The plates were not in contact but it was perfectly obvious that this was *not* action at a distance for the force was obviously transmitted through the medium of the air. Later, when he was concerned with the problem of electrical induction, Faraday could not help but be struck by the analogy.

The mere presentation of Wheatstone's results did not stimulate Faraday to pursue the subject further. There is not one word on sound or acoustical figures in his laboratory *Diary* until the beginning of 1831, and then his attack was extended and vigorous.[112] It is impossible to say precisely what set him off on this tack at that time for he simply leapt into the subject without warning. It is probable that his attention was directed to Chladni figures by an explicit statement of the analogy of sound and light. In 1830 John Herschel's *A Preliminary Discourse on the Study of Natural Philosophy* appeared as the first volume of *The Cabinet Cyclopaedia* conducted by the Rev. Dionysius Lardner.[113] Faraday was deeply impressed by this work. He was not given to flattery and yet his praise of this volume borders on the extravagant. In 1832, he wrote to Herschel:

'When your work on the study of Nat[ural] Phil[osophy] came out I read it as all others did with delight. I took it as a school book for philosophers and I feel that it has made me a better reasoner and even experimenter and has altogether heightened my character and made me if I may be permitted to say so a better philosopher.'[114] Not content with this private tribute, Faraday felt called upon to repeat it in public at the celebration of the centenary of Joseph Priestley's birth.[115]

In his treatise, Herschel returned time and again to the analogy of sound and light. Thus, he pointed out 'that an analogy subsisting between sound and light has been gradually traced into a closeness of agreement, which can hardly leave any reasonable doubt of their ultimate coincidence in one common phenomenon, the vibratory motion of an elastic medium.[116] Herschel called particular attention to the work of Chladni and Savart by which sonorous vibrations were made 'susceptible of ocular examination'.[117] Again, he underlined the importance of this area in terms of the analogy between sound and light.[118]

If, as seems to have been the case, Faraday's interest in light had been aroused by Fresnel's account of his theory, Herschel's stress upon Chladni figures and sound was what led him back to a deeper consideration of the phenomenon. Previously, Wheatstone's work had been suitable for the amusement of the audience at the Royal Institution. Now, acoustical figures appeared to offer a relatively simple means to probe the very nature of light itself. Faraday saw even farther than this. If light and sound were both vibratory motions, was it not possible that electricity also was undulatory in nature? The idea was not original with Faraday. As long ago as 1806 Oersted had suggested exactly the same analogy. He had even specifically cited Chladni figures as analogues of electrical action.[119] Faraday had read and noted the article in which this analogy was put forward.[120]

In February 1831, he began a series of beautiful experiments on acoustical figures. This was clearly no passing whim since he worked intensively on the problems of vibrating surfaces for six months. His goal seems clear; acoustical figures could provide invaluable clues to the nature of vibrations in general. From these clues, it might be possible to clarify the action of electricity. It needs to be baldly stated, however, that *nowhere* in the researches on sound is the word electricity mentioned. It is, indeed, possible that Faraday's work here was simply stimulated by an interest in the figures produced. His deeply felt belief in the unity of force, however, would appear to militate against this isolation of a single phenomenon for such exhaustive study. And, the first appearance in his *Diary* of the notion of electricity as a wave follows so closely upon his acoustical researches that, given the emphasis upon vibrations in Fresnel's and Herschel's works, these experiments must be viewed as the preliminaries to his discovery and unravelling of electromagnetic induction.

From the beginning, Faraday attacked the problem in a way different from his predecessors. Chladni, Oersted, and Savart had all studied only the figures produced by vibrating plates in different modes of vibration. Faraday realized that the situation was more complicated; the surrounding air must be taken into account. On the second day of his experiments he introduced the use of an air pump and examined the resultant figure formed when the plate was made to vibrate under diminished air pressure.[121] The pattern changed and Faraday was able to show that the figures depended upon the strength of the currents of air and the weight of the particles forming the pattern. Where Savart, in particular, had had to invent secondary modes of vibration, Faraday could explain all in terms of the medium.[122] As he pointed out in the published paper, 'The cause of these effects appeared to me, from the first, to exist in the medium within which the vibrating plate and powder were placed, and every experiment which I have made, together with all those in M. Savart's paper, either strongly confirm, or agree with this view.'[123]

The next step was obvious. Instead of merely rarefying the air surrounding the plate, Faraday introduced new media. Water, egg white, and oil were placed on top of plates and then the plate put into vibration. The results were striking. Instead of forming Chladni figures, the liquids formed crispations of singular regularity. How liquids could be thrown into such regular arrangements was clearly seen by Faraday.

> It is very evident [he wrote] that the quadrate form of the crispations or waves is the natural one, for in that form the distance which the particles have to move through is the shortest possible distance i.e. considered in relation to the courses which they would probably take and the number of these courses. In that arrangement the dividing lines are the shortest possible also, and other physical reasons suggest themselves to be considered hereafter.
>
> Again, if as I suspect the elevations are alternating and exist in the manner of stationary undulations, i.e. up and down motion, then linear or triangular or quadrangular – hexagonal? – are the only arrangements that are admissible as capable of alternating – linear are first formed and these readily break up into quadrangular by increased force.[124]

The crispations and the regular figures formed by them must have affected Faraday deeply. In 1821 the discovery of electromagnetic rotations had convinced him that the electric 'current' could not be simply an arrangement of particles, for mere arrangement could not produce continuous motion. Something *must* move through the wire. On the other hand, his experiment with polarized light and a solution undergoing electrochemical decomposition clearly shows his continuing search for some kind of arrangement of particles in the electrical circuit. The two ideas appear to be contradictory; for how is it possible to have an arrangement as well as a progression of force? The answer appeared most dramatically in the crispations. Here one can actually see the arrangements into which the particles of the various fluids were thrown by the vibrations of the plates. Wave *motion* and molecular *arrangement* were now reconciled. If we now add the fact that the vibrations extended beyond the plate into the surrounding medium so that acoustical induction could take place, another dimension may perhaps be added to our understanding of the induction ring experiment.

The analogy between sound and electricity was spelled out by Faraday himself. Some six months after his discovery of electromagnetic induction, he requested J. G. Children, one of the secretaries of the Royal Society to deposit the following sealed note in the Society's safe.

Certain of the results of the investigations which are embodied in the two papers entitled *Experimental researches in Electricity*, lately read to the Royal Society: and the views arising therefrom, in connexion with other views and experiments, lead me to believe that magnetic action is progressive, and requires time; i.e. that when a magnet acts upon a distant magnet or piece of iron, the influencing cause (which I may for the moment call magnetism), proceeds gradually from the magnetic bodies and requires time for its transmission which will probably be found to be very sensible.

I think also, that I see reason for supposing that electric induction (of tension)* is also performed in a similar progressive time.

I am inclined to compare the diffusion of magnetic forces from a magnetic pole, to the vibrations upon the surface of disturbed water, or those of air in the phenomena of sound; i.e. I am inclined to think the vibratory theory will apply to these phenomena, as it does to sound and most probably to light.

By analogy I think it may possibly apply to the phenomena of induction of electricity of tension also.

These views I wish to work out experimentally: but as much of my time is engaged in the duties of my office, and as the experiments will therefore be prolonged, and may in their course be subject to the observation of others; I wish, by depositing this paper in the care of the Royal Society, to take possession as it were of a certain date, and a lone right, if they are confirmed by experiments, to claim credit for the views at that date: at which time as far as I know no one is conscious of or can claim them but myself.

Royal Institution
March 12, 1832   (Signed) M. Faraday.[125]

By 1831, then, Faraday suspected an analogy between sound, light, and electricity. The electric wave was transmitted by the particles of matter and threw these particles into some form of arrangement. The problem now was to detect the wave.

Events in 1831 provided a solution to this difficulty. In an issue of the *Journal of the Royal Institution* for this year, Faraday's friend, Gerritt Moll of Utrecht, remarked upon the interesting behaviour of electromagnets. It appeared that the polarity of an electromagnet could be reversed almost instantaneously merely by reversing the direction of the current.[126]

*[electrostatic induction]

Babbage and Herschel had shown that the alignment of Ampère's electrodynamic molecules took a considerable amount of time; Moll's results
seemed to prove just the opposite. Both could not be correct. Faraday's
scepticism towards the explanation offered by Babbage and Herschel was
reinforced at the same time that confidence in his own ideas was increased.
Waves of force and the resultant arrangements of particles could occur in
the wink of an eye.

Moll also called Faraday's attention to the extraordinary magnetic
power developed by electromagnets. This provided the final element in the
induction ring experiment. An electromagnet could intensify the magnetic
force of the electric current to its utmost. The electric 'wave' would be
accompanied by a magnetic strain of detectable proportions. Such a strain
would be most intense at the poles, and back in 1821 Faraday had experimented with the location of poles in a magnet. He had then written in his
Diary: 'Query the best form for a magnet, i.e. so that the pole may be
nearest the surface: an oblate or oblong spheroid or a sphere or a very
thick ring?'[127]

Since he required an electromagnet, the only one of these forms around
which a wire could be conveniently coiled many times was the ring. In
August 1831, Faraday noted in his *Diary*:

> Have had an iron ring made (soft iron), iron round and ⅞ inches thick and
> ring 6 inches in external diameter. Wound many coils of copper wire round
> one half, the coils being separated by twine and calico – there were 3 lengths
> of wire each about 24 feet long and they could be connected as one length or
> used as separate lengths. By trial with a trough each was insulated from the
> other. Will call this side of the ring A.[128]

When current passed through this coil, if Faraday were correct, it
would create some kind of peculiar state in the iron ring. The forces
associated with this state would be at their most intense on the opposite
side of the ring and near its surface. If these forces had anything to do
with electricity, then they should be detectable at this place by the
presence of a conductor. Since the copper coil on side A intensified the
effect of the current, it was logical to suppose that a similar coil would
multiply the effect of the forces in the ring. Hence 'on the other side but
separated by an interval was wound wire in two pieces together amounting to about 60 feet in length, the direction being as with the former coils;
this side call B'[129] (Figure 9).

All this would have been for nought if coil A had been connected to
the battery before coil B was attached to the galvanometer. Unlike the
experiment in 1825 by which he had tried to induce one current by

another, the effect here was more likely to be a transient than a steady one. He was expecting a 'wave' and if a peculiar state or strain were created in the ring, it would most likely be detected during the instant it was set up by the wave. Faraday was looking at the galvanometer this time. When all was ready, 'connected the ends of one of the pieces on A side with battery; immediately a sensible effect on needle. It oscillated and settled at last in original position. On *breaking* connection of A side with Battery again a disturbance of the needle.'[130]

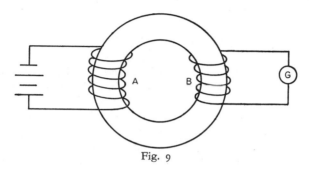

Fig. 9

For almost ten years, Faraday had been searching for some such effect. The movement of the galvanometer indicated that a 'current' had passed in the secondary coil (B) when a 'current' was set up in the primary (A). What this 'current' was he made clear in a description of another experiment made the following day:

> continued the contact of A side [primary] with battery but broke and closed alternately contact of B side [secondary] with flat helix. No effect at such times on the needle – depends upon the change at battery side. Hence is no permanent or peculiar state of wire from B but effect due to a *wave of electricity* caused at moments of breaking and completing contacts at A side.
> Tried to perceive a spark with charcoal at flat helix junction B side but could find none. Wave apparently very short and sudden.[131]

The discovery of electromagnetic induction was not only the culmination of a long search; it was the starting-point for the brilliant series of experimental researches in electricity which were now to occupy him for almost thirty years.

References

1. Article 'Thermo-electricity', *The Edinburgh Encyclopaedia*, 1830. Reprinted in Kirstine Meyer, ed., H. C. Oersted, *Naturvidenskabelige Skrifter . . . Scientific Papers* (3 vols., Copenhagen, 1820), 2, 351 ff. Cited henceforth as *Skrifter*. The quotation is on page 352.

2. For an overall account of Oersted's scientific accomplishments see the excellent essay by Kirstine Meyer which prefaces her edition of Oersted's works cited above.

   Oersted's debt to *Naturphilosophie* is explored by Robert C. Stauffer in 'Speculation and Experiment in the Background of Oersted's Discovery of Electromagnetism', *Isis*, *48* (1957), 33. In an earlier article, 'Persistent Errors Regarding Oersted's Discovery of Electromagnetism', *Isis*, *44* (1953), 307, Dr Stauffer has disposed of the myth of the accidental discovery of electromagnetism.

3. H. C. Oersted, 'Die Reihe der Säuren und Basen', *Gehlen's Jour. für die Chemie und Physik*, 2 (1806), 509, reprinted in Oersted, *Skrifter*, *1*, 289.

4. H. C. Oersted, *Recherches sur l'identité des forces chimiques et electriques*, tr. by Marcel de Serres (Paris, 1813), 243. The passage has been condensed in order to give Oersted's views without undue prolixity. A shorter version of this work was published in German with the title *Ansicht der Chemischen Naturgesetze durch die neueren Entdeckungen gewonnen* (Berlin, 1812). *Skrifter*, *2*, 35 ff. All citations are from the French translation.

5. Ibid., 155.

6. Ibid., 253.

7. *Skrifter*, 356. It should be noted that there is a slight discrepancy between this account and that given in the announcement of the discovery. In the latter, Oersted mentioned 'last winter' as the time when he first made the experiment. In the *Edinburgh Encyclopaedia* no date was given but Oersted said that he put the experiment aside until July, three months later, which would imply that April was the date of the original discovery. The discrepancy may be resolved simply by assuming a late spring in Denmark in 1820.

8. 'Experiments on the Effect of a Current of Electricity on the Magnetic Needle, by John Christian Oersted, Knight of the Order of Danneborg, Professor of Natural Philosophy, and Secretary of the Royal Society of Copenhagen', *Ann. Phil.*, *16* (1820), 276. I have used the English translation because it is the one which Faraday read. The original Latin version may be consulted in *Skrifter*, *2*, 214.

9. Of the two standard histories of electricity, only one pays any significant attention to Prechtl. In E. Hoppe, *Geschichte der Elektrizität* (Leipzig, 1884), Prechtl is barely mentioned. P. F. Mottelay in his *Bibliographical History of Electricity and Magnetism* (London, 1922), devotes two paragraphs to him without discussing his theory of electromagnetic action.

10. Faraday, as has been mentioned before, did not read German. Prechtl's views were presented in English in the *Q.J.S.*, *13* (1822), 160. In volume 1 of his

annotated copy of W. T. Brande's *Manual of Chemistry* (Wellcome Medical Historical Library), opposite page 57, Faraday has written, 'Prechtl on electromagnetism, R.I. Jour., XIII, 160'.

11. M. Faraday, *Experimental Researches in Electricity* (3 vols., London, 1839–55), (283). Although Prechtl is not mentioned by name here, I think it is clear that his theory is the one being referred to.

12. For Prechtl's most direct expression of his adherence to the basic tenets of *Naturphilosophie,* see 'Auszüge aus Briefen an Gilbert . . . von Hrn. Reg. R. Prechtl' in *Gilbert's Ann. der Physik, 67* (1821), 221.

13. J. J. Prechtl, 'Ueber die Wahre Beschaffenheit des magnetischen Zustandes des Schliessungs-Drahte in der Voltaischen Saule', ibid., 260.

14. *Q.J.S., 13* (1822), 160. This is an exact translation of Prechtl's account in ibid., 264.

15. J. Berzelius, 'Lettre à M. Berthollet sur l'Etat magnétique des corps qui transmettent un courant d'électricité', *Ann. de chim. et de phys.,* 1. Ser., *16* (1821), 113 ff.

16. L. de Launay, ed., *Corréspondance du Grand Ampère* (3 vols., Paris, 1936–43), *2, 566. Ampère to Roux-Bordier l'aîné, Paris 21 février 1821.

17. Quoted in Arago's *éloge* of Ampère in François Arago, *Œuvres Complètes* (12 vols., Paris, 1854–9), *2, 50.

18. Ampère, *Corréspondance, 2, 562.

19. For a more detailed account of Coulomb's position and Ampère's modification of it, see L. Pearce Williams, 'Ampère's Electrodynamic Molecular Model', *Contemporary Physics, 4* (1962), 113 ff.

20. Ampère gives no clue anywhere that I have been able to discover as to what led him to suspect that magnetism was really electricity in motion. My reconstruction of the course of his thought is, therefore, entirely conjectural but it does seem to make sense and shed some light on this fundamental concept.

21. A.-M. Ampère, 'De l'action exercée sur un courant électrique par un autre courant, le globe terrestre ou un aimant', *Ann. de chim. et de phys., 15* (1820), 50. All Ampère's memoirs on electrodynamics have been collected together by the Société française de physique, *Mémoires sur l'électrodynamique* (2 vols., Paris, 1885–7). Henceforth all references will be made to these volumes, cited as *Mém. sur l'élect.*

22. A.-M. Ampère, 'Mémoire sur la théorie mathématique des phénomènes électrodynamiques, uniquement déduite de l'expérience', *Mém. sur l'élect., 2,* 1.

23. Burndy Library, Faraday to Ampère, R.I., 17 November 1825.

24. A.-M. Ampère, 'De l'action exercée . . .', *Mém. sur l'élect., 1,* 48.

25. A. Fresnel, 'Note sur des essais ayant pour but de décomposer l'eau avec un aimant', *Mém. sur l'élect., 1,* 76.

26. Ibid., 77.

27. Ibid.

28. A. Fresnel, 'Comparaison de la supposition des courants autour de l'axe avec celle des courants autour de chaque molécule', *Mém. sur l'élect., 1,* 141.

29. A. Fresnel, 'Deuxième note sur l'hypothèse des courants particulières', *Mém. sur l'élect., 1,* 144.

30. *Mém. sur l'élect., 1,* 140, note. Fresnel's first note to Ampère carries no date

but must be before 15 January 1821, for Ampère referred to it at that time. The second note is dated 4 June 1821.

31. A.-M. Ampère, 'Lettre de M. Ampère à M. le comte Berthollet sur la détermination des proportions dans lesquelles les corps se combinent d'après le nombre et la disposition respective des molécules dont les parties intégrantes sont composées', *Ann. de chim., 90* (1814), 43.

32. At the end of February 1806, Ampère wrote to his friend Roux-Bordier in Geneva:

'Je vous dirai que j'ai tellement changé les idées de Maine Biran au sujet de Kant qu'il me disait ce matin que Kant était le plus grand métaphysicien qui eut jamais existé.' Ampère, *Corréspondance, 1*, 298.

Nowhere in Ampère's correspondence or in his printed papers have I encountered mention of Boscovich or his *Theoria naturalis.*

33. The requirement of a minimum of four atoms to form a molecule of ordinary matter marks Ampère's theory off sharply from Boscovich's. Boscovich's atoms, endowed with the forces of attraction and repulsion, do occupy space; Ampère's atoms, as such, do not. The forces associated with Ampère's atoms, similarly, do not appear to be essential to these atoms. Forces were associated with the atoms but were not *inherent* in them.

34. 'Lettre à Berthollet . . .', *Ann. de chim., 90* (1814), 44. From these ideas Ampère independently deduced Avogadro's hypothesis which stated that equal volumes of gases at the same temperature and pressure contained the same number of molecules. It was this hypothesis which, after 1860, was to supply a clue of fundamental importance to the determination of proper atomic weights, and hence to the unravelling of a large number of chemical reactions.

35. For a technical, and not altogether historically trustworthy, account of theories of the ether see, Sir Edmund Whitaker, *History of the Theories of Aether and Electricity* (2 vols., London, rev. ed., vol. *1*, 1951; vol. *2*, 1953).

36. A.-M. Ampère, 'Réponse à la lettre de M. van Beck, sur une nouvelle expérience électromagnétique', *Mém. sur l'élect., 1*, 216.

37. A.-M. Ampère, 'De l'action exercée . . .', *Mém. sur l'élect., 1*, 10.

38. A.-M. Ampère, 'Exposé summaire des nouvelles expériences électro-magnétiques faites par différents physiciens, depuis le mois de mars 1821, lu dans la séance publique de l'Académie royale des sciences, le 8 avril 1822', *Mém. sur l'élect., 1, 249.*

39. A.-M. Ampère, 'Extrait d'une mémoire sur les phénomènes électro-dynamiques', *Mém. sur l'élect., 1, 404.*

40. A.-M. Ampère, 'Réponse à la lettre de M. van Beck . . .', *Mém. sur l'élect., 1*, 214.

41. Ibid., 215.

42. Ibid., 217.

43. Ibid.

44. 'Idées de Mr Ampère sur la chaleur et sur la lumière', *Bibliothèque Universelle, 49* (1832), 225.

45. M. Faraday, 'On the History of the Condensation of the Gases in repiy to Dr Davy, introduced by some remarks on that of Electro-magnetic Rotation'. *Phil. Mag., N.S., 8* (1836), 521.

46. Sir H. Davy, 'On the Magnetic Phenomena produced by Electricity. In a Letter to W. H. Wollaston, M.D., F.R.S.', Davy, *Works*, *6*, 217. The letter was read before the Royal Society, 16 November 1820, and was published in the *Phil. Trans.* for 1821.

47. M. Faraday, 'On the History of the Condensation of the Gases . . .', *Phil. Mag.*, N.S., *8* (1836), 525.

48. 'On the Connexion of Electric and Magnetic Phaenomena', *Q.J.S.*, *10* (1820–1), 363. This article is attributed to Faraday in the Catalogue of the Wheeler Gift. Faraday, however, states quite explicitly that it was by the editor of the *Q.J.S.*, William T. Brande. See 'On the History of the Condensation of the Gases . . .', 522.

49. B.J., *1*, 342. Faraday to Mr Stodart, R.I., Monday, 8 October 1821.

50. The only entry previous to the period when he took up electromagnetism seriously is a very short one describing the effect of a horseshoe magnet upon the electric arc. *Diary*, *1*, 45. This is not altogether conclusive evidence for his lack of interest since there are large gaps in the *Diary* for these early years.

51. 'Historical Sketch of Electro-magnetism', *Ann. of Phil.*, N.S., *2* (1821), 195.

52. Ibid., 196.

53. Ibid., 197. My italics.

54. Ibid., N.S., *3* (1822), 107.

55. Ibid., 108.

56. Ibid., 111.

57. Ibid.

58. Ibid., 112.

59. Ibid., 116.

60. Ibid., 117.

61. *Diary*, *1*, 49. 3 September 1821.

62. Ibid., 50.

63. The first crude apparatus is described in the *Diary*, *1*, 50 ff. The more elegant apparatus which Faraday presented to the world was built by Mr Newman, a scientific instrument maker, and was pictured in the *Q.J.S.*, *12* (1821), 186 and later reprinted in *Exp. Res.*, *2*, 147.

64. For these objections, see below, p. 167.

65. M. Faraday, 'Historical Statement respecting Electro-Magnetic Rotation', *Q.J.S.*, *15* (1823), 288. *Exp. Res.*, *2*, 159 ff. All citations are from the article in *Exp. Res.*

66. Ibid., 160.

67. Even the Fellows of the Royal Society, in 1821, could not always be relied upon to discover scientific distinctions. For an account of the general level of scientific achievement among the F.R.S. in the first quarter of the nineteenth century, see L. Pearce Williams, 'The Royal Society and the Founding of the British Association for the Advancement of Science', *Notes and Records of the Royal Society*, *16* (1961), 221 ff.

68. B.J., *1*, 339, Faraday to James Stodart, R.I., 8 October 1821.

69. Ibid., 340.

70. Ibid.

71. Ibid., 341.

72. B.J., *1*, 344, Wollaston to Faraday, 1 November [1821].

73. 'Historical Statement respecting Electro-Magnetic Rotation', *Exp. Res.*, *2*, 160.

74. B.J., *1*, 346.

75. B.J., *1*, 379.

76. M. Faraday, 'On some new Electro-Magnetic Motions, and on the Theory of Magnetism', *Exp. Res.*, *2*, 132.

77. Ibid., 138.

78. Ibid., 139.

79. Ibid.

80. Ibid., 141.

81. Ibid., 140.

82. Ibid., 144.

83. *Diary*, *1*, 56.

84. Ibid., *1*, 51.

85. *Exp. Res.*, *2*, 131.

86. Bib. pub. et univ. de Génève, MS. 2311, 28 A4, f. 61, Faraday to G. de la Rive, R.I., 12 September 1821. Reproduced (in part) in B.J., *1*, 354.

87. Ibid.

88. Reprinted in *Mém. sur l'élect.*, *1*, 184 ff.

89. Ibid.

90. Ibid., 185.

91. Bib. pub. et univ. de Génève, MS. 2311, 28 A4, f. 65, Faraday to G. de la Rive, R.I., 9 October 1822.

92. The account of his experiments was published in 1822. A.-M. Ampère, 'Expériences relatives aux nouveaux phénomènes électrodynamiques obtenus au mois de decembre 1821', *Ann. de chim. et de phys.*, *20* (1822), 60 ff. *Mém. sur l'élect.*, *1*, 192.

93. Darmstaedter Collection, Preussische Staatsbibliothek, Marburg. Faraday to Ampère, R.I., 2 February 1821. The date is obviously wrong and should be 1822 – a common error in the early months of a new year. This letter has been published, in full, 'A Holograph Letter of Faraday Communicated by Professor L. Darmstaedter', *Trans. of the Newcomen Society*, *3* (1922–3), 119, but as there are a number of small errors in transcribing it, I have followed the original.

94. *Procès-verbaux des séances de l'Académie tenues depuis la fondation de l'Institut jusqu'au mois d'août 1835*, *8* (1824–7), 158.

F. Arago, 'Note concernant les phénomènes magnétiques auxquels le mouvement donne naissance', *Ann. de chim. et de phys.*, 2 ser., *32* (1826), 213 ff.

Samuel Hunter Christie, 'On the Magnetism of Iron arising from its rotation', *Phil. Trans.*, 1825, 347.

Peter Barlow, 'On the temporary magnetic effect induced in iron bodies by rotation. In a letter to J. F. W. Herschel, Esq., Sec. R.S. Communicated April 14, 1825', *Phil. Trans.*, 1825, 317.

95. B.M.Add.MS. 37183, f. 196. Biot to Charles Babbage, Paris, 11 November 1825.

96. A.-M. Ampère, 'Mémoire sur la théorie mathématique des phénomènes

électromagnétiques, uniquement déduite de l'expérience', in *Mém. sur l'élect.*, *2*, 169.

97. C. Babbage and J. F. W. Herschel, 'Account of the repetition of M. Arago's experiments on the magnetism manifested by various substances during the act of rotation', *Phil. Trans.*, 1825, 467 ff.

98. Ibid., 471.

99. Ibid., 481.

100. Ibid., 484.

101. Ibid., 487.

102. R.I., *Davy's Laboratory Notebook*, 30 November 1825.

103. Ibid. These experiments are imperfectly described in *Diary*, *1*, 280.

104. Ibid., 25 November 1825.

105. *Diary*, 71. 10 September 1822.

106. For these truly beautiful memoirs, see Henri de Senarmont, Emile Verdet, and Leonor Fresnel, eds., *Œuvres Complètes d'Augustin Fresnel* (3 vols., Paris, 1866–70). The best account of Fresnel's life and work is still Verdet's 'Introduction aux œuvres d'Augustin Fresnel', *Œuvres*, *1*, ix.

107. Deutsches Museum, Faraday to Eilhard Mitscherlich, R.I., 4 August 1830.

108. *Q.J.S.*, *25* (1828), 173.

109. *Q.J.S.*, *27* (1829), 379.

110. *Q.J.S.*, *29* (1830), 406.

111. *Q.J.S.*, *27* (1829), 383.

112. *Diary*, *1*, 329 ff.

113. J. F. W. Herschel, *A Preliminary Discourse on the Study of Natural Philosophy* (London, 1830). I have used the 1835 edition which does not differ materially from that of 1830.

114. Royal Society, Faraday-Herschel Letters, Faraday to J. F. W. Herschel, R.I., 10 November 1832.

115. *L. & E. Phil. Mag.*, N.S., *2* (1833), 391.

116. Herschel, op. cit., 94. See also 181, 242, 246, 248.

117. Ibid., 248.

118. Ibid., 249.

119. H. C. Oersted, 'Sur la propagation de l'électricité', *J. de Physique*, *62* (1806), 369 ff. In German in *Skrifter*, *1*, 267.

120. Faraday had noted the English account which appeared in *Nich. Jour.*, *15* (1806), 166. See Faraday's annotated copy of Brande's *Manual of Chemistry*, opp. p. 40 (Wellcome Medical Historical Library).

121. *Diary*, *1*, 330, 334.

122. For Savart's work, which Herschel had singled out for particular praise, see Félix Savart, 'Recherches sur les vibrations normales', *Ann. de chim. et de phys.*, 2 ser., *36* (1827), 187.

123. M. Faraday, 'On a Peculiar Class of Acoustical Figures; and on certain Forms assumed by groups of particles upon vibrating elastic Surfaces', *Phil. Trans.*, 1831, 299. Reprinted in and cited from M. F., *Exp. Res. in Chem. and Phys.*, 318.

124. *Diary*, *1*, 337.

125. Royal Society MSS.

126. 'Powerful Electro-magnet constructed by Professor Moll', *Jour. R.I.*, *1*, (1831), 379. See also 609 for an account of the new electromagnet constructed by Joseph Henry.

127. *Diary*, *1*, 56. 8 September 1821.

128. Ibid., 367.

129. Ibid.

130. Ibid.

131. Ibid., 369, my italics.

CHAPTER FIVE

The Nature of Electricity (1)

1. Conditions of the Induction of Electrical Currents

In August of 1831, Faraday had only the slightest intimation of the vast new territory he had opened up. His concern then was to determine as carefully and precisely as possible the causes of the momentary deflection of the galvanometer needle. The first problem that presented itself was to make sure that the galvanometer deflection was caused by electricity, and not some other force. This was no easy task. The effect was so transient that it was exceedingly difficult to study it. No spark could be observed [I–15]; when solutions were placed in the circuit, no chemical decomposition occurred [I–11, 41]. The 'interference of fluid conductors' he thought, 'is enough to stop the wave' [I–41]. He finally had to be satisfied with the transient magnetic effects that could be obtained [I–51] as proof that he was actually dealing with electrical forces. This would have to do for the moment, but it did not really satisfy him. Until he could prove that the effects he was observing were truly electrical there would be an element of uncertainty in his conclusions. Although he did not pause in 1831 to insure the identity of electricities drawn from all sources, he did return to it in 1832 and establish this fact beyond a doubt (265 ff.).

The major question was how the electric wave was generated. Here we see Faraday at his most brilliant, carefully altering circumstances and tracking the facts down until he could enunciate a general law. In the original experiment, Faraday had assumed that the presence of the iron ring was necessary since the iron would intensify the 'strain' and make it detectable. After assuring himself of the reality of the effect, Faraday immediately proceeded to vary the conditions. A number of arrangements of wire were made. These consisted of a flat spiral of covered iron wire containing about 6 feet; a double flat spiral of similar wire about 19 feet long; a spiral of uncovered copper wire of 14 feet in length; a cylindrical round solid helix of covered iron wire containing about 12 feet, and

another with 31 feet of wire; a coil of covered iron wire 35 feet long and
2½ inches mean diameter forming a thick ring: this was then covered by a
helix at right angles to it of two lengths of copper wire 40 feet long; a
short cylinder of iron ⅞ inches thick and 4 inches long around which was
coiled a helix containing 56 feet of wire. With this collection of hollow
helices, spirals, rings, and bars, Faraday began to close in on the cause
of electromagnetic induction. The spirals were similar to the ones he had
used in his work on electromagnetic rotations (see above, Chapter Four,
Figure 5), where he had shown that the magnetic power of an electric
current was greatest at the centre of the spiral. This being so, he now tried
to induce a current in the spiral by subjecting the centre of the spiral
to magnetic forces. The spiral was placed on the table and connected to a
galvanometer. A permanent magnet was then held, pole down, at the
centre of the spiral and suddenly moved away. Nothing happened
[I–25]. The spiral was then put between the N and S poles of two bar
magnets whose opposite poles were in contact. Again nothing happened
(Figure 1). When a copper spiral was substituted for the iron one, there

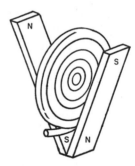

Fig. 1

was still no effect [I–26, 27]. The rationale of these experiments is clear.
Faraday was simply trying to utilize the symmetry of the situation. When
a current flowed, the most intense magnetism was at the centre of the
spiral. Hence a magnet moving towards and away from the centre of the
spiral should give rise to a current. Or, an intense magnetic field (i.e.
from poles on each side of the spiral) ought to induce a current. Faraday
had almost captured the fundamental idea, but not quite. In the one case
he saw the necessity of motion but in the other he had returned again to
his concept of strain.

   On 24 September, the same day as he had performed the above experiments, he was successful but the success still masked the true cause of the

phenomenon. The successful experiment utilized the iron cylinder wound with copper wire. When this was placed lengthwise between the poles of two bar magnets and contact with the cylinder and the magnets made and broken, a current was generated (Figure 2). Faraday triumphantly noted: 'Hence here distinct conversion of Magnetism into Electricity' [I–33]. The experiment is an interesting one for it really served more to becloud the cause of the induced current than to illuminate it. As depicted

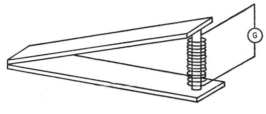

Fig. 2

by Faraday, it was a *magnetic* circuit and Faraday treated it as such. The interposition of the iron bar between the two poles converted the bar magnets, in Faraday's eyes, into a ring and he was working essentially with the original induction apparatus. The only difference was that he was using permanent magnets rather than an electromagnet. Assuming, however, that permanent and electromagnetism were both the result of intermolecular strains of some kind, the effect was to be expected. When the iron rod was placed in the magnetic circuit, the strain was set up and an induced current momentarily existed. This was why Faraday noted the making and breaking of the *magnetic* circuit. 'Every time the magnetic contact at N or S was made or broken there was magnetic motion at the indicating helix, the effect being as in former cases not permanent, but a mere momentary push or pull' [I–33].

The next step followed logically from this experiment. Since induced currents were generated by the conduction of the magnetic strain, what would happen if substances other than iron were used to conduct this strain? When a block of wood was substituted for the iron, the effect was very small. From this experiment Faraday concluded, 'there is an inducing effect without the presence of iron, but it is either very weak or else so sudden as not to have time to move the needle. I rather suspect it is the latter' [I–39]. The particles of iron served to slow the wave down so that it was detectable. The transmission of the force, it should be noted, was from particle to particle, moving far faster in wood or air than in the iron.

The picture was slowly becoming clearer in Faraday's mind. He could now produce induced currents at will. He was becoming more and more convinced of the reality of the strain whose hypothetical existence had started him off on these researches [I–51]. By October he knew that the strain, in and of itself, was not a sufficient condition for the production of induced electrical currents. As he repeated his experiments, it became obvious that it was the *change* in the strain that created the currents. Even the experiment with the wound iron rod in the magnetic circuit showed this. On 17 October 1831, Faraday attacked the problem directly.

> O a cylinder, hollow, of paper, covered with 8 helices of copper wire going in the same direction. . . .
> Expts. with O. The 8 ends of the helices at one end of the cylinder were cleaned and fastened together as a bundle. So were the 8 other ends. These compound ends were then connected with the Galvanometer by long copper wires – then a cylindrical bar magnet $\frac{3}{4}$ inch in diameter and $8\frac{1}{2}$ inches in length had one end just inserted into the end of the helix cylinder – then it was quickly thrust in the whole length and *the galvanometer* needle moved – then pulled out and again the *needle moved but* in the opposite direction. This effect was repeated every time the magnet was put in or out and therefore a wave of Electricity was so produced from *mere approximation of a magnet* and not from its formation *in situ* [I–56, 57].

This was the discovery of magneto-electric induction and was quite different from the discovery of electromagnetic induction. Up to this point, Faraday had been thinking in terms solely of magnetic circuits (as in the ring) through which the magnetic force could be conveyed. The set-up for electromagnetic induction was a means of detecting this wave of force. Magneto-electric induction (the term is Faraday's) was something quite different. It was the creation of a wave of electrical force, not by a wave of magnetic force, but by the mere approximation of a magnet. The inducing force, whatever it might ultimately prove to be, could no longer be looked upon simply as an intermolecular strain. It extended continuously for some distance from the particles of the magnet, yet seemed obviously dependent upon these particles. Whatever peculiar state the particles of a magnet were in, the forces associated with this state extended into the medium surrounding the magnet. The line of force which Faraday had just dimly recognized in his 1821 researches, was becoming ever more real and important.

The basic conditions for the induction of electrical currents were now evident. One needed a magnetic field and the relative motion of magnet and conductor. Pulsating currents could be produced by pushing and pulling a magnet into and out of a helix. Would it be possible to create steady currents by substituting rotary for reciprocating motion? This was

what Faraday set out to discover at the end of October. A copper disc
was rotated between the poles of a magnet and contacts on the edge of
the wheel were made to lead the current (if any) to a galvanometer. All
different kinds of positions of these leads were tried and their effect upon
the current noted (Figure 3). The effect upon the galvanometer was steady

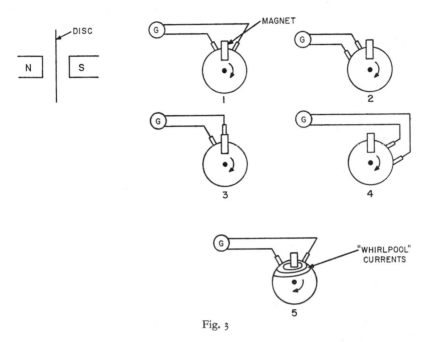

Fig. 3

but feeble. The placement of the leads was intended to find areas of large
current-density but none were to be discovered. Faraday was here looking
for a type of current that did not exist. He felt that the currents should be
like whirlpools, swirling *around* the magnetic poles as centre (Figure 3).
The leads, by completing the circuit should reveal them in all their
power.[1] A most careful search had failed to reveal them and so Faraday
tried another tack.

> Suspected from all this that a single conductor would do more than two, and
> that the condensed imaginary bisected vortex was not so definite as supposed,
> if existing at all. The wire coming from the upper coils of the Galvanometer
> was therefore fastened round the brass axis of the plate as the most neutral
> part of it, and the conductor from the other wire end applied to the edge of
> the wheel [I–116] (Figure 4).

Various other arrangements were investigated [I–116 ff.] and the effects
noted. The results were presented with such little fanfare that it was

impossible to realize at the time the revolution in man's life that would be worked by future developments of this apparatus. In his first paper on *Experimental Researches in Electricity* Faraday simply stated: 'Here, therefore, was demonstrated the production of a permanent current of electricity by ordinary magnets' (90). What Faraday had invented was the

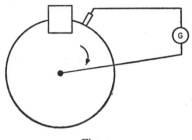

Fig. 4

dynamo. From this simple laboratory toy was to come the whole of the electric power industry and the benefits to everyone that have followed upon the ability to transport electricity to even the smallest village or farm. At the time, of course, no one could foresee all this. Faraday did realize that here was a possible source of cheap electric current, but he was too immersed in discovery to think of pursuing the practical aspects. 'I have rather . . .', he wrote, 'been desirous of discovering new facts and new relations dependent on magneto-electric induction, than of exalting the force of those already obtained; being assured that the latter would find their full development hereafter' (159). The story is told that Sir Robert Peel, the Prime Minister, visited Faraday in the laboratory of the Royal Institution soon after the invention of the dynamo. Pointing to this odd machine, he inquired of what use it was. Faraday is said to have replied, 'I know not, but I wager that one day your government will tax it.' It was to be long after Sir Robert and Faraday had died that this prophecy came true for it was not until after the 1880's that the electrical power industry became large enough to attract the eye of the Treasury.

For Faraday, the dynamo's importance lay in the light that it shed upon that most puzzling phenomenon – Arago's wheel. The induction of currents in the disc immediately explained 'magnetization by rotation' and removed the mystery which had surrounded this peculiar effect since 1824. When a metallic disc was rotated beneath a freely suspended magnetic needle, currents were induced in it. These currents, in turn, created a magnetic field which acted upon the needle. This was why Babbage and Herschel found that only conductors of electricity were subject to magnetization by rotation. It also explained why, when electrical continuity was destroyed by cutting slits in the discs, the effect was destroyed; for if the currents could not be freely generated their accompanying magnetic field could not develop. When continuity was restored by the use of solder, the effect was restored. Metallic powders put in the slits only partially restored the effect for their high electrical resistance cut the strength of the current and hence of the magnetic field. Faraday was able to show that all the observed effects could now be referred to the simple and well-known effects of electricity and magnetism (120 ff.).

By November 1831 Faraday felt he had sufficient material to lay before the Royal Society. On 24 November the First Series of the *Experimental Researches in Electricity* was read to his colleagues in Somerset House. The paper was severely factual, carefully reporting results and concealing almost all the theoretical concepts which had guided him. Even the order of reporting his results was shuffled, so that he could make his points in a more logical fashion. Only occasionally (with but one exception to be noted) did a theoretical idea peep through. As in 1821, it was Ampère who occasioned these remarks. In public, Faraday exercised the utmost caution and his tribute to Ampère's abilities was most carefully couched. He warned his reader at the very beginning that he was still not willing to accept Ampère's ideas. 'Whether Ampère's beautiful theory were adopted, or any other, or whatever reservation were mentally made' (3), was the way he introduced his statement of the probability he had always felt of finding induced currents. The same reservation was held in a passage which praised Ampère.

'The similarity of action, almost amounting to identity, between common magnets and either electro-magnets or volta-electric currents, is strikingly in accordance with and confirmatory of M. Ampère's theory, and furnishes powerful reasons for believing that the action is the same in both cases . . .' (58).

From the *Diary*, it was obvious that Faraday was not thinking along the same lines as Ampère's theory indicated. Actually, this passage was quite explicit, including a fine but necessary distinction. 'Ampère's theory' here can refer only to the identity of electric and magnetic action and this we know Faraday accepted. Moreover, that is just what he said in the phrase, 'that the action is the same in both cases'. It was not intended to be an endorsement of Ampère's electric fluids or electrodynamic molecules. Faraday even went a bit out of his way to point out insufficiencies in Ampère's theory (38). What he appeared to wish to do was to avoid controversy by praising Ampère, at the same time that he developed the results of his own ideas. The sealed note at the Royal Society shows that he was not ready yet to affirm publicly his own views on the nature of electricity and magnetism. By using only that part of Ampère's theory which insisted upon the identity of electricity and magnetism, he was able to present his findings in an easily understandable way, evade a dispute which could be expected to shed little light on the subject at this time, and preserve a line of research to be pursued by himself alone.

Although he carefully refrained from injecting theoretical concepts into his account, there was one effect explicable only in theoretical terms. Here Faraday revealed just how far he was from Ampère's ideas.

The puzzling phenomenon was one that he had noticed from the very beginning. This was the creation of a current when the current in the primary ceased. His explanation of this was one of the ideas which was to guide him through twenty years of research, and to which he was to return time and time again.

> Whilst the wire is subject to either volta-electric or magneto-electric induction, it appears to be in a peculiar state; for it resists the formation of an electrical current in it, whereas, if in its common condition, such a current would be produced; and when left uninfluenced it has the power of originating a current, a power which the wire does not possess under common circumstances. This electrical condition of matter has not hitherto been recognized, but it probably exerts a very important influence in many if not most of the phenomena produced by currents of electricity. For reasons which will immediately appear (71), I have, after advising with several learned friends,[2] ventured to designate it as the *electro-tonic* state.
>
> This peculiar condition shows no known electrical effects whilst it continues; nor have I yet been able to discover any peculiar powers exerted, or properties possessed, by matter whilst retained in this state.
>
> It shows no reaction by attractive or repulsive powers. The various experiments which have been made with powerful magnets upon such metals as copper, silver, and generally those substances not magnetic, prove this point; for the substances experimented upon, if electrical conductors, must have acquired this state; and yet no evidence of attractive or repulsive powers has been observed (60–62).

This is a very peculiar position to find Faraday in. His objections to Ampère's theory had been based on a suspicion of hypothetical entities that had to be deduced from experiment. Yet, here was Faraday suggesting a hypothetical state into which all conducting substances were thrown when under magnetic influence. The state had the very embarrassing property of being totally undetectable! Faraday, nevertheless, clung to it and never gave up looking for evidence of its existence. He was alternately to reject it and then, almost immediately, try once more to detect it. The reason will become obvious as Faraday's ideas unfold before us. The electrotonic state was absolutely fundamental to his ideas on electricity and magnetism. Without it, he would have been forced back to fluids which he was now thoroughly convinced did not exist. With it he could unravel all the mysteries of electricity. In spite of its undetectability, therefore, Faraday held it firmly in his mind.

Although it was undetectable, Faraday had some fairly precise ideas on what the electrotonic state was.

This peculiar state [he wrote] appears to be a state of tension, and may be considered as *equivalent* to a current of electricity, at least equal to that produced either when the condition is induced or destroyed. The current evolved, however, first or last, is not to be considered a measure of the degree of tension to which the electro-tonic state has risen; for as the metal retains its conducting powers unimpaired (65), and as the electricity evolved is but for a moment, (the peculiar state being instantly assumed and lost (68)), the electricity which may be led away by long wire conductors, offering obstruction in their substance proportionate to their small lateral and extensive linear dimensions, can be but a very small portion of that really evolved within the mass at the moment it assumes this condition (71).

Once again, Faraday was at pains to point out the experimental facts that illustrated that the electrotonic state could be measured. If it is a state of tension, can we at least be informed of what is being strained? Faraday can and does answer, but the answer revealed his own hesitancy and uncertainty.

All the results favour the notion that the electro-tonic state relates to the particles, and not to the mass, of the wire or substance under induction, being in that respect different to the induction exerted by electricity of tension. If so, the state may be assumed in liquids when no electrical current is sensible, and even in non-conductors; the current itself, when it occurs, being as it were a contingency due to the existence of conducting power, and the momentary propulsive force exerted by the particles during their arrangement. Even when conducting power is equal, the currents of electricity, which as yet are the only indicators of this state, may be unequal, because of differences as to number, size, electrical condition, etc. etc., in the particles themselves. It will only be after the laws which govern this new state are ascertained, that we shall be able to predict what is the true condition of, and what are the electrical results obtainable from, any particular substance (73).

With this description, fuzzy and muddled as it is, it was now possible for Faraday to understand the odd behaviour of the induction ring. When the current first passed in the primary, it threw the ring into the electrotonic state. This was what caused the galvanometer to deflect. When the current ceased to flow in the primary, the electrotonic state collapsed (i.e. the tension or strain was removed) and the collapse caused the deflection of the galvanometer in the opposite direction. From this, it was possible to hazard a guess on the nature of the electric current. A current might be the rapid build up and break down of the electrotonic state. A wave of strain, transmitted from particle to particle, was what passed down a wire. The strain, too, Faraday suggested, may exist in liquids. The electrotonic state was what he had been looking for back in 1822 when he passed polarized light through an electrolytic solution. It now had more evidence in its favour and Faraday was beginning to see how it might act. As he wrote to his friend Phillips:

> The new electrical condition which intervenes by induction between the beginning and end of the inducing current gives rise to some very curious results. It explains why chemical action or other results of electricity have never been as yet obtained in trials with the magnet. In fact, the currents have no sensible duration. I believe it will explain perfectly the *transference of elements* between the poles of the pile in decomposition. But this part of the subject I have reserved until the present experiments are completed. . . .[3]

Here spoke Faraday the chemist. It was not until 1833 that he was able to turn to the analysis of electrochemical decomposition, but he was to show then how the electrotonic state did, indeed, explain perfectly the transference of elements.

In November 1831 the fertility of the concept of the electrotonic state was not yet apparent. Faraday's ideas were still imprecise and it was with some relief that he left this hypothetical section and returned to the solid ground of experimental fact. Having described all the experiments, he then turned to the law of the production of magneto-electric induction. Here, for the first time, Faraday used the concept and term, line of magnetic force. 'By magnetic curves', he wrote, 'I mean the lines of magnetic forces, however modified by the juxtaposition of poles, which would be depicted by iron filings; or those to which a very small magnetic needle would form a tangent.'[4] The direction and strength of a current was determined by the direction and speed of a conductor passing across these lines of force (114). When put into mathematical form by Clerk Maxwell some forty years later, this law served as the basis of the study of electrical power generation.

The First Series of *Experimental Researches* had been a prodigious achievement. Faraday had, at one and the same time, cleared away a mass of confusion that had threatened to stifle the growth of electrical science. The long-sought converse of Oersted's discovery had been found; the problem of Arago's wheel had been solved; valuable new clues to the nature of electricity and magnetism had been uncovered. Faraday's fame was assured and he had many new leads to follow in his own investigations. He had every reason to be happy and contented, but his achievement was marred by an incident that awakened many bitter memories.

After having read his paper to the Royal Society he had written to Charles Hachette of the French Academy of Sciences, announcing in general terms, the gist of his discoveries. An abbreviated and somewhat garbled version of his letter appeared in the *Annales de chimie et de physique* and *Le Lycée* in Paris.[5] Two Italian physicists, Nobili and Antinori, read this account and immediately set out to explore the exciting new domain opened up by Faraday. Their results, fully acknowledging Faraday's priority, appeared in the *Antologia di Firenze* in the spring of 1832. Unfortunately, the issue of the *Antologia* was dated November 1831 and appeared to antedate Faraday's paper which was not printed in the *Philosophical Transactions* until 1832. It looked as though Nobili and Antinori had discovered electromagnetic induction before Faraday, even though the attentive reader would soon realize the truth. Not all readers were attentive. The editor of the *Literary Gazette* stated rather explicitly that Faraday had been forestalled.[6] This was really too much. Faraday had seen the brilliance of his discovery of electromagnetic rotations tarnished by the charge of plagiarism. Now credit for the most important discovery in electricity and magnetism since Oersted's was to be given over to two other scientists who had merely repeated his experiments! Faraday had to set the record straight. To the editor of the *Literary Gazette*, he wrote:

Will you let me call your attention for a moment to the article Electricity and Magnetism at P. 185 of your last Gazette. You there give an account of Nobili's experiments and speak of them as if independent of or any thing but a repetition of mine. But if you had seen Nobili's paper you would have found that my name is on every page; that the experiments in it were a consequence of his having seen a copy of my letter to Paris, which letter he translates into Italian and inserts, and that he tried and obtained the spark with the magnet, because in my letter, I said that I had obtained the spark in a particular case. Nobili, so far from wishing to imply that the experiments and discovery are his, honors me by speaking of the 'nuove correnti di Faraday'.

I should not have noticed the matter but that in the Gazette it is said 'researches of Mr Faraday which were rapidly tending to the same discovery' whereas they are my own experiments which having gone first to Paris and then to Italy have been repeated and studied by Signori Nobili and Antinori....

Excuse my troubling you with this letter, but I never took more pains to be quite independent of other persons than in the present investigation; and I have never been more annoyed about any paper than the present by the variety of circumstances which have arisen seeming to imply that I had been anticipated.[7]

The idea that he had been anticipated persisted and even grew and Faraday felt it necessary to take extreme measures to prevent it from being accepted. Nobili's and Antinori's paper was translated and published in the *Philosophical Magazine* with notes provided by Faraday in which he set the record straight in no uncertain terms.[8] Still later (1 December 1832) he felt it necessary to write to Gay-Lussac, one of the editors of the *Annales de chimie et de physique*, to request that he publish an account of the discovery of magneto-electric induction.[9] The rumours finally died but much of the joy of discovery had been ruined for Faraday by this incident. Henceforth, he was to be very taciturn in scientific matters. His discoveries were announced by publication, not by private letters to friends.

The proof of his priority, if any were needed, were the papers that continued to flow from the Royal Institution. Faraday had realized that his discoveries in the summer and autumn of 1831 were just the beginning of a long train – hence the title, First Series of *Experimental Researches in Electricity*. Throughout the winter and the spring of 1832 he had continued to work and the Second and Third Series soon appeared in the *Phil. Trans.*

2. The Birth of the Field Concept

After having read his paper to the Royal Society, Faraday plunged back into his magneto-electric researches. His investigation now began to branch off along different lines of inquiry, all of which he worked on at the same time. Basically there were three problems that he wished to solve: he wanted, first of all, to study the production of magneto-electric currents in more detail for there were still some points that bothered him. Then he was fascinated by the contemplation of the earth's magnetic field. He saw the earth as a gigantic magnet spinning on its axis. The effects of this motion must be noticeable and he set out to detect the currents which he was positive were generated by the earth's rotation. Finally, as his ideas grew more precise and his concepts of the nature of electricity matured, he became anxious to prove, once for all, that electricity, no matter how produced, was always the same thing. Then, he hoped, he could show how the diversity of electrical effects could be produced from the unity of the electrical force.

In the earliest investigations of induced currents, Faraday had shown that when a conductor cut the magnetic lines of force, a current was generated. At that time, he had used only solid conductors. Now, to complete the search, he turned to fluid conductors. The results were rather surprising.

A glass dish was mounted on the whirling table, a pole above and below –
then solution put into the dish. The solutions whirled and conductors of
platina introduced into them on each side the place of the pole; but no sensible
current could be obtained when brine and sulphate of copper solution were
used.

   Another form of the experiment was a bent tube into which S[ulphuric]
A[cid] was put, and then the tube, with wires A and B inserted, passed between the poles; but no action took place [I–172–3].

That there should have been some current produced seemed to follow
from the law of induction (114) but there was, of course, one significant
difference. If the electric current were a result of intermolecular strain,
perhaps fluid molecules, which by definition could easily slip over one
another, could not take up the proper stress. It was a point to keep in
mind and Faraday was to return to it later in his work on electrochemistry.
It was such anomalies that provided him with many clues to electrical
action. In December 1831, and the early months of 1832, however, Faraday was primarily interested in those cases where currents were produced.
Specifically he wanted now to determine 'whether it was essential or not
that the moving part of the wire should, in cutting the magnetic curves,
pass into positions of greater or lesser magnetic force; or whether, always
intersecting curves of equal magnetic intensity, the mere motion was
sufficient for the production of the current' (217). To determine the
answer, Faraday took a copper disc and insulating its bottom side with
paper, affixed it to one pole of an ordinary bar magnet. Leads were
attached to the centre and edge of the disc, and the whole thing (disc
and magnet) were rotated around the magnetic axis by means of a cord
passed around the magnet (Figure 5). A current was produced. Then the
disc and the magnet were separated and the magnet alone rotated. No

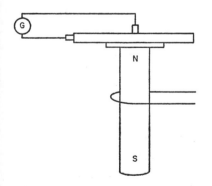
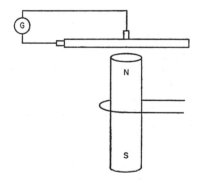

Fig. 5

current was produced [I–255–7] (218). The point was thereby nicely proven for when the disc and magnet were rotated together, there could *not* be movement into regions of larger or smaller magnetic force. The experiment also offered confirmation of the general law of induced currents. As Faraday noted in his *Diary*: 'Hence it appears that, of the metal circuit in which the current is to be formed, different parts must move with different angular velocities' [I–257].

This experiment led him to an even more elegant illustration. A copper cylinder was fixed over the pole of the magnet and the magnet was then dipped into a narrow bottle of mercury. When the magnet and cylinder were now rotated together, a current was formed [I–258]. No disc was required. Indeed, Faraday immediately saw that not even the copper sheath was necessary. 'That the metal of the magnet itself might be substituted for the moving cylinder, disc, or wire, seemed an inevitable consequence, and yet one which would exhibit the effects of magneto-electric induction in a striking form' (220). Accordingly, a little cup into which mercury could be placed was made in the top of the magnet in order to make good electrical contact. The magnet was then rotated and a current produced [I–262–3] (220). These experiments were far more than 'striking', and confirmatory of the conclusions Faraday had drawn from his law of induction. The fact that when the disc or sheath or just the magnet alone was rotated *with* the magnet a current was produced indicated that magnetic curves were being cut. From this only one conclusion could be drawn: the curves or lines of force *did not* rotate with the magnet. Faraday saw this and expressed it with some surprise. 'Thus a *singular independence* of the magnetism and the bar in which it resides is rendered evident' (220). The line of force, which had begun in 1821 as a handy way of visualizing the path that an isolated magnetic pole would follow, had now become much more real. It was an actual entity, somehow associated with matter, but also independent of it. To comprehend this strange entity, Faraday now had to divide his attention between the matter in which the lines of force were seated, and the space surrounding the magnet in which the lines of force acted. It goes without saying that this new property of magnetism appeared incompatible with Ampère's theory, for there the magnetic forces were tied to the molecules of the magnet; when these molecules moved the lines of force had to move with them.[10]

This peculiar situation had great influence upon the course of Faraday's thought. In the same paper in which Faraday noted the independence of the magnetic lines of force, he also introduced a new concept. This was the idea of the field of force generated in time and extending progressively through space. After pointing out that the magnetic curves surrounding a current-carrying wire were exactly analogous to the lines of force surrounding a magnet, Faraday then explained why the starting and stopping of a current in one wire would induce a current in a neighbouring one.

In the first experiments (10, 13), [he wrote] the inducing wire and that under induction were arranged at a fixed distance from each other, and then an electric current sent through the former. In such cases the magnetic curves themselves must be considered as moving (if I may use the expression) across the wire under induction, from the moment at which they begin to be developed until the magnetic force of the current is at its utmost; expanding as it were from the wire outwards, and consequently being in the same relation to the fixed wire under induction as if *it* had moved in the opposite direction across them, or towards the wire carrying the current. Hence the first current induced in such cases was in the contrary direction to the principal current (17, 235). On breaking the battery contact, the magnetic curves (which are mere expressions for arranged magnetic forces) may be conceived as contracting upon and returning towards the failing electrical current, and therefore move in the opposite direction across the wire, and cause an opposite induced current to the first ... (238).

Thus the reasons which induce me to suppose a particular state in the wire (60) have disappeared ... (242).

The abandonment of the 'electrotonic state' appeared to be a necessary consequence of the discovery of the independence of the magnetic curves. He had first assumed that some kind of *material* strain had to exist in order to explain induction when a circuit was broken. He had, however, been quite unhappy with the fact that he had not been able to detect this strain. No such problem existed with the magnetic lines of force. These were clearly strains that could be detected by the use of iron filings. Of their existence, there could be no doubt. What now had to be assumed was the propagation of this force through space (i.e. the build-up and collapse of the field). The electrotonic state gave way to the field. Faraday bade goodbye to his early hypothesis of internal strain with considerable regret. But abandon it he must, for 'though it still seems to me unlikely that a wire at rest in the neighbourhood of another carrying a powerful electric current is entirely indifferent to it, yet I am not aware of any distinct *facts* which authorize the conclusion that it is in a particular state' (242).

The independence of the lines of force introduced a new element into Faraday's researches. For the next thirty years he was to search for essentially two things: the way in which electric and magnetic forces were transmitted through space, and the relation between these forces and ponderable matter. It is no exaggeration to say that a fundamentally new

way of looking at physical reality was introduced into science in this
Second Series of the *Experimental Researches*. Hitherto all that had been
really attended to was the effects of forces acting upon matter. Henceforth, the problem of the way in which the force was transmitted between
particles of matter or even through empty space was to loom ever larger.
Out of the successive answers given by Faraday, James Clerk Maxwell,
and Albert Einstein was to emerge modern field theory.

In 1832 Faraday was only aware of the strange behaviour of the
magnetic curves. At that time it was sufficient for him to recognize the
oddity and investigate its implications. One of the consequences that
followed logically from the behaviour of the lines of force was that the
earth's magnetic field ought to generate a current in a wire even if the
wire (or other conductor) were not moving relatively to the earth.
After first determining that a *moving* wire could react with the earth's
magnetic field to produce a current [I–274] (171 ff.), Faraday went to the
pond before Kensington Palace to see if any electrical effect could be
produced there.

> Experimented in the pond before Kensington Palace. This is a made pond
> with a Stucco or other artificial bottom, and is supplied with water by one of
> the Companies, I believe the Chelsea. There are no springs, hence the water
> is all alike in quality and probably also in temperature.
>   A clean bright copper plate 2 feet by 1 foot had a thick copper wire soldered
> on at one corner. To this was made fast by clean metallic contact a copper
> wire $\frac{1}{20}$ inch thick, and then the plate thrown into the water at the north East
> corner. The water was very clear and the plate quite immersed, depth about
> 2 feet or perhaps more. The wire was then coiled round the eastern side on
> the grass until it reached the south eastern corner, where it was made fast to a
> similar plate as before, and that plate thrown in to water about 2 feet or 20
> inches deep. The plates were nearly N and S of each other and about 160
> yards apart – the wire was of course much longer. The wire was then divided
> in the middle of the eastern side and its ends connected by cups of mercury
> with the ends of a galvanometer wire to observe any induced effect [I–293-4].

It should be noted that this experiment makes sense *only* upon the
supposition of the independence of the lines of force. The plates, wire,
galvanometer, and pond were all at rest relative to one another. Being a
part of the earth, however, all were turning with it at a high rate of speed
and, as the earth turned, the wires and the pond should cut the stationary
lines of terrestrial magnetic force and a current should be generated. Small
currents were generated but Faraday showed that they were caused by
thermal and chemical effects [I–298-9]. Failure to perceive an effect
predicted by his theory of the lines of force did not, however, strike

him as strange. Perhaps it was because there were so many possible sources of disturbance that Faraday merely felt that the effect was masked. Convinced that he was on the right track, he turned to another experiment intended to detect the natural effects of the earth's magnetic field.

Experimented to-day at Waterloo Bridge by leave of Mr Bridell the Secy. Stretched a long copper wire on the Parapet of the Bridge on the western side. It extended from the toll house, Strand side, over six arches and to the sixth pier (these arches are each 140 feet, the piers each about 15 or 20 feet); it was therefore about 960 feet long. One of the plates above mentioned, very clean, was fastened to a wire and let down to the river directly at the toll house. The end of the wire was taken into the toll house by the window. The other plate, fastnd. to a similar wire, was let down into the river at the sixth pier, the other end being connected with the wire just mentioned. The end of the long horizontal wire was taken into the toll house, and thus, these two ends being connected by cups of mercury with the galvanometer wire, the whole became one wire from plate to plate; and the circuit was completed by the water between the plates, which, being in motion up or down, was expected to produce by magneto-electric induction currents rendered sensible at the galvanometer [I–303].

Again this experiment provided only an opportunity for the exercise of his ingenuity in detecting sources of error. A very distinct and powerful current was detected, but one by one Faraday discovered its sources, none of which was the desired one: the solder used to attach the copper wire to the platinum plates caused part of the current, differences in water salinity produced more, and so on [I–318 ff.]. When all these factors were removed, no effect could be found. Faraday still remained undismayed and his ideas now soared into the heavens to contemplate the spinning mass of the earth in space. There, in his mind's eye, he saw the terrestrial globe, surrounded by its magnetic lines of force, revolving on its own axis at a speed of a thousand miles an hour at the equator. As rivers and ocean currents cut through the lines of force, the result *must* be the production of electric currents.

Theoretically, it seems a necessary consequence, that where water is flowing, there electric currents should be formed: thus, if a line be imagined passing from Dover to Calais through the sea, and returning through the land beneath the water to Dover, it traces out a circuit of conducting matter, one part of which, when the water moves up or down the channel, is cutting the magnetic curves of the earth, whilst the other is relatively at rest. This is a repetition of the wire experiment (171), but with worse conductors. Still there is every reason to believe that electric currents do run in the general direction of the circuit described, either one way or the other, according as the passage of the waters is up or down the channel. Where the lateral extent of the moving water is enormously increased, it does not seem improbable that the effect should become sensible; and the gulf stream may thus, perhaps, from electric currents moving across it, by magneto-electric induction from the earth, exert a sensible influence upon the forms of the lines of magnetic variation (190).

The terrestrial electric currents were not only detectable by the variation, they were actually visible! As the earth as a whole cut through its own lines of force, currents moved from the equator through the bowels of the earth to the poles and there they leaped into the air to return to the equator through space. This was an audacious concept and Faraday put it forward with considerable hesitation.

I hardly dare venture, [he wrote] even in the most hypothetical form, to ask whether the Aurora Borealis and Australis may not be the discharge of electricity, thus urged towards the poles of the earth, from whence it is endeavouring to return by natural and appointed means above the earth to the equatorial regions. The non-occurrence of it in very high latitudes is not at all against the supposition; and it is remarkable that Mr Fox, who observed the deflections of the magnetic needle at Falmouth, by the Aurora Borealis, gives that direction of it which perfectly agrees with the present view. He states that all the variations at night were towards the east, and this is what would happen if electric currents were setting from south to north in the earth under the needle, or from north to south in space above it (192).

Faraday's fascination with the lines of force had led him here to adopt a view of terrestrial magnetism quite at variance with the generally accepted view. According to Ampère's theory, the contact of dissimilar metals in the earth created electrical currents parallel to the earth's equator. These currents produced the earth's magnetic field. For Faraday, the earth's magnetic field was the primitive fact. As the earth cut the lines of force, electric currents *perpendicular* to the equator were generated. To be sure, Faraday put his theory forward with great diffidence, but his interest in terrestrial magnetism always remained alive. He returned more than once to the problem of the aurora, convinced that its solution was to be found in the electricity generated by the earth's magnetic field.[11]

Having ascended by hypothesis to interplanetary space and observing, in his mind, the play between our planet and the lines of force, he then descended to the laboratory to examine these lines once more at close quarters. In his first paper he had shown qualitatively what the conditions were for the production of induced currents (114). This had been written before he discovered the independence of the lines of force from the magnets producing them. Now that this had become clear to him, it suggested a further line of inquiry. The line of force represented a peculiar strain, as though a thread were being stretched in space. This line could, so to speak, contain only so much force, so that cutting it would release a definite and constant amount of force. From this consideration it appeared clear that the force released was independent of what was used to cut the line. In modern terms, the electromotive force produced in a conductor cutting the line of force should be exactly the same no matter what substance was used as the conductor. As usual, Faraday turned to experiment for the answer.

> A piece of soft iron bonnet-wire covered with cotton was laid bare and cleaned at one extremity, and there fastened by metallic contact with the clean end of a copper wire. Both wires were then twisted together like the strands of a rope, for eighteen or twenty inches; and the remaining parts being made to diverge, their extremities were connected with the wires of the galvanometer. The iron wire was about two feet long, the continuation to the galvanometer being copper.
> The twisted copper and iron (touching each other nowhere but at the extremity) were then passed between the poles of a powerful magnet arranged horse-shoe fashion ... but not the slightest effect was observed at the galvanometer, although the arrangement seemed fitted to show any electrical difference between the two metals relative to the action of the magnet (194–5).

Various other combinations (copper and tin, copper and zinc, tin and zinc, etc.) were made 'but not the slightest sign of electric currents could be procured' (197). Even a solution of sulphuric acid was ingeniously coupled with a copper wire but here, too, there was no effect.

> From these experiments it would appear [Faraday reported], that when metals of different kinds connected in one circuit are equally subject in every circumstance to magneto-electric induction, they exhibit exactly equal powers with respect to the currents which either are formed, or tend to form, in them. The same even appears to be the case with regard to fluids, and probably all other substances (201).

Faraday, however, was perfectly aware of the fact that certain substances conducted electricity more easily than others. Given, then, the fact that the electromotive *force* was the same in all substances, it should follow that different strength currents would be formed in different substances. For as Faraday saw, 'it seemed impossible that these results could indicate the relative inductive power of the magnet upon the different metals; for that the effect should be in some relation to the conducting power seemed a necessary consequence . . . and the influence of rotating plates upon magnets had been found to bear a general relation to the conducting power of the substance used' (202). The reason for the null effect in the experiments just described was 'that the current excited in iron could not be transmitted but through the copper, and that excited in copper had to pass through iron: i.e. supposing currents of dissimilar strength to be formed in the metals proportionate to their conducting power, the stronger current had to pass through the worst conductor, and the weaker current through the best' (203).

Other more precise and sensitive experiments were then performed, from which Faraday drew a conclusion of great importance.

> These results [he wrote] tend to prove that the currents produced by magneto-electric induction in bodies is proportional to their conducting power. That they are *exactly* proportional to and altogether dependent upon the conducting power, is, I think, proved by the perfect neutrality displayed when two metals or other substances, as acid, water, etc., etc., . . . are opposed to each other in their action. The feeble current which tends to be produced in the worse conductor, has its transmission favoured in the better conductor, and the stronger current which tends to form in the latter has its intensity diminished by the obstruction of the former; and the forces of generation and obstruction are so perfectly balanced as to neutralize each other exactly. Now as the obstruction is inversely as the conducting power, the tendency to generate a current must be directly as that power to produce this perfect equilibrium (213).

This is one of the times when Faraday's lack of mathematical training and his distaste for mathematical formulation prevented a general law from being recognized. What Faraday had stated was clearly Ohm's law. The idea of electromotive force was drawn distinctly from the concept of the line of force. The conducting power was defined specifically as the inverse of the obstruction and the relation between current, e.m.f., and resistance unambiguously presented. Had Faraday taken the one final step of putting his views into the equation $I = \frac{E}{R}$, he would have provided an enormous stimulus to the progress of electrical science. It is true that Georg Simon Ohm had published his famous statement of this law in 1827 but Ohm's results were known only to a very few.[12] It was not until the 1840's that Ohm was 'discovered' and honour paid to him. Had Faraday been able to use mathematical methods for presenting his results, their publication in the Bakerian Lecture would have guaranteed their dissemination. Instead, although its exactitude is evident when one is looking for a specific relationship, the passage could be, and most probably was, read as a qualitative restatement of the relative conducting powers of the various metals. Those who recognized Faraday's intention were confused by his exposition. On 28 February 1833, S. H. Christie delivered the Bakerian Lecture on the 'Experimental Determination of the Laws of Magneto-electric Induction in different masses of the same Metal, and of its intensity in different Metals'.[13] There Christie stated that 'the most conclusive experiment, that of two spirals, one of copper and the other of iron, transmitting opposite currents, was quite consistent with the absolute equality of the currents excited in copper and iron; but, at the same time, the apparent equality of the currents might be due to their inequality being counteracted by a corresponding inequality in the facility of transmission'.[14] For forty-seven pages Christie pursued his quarry, unaware that he had totally misunderstood Faraday. What Faraday had stated was that the electromotive *forces* in the various substances were equal but Christie, not perceiving the reality of the line of force, read current and, in his paper, actually confirmed Faraday's statement. William Ritchie, Faraday's colleague at the Royal Institution, rose to Faraday's defence but based his conclusions on Newton's third law of the equality of action and reaction.[15] All this merely served to draw attention away from the line of force which Faraday considered central to his theoretical views. The failure to understand what Faraday was getting at led, therefore, to increased confusion although it did help to prepare the way for the acceptance of Ohm's views when they were finally discovered by the English.

With the Second Series of *Experimental Researches in Electricity*[16] read as the Bakerian Lecture to the Royal Society on 12 January 1832, the first great burst of Faraday's creativity slackened off. In less than a year he had accomplished prodigies. For eleven years scientists all over the world had sought to discover the induction of electric currents by magnets; Faraday (in his spare time!) had succeeded and for his success was given the highest award in the gift of the Royal Society – the Copley Medal. This had been only the beginning. The strange behaviour of the lines of force had attracted his attention and in his investigations of their properties he had been able to discover fascinating new relationships. Using the concept of the line of force, he was able to delve deeply into the properties of magnetism and electricity to find general laws of electrical and magnetic behaviour. By the spring of 1832 it was time for a brief respite. The tempo of his work slowed as he mulled over some of the problems his first two papers had raised. The spring and summer months of 1832 were ones of consolidation during which he mapped out the course of the next sustained period of intensive experimental work.

3. The Identity of Electricities

Almost from the moment he had discovered electromagnetic induction, Faraday had been concerned to show that the effect he had obtained was truly electrical. On 29 August 1831, the very day on which he had first observed the success of his ring experiment, he described an experiment in which he

> removed the iron and helices and substituted two platina poles to ends of B coil; put these into solution of copper, lead, etc. etc., but could get no evidence of chemical action. Put solution of copper on to one pole and then touched the drop with the other; then connected the battery, then broke connection at drop, and then at battery, and so went on in succession so as to avoid the recurrence of the return or opposite current on the drop; but got no evidence of chemical action [I–11].

This bothered him, and he kept coming back to it, convinced that electro-chemical decomposition must take place [I–41, 92, 386, 387].

This was not the only anomaly. The relations between electricity and magnetism were not as simple as they ought to be, and this obviously gave Faraday pause. In March, after his thorough investigations of magneto-electric induction, he still could not produce magnetism from static electricity although his theory predicted such an effect.

> Conceived that as electricity in passing made magnetism at right angles, so if electricity still and needle moved in opposite directions, should become a magnet, for then the electricity and metal are relatively moving and that seems the only condition required.
> Made a very delicate mag. needle, very feeble. Took other minute needles and passed them near to end of conductor, the needle and its path of motion being perpendicular to each other. The conductor belonged to a small electrical machine and was charged. Could not in this way get a magnet.
> Then held knob near conductor and passed the needle between the two, but could not get signs of magnetism in it.
> When sparks were passed from the conductor to the ball, the needle being near, they did not make it sensibly a magnet, so that evidently could not expect effects from the mere motion of the needle.
> The lines or directions of force between 2 electrical conductors oppositely electrified may be called *electric curves* in analogy to *magnetic curves*. Do they not exist also in the electric current wire? [I–398 ff.].

Thus using static electricity (what Faraday called ordinary electricity or electricity of tension) and arguing by analogy, he was unable to achieve success. There were indications that static and magneto electricity were the same, for both gave a spark [I–46], but there was also enough evidence to cast doubt upon this identity. The problem became particularly acute in 1832 for in the *Philosophical Transactions* for that year the identity of all electricities was strongly challenged. Dr John Davy, the late Sir Humphry's brother, writing on the peculiar electrical power of the torpedo suggested that, 'according to the analogy of the solar ray, ... the electrical

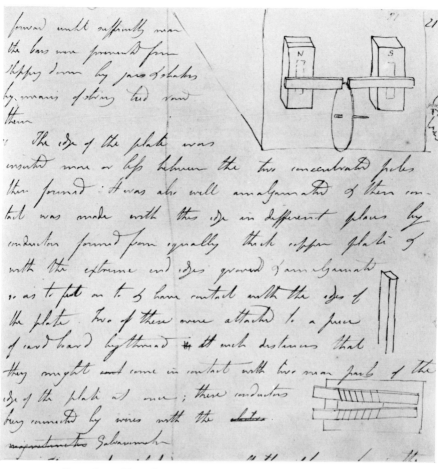

17 Page from Faraday's Diary showing sketch of the first dynamo

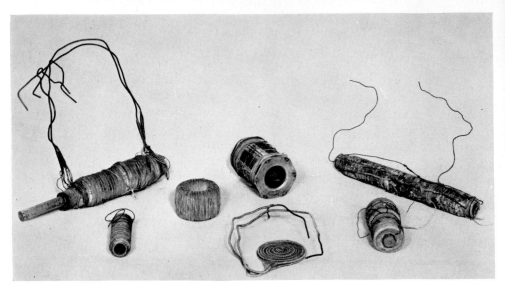

18a R.I. *Electromagnetic induction apparatus*

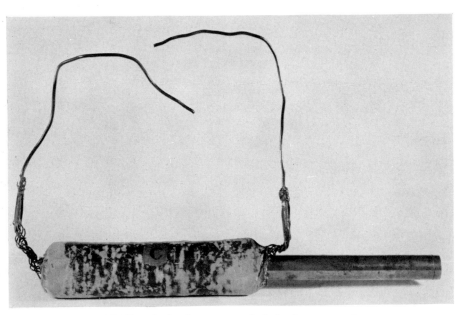

18b Faraday's *electromagnetic induction apparatus*

19a Faraday's electrostatic apparatus

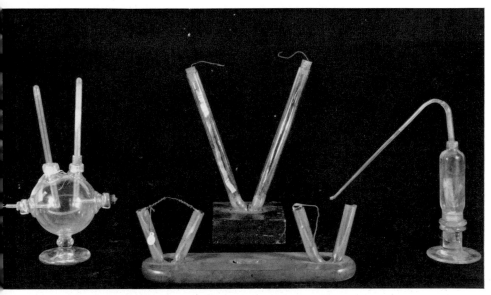

19b Faraday's electrochemical apparatus

20 J. F. *Daniell and Faraday (1841)*

21a J. Hachette

21b William Whewell

22 *The Royal Institution*

23 Charles Augustin Coulomb

24 *Georg Simon Ohm*

power, whether excited by the common machine, or by the voltaic battery, or by the torpedo, is not a simple power, but a combination of powers, which may occur variously associated, and produce all the varieties of electricity with which we are acquainted.'[17] In the same issue, the Rev. William Ritchie also underlined the differences between the various kinds of electricity. Common (static) electricity and voltaic electricity, he claimed, required totally different means of conduction. 'Common electricity is diffused over the surface of the metal; – voltaic electricity exists within the metal. Free electricity is conducted over the surface of the thinnest goldleaf, as effectually as over a mass of metal having the same surface; – voltaic electricity requires thickness of metal for its conduction.'[18] Later in the paper, when discussing the effects of voltaic and static electricity upon the galvanometer, Ritchie added, 'The supposed analogy between common and voltaic electricity, which was so eagerly traced after the invention of the pile, completely fails in this case, which was thought to afford the most striking resemblance.'[19]

Faraday was convinced of the identity of electricities but it would be folly for him to continue his researches without eliminating all sources of ambiguity and confusion. 'The progress of the electrical researches which I have had the honour to present to the Royal Society', he wrote, 'brought me to a point at which it was essential for the further prosecution of my inquiries that no doubt should remain of the identity or distinction of electricities excited by different means' (265). The Third Series of the *Experimental Researches in Electricity* was devoted to this end.

Faraday's approach in this series differed somewhat from that used in the first two papers. Here he was not passing from new discovery to new discovery by means of carefully detailed experiments. Instead, he was intent upon two goals; by criticizing the experiments of others he wanted to remove the seeming obstacles to the admission of the identity of electricities and by utilizing other experiments done by himself and others he wished to establish the identity. For a scientific paper of this period it is heavily footnoted and reveals Faraday's scholarship. The hours spent in searching journals and noting the contents of articles now bore fruit, for he was able to range over more than a half-century of science to muster the evidence for his case.[20] Whenever there was the slightest doubt as to the accuracy of an experiment, Faraday repeated it. The result was overwhelming and there was no doubt that he had proved his point.

Faraday began by listing six effects that electricity in some form produced. These were the attractions and repulsions of static charges, the evolution of heat, magnetism, chemical decomposition, physiological

H

effects, and the spark (267). Voltaic electricity, ordinary (static) electricity, magneto-electricity, thermo-electricity, and animal electricity were then examined to see how far they all could be made to exhibit the same effects.

Voltaic electricity was immediately shown to be able to affect an electrometer. Using the divergence of two gold leaves as a measure of the 'tension' involved, Faraday showed that the reason why a voltaic battery would not discharge into the air through pointed conductors was because the 'tension' was not high enough. A Leyden jar charged to give the same divergence between the gold leaves also would not discharge through the points (268 ff.). The other effects were so well known that Faraday felt it unnecessary to cite any experiments. Yet, in order that he might not be misunderstood he made the difference between current and static electricity clear. Again, this distinction illustrates Faraday's caution and the state of his ideas in the early part of 1833.

> In consequence of the comparisons that will hereafter arise between wires carrying voltaic and ordinary electricities, and also because of certain views of the condition of a wire or any other conducting substance connecting the poles of a voltaic apparatus, it will be necessary to give some definite expression of what is called the voltaic current, in contradistinction to any supposed peculiar state of arrangement, not progressive, which the wire or the electricity within it may be supposed to assume. If two voltaic troughs . . . be symmetrically arranged and insulated, and the ends . . . connected by a wire, over which a magnetic needle is suspended, the wire will exert no effect over the needle; but immediately that the ends . . . are connected by another wire, the needle will be deflected, and will remain so as long as the circuit is complete. Now if the troughs merely act by causing a peculiar arrangement in the wire either of its particles or its electricity, that arrangement constituting its electrical and magnetic state, then the wire . . . should be in a similar state of arrangement *before* . . . [its ends were] connected, to what it is afterwards, and should have deflected the needle, although less powerfully, perhaps to one half the extent which would result when the communication is complete throughout. But if the magnetic effects depend upon a current, then it is evident why they could not be produced in *any* degree before the circuit was complete; because prior to that no current could exist.
>
> By *current*, I mean anything progressive, whether it be a fluid of electricity, or two fluids moving in opposite directions, or merely vibrations, or, speaking still more generally, progressive forces. By *arrangement*, I understand a local adjustment of particles, or fluids, or forces, not progressive (282-3).

Thus, in spite of the sealed note of almost a year previously, Faraday still refused to commit himself in public to *any* theory of electricity. I suspect (but cannot prove) that only part of this was caution. The theory of vibrations had much to recommend it but there were still puzzling aspects of electricity that could not be ignored. Until he had worked out his views in detail, Faraday preferred to leave the way open to more than one theory. At this time he was really only concerned to show that, regardless of *what* theory one adopted, all electrical phenomena could be explained in terms of a single entity, electricity. He went on, therefore, to consider the other kinds, so-called, of electricity.

Magneto-electricity, like the voltaic, was found to exhibit all the characteristics he had picked out to study. M. Pixii, of Paris, one of the first to build a real (though still impracticable) dynamo, had also constructed an apparatus exhibiting electric repulsions and attractions with the magneto-electric current.[21] The ordinary production of heat was observed when the current passed (344). Since the currents were produced from magnetism, their magnetic relations were obvious. By the end of 1832 the decomposition of solutions had still eluded Faraday. Here he had to rely upon others. A number of supposed electrochemical decompositions were cited and shown to be inconclusive.[22] Hachette and Pixii, however, had obtained undoubted decomposition so that the effect could be attributed to the magneto-electric currents.[23] The effect upon frogs was unmistakable [I-389, 390], and when applied to the tongue Faraday pointed out that the sensation 'which I at first obtained only in a feeble degree (56) have been since exalted by more powerful apparatus, so as to become even disagreeable'[24] (347) [I-431-2]. The production of a spark had given some trouble to Faraday. In his first paper, the spark had been described as coming from the presence of an *electro*-magnet in the circuit (32). James D. Forbes of Edinburgh was the first to obtain it from a permanent magnet.[25] In his notes to Nobili's and Antinori's paper, Faraday was able to describe a simple method for obtaining a good-sized one.[26] Magneto-electricity and voltaic electricity were, therefore, identical and could be distinguished from one another only by the ways in which each was produced.

Thermo-electricity did not exhibit all the desired effects. Only its magnetic and physiological action could be observed. This did not alarm Faraday for, as he pointed out, 'only those effects are weak or deficient which depend upon a certain high degree of intensity; and if common electricity be reduced in that quality to a similar degree with the thermo-electricity, it can produce no effects beyond the latter' (350).

The question of animal electricity Faraday answered by an appeal to articles published as far back as 1773. 'No doubt remains on my mind', he reported, 'as to the identity of the electricity of the torpedo with common and voltaic electricity' (351). The evidence, however, was slim. No divergence of gold leaves, no evolution of heat or production of a spark

had been observed, and so Faraday rested upon the physiological, magnetic, and chemical effects emphasized by Dr Davy. There was no easy
answer here, as with thermo-electricity, for the failure to produce the
other effects of electricity, so Faraday simply let it go.[27]

Although it came second in Faraday's list of the kinds of electricity to be
examined, I have left the discussion of static electricity for last because it
is by far the most interesting. Unlike the other sections, the examination
of static electricity was solidly based on Faraday's own researches. In the
course of his attempt to prove the identity of static and voltaic electricity,
he resorted to many and clever experiments which succeeded in their
object. They also raised certain questions which were to lead him on to
other investigations of primary importance. As we shall see, the first
glimmerings of his revolutionary ideas on the mechanism of electrochemical decomposition arose out of these experiments. His great quantitative generalization known today as Faraday's Laws of Electrolysis also
were to emerge from the results of some of his work during this period.

His starting-point was an obvious one. By the summer of 1832 he had
become convinced of the necessity of proving the identity of electricities.
As his published paper shows, most of the 'electricities' could be attacked
by citing articles; magneto-electricity had just been successfully shown to
be like other forms of electricity by Faraday himself. The one really stubborn hold-out from this reduction to the same entity was static electricity.
Two of the effects of voltaic electricity that static electricity ought to
produce but did not were electrochemical decomposition and magnetism.
There were, of course, many reports of the production of both, but upon
close examination these reports always revealed serious flaws. The
standard experiment, for example, that was always cited to illustrate the
decomposing power of static electricity was one performed by William
Hyde Wollaston in 1801. It consisted of embedding two thin wires in
glass leaving only the ends exposed. When an electrostatic generator was
discharged through these wires, and the wires were immersed in water,
the water was decomposed. But, as Wollaston had pointed out, hydrogen
and oxygen both bubbled up at both wires.[28] This was only superficially
similar to voltaic decomposition where hydrogen appeared at one pole
and oxygen at another.

Similarly, the power of electrostatic discharges to magnetize needles
was well attested to. But the deflection of magnetic needles by electrostatic discharges was somewhat in doubt. Faraday's failure to produce a
magnet from an electrostatic field[29] underlined this anomaly.

In August 1832 Faraday set out to remove, once for all, any doubts that might be entertained of the identity of static and other forms of electricity. He began by concentrating on the problem of the magnetic effect of static electricity. The simplest way to show this was to record the deflection of a galvanometer needle by electric discharge. Almost immediately he ran into difficulties. The galvanometer was susceptible to electrostatic induction and his first successes had to be written off for this reason [4]. He found, too, that when the discharge was too strong it affected the magnetism of the galvanometer needles [5]. By constructing a galvanometer which was not affected by ordinary electrical attraction and repulsion, he was able to avoid the first difficulty; by slowing down the discharge by interposing poor conductors (water and wetted thread) between the generator and the galvanometer he solved the second problem [7–11]. The result was all he could hope for.

> Now exptd. by passing electricity of battery through water. A thick thread about four feet long was thoroughly wetted and then one end attached to the A end of the galvanometer, containing 36 feet of wire, and the other end to a discharger. The end B of galvanometer wire was connected with the discharging system.... The battery of 15 Jars was then connected, its outside with the discharging train, which is the same thing as being connected with the end B of the galvanometer, and its inside with the Electrical machine. A Henly's Electrometer was put upon the general conductor and the machine worked and the battery charged until the electrometer stood at about 40° or 35° of inclination with the stem. Then the discharger was brought in contact with the conductor and so the discharge made through water in the thread and through the galvanometer in the direction from A to B.
>
> On these occasions the needle was deflected, and by continuing the machine at work and discharging the charge in the battery each time the needle in swinging returned in the direction of the first impulse, the deflection was soon raised to 40° or more [11, 12].

When the leads were reversed, the deflection was also reversed [17, 18]. Various changes were rung on this experiment, all to Faraday's satisfaction. Wire was substituted for string, different size strings were used, and the influence of points was investigated. These were used to 'slow down' the discharge and thus permit the effect of the current to have time enough to affect the galvanometer. Again, his point was driven home by Faraday becoming a part of the circuit: 'When water formed part of the circuit', he noted, '. . . then the shock of the battery charged by eight turns of the machine was such as I could easily support, caring indeed nothing about it. But when no water was there, I could not well bear four or five turns, the sensation then being general through the arms and chest and very much indeed greater than the former' [34].

At this point, Faraday had amply proved his point. The evidence of the magnetic (and physiological) effects of static electricity could not be denied, and the problem could now be considered solved. Yet, as so often happened with Faraday, the mere act of experimenting set off a train of thought that led to further experiments. In this case, he saw the opportunity for making the comparison between voltaic and static electricity even more detailed. Since the galvanometer could be deflected by static electrical discharge, would it not be possible to compare the actual *quantities* of electricity that passed in voltaic circuits and in electrostatic discharge by comparing their effects on the galvanometer?[30] The answer to this question required two separate lines of investigation; one was to correlate the throw of the galvanometer needle with the quantity of electricity passed. The other was to compare the effects of voltaic and static electricity on the galvanometer.

The first problem was solved quite easily by Faraday. He took a battery of fifteen Leyden jars, all of equal size and, in modern terms, of equal capacitance. Seven were disconnected, leaving eight in the circuit.

On working the machine the battery charged up to the 38th turn but discharged spontaneously at the 39th. Then charged the battery with 30 turns and discharged it through the string and galvanometer. The needle was deflected, passing to the left to the 2½ and then swinging to the right to the 3 division or line of an arbitrary and irregular scale of large degrees placed under it. The marks were, however, quite sufficient to determine what extent the vibration occupied.

Then connected the other seven jars and charged the whole fifteen with 30 turns of the machine. The Henly's electrometer stood now not quite half so high as before; but on passing this charge through the string and galvanometer, the needle of the latter swung to the left to the 2½ and then back to the right to the 3 division as before.

Repeated this experiment with exactly the same result [123-5].

From this experiment, Faraday drew a conclusion of far-reaching importance. 'Hence,' he pointed out in the published paper, 'it would appear that *if the same absolute quantity of electricity pass through the galvanometer, whatever may be its intensity, the deflecting force upon the magnetic needle is the same*' (366).

This passage, with italics supplied by Faraday, was intended to strike the reader forcefully. The modern reader is both struck and knocked down by it. It is so palpably false that shock must be followed immediately by astonishment that such an astute theorist and experimenter as Faraday could be its author. Astonishment must give way to analysis and then the realization comes of the enormous good fortune that Faraday enjoyed.

For, on the basis of his experiment, he was quite right. His galvanometer, by the grace of God, was a ballistic galvanometer and, in the experiment he described, did react as Faraday described it. In both cases (i.e. with seven and with fifteen jars in the battery), the discharge was extremely rapid and the 'throw' of the galvanometer was, indeed, the same. The voltages or 'tensions' here were in the thousands of volts. When this was not the case, or when the first impulse was not being measured, Faraday's 'law' does not hold. What the ordinary galvanometer measures, after the circuit is closed and a steady state obtained, is not the quantity of electricity that flows but the *rate* of current flow. Thus, the 'error' committed by Faraday is one that depends upon the conditions of the electric flow in a circuit. It is quite valid for the experiment he cited; it is invalid for ordinary steady-state electrical flow.

It was, however, an error that bore precious fruit. Faraday had produced the first really accurate measurement of a quantity of electricity. If connected up, as it soon would be by Faraday, to other measurable quantities, it provided a basis for the absolute measurement of electrical quantities. As will be shown, it was the basis for Faraday's Laws of Electrolysis.

At the time of its formulation, however, Faraday was not thinking in such universal terms. All it was to him, then, was an experimental demonstration of the possibility of measuring the quantity of electricity involved in static electrical discharge. His concern was to find an equivalent measure of voltaic electricity. This had to be done by trial and error, but it was done with great rapidity. From the failure of electrostatic discharges to decompose electrolytic solutions Faraday knew that voltaic electricity involved far greater quantities of electricity than were present in electrostatic phenomena. If he were to find a voltaic equivalent of the electrostatic discharge he had measured, he knew he would have to work with extremely small elements.

Now drew some platina and zinc wire through the same hole in a draw plate – it rendered them very nearly $\frac{1}{18}$ of an inch in diameter – fastened these to a piece of wood so that their lower ends projected beyond the wood and were parallel to each other and $\frac{5}{16}$ of an inch apart. These are to be immersed in acid to constitute a standard voltaic arrangement. The other ends were directly connected with the ends of the galvanometer wire and bound round with clean copper wire to make the contact good.

Put one drop of Sulphuric acid in 4 oz. of water, mixed well, then brought it under the ends of plat. and zinc wire, lifted it up until the wires were immersed about $\frac{5}{8}$ of an inch and instantly took it away again. The galvanometer needle swung to the right hand beyond the 3rd division. So that in that moment the two wires in such weak acid produced as much electricity as the battery contained after 30 turns of the machine [129–30].

Now that the possibility of comparison between voltaic and static electricity was shown to be possible, Faraday further refined his experiments. He recognized the 'throw' of the galvanometer and so carefully noted how long the zinc and platinum wires had to be immersed in the sulphuric acid solution to produce a 'throw' equivalent to the discharge of the electrostatic battery. This time, without italics, Faraday recognized the true law. 'Hence,' he wrote, 'a permanent deflection to that extent might be considered as indicating a constant voltaic current, which in eight beats of my watch ... could supply as much electricity as the electrical battery charged by thirty turns of the machine' (372). Here the time element involved in the *rate* of flow was explicitly stated. This is an instructive example for inside of six paragraphs (see 366) Faraday had completely contradicted himself. Not only this, but if (366) and (373) are placed side by side, it is equally clear that Faraday did not apply his version of Ohm's law which had been put forth in (213). To those who like to take their science neat and accurate, this is an intolerable muddle. Doesn't Faraday know his own mind? The answer is no! These passages show beautifully how Faraday was wrestling with a whole series of new ideas and trying to make sense of a host of strange effects. The papers were written at white heat, entire passages being lifted, almost unchanged, from his laboratory notes. That the papers were muddled is not surprising; Faraday, too, was muddled. New concepts and theories were struggling to be born. As he juggled magnetic and electric lines of force, electrical quantities (of what? fluids, vibrations, forces?), chemical effects, and a dozen other phenomena in his mind and endeavoured to connect them together, the details inevitably escaped him. In the next six years, he was to achieve the unity and harmony that he now sought. But at this point he was floundering. His finished theory was in much the same form in 1832 as the flawless block of Carrara marble from which Michelangelo's 'David' was to emerge. Each new discovery was like a blow of the hammer upon the chisel modifying, clarifying, and forming the ultimate creation. It would be churlish to suggest to Michelangelo after a few hammer blows that the result was imperfect. Faraday, surely, deserves the same respect.

In spite of contradictions and errors, Faraday's eyes were firmly fixed upon his goal. He had shown up to this point only that a similar galvanometer reaction indicated equal amounts of current. The next step was, again, an obvious one to take. Could not the chemical effect of similar quantities of static and voltaic electricity be compared? By passing equal quantities of electricity (static and voltaic) through water, Faraday discovered that the *same* amount of electrochemical decomposition took place. This was the germ of Faraday's First Law of Electrolysis, although it was to be stated more forcefully in a later series of the *Electrical Researches*. At the end of 1832 Faraday contented himself with a simple summary of his results:

> Hence it results that both in *magnetic deflection* . . . and in *chemical force,* the current of electricity of the standard voltaic battery for eight beats of the watch was equal to that of the machine evolved by thirty revolutions.
> It also follows that for this case of electrochemical decomposition, and it is probable for all cases, that the *chemical power, like the magnetic force* . . . *is in direct proportion to the absolute quantity of electricity which passes* (376–7).

The electrochemical decompositions which Faraday had studied, and upon which his above conclusions were based, were carefully detailed in the published paper. There was no doubt that Faraday had succeeded in his aim; static electricity, by its ability to decompose chemical compounds, was shown to be identical with the magneto and voltaic varieties.

In his *Diary*, the story was much more dramatic. He had begun by seeking for the effect of chemical decomposition. Again, one experiment led to another and the result was so unthinkable that Faraday himself shrank from it. It is a story worth looking at in some detail.

He began by repeating one of Wollaston's experiments in which copper sulphate solution was decomposed by passing the discharge of an electrostatic machine through two thin silver wires immersed in the solution [39]. Copper was plated out on the negative wire, but Faraday was somewhat dissatisfied with the results. 'The decomposing action', he noted, 'is however very minute – very little copper is precipitated and no sensible trace of silver appeared in the solution of copper' [42]. It was obviously of little use to add still one more ambiguous account to those already existing for it would not convince those who held that static electricity did not decompose chemical compounds. Faraday set out, therefore, to intensify and clarify the effect.

> Experimented on chemical action of common electricity in another way and obtained beautiful results.
> Bent two small platina wires twice at right angles nearly, thus [Figure 6], so that the part [CD] would be nearly upright whilst the whole stood upon the three bearing places [A], [B], [C]. Put a glass valve or plate on a table, placed a piece of tin foil on that and then let the end of a wire connected with the electrical machine by 8 inches of wet string rest on the tin foil. Then one of the bent platina wires was so placed that [B] and [C] rested on the other end

of the same tin foil and [A] on a second glass plate. The second platina wire was placed with its end [A] near [A] of the former and the rest in connection by tin foil or otherwise with the discharging train. Thus the connection could be arranged or broken at pleasure, being discontinued only between the two points [A], [A] when the experiments were in progress. In this way surfaces of contact as minute as possible could be obtained at pleasure, as will soon be seen.

A mixture of half pure Mur.[iatic] acid and half water was rendered deep blue by sulphate of indigo and then a moist strip or place made with it on the larger glass plate and the two ends [A], [A] arranged so as to be about $\frac{1}{2}$ an inch apart and connected together by it. Immediately on turning the machine a decolouring effect was seen at the end [A] connected with the machine, i.e. the positive side, and after 20 or 30 turns the bleached portion of solution was so large and powerful that when the wires were removed and the whole of the solution stirred together the chlorine evolved by the machine was enough to bleach the whole [46-8].

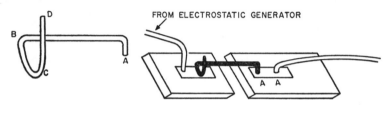

Fig. 6

Having found an unequivocal answer to the question posed, most other investigators would have stopped there and written the paper on the identity of electricities. This was never Faraday's way. Having found a new effect, he tried to look at it from all angles and discover new facets if possible. The unexpected, it has been said, happens only to the expectant. So Faraday played with his new experiment. Different solutions were tried, different means of connecting up the battery were used, and different 'tensions' applied. One of the variations involved replacing the bent platinum wires with simple arcs of wire, as in Figure 7.

On working the machine a few turns, the litmus under 1 and 3 was reddened by acid and the turmeric under 2 and 4 also reddened by the alkali.

Then let the positive *a* rest on litmus paper moistened by the sul.[phate of] soda and touched the paper itself with moist string held in the hand, so as in fact to have a positive pole active but no definite decomposing pole near; still the decomposing effect took place there as well as if a negative pole had been active [73-4].

In effect, Faraday had really eliminated the poles. All he had was a path through which electricity could pass. He did not understand this at first for he was still thinking of the poles as centres of attraction and repulsion which tore the molecules of the interposed solution apart. Thus, at this time, he asked only, 'In this case what becomes of the alkali repelled from the positive pole?' [75]. Since decomposition appeared to take place when only one 'pole' was present, he set out to investigate this peculiar

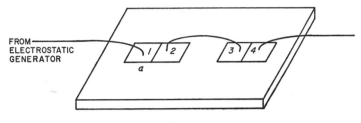

FROM
ELECTROSTATIC
GENERATOR

Fig. 7

fact. Instead of a circuit, Faraday set up a discharge train in which the ultimate discharge was into the air as a spark. The only metallic 'pole' existed where the electricity entered the conducting solution. Still decomposition took place. The electricity was, however, led off by a piece of wet string before discharge. To eliminate the possibility that the string was acting as a pole, Faraday reduced the experiment to its utmost simplicity. A long piece of indicating paper was soaked in sodium sulphate solution. One end of the strip was cut into a point and the other end was connected to the electrostatic generator. The electricity, therefore, merely passed through the paper and discharged into the air. There were no poles at all. The conclusion Faraday drew from this experiment was to serve as the starting-point of his magnificent electrochemical researches.

> Hence it would seem that it is not a mere repulsion of the alkali and attraction of the acid by the positive pole, etc. etc. etc., but that as the current of electricity passes, whether by metallic poles or not, the elementary particles arrange themselves and that the alkali goes as far as it can with the current in one direction and the acid in the other. The metallic poles used appear to be mere terminations of the decomposable substance.
> The effects of decomposition would seem rather to depend upon a relief of the chemical affinity in one direction and an exaltation of it in the other, rather than to direct attractions and repulsions from the poles, etc. etc. [103-4].

Innocent enough words, and how tentatively put forward! Faraday could not foresee that in following out these ideas he would not only provide a solid foundation for the science of electrochemistry, but would also throw down a challenge to the physicists of his day. For here, for the first time in his work, was the denial of action at a distance.

References

1. On 24 October he had tried to produce these whirlpools by moving a copper strip rapidly back and forth over a bar magnet [I–77]. 'The hopes were that the pole being at N a semi-vortex would be formed and electricity gathered up by the conductors at the section of the vortex occasioned at the edge of the plate.' It is obvious that the experiments with the copper discs are simple modifications of this one.

2. From 1831 on, Faraday was in constant need of new terms. The two people to whom he turned for the coining of these words were Whitlock Nicholl, M.D., his personal physician, and William Whewell, the great Master of Trinity College, Cambridge. For the history of the contributions made by these men, see Sydney Ross, 'Faraday Consults the Scholars: The Origins of the Terms of Electrochemistry', *Notes & Records of the Royal Society, 16* (1961), 187 ff.

3. Faraday to R. Phillips, Brighton, 29 November 1831, B.J., *2*, 8. The original is in the Burndy Library, Norwalk, Conn. See Bern Dibner, *Faraday Discloses Electro-magnetic Induction*, Burndy Library, 1949.

4. *Exp. Res., 1*, 32, note.

5. 'Extrait d'une lettre de M. Faraday à M. Hachette, communiquée à l'Académie des sciences le 17 decembre', *Ann. de chim. et de phys.*, 2 ser., *48* (1831), 402. *Le Lycée*, Jeudi, 29 dec. 1831.

6. *The Literary Gazette; and Journal of Belles Lettres, Arts, Sciences, etc. for the year 1832*, 185.

7. Burndy Library, Faraday to – –, R.I., 27 March, 1832.

8. 'On the Electro-motive Force of Magnetism. By Signori Nobili and Antinori', *Exp. Res., 2*, 164.

9. *Ann. de chim. et de phys., 51* (1832), 404 ff. Translated and republished in *Exp. Res., 2*, 179 ff.

10. The theory of the unipolar generator (which was what Faraday was working with in these experiments) did not become clear until the present century. It involves the consideration of Lorentz forces acting upon the electrons of the disc or of the rotating magnet. For a discussion of the theory, see Wolfgang H. Panofsky and Melba Phillips, *Classical Electricity and Magnetism* (Reading, Mass., 1955), 148–50 and 344.

In 1832, the conclusion seemed inescapable that the lines of force did not rotate with the magnet.

11. In the collection of his own papers which he annotated (now at the R.I.) his continuing interest in the aurora can be seen. He has jotted down opposite paragraph 192 of his *Experimental Researches* some seven references to the aurora, ranging in time from 1832 to 1849.

12. G. S. Ohm, *Die galvanische kette mathematische bearbeitet* (Berlin, 1827).

The book was published in a very small edition and is today exceedingly scarce. Its style is dense and oftentimes confused so that even its few readers were not convinced of its importance. It was reviewed only in one journal – the *Jahrbücher für wissenschaftliche Kritik* – and it was there heavily criticized by G. F. Pohl for its highly theoretical approach. That Ohm went unread can be seen by the fact that Ampère never mentioned his name either in his published works or his correspondence. It was not that Ampère consciously ignored Ohm: he simply had never heard of him.

13. *Phil. Trans.*, 1833, Part I, 95 ff.

14. Ibid.

15. Rev. William Ritchie, 'On the Reduction of Mr Faraday's Discoveries in Magneto-Electric Induction to a general Law', *L. & E. Phil. Mag.*, N.S., *4* (1834), 11.

16. It should be noted that between the time of reading the lecture and its publication, Faraday continued to experiment and added new material. Thus one finds experiments performed in February [I–358] reported in the published paper (247 ff.).

17. Dr John Davy, 'An Account of Some Experiments and Observations on the Torpedo (*Raia Torpedo*, Linn.)', *Phil. Trans.*, 1832, 259 ff. The quotation is on page 275.

18. Rev. William Ritchie, 'Experimental Researches in Voltaic Electricity and Electro-Magnetism', *Phil. Trans.*, 1832, Part II, 279 ff. The quotation is on page 280.

19. Ibid., 291, note. All these statements were cited by Faraday, 'to show that the question is by no means considered as settled' (265).

20. Most of the articles appearing before 1825, cited by Faraday in this paper were noted in his copy of Brande's *Manual*.

21. 'Nouvelle construction d'une Machine électromagnétique', *Ann. de chim. et de phys.*, 2 ser., *50* (1832), 322.

22. *L. & E. Phil. Mag.*, *1* (1832), 161.

Professor Botto, 'Notice on the Chemical Action of the Magneto-electric Currents', ibid., *1* (1832), 441.

23. M. Hachette, 'De l'action chimique produite par l'Induction électrique; Decomposition de l'Eau', *Ann. de chim. et de phys.*, *51* (1832), 72.

'Note de M. Ampère, sur une Expérience de M. Hippolyte Pixii', ibid., 77.

24. This method of detecting electricity had a long and honourable history. Every since 1736 when Muschenbroek first detected the power of the Leyden jar by becoming a part of the circuit and vowed that he would not take another such shock for the kingdom of France, electrical researchers had reassured themselves of the reality of their subject by direct application to themselves. Cavendish, it may be remembered, used himself as a voltmeter but he had no other instrument at his disposal. Faraday could plead no such excuse yet he seemed determined to prove his fortitude by constant application of live leads to his arms, eyes and tongue. His *Diary* is filled with casual remarks to the effect that the shock of current was almost unbearable. Although a small point, it is worth noting as one of the differences between present-day and nineteenth-century science.

25. James D. Forbes, 'On the Obtaining of an Electric Spark from a Natural Magnet', *L. & E. Phil. Mag.*, N.S., *11* (1832), 359.

26. *Exp. Res.*, *2*, 169.

27. There is an interesting letter from Dr (later Lord) Lister to Faraday in which Lister cited references to the Gymnotus electricus and the production of

the spark. It appears opposite the *Third Series* bound in Faraday's own annotated copy of his researches at the Royal Institution.

28. W. H. Wollaston, 'Experiments on the chemical Production and Agency of Electricity', *Phil. Trans.*, 1801, 427 ff. See p. 432 for the distinction here made.

29. See above, p. 212.

30. In fact, Faraday did stop, momentarily, at the point where he had shown the magnetic effect of an electrostatic discharge (29 August). He picked it up again, however, two weeks later (14 September) so that while historical continuity here has been violated, I do not think that the violation is a serious one.

CHAPTER SIX

The Nature of Electricity (2)

1. Electrochemistry before 1833

The problem of the mechanism of the decomposition of chemical compounds by the agency of electricity was one which, by 1832, had intrigued chemists for a generation. When William Nicholson and Anthony Carlisle discovered in 1800 that a voltaic current would decompose water they created a whole new set of questions begging for answers.[1] The most important was, how the constituents of water, both gases, were able to travel undetected through a solution and bubble up only at the poles. Nicholson's words are worth citing again: 'it was with no little surprise', he wrote, 'that we found the hydrogen extricated at the contact with one wire, while the oxigin fixed itself in combination with the other wire at the distance of almost two inches.'[2]

Such a strange and inexplicable effect immediately attracted universal attention. Chemists everywhere set up their little voltaic piles, immersed the connecting wires in cups of slightly saline water and watched, with puzzled frowns, as hydrogen appeared mysteriously at the negative pole. The young Faraday, some twelve years later, as we have seen, also seized immediately upon the basic problem when he observed that the zinc discs of his home-made pile were covered lightly with copper and that the copper discs had a coating of zinc oxide. 'In this case', he wrote, 'the metals must both have passed through the flannel disc holding the solution of muriate of soda, and they must have passed by each other.'[3] Both this transfer of metals and the transfer of hydrogen and oxygen through an aqueous solution were unlike any previously observed effect. What was the strange power of electricity which allowed such curious activity to take place?

The problem of electrochemical transfer of matter, by itself, was sufficiently important to guarantee that it would be thoroughly investigated. Almost from the beginning, however, the effect was given a theoretical aspect which forced every chemist to focus his attention upon it

A small group of German chemists pounced upon the strange behaviour of water undergoing electrochemical decomposition and used it as their main offensive piece in an attempt to blow up Lavoisier's new system of chemistry.

The foremost aggressor was Johann Ritter of Jena. As a Kantian, he had long resented Lavoisier's philosophical bias which would reduce all chemistry to measurable entities. As a German, he took a certain national pride in the phlogistic theory of chemistry developed by his countrymen Becher and Stahl. As an enthusiast whose ideas often outdistanced his experimental abilities, the problem of the electrochemical decomposition of water offered him the opportunity to liberate himself from the precision of the new chemistry.[4] The experiments upon which he based his attack on the new chemistry were both simple and dramatic. First he took a simple V-tube and filled it with water. The wires from the terminals of a voltaic pile were then plunged into each branch of the tube. As Nicholson and Carlisle had shown, hydrogen and oxygen were produced at the two wires but the use of the V-tube made the phenomenon stand out more clearly. There could be no doubt that the gases were actually *produced* at the poles and that the transfer of matter involved was not due to convection currents or mechanical agitation. Ritter then proceeded to connect two filled V-tubes in series (Figure 1) and plunged the terminal wires of the battery into the end branches. Again, hydrogen and oxygen were produced. Finally, he partially filled the V-tube with sulphuric acid and then carefully poured water on the top of the acid in each branch. Now, when the leads were dipped into the water *only*, hydrogen and oxygen again were produced.[5]

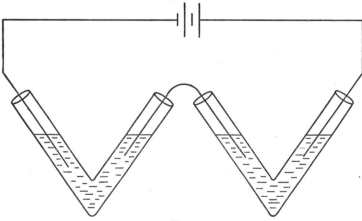

Fig. 1

25 Faraday lecturing before the Prince Consort and the Prince of Wales

26a *Davies Gilbert, P.R.S.*   26b *Charles Babbage*

26c *Sir William Rowan Hamilton*

27a Justus von Liebig

27b Carlo Matteucci

27c Gerritt Moll

27d J. B. Dumas

28 The Royal Institution's great electromagnet

The question Ritter posed was, how, on the supposition that water was a compound of oxygen and hydrogen, could these experiments be explained? Consider a molecule of water which, for simplicity's sake, may be assumed to consist of one atom of hydrogen and one of oxygen. When subjected to the force of the pile, the molecule must be torn apart and the hydrogen and oxygen atoms must begin to travel in opposite directions through the solution. Why these atoms did not simply bubble up when and where the water molecule was torn apart was the first unanswerable question. Ritter, however, had made the problem even more difficult of solution. What happened when the V-tubes were connected in series? Suppose a molecule of water in the left branch of the first tube. Its oxygen could perhaps reach the positive wire close by, but what happened to the hydrogen? Unless it be assumed that it could travel *through* the wire between the tubes, it could not possibly get to the negative terminal. Hence, argued Ritter, one could only conclude that the oxygen was literally produced at the positive pole and hydrogen at the negative. The same conclusion followed from the experiment with the sulphuric acid for the bulk of the water in each branch of the V-tube was prevented from moving from one side to the other.

If the hydrogen and oxygen were *not* the result of the decomposition of a water molecule, then what were they? Ritter's triumph could not be disguised and to underline it he set his conclusion off on a separate line by itself. The real truth was that

'Water is an element.'[6]

From this it followed that hydrogen and oxygen were compounds of water and electricity. Oxygen thus became water plus positive electricity and hydrogen was water plus negative electricity. From here Ritter gave free rein to his imagination and proceeded to revive the phlogiston theory. He had long sought for the interconnexions of the so-called imponderable fluids and was convinced that they could all be reduced to some simple entity or force. This was now discovered to be electricity which could henceforth be called phlogiston. Like phlogiston it could be used to account for a whole host of chemical reactions if only one ignored the dictum of the new chemistry that a material balance in a reaction was the primary guide to chemical truth.[7]

Ritter's views achieved widespread notoriety. Oersted early became a disciple and was instrumental in spreading news of Ritter's activities in France.[8] The English journals reported his experiments, usually taking their information from the French.[9] The French chemists, as was to be expected, received Ritter's views with considerable chilliness. The editors of the *Annales de Chimie* noted that the 'heat and enthusiasm which fills M. Ritter's memoir', indicated that extreme caution should be exercised before Ritter's views were taken seriously. The experiments, however, were so simple and the results were so clear-cut that it was difficult to find a flaw in Ritter's argument. Georges Cuvier, chairman of a committee appointed by the French National Institute to look into the new galvanic effects, could do little more than report his and the committee's puzzlement. 'How', Cuvier asked, 'can oxygen and hydrogen, both coming from the same molecule of water, appear at widely separated points? And why should each appear only at one of the wires connected to the ends of the pile and not the other?' This fact, plus Ritter's demonstration of the appearance of hydrogen and oxygen in separate portions of water, joined only by a conductor, drove Cuvier to list the (seemingly) only ways in which this strange effect could be explained.

> It is clear [Cuvier wrote] that there are only three possible ways of explaining these facts.
>
> Galvanic action tends to remove one of its constituents from each portion of water, leaving the other in excess;
>
> [Galvanic action] decomposes the water, permitting the disengagement of one of the gases at the end of the wire, and conducting the other gas in some invisible manner to the end of the other in order to release it there;
>
> Or, finally, the water does not decompose at all; rather, its combination with some principle, emanating from the positive end of the pile, produces oxygen, and with that [principle] which emanates from the negative side, hydrogen.[10]

Such a group of alternatives offered little cheer to the orthodox. The first involved a denial of the constant composition of water and could lay claim to a certain authority in Claude Louis Berthollet, France's foremost chemist. Long an opponent of the doctrine of constant proportions, Berthollet seized upon Ritter's experiments as direct proof of his ideas of variable chemical composition. 'It would appear', he wrote triumphantly, 'that unless one wishes to admit properties irreconcilable with those which have been long established in Physics, this isolated disengagement of each of the elements of water must be explained . . . by the property which water, as well as all other compounds, has of being composed of different proportions of the substances forming it.'[11] Ever since Lavoisier had realized the importance of the composition of water, however, this compound had been so thoroughly analysed, always with the same results, that even Berthollet's justly deserved reputation could not convince anyone.

The second alternative was really only a statement of the facts. The constituent gases of water did seem to travel invisibly through the solution. The real problem was to discover some way of accounting for this.

The third alternative involved nothing less, as Ritter and Cuvier both knew, than the suppression of Lavoisier's Chemical Revolution. To Cuvier and the French, this German counter-revolution was anathema. There is more than cool scientific objectivity in Cuvier's advice to his fellow *savants*. 'The third [alternative] is advocated by a few foreigners, especially M. Ritter of Jena. It seems so to contradict the ensemble of all chemical phenomena that it would be almost impossible to accept it, even if a satisfactory explanation of the experiment in question cannot be found.'[12]

The honour of rescuing the French chemists from the embarrassment into which Ritter had plunged them went to a young German nobleman residing in Rome. Freiherr Theodor von Grotthus,[13] at the age of 20, hit upon a way in which all the apparent difficulties of Ritter's experiments could be explained without sacrificing the new chemistry.

Grotthus was struck by the resemblance between the metallic deposits produced on the wires from the ends of a voltaic pile when placed in a solution of a metallic salt, and the metallic crystals long known as arbors. Arbors were the result of the displacement of one metal in solution by another. Thus, if a piece of clean copper were placed in a solution of silver nitrate, the silver would gradually come out of solution and form a beautiful fern-like structure known as the *Arbor Dianae*.[14] Grotthus noticed that the arbor always formed 'a symmetrical arrangement which extends along the direction of the galvanic current'.[15] From this clue he deduced that the forces exerted by the electrical fluids must act along the line joining the positive and negative poles. The metallic molecules in solution reacted to this force by moving in the direction of the negative pole. The situation was analogous to the pointing of a magnetic needle to a magnetic pole. In fact, the analogy was an identity. 'The Voltaic column', he remarked, 'which has immortalized the genius of its inventor, is an electric magnet, of which each element (that is, each pair of discs) has a positive and a negative pole. The contemplation of this polarity suggested to me the idea that a similar polarity might well be induced among the elementary molecules of water by the same electrical agent; and I confess that suddenly the whole problem was clarified.'[16]

The assumption that the voltaic pile was an electric magnet only indicated to Grotthus how the problem should be attacked. Before actually describing the way in which oxygen and hydrogen were transported through the solution, he had to solve another important problem.

This was the question of how the oxygen and hydrogen in the water molecule could undergo an induced polarity whereas when in the gaseous state no such polarity had ever been observed. The solution actually was very simple. Given a water molecule, all that was necessary was to get the total electricity contained within the molecule distributed in such a way that the hydrogen had an excess of the positive and the oxygen an excess of the negative. This could be done either by friction between the hydrogen and oxygen, or, better yet, by their contact. Just as the contact of two dissimilar metals in the voltaic pile created a polarity, so the contact of two dissimilar atoms created a molecular polarity.[17] When no electrical forces were applied to these molecules, they exhibited perfect electrical neutrality. The minute the polarity of the pile was communicated to the water through the wires introduced into it, the polarity became manifest. The hydrogen part of each water molecule was immediately attracted towards the negative pole and repelled from the positive. The oxygen half was drawn in the opposite direction. The electrical forces, *acting at a distance according to the inverse square law,* sheared the water molecules in half. Why, then, didn't the two gases, once separated from one another, bubble up all over the solution? The answer now was simple. Before a hydrogen atom could begin to bubble, it met another oxygen atom going the other way. Since they were oppositely charged, they joined together to form a water molecule. The electrical forces from the pile had not ceased to act, however, and so this new molecule of water was, in turn, torn apart, and the hydrogen and oxygen continued to move towards their respective attracting poles. 'It is clear that in this whole operation', Grotthus noted, 'only the molecules of water at the extremities of the connecting wires [near each pole] will be decomposed, while all those in the middle will exchange the composing principles reciprocally and alternately without changing their character [as water].'[18]

The Chemical Revolution was saved. Grotthus showed beautifully how it was possible to preserve the compound nature of water and also understand the transfer of two gases through a solution without any visible sign of them. One had only to close one's eyes to see vividly the dance of the molecules as they clasped and released one another along the path laid out by the poles. In fact, the ease of comprehension of this theory and the simplicity with which the decomposition of water was reduced to familiar mechanical terms tended to obscure the questions the theory raised. The first was that decomposition of metals on the negative pole was *not* as Grotthus described it. There was no clear-cut tendency for the metals to build up along the line joining the poles. Faraday was later to call attention to this error for, to him, it was a crucial one. The origin of molecular polarity was also to come under attack later when Volta's whole theory was assailed. Finally, there was the problem of what actually happened at the poles. In his first memoir, Grotthus focused his attention on what took place in the water, merely assuming that when the oxygen and hydrogen got to the poles they bubbled off. He was quite explicit, however, in pointing out that the material molecules were not the only things moving through the solution. He described the negative pole as 'the pole from which resinous [positive] electricity pours endlessly'[19] and this electricity presumably had to pass to the positive pole, just as positive electricity passed to the negative pole. What happened *at* the pole where charged particle met electrical stream was not described until a later memoir. There Grotthus achieved an elegant synthesis. Each particle of oxygen and hydrogen combined with the electricity of the pole that attracted it, thus neutralizing its charge. These neutral particles then assumed the gaseous state but the sum of their electricities was greater than that of the water molecule from which they came. So, Grotthus pointed out with pride, when the two particles were brought together again (by ignition) to form water, the excess electricities combined with great light and heat.[20] What Grotthus and no one else saw at the time was that the independent currents of electricity from the two poles were totally superfluous. As long as the particles combined with the electricities of the two poles, the result was equivalent to the transfer of positive electricity to the negative pole and of negative electricity to the positive pole. Again, Faraday was to point out this fault and use it to criticize Grotthus' theory of electrochemical composition.

At the same time that Grotthus was perfecting his ideas on electrochemistry, another chemist was at work on the same subject. Humphry Davy was drawn to the problem of electrochemical action from the analytical side. The effects of the galvanic current on aqueous solutions, usually contaminated by other chemicals, had led many chemists to publish wild hypotheses and sheer nonsense.[21] Among these was the report by Pacchiani in Italy that the decomposition products of water were not just oxygen and hydrogen, but muriatic (hydrochloric) acid as well.[22] If Pacchiani were correct, then this should prove to be a fact of capital importance. As we have seen, muriatic acid was the one really stubborn fact that could not be fitted into Lavoisier's theory. Any approach that promised to shed light upon its composition, therefore, was eagerly sought by chemists everywhere.

Davy began his investigations of this supposed electrochemical result with a frankly sceptical attitude. From the beginning he was convinced that the production of acid was caused by minute traces of contaminants and he tracked them down relentlessly.[23] In the process, his attention was caught by the seemingly strange behaviour of solutions subjected to the passage of an electrical current. To explain the facts that emerged from his investigations of this behaviour, Davy suggested a theory of electro-

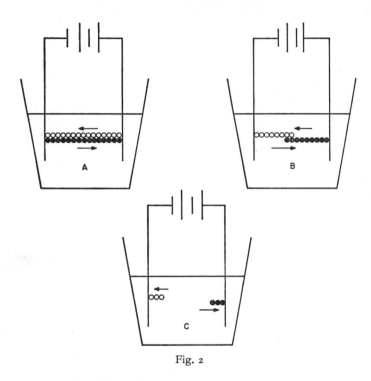

Fig. 2

chemical action that differed in many important points from that proposed by Grotthus.[24] Davy's ideas were set forth in what was probably the finest paper he ever wrote, the Bakerian Lecture for 1806, 'On some chemical Agencies of Electricity'.[25]

From the start, he took a wider view of the problem than had Grotthus. As he had traced the contaminants in Pacchiani's experiments, it was borne in upon him that the effect of the galvanic current was by no means confined to the molecules of water. Most neutral salts underwent decomposition and the problem of how the constituents of these salts migrated through a solution could be added to the problem of the migration of oxygen and hydrogen.[26] This generalization of the problem immediately suggested a question to Davy. 'I made several experiments', wrote Davy, 'with the view of ascertaining whether, in the decompositions by electricity, the separation of the constituent parts was complete from the last portions of the compound; and whenever the results were distinct, this evidently appeared to be the case.'[27] His description of one of these experiments leaves no doubt as to his train of thought. A dilute solution of potassium sulphate was placed in two agate cups and the cups then connected by a strip of moistened asbestos. A current was passed through the two cups for three days, at the end of which time their contents were analysed. The one cup held potash, the other sulphuric acid. The separation of the two components of the salt was complete.[28]

Davy glimpsed the theoretical importance of this experiment only vaguely. Yet it was fundamental and was to prove a stumbling block to Faraday. The implication was clear; the kind of molecular chain envisioned by Grotthus was impossible. Somewhere along the line, there was a last link of each component of the salt and the two last links *must* travel as free agents for part of the distance through the solution (see Figure 2). Davy did not fully comprehend this fact, but the experiment did suggest to him a series of further investigations in which he tried to unveil the mechanics of ionic transfer. The results were apparently contradictory but Davy was ultimately able to resolve them.

If the transfer of the constituent parts of a neutral salt involved even the momentary existence of these constituents as free chemical agents, then it seemed logical that they should be detectable by ordinary chemical means. When this was tried, the results were surprising.

> I endeavoured to ascertain the progress of the transfer [Davy wrote] and the course of the acid or alkaline matter in these decompositions, by using solutions of litmus and turmeric, and papers coloured by these substances: and these trials led to the knowledge of some singular and unexpected circumstances.
>
> Two tubes, one containing distilled water, the other solution of sulphate of potash, were each connected by amianthus with a small ounce measure filled with distilled water tinged by litmus: the saline solution was negatively electrified; and as it was natural to suppose, that the sulphuric acid in passing through the water to the positive side would redden the litmus in its course, some slips of moistened paper tinged with litmus were placed above and below the pieces of amianthus, directly in the circuit. The progress of the experiment was minutely observed; the first effect of reddening took place immediately above the positive surface, where I had least expected it; the red tint slowly diffused itself from the positive side to the middle of the vessel, but no redness appeared above the amianthus, or about it, on the negative side, and though it had been constantly transmitting sulphuric acid, it remained unaffected to the last.[29]

There seemed only one possible conclusion to be drawn from this experiment. In some way, the electric current interfered with the ordinary course of chemical reactions, preventing them from taking place. Thus, the litmus was unaffected in the middle of the solution, even though sulphuric acid was present. The next step was clear:

> As acid and alkaline substances during the time of their electrical transfer passed through water containing vegetable colours without affecting them, or apparently combining with them, it immediately became an object of inquiry whether they would not likewise pass through chemical menstrua, having stronger attractions for them; and it seemed reasonable to suppose, that the same power which destroyed elective affinity in the vicinity of the metallic points would likewise destroy it, or suspend its operation, throughout the whole of the circuit.[30]

The results were quite dramatic! Acids could be passed through bases, and bases through acids without a reaction occurring. The power of chemical affinity was suspended by the forces emanating from the poles of the electrochemical cell. But this was only an appearance. When the attempt was made to pass sulphuric acid through a solution of a barium salt, the result was a precipitate of barium sulphate. The affinity between the barium and the sulphuric acid was clearly not suspended. To account for all these facts, Davy suggested a theory that deserves to be quoted in its entirety.

> It will be a general expression of the facts that have been detailed, relating to the changes and transitions by electricity, in common philosophical language, to say that hydrogen, the alkaline substances, the metals, and certain metallic oxides, are attracted by negatively electrified metallic surfaces, and repelled by positively electrified metallic surfaces; and contrariwise, that oxygen and acid substances are attracted by positively electrified metallic surfaces, and repelled by negatively electrified metallic surfaces; and these attractive and repulsive forces are sufficiently energetic to destroy or suspend the usual operation of elective affinity.
>
> It is very natural to suppose, that the repellent and attractive energies are communicated from one *particle to another particle* of the same kind, so as to establish a conducting chain in the fluid; and that the locomotion takes place in consequence; and that this is really the case seems to be shown by many facts. Thus, in all the instances in which I examined alkaline solutions through which acids had been transmitted, I always found acid in them whenever any acid matter remained at the original source. In time, by the attractive power of the positive surface, the decomposition and transfer undoubtedly becomes complete; but this does not affect the conclusion.
>
> In the cases of the separation of the constituents of water, and of solutions of neutral salts forming the whole of the chain, there may possibly be a succession of decompositions and recompositions throughout the fluid. And this idea is strengthened by the experiments on the attempt to pass barytes

through sulphuric acid, and muriatic acid through solution of sulphate of silver, in which, as insoluble compounds are formed and carried out of the sphere of the electrical action, the power of transfer is destroyed.[31]

This general view of the mechanism of electrochemical decomposition, it must be confessed, is hardly a satisfying one. It abounds in contradictions that Davy either could not or would not see. Yet, the separate parts were all important. How, for example, did the electrified metallic surfaces really act upon the components of a neutral salt? The action, Davy said, was passed from one particle to another particle so that it was, strictly speaking, not action at a distance. But, there was a series of decompositions and recompositions in which the components *were* free for a moment, and then the attractive and repellent forces must act at a distance. There was, too, a chain of particles stretching between the two poles, but the last sentence of the first paragraph recognized that the chain must have an end, and that the final particles must traverse some of the solution as free chemical agents. What, then, was to be made of the description of the precipitation of barium sulphate or of silver chloride. Why should these compounds be 'carried out of the sphere of the electrical action' if they were only chemical compounds like the others? When Faraday re-read this paper in 1833, he was led to remark that, 'the *mode of action* by which the effects take place is stated very generally, so generally, indeed, that probably a dozen precise schemes of electro-chemical action might be drawn up, differing essentially from each other, yet all agreeing with the statement there given' (482).

If Davy's theory of electrochemical action did not serve to clarify all the problems involved, his approach was of basic importance to the further elucidation of this action. What Davy had done was to introduce chemistry into the problem by identifying the electric forces with chemical affinity. He was thereby able to avoid the confusion of Grotthus who had to direct streams of electrical fluids passing in opposite directions while also keeping his molecular fragments on the right road to ultimate freedom. Davy, to be sure, was hesitant, but he did perceive that the forces present in the poles of the voltaic cell had an immediate effect upon the forces binding compounds together. Thus he could write: 'In the present state of our knowledge, it would be useless to attempt to speculate on the remote cause of the electrical energy, or the reason why different bodies, after being brought into contact, should be found differently electrified; its relation to chemical affinity is, however, sufficiently evident. May it not be identical with it, and an essential property of matter?'[32]

The identification of electricity as an inherent property of matter, introduced a new and potentially fruitful concept into chemistry. It offered the hope that if the electrical state of a chemical substance could be known in detail, then full predictions of its reactions with other substances could be made. Chemistry would pass from a highly empirical art to a fully deductive science. This identification of electricity and chemical activity was explicitly made by Davy. At the end of his paper on the decomposition of the earths, he wrote:

> Other hypotheses might be formed upon the new electro-chemical facts, in which still fewer elements than those allowed in the antiphlogistic or phlogistic theory might be maintained. Certain electrical states always coincide with certain chemical states of bodies. Thus acids are uniformly negative, alkalies positive, and inflammable substances highly positive; and as I have found, acid matters when positively electrified, and alkaline matters when negatively electrified, seemed to lose all their peculiar properties and powers of combination. In these instances the chemical qualities are shewn to depend upon the electrical powers; and it is not impossible that matter of the same kind, possessed of different electrical powers, may exhibit different chemical forms.[33]

It needs little effort of the imagination to realize the next step that should be taken by any of Davy's disciples. If chemical identity depended upon the quality of electrical force of a substance (+ or −), it must also depend upon its quantity. Faraday's law of electrochemistry by which he showed the identity between electrical quantity and chemical equivalents was an extension of Davy's insight into the nature of matter. As Faraday remarked, however, Davy's insight was never made precise enough to be called a scientific theory.

Between 1806 and Faraday's paper on electrochemistry in 1833, a third theory of electrochemical action was proposed.[34] Its leading exponent was Auguste de la Rive of Geneva, Faraday's friend and correspondent for many years. Faraday took it seriously enough to discuss it and refute it.

De la Rive developed his ideas in a number of articles published in the *Annales de chimie et de physique* and in the *Mémoires de la Société de physique et d'histoire naturelle de Génève* during the 1820's. Each article raised new questions which de la Rive tried to answer in the succeeding one. The result, therefore, was not a coherent theory but a kind of patchwork affair in which specific problems were treated but electrochemistry never dealt with as a whole.

In his first article, de la Rive focused on the problem of the transfer of substances through solutions. He first assured himself that the transfer was really invisible by turning the new achromatic microscope developed by Amici on a solution and observing nothing.[35] Grotthus' hypothesis was then examined and found wanting. How, asked de la Rive, could a chain of decompositions and recompositions account for the migration of different substances that occurred when the solution contained more than one salt? Thus if zinc sulphate were placed in one cup, connected to another cup containing sodium chloride, how could the zinc oxide form a chain with the chlorine?[36] Davy's solution to this problem was rejected out of hand since de la Rive, like Ampère, was a firm believer in the existence of two electrical fluids. Given these fluids, de la Rive then suggested a scheme whereby the transfer of substances could be accomplished.

> These two elementary currents, each endowed with a very strong affinity for molecules of different and opposed nature, are established as soon as the two poles of the pile are placed in a fluid conductor. The current which flows from the + pole attacks the molecule near it, grasps its hydrogen if it is water, or its base if it is a salt, and leaves behind the oxygen or the acid, which is then liberated. This current, attracted by the − pole, carries with it through the liquid conductor, the molecules with which it has united. Not being able to carry them through a dry conductor, like a metal, however, it abandons them when it enters the [−] pole.[37] The negative current acts in the same way on the oxygen or the acid of the molecule that it meets as it leaves its pole. Thus, according to this hypothesis which seems to me to encompass all the observed phenomena, the substances which collect around each pole come from two sources; 1. from one of the elements of a molecule whose other part has been taken away by the escaping current; 2. from the same element carried in by the current arriving from the opposite pole.[38]

De la Rive did not expand upon the curious action of the two electricities, but he did throw out a hint to indicate how he, himself, was tempted to view it.

> What force [he asked] can give rise to this attraction of currents for molecules? is it a result of the attraction of the two electricities for one another? or is it the result of the attraction of the electric currents existing in each molecule, for the similar currents flowing in the liquid? Is it the result of another, unknown force? I shall not attempt to deal with these questions, whose answers are in no way necessary for the explanation of the facts: I shall only remark that the explanation which suggests that the affinity of the currents for the molecules of the [decomposed] substances results from the similar currents in these molecules can be supported by the works and interesting observations made on this subject by M. Ampère.[39]

Even Ampère had not realized that his electrodynamic molecular model could serve to explain electrochemistry. But de la Rive, who had witnessed and even aided Ampère in his brilliant discoveries, was now able to press his friend's concepts into use in this new area. The point is an important one for it helps to explain why Faraday took the pains he did to refute de la Rive. More was at stake than a simple hypothesis; de la Rive's ideas implied the existence of Ampère's electrodynamic molecules and Faraday, by 1833, was convinced these molecules did not exist.[40]

There is one interesting consequence of the introduction of Ampère's molecular model into electrochemistry. The currents surrounding each molecule, it will be remembered, were the results of the decomposition of the neutral ether by the atoms of which the molecules were composed. The electricity, therefore, was not, as Davy had suggested, an inherent part of the molecule but was produced by the molecule from the ether. The independent existence of electricity and matter was made quite explicit by de la Rive.

> In this theory [he wrote of his own work] the production of electricity in the voltaic cell is not due to an electrical principal inherent in each body and proper to its nature, as it is customary to suppose in saying that copper is a metal negative in respect to zinc which is positive; an acid, a body eminently negative; an alkali, a positive substance. Electricity, however, comes from an action, and this action is that which a chemical agent exercises on the surface of a solid body; it is this which gives rise to the separation of the two electrical principles, an effect analogous to that of friction and pressure; in short, of all the mechanical actions which cause motion in all or part of the molecules of a body. . . .[41]

It was while investigating this chemical action that de la Rive was forced to abandon the simplicity of his earlier hypothesis of material transfer, and so complicate his theory as to make it almost incomprehensible. Instead of the simple migration of substances caused by electricity riding piggy-back on them, he had to introduce currents going in two directions at the same time, some carrying matter, others not.[42] It is difficult to believe that anyone really took this later theory seriously, for it is almost impossible to understand what de la Rive meant. Even in the midst of this confusion, however, de la Rive did manage to drive home one further point of considerable importance. Although he could not elucidate the mechanism of chemical action by which the electricity of the pile was produced, he could and did argue forcefully and well that the electricity developed by the pile was the result *solely* of this chemical action. Where Volta, Grotthus, and even Davy had insisted that the mere contact of two dissimilar substances produced an electromotive force, de la Rive showed with equal vigour that in all cases chemical changes were paramount. This was a controversy into which Faraday was to throw himself enthusiastically. In his arguments, he was to draw heavily upon his friend's facts while rejecting his theory absolutely.

When Faraday's attention in 1832 was drawn back again to electrochemistry by the seemingly anomalous decomposing action of a static electrical discharge, he was well aware of the theories then prevalent. They all shared the basic point of view that poles acted at a distance upon the elements of the decomposing bodies, but beyond this there was no agreement. Was electricity a 'power' inherent in bodies or was it a set of fluids existing independently of matter? Did mere contact create electromotive force? or was some chemical action necessary to create the electric current? And, conversely, did chemical action depend upon the electrical state of the reagents, or were chemical affinity and electrical attraction two basically and fundamentally different things? All these questions cried out for answers. Only gradually, however, did Faraday come to realize just how important they were. But, as he penetrated ever more deeply into the subject of electrochemistry, he began to see that nothing less than a revolution was required. When he had finished his second great paper on electrochemical reactions in December 1833, the science stood on new foundations erected by him.

2. Faraday's Theory of Electrochemical Action

Faraday's discovery that electrochemical decomposition could take place when no 'poles', as such, were present, intrigued him. On 7 September 1832, he hesitantly suggested that electrochemical effects 'would seem' to be something other than the result of attraction and repulsion at the poles [103]. This was not a conclusion but a hypothesis and deserved to be tested. Because it also ran counter to every electrochemical theory of the day, Faraday felt it necessary to take a long look at the theories which had been put forward since 1800. His 'reading list' is included in the *Diary* [108½] and illustrates the thoroughness with which Faraday approached every new problem. As he read, some of the contradictions that had earlier escaped his notice appeared and the insufficiencies of the current theories were revealed. These encouraged him to pursue his own tentative conjectures. No doubt, too, his daring was reinforced by the fact that most of the theories with which he now found cause to quarrel were founded on the assumption of electrical fluids. Faraday was still willing to entertain the *possibility* that fluids existed, although his own experimental researches appeared to indicate the opposite. He was not willing to give exclusive allegiance to this idea. At the very beginning of his electrochemical researches, he once more defined his concept of a current. 'By current I mean any thing progressive, whether it be a fluid of Electricity or vibrations or generally progressive forces' [116].

The fundamental question that Faraday now set out to answer was, how could such a 'current' cause electrochemical decompositions? Stated in such a naked fashion, the question was of little help in the design of either experiments or theory. It could, however, be broken down into subsidiary questions to which specific answers could be given. First of all, and the one which was uppermost in Faraday's mind at the commencement of his electrochemical researches, was whether the forces of attraction and repulsion, acting at a distance, were essential, or even possible, in electrochemical reactions. Then, if it could be shown that such forces did not, in fact, act in the voltaic circuit, what kind of forces could be substituted for them? And how would these forces act, if not at a distance, to achieve the observed results? The answers to these questions were to lead Faraday to a radically new view of electrochemical action. All were present in his mind from the very beginning of his researches and they are inextricably intertwined in his laboratory record. For clarity's sake we shall here trace them out individually and combine them only at the end when the fully developed theory emerged.

The problem of the action of the electrical current at a distance was attacked in a number of ingenious ways. The first was a variation of the original experiment which had called Faraday's attention to the possibility of the non-existence of poles. In his original experiment, he had discharged electricity from a static electricity generator through turmeric paper soaked in sodium sulphate solution and from thence into the air. This he interpreted as indicating the absence of poles or centres of attraction. It said nothing, however, about action at a distance and it was conceivable that some poles did exist which had escaped his attention. The thing to do, therefore, was to attack the problem directly. Two pieces of litmus and turmeric paper were each placed upon separate pieces of glass and connected by a string four feet long soaked in the solution of sodium sulphate. Wires from the electrostatic generator were now placed upon the two papers and the machine was put into operation.

> On working the machine, [Faraday reported] the same evolution of acid and alkali appeared as in the former instance, and with equal readiness, notwithstanding that the places of their appearance were four feet apart from each other. Finally, a piece of string, seventy feet long, was used. It was insulated in the air by suspenders of silk, so that the electricity passed through its entire length: decomposition took place exactly as in former cases, alkali and acid appearing at the two extremities in their proper places (455).

The conclusion to be drawn from this experiment fairly leaped from the page. *Electrochemical decomposition was independent of the distance separating*

the 'poles'. This was a direct refutation of Davy's position. In his great
1806 paper he had specifically referred to the diminution of force with
distance in the electrochemical solution, and backed it up by experiment.
'He states', wrote Faraday, 'that in a circuit of ten inches of water, solution
of sulphate of potassa placed four inches from the positive pole, did not
decompose; whereas when only two inches from that pole, it did render
up its elements' (483).[43]

Faraday's experiment did not *prove* that the electric forces did not act at
a distance but only that the quantity of action did not vary with the distance. Since no other force acting at a distance obeyed this kind of law, it
was certainly a presumptive proof that the force was not akin to that of
gravity and must depend on the particles of the solution rather than upon
the mere space separating the particles from the poles. There was a way,
however, to penetrate to the molecular level itself and Faraday seized
upon it. Suppose that the 'poles' did somehow exert a force across empty
space upon the molecules in solution. Then grant Grotthus' mechanism of
decomposition. The force, emanating from the poles, would tear the
molecule apart and the two fragments would move in opposite directions
until they met other fragments with which they could combine. During
this interval, however brief, the fragments would be free chemical agents
and should act as such. Davy had tried to detect them, but had failed.
Faraday now made the attempt in a most beautifully conceived and
executed experiment. He took ordinary gelatine and made a series of
slices of different composition; some were made with distilled water,
while others were mixed with a sodium sulphate solution. He then
connected two metal plates to a voltaic battery and interposed between
them the gelatinous discs in the following order: plate, litmus paper, pure
jelly, litmus paper, saline jelly, turmeric paper, pure jelly, turmeric
paper, plate (see Figure 3). When the circuit was closed, the turmeric and

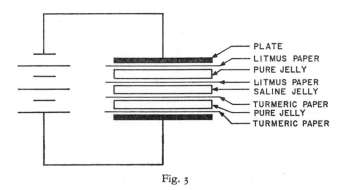

Fig. 3

litmus paper in the middle of the 'jelly sandwich' remained unchanged while those next to the plates changed colour. Faraday's thinking here appears perfectly clear. If the molecular fragments did exist as free chemical agents, they had probably not been detected because they moved too rapidly through the solution, and the interval between decomposition and combination was too short. The jellies, however, should slow up this process sufficiently to permit evidence of the chemical presence of the fragments to become visible. No such evidence was forthcoming and Faraday was able to conclude: 'the transference was good, ready and effective, but the evolution seemed to be altogether at the poles. No signs of the free acid or alkali in its transit appeared' [169].

He immediately repeated a variant of his original experiment of discharging static electricity through a conducting solution.

> Now worked with large electrical machine as at [135], repeating that experiment.
> Then instead of connecting the discharging train wire directly with the paper moistened with hyd. pot. on which the wire rested, that paper was put on a glass plate and connected with the discharging train by 4 feet of wet string, insulated through its course in the air. The platina wire of $\frac{1}{12}''$ diameter resting as before on the paper moistened with the hydriodate solution. On turning the machine 30 times the spot of iodine was as brown as before.
> Now the hyd. pot. paper was made to touch a piece of paper moistened in pure water and the end of the wire put upon the latter. Upon turning the machine *no spot* of iodine was produced. When the wire was gradually brought on the paper nearer and nearer to that containing the hyd. pot., still no spot of iodine was produced until it actually touched it [172-4].

From this it followed that any 'action at a distance' of the platinum wire 'pole' was insufficient to cause decomposition *until* a current of electricity actually passed through the potassium iodide solution. Only when the distance between the 'pole' and the solution became zero, i.e. when contact was made, did the solution decompose and free iodine appear. 'Thus', Faraday noted, 'the iodine is not transferred instantly and in a free state, but gradually and by successive combination and decomp., and the experiment corresponds with those w[h]ere jelly and the Volt. battery was used in proving the successive combination, etc., etc. of the elements moving between the metallic poles' [175]. Faraday's first question had been answered definitely: the forces involved in electrochemical decomposition did *not* act at a distance upon the molecules of a solution and they did not vary as the inverse square of the distance separating any particular molecule from a pole. This knocked all existing theories into a cocked hat and Faraday found himself faced with the problem of devising a new one to take their place.

The nature and mode of action of the forces involved in electrochemical decomposition had already suggested themselves to Faraday in his earliest experiment. There he had noted that 'the effects of decomposition would seem rather to depend upon a relief of the chemical affinity in one direction and an exaltation of it in the other' [104]. As with Davy, Faraday suspected that the electricity involved in any electrochemical operation was an inherent property of matter and not a separate fluid. The action of the voltaic circuit served to distort the electrical force of chemical combination and the electric 'current' was, in reality, the progressive passage of this distortion through the solution. It was one thing to speculate in this fashion but it was quite another to reduce these speculations to a coherent theory of electrochemical action. It took Faraday from September of 1832 until August of 1833 to achieve this feat.

His early experiments intended to test his hypothesis were aimed primarily at strengthening his own conviction of the correctness of the path he was following and the falsity of that of his predecessors. Thus, he wondered what would happen when a single element, uncombined with any other, were placed within the circuit. If there were poles and they acted at a distance upon such elements, should there not be a migration of these suspended or dissolved particles to one of the poles? If, on the other hand, the passage of the 'current' merely distorted the pattern of the forces of affinity surrounding the element there would be no reason for the element to move since no other substance existed nearby to seize upon this distortion and bring about combination [118]. When the experiments were carried out [647–9] his supposition was shown to be true (546). The reasoning here should be carefully noted for it reveals clearly Faraday's continuing use of the hypothesis of point atoms. He was thinking in terms of patterns of force which unlike the forces associated with Daltonian atoms, were changeable and variable under different conditions. A Daltonian could never conceive of an 'exaltation' of the force of affinity whereas to Faraday the addition and subtraction of the forces represented by Boscovich's curve was a necessary concomitant of all chemical action.

A more direct test of his hypothesis suggested itself to Faraday in December of 1832. If he were correct, the exaltation of affinity on one side and its reduction on the other in the elements of a chemical compound should cause them to separate and combine with other neighbouring particles in much the same way as Grotthus had suggested. Thus there

I

would be a chain of decompositions and recompositions provided the substances were free to move. So, asked Faraday, 'Can an electric current, voltaic or not, decompose a solid body, ice, etc., etc. If it can, does it give structure at the time' [218–19]. There was little doubt in Faraday's mind that decomposition would take place, for it was perfectly obvious that the force of chemical affinity was stronger by far than that of solid cohesion. He was, therefore, extremely surprised to discover that an electric current would not pass through a thin sheet of ice and that no decomposition products were formed even when fairly high voltages were applied [222 ff.].[44] Faraday always profited from his surprises and this case was no exception. Two new lines of investigation immediately came to his mind. The one was based on analogy and proved simple to follow. If water, when solid, would not conduct electricity, would other solids, when melted, prove to be conductors and decompose with the passage of an electric current? When a large number of substances were tried, many were found to behave like water. This, too, was unexpected for previous investigators had insisted that no electrochemical decomposition could take place unless water were present. Faraday was now able to refute this and, more importantly, to suggest that the ability to conduct electricity and be decomposed by it would provide clues of basic importance to the understanding of chemical combination.

This *general assumption of conducting power* by bodies as soon as they pass from the solid to the liquid state [he remarked], offers a new and extraordinary character, the existence of which, as far as I know, has not before been suspected; and it seems importantly connected with some properties and relations of the particles of matter which I may now briefly point out (412).

In almost all the instances as yet observed, which are governed by this law, the substances experimented with have been those which were not only compound bodies, but such as contain elements known to arrange themselves at the opposite poles; and were also such as could be *decomposed* by the electrical current. When conduction took place, decomposition occurred; when decomposition ceased, conduction ceased also; and it becomes a fair and an important question, Whether the conduction itself may not, wherever the law holds good, be a consequence not merely of the capability, but of the act of decomposition? And that question may be accompanied by another, namely, Whether solidification does not prevent conduction, merely by chaining the particles to their places, under the influence of aggregation, and preventing their final separation in the manner necessary for decomposition? (413).

Again, there are many substances which contain elements such as would be expected to arrange themselves at the opposite poles of the pile, and therefore in that respect fitted for decomposition, which yet do not conduct. Amongst these are the iodide of sulphur, per-iodide of zinc, per-chloride of tin, chloride of arsenic, hydrated chloride of arsenic, acetic acid, orpiment, realgar, artificial camphor, etc.; and from these it might perhaps be assumed that decomposition is dependent upon conducting power, and not the latter upon the former. The true relation, however, of conduction and decomposition in those bodies governed by the general law which it is the object of this paper to establish, can only be satisfactorily made out from a far more extensive series of observations than those I have yet been able to supply (415).

At this moment, Faraday could not really spare the time to follow up the important distinction between those substances which would conduct and decompose when liquid and those which would not, although theory appeared to require they should. Instead he had to content himself with the 'Query – are not all compounds of single proportionals conductors, or how far does it hold?' [299]. The answer to this question and its corollary concerning compounds containing more than single proportionals was to be of fundamental importance to the evolution of modern chemistry. Faraday's later ideas on this subject contained the germ of the distinction between ionic and co-valent bonding although the full utilization of this concept in chemistry did not come until the generation after his death.[45]

In 1833, however, the problem that concerned him deeply was the one involving conduction and decomposition. The current theories made the conduction of electricity in a voltaic circuit the result of the decomposition of the substances in the circuit. Faraday now felt that precisely the opposite must be the case. His *Diary* vividly recorded his struggles to clarify his thought. Thus on 24 January 1833, he wrote: 'If ice will not conduct, is it because it *cannot* decompose?' [248] and again on 15 February: 'Does not insulation by solid shew that decomposition by V. pile is due to slight power super added upon previous chemical attractive forces of particles when fluid? Since mere fixation of particles prevents it, must be slight' [286]. At first glance, the distinction Faraday wished to draw appears trivial. Does it really matter whether the passage of electricity caused the decomposition or whether the decomposition was what permitted the passage of the electricity? To Faraday it made all the difference in the world. Both Grotthus and de la Rive had employed material agents for electricity and it was the decomposition of the substances in the circuit that permitted the electric fluids to pass. To reverse the process was to deny the materiality of electricity and this Faraday was quite willing to do. 'Does it [insulation by solid] not shew very important relation between the decomposability of such bodies and their conducting power, as if here the electricity were only a transfer of a series of alternations or vibrations and *not* a body transmitted directly. May settle or relate to question of materiality or fluid of Electricity' [287].

There is no doubt that Faraday took seriously the idea of the passage of vibrations as the equivalent of the electric current. In December of 1832 he had tried to decompose water by introducing a rapidly vibrating wire into a glass filled with distilled water. 'The sounds were high and vibration powerful, but no bubbles appeared,' he noted with obvious disappointment [190]. Nevertheless the concept of the electric 'current' as a wave transmitted through a conductor, had a firm hold upon his mind. It had already led him to the discovery of electromagnetic induction and he was not, as yet, prepared to abandon it. Rather, he now found it relatively easy to reconcile this hypothesis with his other conjectures. Given the 'fact' that during electrochemical processes the chemical affinities of the elements of the compound undergoing decomposition were 'exalted' in opposite directions: given also the fact that the field of action of these elements was larger than that granted by conventional atomists (i.e. given point atoms), Faraday could erect a general theory of electrochemistry which did not require poles, action at a distance in the conventional sense, or electrical fluids. No one can present this theory more clearly than the creator of it and a somewhat lengthy quotation may, therefore, perhaps be forgiven.

> *Judging from facts only,* there is not as yet the slightest reason for considering the influence which is present in what we call the electric current, – whether in metals or fused bodies or humid conductors, or even in air, flame, and rarefied elastic media, – as a compound or complicated influence. It has never been resolved into simpler or elementary influences, and may perhaps best be conceived of as *an axis of power having contrary forces, exactly equal in amount, in contrary directions.*
>
> Passing to the consideration of electro-chemical decomposition, it appears to me that the effect is produced by an *internal corpuscular action,* exerted according to the direction of the electric current, and that it is due to a force either *superadded to,* or *giving direction to the ordinary chemical affinity* of the bodies present. The body under decomposition may be considered as a mass of acting particles, all those which are included in the course of the electric current contributing to the final effect; and it is because the ordinary chemical affinity is relieved, weakened, or partly neutralized by the influence of the electric current in one direction parallel to the course of the latter, and strengthened or added to in the opposite direction, that the combining particles have a tendency to pass in opposite courses.
>
> In this view the effect is considered as *essentially dependent* upon the *mutual chemical affinity* of the particles of opposite kinds. Particles *aa* . . . could not be transferred or travel from one pole N towards the other P, unless they found particles of the opposite kind *bb*, ready to pass in the contrary direction: for

it is by virtue of their increased affinity for those particles, combined with their diminished affinity for such as are behind them in their course, that they are urged forward; and when any one particle a . . ., arrives at the pole, it is excluded or set free, because the particle b of the opposite kind, with which it was the moment before in combination, has, under the superinducing influence of the current, a greater attraction for the particle a', which is before it in its course, than for the particle a, towards which its affinity has been weakened (517–19).

Thus while the elements migrated in opposite directions the electrical force was transmitted in waves of combination and decomposition. The action was from particle to particle (provided *particle* be understood in the Boscovichean sense), and there was no need to call upon extraneous fluids for explanation. Just how the current as an 'axis of power' accomplished the observed decompositions, however, did require further explanation for the idea of an *axis* implied action along the line connecting the poles. The simplest fact of electrochemistry contradicted this. If wires were used as poles, the deposition of substances upon these poles was uniform and not, as might be expected, greater on the sides of the wires facing one another. This, as a matter of fact, is what Grotthus had suggested really did happen, so Faraday was at pains to refute it.

It is not here assumed that the acting particles must be in a right line between the poles. The lines of action which may be supposed to represent the electric currents passing through a decomposing liquid, have in many experiments very irregular forms; and even in the simplest case of two wires or points immersed as poles in a drop or larger single portion of fluid, these lines must diverge rapidly from the poles; and the direction in which the chemical affinity between particles is most powerfully modified . . . will vary with the direction of these lines, according constantly with them. But even in reference to these lines or currents, it is not supposed that the particles which mutually affect each other must of necessity be parallel to them, but only that they shall accord generally with their direction. Two particles, placed in a line perpendicular to the electric current passing in any particular place, are not supposed to have their ordinary chemical relations towards each other affected; but as the line joining them is inclined one way to the current their mutual affinity is increased; as it is inclined in the other direction it is diminished; and the effect is a maximum, when that line is parallel to the current (521).

The reader will immediately recognize the introduction of the line of force into electrochemistry. These lines, now of electric force, did not have the regularity and symmetry of their magnetic cousins for they might be varied according to the location, magnitude, and disposition of the poles. Suppose, however, that the poles could be reduced to mere points at the longitudinal extremities of a perfectly homogeneous solution capable of undergoing electrochemical decomposition. Now imagine, using Faraday's theory that the transmission of the electric force was directly from particle to particle, what the ensemble of these lines of electric force would be. They would, in fact, be the same as the magnetic lines of force. In 1833 Faraday did not realize this consequence clearly but what he did see was to influence the whole course of his future thought. That the action was from particle to particle he felt he had proven; the lines of transmission of this action were curves, whereas action at a distance took place in straight lines. From this he concluded, and was to insist upon it time and time again, that when it could be shown that force was transmitted in curved lines *it must be the result of the action of contiguous particles.*

The character of the action of contiguous particles had enough oddness about it to deserve an explanation. What Faraday was proposing made little sense in terms of conventional Daltonian atoms which could act upon one another only in two ways: by direct impact or at a distance according to the fixed laws of Newtonian dynamics. Faraday, as we have insisted upon so often, preferred the force-atoms of Boscovich in which atomic, or better, molecular, dimensions were to be defined in terms of a volume of (varying) force, rather than in terms of solid, material boundaries. Thus 'contiguous' particles could have their centres quite far apart and still be 'contiguous'. This 'fact' was incomprehensible to the Daltonian who visualized contiguity in terms of material contact. Faraday knew this and felt it necessary to explain himself more explicitly.

> The theory which I have ventured to put forth (almost) requires an admission, that in a compound body capable of electro-chemical decomposition the elementary particles have a mutual relation to, and influence upon each other, extending beyond those with which they are immediately combined. Thus in water, a particle of hydrogen in combination with oxygen is considered as not altogether indifferent to other particles of oxygen, although they are combined with other particles of hydrogen; but to have an affinity or attraction towards them, which, though it does not at all approach in force, under ordinary circumstances, to that by which it is combined with its own particle, can, under the electric influence, exerted in a definite direction, be made even to surpass it. This general relation of particles already in combination to other particles with which they are not combined, is sufficiently distinct in numerous results of a purely chemical character; especially in those where partial decompositions only take place, and in Berthollet's experiments on the effects of quantity upon affinity: and it probably has a direct relation to, and connexion with, attraction of aggregation, both in solids and fluids. It is a remarkable circumstance, that in gases and vapours, where the attraction of aggregation ceases, there likewise the decomposing powers of electricity apparently cease, and there also the chemical action of quantity is no longer

evident. It seems not unlikely, that the inability to suffer decomposition in these cases may be dependent upon the absence of that mutual attractive relation of the particles which is the cause of aggregation (523).[46]

To chemists still visualizing chemical combination in terms of hooks and eyes, such playing with complex patterns of force to explain physical and chemical actions must have seemed like gibberish. The coolness of the reception given Faraday's theoretical concepts may be felt in the remarks of one of his close friends and himself a practising chemist. Richard Phillips, orthodox Daltonian, wrote to Charles Babbage in 1832: 'Mistakes have led to some theories which are caricatures of nature, and really the greedy recognition of gratuitous powers and fanciful modes of action is a libel on the soi-disant philosophers of the day. Farraday [*sic*] would do more if he would not work under the silly theories of the last ages.'[47]

Faraday's 'silly theories' had the amazing ability to lead him to discovery after discovery. People like Phillips might find his theoretical views odd and even unacceptable, but they could not deny the force of the conclusions Faraday drew from them. So it was with his theory of electrochemical decomposition. He had not only devised it in order to circumvent the objections that he himself had raised against the existing theories; he had also realized its power as an instrument of explanation and discovery. On the level of explanation, Faraday pointed to a number of difficulties inherent in the older theories which vanished in his. Thus, for example, he was able neatly to dispose of the strange action of poles which, after attracting a body across the space of the decomposing solution, suddenly became indifferent to it when it arrived at the pole.

The theory I have ventured to put forth [he wrote] appears to me to explain all the prominent features of electro-chemical decomposition in a satisfactory manner.

In the first place, it explains why, in all ordinary cases, the evolved substances *appear only at the poles*; for the poles are the limiting surfaces of the decomposing substance, and except at them, every particle finds other particles having a contrary tendency with which it can combine.

Then it explains why, in numerous cases, the elements or evolved substances are not *retained* by the poles; and this is no small difficulty in those theories which refer the decomposing effect directly to the attractive power of the poles. If, in accordance with the usual theory, a piece of platina be supposed to have sufficient power to attract a particle of hydrogen from the particle of oxygen with which it was the instant before combined, there seems no sufficient reason, nor any fact, except those to be explained, which show why it should not, according to analogy with all ordinary attractive forces, as those of gravitation, magnetism, cohesion, chemical affinity, etc., *retain* that particle which it had just before taken from a distance and from previous combination. Yet it does not do so, but allows it to escape freely. Nor does this depend upon its assuming the gaseous state, for acids and alkalies, etc., are left equally at liberty to diffuse themselves through the fluid surrounding the pole, and show no particular tendency to combine with or adhere to the latter. And though there are plenty of cases where combination with the pole does take place, they do not at all explain the instances of non-combination, and do not therefore in their particular action reveal the general principle of decomposition (534–6).

In his theory, Faraday was quick to point out, there was no such problem.

The evolved substances are *expelled* from the decomposing mass . . . not *drawn out by an attraction* which ceases to act on one particle without any assignable reason, while it continues to act on another of the same kind: and whether the poles be metal, water, or air, still the substances are evolved, and are sometimes set free, whilst at others they unite to the matter of the poles, according to the chemical nature of the latter, i.e. their chemical relation to those particles which are leaving the substance under operation (537).

There was another circumstance in electrochemistry which had long puzzled chemists. Bodies which had the strongest affinity for one another were the most easily decomposed in the voltaic circuit. Sir Humphry Davy's most spectacular experiments had been those in which he had passed acids through bases, without combination taking place, by the mere instrument of the electric current. This was a strange force, indeed, which was able to separate elements bound to one another with the strongest bonds and yet unable to decompose compounds whose elements could be dissociated by the gentle heat of a candle. But, as Faraday triumphantly stated, 'if I be right in the view I have taken of the effects, it will appear, that that which made the *wonder*, is in fact the *essential condition* of transfer and decomposition . . .' (550). For if Faraday's views were correct, the passage of the electric current 'exalted the affinity on one side and reduced it on the other'. A binary compound in which the forces of affinity were extraordinarily strong would then easily be decomposed for as the affinity of element a in the molecule ab were exalted in one direction, it would become enmeshed with the affinity of b' of molecule $a'b'$ which had been exalted in the other. Thus a and b' would combine and the chain of decompositions and recombinations would begin. If, on the other hand, a and b were united by weak forces, the exaltation and reduction would be correspondingly weak and the disturbance of the equilibrium of molecular forces might not be sufficient to cause decomposition. In this case more outside force (i.e. a stronger current) would have to be applied before the process could proceed.[48]

In all these cases, Faraday's theory was more simple, more in accord with the facts, and more elegant than those he was combating. But, it might be argued (and was), it is really only the facts that count. Theories are interpretations and, as such, a thousand theories could be devised to account for a single set of facts. Faraday's theory might be superior to the others in explanatory power but this was of little importance; what was of fundamental interest was the discovery of new facts which led, in turn, to new laws summing up these facts. For a theory to be considered as approaching 'Truth' it had to be shown that it led to the discovery of new facts. This Faraday's theory was quite capable of doing; the two laws of electrolysis which now go under his name were directly deducible from his theory of electrochemical action.

In his investigations of the identity of electricities, Faraday had discovered the direct proportionality between the quantity of current that passed through a solution and the amount of hydrogen and oxygen evolved.[49] This was easily explained on the basis of the new theory. The passage of the electric current, after all, was nothing more than the successive distortions of the chemical affinity of the particles of oxygen and hydrogen. The forces of affinity, as the law of combining proportions showed, were perfectly definite; hence, it followed that the action of the electric force must be directly proportional to the number of decompositions and recompositions which occurred in the solution during any given period of time. This number, in turn, was reflected in the quantities of the gases evolved.

The next step was not a large one to take. 'Is it possible,' Faraday asked, 'it may generalise so far as to give equal chemical action estimated on the same elements on variable media? Ought it not be so if decomposition essential to conduction?" [522]. This query was the starting-point for a series of experiments.

> By putting cups and expts. in succession and sending the same electrical current through both or all, are sure that each is submitted to an equal force. Can try well this way whether the same quantity of different intensity does the same chemical work using *same dilute* S[ulphuric] A[cid] but *different sized poles,* and collecting gas, and that will tell – some poles mere wires, others large plates [543].

These experiments were performed at the end of May 1833, and gave the answers Faraday expected. The length of the path taken by the electric current through the solution and the size of the poles were irrelevant to the final effect. The quantity of the decomposition products depended *solely* upon the quantity of electricity that passed. Such a conclusion could not be reconciled with any theory that required action of the poles at a distance for there the electrical force must diminish with the distance. Faraday saw the situation quite differently. 'Expect that a plate placed any ways across a decomposing portion will give same decomposing effect,' he wrote in his *Diary*, 'if the quantity of electricity retained the same, i.e. expect that the chemical action in any possible section, plane or curved or oblique, between the poles is a constant quantity' [548].

When experiment justified these expectations, Faraday was in possession of the first law of electrolysis.[50] Electrochemical action depended solely upon the *quantity* of electricity which passed through a solution. Or, to put it in Faraday's words, 'chemical action or decomposing power is exactly proportional to the quantity of electricity which passes in solution' [638] (821).

While the first law thus stated the dependence of the electrochemical action solely upon the amount of current, the second law related this action more precisely to the chemical properties of the elements themselves. It, too, followed directly from Faraday's theory of electrochemical action.

We must now look at Faraday's theory from a purely chemical viewpoint. The elements may be visualized as composed of a number of point atoms whose force fields mesh to produce a complex pattern of forces which determined the affinity of these elements for each other. It was this pattern which determined the combining power of the elements with one another. Ever since the work of Proust and Dalton at the beginning of the nineteenth century it had been known that this power was specific for each element and that there were quite definite combining ratios, by weight, to be found in all chemical processes. The specific combining weights by which elements entered into compounds were known as equivalent weights. Thus 1 gramme of hydrogen always combined with 8 grammes of oxygen to form water and if hydrogen were assigned the arbitrary relative weight of 1, then 8 became oxygen's equivalent weight. Largely through the efforts of J. J. Berzelius and his pupils, it was shown that a general table of equivalent weights could be created so that these weights were considered to be constant in all chemical processes. This invariability of combining weights was the strongest argument that could be brought forward to prove that the so-called chemical elements were atoms (i.e. indivisible and ultimate particles). Davy and Faraday, we know, preferred to assign the cause of the invariability to the constancy of the forces associated with the molecules made up of point atoms. In their view, equivalent weights were the direct consequence of the chemical affinity of the particles of the elements.

By 1833 Faraday had proven to his own satisfaction that the electric 'current' acted upon the chemical substances which underwent electrochemical decomposition *solely* by distorting the field of force which *was* the affinity of these elements. The process of electrochemical decomposition he viewed as the successive distortion and restoration of this pattern of force. No new force or substance was permanently added and the phenomena could be accounted for in terms of this play of affinities. In other words, electrochemical decomposition was a *purely* chemical affair stimulated by the application of electrical force. Therefore, it followed that the ordinary laws of chemistry must apply to electrochemistry. The first law of electrochemistry then made it possible for Faraday to state specifically how these laws did apply.

The first law stated that chemical action was exactly proportional to the quantity of electricity which passed through the solution undergoing decomposition. Faraday's theory attributed the decomposition to the distortion of the forces of affinity. The laws of chemistry, as Faraday understood them, correlated the forces of affinity with the combining or equivalent weights of the elements. The second law was now obvious: The amounts of different substances deposited or dissolved by the same quantity of electricity were proportional to their chemical equivalent weights.[51]

This law, as deduced from theory, now required experimental verification, and the experimental path was both clear and obvious. All Faraday had to do was to show that for equal quantities of electricity, the weights of the evolved substances in electrochemical decomposition were in the same ratio as their equivalent weights. Two measurements on a large number of different compounds were, therefore, necessary; the total quantity of electricity had to be measured, and the weights of the evolved substances determined. The first law provided an easy method for measuring the quantity of electricity and Faraday constructed a new instrument based upon it. He called it a volta electrometer, for it was intended to measure voltaic electricity (i.e. electricity generated by a voltaic pile). It had a number of different forms but the principle was the same in all. A tube in which two platinum plates were affixed by wires extending through the walls was filled with slightly acidic water and inserted in the voltaic circuit. The electricity had to pass through the water before it could reach the cell in which the electrochemical decomposition occurred.

As it passed, it decomposed the water and the two gases thus evolved rose to the top of the tube. By calibrating the tube, the relative amounts of gas evolved in different experiments could easily be determined. Since these amounts were directly proportional to the quantity of electricity which had passed, a direct comparison in two or more experiments could be made.

The measurement of the weights of the evolved substances was a straightforward problem in quantitative analysis of which Faraday was a master. During the autumn of 1833 Faraday carefully experimented on a large number of substances. He realized very early the necessity of distinguishing between primary and secondary effects (i.e. between substances that were produced directly by the decomposing effects of the current and those produced by the materials of which the poles were composed) and with great care examined the results. With his usual ability to detect sources of error he was able to explain those cases which appeared to deviate from the law. By December the evidence was overwhelming; the second law of electrochemistry was not only theoretically sound but was supported by the experimental evidence (751 ff.).

There is a curious point connected with Faraday's discovery of the second law of electrochemistry. In his Faraday Memorial Lecture of 1881, the great German physicist, Hermann von Helmholtz, suggested that the second law of electrochemistry clearly implied the atomic nature of electricity.[52] The reason for this is clear. If elements were distinguished from one another solely by their atomic weight as Dalton had said, and if the same amount of electricity deposited amounts of these elements upon the poles in ratios of their equivalent weights, then it is seen that on the atomic level each element received the same quantum of electricity. This quantum is what we would today call the electron. It has been asked why Faraday failed to see this. The answer has two parts. In the first place, Faraday was loath to associate a certain quantum of force with a new particle and, hence, did not even think in these terms. Secondly, the discovery that there was a specific electrical force associated with the particles of matter was used by Faraday to drive home the faults in previous theories, such as that of Ampère and de la Rive, which had considered electricity and matter to be two separate things. As Faraday himself put it:

... considering the definite relations of electricity as developed in the preceding parts of the present paper, the results prove that the quantity of electricity which, being naturally associated with the particles of matter, gives them their combining power, is able, when thrown into a current, to separate those particles from their state of combination; or, in other words, that *the electricity which decomposes, and that which is evolved by the decomposition of, a certain quantity of matter, are alike.*

The harmony which this theory of the definite evolution and the equivalent definite action of electricity introduces into the associated theories of definite proportions and electro-chemical affinity, is very great. According to it, the equivalent weights of bodies are simply those quantities of them which contain equal quantities of electricity, or have naturally equal electric powers; it being the ELECTRICITY which *determines* the equivalent number, *because* it determines the combining force. Or, if we adopt the atomic theory or phraseology, then the atoms of bodies which are equivalents to each other in their ordinary chemical action, have equal quantities of electricity naturally associated with them. But I must confess I am jealous of the term *atom*; for though it is very easy to talk of atoms, it is very difficult to form a clear idea of their nature, especially when compound bodies are under consideration (868–9).

It would seem, after this, that one of two developments had to take place. Those people who were adherents of the fluid theory of electricity should have discovered the electron, or at least seen that electricity came in discrete bundles. Or, it should have been recognized that since chemical effects depended upon electricity, then electricity was an inherent power of matter. Nothing of the sort happened. The fluidists continued much as they had before, simply ignoring the implications of Faraday's work while utilizing the results. And Faraday, almost alone among his contemporaries, continued to prefer forces to material fluids to explain electricity.

3. The New Electrochemical Nomenclature[53]

In 1810, when Faraday had turned to the inestimable Dr Watts for guidance through the maze of learning, he had read one of Dr Watts's exhortations and had never forgotten it. The good Doctor had stressed above all else the necessary connexion, if one were to think clearly, between words and the things they were to represent. 'The first direction for youth is this,' he wrote, 'learn betimes to distinguish between words and things. Get clear and plain ideas of the things you are set to study. Do not content yourselves with mere words and names lest your laboured improvements only amass a heap of unintelligible phrases, and you feed upon husks instead of kernels.'[54] Ever since 1821, when his ideas on the nature of electromagnetic force challenged those of Ampère, Faraday had been conscious of the ever-widening gap between current terminology and his theories. For practical reasons he had continued to use terms which meant quite different things to him and to his readers. The primary example is the term *current*; as we have seen, Faraday constantly felt it necessary to underline the fact that when he used the term he did not necessarily mean the flow of the electric fluids, but wished to be understood in quite another sense. There had been occasions, too, when he had had to invent new terms in order properly to express his ideas. In his first paper on electromagnetic induction, he had introduced the 'electrotonic state' as an essential condition for electromagnetic induction. His diffidence about being the inventor of new terms was revealed in a passage in the letter to Richard Phillips which announced the discovery of electromagnetic induction. '*The Electro-tonic state*. What do you think of that; am I not a bold man, ignorant as I am, to coin words – but I have consulted the scholars.'[55]

Until 1833, the problem of correct terminology was not a serious one. Faraday was able to use the generally accepted terms, even if he did have sometimes to warp their meanings to suit his own ideas. It was only rarely that he had to 'consult the scholars'. As his ideas on the mechanism of electrochemistry developed, however, he found it increasingly difficult to remain within the conventional terminological framework. From the very beginning he was in serious trouble. Having discovered that electrochemical decomposition could take place when no 'poles', as such, were present, what sense did it make to continue to talk of 'poles'? Here, too, was a very clear case where no amount of modification or explanation would suffice. The very word 'pole' carried with it an entire theory; 'poles', almost by definition, were the centres of attraction and repulsion which accomplished the decomposition of the solutions in which they were plunged. For Faraday this was a good case of kernels that had been turned into husks. The word 'poles' was so overladen with theory that it would be impossible to use it and not have the reader almost automatically assume centres of attraction and repulsion. Since Faraday was attempting to refute this very view, his need for new terms for the poles was vital.

There was another set of terms which had become common in electrochemistry by the 1830's. These were *electro-negative* and *electro-positive* which had received official recognition in J. J. Berzelius' *Essai sur la théorie des proportions chimiques et sur l'influence chimique de l'électricité*.[56] If used merely to indicate to which 'pole' certain elements migrated, the terms were unexceptionable. Berzelius, however, had erected a general theory of the relation of the electric fluids to the atoms of bodies upon this distinction. To use the terms meant, to most of Faraday's readers, that Berzelius' theory was also to be the basis of the discussion. This, too,

Faraday could not permit for, as he pointed out in the Seventh Series, he was jealous of the term *atom*, and was certainly no ardent partisan of the fluid theories of electricity.

To recognize that certain terms were loaded with a theoretical significance which made them inapplicable to other theories of electrochemical action was only part of the problem. By recognizing that terms often carried theoretical overtones Faraday was made aware of the difficulties that awaited him when the attempt would be made to substitute new terms. The last thing he wanted to do was to tie the new terms to a new theory, even his own, for he was very conscious of the ephemeral nature of theories. He was, of course, convinced that he was on the right track but he also knew that all promulgators of theory felt the same way. What he wanted to do was to devise terms which did no more than describe the observed effects and implied no theory whatsoever. There were two ways to approach this problem. One he had already utilized in the paper on the identity of electricities and may be termed the operational approach. It involved giving new names which referred only to the operations by which the effect was produced. The advantages of this mode of proceeding were outlined by Faraday in a letter to William Whewell of Trinity College, Cambridge, in answer to Whewell's criticism of the new terms.

> Your remarks on my phraseology [he wrote] I am quite willing to admit; but let me remind you that I and Ampère use words, i.e. names, in very different ways. My words *Volta-induction – magneto-electric-induction – magneto-electricity – electro-magnetism*, etc., are merely intended to indicate how the effects included under them are obtained whereas Ampère by the word 'Electrodynamic' essentially implies a theory which theory may be wrong. The origin of all these effects may be something in such a state that when we come to know what it is the word *electrodynamic* may not apply.[57]

Even these terms were not without fault as Faraday immediately noted. 'Perhaps I may be equally wrong,' he wrote, 'nay more so by far, in the word induction but at all events the prefixes, *Volta, magneto, magneto electric, electro magnetic,* pledge me to no theory, and yet have a certain distinctness of sense which makes them useful.'[58]

This principle of nomenclature was, unfortunately, inapplicable to electrochemistry. There were no operations which could serve the function of name-givers. New terms had to be invented and for this purpose Faraday once more had to consult the scholars. In the introduction to the Seventh Series of the *Experimental Researches*, he warned the reader that he was going to introduce a new set of terms in place of the old since he was intent upon attacking the older theories implied by these terms. 'To avoid, therefore, confusion and circumlocution, and for the sake of greater precision of expression than I can otherwise obtain, I have deliberately considered the subject with two friends, and with their assistance and concurrence in framing them, I purpose henceforward using certain other terms . . .' (662). The two friends were Dr Whitlock Nicholl and the Rev. Robert Willis, of Caius College, Cambridge. There is little doubt that Dr Nicholl played by far the major role.[59]

Dr Nicholl was Faraday's personal physician and friend. He was far more than an ordinary physician, possessing an intellectual appetite and curiosity which led him into areas far beyond the bounds of medicine. His interests in scripture, which must have endeared him to Faraday, led him to the study of comparative philology and it was as a philologist that Faraday now consulted him. Precisely when the consultation took place is impossible to determine. Dr Nicholl used to drop in frequently to the laboratory of the Royal Institution where he and Faraday would discuss whatever problem Faraday was working on. It is probable that Dr Nicholl was made aware of Faraday's difficulty with terms sometime in the autumn of 1833. It was not until then that Faraday was convinced beyond doubt that the 'poles' did not act as centres of attraction and re-pulsion at a distance. The first new terms to be devised were those intended to replace 'poles'. The first use of these terms occurred on 17 December 1833, when Faraday wrote in his *Diary*: 'Hence 1·76 of tin had been electro-chemically evolved at the *exode* and of course a corres-ponding proportion of chlorine at the *eisode*, which had formed *bi-chloride* of tin as a secondary result' [1175]. On 19 December a new term, *electro-beids*, was used [1204]. On 20 December *electrode* was introduced [1219]. Terms such as *electrolyte, electrolyzed* and *electrolytical* which were defined in the published paper (dated 31 December 1833) did not appear in the *Diary* until 1834. They were, however, probably formed before the paper was read to the Royal Society.

The etymology of these terms shows the goal towards which Faraday was striving. Instead of centres of attraction and repulsion, Faraday wished the 'poles' to be considered merely as portals by which the electric current, whatever it might be, entered and left the solution. Hence *electrode* from ἤλεκτρον (for 'electricity') and ὅδος (for 'a way') by which Faraday merely wished to indicate that the electricity passed by way of the electrodes. *Electrolyte* was derived from ἤλεκτρον and λύω ('I dissolve') and was intended to designate 'bodies [which] are decomposed directly by the electric current' (664). *Electrolyzed* and *electrolytical* were obvious forms of the new term which, by analogy with analysed and analytical, could not be misunderstood. All these terms were strictly non-theoretical with no overtones concerning the nature of the electrical current or the mechanism of electrochemical decomposition. Furthermore, they were euphonious, involving no peculiar sounds which would prevent their easy and rapid adoption.

The same could not be said for *electrobeids*. How was it to be pronounced? Was it to be electro*beeds* to rhyme with deeds? or should it be electro*bē*-ids, or even electro*bides*? The derivation from ἔβην the aorist tense of the verb βαίνω would indicate that the correct pronunciation was electro*bādes* but Faraday, who knew no Greek, must have felt that other chemists, similarly placed, would have difficulties. Even if the word were correctly pronounced, it was not a very pretty one and Faraday was very sensitive to the sound of language. In 1840 he wrote to Whewell commenting upon the invention of the word *scientist*. 'I perceive also another new and good word, the *scientist*. Now can you give us one for the french physicien? physicist is both to my mouth and ears so awkward that I think I shall never be able to use it. The equivalent of three separate sounds of *s* in one word is too much.'[60]

Eisode (from εἰς – into) and *exode* (from εχ – to leave) presented more serious problems. What Faraday really meant to convey was direction, not a process. By defining the electric current as '*an axis of power having contrary forces, exactly equal in amount, in contrary directions*' (517), he had wanted to indicate merely a general polarity, extending throughout the electrolyte, of which the poles were the termini. 'Into' and 'out of', however, implied that something material was passing through the electrolyte, and this was precisely what Faraday wished to avoid. Nevertheless, he and Dr Nicholl were unable to find any substitute and these terms were used when Faraday read his paper to the Royal Society.[61] Faraday's dissatisfaction remained and it was then that he turned to the Rev. Robert Willis. Willis had recently required new terms for his work, *Remarks on the Architecture of the Middle Ages*, and had asked his colleague the Rev. William Whewell of Trinity College for help.[62] By 1834 Whewell was an expert at coining new terms. It was he who supplied Charles Lyell with *pliocene, miocene* and *eocene* for his *Principles of Geology*. He had also shown his conservative good sense in an article 'On the employment of notation in chemistry' which was published in the *Journal of the Royal Institution* and which drew Faraday's praise.[63] Thus, it was only natural for Faraday to call upon Whewell for aid when all other help failed. The Whewell–Faraday correspondence is preserved at Trinity College, Cambridge. Ross has published the letters pertaining to electrochemical nomenclature but they are of such interest that it will, perhaps, be forgiven if they are cited here at some length.

Faraday's appeal for help was dated 24 April and began by explaining his problem.

I am in a trouble [he wrote] which when it occurs at Cambridge is I understand referred by every body in the University to you for removal and I am encouraged by the remembrance of your kindness and on Mr Willis' suggestion to apply to you also. But I should tell you how I stand in the matter.

I wanted some new names to express my facts in Electrical science without involving more theory than I could help and applied to a friend Dr Nicholl who has given me some that I intend to adopt for instance a body decomposable by the passage of the Electric current I call an '*electrolyte*' and instead of saying that water is *electrochemically decomposed*, I say it is '*electrolyzed*'. The intensity above which a body is decomposed beneath which it conducts without decomposition I call the 'Electrolytic intensity', etc., etc. What have been called the poles of the battery I call the *electrodes*. They are not merely surfaces of metal but even of *water* and *air* to which the term poles could hardly apply without receiving a new sense. *Electrolytes* must consist of two parts which during the *electrolyzation* are determined the one in one direction the other in the other towards the electrodes or poles where they are evolved. These evolved substances I call *zetodes* which are therefore the direct constituents of electrolytes.

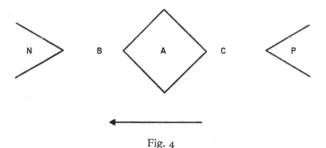

Fig. 4

All these terms I am satisfied with but not with two others which I have used this far. It is essential to me to have the power of referring to the two surfaces of a decomposable body by which the current enters into and passes out of it without at the same time referring to the electrodes. Thus let [A] be a decomposable body and P and N the pos. and neg. poles which may or may not be in contact with [A] at the points [B] [C] and shall yet transmit the electricity which passes through [A] [See Figure 4]. Admitting the usual mode of expression and talking of a current of Electricity proceeding from the positive pole P through [A] to the negative pole N my friend suggested and I have used the terms *eisode* for [C] and *exode* for [B], the points where the *zetodes* are rendered and a zetode going to [C] I have called a *zeteisode* and another going to [B] a *zetexode*.

But the idea of a current especially of *one* current is a very clumsy and hypothetical view of the state of Electrical forces under the circumstances. The idea of *two* currents seems to me still more suspicious and I have little doubt that the present view of electric currents and the notions by which we try to conceive of them will soon pass away and I want therefore names by which I can refer to [C] and [B] without involving any theory of the nature of electricity. In searching for a reference on which to found these I can think of nothing but the globe as a magnetic body. If we admit the magnetism of the Globe as due to Electric currents running in lines of latitude their course must be according to our present modes of expression from East to West and if a portion of water under decomposition by an electric current be placed so that the current through it shall be parallel to that considered as circulating round the earth then the oxygen will be rendered towards the east as at [C] in the figure and the hydrogen towards the west or at [B] in the figure. I think therefore that if I were to call [C] the *east-ode* and [B] the *west-ode* I should express these parts by reference to a natural standard which whatever changes take place in our theories or knowledge of Electricity will still have the same relation. But Eastode and Westode or Oriode and Occiode are name[s] which a scholar could not suffer I understand for a moment and *Anatolode* and *dysiode* have been offered me instead.

Now can you help me out to two good names not depending upon the idea of a current in *one direction only* or upon Positive or negative and to which I may add the prefixes zet or zeto so as to express the class to which any particular zetode may belong.[64]

Faraday's rejection of the fluid theories of electricity is nowhere more firmly stated than in this letter. His intentions, too, were equally clear. He wished merely to convey an idea of direction yet he went about it in a most curious fashion. Having strongly suggested that electrical currents do not exist, he then proposed a model which depended upon such currents. Furthermore, it was a model which he had rejected in the Second Series of the *Experimental Researches*. There, it will be remembered that he had spoken as though currents of terrestrial electricity travelled perpendicularly to the earth's equator and not parallel to it. What lay behind this rather peculiar behaviour, Faraday does not say but it is probable that he knew that Ampère's model was almost universally accepted. It would, therefore, be easily called to mind by his readers and its combination of electricity and direction, even though a theory of electricity was involved, would make his own terminology more comprehensible and acceptable. This illustrates a facet of Faraday's career that is of some importance. All his life, except at the very end, he was able to disagree completely with current theories, yet put his own results in such form that his contemporaries accepted a good part of them. The history of science is strewn with the bones of geniuses who were misunderstood at the time of their discoveries and were only awarded their due honour after they had died. Faraday could have been one of these. The care with which he prepared his papers, however, and the subtlety with which he disguised his opposition to current theories led to the acceptance of much of what he did, even as he did it.

Whewell received Faraday's letter the next day and immediately sat down to answer it. He had heard the paper when Faraday had read it at the Royal Society and was very taken with it. Even the new terms pleased him for, as he wrote,

> I saw or thought I saw that these novelties had been forced upon you by the novelty of extent and the new relations of your views. In cases where such causes operate new terms inevitably arise, and it is very fortunate when those upon whom the introduction of these devolves look forward as you do to the general bearing and future prospects of the subject; and it is an additional advantage when they humour philologists so far as to avoid gross incongruities of language.[65]

As a philologist (among other things) Whewell was eager to help.

> I have considered [he continued] the two terms you want to substitute for *eisode* and *exode,* and upon the whole I am disposed to recommend instead of them *anode* and *cathode*; these words may signify eastern and western way, just as well as the larger compounds which you mention, which derive their meaning from words implying rising and setting, notions which anode and cathode imply more simply. But I will add that as your object appears to me to indicate opposition of direction without assuming any hypothesis which may hereafter turn out to be false, *up* and *down,* which must be arbitrary consequences of position on any hypothesis, seem to be free from inconvenience, even in their simplest sense. I may mention too that *anodos* and *cathodos* are good genuine Greek words, and not compounds coined for the purpose.[66]

Whewell went on to suggest other terms that might serve, such as *dexiode* and *sceode* (right and left) and *orthode* and *anthode* (direct and opposite) but he was obviously in favour of anode and cathode which Faraday ultimately accepted and used.

Although generally pleased with Faraday's new words, Whewell did take issue with *zetode.*

> My objections are these [he wrote]. This word being grouped with others of the same termination might be expected to indicate a modification of electr*ode,* as eis*ode* and ex*ode,* or an*ode* and cath*ode* do. Instead of this it means a notion altogether heterogeneous to these, and the *ode* is here the object of a verb *zete,* contrary to the analogy of all the other words. It appears to me that as what you mean is an element, all that you want is some word which implies an element of a composition, taking a *new* word, however, in order that it may be

recollected that the decomposition of which you speak is of a peculiar kind, namely *electrolytical* decomposition. Perhaps the Greek word stecheon (or stoicheion) would answer the purpose. It has already a place in our scientific language in the term *stoicheiometry*; and has also this analogy in its favour, that whereas your other words in *ode* mean *ways*, this word *stecheon* is derived from a word which signifies to *go* in a row. . . . If you were to take anode and cathode and adopt stecheon, I think *anastecheon* and *catastecheon* might indicate the two *stecheons*. If you stick to zetode, *anazetode* and *catazetode* would be proper terms but perhaps *zetanode* and *zeto cathode* would be more analogous to zetode, which is a word, that, as I have said, I do not much like.[67]

Faraday was not too favourably impressed with Whewell's suggestions. His objections were based on a combination of aesthetics and fear of misunderstanding.

All your names I and my friend approve of or nearly all as to sense and expression but I am frightened by their length and sound when compounded. As you will see I have taken *dexiode* and *skaiode* because they agree best with my natural standard East and West. I like Anode and Cathode better as to sound but all to whom I have shewn them have supposed at first that by *Anode* I meant *No way*.

Then Stechion I have taken although I would rather not have had the hard sound of *ch* here especially as we have similar sounds in both the former words. But when we come to combine it with the two former as *dexio-stechion* and *skaiostechion* especially the latter I am afraid it becomes inadmissible simply from its length and sound forbidding its familiar use. For I think you will agree with me that I had better not give a new word than give one which is not likely to enter into common use.

It is possible perhaps that by this time some other shorter word may have occurred for *Stechion*. If so will you favour me with it. If not I think I must strike out the two compounds above and express my meaning without the use of names for the two classes of stechions though they are very very much want[ed].

It was the shortness and euphony of *zeteisode* and *zetexode* which were their strong recommendations to me.[68]

Before Whewell could answer, Faraday sent off another letter with what he hoped would solve all problems. 'Hoping that this sheet of paper will reach you before you write to me I hasten to mention two names instead of eisode and exode which are free I think from objection as to involving a point of theory, namely *Voltode* and *Galvanode*.

My friend Dr Nicholl proposes *Alphode* and *Betode*.

Then the compounds are good in sound *Volta stechion*, *Galva-stechion* or *Alphastechion* and *Beta-stechion*.'[69]

Whewell quickly agreed that *stechion* was too awkward and he abandoned his advocacy of it. Anode and cathode, however, had grown upon him since he had first suggested them. To Faraday's objection that *anode* implied a negative Whewell replied in his best schoolmasterly way.

> . . . *anodos* does not and cannot mean the absence of way: and if it did mean this as well as a way up, it would not cease to mean the latter also; and when introduced in company with *cathodos* no body who has any tinge of Greek could fail to perceive the meaning at once. The notion of *anodos* meaning *no way* could only suggest itself to persons unfamiliar with Greek, and accidentally acquainted with some English words in which the negative particle is so employed; and those persons who have taken up this notion must have overlooked the very different meaning of negatives applied to substantives and adjectives. Prepositions are so very much the simplest and most decisive way of expressing opposition or other relations that it would require some very strong arguments to induce one to adopt any other way of conveying such relations as you want to indicate.[70]

Whewell's spirited defence of *anode* was occasioned by what he considered a most elegant solution to the whole problem which had so vexed Faraday. He had been able to eliminate *stechion* and set up a beautiful and simple nomenclature.

> If you take *anode* and *cathode* I would propose for the two elements resulting from electrolysis the terms *anion* and *cation* which are neuter participles signifying *that which goes up* and *that which goes down*; and for the two together you might use the term *ions* instead of zetodes or *stechions*. The word is not a substantive in Greek, but it may easily be so taken, and I am persuaded that the brevity and simplicity of the terms you will thus have will in a fortnight procure their universal acceptance. The *anion* is that which *goes* to the *anode,* the cation is that which *goes* to the *cathode.* The *th* in the latter word arises from the aspirate in *hodos*, *way*, and therefore is not to be introduced in cases where the second term has not an aspirate as *ion* has not.[71]

This was exactly what Faraday had been looking for and he adopted the terms immediately.[72] They were then introduced into the proofs of the printed paper. The eleven propositions of electrochemistry with which Faraday closed his Seventh Series were couched in the new terms which are now so familiar to us. These propositions represented the starting-point for a whole series of researches throughout the nineteenth century and, as such, they deserve restatement here in their original form.

> i. A single *ion*, i.e. one not in combination with another, will have no tendency to pass to either of the electrodes, and will be perfectly indifferent to the passing current, unless it be itself a compound of more elementary *ions,* and so subject to actual decomposition. Upon this fact is founded much of the proof adduced in favour of the new theory of electro-chemical decomposition, which I put forth in a former series of these Researches. . . .
>
> ii. If one *ion* be combined in right proportions (697) with another strongly opposed to it in its ordinary chemical relations, i.e. if an *anion* be combined

with a *cation,* then both will travel, the one to the *anode,* the other to the *cathode,* of the decomposing body. . . .

iii. If, therefore, an *ion* pass towards one of the electrodes, another *ion* must also be passing simultaneously to the other electrode, although, from second-ary action, it may not make its appearance. . . .

iv. A body decomposable directly by the electric current, i.e. an *electrolyte,* must consist of two *ions,* and must also render them up during the act of decomposition.

v. There is but one *electrolyte* composed of the same two elementary *ions*; at least such appears to be the fact (697), dependant upon a law, that *only single electro-chemical equivalents of elementary ions can go to the electrodes, and not multiples.*

vi. A body not decomposable when alone, as boracic acid, is not directly decomposable by the electric current when in combination (780). It may act as an *ion* going wholly to the *anode* or *cathode,* but does not yield up its elements, except occasionally by a secondary action. Perhaps it is superfluous for me to point out that this proposition has *no relation* to such cases as that of water, which, by the presence of other bodies, is rendered a better conductor of electricity, and *therefore* is more freely decomposed.

vii. The nature of the substance of which the electrode is formed, provided it be a conductor, causes no difference in the electro-decomposition, either in kind or degree (807, 813): but it seriously influences, by secondary action (744), the state in which the *ions* finally appear. Advantage may be taken of this principle in combining and collecting such *ions* as, if evolved in their free state, would be unmanageable.

viii. A substance which, being used as the electrode, can combine with the *ion* evolved against it, is also, I believe, an *ion,* and combines, in such cases, in the quantity represented by its *electro-chemical equivalent.* All the experiments I have made agree with this view; and it seems to me, at present, to result as a necessary consequence. Whether, in the secondary actions that take place, where the *ion* acts, not upon the matter of the electrode, but on that which is around it in the liquid (744), the same consequence follows, will require more extended investigation to determine.

ix. Compound *ions* are not necessarily composed of electro-chemical equivalents of simple *ions.* For instance, sulphuric acid, boracic acid, phos-phoric acid, are *ions,* but not *electrolytes,* i.e. not composed of electro-chemical equivalents of simple *ions.*

x. Electro-chemical equivalents are always consistent; i.e. the same number which represents the equivalent of a substance A when it is separating from a substance B, will also represent A when separating from a third substance C. Thus, 8 is the electro-chemical equivalent of oxygen, whether separating from hydrogen, or tin, or lead; and 103·5 is the electro-chemical equivalent of lead, whether separating from oxygen, or chlorine, or iodine.

xi. Electro-chemical equivalents coincide, and are the same with ordinary chemical equivalents (826–36).

The Seventh Series of the *Experimental Researches* marked a second milestone in Faraday's investigations of electricity. The ordering of the mass of electrochemical facts was only part of the achievement. Of equal importance was the confidence which he gained from the congruence of these facts with his hypothetical ideas. From his apprentice days with Sir Humphry Davy he had been exposed to the idea that electricity was an inherent power of matter; now he knew it. The concept of the electric current as some form of vibration had led him to the discovery of electro-magnetic induction; his electrochemical researches seemed to bolster this hypothesis. Moreover, the vibration appeared to be one that involved the mutual interaction of 'contiguous' particles. This interaction, in turn, was directly related to two molecular forces; the force of cohesion and the force of chemical affinity. Finally, and perhaps most importantly, Faraday had been led to postulate a scientific heresy by insisting that electro-chemical action was *not* action at a distance. There appears to have been no reaction to this at the time from physicists for they were not greatly concerned with chemical problems. Nevertheless the seed had been sown and when the full-grown plant emerged, there were to be screams of pain and anger from those who felt that the whole edifice of Newtonian mechanics was threatened. This day was not far distant for as Faraday focused upon the molecular forces of matter he was led by a chain of inexorable logic to challenge action at a distance in electrostatics where physicists *did* care and had constructed a lovely theory.

Faraday's investigations of intermolecular forces was also to help to clarify his concept of the nature of electricity. We have insisted upon his rejection of the fluid theories and have, for the sake of clarity, perhaps made his own hypothesis seem more definite and free from contradiction than it actually was in his mind. Thus, it may be fitting to end this chapter with a letter written by Faraday in 1834 to Sir C. Lemen, Bart., M.P., who had asked Faraday to comment on the views of electricity held by his fellow F.R.S., Mr Fox.

> I am much obliged to you [he wrote] for a sight of Mr Fox's letter. At present my mind is very unsettled with regard to the nature of the Electric agent. The usual notions attached to Positive and negative and to the term current I suspect are altogether wrong but I have not *a clear view* of what ought to be put in their places.
>
> It is very easy to imagine forces with certain directions as a kind of abstract notion of electricity but that is saying little or nothing although all the phenomena may be accounted for in such a way. It is the cause of the forces that one wants to lay hold of. I have one idea that in what we call the current in the decomposition of bodies anything but a resolution and recombination of forces seems between contiguous particles but I want to see clearly *how* these changes come about and as yet cannot.[73]

So it was to the intensified study of the forces of particles and, particularly, to the way in which force was transmitted between particles, that Faraday turned. The results were to be revolutionary and feed back to the development of field theory. Electromagnetism, electrochemistry, and electrostatics were to be found merely to be different manifestations of one general and universal law.

References

1. See above, Chapter Two.
2. W. Nicholson, 'Account of the new Electrical or Galvanic Apparatus of Sig. Alex. Volta, and Experiments performed with the same', *Nich. Jour.*, 4to, *4* (1800), 183.
3. See above, Chapter One.
4. Ritter's works are extremely rare outside Germany. His complete works are not to be found in any of the great national libraries – the Library of Congress, British Museum, Bibliothèque nationale, Biblioteca nazionale. They are, to my knowledge, only in the Ronalds Library of the Institution of Electrical Engineers, London. A list of the titles of these volumes might, therefore, be of some value.

J. Ritter, *Beweis, dass ein beständiger galvanismus den Lebensprocess in dem Theirreich begleite* (Weimar, 1798).
—— *Das electrische System der korper, Ein Versuch* (Leipzig, 1805).
—— *Physische-chemische Abhandlungen in chronologischer Folge* (3 vols., Leipzig, 1806).
—— *Beyträge zur nähern kenntniss des Galvanismus und der Resultate Seiner Untersuchung* (5 vols., Jena, 1800–5).
—— *Neue Beyträge zur nähern kenntniss des Galvanismus und der Resultate seiner Untersuchung* (Tubingen, 1808).
—— *Fragmente aus dem Nachlasse eines jungen Physikers, Ein Taschenbuch für Freunde der Natur* (Heidelberg, 1810).

5. J. Ritter, 'Galvanische Versuche über die chemische Natur des Wassers', *Crell's Chemische Annalen*, *1* (1801), 41 ff. Reprinted in *Physische-chemische Abhandlungen*, *1*, 245 ff.
6. Ibid., 59, or in reprint, 261.
7. Modern chemical texts today emphasize the fact that Lavoisier's greatest contribution to the development of modern chemistry was the use of the balance to analyse chemical reactions. At the beginning of the nineteenth century this point was by no means grasped by all chemists. The seeming impossibility of explaining the electrochemical decomposition of water made a far greater impression than did the fact that specific quantities of hydrogen and oxygen combined together to give a quantity of water exactly equal to the sum of the weights of the two gases.
8. See, for example, the series of papers Oersted published in the *Jour. de*

Phys. in 1804, in which he reported enthusiastically on the work of Ritter. Also, *Skrifter, 1*, 214 ff. His acceptance of Ritter's chemical theories was contained in 'Betrachtungen über die Geschichte der Chemie', *Gehlen's Jour. für die Chemie und Physik, 3* (1807), 194, *Skrifter, 1*, 315.

9. *Nicholson's Journal*, volumes 5–24 (1803–9) contained announcements of Ritter's work. These were carefully noted by Faraday in his copy of Brande's *Manual of Chemistry*.

10. G. Cuvier, 'Rapport sur le galvanisme fait à l'Institut national', *Jour. de Phys., 52* (1801), 320.

11. C. L. Berthollet, *Essai de statique chimique* (2 vols., Paris, 1803), *1*, 216.

12. Cuvier, loc. cit.

13. Grotthus' name is variously spelled in the literature. The memoir in the *Annales de chimie* (see below) gives Grotthuss but the French at this time were notoriously incapable of dealing with the names of foreigners. W. Ostwald in *Der Werdegang einer Wissenschaft* (Leipzig, 1908), 171, gives Grotthus. E. Hoppe in his *Geschichte der Elektrizität* (Leipzig, 1884), uses both Grotthus and Grothuss (67 and 278). Ostwald seems to be the greater authority.

14. The various *Arbors* depended for their complete names upon what metal formed the tree. Silver, associated with the moon by the alchemists, formed the *Arbor Dianae*. Copper would form an *Arbor Martis* (copper being red, it suggested the God of War), etc.

15. J. T. de Grotthus, 'Mémoire sur la décomposition de l'eau et des corps qu'elle tient en dissolution à l'aide de l'électricité galvanique', *Ann. de Chim., 58* (1806), 55.

16. Ibid., 65.

17. Ibid. In a later memoir, 'De l'influence de l'électricité galvanique sur les végétations métalliques', *Ann. de chim. et de phys., 63* (1807), 25, Grotthus definitely attributed the molecular polarity to this contact.

18. Ibid., 68.

19. Ibid., 65.

20. J. T. de Grotthus, 'De l'influence galvanique . . .', *Ann. de chim. et de phys., 63* (1807), 34.

21. See above, Chapter Two.

22. M. Pacchioni, *Phil. Mag., 22* (1805), 178 ff.

23. See Davy's early electrochemical papers in *Works, 2*. For a general account of these researches, see L. Pearce Williams, 'Humphry Davy', *Scientific American*, June 1960.

24. It is curious that Davy never mentioned Grotthus or his theory. It seems inconceivable that he had not read Grotthus' papers which appeared in the *Annales de chimie*, the most important chemical journal of the day, yet unless one wishes to suggest a conscious ignoring of Grotthus' work, this appears to be the only explanation.

25. Davy, *Works, 5*, 1 ff.

26. The classic paper on the decomposition of neutral salts was that of J. J. Berzelius and W. Hisinger, published first in Swedish in 1804 but not generally known until it was translated into French and German, *Ann. de chim. et de phys., 51* (1804), 167; *Gilbert's Annalen der Physik, 27* (1807), 269 ff.

27. *Works*, *5*, 19.

28. Ibid.

29. Ibid., 22.

30. Ibid., 24.

31. Ibid., 28.

32. Davy, *Works*, *5*, 39.

33. H. Davy, 'Electrochemical Researches on the Decomposition of the Earths; with observations on the Metals obtained from the alkaline earths, and on the amalgam procured from Ammonia', *Works*, *5*, 136.

34. I have omitted a discussion of Berzelius' theory, even though it had a long vogue and enormous influence in the history of nineteenth-century chemistry. The reason is that, in essence, it was identical with Grotthus' hypothesis. It relied upon the two electrical fluids associating with ponderable matter and raised no new and fundamental problems. It merely extended Grotthus' ideas from water to all matter.

35. Auguste de la Rive, 'Mémoire sur quelques-uns des phénomènes que présente l'électricité voltaïque dans son passage à travers les conducteurs liquides', *Ann. de chim. et de phys.*, *28* (1825), 199.

36. Ibid.

37. De la Rive has written + but this is an obvious impossibility and must be a mistake.

38. Ibid., 201.

39. Ibid., 202.

40. This does not mean that Faraday had shut his mind to Ampère's concepts. As he refined his experimental techniques, he continued to test the consequences of Ampère's theory. Thus, in 1833, Faraday attempted to detect the change in dimensions of an iron bar which, upon the hypothesis of molecular currents, ought to occur when the bar was magnetized [702].

41. A. de la Rive, 'Analyse des circonstances qui déterminent le *sens* et *l'intensité* du courant électrique dans un élément voltaïque', *Ann. de chim. et de phys.*, *37* (1828), 248.

42. A. de la Rive, 'Recherches sur la cause de l'électricité voltaïque', *Mém. de la Soc. de Phys. . . . . de Génève*, *4* (1828), 285 ff.

43. For Davy, see *Phil. Trans.* (1807), 42.

44. The Fourth Series of the *Experimental Researches* was concerned with this effect.

45. Faraday himself was to hint at this distinction in fairly clear language. See L. Pearce Williams, 'Boscovich and the British Chemists' in L. L. Whyte, ed., *Roger Joseph Boscovich, S.J.* (London, 1961).

46. 'Berthollet's experiments' and 'the chemical action of quantity' refer to the Law of Mass Action.

47. B.M.Add.MSS. 37187, f. 113, R. Phillips to Charles Babbage, 45 Brompton Row, 4 September 1832. This clearly refers to Faraday's adherence to Boscovich's theory and although written before the publication of Faraday's theory of electrochemistry nevertheless reveals Phillips' attitude towards Faraday's whole theoretical framework.

48. It should be noted here that Faraday's theory required, in the case of weak

electrolytes, a certain 'threshold' voltage under which no decomposition took place [551–60]. In the 1850's Hittorf was to show that this was not the case and thus refute Faraday as Faraday had refuted his predecessors. Science, it may be remarked, is like that.

49. See above, Chapter Five.

50. The experiments, which were variations of those devised by Faraday in May, were performed in the summer of 1833. By 2 September Faraday was convinced of the accuracy of the new law.

51. I have here used a modern definition since Faraday never formulated the second law as a distinct statement. To him, it followed so naturally from the first law and his theory that it was not necessary to enunciate it as a separate law. Instead, he included it in the series of propositions on electrochemistry which he inserted in the Seventh Series of his *Experimental Researches*. See (826–36).

52. 'Now the most startling result of Faraday's law is perhaps this. If we accept the hypothesis that the elementary substances are composed of atoms, we cannot avoid concluding that electricity also, positive as well as negative, is divided into definite elementary portions, which behave like atoms of electricity.' Hermann von Helmholtz, 'On the Modern Development of Faraday's Conception of Electricity', *Faraday Lectures, 1869–1928* (London, 1928), 145.

53. I have drawn heavily for this section on Sydney Ross's excellent article, 'Faraday Consults the Scholars: The Origin of the Terms of Electrochemistry', *Notes and Records of the Royal Society, 16* (1961), 187 ff.

54. Dr Isaac Watts, *The Improvement of the Mind*, 18.

55. B. Dibner, *Faraday discloses Electro-magnetic Induction*, 12.

56. J. J. Berzelius, *Essai sur la théorie des proportions chimiques et sur l'influence chimique de l'électricité* (Paris, 1819).

57. Trinity College, Cambridge, Whewell–Faraday Correspondence, 8, Faraday to W. Whewell, R.I., 19 September 1835.

58. Ibid.

59. See Ross, op. cit. The information on Nicholl and Willis is taken from Ross.

60. Trinity College, Cambridge, Whewell–Faraday Correspondence, 13, Faraday to Whewell, R.I., 20 May 1840.

61. These terms do not appear in the printed paper, but it is obvious that Faraday changed them before the paper was published in the *Phil. Trans.* The terms were used in the account of the paper published in the *Proc. R.S., 3* (1837), 261.

62. Ross, op. cit.

63. Ibid. Trinity College MSS., Faraday–Whewell Correspondence, 2, Faraday to Whewell, R.I., 21 February 1831.

64. Trinity College, Faraday–Whewell Correspondence, 4, Faraday to Whewell, R.I., 24 April 1834. I have not followed Ross in adding punctuation so that there are slight variations between his and my versions.

65. Published originally in I. Todhunter, *William Whewell, an Account of his Writings, with Selections from his Literary and Scientific Correspondence* (2 vols., London, 1876), 2, 177. I have used the original so again my punctuation differs from that given by both Todhunter and Ross. Whewell's handwriting is quite

difficult and there are occasions where I have disagreed with Ross's and Tod-hunter's interpretations of a word. For this letter, see Trinity College, Faraday–Whewell Correspondence, 2, Whewell to Faraday, Trinity College, Cambridge, 25 April 1834.

66. Ibid.

67. Ibid.

68. Trinity College, Faraday–Whewell Correspondence, 5, Faraday to Whewell, R.I., 3 May 1834.

69. Trinity College, Faraday–Whewell Correspondence, 1, Faraday to Whewell, R.I., Monday [5 May 1834].

70. Trinity College, Whewell–Faraday Correspondence, 3, Whewell to Faraday, Trinity College, Cambridge, 5 May 1834.

71. Ibid.

72. Trinity College, Faraday–Whewell Correspondence, 6, Faraday to Whewell, R.I., May 1834.

73. Faraday to Sir C. Lemen, Bart., M.P., R.I., 25 April 1834. This letter is in the possession of Mr W. H. Browning, 'Chiddingstone', Bexley Road, Eltham, S.E.9 with whose kind permission it is cited.

CHAPTER SEVEN

The Nature of Electricity (3)

---

1. Intermolecular Forces

On 25 November 1833, in the middle of his researches on electro-chemistry, Faraday noted in his *Diary*, 'I am convinced that the superficial actions of matter and the action of particles not directly or strongly in combination are becoming daily more and more important in Chemical as well as in Mechanical Philosophy. I have therefore pursued this matter more closely' [1109]. The occasion for the interruption of his electro-chemical labours was the realization that he was being deceived in his measurements by the peculiar reaction of platinum with the gaseous products of electrochemical decomposition. When platinum electrodes were used in the electrolytic decomposition of water, Faraday found that his second law of electrochemistry was apparently violated. The relation between the amount of hydrogen and oxygen produced and the quantity of current that passed did not follow that which he had proved to be the case when other materials were used for poles.

Faraday did not have to seek far for the cause. Some ten years before he had himself reported upon the discovery by Döbereiner that platinum could cause the combination of hydrogen and oxygen below the ignition temperature. His wonderment at the time was communicated vividly to his readers.

A most extraordinary experiment has been made by M. Döbereiner [he wrote]. It was communicated to me by M. Hachette, and having verified it, I think every chemist will be glad to hear its nature. It consists in passing a stream of hydrogen against the finely divided platina, obtained by heating the muriate of ammonia and platina. In consequence of the contact, the hydrogen inflames. Even when the hydrogen does not inflame, it ignites the platina in places; and I find that when the hydrogen is passed over the platinum in a tube, no air being admitted, still the platinum heats in the same manner. What the change can be in these circumstances, M. Döbereiner has, no doubt, fully investigated; and the scientific world will be anxious to hear his account of this remarkable experiment, and the consequences it leads to.[1]

Faraday was no less anxious than his colleagues to find out the reasons for this extraordinary behaviour of platinum. In the next issue of the *Quarterly Journal of Science* he reported on what he had been able to discover. This consisted mostly of a digest of the numerous articles which had been published on this topic. All seemed more or less agreed that the phenomenon was electrical in nature. Döbereiner felt it was a simple case of voltaic action, and the authors of the other articles seemed to think that this was the correct way of viewing the action.[2] Döbereiner, Faraday reported, 'considers the phenomenon as an electric one, and that hydrogen and platina form a voltaic combination, in which the former represents the zinc'.[3] Superficially, the analogy appeared to be a valid one, although it was curious that no one seemed to bother to ask why the result was combination rather than decomposition. But, in 1823, that was where the matter rested.

It was not until 1833 when Faraday was probing to the very foundations of electrochemistry that the catalytic action of platinum became once more the subject of research.[4] The peculiar behaviour of platinum could not now be ignored. If it were, indeed, an electrical effect it was a most curious one for it did not fit into the theory which Faraday was developing. It, therefore, required him to halt momentarily his work on the action of the voltaic pile and to turn his attention to discovery of the mechanism by which platinum could bring about the combination of two gases which, in the absence of platinum, could be stored together for years without ever combining. The results of this research were to be reported in the Sixth Series of the *Experimental Researches in Electricity*. More importantly, they were to strengthen his conviction of the correctness of his views of molecular action and on the value of the theory of point atoms as an aid to discovery.

It is obvious from his laboratory *Diary* that the disappearance of the oxygen and hydrogen produced in the electrolysis of water took Faraday completely by surprise. His first reaction was that this was a completely new phenomenon that deserved investigation. Even in the published paper where he later showed that it was the same as that Döbereiner had discovered, he reported that 'the effect is, as far as I am aware, altogether new' (568). What was really strange about it was that the effect was not exhibited equally by the two platinum electrodes. Only the one that served as the positive electrode appeared capable of bringing about the combination of hydrogen and oxygen below the ignition temperature.

On 10 October 1833, Faraday began the task of penetrating the mystery of this strange action. His first step, as always, was to assure himself that the effect really did exist, and was not the result of other unknown circumstances. Three platinum plates were placed in sulphuric acid and made the positive plates in their circuits. When removed from the acid after five minutes and inserted in mixtures of oxygen and hydrogen, they caused an immediate diminution of the gas volume. The plates were then removed, re-'electrified' and then placed after washing into dilute sulphuric acid, distilled water, and air. They still retained their power of causing gaseous combination [885–6]. This appeared to rule out simple chemical action involving the residual sulphuric acid from the circuit. Other gases were then tried, but the action if present at all, was very feeble [888–90]. Other acids were substituted for sulphuric acid and, with but few exceptions, these served as well as the sulphuric to preserve the peculiar property of the positive platinum pole. The effect, no doubt about it, was real and appeared to be dependent upon the peculiar chemical properties of oxygen and hydrogen as well as whatever odd *state* the positive pole was thrown into by the electric current.

From the very beginning, Faraday could not bring himself to believe that positive electricity could have a peculiar effect which was not exhibited by negative electricity. If the electric current were an axis of power, this violation of symmetry was impossible. There was one faint clue that Faraday now seized upon in an effort to explain the effect without having to grant separate properties to the two electric powers. In the sulphuric acid solution, the positive electrode was the one to which the sulphate ion was attracted and sulphuric acid was constantly being generated there.[5] If there were any metallic impurities in the solution (and it was almost impossible for there not to be) they would be attracted to the negative electrode where they would plate out in such a thin film that they would not be noticeable. Faraday, who was extremely sensitive to the action of contaminants in electrical experiments,[6] was led naturally to ask if the difference between the action of negative and positive electrodes was caused by the fact that the positive pole was constantly being cleansed by sulphuric acid while the negative was coated with a film of impurities.

Yesterday [he wrote in his *Diary* on 12 October] a piece of amalgamated Zinc and a platina spatula were put into dilute Sul. Acid and left all night for the electric action to proceed. This morning, the platina was dull in most places but in some parts amalgamated. There had been precipitation in fact upon it. It was put up into a tube of O. and H. and left there for $2\frac{1}{2}$ hours, but no action ensued. It was then taken out and heated red hot, then cleaned by a cork, water and emery and returned into the gas. It instantly began to act and condense the gas, yet it had been a negative pole all night [913].

This experiment led Faraday to see clearly precisely what elements were involved in the effect. The action 'was not essentially dependent upon the action of the pile, or upon any structure or arrangement of parts it might receive whilst in association with it, but belonged to the platina *at all times*, and was *always effective* when the surface was *perfectly clean*' (590).

The effect of heat was then investigated. Sometimes heating the plates increased their ability to stimulate the production of water from hydrogen and oxygen;

> but it happened not unfrequently that plates, after being heated, showed no power of combining oxygen and hydrogen gases, though left undisturbed in them for two hours. Sometimes also it would happen that a plate which, having been heated to dull redness, acted feebly, upon being heated to whiteness ceased to act; and at other times a plate which, having been slightly heated, did not act, was rendered active by a more powerful ignition (597).

The cause of this anomalous behaviour was now easily discovered. In general, heating a platinum plate cleansed it of impurities. Occasionally, however, the heat caused the impurities to adhere more closely and thus prevent the action. Even the source of the heat could be the cause as Faraday demonstrated by showing that the carbon from the flame of the spirit lamp could so mask the platinum surface that the plate was rendered inert (598).

On the basis of these experiments Faraday was now able to challenge Döbereiner's electrical theory of the catalytic action of platinum. No electricity was required nor was any evolved and Faraday was certainly not eager to find electricity whose source his newly devised theory would find it difficult to explain.

Another theory proposed by Dr Fusinieri of Italy in 1825 also met with opposition from Faraday. In the Sixth Series, Faraday quoted him as follows: 'The platina determines upon its surface a continual renovation of *concrete laminae* of the combustible substance of the gases or vapours, which flowing over it are burnt, pass away, and are renewed: this combustion at the surface raises and sustains the temperature of the metal' (613).[7] According to Fusinieri, the creation of these *laminae* was what caused the action, for the combustible gas lost its gaseous elasticity and thus was in a peculiarly fit condition for combination. The problem, of course, was why the loss of elasticity took place? As Faraday interpreted Fusinieri,

> The power or force which makes combustible gas or vapour abandon its elastic state in contact with a solid, that it may cover the latter with a thin

K

stratum of its own proper substance, is considered as being neither attraction nor affinity. It is able also to extend liquids and solids in concrete laminae over the surface of the acting solid body, and consists in a *repulsion*, which is developed from the parts of the solid body by the simple fact of attenuation, and is highest when the attenuation is most complete. The force has a progressive development, and acts most powerfully, or at first, in the direction in which the dimensions of the attenuated mass decrease, and then in the direction of the angles or corners which from any cause may exist on the surface. This force not only causes spontaneous diffusion of gases and other substances over the surface, but is considered as very elementary in its nature, and competent to account for all the phenomena of capillarity, chemical affinity, attraction of aggregation, rarefaction, ebullition, volatilization, explosion, and other thermometric effects, as well as inflammation, detonation, etc., etc. It is considered as a form of heat to which the term *native caloric* is given, and is still further viewed as the principle of the two electricities and the two magnetisms' (614).

If the reader finds himself confused by this strange force, he should be consoled by the fact that Faraday was equally at a loss to understand it. 'I cannot form a distinct idea of the power to which [Fusinieri] refers the phenomena' (615), he wrote, but he had made a gallant attempt to describe it so that the public could estimate its value. Even if he had understood it, it is probable that he would not have been happy with it. The introduction of new forces or new substances (or, one might add parenthetically, new fluids) to explain every new fact was never Faraday's way. Until it was shown that the known forces or substances were insufficient to account for the fact, every effort should be made to bring the new phenomena within the framework of known theories. What Faraday now attempted to do was to show how the catalytic action of platinum could be explained according to the known nature of molecular forces. The only real difficulty with his explanation was that very few of his contemporaries viewed molecular forces as he did. The chemists and physicists of his day considered molecular forces to act in two different ways. There was the force of chemical affinity which acted at insensibly small distances and there was the force of universal attraction which acted at all distances. What appeared to be indisputable was that there was a difference in kind between these two forces.[8] There was a definite discontinuity involved for the force of chemical affinity was assumed to end rather abruptly at a very small distance from the molecule. One of the advantages of the theory of point atoms was that it avoided this discontinuity and permitted the chemist to view chemical combination and physical aggregation as the result of the same, not different, forces. It was this fact that Faraday felt it was necessary to insist upon, for without it his theory fell to the ground.

Before detailing his theory, therefore, he reminded his readers of the framework within which his ideas had been born.

All the phenomena connected with this subject press upon my mind the conviction that the effects in question are entirely incidental and of a secondary nature; that they are dependent upon the *natural conditions* of gaseous elasticity, combined with the exertion of that attractive force possessed by many bodies, especially those which are solid, in an eminent degree, and probably belonging to all; by which they are drawn into association more or less close, without at the same time undergoing chemical combination, though often assuming the condition of adhesion; and which occasionally leads, under very favourable circumstances, as in the present instance, to the combination of bodies simultaneously subjected to this attraction. I am prepared myself to admit (and probably many others are of the same opinion), both with respect to the attraction of aggregation and of chemical affinity, that the sphere of action of particles extends beyond those other particles with which they are immediately and evidently in union, ... and in many cases produces effects rising into considerable importance: and I think that this kind of attraction is a determining cause of Döbereiner's effect, and of the many others of a similar nature (619).

Faraday enumerated some of these other cases of molecular interaction. Many substances, for example, which did not combine chemically with water did tend to pull water vapour out of the air and condense it upon their surfaces. Air will adhere so tenaciously to glass that this layer will interfere seriously with the proper working of mercury barometers. Foreign substances, introduced into saturated solutions of salts, will initiate crystallization of the dissolved substance by bringing the particles into closer relationship with one another. Thus

it would appear [wrote Faraday] from many cases of nuclei in solutions, and from the effects of bodies put into atmospheres containing the vapours of water, or camphor, or iodine, etc., as if this attraction were in part elective, partaking in its characters both of the attraction of aggregation and chemical affinity: nor is this inconsistent with, but agreeable to, the idea entertained, that it is the power of particles acting, not upon others with which they can immediately and intimately combine, but upon such as are either more distantly situated with respect to them, or which, from previous condition, physical constitution, or feeble relation, are unable to enter into decided union with them' (624).

The intermolecular forces, which Faraday felt it necessary to mention twice in the same short paper, had peculiar properties. They shared in the specificity of elective affinity but acted at greater distances than their more purely chemical cousins. They can be easily visualized if one refers to Boscovich's curve of forces associated with elementary particles. Just as chemical affinity was the result of the intermeshing of the forces represented by a number of these curves at a small distance from the centre of the system of particles, so was the intermolecular force the result of a similar addition of force-curves, at a greater distance from the centre. It was these forces which were the ones responsible for the creation of regular crystalline bodies for, as Faraday was careful to point out, the attractive force was 'in part elective'. Thus only certain regular and stable molecular configurations would be formed and regularity was a characteristic of crystalline bodies.[9]

Utilizing these intermolecular forces, Faraday was able to give a coherent theory of catalytic action. Since catalysis is a process which still mystifies chemists, Faraday's view of it may properly be given in his own words.

> . . . of all bodies, the gases are those which might be expected to show some *mutual* action, whilst *jointly* under the attractive influence of the platina or other solid acting substance. Liquids, such as water, alcohol, etc., are in so dense and comparatively incompressible a state, as to favour no expectation that their particles should approach much closer to each other by the attraction of the body to which they adhere, and yet that attraction must (according to its effects) place their particles as near to those of the solid wetted body as they are to each other, and in many cases it is evident that the former attraction is the stronger. But gases and vapours are bodies competent to suffer very great changes in the relative distances of their particles by external agencies; and where they are in immediate contact with the platina, the approximation of the particles to those of the metal may be very great. In the case of the hygrometric bodies referred to . . . it is sufficient to reduce the vapour to the fluid state, frequently from atmospheres so rare that without this influence it would be needful to compress them by mechanical force into a bulk not more than $\frac{1}{10}$th or even $\frac{1}{20}$th of their original volume before the vapours would become liquids.
>
> Another most important consideration in relation to this action of bodies, and which, as far as I am aware, has not hitherto been noticed, is the condition of elasticity under which the gases are placed against the acting surface. We have but very imperfect notions of the real and intimate conditions of the particles of a body existing in the solid, the liquid, and the gaseous state; but when we speak of the gaseous state as being due to the mutual repulsions of the particles or of their atmospheres, although we may err in imagining each particle to be a little nucleus to an atmosphere of heat, or electricity, or any other agent, we are still not likely to be in error in considering the elasticity as dependent on *mutuality* of action. Now this mutual relation fails altogether on the side of the gaseous particles next to the platina, and we might be led to expect *a priori* a deficiency of elastic force there to at least one half; for if, as Dalton has shown, the elastic force of the particles of one gas cannot act against the elastic force of the particles of another, the two being as vacua to

each other, so is it far less likely that the particles of the platina can exert any influence on those of the gas against it, such as would be exerted by gaseous properties of its own kind (625, 626).

Here was Faraday's theory. Its main provisions were clear; solid bodies, especially clean platinum, had a strong power of attraction near its surface precisely because it was in the solid state. In Boscovichean terms, the association of the particles of platinum created an extraordinarily powerful force field near the surface where these forces were not balanced by the force of other platinum particles. This attraction 'condensed' the gases on the platinum surface. This is all contained in the first paragraph, but it is the *second* paragraph which is really rather startling for it seems superfluous. If the strength of the attractive force emanating from the platinum surface was sufficient, why did Faraday bother about the destruction of the mutual *repulsion* of the gaseous particles? The clue would appear to be in his pointing out what was new in his approach – namely that repulsion had to be mutual. Here Faraday was subtly and gently attacking the current theories of the gaseous state. And what makes it even more interesting is that he did it in the name of Dalton who represented orthodoxy! The Daltonian atomic theory had endowed atoms with atmospheres of heat or caloric. It was these atmospheres which kept the atoms from touching and, since caloric repelled caloric, the atoms of gases were surrounded by quite extensive atmospheres. What the person who is accustomed to the modern kinetic theory of gases must realize is that this was a totally static picture. If a gas could be magnified so that its atoms became visible, it would resemble a bowl of gelatine (caloric) in which the gas atoms were imbedded like raisins. It was in this sense that caloric exercised repulsive powers, just as the gelatine resists compression. Hence, in Dalton's theory, there was not really any mutuality of action. Resistance to compression, or better, elasticity, was a function of the quantity of caloric present, not of the spatial configuration of the atoms. Faraday found the fatal flaw in this scheme. Dalton, in his work on the law of partial pressures, had shown that gases acted in such a way that the partial pressure of a specific gas in a closed receiver depended solely upon the quantity of *that* gas which was in the vessel. In other words, if one gramme of both hydrogen and oxygen were introduced into a one litre jar, the total pressure on the walls of the jar would be the sum of the pressures which one gramme of hydrogen and one gramme of oxygen would exert if each were placed *alone* in the jar. Thus, the hydrogen and oxygen *did not* repel one another as they should if the cause of repulsion were caloric which, by Dalton's own theory, must surround each atom of both gases. Oxygen and hydrogen *must* repel one another, however, or else their combination would take place at ordinary room temperature. This dilemma could be avoided if the theory of point atoms were adopted and the situation viewed as the result of the interaction of molecular forces. The interplay of forces also enabled Faraday to give a qualitative account of catalytic action.

> The course of events when platina acts upon, and combines oxygen and hydrogen, may be stated, according to these principles, as follows. From the influence of the circumstances mentioned . . . *i.e.* the deficiency of elastic power and the attraction of the metal for the gases, the latter, when they are in association with the former, are so far condensed as to be brought within the action of their mutual affinities at the existing temperature; the deficiency of elastic power, not merely subjecting them more closely to the attractive influence of the metal, but also bringing them into a more favourable state for union, by abstracting a part of that power (upon which depends their elasticity,) which elsewhere in the mass of gases is opposing their combination. The consequence of their combination is the production of the vapour of water and an elevation of temperature. But as the attraction of the platina for the water formed is not greater than for the gases, if so great, (for the metal is scarcely hygrometric,) the vapour is quickly diffused through the remaining gases; fresh portions of the latter, therefore, come into juxtaposition with the metal, combine, and the fresh vapour formed is also diffused, allowing new portions of gas to be acted upon. In this way the process advances, but is accelerated by the evolution of heat, which is known by experiment to facilitate the combination in proportion to its intensity, and the temperature is thus gradually exalted until ignition results (630).

The investigation of catalysis also served to shed light on the general problem which occupied Faraday in the 1830's. Behind the specific researches on electromagnetic induction and electrochemical decomposition, was the larger question of the means of transmission of the electric force. The work on catalysis drew Faraday's attention to the intermolecular forces operating in nature. He was already convinced that the transmission of force in electrochemistry was accomplished by the action of the force of affinity. The necessary consequence of this mode of transmission was chemical decomposition. The catalytic action of platinum revealed that force could be transmitted in much the same way, but without necessitating the introduction of affinity. The intermolecular forces, like those of chemical affinity, were elective but the breaking of the bonds so formed between molecules did not result in chemical decomposition but only in molecular separation. The intermolecular forces, therefore, filled the void between the force of affinity operating only at insensible distances and that of gravity which was not elective but universal. Having shown that electric force could be transmitted by means of the force of chemical affinity, the next step for Faraday was clear. Could the electric force be transmitted by the intermolecular forces? It was well known that electrostatic forces could act *through* many substances but was this merely action at a distance which had no effect upon the substances interposed between two charged particles or did the force have to be transmitted by the particles of which the substances were composed? The answers to these questions were what Faraday now sought.

2. The Nature of Electrostatic Force

Faraday read his paper on the catalytic action of platinum to the Royal Society on 11 January 1834. Only ten days later, he commenced the reading of the masterly Seventh Series on electrochemistry, finishing on 13 February 1834. In April, the Eighth Series was sent to the Royal Society where it was read on 5 June. The Ninth and Tenth followed in December and June 1835.[10] Then a curious thing happened. Although his laboratory *Diary* shows that Faraday was working away at a furious pace, no further paper appeared for over two years. The Eleventh Series dealing with electrostatic induction was not received by the Royal Society until 30 November 1837. Faraday's well-known motto 'Work, finish, publish' was here violated for the first time and the two-year silence was most uncharacteristic of him. The reason is not difficult to discover. Faraday's papers on induction contained a most serious challenge to classical physics; for what Faraday was doing was undermining the very basis of the mathematical physics of the 1830's. It was in these papers that Faraday flatly denied electrical action at a distance. It may be objected that he had already done this in his electrochemical theory but there was a vast difference in the two cases. Electrochemistry, before Faraday's researches, was in a state of almost total confusion. Theoretical models abounded and, most importantly, the phenomena had not been successfully subjected to mathematical analysis. Electrochemical action at a distance had only been suggested as an analogy with electrostatic action at a distance with the hopes that this would help to clarify matters. Certainly the mathematical physicist felt that almost anything could happen in chemistry which steadfastly refused to bow before the analytical powers of his mathematical tools. So, when Faraday showed how clear things became if action at a distance were denied, the mathematical physicist merely shrugged his shoulders and went about his work, never dreaming that one of his most valuable and cherished concepts was about to be attacked. A criticism of action at a distance, indeed, seemed to be something almost beyond imagining. Coulomb's experimental researches in the 1780's had shown conclusively that electrostatic forces depended solely upon the product of the electrical 'masses' (i.e. quantity of electrical charge) and the square of the distances separating the charged bodies. This, Coulomb had explicitly stated, was exactly the way gravitational forces worked and if the one were action at a distance, so, too, was the other. The exactitude of Coulomb's measurements and the clarity of his deductions were impressive. Even more impressive was the work of Denis Poisson in the early years of the nineteenth century. Using Coulomb's experimental results on the distribution of electrical charge on bodies, and developing the concept of electrical potential, Poisson constructed a mathematical theory of great beauty. His theory appeared to place action at a distance beyond the reach of criticism. If anyone were to succeed in questioning action at a distance in electrostatic induction, he would have to stand up to one of the great theoretical physicists of the nineteenth century. This Faraday knew full well. In 1837, he met this difficulty head on.

> As a test of the probable accuracy of my views, [he wrote at the conclusion of the Eleventh Series] I have throughout this experimental examination compared them with the conclusions drawn by M. Poisson from his beautiful mathematical inquiries. I am quite unfit to form a judgment of these admirable papers; but as far as I can perceive, the theory I have set forth and the results I have obtained are not in opposition to such of those conclusions as represent the final disposition and state of the forces in the limited number of cases he has considered. His theory assumes a very different mode of action in induction to that which I have ventured to support, and would probably find its mathematical test in the endeavour to apply it to cases of induction in curved lines. To my feeling it is insufficient in accounting for the retention of electricity upon the surface of conductors by the pressure of the air, an effect which I hope to show is simple and consistent according to the present view; and it does not touch voltaic electricity, or in any way associate it and what is called ordinary electricity under one common principle (1305).

By 1837, therefore, Faraday was able to suggest that Poisson might be wrong and even to delineate those areas in which he felt his theory was clearly superior. But this decision to challenge orthodox physics had not been made lightly and the reason for the long delay in publication now becomes clear. Each step had to be checked, and re-checked and then checked once more before Faraday could proceed. Each part of his new theory had to be subjected to the most intense experimental tests he could devise. Finally the whole chain of his argument had to be examined with the greatest care. What a fool he would appear if his rejection of one of the most sacred doctrines of physics was found to be based on a silly experimental or theoretical error! There were many who felt strongly that no mathematically illiterate person should be allowed to meddle with physics and Faraday knew only too well how pleased they would be if he should stumble and fall. The Eleventh Series of the *Experimental Researches* was prepared, therefore, with infinite care and brought before the public only when Faraday felt certain that he had done all he could do to buttress his theory.

The origin of Faraday's extraordinary investigations of the transmission of electrostatic force lay in his electrochemical research. Having explained electrochemical decomposition in the Seventh Series, he turned his attention to the generation of electricity by a voltaic cell. There the play of chemical affinities was viewed from another angle. Instead of passing on a force the associated particles had somehow to be viewed as causing a tension or distortion in the molecular fields. The electromotive force Faraday found in the action of the forces of chemical affinity of two substances which could combine with one another (921, 924). This action was vividly described in the Eighth Series.

Assuming it sufficiently proved, by the preceding experiments and considerations, that the electro-motive action depends, when zinc, platina, and dilute sulphuric acid are used, upon the mutual affinity of the metal zinc and the oxygen of the water, . . . it would appear that the metal, when alone, has not power enough, under the circumstances, to take the oxygen and expel the hydrogen from the water; for, in fact, no such action takes place. But it would also appear that it has power so far to act, by its attraction for the oxygen of the particles in contact with it, as to place the similar forces already active between these and the other particles of oxygen and the particles of hydrogen in the water, in a peculiar state of tension or polarity, and probably also at the same time to throw those of its own particles which are in contact with the water into a similar but opposed state. Whilst this state is retained, no further change occurs; but when it is relieved, by completion of the circuit, in which case the forces determined in opposite directions, with respect to the zinc and the electrolyte, are found exactly competent to neutralize each other, then a series of decompositions and recompositions takes place amongst the particles of oxygen and hydrogen constituting the water, between the place of contact with the platina and the place where the zinc is active; these intervening particles being evidently in close dependence upon and relation to each other. The zinc forms a direct compound with those particles of oxygen which were, previously, in divided relation to both it and the hydrogen: the oxide is removed by the acid, and a fresh surface of zinc is presented to the water, to renew and repeat the action (949).

The electrotonic state which Faraday had reluctantly abandoned in his electromagnetic researches was reintroduced in electrochemistry. As in

1831, he again attempted to discover experimental evidence for the existence of this state. Polarized light was passed through electrolytic solutions
but to no avail (951, 952, 953). There was not the slightest effect. These
experiments had been carried out in May of 1833 and Faraday had then
written in his *Diary* that he did 'not think therefore that decomposing
solutions or substances will be found to have (as a consequence of decomposition or arrangement for the time) any effect on a polarized ray'
[493]. The very next paragraph, however, indicated that he had not lost
hope of finding the electrotonic state. 'Should now try non decomposing
bodies, as solid nitre, nit. silver, borax, glass, etc. whilst solid, to see if
any internal state induced which by decomposition is destroyed, i.e.
whether when cannot decompose any state of electrical tension is preserved. My Borate of Lead glass good, and common electricity better
than voltaic – higher intensity' [494]. This arrangement, using an electrostatic generator rather than the poles of a voltaic cell to provide the
'tension', also failed to produce a result [501].[11] In his experiment Faraday
obviously expected the electrostatic force to be transmitted from particle
to particle and to become manifest as an intermolecular strain. This was
the case in his later theory of induction and it is not too much to say that
the electrotonic state was the fundamental concept upon which his whole
electrical theory was based. Here all action was from particle to particle
and the care with which Faraday sought for confirmation of this action
revealed how important it was to him. In 1834 he thought he had the
proof (956, 957), but more careful experimenting dashed his hopes
(1074). The hold this view of electrical action had over him can be appreciated from the published account he gave of the unsuccessful experiment
with his borate of lead glass.

> Hence I conclude, [he wrote after reporting that polarized light was unaffected
> by the electric field placed across the glass] that *notwithstanding the new and
> extraordinary state* which *must* be assumed by an electrolyte, either during
> decomposition (when a most enormous quantity of electricity must be
> traversing it), or in the state of tension which is assumed as preceding
> decomposition, and which might be supposed to be retained in the solid form
> of the electrolyte, still it had no power of affecting a polarized ray of light; for
> no kind of structure or tension can in this way be rendered evident (955)
> [Italics mine].

In a letter to William Whewell, Faraday went even further. 'I have given
up this electrotonic state for the time as an experimental result (remember
my researches are *experimental*) because I could find no fact to prove it
but I cling to it in fancy or hypothesis . . . from general impressions
produced by the whole series of results.'[12]

In his retention of the electrotonic state in spite of the lack of experimental evidence for it Faraday would seem to have violated the first commandment of the experimentalist – to admit no effects which are incapable of experimental detection. What is often forgotten about Faraday, however, is that he was a daring theorist as well as a brilliant experimentalist. It should never be lost sight of that the new facts and laws that Faraday announced in a constant stream throughout thirty years were deduced by him from theories of his own devising and confirmed by experiment. His extraordinary experimental talent lay in being able to devise sensitive laboratory tests by which the particular effect he expected from theory could be detected. It was his theoretical genius that led him onward and the most important part of his theoretical vision from 1832 onwards was his conviction that the transmission of force was an intermolecular process and not action at a distance. The concept of the electrotonic state had led him to the laws of electrochemistry and he had, therefore, to 'cling to it in fancy or hypothesis' for it was the very cornerstone of the theoretical edifice he was building. Thus, in spite of all failures to detect it, Faraday stubbornly refused to abandon his hypothesis and continued to use it to help divulge the secrets of electrical action. Some day, he was sure, his faith would be justified and the electrotonic state would be revealed as clearly in the laboratory as it was in his mind.

The application of the concept of the electrotonic state to electrostatics first occurred in February of 1834 when Faraday was marshalling his evidence for the Eighth Series of the *Electrical Researches*. We have already quoted the section in that Series where Faraday discussed the state of tension created in a mixture of zinc, water, and sulphuric acid by the play of chemical affinity. In the *Diary* the analogy with electrostatics was tentatively drawn.

Is not rubbed glass and the rubber [Faraday asked] exactly in the state of Zinc and the oxygen of water in an electromotive circle, i.e. when the rubbed glass and the rubber are separated are they not in the state assumed by the zinc and the oxygen before they combine and before the contact is made in a single voltaic circle. They probably give an exalted view of the conditions of the particles of the zinc and oxygen, a permanent view as it were. How do the states agree?

Would not this view, if supported, reduce both modes of evolution to one common principle. The mutual influence of neighbouring particles – in the glass not proceeding to a full effect: in the voltaic circle being completed and being followed in succession by a multitude of others of the same kind. In the last it is the attraction of the Zinc for the oxygen of the oxide, and this would tell in well for the instances of induction, etc. perhaps, of common electricity [1646, 1647].

It was not until some twenty months later that Faraday was able to begin to explore the consequences of his supposed analogy. On 3 November 1835, he began his electrostatic researches by remarking: 'Have been thinking much lately of the relation of common and voltaic electricity: of induction by the former and decomposition by the latter, and am quite convinced that there must be the closest connexion. Will be first needful to make out the true character of ordinary electrical phenomena' [2468]. This was the modest beginning from which Faraday's monumental work was to grow.

The first 'true character' of electrostatic action to which Faraday turned his attention was one he considered crucial in deciding for or against his hypothesis. An 'ever-present question' on his mind, he remarked in the Eleventh Series, was 'whether electricity has an actual and independent existence as a fluid or fluids, or was a mere power of matter like what we conceive of the attraction of gravitation' (1168). This basic question had always occupied him but now it assumed overpowering importance. In essence it involved the crux of the difference between his theory of electrical action and that held by the overwhelming majority of his contemporaries. All the classical theories – Coulomb's, Poisson's, Ampère's – supposed that electrical phenomena could be accounted for by assuming fluids separable from matter, endowed with certain powers. Faraday almost alone among creative scientists believed that the electrical powers were inextricably connected with matter itself. According to the one theory, the two fluids of electricity should be capable of separation and each ought then to be susceptible to study by itself. According to Faraday's theory, the two electricities were merely manifestations of the powers of matter and could no more be separated from it than could chemical affinity or gravity. The best defence, Faraday always felt, was an offence mounted against his own ideas. Thus he wrote:

> It was in attempts to prove the existence of electricity separate from matter, by giving an independent charge of either positive or negative power only, to some one substance, and the utter failure of all such attempts, whatever substance was used or whatever means of exciting or *evolving* electricity were employed, that first drove me to look upon induction as an action of the particles of matter, each having *both* forces developed in it in exactly equal amount (1168).

The first lengthy series of experiments on induction was, therefore, devoted to answering the question: 'Can matter, either conducting or non-conducting, be charged with one electric force independently of the other, in any degree, either in a sensible or latent state' (1169).

In 1786 Coulomb had shown that 'in conducting bodies, the [electrical] fluid in a stable state, is spread over the surface of bodies, and does not penetrate into them'.[13] This fact, known and even cited by Faraday, would appear at the very beginning to settle the question. An insulated metal globe can be charged positively or negatively very simply. Yet Faraday cited this fact to prove his point. The course of his thought here is rather obscure. In the published paper, he cited Coulomb's result and commented that Coulomb's experiments were 'sufficient, if properly viewed, to prove that *conductors cannot be bodily charged*' (1170). Presumably, then, the electricity could not enter into the body of the conductor or, put another way, could not be the result of any peculiar state of tension in the particles of the conductor. This cannot, of course, be Faraday's meaning since he was convinced that electricity *was* the result of such a state. Some light is shed upon this statement by a comment in the *Diary* early in the course of his research.

> Consider the supposed existence of Electricity upon the electric [i.e. non-conductor] and not upon the conductor, in relation to the *nature of that electric*.
>
> Thus, will the same conductor in different Electrics have the same intensity and quantity with the same quantity of electricity?
>
> A metal globe in Air; rare air; glass (a body so as to avoid what is called induction); Wax; Oil; Oil turpentine, and other electrics, electrified from the same common source, and then brought in contact with an Electrometer – the divergences observed. If the results are constant for the same body, but vary with different bodies, then a proof that the electricity is related to the electric, not to the conductor [2495-7].

We may note in passing that the idea of what was later to be called specific inductive capacity was the basis for Faraday's attack on the problem of the relationship between electricity and a conductor. What is of more importance at this point was his view of this relationship. If electricity were related to the insulator, then how could a conductor be electrified? The answer was that it could not. The *apparent* charge resulted from the fact that the conductor was merely the terminus of a chain of induction which extended from the conductor to other nearby bodies. In most cases this would be the walls of the room in which the electrification took place. Even in the open air the effect would occur since the conductor would be surrounded by a non-conductor – Air. Faraday carried out the experiments and found the situation as he expected [2741 ff.]. The point was an important one as Faraday was to show when he considered the nature of electrical conduction. Conductors cannot take on much strain – that is why they are conductors. Hence electrostatic induction will not pass *through* conducting bodies but will terminate there. To illustrate this point, Faraday performed a spectacular experiment which had its proper effect on his audience at the Royal Institution. He built a cube twelve feet on an edge. Copper wire was passed over it in all directions until a mesh had been formed. Paper upon which tinfoil bands had been fastened was then used to cover the cube so that the whole was an excellent conductor. Faraday then entered the cube carrying instruments used for detecting electrostatic charge. When the cube was charged to such an extent that sparks flew off at the corners and the tinfoil strips stood straight out with brushes of electricity surrounding their ends, Faraday could detect not the slightest effect. 'The conclusion I have come to,' he wrote in the published paper, 'is, that non-conductors, as well as conductors, have never yet had an absolute and independent charge of one electricity communicated to them, and that to all appearance such a state of matter is impossible' (1174).[14] Not only was electricity inseparable from matter, but one kind was always accompanied by the other kind. This served to reinforce Faraday's previous definition of the electric current as an 'axis of power', for induction could now be viewed as the initial orientation of this axis along which the force was transmitted. In August 1836, he was able to arrive at certain fundamental conclusions concerning the electric forces drawn from his experiments on the inability to produce an absolute electric charge.

> After much consideration (here at Ryde) of the manner in which the electric forces are arranged in the various phenomena generally, I have come to certain conclusions which I will endeavour to note down, without committing myself to any opinion as to the cause of electricity, i.e. as to the nature of the power. If electricity exist independantly of matter, then I think that the hypothesis of one fluid will not stand against that of two fluids. There are, I think, evidently what I may call two elements of power of equal force and acting towards each other. These may conventionally be represented by Oxygen and Hydrogen, which represent them in the voltaic battery. But these powers may be distinguished only *by direction*, and may be no more separate than the North and south forces in the elements of a magnetic needle. They may be the polar points of the forces originally placed in the particles of matter, and the description of the current as an axis of power, which I have formerly given, suggests some similar general expression for the forces of quiescent electricity. *Line of electric tension might do*; and though I shall use the terms Pos. and Neg., by them I merely mean the *termini* of such lines [3423].

The reasons for the equality of positive and negative electricity, and for the absence of absolute charge now become apparent. The so-called

charges were really only tensions and could be detected anywhere along
the line of electric tension. Since this line was static, the positive 'charge'
must always equal the negative or else there would be electric displacement. It is as though one stretched a rope between two stationary points
and measured the tension at these points. The two would have the same
tension (charge) but the forces would be in opposite directions. Electric
charge, then, was necessarily bound up with induction and Faraday now
realized that induction must lie at the bottom of *all* electrical phenomena.

> Bodies cannot be charged absolutely [he wrote in his *Diary*] as far as my ex-
> perience goes, only relatively, and by a principle which is the same with that
> of induction. All *charge* is sustained by induction. All phenomena of *intensity*
> includes the principle of induction. All *excitation* is dependant as far as I can
> see on induction. All *currents* involve previous intensity and therefore
> previous induction. *Induction* appears to be the essential principle of the
> development of electricity [3425].[15]

Since induction was the basic phenomenon in all electrical science,
it deserved the closest study. Such study necessarily involved Faraday in
an investigation of the state of the molecular forces in a body undergoing
induction, for it was upon these forces that induction depended. By 1836
his ideas on the nature and character of these forces were highly developed
and he was able to reason clearly upon them. One of the necessary consequences of his theoretical views was that there ought to exist differences
in the transmission of electrical force by different materials. Or, to put it
in his own words, 'if induction be an action of contiguous particles, and
also the first step in the process of electrolyzation . . . there seemed reason
to expect some particular relation of it to the different kinds of matter
through which it would be exerted, or something equivalent to a *specific
electric induction* for different bodies, which, if it existed, would unequi-
vocally prove the dependence of induction on the particles' (1167). Two
points should be underlined in this statement: first, the existence of a
specific inductive capacity would *prove* that electrostatic action was *not* at a
distance but from particle to particle and, second, that if the action were
from particle to particle, a specific inductive capacity should exist. It is not
Faraday's circularity of reasoning that is noteworthy here, but, as we shall
see, the fact that *only* in the theory of point atoms can one be led to these
two conclusions. This Faraday knew and we shall see with what eagerness
he accepted a theory of molecular forces forthcoming in 1836 which supported his views.

To understand Faraday's derivation of specific inductive capacity from
his theory of molecular forces, we must go back to his work on catalysis.

There he had shown that the elective nature of chemical affinity was to be found also at distances larger than those at which chemical combination took place. Intermolecular forces were, therefore, both specific in terms of the nature of the substance and of a peculiar strength for each material. Let us now represent these forces in terms of arcs of the Boscovichean curves. Some will be sharp and strong; others will show a more gradual change with distance, while still others may combine large forces with considerable latitude of action. Each substance, however, will be represented by a unique curve, and only rarely will two such curves be found to be identical. Now, when the electric force is applied across a chain of particles tied together by these intermolecular forces, the reaction of the chain will be specific for each substance. Such specificity of action was insisted upon *only* by the theory of point atoms and from this theory Faraday had deduced the existence of specific inductive capacity. Showing that such an effect really existed was something else again for it involved experiments of the most delicate nature.

Faraday's inductive apparatus may be seen in Figure 1. His description cannot be improved upon.

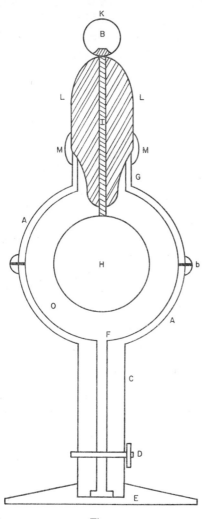

Fig. 1

The apparatus used may be described in general terms as consisting of two metallic spheres of unequal diameter, placed, the smaller within the larger, and concentric with it; the interval between the two being the space through which the induction was to take place.... [A], [A] are the two halves of a brass sphere, with an air-tight joint at *b*, like that of the Magdeburg hemispheres, made perfectly flush and smooth inside so as to present no irregularity; [C] is a connecting piece by which the apparatus is joined to a good stop-cock [D], which is itself attached either to the metallic foot [E], or to an air pump. The aperture within the hemisphere at [F] is very small: [G] is a brass collar fitted to the upper hemisphere, through which the shell-lac support of the inner ball and its stem passes; [H] is the inner ball, also of brass; it screws on to a brass stem [I], terminated above by a brass ball B; [L], [L] is a mass of shell-lac, moulded carefully on to [I], and serving both to support and insulate it and its balls [H], B. The shell-lac stem [L] is fitted into the socket [G], by a little ordinary resinous cement, more fusible than shell-lac, applied at [M] [M] in such a way as to give sufficient strength and render the apparatus air-tight there, yet leave as much as possible of the lower part of the shell-lac stem untouched, as an insulation between the ball [H] and the surrounding sphere [A], [A] (1188). . . .

The inductive apparatus described is evidently a Leyden phial, with the advantage, however, of having the *dielectric* or insulating medium changed at pleasure (1195).[16]

In order to detect the slightest difference in the inductive capacity of substances introduced into the space between the two brass spheres, Faraday utilized the equilibrium method by which, under identical circumstances, two such instruments would show identical results. Two instruments as nearly alike as possible were constructed. To check the sensitivity of this method, Faraday charged one instrument and measured this charge with a Coulomb torsion electrometer. The charged instrument was then touched to the uncharged and the resultant charge on both was measured. When the space between the two brass balls was filled with the same dielectric such as air, the charge was evenly divided. Hence, it could be reasonably assumed that when different dielectrics were present, if there were such a thing as a specific inductive capacity, it ought to become evident by a difference in the partition of charge.[17]

Once again, as was the case with the question of the absolute charge on a conductor, when Faraday began to experiment he got results that seemed to contradict his hypothesis. When different gases were used in the space between the two brass balls, absolutely no difference in charge could be detected. Where, then, was the specific inductive capacity? It is even more disconcerting to find Faraday looking for errors in the experiment when a difference *was* detected [3706, 3707] as though this were an unexpected, rather than a predicted, result. A moment's reflection will resolve the difficulty. What conclusion should be drawn from an equality of inductive capacity in all the gases? It would seem inescapable that one of two situations must obtain: either the induction is an action at a distance in which the nature of the interposed medium was irrelevant, or the intermolecular forces between the particles of gases were the same for all gases. Faraday, by 1837 when he performed these experiments, was certainly not prepared to accept the first alternative, so he must have chosen the second.

As a matter of fact, the second is obviously true; Boyle's law stated it as succinctly as it could be stated. This is why he was surprised when his results seemed to indicate that a difference in inductive capacity existed.

When solid or liquid bodies were introduced into the space between the spheres, the results were all that Faraday expected. A hemisphere of shellac was made which just fitted between the two brass spheres. The apparatus containing air only was charged. This charge was then shared with the apparatus in which the space was half-filled with shellac. The air instrument lost more than half its charge but the shellac gained less than half of the original charge [4182]. From this it followed, Faraday argued, that if the difference in the charge of the two instruments after the charges were shared were assumed to depend 'entirely on the greater facility possessed by shell-lac of allowing or causing inductive action through its substance' (1259) then this difference could be used to compute the specific inductive capacity. In the case of shellac, Faraday found this capacity to be 1·55, a figure which indicated the relative superiority of shellac to air in taking up the strain of the electric tension.

Experiments with other substances such as glass and wax served to generalize Faraday's theory of specific inductive capacity. There could be no doubt that the new effect existed and that its existence was of the utmost importance in the arguments Faraday directed at electrostatic action at a distance. The effect also seemed inexplicable on any other but Bosco-vichean terms. Here, it would seem, was the perfect place for Faraday publicly to acknowledge his debt to the theory of point atoms and to establish that theory as a respectable one. There is, however, not one word even hinting at Faraday's deepest concepts. The reason for this is not difficult to discover. It is plain that Faraday wished to avoid a theoretical fight at almost all costs. He was, after all, exploding a fundamental hypothesis of contemporary physics by denying electrostatic action at a distance. It would be enough for his readers to accept this without being asked, as well, to accept a theory which appeared to deny the evidence of their own senses. Faraday even avoided conflict over the nature of electricity. Although his whole paper was couched in terms which denied the existence of electrical fluids, he insisted in a footnote that 'the theory of induction which I am stating does not pretend to decide whether electricity be a fluid or fluids. . . .'[18]

There is evidence, fortunately, to show that Faraday's enthusiasm for the theory of point atoms had by no means lessened. In December 1836, he received a short paper from Signor Mossotti of Turin and immediately upon reading it, dashed off a letter to his friend Whewell which reveals his excitement.

> I cannot refrain from writing to you. I have just received a short memoire from Sig. Mossotti of Turin on the forces which govern matter. Have you seen it. I have been exceedingly struck with it and hope it is correct in its mathematical part of which I am no judge. It relates essentially to electricity and deduces all the phenomena of gravitation from it and it is this which makes the interest to me for his view jumps in with my notion which I think I mentioned to you that Universal Gravitation is a mere residual phenomenon of Electrical attraction and repulsion.
>
> He first proceeds to shew that Poissons investigations do nothing as to the settlement of the question whether there be one or two fluids of Electricity. He then goes on to shew that the supposed difficulty of allowing that matter (according to the theory of Æpinus and Cavendish) has repulsive powers which are inversely as the square of the distance and also attractive powers in the same ratio does not in reality exist. But that on the assumption of one electric fluid having repulsive powers inversely as the square of the distance – of matter also having repulsive powers in the same ratio whilst the attraction of matter and electricity for each other is in the same ratio but with this addition that the repulsive power of the particles of matter for each other is a little less than the repulsive power of electricity or than the mutual attraction of electricity and matter – then all the phenomena of gravitation – those of statical electricity and likewise that condition of the particles of bodies by which they are (though not in contact) prevented from approaching each other or receding from each other – flow as natural consequences – the electrical phenomena being as fully explained as they are in Poissons theory.
>
> What I want to ask you is your opinion of this paper and of the correctness of the mathematical reasoning. I dare say you have had copies of it sent to Cambridge but if not let me know how I can convey mine to you or let me know that you wish to see it and I will find means of sending it. But I cannot give it to you.[19]

Faraday's enthusiasm did not stop here. He delivered a lecture on Mossotti's theory at the Royal Institution[20] and sent his copy of the paper to Richard Taylor for publication in the first volume of *Scientific Memoirs, selected from the Transactions of Foreign Academies of Science and Learned Societies and from Foreign Journals.*[21]

Mossotti's theory[22] differed in many ways from Boscovich's – not least in its clinging to fluids and matter as the substratum of force – but it did contain certain other ideas which Faraday was eager to spread. Most important was the association of both attractive and repulsive forces with 'matter' for this was essential to his theory of the propagation of force through the action of contiguous particles. Mossotti's memoir also had the advantage of being filled with mathematical equations which guaranteed it a respectful reading by physicists. In 1836 Faraday had not yet published his views on induction and there is little doubt that he welcomed the assistance that Mossotti offered. He must, too, have been pleased with the result of his efforts. Mossotti's ideas, so similar to his own, became a popular topic of scientific conversation and even Boscovich returned briefly to the public stage. The editors of *The London and Edinburgh Philosophical Magazine and Journal of Science* took this opportunity 'of referring those who are interested in the philosophy of molecular action, to the account of the theories of Father Boscovich and Mr Michell, in Dr Priestley's Disquisitions on Matter and Spirit. . . . This account, we think, may be advantageously read in connexion with the memoir of M. Mossotti.'[23]

Faraday's philosophy of molecular action, strengthened by the discovery of specific inductive capacity, led him in 1837 to the final proof he required that electrostatic induction was not action at a distance. This was the discovery that induction took place along curved rather than straight lines.

Faraday was led to this hypothesis both by theoretical and experimental considerations. On the theoretical side, it seemed a necessary consequence of his ideas concerning the mutual relations of particles of matter. These 'particles' were, so to speak, suspended in a plenum of force so that the centres of force were considerably removed from one another, but the particles themselves were 'contiguous'.[24] This was what Faraday meant in his letter to Whewell by the 'condition of the particles of bodies by which they are (though not in contact) prevented from approaching each other or receding from each other'. If an inductive force was now imposed upon such an agglomeration of particles, the transmission of the force would have to be along curved lines as the forces of the individual particles took up the strain (Figure 2). That such was, indeed, the case Faraday had shown experimentally in his electrochemical researches. He noted in his *Diary* for 16 January 1836, that 'Induction therefore may doubtless take place in curved lines. It does so in decomposing solutions, as is easily

Fig. 2

shewn by its turning a corner . . .' [2867]. The problem now was to map these electrostatic lines of force so that their curvature could become apparent to all.

The apparatus Faraday devised for this purpose was simplicity itself. It consisted of a column of shellac upon which a brass ball or a metal plate could be placed. Since he had earlier shown that conductors of electrical currents could not conduct the electrostatic inductive force, the metallic objects served as efficient screens of this force. When the shellac column was given a charge by rubbing it with a flannel cloth, there ought to be a 'shadow' cast by the ball or the plate. If induction were really action at a distance and occurred in straight lines, then the 'shadow' should be as well defined as an optical one and no inductive action should take place behind the plate or the ball. If, on the other hand, induction was the result of the action of contiguous particles, such action ought to be detectable in the 'shadow' (Figure 3). When a Coulomb electrometer was used to

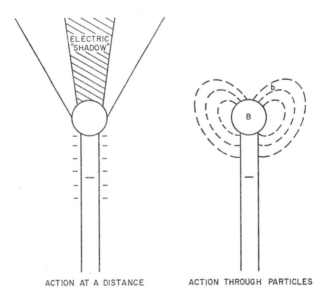

ACTION AT A DISTANCE   ACTION THROUGH PARTICLES

Fig. 3

detect inductive action, Faraday's supposition was proven correct. At *b* in the figure a charge was detected and Faraday insisted upon its meaning: 'it is clearly a charge by induction, but *induction* in *a curved line*; for the carrier ball whilst applied to *b*, and after its removal to a distance of six inches or more from B, could not in consequence of the size of B, be connected by a straight line with any part of the excited and inducing shell-lac' (1219). These experiments were multiplied with all possible precautions taken, so that it was impossible to deny the reality of induction in curved lines. In unusually strong terms Faraday hammered his point home.

> As argument against the received theory of induction [he wrote] and in favour of that which I have ventured to put forth, I cannot see how the preceding results can be avoided. The effects are clearly inductive effects produced by electricity, not in currents but in its statical state, and this induction is exerted in lines of force which, though in many experiments they may be straight, are here curved more or less according to circumstances. I use the term *line of inductive force* merely as a temporary conventional mode of expressing the direction of the power in cases of induction; and in the experiments with the hemisphere (1224), it is curious to see how, when certain lines have terminated on the under surface and edge of the metal, those which were before lateral to them *expand and open out from each other*, some bending round and terminating their action on the upper surface of the hemisphere, and others meeting, as it were, above in their progress outwards, uniting their forces to give an increased charge to the carrier ball, at an *increased distance* from the source of power, and influencing each other so as to cause a second flexure in the contrary direction from the first one. All this appears to me to prove that the whole action is one of contiguous particles, related to each other, not merely in the lines which they may be conceived to form through the dielectric, between the *inductric* and the *inducteous* surfaces (1483), but in other lateral directions also. It is this which gives an effect equivalent to a lateral repulsion or expansion in the lines of force I have spoken of, and enables induction to turn a corner (1304). The power, instead of being like that of gravity, which causes particles to act on each other through straight lines, whatever other particles may be between them, is more analogous to that of a series of magnetic needles, or to the condition of the particles considered as forming the whole of a straight or a curved magnet. So that in whatever way I view it, and with great suspicion of the influence of favourite notions over myself, I cannot perceive how the ordinary theory applied to explain induction can be a correct representation of that great natural principle of electrical action (1231).

This extraordinary paragraph deserves to be carefully read and thoroughly digested. In it Faraday flatly denied action at a distance and threw down a challenge to orthodox physics that could not be ignored. The challenge, furthermore, was directed (seemingly) at the very cornerstone of Newtonian theoretical physics for it was upon the concept of action at a distance that the great French theorists, particularly Laplace, had built. Faraday also, with astonishing calm, and almost in passing, demolished the experimental basis of electrostatics. Coulomb's law relating charge, force, and distance was discovered to be only a quite special case of the action of the contiguous particles. If it were still to be retained, it would have to be restated in terms which took into account the nature of the medium or media through which the force was propagated. The force varied inversely as the square of the distance *only* under special conditions which now had to be stated explicitly.

The paragraph also called attention to the lateral action of repulsion between particles along the line of inductive force. We can now see why Mossotti's ideas were so welcome for they helped Faraday to preserve his hypothesis of particulate action. Finally, the analogy of electrostatic induction with magnetic action is worthy of notice. Faraday's theories had led him closer to the connexion between electric and magnetic phenomena and he was, in the 1840's, to achieve brilliant new results by applying these ideas to magnetism. At this time, however, his thoughts on the process of induction had opened up exciting prospects of unifying all electrical action. In spite of the fact that his ideas were bound to lead to intense attacks upon him, he had to publish them for he was eager to press onward and apply them to other areas. Thus he closed the Eleventh Series with the warning that a good deal more was yet to come.

> Finally, I beg to say that I put forth my particular view with doubt and fear, lest it should not bear the test of general examination, for unless true it will only embarrass the progress of electrical science. It has long been on my mind, but I hesitated to publish it until the increasing persuasion of its accordance with all known facts, and the manner in which it linked together effects apparently very different in kind, urged me to write the present paper. I as yet see no inconsistency between it and nature, but, on the contrary, think I perceive much new light thrown by it on her operations; and my next papers will be devoted to a review of the phenomena of conduction, electrolyzation, current, magnetism, retention, discharge, and some other points, with an application of the theory to these effects, and an examination of it by them (1306).

He aimed, in short, at revolutionizing the whole of the theory of electricity.

3. The Unity of Electrical Action

The Eleventh Series provided Faraday with a firm experimental and theoretical foundation upon which to build a complete theory of electrical action. It seemed impossible now to deny that electrical action involved the particles through which the electrical forces acted. Having proved this point, it remained for Faraday to illustrate how action between particles, rather than at a distance, could explain all electrical effects. Part of this task he had already accomplished. The papers on electrochemistry had shown how the transmission of force from molecule to molecule could give rise both to an electrolytic 'current' and to chemical decomposition. What remained to be done was to extend his theory to areas such as electrostatic discharge and the conduction of electricity in good conductors. The Twelfth, Thirteenth, and Fourteenth Series were devoted to an examination of these subjects.

There is no more dramatic evidence for the passage of an electrical substance of some kind than the electric spark. It seems, literally, to provide visible proof of the materiality of electricity as it leaps from point to point. The thunderbolt of Zeus could be nothing else than some real transfer of matter carrying with it enormous energies. To prove that the spark and lightning were merely the collapse of a previous inductive state of strain was to be no easy task.

Faraday began by assuming the correctness of his theory of electrical action. His method, then, was to examine a whole host of effects and compare his explanation with that offered by the theory that assumed action at a distance. This section, therefore, was not 'experimental' but dialectical and Faraday here called upon the history of electricity and upon other people's experimental results to support his case.

The stage for the dispute was set by a careful description of conditions and definition of terms. The creation of a disruptive discharge or spark required certain conditions.

> An insulating dielectric must be interposed between two conducting surfaces in opposite states of electricity, and then if the actions be continually increased in strength, or otherwise favoured, either by exalting the electric state of the two conductors, or bringing them nearer to each other, or diminishing the density of the dielectric, a *spark* at last appears, and the two forces are for the time annihilated, for *discharge* has occurred (1360).

This was intended simply as a bare statement of the facts, but it is not difficult to discern Faraday's theory peeping through. The appearance of the spark depended upon the condition of the dielectric and, as Faraday went on to remark: 'In my view of induction . . . every dielectric becomes of importance, for as the results are considered essentially dependent on these bodies, it was to be expected that differences of action never before suspected would be evident upon close examination, and so at once give fresh confirmation of the theory, and open new doors of discovery into the extensive and varied fields of our science' (1361). Before exploring these new fields Faraday wished to explain himself again on the mechanism of induction and of eventual discharge. The point was an important one for he was to use it time and again to explain particular results. Induction,

as the Eleventh Series had pointed out, was a condition of strain imposed
on the molecules of the dielectric, by the electric forces.

> Whilst the induction continues, it is assumed that the particles of the dielectric
> are in a certain polarized state, the tension of this state rising higher in each
> particle as the induction is raised to a higher degree, either by approximation
> of the inducing surfaces, variation of form, increase of the original force, or
> other means; until at last, the tension of the particles having reached the
> utmost degree which they can sustain without subversion of the whole
> arrangement, discharge immediately after takes place.
>
> The theory does not assume, however, that *all* the particles of the dielectric
> subject to the inductive action are affected to the same amount, or acquire
> the same tension. What has been called the lateral action of the lines of in-
> ductive force (1231, 1297), and the diverging and occasionally curved form of
> these lines, is against such a notion. The idea is, that any section taken through
> the dielectric across the lines of inductive force, and including *all of them*,
> would be equal, in the sum of the forces, to the sum of the forces in any other
> section; and that, therefore, the whole amount of tension for each such
> section would be the same.
>
> Discharge probably occurs, not when all the particles have attained to a
> certain degree of tension, but when that particle which is most affected
> has been exalted to the subverting or turning point. . . . For though *all* the
> particles in the line of induction resist charge, and are associated in their
> actions so as to give a sum of resisting force, yet when any one is brought
> up to the overturning point, *all* must give way in the case of a spark between
> ball and ball. The breaking down of that one must of necessity cause the
> whole barrier to be overturned, for it was at its utmost degree of resistance
> when it possessed the aiding power of that one particle, in addition to the
> power of the rest, and the power of that one is not lost (1368–70).

With this picture firmly fixed in his mind, Faraday ticked off the facts
his theory could explain. When the distance between the two inducting
plates was decreased, the induction increased, 'for there are then fewer
particles in the line of inductive force to oppose their united resistance to
the assumption of the forced or polarized state, and *vice versa*' (1371).
The same reasoning applied to discharge across a shorter distance. It had
been shown that when the interval between the plates was halved, it took
only half the voltage (or tension) to bring about discharge. Such a result
followed directly from Faraday's theory since 'at that time there are only
half the number of interposed molecules uniting their forces to resist the
discharge' (1371). If the areas of the inducing plates were increased, the
intensity of the induction diminished, as would be expected since the
inducing force would then be diffused among a larger number of particles
(1372). When the areas were drastically reduced, as with a point, Faraday
was equally successful for he was able to show that the particles near the

point suffered extraordinary forces and tended, therefore, to give way. This was why points were so efficient in discharging electrical tension (1374). The fact that it was easier to cause a spark to jump a given distance in rarefied air than in air at atmospheric pressure offered no difficulties in Faraday's theory. '. . . As there are only half the number of dielectric particles in the rarefied atmosphere, so these are brought up to the discharging intensity by half the former quantity of electricity . . .' (1375).

Faraday again took the opportunity to call attention to the superiority of his theory *physically* (as opposed to mathematically) over that developed by Poisson and Biot in France. This theory had to wrestle with the paradox that the electrical fluids did not have any effect whatsoever upon ponderable matter and yet were retained upon the surface of charged bodies by the pressure of the air.[25] Faraday proved experimentally that discharge was not a simple function of pressure [4340 ff.] and in the published paper introduced a simple experimental refutation of this hypothesis. If a solid dielectric such as sulphur or shellac were introduced into *part* of the space separating two charged concentric spheres, the diffusion of electricity upon the inner sphere became unequal 'although', as Faraday noticed, 'the form of the conducting surfaces, their distances, and the *pressure* of the atmosphere remain perfectly unchanged' (1378).

> Here I think my view of induction has a decided advantage over others [Faraday wrote], especially over that which refers the retention of electricity on the surface of conductors in air to the *pressure of the atmosphere*. The latter is the view which, being adopted by Poisson and Biot, is also, I believe, that generally received; and it associates two such dissimilar things, as the ponderous air and the subtile and even hypothetical fluid or fluids of electricity, by gross mechanical relations; by the bonds of mere static pressure. My theory, on the contrary, sets out at once by connecting the electric forces with the particles of matter; it derives all its proofs, and even its origin in the first instance from experiment;[26] and then, without any further assumption, seems to offer at once a full explanation of these and many other singular, peculiar, and, I think, heretofore unconnected effects (1377).

The claim that a theory is drawn more directly from experimental facts and that it contains a greater economy of supposition than a rival is always a good one to advance. It is often impressive, but rarely decisive. For the theory to gain a significant advantage over another, it must reveal an ability to cope with facts inexplicable in other terms. If it can, as well, correlate seemingly disconnected effects and show that they are but modifications of a single law, the theory will have become a formidable contender for general acceptance. Faraday, therefore, set out to show how his theory could accomplish precisely this.

In 1834, Faraday's friend W. Snow Harris, had reported a fact that puzzled him and could not be explained in terms of electrical action at a distance. In his studies of electrical discharge, especially as it related to lightning bolts at sea, Harris found a peculiar effect. 'At the instant before which the discharge takes place', he wrote, 'the stream of electricity in the act of moving to restore the equilibrium of distribution, seems, by a wonderful influence, to *feel its way*, and *mark out, as it were, in advance*, the course it is about to follow which course is *invariably through the line or lines of least resistance between the points of action.*'[27] Harris was an orthodox adherent of the two-fluid, action-at-a-distance school and his description of the odd prescience of the lightning bolt reflected his amazement. When he treated of the redistribution of electric matter to effect equilibrium, he again called attention to the phenomenon. In order to effect equilibrium, the electrical fluid '*marks* out, as it were, *in advance*, by a wonderful influence, operating at a distance, the course it is about to follow'.[28] On 21 October 1837, Faraday had noted in his *Diary*: 'By my theory, Harris' wonderful foreknowledge of electricity in making out its easiest passage very easily explicable' [4154]. In the Twelfth Series he proceeded to the explanation. The note of triumph could not be disguised.

> The *path of the spark*, or of the discharge, depends on the degree of tension acquired by the particles in the line of discharge, circumstances, which in every common case are very evident and by the theory easy to understand, rendering it higher in them than in their neighbours, and, by exalting them first to the requisite condition, causing them to determine the course of the discharge. Hence the selection of the path, and the solution of the wonder which Harris has so well described as existing under the old theory. All is prepared amongst the molecules beforehand, by the prior induction, for the path either of the electric spark or of lightning itself (1407).

In search of instances which would support his theory, Faraday was led to a series of experiments which could never have even occurred to an exponent of the orthodox theory. The role of the air, or any other gas, in this theory, was simply to supply the pressure needed to retain the electrical fluids on charged conductors. At the same pressures, discharge should occur in air, oxygen, nitrogen, etc., when the tension (voltage) across the discharge gap reached a certain value which would be the same regardless of what gas filled the gap. In Faraday's theory, there was room for doubt about this. He had seen that the specific inductive capacity was the same for all gases and this was to be expected given the obedience of all gases to Boyle's law. Disruptive discharge, however, involved the absolute forces between the molecules making up the gas. In his electrochemical researches, Faraday had demonstrated the specificity of these forces when electrolytes were involved, and he had been able to relate them directly to chemical affinity. Was it not possible that gases would reveal some similar specificity when discharge was involved? Faraday immediately set to work to test this hypothesis. Using air as a standard of comparison, he compared the insulating power of a number of different gases [4340 ff.]. The results revealed a definite difference, specific for each gas. The first conclusion Faraday drew from this fact was, once again, that 'it cannot be mere pressure of the atmosphere which prevents or governs discharge' (1398) [4356]. The second was more in the nature of a hope and a dream of unity. It was speculative, but it was a speculation that had led Faraday to the frontier of physics and was to guide him onwards for another fifteen years. This was the dream of reducing all observed effects of the various forces of nature to the manifestation, under different conditions, of the primal forces of attraction and repulsion. Thus the force needed to create disruptive discharge must, in Faraday's mind, bear some relation to the other intermolecular forces.

> It seems probable [he pointed out], that the tension of a particle of the same dielectric, as air, which is requisite to produce discharge, is a *constant quantity*, whatever the shape of the part of the conductor with which it is in contact, whether ball or point; whatever the thickness or depth of dielectric throughout which induction is exerted; perhaps, even, whatever the state, as to rarefaction or condensation of the dielectric; and whatever the nature of the conductor, good or bad, with which the particle is for the moment associated. In saying so much, I do not mean to exclude small differences which may be caused by the reaction of neighbouring particles on the deciding particle, and indeed, it is evident that the intensity required in a particle must be related to the condition of those which are contiguous. But if the expectation should be found to approximate to truth, what a generality of character it presents! and, in the definiteness of the power possessed by a particular molecule, may we not hope to find an immediate relation to the force which, being electrical, is equally definite and constitutes chemical affinity? (1410).

Faraday's description of spark discharge in terms of his theory was a model of clarity. The whole process was easily visualized, and the deductions Faraday drew, beautifully supported by experiments, followed simply and logically from the basic assumptions of intermolecular action. The same cannot be said of his discussion of brush discharge. The imprecision of his terms, especially that much abused word force, here served to muddy his ideas and led to a section of the Twelfth Series which was something less than satisfactory. The reason for this was that with the brush, Faraday was deprived of the chain of particles by which he had accounted for the transmission of force in all his previous investigations. This chain had existed between the electrodes of the voltaic cell, as well as between the two conductors between which the electrostatic spark jumped. Brush discharge, however, simply went into the air. Faraday tried to preserve the chain, but it was only at the expense of clarity. Thus describing the brush, he wrote:

> The *brush* is in reality a discharge between a bad or a non-conductor and either a conductor or another non-conductor. Under common circumstances, the brush is a discharge between a conductor and air, and I conceive it to take place in something like the following manner. When the end of an electrified rod projects into the middle of a room, induction takes place between it and the walls of the room, across the dielectric, air; and the lines of inductive force accumulate upon the end in greater quantity than elsewhere, or the particles of air at the end of the rod are more highly polarized than those at any other part of the rod, for the reasons already given (1374). The particles of air situated in sections across these lines of force are least polarized in the sections towards the wall, and most polarized in those nearer to the end of the wires [from which the brush proceeds]: thus, it may well happen, that a particle at the end of the wire is at a tension that will immediately terminate in discharge, whilst in those even only a few inches off, the tension is still beneath that point. But suppose the rod to be charged positively, a particle of air A, . . . next it, being polarized, and having of course its negative force directed towards the rod and its positive force outwards; the instant that discharge takes place between the positive force of the particle of the rod opposite the air and the negative force of the particle of air towards the rod, the whole particle of air becomes positively electrified; and when, the next instant, the discharged part of the rod resumes its positive state by conduction from the surface of metal behind, it not only acts on the particles beyond A, by throwing A into a polarized state again, but A itself, because of its charged state, exerts a distinct inductive act towards these further particles, and the tension is consequently so much exalted between A and B, that discharge takes place there also, as well as again between the metal and A (1434).

All is familiar here until we discover that 'the whole particle of air becomes positively electrified'. How can this be? Was not a good part of the Eleventh Series devoted to proving that an absolute charge was impossible? Where is the other 'power' which Faraday always insisted had to be present?

Faraday also seemed to have forgotten his opposition to action at a distance, as well as to absolute charge.

> The particles that are charged are probably very highly charged, [he noted] but, the medium being a non-conductor, they cannot communicate that state to their neighbours.[29] They travel, therefore, under the influence of the repulsive and attractive forces, [!] from the charged conductor towards the

nearest uninsulated conductor, or the nearest body in a different state to themselves, just as charged particles of dust would travel, and are then discharged; each particle acting, in its course, as a centre of inductive force upon any bodies near which it may come (1442).

Where is the action of the contiguous particles upon which all electrical action supposedly depended? Indeed, except for the last phrase about centres of induction, Faraday's treatment of brush discharge differs in no way from that of an orthodox fluidist. Merely substitute fluid for force and this account could have been drawn from Biot's *Traité de Physique*.

This apparent contradiction by Faraday of his own theory was picked up almost immediately by his contemporaries. Robert Hare, of the University of Pennsylvania, put the question to Faraday quite bluntly:

> . . . I cannot avoid considering it inevitable that each particle must have at least two poles. It seems to me that the idea of polarity requires that there shall be in any body possessing it, two opposite poles. Hence you correctly allege that agreeably to your views it is impossible to charge a portion of matter with one electric force without the other (see par. 1177). But if all this be true, how can there be a 'positively excited particle'? (See par. 1616). Must not every particle be excited negatively, if it be excited positively? Must it not have a negative, as well as a positive pole?[30]

Faraday's reply did not (to put it mildly) altogether remove the difficulty. He first showed how a sphere could be charged positively according to his theory of induction.[31] This charge, however, must simply be the result of the chain of the strained particles constituting the inductive lines of force (see Figure 4) and did not, therefore, imply the polarity of the sphere. *But*, the particles in the inductive chain must be polar by Faraday's theory. A strange picture emerges from this 'explanation' when combined with the original description. There Faraday had specifically mentioned that the particle *was* polarized by the inductive force, at the same time that it was positively charged. We are, in short, back where we started from.

There are now two things that can be done. The simplest is to declare that Faraday really was hopelessly confused and finally caught up in the ambiguities involved in his use of the term 'force'. As the various passages cited show, there is a good deal to recommend this course. One fact, however, must give us pause. Faraday's writings are filled with errors which he willingly corrected when his papers were reprinted. The fact that the confusion had been pointed out to him publicly and that he publicly chose to defend his view would indicate that he saw something here that escaped his readers. If this is so, does he give any further clues to the solution of this mystery of molecular action?

The starting-point for the solving of this problem must be Faraday's views on molecular force and, especially, this force as related to chemical affinity. It was here after all that the theory of electrical action by contiguous particles had been born. The electrical force in electrochemical reaction, it will be remembered, had served to exalt the affinity in a certain direction and lower it in the opposite direction. The particle so affected then migrated in a direction determined by its 'charge'. Properly speaking, this particle was not polarized in Hare's sense of the word, but distorted and this distortion seems to be what Faraday meant by polarization

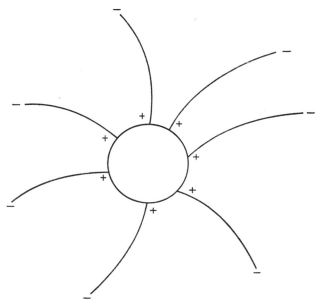

Fig. 4

throughout his researches. There was not, in short, a *separation* of the forces so that equal quantities of positive and negative force were concentrated at each end of the particle. Rather the distortion created a complex pattern of forces, the resultant of which determined the direction in which the particle moved. Faraday was quite explicit on this point.

> The modes of polarization, as I shall have occasion hereafter to show, [he wrote in the Thirteenth Series] may be very diverse in different dielectrics. With respect to common air, what seems to be the consequence of a superiority in the positive force at the surface of the small ball, may be due to the more exalted condition of the negative polarity of the particles of air, or of the nitrogen in it (the negative part being, perhaps, more compressed, whilst the positive part is more diffuse, or *vice versa* . . .) (1503).

Thus each species of matter had its own mode which gave it its specific properties when subjected to the electrical forces. This view of molecular action was even more explicitly stated in the Fourteenth Series. There Faraday summed up the results of his electrical researches, and stated the theoretical conclusions to which these researches had led him.

> The theory assumes that all the *particles*, whether of insulating or conducting matter, are as wholes conductors.
>
> That not being polar in their normal state, they can become so by the influence of neighbouring charged particles, the polar state being developed at the instant, exactly as in an insulated conducting *mass* consisting of many particles.
>
> That the particles when polarized are in a forced state, and tend to return to their normal or natural condition.
>
> That being as wholes conductors, they can readily be charged, either *bodily* or *polarly*.
>
> That particles which being contiguous are also in the line of inductive action can communicate or transfer their polar forces one to another *more or less* readily (1669–73).

Faraday now has introduced a new concept into his theory of molecular action. Hitherto the transmission of force had been intermolecular in the sense that a chain of molecules could be subjected to strain. Force could then be applied along the chain. When the chain broke, the molecules which had been pulling on *one another* returned to their normal unstrained state. The strain, therefore, was *inter*molecular and the transmission of force depended upon the mutual relations of a number of particles. Now what Faraday appears to be saying is that a single particle can be strained by the application of electrical force. When the force is applied, a semipermanent 'set' is given to the forces surrounding the molecule and until the molecule can find other particles which can relieve it of this 'set', it is destined to wander throughout space. It is in a metastable state, able to regain stable equilibrium only under certain conditions. It is, in short, a charged particle in which the energy of the charge was contained in the distortion of its normal pattern of force. Precisely *how* it was able to pass on this energy was not discussed by Faraday but that it could do so, he thought was certain. Electrical force, therefore, could be transmitted in two ways: either by the intermolecular strain of a chain of particles, or by the intramolecular distortion of a single particle. In both cases, the action was not at a distance, but from particle to particle.

Given this new aspect of electrical action, the mechanism of brush discharge may easily be seen. The first effect of the presence of a charged metallic rod was to set up lines of induction between the rod and the walls of the room. These lines consisted of particles of air, linked together by polar strain and transmitting this strain from the rod to the walls. Thus if the rod were negatively charged, the particles of the surface of the wall which anchored the ends of the lines of inductive force, had to be positive. The air particles nearest the rod were under the greatest strain, for here the lines of inductive force converged and the individual particle bore a larger share of the total force. There was, then, a gradient of strain which fell off sharply from the rod as one passed towards the walls. When the electrical tension was heightened, a particle of air (which was in a polar state of strain) next to the rod somehow was able to lose its strain at the end nearest the metal and the metal, being a conductor, was able to absorb this force. The situation was completely analogous to that involving the catalytic action of platinum. There, too, the repulsive forces of the molecules of the oxygen and hydrogen were somehow relieved on the sides nearest the metal. The result then had been chemical combination; the result now was the creation of a distorted particle. This particle, precisely because of its distortion, became a centre of inductive action and imparted its strain to others and thereby created another chain of inductive action. The total quantity of positive and negative force, therefore, remained constant although the force had been transferred from one particle to the rod on the one side, and to other particles (as strain) on the other. When the initial strain on the particle was relieved by the metal rod, the inductive chain from the rod to the wall was broken. The particles nearer the rod, which had been in a highly exalted state, lost their exaltation and gave off light. Those particles near the wall, suffering only minor tension, regained their original condition without any show of light. The particle which had touched all this off, still carrying its charge, drifted about until it could also resume a normal mode. It was particles of this kind that Faraday utilized to explain convection, or carrying discharge (1562 ff.).

Faraday's use of the theory of point atoms was here so basic that the presentation of his own ideas suffered seriously from his failure to make his debt to this theory explicit. Hare's objections illustrate this well. To Hare, for example, polarization implied the existence of poles where forces were localized and he specifically called Faraday to task on this point.

As the theory which you have proposed gives great importance to the idea of polarity, I regret that you have not defined the meaning which you attach to this word. As you designate that to which you refer, as a 'species of polarity', it is presumable that you have conceived of several kinds with which ponderable atoms may be endowed. I find it difficult to conceive of any kind which may be capable of as many degrees of intensity as the known phenomena of

electricity require; especially according to your opinion that the only difference between the fluid evolved by galvanic apparatus and that evolved by
friction, is due to opposite extremes in quantity and intensity; the intensity of
electrical excitement producible by the one being almost infinitely greater
than that which can be produced by the other. What state of the poles can
constitute quantity – what other state intensity, the same matter being capable
of either electricity, as is well known to be the fact? Would it not be well to
consider how, consistently with any conceivable polarization, and without the
assistance of some imponderable matter, any great difference of intensity in
inductive power can be created?[32]

As we have seen, polarity to Faraday meant something quite different
from what it meant to Hare. He did not, however, at this time make this
difference clear and while he continued to think of patterns of forces,
others either interpreted him in terms of the fluid theory or, like Hare,
confessed their inability to understand what he was talking about.

There is one other example of the confusion generated by Faraday's use
of point atoms and his refusal to tell his reader about them which must be
given. One of the aspects of electrical action that Faraday felt obligated to
discuss was the possibility of electrical discharge *in vacuo* for, as he noted,
'it would seem strange, if a theory which refers all the phenomena of
insulation and conduction, i.e. all electrical phenomena, to the action of
contiguous particles, were to omit to notice the assumed possible case of a
vacuum' (1613). After suggesting that no perfect vacuum had yet been
obtained experimentally, Faraday proceeded to discuss the theory of
electrical discharge in a vacuum.

> . . . assuming that a perfect vacuum were to intervene in the course of the
> lines of inductive action (1304), it does not follow from this theory, that the
> particles on opposite sides of such a vacuum could not act on each other.
> Suppose it possible for a positively electrified particle to be in the centre of a
> vacuum an inch in diameter, nothing in my present views forbids that the
> particle should act at the distance of half an inch on all the particles forming
> the inner superficies of the bounding sphere, and with a force consistent with
> the well-known law of the squares of the distance (1616).

This was really more than Hare could bear and his impatience was
evident in his query:

> . . . you believe ordinary induction to be the action of *contiguous* particles [he
> wrote] consisting of a species of polarity, instead of being an action of either
> particles or masses at '*sensible distances*' . . . I beg leave to inquire how a
> positively excited particle, situated as above described, can react 'inductrically'
> with any particles in the superficies of the surrounding sphere, if this species
> of reaction require that the particles between which it takes place be contig-
> uous. Moreover if induction be not 'an action either of particles or masses at

sensible distances', how can a particle, situated as above described, '*act at the distance of half an inch on all the particles forming the disk of the inner superficies of the bounding sphere?*' What is a sensible distance, if half an inch is not ?[33]

Faraday's answer was not calculated to satisfy Hare. Faraday evidently felt that the confusion arose from the use of the term 'contiguous' so he proceeded to repeat the note he had appended to (1665). 'I mean by contiguous particles those which are next to each other, not that there is no space between them.'[34] Hare's reaction to this explanation is not recorded but it must have been one of total frustration. Yet each man was right according to his own theoretical views. To Hare, a vacuum was empty space and anything acting across it must be acting at a distance. To Faraday, a vacuum was space empty of all matter, i.e. containing no point atoms or molecules composed of these atoms. The space, however, was filled with the forces of the particles surrounding the vacuum and these forces were in contact. When one particle acted upon another, therefore, the action was not at a distance but from particle to particle even though a sensible distance between the points of origination of the forces existed.[35] It was this web of force which he saw in his mind's eye that enabled him to analyse the nature of electrical action. The success of this concept when applied to electrochemical decomposition, and now to electrostatic induction and discharge only strengthened his belief in its essential truth. It only remained to be seen whether it would serve to elucidate the problem of the conduction of electricity in ordinary conductors.[36]

In his discussion of the common electric current Faraday levelled his most devastating criticism yet at the fluid theory of electricity. Its power was intensified by the subtlety with which the attack was driven home. After first objecting mildly to the term, current, because it implied the passage of some fluid (1617), Faraday considered some of the characteristics of the electric current. To these we shall return. It was at the end of this section that he demonstrated the difficulties inherent in the fluid theory.

'*As long as* the terms *current* and *electro-dynamic* are used to express those relations of the electric forces in which progression of either fluids or effects are supposed to occur . . . *so long* will the idea of velocity be associated with them; and this will, perhaps, be more especially the case if the hypothesis of a fluid or fluids be adopted' (1648). This being so, Faraday turned to the attempts at measuring this velocity. In his electrochemical research, he had shown that a definite quantity of electricity was associated with the particles of matter. The transfer of the electrical force inherent in these particles could be followed by following the particles and the rate of transfer could easily be timed. Charles Wheatstone had, in 1834, made some rough measurements of the velocity of the electric current in wires, and Faraday now put these two things together. If an electrolytic process occurred in a circuit, what would be the relation between the velocity of the 'electricity' in the solution to that of the 'electricity' in the wires? The 'electricity' in the wire travelled at a rate of 576,000 miles per second,[37] that in the electrolytic solution at less than one tenth of an inch per hour! Yet all the 'electricity' that went through the wires went, also, through the solution (1652). Faraday merely reported the result, leaving it to the proponent of the fluid theory to explain how such a thing could happen.

For Faraday, there was no difficulty. The application of the electrical force caused the oxygen and the hydrogen of the water and even the particles of metal in the wire to assume a state of strain. When the strain was sufficient for the oxygen and hydrogen to slide by one another, the strain was relaxed, only to be almost immediately restored as new combinations of oxygen with hydrogen particles were formed (1621 ff.). Thus, the particles migrated at a slow rate, while waves of force passed through the wire at high speeds. No fluids were needed nor even, it seemed, possible.

From this it followed that 'it is a most important part of the character of the current, and essentially connected with its very nature, that it is always the same. The two forces are everywhere in it. There is never one current of force or one fluid only' (1627). Polar strain obviously required two equal forces, acting in opposite directions in order for the strain to exist. Once again, therefore, Faraday felt it necessary to insist that 'the current is an indivisible thing; an axis of power, in every part of which electric forces are present in equal amount' (1642).

With the examination of the electric current, Faraday was ready to bring all his researches together under a single law. Electrolysis, conduction, induction, sparks, brushes, flows – all were to be shown to be but mere variations of a single process. We have already cited a number of his conclusions in the discussion of polarity, but since they are all necessary if we are to understand his ideas, they must be cited again.

The theory [Faraday wrote in June 1838] assumes that all the *particles*, whether of insulating or conducting matter, are as wholes conductors.
  That not being polar in their normal state, they can become so by the influence of neighbouring charged particles, the polar state being developed at the instant, exactly as in an insulated conducting *mass* consisting of many particles.

That the particles when polarized are in a forced state, and tend to return to their normal or natural condition.

That being as wholes conductors, they can readily be charged, either *bodily* or *polarly*.

That particles which being contiguous are also in the line of inductive action can communicate or transfer their polar forces one to another *more or less* readily.

That those doing so less readily require the polar forces to be raised to a higher degree before this transference or communication takes place.

That the *ready* communication of forces between contiguous particles constitutes *conduction*, and the *difficult* communication *insulation*; conductors and insulators being bodies whose particles naturally possess the property of communicating their respective forces easily or with difficulty; having these differences just as they have differences of any other natural property.

That ordinary induction is the effect resulting from the action of matter charged with excited or free electricity upon insulating matter, tending to produce in it an equal amount of the contrary state.

That it can do this only by polarizing the particles contiguous to it, which perform the same office to the next, and these again to those beyond; and that thus the action is propagated from the excited body to the next conducting mass, and there renders the contrary force evident in consequence of the effect of communication which supervenes in the conducting mass upon the polarization of the particles of that body.

That therefore induction can only take place through or across insulators; that induction is insulation, it being the necessary consequence of the state of the particles and the mode in which the influence of electrical forces is transferred or transmitted through or across such insulating media (1669–78).

In these ten propositions, Faraday had summed up seven years of the most intense experimental activity. He could now boldly answer the fundamental questions he had posed to himself years before. What was the nature of electricity? Strain. How did electricity act? By the transmission of this strain. How was the strain transmitted? From particle to particle. How could differences in particles serve to explain the different electrical phenomena? Simply. When particles were able to communicate the strain easily to contiguous particles, the result was conduction. When the particles were free to move by one another but were closely associated in chemical combination, the result was electrolytic conduction in which both matter and force was transmitted. When the particles were fixed by other forces such as that of solid cohesion, or when it was difficult for them to transmit their forces to other particles, the result was a polar stress that was called induction. The relief of this stress was disruptive discharge. Thus, all electrical phenomena could be viewed as the setting up of a strain, followed by the relief of the strain. Induction, therefore, was always the first result of the application of electrical force. The other electrical effects depended upon the way in which the inductive state was removed.[38] In the realm of electricity, at least, Faraday had finally discovered that unity of action which he was convinced must underlie all phenomena.

It is characteristic of Faraday's researches that they always led on to something else. Even when he had wrapped up the whole of electrical science in one neat bundle, there was still one thread sticking out which might lead to exciting new discoveries.

The similarity between the electric and magnetic lines of force could not help but impress Faraday. Surely they must have a great deal in common, and this led him to attempt to find at least one similar effect. His deep faith in the unity of forces led him to some speculative notions which were to bear fruit seven years later. It is worth recounting the thoughts he set on paper in 1838, for we shall return to them later.

> The phenomena of induction amongst currents which I had the good fortune to discover some years ago (6, etc., 1048),[39] may perchance here form a connecting link in the series of effects. When a current is first formed, it tends to produce a current in the contrary direction in all the matter around it; and if that matter have conducting properties and be fitly circumstanced, such a current is produced. On the contrary, when the original current is stopped, one in the same direction tends to form all around it, and, in conducting matter properly arranged, will be excited.
>
> Now though we perceive the effects only in that portion of matter which, being in the neighbourhood, has conducting properties, yet hypothetically it is probable, that the non-conducting matter has also its relations to, and is affected by, the disturbing cause, though we have not yet discovered them. Again and again the relation of conductors and non-conductors has been shown to be one not of opposition in kind, but only of degree . . . ; and, therefore, for this, as well as for other reasons, it is probable, that what will affect a conductor will affect an insulator also; producing perhaps what may deserve the term of the electrotonic state. . . .
>
> It is the feeling of the necessity of some lateral connexion between the lines of electric force . . .; of some link in the chain of effects as yet unrecognized, that urges me to the expression of these speculations. The same feeling has led me to make many experiments on the introduction of insulating dielectrics having different inductive capacities . . . between magnetic poles and wires carrying currents, so as to pass across the lines of magnetic force. I have employed such bodies both at rest and in motion, without, as yet, being able to detect any influence produced by them; but I do by no means consider the experiments as sufficiently delicate, and intend, very shortly, to render them more decisive (1660 ff.).[40]

Faraday was obviously hoping to find that the material interposed between the poles of a magnet would affect the transmission of the magnetic force in the same specific way that non-conductors affected the electric lines of force. These substances were dielectrics; should there not also be diamagnetics? He was not to find the answer to this question until 1845.

In 1839 the effects of eight years of constant and unremitting effort were beginning to tell on him. He could no longer sustain the pace; his mind wandered, and he was unable to concentrate. Rest was imperative and so, reluctantly, he laid aside his apparatus and allowed his mind to gather its forces for what was to prove his last sustained assault upon nature's mysteries. Between 1838 and 1845 only four new Series in the *Experimental Researches* appeared in the *Philosophical Transactions*. The fifth was to announce the discovery of diamagnetism.

The reader, like Faraday, no doubt needs a respite here. We have followed Faraday's thoughts now unremittingly through four chapters. It is time to look once more at Faraday the man.

References

1. 'Miscellaneous Intelligence', *Q.J.S.*, *16* (1823), 179. The article is signed only with Faraday's initials.

2. For the articles dealing with the catalytic action of platinum, see 'On the Action of Platina on Mixtures of Oxygen, Hydrogen, and other Gases', *Q.J.S.*, *16* (1823), 375 ff. The article, although unsigned, is most probably by Faraday since it refers in personal terms to the article by Faraday cited in the previous footnote.

3. Ibid., 375.

4. The term *catalysis* was not coined until 1836 when Berzelius introduced it into the vocabulary of chemistry.

5. I am using modern terminology here in order to make the problem clear. These were not the terms used by Faraday, although he was aware of the regeneration of the sulphuric acid at the positive pole.

6. See above, on the experiments in Kensington Pond, where he was able to trace the currents to contaminations.

7. The original is to be found in the *Giornale di Fisica*, *8* (1825), 259.

8. Thomas Thomson, *A System of Chemistry*, 2nd ed., *3*, 184 ff.

9. Faraday noted what happened when this regularity (and consequent disturbance of force) was destroyed. *Exp. Res.*, *1*, 191, note.

'As a curious illustration of the influence of mechanical forces over chemical affinity, I will quote the refusal of certain substances to effloresce when their surfaces are perfect, which yield immediately upon the surface being broken. If crystals of carbonate of soda, or phosphate of soda, or sulphate of soda, having no part of their surfaces broken, be preserved from external violence, they will not effloresce. I have thus retained crystals of carbonate of soda perfectly transparent and unchanged from September 1827 to January 1833; and crystals of sulphate of soda from May 1832 to the present time, November 1833. If any part of the surface were scratched or broken, then efflorescence began at that part, and covered the whole.'

10. The Eighth, Ninth and Tenth Series will be treated in following sections.

11. The voltages used by Faraday must have been just a bit too weak for the effect he had anticipated does occur. It was discovered by John Kerr in 1875.

12. Trinity College MSS., Faraday–Whewell Correspondence, Faraday to Whewell, R.I., 19 September 1835.

13. C. Coulomb, 'Quatrième Mémoire où l'on demontre deux principales propriétés due fluide électrique', in *Mem. Soc. de Phys.*, *1* (1884), 173.

14. Faraday was so cautious in his attack on induction that he repeated and varied his experiments almost endlessly. It would be both tiresome and unnecessary to relate all that he did experimentally. Instead I have chosen those experiments which shed light on the development of his ideas. In the references mention will be made of the other experiments which merely served to confirm what the more important experiments had shown. Thus, in this section dealing with the separability of electricity and its relation to conductors see [2664–2704] and [2709–27]. The same results were provided, but with greater clarity, by the large cube.

15. This paragraph was repeated almost word for word in the Eleventh Series (1178).

16. The word *dielectric* was here introduced into electrical science. Like so many of his other new technical terms, Faraday had received this one from Whewell. In a letter to Faraday, Whewell wrote:

'Thinking over your intended experiments a word occurs to me which, if I understand your arrangements may do very well to express the non-conducting body interposed between two inductive conductors. Call it a *Dielectric*: *Dia* means *through* and we are familiar with it in scientific words as dioptrice, diaphragm, and recently diathermal', Trinity College MSS., Faraday–Whewell Correspondence, Whewell to Faraday, 29 December 1836.

17. (1195). The actual difficulties encountered by Faraday in attempting to carry out what appeared to be the simplest kind of experiment are detailed both in the published paper (1196 ff.) and in the *Diary* [3755–57, 3783, 3794–3800]. Faraday was plagued by all kinds of trouble: leakage, conduction, breaks in the apparatus, casual charges, etc. Once again, his extraordinary ability to detect the sources of error permitted him to eliminate them and to achieve results that were clear-cut and decisive.

18. *Exp. Res.*, *1*, 409, note.

19. Trinity College MSS., Faraday–Whewell Correspondence. Faraday to Whewell, R.I., 13 December 1836.

20. *L. & E. Phil. Mag.*, N.S., *10* (1837), 317.

21. (London, 1837). Taylor edited five volumes in all (1837–52). This series helped to call the attention of British scientists to work being done on the Continent, especially that of German scientists. G. S. Ohm's great paper, *Die galvanische kette, mathematisch bearbeitet*, for example, made its first appearance in English in this series.

22. O. F. Mossotti, 'On the Forces which regulate the Internal Constitution of Bodies', *Sci. Mem.*, *1*, 448.

23. *L. & E. Phil. Mag.*, N.S., *10* (1837), 357.

24. This term was to cause Faraday some difficulty for it is hard to see (unless one realizes that the particles are 'force' particles) how particles can be contiguous and yet be some distance apart. This problem will be considered in the next section.

25. This was a serious problem in Poisson's theory, at least as it was presented in England. In the account of this theory offered in the *Supplement* to the *Encyclopaedia Britannica* (*4*, Edinburgh, 1824), the role of the air as container for the electrical fluids was insisted upon time and time again. (See 80, 81, 82, 86). The physical problem was also raised:

'. . . The last element to be considered, and which is a consequence of the preceding ones, is the *pressure* which the electricity exerts against the external air in each point of the surface of the electrified body. The intensity of this pressure is proportional to the square of the thickness of the electric stratum.

'By adhering strictly to these denominations, there will be no risk of falling into error from vague considerations; and if we also keep in mind the developement of electricity by influence at a distance, we shall then find no difficulty in explaining all the electric phenomena.

'To place this truth in its full light, we shall apply it to some general phenomena which, viewed in this manner, can be conceived with perfect clearness, but which, otherwise, do not admit but of vague and embarrassed explications. These phenomena consist in the motions which electrified bodies assume, or tend to assume, when they are placed in presence of each other, and in which they appear as if they really acted upon each other by attraction or by repulsion. But it is extremely difficult to conceive the cause of these movements, when we consider that, according to the experiments, the attraction and repulsion are only exerted between the electric principles themselves, without the material substance of the body, provided it be a conductor, having any influence on their distribution or their displacement. We cannot hence admit, that the particles of the electric principles, whatever they may be, really attract or repel the material particles of the bodies. It is absolutely necessary, therefore, that the attractive and repulsive actions of these principles, whatever they are, be transmitted indirectly to the material bodies, by some mechanism which it is of extreme importance to discover, as it is the true key to these phenomena. But we will see that this mechanism consists in the reaction produced by the resistance which the air and non-conducting bodies in general oppose to the passage of electricity' 86.

It is worth noting that Poisson's theory appeared to prove beyond doubt the existence of the two electrical fluids. The elegance of the mathematical analysis, plus the ability of the theory to predict new *quantitative* relations were formidable arguments in favour of the theory. The *Britannica* account also underlined this aspect.

'When we now consider how various, how delicate, and how detached from each other, are the phenomena this theory embraces; with what exactness, also, it represents them, and follows, in a manner, all the windings of experiment, we must be convinced that it is one of the best established in physics, and that it bestows on the real existence of the two electric fluids the highest degree of probability, if not an absolute certainty' 85.

26. Presumably this refers to the experiment in which electrical discharge was made through a pointed piece of filter paper soaked with a solution of potassium iodide. This experiment, the reader will recall, first led Faraday to suspect action at a distance. It has been the author's thesis that it was Faraday's theory of matter which permitted him to exploit this experiment.

27. W. Snow Harris, 'On the Protection of Ships from Lightning', *The Nautical Magazine, 3* (1834), 151, 225, 353, 477, 739. The quotation is on 229.

28. Ibid., 357.

29. One wonders why not? What happened to specific inductive capacity?

30. 'A Letter to Prof. Faraday, on certain Theoretical Opinions, by R. Hare, M.D., Professor of Chemistry in the University of Pennsylvania', *Exp. Res.*, *2*, 254. Further references will be made to this reprint. The letter first appeared in Silliman's, *American Journal of Science and Arts, 38* (1840), 1 ff. and was then reprinted in the *L. & E. Phil. Mag.*, N.S., *17* (1840), 44.

31. 'An Answer to Dr Hare's Letter on certain Theoretical Opinions', *Exp. Res.*, *2*, 262 ff.

32. Hare, loc. cit., 253. Faraday did not reply specifically to this objection.

33. Ibid., 251. This composite quotation which merely eliminates repetitious material, is taken from paragraphs 3 and 4.

34. 'An Answer to Dr Hare's Letter . . .', *Exp. Res.*, *2*, 266.

35. It can be immediately objected that this is mere quibbling over words. If the 'forces' affect one another, is this not, then, action at a distance? Boscovich would have answered, yes, for to him, the forces associated with his particles became manifest only when they acted upon another body and this action was at a distance. To Faraday, however, the forces were real and had an existence of their own. They did not, therefore, act at a distance but only where they were. This point will become clearer when Faraday's concept of the conservation of force is discussed.

36. I have not treated electrical discharge in evacuated tubes here because it involves no new concepts. Faraday saw this effect, brushes, and sparks as all coming from the same actions described in the text. His discovery of what later was known as Faraday's dark space in these investigations was of little importance to him at this time. Those interested in these researches may consult the relevant sections of the Fourteenth Series (1526 ff.).

37. According to Wheatstone's figures.

38. It is extremely difficult to understand what Faraday meant by the communication of force from one particle to another when conduction occurred. I have visualized it as a rapid build-up and break-down of the inductive or electrotonic state. Metallic particles, in this interpretation, cannot bear much tension so that a small force, constantly applied, will set up a state of rapid vibration in the wire as the strain is built up (to a low tension) and then breaks down, only to build up again. The waves thus generated would constitute the current, and be transmitted rapidly down the wire. This seems to me to be a possible, but not necessarily the only, interpretation. No such difficulties appear

with the disruptive discharge since here the chain of strained particles does give way with a snap.

39. (1048) refers to the first paragraph of the Ninth Series in which Faraday reported the discovery of self-induction. While self-induction is a fact of great significance in electrical practice, I have not discussed it here. Faraday was led to it at the suggestion of a Mr Jenkin and it did not follow, as did his other discoveries, from his theoretical views. In the tracing of Faraday's ideas, therefore, it is only of peripheral interest. This would not be the case for Joseph Henry who discovered self-induction independently of Faraday and seems to have deduced the effect from *his* theoretical concepts.

40. For these experiments, see [4886 ff.].

CHAPTER EIGHT

Faraday in the World

1. The Royal Institution

Dr Henry Bence Jones in his history of the early years of the Royal Institution has described the troubles with which the early Managers had to struggle. The basic problem involved an internal flaw present from the very beginning and only eliminated permanently by Faraday and the tradition he did so much to create.

Benjamin Thompson, Count Rumford, from whose fertile brain the original idea of the Royal Institution had sprung, had envisioned building an institution 'for diffusing the knowledge and facilitating the general introduction of useful mechanical inventions and improvements, and for teaching by courses of philosophical lectures and experiments the application of science to the common purposes of life. . . .'[1] The financial support for this undertaking was supposed to come from those wealthy persons by whom 'the application of science to the common purposes of life' was usually left to mechanics and artisans. The early history of the Royal Institution was to reveal that here was the really fundamental problem. When the lectures given dealt with the useful application of science to the arts, the number of subscribers dwindled and the Royal Institution plunged into debt. In order to get out of debt, lectures had to be offered which appealed to the members of the higher ranks of society. Then the number of subscribers increased and coffers were filled.[2]

A temporary solution to this problem was provided by the genius of Humphry Davy. He, and he alone, seemed able to attract the *haut monde* with lectures on such subjects as the art of tanning or the elements of agricultural chemistry. And, too, the series of discoveries announced from the laboratory in Albemarle Street served in the years from 1806–12 to make the Royal Institution the centre of English science. The membership of the Royal Institution grew, even though Davy's lecturing efforts became more and more sporadic as he, himself, was seduced by the society which so admired his talents. When he resigned his professorship in 1812, the Royal Institution suffered a nearly mortal blow. In 1814, Faraday wrote to his friend Benjamin Abbott from Geneva, that he had heard that the Royal Institution was in imminent danger of collapse.[3] He could do nothing about this but he did not wish his books to be sold at the auction which seemed likely if the Royal Institution did fail to meet its obligations. Through heroic efforts on the part of the Managers and members, financial ruin was avoided, and Abbott was able to inform his friend, 'Respecting the R.I. you need be under *no* apprehensions.'[4] Yet, as Abbott went on to explain, the solution contrived by the Managers could be, at best, a temporary one. 'The members', Abbott wrote, 'have this summer submitted to a great sacrifice and all the debts are paid off so that altho' eventually the expences will eat up the Principal of their funds, yet a dissolution in consequence cannot take place within a period of time much larger than it is even probable you will be absent.'[5]

When Faraday returned from his tour of the Continent with Sir Humphry Davy, he was immediately appointed to a new position at the Royal Institution. He was named Assistant in the laboratory and mineralogical collection, and superintendent of the laboratory and lecture apparatus. He could not have been unaware of the general state of the Royal Institution's finances but again there was little he could do about it. He performed his duties as well as he could; he helped William Thomas Brande edit the *Quarterly Journal of Science* which, though not officially the journal of the Royal Institution, nevertheless brought credit to it. He assisted Davy in the laboratory when Davy worked at the R.I. and, perhaps most importantly, he assisted Brande in his lectures. These lectures had been begun in 1815 when Brande was appointed to replace Davy as Professor of Chemistry and continued until 1848. The fees paid by his students were an important source of income to the R.I. for Brande was always, in the early years, assured of a goodly audience. In 1852, he could say with pride, that 'they were the first lectures in London in which so extended a view of chemistry, and of its applications, including technical, mineralogical, geological, and medical chemistry was attempted'[6] and because they had particular relevance to the study of medicine, Brande could always count on a full class.

In addition to these lectures, Brande gave shorter courses of a more popular kind intended to edify the members of the Royal Institution and their families and guests. In both series of lectures, Brande was always competent but almost totally lacked that brilliance which had so marked Davy's similar efforts. In spite of the evident utility of Brande's courses, in spite of the clarity which Faraday's manipulative skill brought to the lecture demonstrations, Brande simply could not fill Davy's shoes and the financial situation of the Institution steadily worsened. Dr Bence Jones lists the grim statistics.

The bill for coals for 1816 could not be paid until 1818. In the same year, part of the endowment had to be utilized to meet the Institution's debts. In 1822 the treasurer had to advance £1,000 to pay the bills. In 1823, the members again rose generously to meet impending catastrophe by lending £4,000 without interest to the Royal Institution.[7] The situation was the same as it had been ten years previously when Faraday's anxiety about the success of the R.I. prompted him to inquire of its future from Abbott.

It must have been perfectly obvious to everyone associated with the Royal Institution that things could not long go on this way. Two things were absolutely vital if the Institution were to survive: The immediate financial problem had to be solved and the Institution had to find the public support necessary for its continuance. Faraday was to be the moving power behind both solutions offered to these problems.

The immediate difficulties were overcome largely through Faraday's placing his skill as a practising chemist at the disposal of the Royal Institution. The use of the laboratory in the researches on the alloys of steel, and more particularly, for the thousands of analyses performed by Faraday in the 1820's brought in the necessary funds to keep the R.I. going.[8] In 1827 Faraday declined the offer of the Professorship of Chemistry at the newly-created University of London because his efforts on behalf of the R.I. seemed almost enough to guarantee its survival.[9]

Faraday had no intention, however, of leaving trade to trade in science. The extraordinary exertions required by innumerable analyses and the work on glass tired both his body and his mind. Throughout the 1820's he wanted to get back to more philosophical researches but his concern for the success of the R.I. could permit him to do this only when some substitute could be found for his laboratory skill as a means of making money. The search for such a substitute could not have been an arduous or long one for Faraday. The Royal Institution had prospered under Davy because Davy had been a brilliant lecturer. Faraday had been preparing himself to replace Davy for a decade and it was to be his ability to reach a lay audience which was, over the course of some thirty-seven years, to give the Royal Institution that popularity and financial security it had so long needed.

From his earliest association with the Royal Institution, Faraday had been deeply interested in the art of lecturing. Davy's lectures had excited him tremendously, and, as an amateur lecturer at the City Philosophical

Society, he was eager to find the secrets of the art. Here, again, he laboured under severe handicaps. Davy, it would appear, was one of those natural teachers who combined felicity of phrase, liveliness of motion and of language, and an instinct for the dramatic in both demonstrations and in structure of the lecture in such proportions as to captivate any audience. Faraday, as a young man, felt no such power. His first lecture was carefully written out beforehand as though he were fearful of trusting himself upon the unknown waters of extemporary expression. What strides he had to make before he could advise a lecturer in 1862 that 'as we are sure that you would do it better the less you read, so I venture to express a hope that you will not read more than you may find quite necessary for your own convenience'.[10]

His education as a lecturer followed the same pattern as his education as a natural philosopher. His critical faculty, always his most acute sense, was first exercised upon the lecturers he heard. He then turned to the acquisition of whatever skills could be learned of others, and then polished his techniques by the actual practice of lecturing. One finds him, therefore, in 1813 setting down his ideas of the general attributes of a good lecture and a good lecturer. Then, in 1818, when the possibility of giving lectures at the Royal Institution in the future must have first arisen, he attended and noted carefully a series of lectures on oratory.[11] Finally, in 1824 he lectured in the laboratory of the Royal Institution and, in 1825, was instrumental in creating the Friday Evening Discourses which did so much to popularize science in Victorian England and which also served to save the Royal Institution from bankruptcy.

In the summer of 1813, Faraday addressed four letters to Benjamin Abbott concerning the art of lecturing which contain so much good sense, and reveal Faraday's philosophy of the art so well, that they deserve close attention. He began his exposition by a passage so characteristic of his outlook throughout his entire life that I cannot help but cite it.

It may perhaps appear singular and improper [he wrote] that one who is entirely unfit for such an office [of lecturer] himself and who does not even pretend to any of the requisites for it should take upon him to censure and to commend others, to express satisfaction at this, to be displeased with that, according as he is led by his judgment when he allows that his judgment is unfit for it; but I do not see, on consideration, that the impropriety is so great. If I am unfit for it 'tis evident that I have yet to learn and how learn better than by the observation of others? If we never judge at all we shall never judge right and it is far better to learn to use our mental powers (tho' it may take a whole life for the purpose) than to leave them buried in idleness, a meer void.[12]

The education of his judgement was ever his primary concern[13] and this inevitably involved the probability of error. Others might strive always to be right; Faraday was content to learn from being wrong. His views on lectures and lecturers were intended (as were all his writings) to serve more as a basis for discussion than as a prescription of what was right.

The physical attributes of a lecture hall first engaged Faraday's attention. The theatre of the Royal Institution he found the best he had ever seen. The lecturer was clearly visible from all seats, the slope of the banks of seats was steep enough so that every person had an unobstructed view of the demonstrations and charts utilized by the lecturer to illustrate his words. Best of all, the ingenious dome suggested by Count Rumford permitted illumination of the room by sunlight, which Faraday considered vastly superior to artificial light, and also allowed for the darkening of the room when the lecturer wished to show effects in the dark. Finally, Faraday called attention to a fact which particularly bothered him. He never could bear stale or dirty air. Throughout his life he sniffed around the Royal Institution, or the Athenaeum, or the rooms of the Royal Society trying to locate the source of smells which quite literally oppressed him.[14] A failure of fresh air in a lecture could nullify the efforts of even the finest lecturer.

> How often [he wrote feelingly] have I felt oppression in the highest degree when surrounded by a number of other persons and confined in one portion of air! How have I wished the lecture finished, the lights extinguished, and myself away merely to obtain a fresh supply of that element! The want of it caused the want of attention, of pleasure, and even of comfort, and not to be regained without its previous admission. Attention to this is particularly necessary in a lecture room intended for night delivery as the lights burning add considerably to the oppression produced on the body.[15]

The subject-matter for lectures, Faraday considered to be almost infinite, excluding only politics. Yet, science was, he felt, 'undeniably the most eminent in its fitness for this purpose'.[16] Every branch of it could be presented and illustrated to an audience and the use of experiments and demonstrations gave added value, for the listener not only heard but saw as well. Subjects for lectures, however, had to be chosen with a view of the audience in mind. In his description of the kinds of audiences, Faraday permitted himself one of his few comments on the classes of English society.

> A lecturer may consider his audience as being polite or vulgar. . . . learned or unlearned (with respect to the subject) listeners or gazers. Polite company

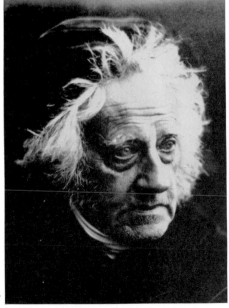

29a Edward Sabine
29c Sir John F. W. Herschel

29b Wilhelm Weber
29d John Tyndall

a

b

c

d

30a Lord Kelvin
30c Heinrich D. Ruhmkorff

30b Sir George B. Airy
30d Henry Bence Jones

a

b

c

d

31 a, b, c, d Faraday in later life

32 a, b, c, d Faraday in later life

33a

33b Faraday in later life

34 Michael and Sarah Faraday

35b Faraday in later life

35a Faraday at the Royal Institution

35c Faraday in later life

36 The library of the Royal Institution

expect to be entertained not only by the subject of the lecture, but by the manner of the lecturer; they look for respect, for language consonant to their dignity and ideas on a level with their own. The vulgar – that is to say in general those who will take the trouble of thinking and the bees of business – wish for something that they can comprehend. This may be deep and elaborate for the learned but for those who are as yet tyros and unacquainted with the subject must be simple and plain. Lastly listeners expect reason and sense, whilst gazers only require a succession of words.[17]

From the conditions under which lectures should, ideally, be given, Faraday passed to the methods utilized by the lecturer to drive his points home. Here Faraday laid down a principle drawn from his own experience and followed without exception throughout his life. For Faraday, a truth did not become evident until he had seen it with his own eyes. The nature of chlorine, for example, did not become clear to him until he had *seen* Davy's demonstrations and then, and only then, was he convinced. He could have read about chlorine in any number of articles, or could have listened to a multitude of lecturers without giving his assent to the new idea, but seeing was believing.

Apparatus therefore is an essential part of every lecture in which it can be introduced but to apparatus should be added, at every convenient opportunity, illustrations that may not perhaps deserve the name of apparatus and of experiments and yet may be introduced with considerable force and effect in proper places. Diagrams and tables too are necessary or at least add in an eminent degree to the illustration and perfection of a lecture.[18]

Faraday felt strongly the appeal to the aesthetic sense that an experimental lecture should make. When a lecture is profusely illustrated by experiments, there is always the possibility of the lecturer's activity being confused with frenzy. Thus,

when an experimental lecture is to be delivered and apparatus is to be exhibited some kind of order should be observed in the arrangement of them on the lecture table. Every part illustrative of the lecture should be in view, no one thing should hide another from the audience nor should anything stand in the way of or obstruct the lecturer. They should be so placed, too, as to produce a kind of uniformity in appearance. No one part should appear naked and another crowded unless some particular reason exists and makes it necessary to be so. At the same time the whole should be so arranged as to keep one operation from interfering with another. If the lecture table appears crowded, if the lecturer (hid by his apparatus) is invisible, if things appear crooked or aside or unequal or if some are out of sight and this without any particular reason, the lecturer is considered (and with reason too) as an awkward contriver and a bungler.[19]

All these remarks, important as their subjects were, were directed at the mechanics of lecturing. Care and attention to detail were all that was necessary to insure that these aspects of the lecture went well. It is hardly necessary to add that such care and attention were always lavished upon his lectures by Faraday. All that could be done for the comfort of the audience was done, and every point that could be illuminated by experiment was so illuminated. There is, however, far more to a lecture than this. There is, as the most important element, the lecturer's art. Here Faraday had the true instinct of the theatre without which no lecturer can ever really succeed. Although not presented in the same glowing language, Faraday's remarks are distinctly reminiscent of Hamlet's speech to the players. Just as Shakespeare's words are still the finest advice that can be offered to the aspiring actor, so are Faraday's words well worth heeding by the young lecturer.

> The most prominent requisite to a lecturer tho' perhaps not really the most important is a good delivery for tho' to all true philosophers science and nature will have charms innumerable in every dress, yet I am sorry to say that the generality of mankind cannot accompany us one short hour unless the path is strewed with flowers. In order, therefore, to gain the attention of an audience (and what can be more disagreeable to a lecturer than the want of it?) it is necessary to pay some attention to the manner of expression. The utterance should not be rapid and hurried and consequently unintelligible but slow and deliberate conveying ideas with ease from the lecturer and infusing them with clearness and readiness into the minds of the audience. A lecturer should endeavor by all means to obtain a facility of utterance and the power of cloathing his thoughts and ideas in language smooth and harmonious and at the same time simple and easy. His periods should be round, not too long or unequal; they should be complete and expressive, conveying clearly the whole of the ideas intended to be conveyed. If they are long or obscure or incomplete they give rise to a degree of labour in the minds of the hearers which quickly causes lassitude, indifference and even disgust.[20]

But, a lecturer must not stand like a wooden stick and merely mouth phrases; he must, in Hamlet's phrase, 'suit the action to the word, and the word to the action'. In the lecture hall, action must necessarily differ from that of the theatre, but

> it is requisite that [the lecturer] should have some though it does not here bear the importance that it does in other branches of oratory. For tho' I know of no species of delivery (divinity excepted) that requires less motion, yet, I would by no means have a lecturer glued to the table or screwed on the floor. He must by all means appear a body distinct and separate from the things around him and must have some motion apart from that which they possess.
> A lecturer should appear easy and collected, undaunted and unconcerned, his thoughts about him and his mind clear and free for the contemplation

and description of his subject. His action should not be hasty and violent but slow, easy and natural consisting principally in changes of the posture of the body in order to avoid the air of stiffness or sameness that would otherwise be unavoidable. His whole behaviour should evince respect for his audience and he should in no case forget that he is in their presence. No accident that does not interfere with their convenience should disturb his serenity or cause variation in his behaviour. He should never, if possible, turn his back on them but should give them full reason to believe that all his powers have been exerted for their pleasure and instruction.[21]

The lecturer who illustrates his discourse with experiments or demonstrations faces the hazard of momentary failure which can be most embarrassing. 'On these occasions', Faraday wrote, 'an apology is sometimes necessary, but not always. I would wish apologies to be made as seldom as possible, and generally, only when the inconvenience extends to the company. I have several times seen the attention of by far the greater part of the audience called to an error by the apology that followed it.'[22]

The principles of an experimental lecture were clearly laid down. The experiments the lecturer chose

should be important, as they respect the science they are applied to, yet clear, and such as may easily and generally be understood. They should rather approach to simplicity, and explain the established principles of the subject, than be elaborate, and apply to minute phenomena only. . . .

Apt experiments . . . ought to be explained by satisfactory theory, or otherwise we merely patch an old coat with new cloth, and the whole (hole) becomes worse. If a satisfactory theory can be given, it ought to be given. If we doubt a received opinion, let us not leave it unnoticed, and affirm our own ideas, but state it clearly, and lay down also our objections. If the scientific world is divided in opinion, state both sides of the question, and let each one judge for himself, assisting him by noticing the most striking and forcible circumstances on each side. Then, and then only, shall we do justice to the subject, please the audience, and satisfy our honour, the honour of a philosopher.[23]

It was always as a philosopher that Faraday faced an audience and for a lecturer to degrade the art was reprehensible. Just as Hamlet castigated those players who tore a passion to tatters, or clowns who forgot the business of the play in order to secure a few more laughs, so, too, did Faraday pour scorn on the lecturer who used a lecture in order to elevate his own ego.

A lecturer [Faraday pointed out] falls deeply beneath the dignity of his character when he descends so low as to angle for claps, and asks for commendation. Yet have I seen a lecturer even at this point. I have heard him causelessly condemn his own powers. I have heard him dwell for a length of time on the extreme care and niceness that the experiment he will make requires. I have heard him hope for indulgence when no indulgence was wanted, and I have even heard him declare that the experiment now made cannot fail from its beauty, its correctness, and its application, to gain the approbation of all.[24]

For a young man of only twenty-three, these remarks are really quite acute. All experienced lecturers will recognize their aptness and applicability to the problem of lecturing today. Indeed, if Faraday's advice were made required reading for all university and college lecturers, some of the modern problem of 'the large lecture class' might be found to vanish.

Faraday, in 1813, was unable to live up to his own advice. He could tell what was the matter with other lecturers, and he could even see how their faults could be remedied. But that he, an uneducated tyro in science and lecturing, should ever really master the art must have seemed most unlikely to him. After his return from his continental tour with Davy, however, the possibility that he should be called upon some day to fill the office of lecturer at the Royal Institution no longer appeared so remote. Brande was competent but dull and the void left by Davy's absence served as a constant invitation to Faraday to strive to fill it. Faraday, therefore, began his serious training in lecturing. As Brande's assistant, he prepared and carried out the demonstrations for the course in practical and theoretical chemistry. The notes on the course in oratory which he attended reveal the interest with which he pursued this subject. At one and the same time, his thoughts on the proper manner of a lecturer were confirmed and the intricacies and suppleness of the English language were made manifest. It was in these years, too, that Edward Magrath helped him with grammar and writing so that all forms of expression were explored and refined. From 1817 to 1819 he also had the opportunity to try out his fledgeling talents. The lectures on chemistry delivered at the City Philosophical Society reveal his progress. The early ones were all written out in complete sentences. As he gained confidence, these give way to notes and finally to mere jottings. By 1819 he had adopted the form of lecture notes that were to serve him well for so many years. Rarely did these notes extend over more than two large sheets of paper. On the right-hand side were the notes for the delivery of the lecture. On the left, keyed by an X into the notes, were the experiments and demonstrations.

By 1820, only one element was lacking in Faraday's preparation as a public lecturer, and it was a vital one. No one in London beyond his immediate circle of acquaintances would ever have come to hear him. What, after all, might one expect of the laboratory assistant of the R.I.? He might be able to illustrate an analysis or two but to suggest that he could ever rival the breadth, depth, and brilliance of Davy was absurd. The years from 1820 to 1824 removed this final obstacle. By 1824, Faraday was no longer an obscure toiler in the lesser fields of chemistry. He was the discoverer of electromagnetic rotation which had eluded the experimental wizardry of Wollaston and the theoretical sagacity of Ampère. He was also the condenser of the permanent gases and a F.R.S.

In 1824 Faraday made his professional début as a lecturer in Brande's course. The audience was composed of students, not the general public, and there is no record of their response. In 1825 Faraday took steps to enlarge his audience. On 7 February 1825, at Davy's suggestion, Faraday was appointed Director of the Laboratory of the Royal Institution.[25] Among his early acts as Director was to issue an invitation to the Members to visit the R.I. on certain evenings to hear of the latest novelties in science and to inspect various instruments or curiosities arranged in the library. Only a few meetings took place in 1825, at one of which Faraday illustrated and analysed the electromagnetic rotations which he had discovered in 1821. In 1826 the meetings moved from the laboratory to the theatre of the R.I. and were held on Friday evenings during the winter and spring. Thus was born the famous Friday Evening Discourses at which scientists and non-scientists alike have for over a century described their work to lay audiences. It would be an exaggeration to suggest that these meetings directly affected the development of science or the arts, but by informing the public which supported intellectual endeavour of what the major lines of activity and research were at any given time, they did contribute to an understanding of what was being done. I think it not unfair to suggest that those who had attended the Friday Evenings were more sympathetic to the cause of science than they otherwise might have been.

The early meetings were quite informal. In a lecture on Arago's wheel delivered on 26 January 1827, Faraday explained the purpose of the meetings.

> I shall be permitted to refer to the Friday evenings, I trust, as I was actively engaged in them at their first institution and now serve as secretary of the Committee.
> They are intended as meetings of an easy and agreeable nature to which members have the privilege of bringing friends and where all may feel at ease. It is desirable that all things of interest, large or small, be exhibited here either in the library or in the lecture room. In the lecture room, the lecturer and the audience are relieved of all formalities except those essential to secure the attention and freedom of all. The lecture may be long or short, so it contain good matter and afterwards, everyone may adjourn for tea and talk.[26]

One anecdote told by Benjamin Abbott must suffice to illustrate this informality.

> When circumstances permitted me to do so [Abbott wrote many years later] I not unfrequently attended the Friday Evening Meetings to which [Faraday] always kindly gave me admission. This was especially pleasant to me when *he* was the Lecturer and I remember well his pausing at a point in his explanation of Ericson's Air Engine on which a sudden doubt occurred to him. Referring to this long afterwards he told me that from that time he heard no more on the subject, and I believe the circumstance proved fatal to the success of the Machine. It was I think on that occasion when a large number of Engineers being present Mr M. Fuller,[27] who sat in a front seat, fell asleep and snored loudly. The Lecturer paused – when someone near the old gentleman commenced clapping. This extending to all the company awakened Mr F. who, ignorant of the cause of the noise joined heartily in it, at the same time shouting out 'Bravo' in his usual deep and sonorous tones. A general burst of laughter succeeded, at the subsidence of which the Lecturer resumed his discourse.[28]

From 1825 until his retirement in 1862, Faraday gave well over a hundred of the Friday Evening Discourses.[29] The range of subjects strikes one at first as astonishing. There is a lecture on the reproduction and regeneration of planaria; one on lighthouse illumination utilizing the electric light; another on an electric silk-loom; one on the artificial production of rubies; a lecture on the physical lines of magnetic force; an evening given over to the condition and ventilation of the coal-mine goaf; a report on improvements in the manufacture and silvering of mirrors; a lecture on the strange motions of small particles discovered by the botanist Robert Brown; and so on over the years. Electricity and its applications we expect, but zoology and botany seem rather far afield for Faraday to be wandering. As a first-rate experimentalist, however, Faraday easily mastered the experimental part of any subject. When the subject was a technological one, the theory was usually quite simple and the interest lay in its application. When, as with Brownian motion or the regeneration of planaria, the theory was obscure and difficult, Faraday was helped by this very fact. It was the facts that had attracted attention. These Faraday could present; he could then expound the various theories together with their experimental evidence, and allow the audience to choose amongst them.

Faraday's Friday Evening Discourses may be roughly classified into three groups. Many lectures were devoted to expounding his own theories. After 1831, these made news and the Members had a right to hear about them from the discoverer rather than sit down with the latest volume of the *Philosophical Transactions* and go through the original paper. These lectures always followed the publication of the original paper, so they served merely to disseminate knowledge rather than announce something new. Occasionally, however, the Friday evening meeting served as a place where Faraday could speculate more freely than he could in a published paper. Many of his later thoughts on the nature of magnetism and the lines of force were presented first at the Royal Institution. Not all such speculations were the result of plan; the story is still told at the Royal Institution of the evening Sir Charles Wheatstone was supposed to deliver his own Discourse instead of having Faraday do it for him as he had done so many times before. As Faraday and Wheatstone neared the open doors of the theatre, Wheatstone panicked, dashed down the stairs, and ran down Albemarle Street, leaving Faraday with an expectant audience and no lecturer. To fill in, Faraday spoke for as long as he could on the announced subject, and then gave his 'Thoughts on ray vibrations' which may be considered as the first hint of the electromagnetic theory of light.[30] This incident has had a permanent effect upon the organization of the Friday meetings. Today, as the lecturer is escorted from the library to the theatre, the Director of the R.I. stands between him and the stairs, presumably ready to trip him up before he can reach the stairway and gain release from the fear that suddenly wells up within him as he hears the clock strike the hour of nine.

A second group of lectures concerned those discoveries or practices of others which were particularly newsworthy. It must be remembered that the Friday evenings were first conceived of as a means of keeping the Members of the R.I. abreast of advances in science and technology, so that when some particularly striking discovery or event was announced, Faraday felt honour bound to give some account of it. Thus, for example, the new tunnel under the Thames, built under the direction of I. K. Brunel was the subject of three discourses between 1826 and 1828. All members of the audience knew of it and, presumably, were curious as to *how* a tunnel could be built under a river. Faraday showed them. Similarly, the discovery of Brownian movement by Robert Brown caused a considerable stir at the time. For almost two centuries a debate had been carried on over the activity or passivity of matter. Should matter be shown to be *inherently* active, then this must lead inevitably to atheism. Atomism, indeed, had been made acceptable in England only because matter was stripped of all active attributes and rendered totally passive, reacting to forces (presumably spiritual) but never originating them. Now it appeared that matter, by and of itself, was constantly initiating peculiar motions from which all other activity might be derived. Faraday's presentation was a model of objectivity: the phenomenon was shown, the various theories were passed in review, a few cautionary words were spoken about leaping to conclusions, and the audience sent home hopefully to make up its own mind on what it had seen and heard.[31]

The third group of discourses were those dealing with applied science. Faraday has so often been portrayed as a pursuer of pure science who willingly passed by the practical applications of his own discoveries, that it is necessary here to insist that he did not scorn applied science. Rather, he delighted in the ways in which science could lighten or brighten man's burden in life. He knew full well that there would be others who would develop his ideas and forge them into practical inventions. It was his destiny to pursue his ideas as far as he could into the wilderness of the unknown. But, that these discoveries must bear practical fruit he felt was both inevitable and desirable. As he wrote to the physicist Jacobi who had developed a practical electric motor for transportation purposes, 'To think only of putting an electromagnetic machine into the *Great Western* or the *British Queen* and sending them across the Atlantic by it or even to the East Indies! What a glorious thing it would be.'[32] Faraday went out of his way to point out to his audience, many of whom were men of affairs, how the application of the simplest scientific principles could have far-reaching economic results. The process of anastatic (a form of lithographic) printing was described; an electric silk-loom which was actually a primitive device for automation was analysed in the simplest terms. The problem of mine explosions, with which the name of the Royal Institution had been associated since Davy's time, was again explored in 1845 after Faraday together with Sir Charles Lyell, had visited the scene of a tragic explosion in Durham.

His intention throughout seems clear; it was to reveal to his audience the beauty, charm, and utility of science. By lecturing on his own researches, he laid bare the mind of a creative scientist; by discoursing upon topics of current interest, he showed how science could react upon a world largely indifferent to it; and by pointing out the practical applications of science, he could glorify it in terms that were easily grasped in the early Victorian age.

These may have been Faraday's intentions; it is legitimate to ask to what extent they were achieved. The answer cannot be given in specific terms, but there can be no question of Faraday's success as a lecturer. Whether or not his listeners perceived the point of the lessons he sought to teach, there can be no doubt of his brilliance as a teacher. The testimony of his auditors must be heard if we are to see him as he was. From the scores of persons willing to testify, two have been chosen. One, Frederick von Raumer, Professor of History at the University of Berlin, was, as a foreigner, uniquely qualified to judge Faraday's technical skill as a lecturer. Not only was English a foreign tongue, but science too was strange to him and, as a lecturer himself, he would be able immediately to detect any flaws.

> Mr Faraday is not only a man of profound chemical and physical science (which all Europe knows), but a very remarkable lecturer. He speaks with ease and freedom, but not with a gossiping, unequal tone, alternately inaudible and bawling, as some very learned professors do; he delivers himself with clearness, precision and ability. Moreover, he speaks his language in a manner which confirmed me in a secret suspicion I had, that a great number of Englishmen speak it very badly. Why is it that French in the mouth of Mdlle Mars, German in that of Tieck, English in that of Faraday, seems a totally different language? Because they articulate, what other people swallow or chew.[33]

The other description, by Lady Holland, described how the audience at the Royal Institution saw Faraday. Though long, it nevertheless conveys the flavour of an evening spent in his presence and permits us to see, however dimly, the charm and greatness of Faraday, the teacher. Faraday should be remembered, Lady Holland wrote:

> in his characteristic phases; first, as he stood at the lecture table, with his voltaic batteries, his electro-magnetic-helix, his large electrical machine, his glass retorts, and all his experimental apparatus about him, – the whole of it being in such perfect order that he could without fail lay his hand upon the right thing at the right moment, and that, if his assistant by any chance made a blunder, he could, without a sign of discomposure, set it right. His instruments were never in his way, and his manipulation never interfered with his discourse. He was completely master of the situation; he had his audience at his command, as he had himself and all his belongings; he had nothing to fret him, and he could give his eloquence full sway. It was an irresistible eloquence, which compelled attention and insisted upon sympathy. It waked the young from their visions and the old from their dreams. There was a gleaming in his eyes which no painter could copy and which no poet could describe. Their radiance seemed to send a strange light into the very heart of his congregation; and when he spoke, it was felt that the stir of his voice and the fervour of his words could belong only to the owner of those kindling eyes. His thought was rapid, and made itself a way in new phrases, if it found none ready made, – as the mountaineer cuts steps in the most hazardous ascent with his own axe. His enthusiasm sometimes carried him to the point of ecstasy when he expatiated on the beauty of nature, and when he lifted the veil from her deep mysteries. His body then took motion from his mind; his hair streamed out from his head, his hands were full of nervous action, his

light lithe body seemed to quiver with its eager life. His audience took fire with him, and every face was flushed. Whatever might be the after-thought or the after-pursuit, each hearer for the time shared his zeal and his delight; and with some listeners the impression made was so deep as to lead them into the laborious paths of philosophy, in spite of all the obstacles which the daily life of society opposes to such undertakings. . . .

A pleasant vein of humour accompanied his ardent imagination, and occasionally, not too often, relieved the tension of thought imposed upon his pupils. He would play with his subject now and then, but very delicately; his sport was only just enough to enliven the effort of attention. He never suffered an experiment to allure him away from his theme.[34]

Even allowing for the exaggeration inherent in a eulogy, the main outlines of Faraday's greatness as a teacher emerge clearly from this description. Suppose he had accepted the chair of chemistry at the University of London, would he have created a great school like that of Leibig at Giessen? Would England, rather than Germany, have dominated chemistry in the second half of the Victorian age? Futile questions! yet how tantalizing they are and how fortunate that we shall never answer them.

Although Faraday did not create a school, it would be wrong to dismiss him as a teacher. He held very strong ideas on education and these ideas were put into practice at the Royal Institution. The Friday evening meetings were intended primarily for the entertainment of the Members and their guests. There were, however, regular courses which Faraday taught whose purpose was somewhat more serious. There were, as well, the juvenile lectures and here Faraday's genius could really exercise itself.

2. Faraday, the Educator

The process of education was one that had long fascinated Faraday. His interest had been born of necessity when, as a young man, he had set out to educate himself. As we have seen,[35] it was early made apparent to him that education involved far more than the accumulation of factual information. True education was the result of the development of the faculty of the judgement for it was this faculty that permitted one to sift out the raw impressions of the senses and bring order to them. In his essay 'On Imagination and Judgment', written in 1818, he had discussed the way in which this was accomplished.[36] The function of the imagination was to produce all kinds of possibilities and analogies and lay them before the mind. The senses provided the means for the examination of the external world. The judgement was the key faculty. It was the judgement which accepted the gifts of the imagination, but then subjected them to the most intense critical scrutiny. The evidence provided by the senses allowed the judgement to control the imagination and extract from its offerings what appeared reliable and reject what could not pass the acid test of experience. Education, as Faraday conceived it, was the process of training the judgement. This was achieved by exercising it and forcing it to mediate between the illusions of the imagination and the confusions of the senses. The result was the constant interplay between mind and the external world of fact in which facts were not defined as a fundamental 'given' of existence but, rather, were called forth by the judgement in order to test the claims of the imagination. In a very real sense, therefore, it was the imagination which gave rise to the knowledge of facts for until the imagination had suggested some relationship, the judgement could not be exercised in singling out those facts relevant to the relationship to be used for testing its validity. It was in this sense that Faraday was empirical; his theories did not *arise* from facts but the experimental facts were the evidence upon which his judgement relied for accepting or rejecting an idea suggested to it by the imagination.

In the years following 1818, these were the principles that guided Faraday in his own development. They were also the guide lines for his teaching, both in his courses offered to adults and before a juvenile audience. It was not until the 1850's, however, that the occasion arose to publicize his views. At that time, as debate raged over the desirability of introducing the teaching of science into the secondary schools and expanding the science offerings of the two older English universities, Faraday stepped forward to educate his contemporaries.

In 1854, Faraday organized a series of discourses at the Royal Institution on the general subject of education. He delivered one of these lectures on 6 May 1854, entitled, 'Observations on Mental Education', before a brilliant audience which included His Royal Highness, Prince Albert. In 1859, when he gathered his papers on non-electrical subjects together for publication, he included this lecture with the comment: 'These observations . . . are so immediately connected in their nature and origin with my own experimental life, considered either as cause or consequence, that I have thought the close of this volume not an unfit place for their reproduction.'[37]

Faraday's observations were intended as a sharp criticism of prevailing mental attitudes. The disease affecting all Victorian society was, with Faraday's emphasis, a *deficiency of judgment*[38] and his task at this time was to reveal the syndrome to his audience. He first challenged the simplistic notion that the senses were built-in and automatic checks against error.

Our sense-perceptions are wonderful [he admitted]. Even in the observant, but unreflective infant, they soon produce a result which looks like intuition, because of its perfection. Coming to the mind as so many data, they are stored up, and without our being conscious, are ever after used in like circumstances in forming our judgment; and it is not wonderful that man should be accustomed to trust them without examination. Nevertheless, the result is the effect of education: the mind has to be instructed with regard to the senses and their intimations through every step of life; and where the instruction is imperfect, it is astonishing how soon and how much their evidence fails us. Yet, in the latter years of life, we do not consider this matter, but, having obtained the ordinary teaching sufficient for ordinary purposes, we venture to judge of things which are extraordinary for the time, and almost always with the more assurance as our powers of observation are less educated.[39]

Faraday had only recently witnessed an example of this want of judgement in the craze for 'table-turning' that swept through London in 1853 and 1854. Sensible, educated (according to the standards of the day) people suddenly appeared to abandon common sense and insist upon the 'spirits' and other immaterial agents and powers that supposedly caused the motions of tables and chairs. Here the senses deceived and the judgement was faulty in permitting this deception to pass unnoticed. The judgement, in turn, erred because it had been improperly trained. Had there been a real knowledge of the laws of nature, table-turning would not have been accepted so easily. It was not that Faraday felt that natural laws were absolute, but that they were, at any given time, the best guide the judgement had.

The *laws of nature*, as we understand them, are the foundation of our knowledge in natural things. So much as we know of them has been developed by the successive energies of the highest intellects, exerted through many ages. After a most rigid and scrutinizing examination upon principle and trial, a definite expression has been given to them; they have become, as it were, our belief or trust. From day to day we still examine and test our expressions of them. We have no interest in their retention if erroneous; on the contrary, the greatest discovery a man could make would be to prove that one of these accepted laws was erroneous, and his greatest honour would be the discovery. Neither should there be any desire to retain the former expression: – for we know that the new or amended law would be far more productive in results, would greatly increase our intellectual acquisitions, and would prove an abundant source of fresh delight to the mind.[40]

The function of the judgement was clearly revealed in this passage. It was constantly to be on the alert and critical of its own (and other's) conclusions. Science was not 'an organized body of knowledge' but a series of guides permitting the judgement to analyse, examine, and reject notions that could not meet the severest tests the judgement could devise. This was why Faraday felt so strongly about table-turning. It was *not* that table-turning was necessarily impossible. Faraday, himself, had discovered so many new facts of nature which conventional theories had failed to predict, that he was not prepared to eliminate table-turning because it was a novelty. Rather, as he wrote,

> I do not object to table-moving, for *itself*; for being once stated, it becomes a fit, though a very unpromising subject for experiment; but I am opposed to the unwillingness of its advocates to investigate; their boldness to assert; the credulity of the lookers-on; their desire that the reserved and cautious objector should be in error; and I wish, by calling attention to these things, to make the general want of mental discipline and education manifest.[41]

These were harsh words and demanded justification. In the second half of his discourse, Faraday addressed himself to the possible remedies for the widespread failure of judgement. His point of view reflected his feelings on the laws of nature, but to the objection that science was too narrow to be used as an example of proper thinking, Faraday opposed the dubious argument that the failure of the judgement in one area indicated a habit of mind that would carry over into other areas.

> I can only repeat my conviction, [he wrote] that society occupies itself now-a-days about physical matters and judges them as common things. Failing in relation to them, it is equally liable to carry such failures into other matters of life. The proof of deficient judgment in one department shows the habit of mind, and the general want, in relation to others. I am persuaded that all persons may find in natural things an admirable school for self-instruction, and a field for the necessary mental exercise; that they may easily apply their habits of thought, thus formed, to a social use; and that they ought to do this, as a duty to themselves and their generation.[42]

The study of natural science, then, was to be Faraday's cure for the educational ills of his day. The idea that the study of science would lead to the liberation of man's mind from prejudice and preconceptions was by no means new. It had been discussed and utilized by educators in the eighteenth century, and had even been applied on a large scale in France in the Revolutionary period.[43] One need only glance at Condorcet's *Sketch of a Tableau of the Progress of the Human Mind* to realize the allure of this dream. What *is* new with Faraday is his insistence upon the inevitability of error. Almost alone among his contemporaries Faraday realized the provisional nature of all knowledge. He did not share the Victorian confidence in the eventual triumph of Truth, for he well knew that Truth was reserved for God alone. Humanity must learn to live with a mixture of truth and error; the well-educated judgement could be used to mini-mize, but never eliminate, error. His programme for the education of the judgement had, therefore, to be based upon this fact. Education meant self-criticism. 'It is necessary that a man *examine himself*, and *that* not care-lessly. On the contrary, as he advances, he should become more and more strict, till he ultimately prove a sharper critic to himself than any one else can be; and he ought to intend this, for, so far as he consciously falls short of it, he acknowledges that others may have reason on their side when they criticise him.'[44] This was Faraday's main point; education meant *self*-education and particularly, self-criticism.

> This education has for its first and its last step *humility*. It can commence only because of a conviction of deficiency; and if we are not disheartened under the growing revelations which it will make, that conviction will become stronger unto the end. But the humility will be founded, not on comparison of our-selves with the imperfect standards around us, but on the increase of that internal knowledge which alone can make us aware of our internal wants. The first step in correction is to learn our deficiencies, and having learned them, the next step is almost complete: for no man who has discovered that his judgment is hasty, or illogical, or imperfect, would go on with the same degree of haste, or irrationality, or presumption as before. I do not mean that all would at once be cured of bad mental habits, but I think better of human nature than to believe, that a man in any rank of life, who has arrived at the consciousness of such a condition, would deny his common sense, and still judge and act as before.[45]

Such a man as this, Faraday clearly implied, is to be considered educated although he has not, perhaps, been exposed to what the rest of society considers an education. When one realizes that he was addressing an audi-ence that was composed of 'educated' people to whom Faraday's standards must have been totally foreign, it is almost impossible not to admire his courage and moral fervour. Worse, however, was yet to come for Faraday quite explicitly set out to jolt his listeners out of whatever complacency might still be left to them.

> And now [he concluded] a few words upon the mutual relation of two classes, namely, *those* who decline to educate their judgments in regard to the matters on which they decide, and those who, by self-education, have endeavoured to improve themselves; and upon the remarkable and somewhat unreasonable manner in which the latter are called upon, and occasionally taunted, by the former. A man who makes assertions, or draws conclusions, regarding any given case, ought to be competent to investigate it.[46]

Again the emphasis was upon the criticism of one's own ideas. Everyone may have a right to his own opinion, but he has no right to expect others to listen to him unless he has taken the trouble first to subject his opinion to the test of his own critical judgement. Where such judgement is lacking, Faraday felt, the ideas can be of only passing interest.

In this discourse, Faraday has presented us, as he himself avowed, with an intellectual self-portrait. To him, the judgement was paramount and he told his audience how and why he had trained it over the years. Again and again he insisted that education was *self*-education and must be based upon an awareness of fallibility. Such a position, while laudable, was hardly of much value to those involved in the practical task of educating Britain's youth. To the conscientious schoolmaster who sincerely wished to improve his teaching, Faraday's advice in this lecture must have seemed totally worthless. What he needed was some hint as to how to approach the education of the young, not merely the injunction that the young should learn how little they knew. Faraday, it must be remembered, was a brilliant teacher of the young, and so it was that he could offer such hints, although they do not seem to have been much heeded at the time. His views on the teaching of science were laid out in another discourse, 'On Wheatstone's Electric Telegraph . . .'[47] and in his testimony before 'H.M. Commissioners appointed to inquire into the revenues and management of certain colleges and schools and the studies pursued and instruction given therein'.[48]

Between his lecture on mental education of 1854 and his discourse on Wheatstone's telegraph in 1858, it is highly doubtful that Faraday's ideas on education underwent any significant change. What did change was the manner in which he presented them. In 1854 he had been primarily concerned with the lack of good judgement shown by the majority of men and he had prescribed a cure based upon self-criticism. By 1858 the controversy over the place of science in an educational system had become far more heated and the issues had become much more precisely defined. The question to which Faraday addressed himself in 1858 was no longer the general one of the formation of the judgement, but the specific one of what role, if any, science should play in education. Wheatstone's new telegraph provided him with an opportunity to plead for science by emphasizing its utility.

The development of the applications of physical science in modern times [he wrote] has become so large and so essential to the well-being of man that it may justly be used, as illustrating the true character of pure science, as a department of knowledge, and the claim it may have for consideration by Governments, Universities, and all bodies to whom is confided the fostering care and direction of learning. As a branch of learning, men are beginning to recognize the right of science to its own particular place; – for though flowing in channels utterly different in their course and end to those of litera-ture, it conduces not less, as a means of instruction, to the discipline of the mind; whilst it ministers, more or less, to the wants, comforts, and proper pleasure, both mental and bodily, of every individual of every class in life.[49]

Faraday's appeal to the utility of science as an argument in favour of public support of science was not used by him merely to introduce his subject. God had given man dominion over the earth; man's mind could comprehend the laws of nature and through comprehension, gain mastery over her. To Faraday it was almost a sacred duty to reveal these laws and use them for the betterment of mankind. Today, when it is fashionable in some quarters, to look at applied science as though it should be the con-cern only of mechanics and rude artisans, it is well to keep Faraday's attitude in mind. The cause of science, which appears to need pleading in every generation, would gain were Faraday's attitude more widespread.

The utility of science, of course, was not its only claim to public attention. As an educational device, it formed the mind in a way no other study could. Literature and literary studies refined the taste and, hope-fully, improved morals but since the ultimate object of belles-lettres was man, the breadth of vision contemplated by Faraday could not be gained here. In a passage remarkable for its zeal and fervour, Faraday revealed that vision as it had guided him throughout his life and offered it to others for their own use.

> . . . if the term education may be understood in so large a sense as to include all that belongs to the improvement of the mind either by the acquisition of the knowledge of others or by increase of it through its own exertions, we learn by them what is the kind of education science offers to man. It teaches us to be *neglectful* of nothing; – not to despise the small beginnings, for they precede of necessity all great things in the knowledge of science, either pure or applied. It teaches a continual comparison of the *small* and *great*, and that under differences almost approaching the infinite: for the small as often contains the great in principle as the great does the small; and thus the mind becomes comprehensive. It teaches to deduce principles carefully, to hold them firmly, or to suspend the judgment: – to discover and obey *law,* and by it to be bold in applying to the greatest what we know of the smallest. It teaches us first by tutors and books to learn that which is already known to others, and then by the light and methods which belong to science to learn for ourselves and for others; – so making a fruitful return to man in the future for that which we have obtained from the men of the past. Bacon, in his instruc-tion, tells us that the scientific student ought not to be as the ant who gathers merely, nor as the spider who spins from her own bowels, but rather as the bee who both gathers and produces.

All this is true of the teaching afforded by any part of physical science. Electricity is often called wonderful – beautiful; – but it is so only in common with the other forces of nature. The beauty of electricity, or of any other force, is not that the power is mysterious and unexpected, touching every sense at unawares in turn, but that it is under *law*, and that the taught intellect can even now govern it largely. The human mind is placed above, not beneath it; and it is in such a point of view that the mental education afforded by science is rendered supereminent in dignity, in practical application, and utility; for, by enabling the mind to apply the natural power through law, it conveys the gifts of God to man.[50]

By 1862, when he gave evidence before H.M. Commissioners, Faraday had become increasingly critical of the traditional modes and subjects of education. The dispute over science and its place in education had now been occupying the English for well over five years with no significant progress being made by the advocates of science. There was a note of impatience in Faraday's testimony quite foreign to his usual attitude.

I am not an educated man, according to the usual phraseology [he informed the Commissioners] and, therefore can make no comparison between languages and natural knowledge, except as regards the utility of language in conveying thoughts; but that the natural knowledge which has been given to the world in such abundance during the last 50 years, I may say, should remain untouched, and that no sufficient attempt should be made to convey it to the young mind growing up and obtaining its first views of these things, is to me a matter so strange, that I find it difficult to understand. Though I think I see the opposition breaking away, it is yet a very hard one to overcome. That it ought to be overcome, I have not the least doubt in the world.[51]

This opposition, Faraday felt, was supported by ignorance and tradition rather than any conscious hostility, but that it was a powerful opposition Faraday had no doubt. Hopefully it would fade when the real value of science was realized. He repeated the arguments used in the two R.I. discourses, calling the attention of H.M. Commissioners both to the utility of science and to its use as a former of the judgement.[52] What was new in Faraday's testimony was his comparison of science and the classics as means of educating the judgement and his suggestions on how science should be taught. Lord Clarendon put the questions to Faraday which enabled him to draw the distinction he wished between the result of a classical and scientific education. The problem is still with us and since this exchange contains many elements of arguments which are still to be heard today, it is, perhaps, worth attending to in some detail.

Lord Clarendon began by asking Faraday if he did not feel that the study of the classics and of pure mathematics afforded the 'best training of the mind' that can be given. Faraday's reply was eloquent:

M

The phrase 'training of the mind' has to me a very indefinite meaning [he testified]. I would like a profound scholar to indicate to me what he understands by the training of the mind; in a literary sense, including mathematics. What is their effect on the mind? What is the kind of result that is called the training of the mind? or what does the mind learn by that training? It learns things I have no doubt. By the very act of study it learns to be attentive, to be persevering, to be logical according to the word logic. But does it learn that training of the mind which enables a man to give a reason in natural things for an effect which happens from certain causes; or why in any emergency or event he does or should do this, that, or the other? It does not suggest the least thing in these matters. It is the highly educated man that we find coming to us again and again, and asking the most simple question in chemistry or mechanics; and when we speak of such things as the conservation of force, the permanency of matter, and the unchangeability of the laws of nature, they are far from comprehending them, though they have relation to us in every action of our lives. Many of these instructed persons are as far from having the power of judging of these things as if their minds had never been trained.[53]

Although he expressly denied any hostility towards the classics, it is perfectly clear that he felt that the exclusive study of them did not train the mind as he would have it trained. The classics and pure mathematics, he implied, could fill the mind with facts, could even lay down a method of procedure within areas where the rules of procedure were known and followed. What Faraday missed, and what he felt the proper study of science could provide, was a training for action when the outcome of such action was unknown and where there were no common rules. Because of its self-corrective nature, science best equipped men for those areas of life in which action and reaction could be known only through experience. For this reason, Faraday was not eager merely to cram students' heads full of facts about the natural world. This would be of as little use as cramming them full of Greek or Latin words. What he wanted was to teach science as a living study in which facts were but the bricks from which the structure of science was built.[54]

If this programme were admitted, the next question that arose was, when and how should science be taught? Should there be a course of, say, ten lectures on various subjects throughout the term or should there be more intensive instruction? Could young boys really follow and understand the intricacies and jargon of science? What kind of instruction and instructors would suffice to give the kind of training Faraday had in mind?

Faraday immediately underscored the real problem involved here. The successful introduction of science into England's educational system depended upon far more than a decision by headmasters to do so. Science masters could be hired, for nothing is easier than to get up a course in natural science resembling one in classics. All that is required is to stay one step ahead of the class and drill the students in memorizing laws, or names, or properties, or what have you. This was not what Faraday desired: to achieve his aim required a long course of social re-education. For, there would not be good science masters until science was recognized as valuable.

> You want men who can teach [he informed the commissioners] and that class has to be created. Without such channels the stream of knowledge is cut off from the young mind. I have no doubt that you will find such exceedingly hard to obtain, because up to this time habit and prejudice has not been for such men, and teachers have not even learnt by practice what they ought to learn and could learn even in that way. . . . I do not know any other way of obtaining the desired end than to honour and encourage natural knowledge, gradually to introduce it into the general system of education, and whilst so doing to create, in the manner progressive experience may decide, a willing and competent set of teachers.[55]

Faraday was, himself, the best proof that science could be taught the way he wished it to be. Since the 1820's he had offered courses at the Royal Institution which, while not serving particularly to advance scientific knowledge, had achieved the goal of creating an interest in and respect for science.

These courses underwent a slow transformation over the years which reflected the gradual penetration of science into education, at least in London. In the early years, the lectures were directed at students who were serious students of chemistry and for whom Faraday's lectures were an integral part of their training. In 1827, for example, Faraday delivered twelve lectures on 'the philosophy and practice of chemical manipulation'. These lectures were quite highly technical and formed the basis of his book on the same subject. In the 1830's and 1840's facilities for the study of chemistry were greatly expanded in London and the clientele served by the Royal Institution changed radically. Serious students of science were no longer to be found there; the audience in the laboratory tended more and more to consist of the wives of members who found an afternoon with Mr Faraday both amusing and instructive. The subjects of the lectures changed accordingly, as did their purposes. After 1830, no technical subjects such as chemical manipulation appear in the syllabi. Instead, one finds Faraday using these courses to introduce his listeners to the grand and great phenomena of our globe. There were, as was only to be expected, many, many lectures on electricity and on the connexion between electricity and chemistry. The other forces of matter – heat, magnetism, cohesion, and gravity – also were passed in review periodically. Other courses were designed to catch and hold the attention of his listeners by appealing directly either to their curiosity or to their immediate interests. Thus there was a 'course of six lectures on the ancient elements Earth, Air, Fire and Water' and another 'upon some points of Domestic Chemical Philosophy'.[56] This latter course well illustrates Faraday's method. Each of the six lectures dealt with a familiar aspect of the home: a fire, a candle, a lamp, a chimney, a kettle, and ashes. Each object was used to illustrate some basic chemical or physical principle in such a way that it could never be forgotten. Many in Faraday's audience must have been delighted by the discovery that they had been doing chemistry for years but hadn't known it.

It is impossible to evaluate the effect of these courses. They were always well attended and they must have done something to spread respect, even a liking, for science. Nor should one of their main functions be neglected. They were open to the public for a payment of two guineas (for non-subscribers to the R.I.) and one guinea for ladies. While the coffers of the Royal Institution were never filled to overflowing by these courses, they were, nevertheless, a steady source of much-needed income.

Faraday was to be seen at his best as a lecturer in the famous Christmas Lectures for children. His love of simplicity and his sense of the dramatic were enthusiastically echoed by his audience who entered wholeheartedly into the world of science with him as guide. Who could ever lose the sense of wonder at the strange power of a magnet after they had seen Mr Faraday suddenly, and without warning, hurl a scuttle of coals at the Royal Institution's great electromagnet, and then follow this with the fire tongs and poker – all reaching their target and sticking there!

The Juvenile Lectures appear to have been suggested by Faraday in 1826 and were, most probably, looked upon by Faraday and the Managers of the Royal Institution as an additional means of raising funds for the continuance of the Institution. Over the course of the years, Faraday gave nineteen of these courses of lectures. In the 1820's and 1830's, when he was pursuing his theoretical speculations feverishly, one, sometimes two years would pass between his appearances before the 'juvenile auditory'. After the 1840's, however, when his last great discoveries had been made and when his theoretical ideas were considered most unorthodox, he gave the lectures year after year. Children still could react enthusiastically to the wonders of the cosmos, and, most importantly, because they had not yet committed themselves to orthodox ideas, they would listen to the unorthodox ones that Faraday presented. The Christmas Lectures very rapidly became popular among the higher classes of London society; even the Prince of Wales attended and was introduced to the mysteries of electricity.[57]

Two of these courses of lectures were taken down by professional stenographers and published with Faraday's consent. They have become deservedly famous and have run into many, many editions. The more famous of the two, *The Chemical History of a Candle*, has been translated into all the European languages and has even earned the distinction of being the first complete book on science to be put into Basic English.[58] There is an English edition published in the Soviet Union with which Soviet youth learns both English and science in the early grades.

In both *The Chemical History of a Candle* and the *Lectures on the Various Forces of Matter*[59] Faraday followed the same pedagogical procedure. He began with the simple, the everyday, and the commonplace. In the one case, it was an ordinary candle; in the other, with the youngsters themselves and the fact that they were firmly anchored to their seats and not flying about the room. From this point, he led his audience by simple steps up to the contemplation of fundamental laws of nature. The *Lectures on the Various Forces of Matter* illustrate his method so well and, being relatively less widely read than *The Chemical History of a Candle*, provide such a clear picture of Faraday as a practical and practising educator, that it is worth examining them in some detail.

The first task Faraday set himself was to awake a sense of wonder in his listeners. This, he knew, was an inexhaustible source of inspiration and once a person could be made to wonder about the world, it was only a short step from there to investigating it. Thus Faraday strove to point out that if one considered the most ordinary thing closely, it ceased to be ordinary and took on the character of the miraculous.

Let us now consider, for a little while [he said to his youthful group] how wonderfully we stand upon this world. Here it is we are born, bred, and live, and yet we view these things with an almost entire absence of wonder to ourselves respecting the way in which all this happens. So small, indeed, is our wonder, that we are never taken by surprise; and I do think, that, to a young person of ten, fifteen, or twenty years of age, perhaps the first sight of a cataract or a mountain would occasion him more surprise than he had ever felt concerning the means of his own existence; how he came here; how he lives; by what means he stands upright; and through what means he moves about from place to place. Hence, we come into this world, we live, and depart from it, without our thoughts being called specifically to consider how all this takes place; and were it not for the exertions of some few inquiring minds, who have looked *into* these things and ascertained the very beautiful laws and conditions by which we *do* live and stand upon the earth, we should hardly be aware that there was anything wonderful in it. These inquiries, which have occupied philosophers from the earliest days, when they first began to find out the laws by which we grow, and exist, and enjoy ourselves, up to the present time, have shown us that all this was effected in consequence of the existence of certain *forces*, or *abilities* to do things, or *powers*, that are so common that nothing can be more so: for nothing is commoner than the wonderful powers by which we are enabled to stand upright – they are essential to our existence every moment.[60]

The nature of force was then explained in increasingly abstract ways. First Faraday illustrated it by a simple push and pull, halting to call attention to the 'remarkable' way in which force was transmitted through a string when the string was pulled.[61] Then electric attraction and repulsion were illustrated. Finally the power of heat was shown. In a few short minutes, Faraday had called attention to the existence of 'powers' upon which the very existence of the world depended, had illustrated some of their effects, and had hinted at their common basis. An element of unity was thereby injected into the discussion and was to serve as the guiding thread for the whole course of lectures.

As the most immediately perceptible of the powers (once the attention was called to it) gravity was the first to be investigated. The centre of gravity of a body was described and a means for locating it was illustrated. Then, ever willing to bring science down to everyday life, Faraday asked the audience what had to be done if he were to stand upon one leg. Matching action to the question, he showed by example that he had to shift his body so that his centre of gravity fell over the leg he was standing on. What boy could fail to repeat this 'experiment' at home both to convince himself and to illustrate the lecture to parents and brothers and sisters? To stimulate further the almost innate desire among the adolescent to do things for himself, Faraday arranged to have materials on his desk for his students to take home. Thus, when speaking of the force of molecular cohesion, he brought in pieces of calcareous spar and invited his audience to take one home and see the various ways in which it could be split.[62] And, when speaking of static electricity, he showed the group how they, themselves, could make a static electricity generator and an electrometer using only a piece of sealing wax, a watch and a small piece of wooden board.[63] The facts and laws of science *could* be illustrated and Faraday did all he could to urge his audience to see and judge for themselves. From the first surge of wonder, he gently led them to the first principle of critical control of this wonder. Experiment – the direct questioning of nature – should follow the first realization that one has discovered something out of the ordinary.

The lecture on gravity also permitted Faraday to describe one of the general laws which some of the forces obeyed. The law of gravitational action was introduced by a history of the recent discovery of Neptune – a true marvel of science! The law that permitted Leverrier and Adams to calculate the position of Neptune so that astronomers could direct their telescopes at this portion of the sky was the inverse square law – 'a sad jumble of words until you understand them', as Faraday quickly pointed out. Instead of merely writing an equation on the blackboard, or simply stating that the force of gravitation varied inversely with the square of the distance, Faraday illustrated a case where a power evidently did vary, visibly, with the square of the distance. He chose light as his example and showed, simply and elegantly, how the intensity of light followed the same law.[64] To be able to *see* a law is always so much better than merely being able to state it.

From gravity, Faraday passed on to the force of intermolecular cohesion. This force resembled gravity in many respects, except that it acted only at very short distances. The difference, however, was so slight that the student had no difficulty in assimilating the concept of cohesive force to that just gained of gravitational force. The result of varying the distances at which this force operated was easily illustrated by the phenomenon of change of state. Just as the audience was beginning to believe that cohesive force was like gravitational force, only restricted in its range, Faraday dramatically called its attention to a peculiarity of the force of cohesion. Taking a sheet of mica, he beat it with a hammer on its broad face, without breaking it. He then turned it on edge and easily peeled off sheets of it. The force of cohesion, unlike that of gravity, did not act equally in all directions. This fact was then driven home by examining the cleavage planes of a number of crystalline substances. The ways in which the force varied was then illustrated by utilizing plane polarized light to reveal the optical axes. Again, the law could be *seen* and the effect appreciated.

There was a more subtle lesson to be learned from the lecture on cohesion. It was not pressed by Faraday, yet the perceptive must have understood it. It was, not to confuse analogy and identity. Just because two forces acted alike in some situations was no reason to assume they were really the same. There *was* a difference, as Faraday pointed out, between cohesion and gravity and this difference was well worth thinking about since it might lead to some new insight into the nature of all forces.

Having made this point in Lecture II, Faraday went on in the third lecture specifically to underline the difference between cohesive force and the force of chemical affinity. Here he was able to probe even more deeply into the relation between matter and force. The force of chemical affinity, he showed, was even more selective than that of cohesion and upon this selectivity depended the science of chemistry. The way in which this force acted was illustrated copiously so that, again, the basic principles were firmly impressed upon his hearer's mind.

The transference of this force was then illustrated by the use of the voltaic cell, and so the audience was led by logical, but slow, degrees to the forces of electricity. Then, from this force, Faraday moved to the correlation of the physical forces. Force, he stated, can neither be created nor destroyed[65] and, therefore, the various forces must be seen as but different manifestations of a single, overall, power. And, thus, at the end of the series, Faraday came back to that hint that he had thrown out in the beginning about the essential unity of force. He had presented to his listeners a truly artistic picture of the universe in which they lived. Behind the infinity of appearances in this world, he had uncovered a unity of action. The existence of this unity, he had stressed, had taken the work of generations to discover but the panorama thus revealed was worthy of the labour. After all, the noblest creation of God was man, and, by implication, the noblest creation of man was knowledge of God's universe. Not only had Faraday ably presented this vision of a *uni*verse to his auditors, he had also subtly implanted in them the seed of future investigations. Whether the seed would germinate and grow would depend upon factors outside his control but, given proper circumstances, the lessons learned at the Christmas Lectures might be expected to influence the course of a man's life. Looking back upon these lectures from a hundred years away, the professional educator certainly should discern the outlines of a method which might be profitably applied today to the teaching of science.

3. Faraday and British Science

During the 1820's the state of science in England was the cause of considerable concern to many of its practitioners. In some quarters there was the feeling that there was insufficient patronage by the Government and an almost total lack of understanding of the importance of science by the educated public. Even the dignity of F.R.S. seemed to have been degraded under the long reign of Sir Joseph Banks who, as President of the Royal Society, had permitted its ranks to swell and had lowered the scientific standards of admission. The feelings of disquiet thus engendered only rarely were made explicit by members of the scientific community.

Occasionally a pamphlet would appear attacking this or that aspect of the problem but the combined conservatism of the Council and President of the Royal Society and of the English public was always sufficient to stifle these isolated cries. Even John Herschel, with all the prestige of his name and of his scientific achievements, was reduced to lamenting what appeared to be the incurable disease afflicting English science. And, when science in England was compared to science in other lands, the situation became almost too painful to bear. In his *Treatise on Sound,* in the *Encyclopaedia Metropolitana,* Herschel spelled out his diagnosis of the illness.

We have drawn largely [he wrote] both in the present Essay, and in our article on Light, from the Annales de Chimie, and we take this only opportunity distinctly to acknowledge our obligations to that most admirably conducted work. Unlike the crude and undigested Scientific matter which suffices (we are ashamed to say it) for the monthly and quarterly amusement of our own countrymen, whatever is admitted into its pages, has at least been taken pains with and, with few exceptions, has sterling merit. Indeed, among the original communications which abound in it, there are few which would misbecome the first academical collections; and if any thing could diminish our regret at the long suppression of those noble memoirs, which are destined to adorn future volumes of that of the Institute, it would be the masterly abstracts of them which from time to time appear in the Annales, either from the hands of the authors, or from the reports rendered by the committees appointed to examine them; which latter, indeed, are universally models of their kind, and have contributed, perhaps more than any thing, to the high scientific tone of the French savants. What author, indeed, but will write his best when he knows that his work, if it have merit, will immediately be reported on by a committee, who will enter into all its meaning; understand it, however profound: and, not content with merely understanding it, pursue the trains of thought to which it leads; place its discoveries and principles in new and unexpected lights; and bring the whole of their knowledge of collateral subjects to bear upon it. Nor ought we to omit our acknowledgments to the very valuable Journals of Poggendorf and Schweigger. Less exclusively national than their Gallic compeer, they present a picture of the actual progress of physical science throughout Europe. Indeed, we have been often astonished to see with what celerity every thing, even moderately valuable in the scientific publications of this country, finds its way into their pages. This ought to encourage our men of science. They have a larger audience, and a wider sympathy than they are perhaps aware of; and however disheartening the general diffusion of smatterings of a number of subjects, and the almost equally general indifference to profound knowledge in any, among their own countrymen, may be, they may rest assured that not a fact they may discover, nor a good experiment they may make, but is instantly repeated, verified, and commented upon in Germany, and, we may add too, in Italy. We wish the obligation were mutual. Here, whole branches of continental discovery are unstudied, and indeed almost unknown, even by name.

It is in vain to conceal the melancholy truth. We are fast dropping behind. In mathematics we have long since drawn the rein, and given over a hopeless race. In chemistry the case is not much better. Who can tell us anything of the Sulfosalts? Who will explain to us the laws of Isomorphism? Nay, who among us has even verified Thenard's experiments on the oxygenated acids, Oersted's and Berzelius's on the radicals of the earths, – Balard's and Serrulas's on the combinations of Brome, – and a hundred other splendid trains of research in that fascinating science? Nor need we stop here. There are, indeed, few sciences which would not furnish matter for similar remark. The causes are at once obvious and deep-seated; but this is not the place to discuss them.[66]

A dismal picture, if true, and Herschel's plaintive cry has the note of despair and of defeat in it. Its effect upon those who might be expected to do something about the low state of English science was nil. There were, undoubtedly, some other Fellows of the Royal Society who agreed with Herschel, but what could these isolated individuals do? There must have been members of the public who shared Herschel's concern, but they, too, were powerless to act in the face of general apathy. If anything were to be done, what was required was not a post-mortem but a cry to arms. No sad and polite preface would do – there must be a thunderclap, an earthquake, and whatever other violent effects an author could produce if lethargy were to give way to reform.

In 1830 such a work was published. Its author was Charles Babbage, Lucasian Professor of Mathematics at Cambridge, and the instigator, with Herschel, of the reform of English mathematical notation. Babbage's boiling-point was notoriously low, his skill as a polemicist almost unmatched, and, he felt, his cause was just.[67] The combination of these factors led to the production of a work with the misleadingly mild title of *Reflections on the Decline of Science in England* which had the desired effect of calling general attention to the state of English science.

Babbage, often without reflection, flailed about him with a right good will. Very little escaped his notice and the bludgeon of his pen. The Government was assailed because it did not honour scientists with titles as it did soldiers and sailors. It was also attacked because it failed to provide financial support in the form of pensions. John Dalton, Babbage pointed out, had to teach school in order to live, whereas a person who had made the contribution to science that Dalton had, would have been freed from such financial worries in another country.[68] The public was accused of being indifferent, if not hostile, to science. The universities were bluntly shown the errors of their ways. The Royal Society, finally, was treated to a searching criticism in which few aspects of it were spared.

From a scathing attack on the non-productive members who used their appellation of F.R.S. for personal or professional gain to an outright accusation of dishonesty directed at the President and Secretary, Babbage raked the Royal Society from stem to stern.[69]

Babbage's work could not be ignored. Letters to *The Times* signed by 'F.R.S.' and others debated Babbage's points publicly. The President and the Secretary of the Royal Society, Davies Gilbert and P. M. Roget, were obliged to answer Babbage's charges in the *Philosophical Magazine*.[70] Sir David Brewster called the attention of the literary public to the situation in science in a laudatory review of Babbage's book in the *Quarterly Review*, adding his experience in Scotland to Babbage's.[71]

There is no doubt that some of Babbage's missiles hit the mark but his blanket condemnation of English science was not justified by the facts. The anti-declinarians (as Brewster christened them) made less noise than Babbage but they did serve to restore some balance to the argument. Faraday was one who felt that Babbage had gone too far although he did not enter into controversy directly with him. What he did do was to publish, at his own expense,[72] a remarkable pamphlet challenging Babbage's conclusions. This pamphlet was the work of G. Moll of Utrecht who took serious issue with the idea of the decline of science in England and attempted to show the other side of the coin. Faraday wrote a short introduction and, in spite of his disclaimer that he was not taking sides, it seems reasonable to assume that he was in general agreement with Moll. If this assumption be granted, then *On the Alleged Decline of Science in England, by a Foreigner*[73] provides a valuable insight into Faraday's ideas of the mutual relations of scientists and the society of which they were a part.

Moll attacked both Babbage and Herschel. Where Herschel had suggested that English chemistry was rapidly declining, Moll pointed out that English chemists, namely Faraday and Wollaston, had made significant advances in electromagnetism which they chose to consider a part (and an important part) of chemistry. Rather than illustrating its decline, this seemed to show the vigour of English chemistry.[74] Moll did not stop here, however, and his further pursuit of the argument must have pleased Faraday who considered himself a natural philosopher, not a physicist (a word he could not abide) or a chemist or any other kind of -ist. In France, which Herschel and Babbage seemed to admire so much, there was far more specialization than in England. A mathematician there knew mathematics and nothing else; chemists stuck closely to chemistry and so on.[75] In England, however, Moll stated, the case was entirely different. Wollaston, for example, had been an expert chemist, a more than competent astronomer and an investigator of physical optics. Babbage and Herschel themselves were living examples of how a keen mind could investigate a number of fields without losing any of its power.

The desire that Babbage felt to have men of scientific attainments appointed to high governmental posts met only with scorn from Moll. Some of the men of science who did hold such positions did so because of their high rank, not because of their scientific attainments. Alexander von Humboldt, for example, was a baron by birth and, because of this, held the post of Chamberlain to the King of Prussia.[76] But, Moll asked of Babbage, did he really feel that the post of chamberlain, no matter to whom, was really a post of honour? We need have no doubt of Faraday's answer; he had, after all, served as chamberlain to a prince of science and left us in no doubt as to his opinion of the post.[77] As for the great French scientists who had been ennobled by Napoleon, had they really been honoured? Moll's indictment here deserves to be cited for there are still those who feel that Napoleon had been a great patron of science.

> With the Marquis La Place [Moll wrote] the Counts Carnot and Chaptal, and the Baron Cuvier, the case is widely different. When Napoleon abolished the Republic, he endeavoured to strengthen his new government by the co-operation of all the men of talent whom he could bring over to his party. With this view La Place was created a minister of the interior; but so far from its being found that a man 'does not make a worse minister because he has directed an observatory, or had added by his discoveries to the extent of our knowledge of animated nature', the author of the 'Méchanique Céleste' proved quite inadequate to the task, and after a few months' trial it became absolutely necessary to give him a successor. He was then made, not President as Mr Babbage erroneously states, but Chancellor to that senate whose duty it was to watch over the conservation of the liberties of the French people. That the office of keeping the liberties of France, under the reign of Napoleon, was a sinecure, need scarcely be told; it required only in the chancellor the necessary abnegation to put his signature indiscriminately under any decree, however unjust or oppressive. Indeed the chancellor of the senate was in fact its secretary. How these functions can be accounted *honourable* I am at a loss to conceive – profitable they certainly were; for the salary of the chancellor was, I believe, 36,000 francs, exclusive of the donation on foreign and conquered countries, with which the Emperor used to reward his faithful followers. Wealth and dignities, acquired at such a price, cannot be objects of envy in the eyes of a philosopher.[78]

Faraday's opinion on this matter was expressed in the strongest terms in a letter he wrote in 1843 to his friend Dr Andrews. 'I have always felt', he stated, 'that there is something degrading in offering rewards for intellectual exertion, and that societies or academies, or even kings and emperors, should mingle in the matter does not remove the degradation, for the feeling which is hurt is a point above their condition, and belongs to the respect which a man owes to himself.'[79] And in another, later, letter to Lord Wrottesley who had asked him what course Government should follow, Faraday replied that 'a Government *for its own sake* [should] honour the men who do honour and service to the country. I refer now to honours only, not to beneficial rewards, of such honours I think there are none.'[80] It is inconceivable that a Government could have used Faraday as Napoleon did Laplace and, from his laudatory remarks, could have used Babbage. Faraday's sense of honour was far too high for this. It is well illustrated by the famous incident in 1835 when Faraday was asked by Lord Melbourne to call upon him in regard to the granting of a pension. It was reported that at the interview, Melbourne referred to the practice of granting pensions to literary and scientific persons as 'a piece of gross humbug'.[81] Faraday thereupon excused himself and returned to the Royal Institution. The reports of this event became rather embarrassing to Melbourne and he finally felt it necessary to apologize for his hasty words. Faraday accepted both the apology and the pension for he had clearly made his point; *he* was honouring the Government, not vice versa.[82]

In all important respects Faraday agreed with Moll and could be listed as an 'anti-declinarian'. He was certainly treated as such by the 'declinarians'. In a scathing review in *The Edinburgh Journal of Science*, David Brewster set out to demolish Moll's argument. He also attacked Faraday personally for what he considered little less than treason to the cause of science.[83] The purpose of Babbage's book and of Brewster's strong support of it, was to effect reforms in English institutions and particularly in the Royal Society, the 'guardian of British science'. Both Babbage and Brewster clearly felt very strongly that such reforms could be justified only by showing how the whole of English science was declining because of the decline of the Royal Society. It was this overall condemnation with which Faraday could not agree and which had led him to publish Moll's pamphlet. In spite of Brewster's attack, however, Faraday was to be counted on the side of the reformers when the attack was focused specifically on the Royal Society. He obviously did not feel that the illness of the institution had infected the body of English science.

The attack launched by Babbage against the Royal Society began by accusing the President and Secretary of the Royal Society of having falsified the minutes of the Council on at least one occasion.[84] The charge was pressed home and Davies Gilbert, P.R.S., found himself in a most awkward position. He could resign but this would open the way to a successful campaign by the reformers and the decline of the influence of a large group within the Royal Society. The basic issue between the two parties was a simple one; should the Royal Society be run by those who were professional scientists, who contributed actively to the advance of science and who would attempt to shape the Royal Society according to the professional demands of the scientist, or should the Royal Society continue to be guided by the amateurs whose interest in science was peripheral and who could not be counted upon to throw their weight behind serious scientific proposals? Davies Gilbert represented the amateurs, and the professionals began to sense victory as Gilbert's position rapidly became untenable. When *The Times* joined the *Phil. Mag.* and other organs of opinion in demanding some kind of justification of the actions of the President, he began to lay out his route of retreat.[85] He made overtures to H.R.H. the Duke of Sussex offering him his support and the support of the Council if His Royal Highness wished to assume the Presidency of the Royal Society. This was done without the knowledge of the Council and reveals the confidence Mr Gilbert had in his support amongst the Fellows at large.[86]

The party of reform was headed by Babbage, but counted Faraday among its supporters. When the reformers took the offensive, Faraday was prominent in executing the moves intended to bring victory. At a special meeting of the Council, occasioned by rumours of Gilbert's overtures to H.R.H., the reformers were able to force through a resolution to the effect that 'the Officers and Council should be selected from among such members of the Society as are, by their acquaintance with the condition and interests of Science, best qualified to discharge such offices'.[87] This was clearly aimed at the amateurs. In order to exclude any nominee of the President, it was moved by Mr Herschel and seconded by Mr Faraday, that a list of fifty names be drawn up so that the Fellows would have a real choice for members of the Council and for President instead of merely approving the list drawn up by the Council itself. This, too, was passed; the joy of the reformers can only be imagined when the list was found not to contain the name of the Duke of Sussex. The party of the amateurs appeared to be totally beaten and the path of reform seemed smooth.

Davies Gilbert was not willing to concede defeat and soon found a way around the various resolutions passed by the reformers. According to the statutes of the Royal Society, none of the actions of the reformers had any legal standing whatsoever and so Mr Gilbert very calmly renewed his campaign in favour of His Royal Highness. The reformers were taken aback by this manœuvre and immediately began a campaign to elect John Herschel President. Faraday signed the requisition in Herschel's favour and undoubtedly voted for him. The campaign, however, was lost by Babbage. He had managed Herschel's candidacy, had solicited support, and seemingly had victory in his grasp. In fact, he was so confident of success that he wrote to a number of Fellows who resided some distance from London that they need not come to London since Herschel's election did not seem in doubt.[88] The vote was 119 for the Duke of Sussex and 111 for Herschel. The cause of reform had failed.

The result of this failure was the creation of the British Association for the Advancement of Science in 1831. The members of the reform group were charter members and they set out to create an association run for professionals by professionals. Thus, the political manœuvring and the social prestige that were to be found in the Royal Society were kept to a minimum. The purpose of the association was to facilitate communication between professionals, call the needs of scientists to the attention of Government, and serve as a powerful spokesman for British science.

Despite the defeat of his hopes for reform of the Royal Society, Faraday did not (as did Babbage) cut off his relations with it. He faithfully observed the desire of the Royal Society that its members publish their papers only (or at least first) in the *Philosophical Transactions*. Nevertheless, he did withdraw somewhat from involvement in the affairs of the Society. In 1832 he respectfully declined the nomination to the Council, although he was to accept election in 1833 and 1834.[89] His attitude was made clear in a letter to Carlo Matteucci in 1843.

> I think you are aware [he wrote] that I have not attended at the Royal Society, either meetings or council, for some years. Ill health is one reason, and another that I do not like the present constitution of it, and want to restrict it to scientific men. As these my opinions are not acceptable, I have withdrawn from any management in it (still sending scientific communications if I discover anything I think worthy). This of course deprives me of power there.[90]

In 1857, he was offered the presidency of the Royal Society, but by that time, even though most of the reforms which he had so long desired had been made, he knew the post to be beyond his strength.

Although he was a charter member of the British Association, Faraday did not play a prominent role in either its organization or its development. He attended the meetings when he felt able to or when this would not interfere with his work. The glimpses we catch of him there are characteristic of him, and show that he went to participate as a scientist, and not to become involved in the administration or politics of science. In 1837, for example, he presided over the Chemistry Section on one day, and on another, together with Sir William Rowan Hamilton led an assault upon the use of the term 'atom' in chemistry.[91] Hamilton presented a straightforward Boscovichean attack on material atoms and Faraday's concurrence was his first public acknowledgment of his adherence to this theory. At the same meeting, he had the opportunity of speaking with Andrew Crosse who claimed to be able to create insects from nothing but a saline solution and an electric current. As Faraday wrote to Schoenbein, 'I do not think anybody believes in them here except perhaps himself and the mass of wonder-lovers. I was said in the English papers to have proved the truth of his statement, but I immediately contradicted the matter publicly and should have thought that nobody who could judge in the matter would have suspected me of giving evidence to the thing for a moment.'[92] Nevertheless, Faraday could defend Crosse. 'It is but fair of me to say', he continued, 'that in conversation with Mr Crosse I was very much pleased with him and with the readiness with which he received my critical remarks. As regards the cristallization supposed as real he was lugged into view and must not be charged with having pressed himself forward. He is in fact a very modest man but has been dragged into an unkind situation.'[93]

In 1848, it was Faraday's manipulative skill that led him to take the floor. Dr Plücker of Germany had read a paper on the relation of magnetic and crystalline forces, but much of it seemed to have been lost on the audience.

> Prof Faraday [*The Athenaeum* reported] contrived to convert two raw potatoes into representatives of the poles of an electro-magnet, and by a slice of another, with a quill stuck through it, represented the magnetic or diamagnetic crystal with its optic axes – and thus contrived to convey a distinct idea of the exact results of Prof. Plücker's discoveries of the relations of the optical axes of magnetic and diamagnetic crystals and the changes of distance to the nature and laws of the attractions and repulsions exhibited under the several circumstances detailed.[94]

Why Faraday had three raw potatoes with him the reporter for *The Athenaeum* did not see fit to recount, but there was no doubt of his ability to make a complex point clear by using them.

Faraday's participation in the British Association was of this nature. It was sporadic and purely personal. He represented no special interests and pleaded no special causes. When he attended, he spoke with others, raised a point when one occurred to him, and then retired into the background.

He took no part in the increasing financial activities of the Association; he does not appear to have been consulted for advice when the B.A.A.S. served as a consultant to the Government. He had no desire to become involved in the politics of science.

4. Faraday and Politics

Faraday's unwillingness to play an active part in the internal politics of either the Royal Society or the British Association was merely a reflection of his general lack of interest in politics of all kinds. Although his political views were firm, there is no evidence that he ever, like Babbage, actively worked to implement them.

Not surprisingly in a firm believer in rendering unto Caesar that which was Caesar's, and in the essential frailty of the human race, Faraday was a Tory. A man's lot in life was what God granted him and Faraday was always suspicious of attempts to interfere here with the Divine Will. His reaction to the wave of revolutions that swept over Europe in 1848 was typical. They were not, for Faraday, an expression of a deep desire for liberty and freedom from tyranny. They were, rather, the result of man's basest passions.

> What a delight it is to think that you are quietly and philosophically at work in the pursuit of science. . . . [he wrote to his friend, Schoenbein in 1848] rather than fighting amongst the crowd of black passions and motives that seem now a days to urge men every where into action. What incredible scenes every where, what unworthy motives ruled for the moment, under high sounding phrases, and at the last what disgusting revolutions. Happy are we here who have thus far been kept from these things and hope to be so preserved in the future.[95]

To Auguste de la Rive he pointed out, 'For me, who never meddle with politics and who think very little of them as one of the games of life, it seems sad that Scientific men should be so disturbed by them and so the progress of pure [science and] philosophy be much and so often disturbed by the passions of men.'[96]

Faraday did not only object to revolutions but even to the ultimate political form at which the revolutions of the nineteenth century aimed. The only republic of which he approved was the republic of science. 'When science is a republic, then it gains;' he wrote to John Tyndall in 1850, 'and though I am no republican in other matters, I am in that.'[97] Even the great republic across the Atlantic which had seemed to prove that republicanism was not inconsistent with law and order failed to impress him. Where his colleagues, men such as Babbage, Herschel, Lyell, entered passionately into the debate in the 1860's over the ordeal of the Union and the freeing of the slaves, Faraday merely saw a necessary chastisement of American exuberance.

> As with you, so with us [he wrote to Miss Moore just as the United States plunged into Civil War] the harvest is a continual joy: all seems so prosperous and happy. What a contrast such a state is to that of our friends the Americans, for notwithstanding all their blustering and arrogance, selfwilledness, and nonsense, I cannot help but feel drawn towards them by their affinity to us. The whole nation seems to me as a little impetuous, ignorant, headstrong child under punishment, and getting a little sobering experience, quite necessary for its future existence as a decent well-behaved nation among nations.[98]

Such expressions of political point of view were extremely rare. They reveal only how Faraday viewed the world of politics, not what he did in it. There is no evidence to indicate that he ever did anything. He was a loyal subject of his Queen who frowned upon any activity that threatened to upset the even tenor of life anywhere. His research and duties at the Royal Institution took all his time. Furthermore, in just those years when the political climate of Europe was becoming ever more torrid, Faraday's health failed. Even had he wished to he could not have played an active part on the British political scene. Indeed, from about 1839 until the time of his death, the state of his health was the determining factor regulating his research as well as his other activities. Although he had suffered from giddiness in previous years, he underwent a serious breakdown in 1839 from which he never fully recovered.

From 1839, Faraday seems to have been plagued with almost constant and severe headaches. In December of 1839, he went to Brighton under the orders of Dr Latham to try and rid himself of one.[99] Nearly a year later, he wrote to Babbage that he was leaving town again for Brighton 'and hope to get rid of a headache there which as some people say I have *enjoyed* for the last four months'.[100] His condition steadily deteriorated. In the summer of 1841, he and Mrs Faraday went to Switzerland where he hoped to regain his health. There he appeared to improve somewhat for Mrs Faraday reported that he often took daily walks of thirty miles and once did forty-five miles 'which I protested against his doing again though he was very little the worse for it'.[101] Still, he was subject to fits of giddiness and failing memory that prevented him from doing much. In the spring of 1843 he was still lamenting to Schoenbein the poor state of his mental faculties. 'I must begin to write you a letter, though feeling, as I

do, in the midst of one of my low, nervous attacks, with memory so
treacherous, that I cannot remember the beginning of a sentence to the
end – hand disobedient to the will, that I cannot form the letters, bent
with a certain crampness, so I hardly know whether I shall bring it to a
close with consistency or not.'[102]

By 1844 his condition improved enough to permit him to begin serious
work again. After almost five years of constant physical debility, the
return of comparative health was greeted by Faraday with both joy and a
consciousness of its ephemeral nature. His leanings towards isolation from
the world were reinforced by his awareness of the delicate balance of his
condition. His mental resources must be carefully husbanded. To spend
them in the world would mean to lose them in the laboratory. Faraday had
no choice. He must now sever *all* his social connexions except those which
he owed to the Royal Institution. As he withdrew entirely from society,
he began again to discern the path that led to new discoveries. In 1845 he
was to begin another series of Experimental Researches which were to be
as revolutionary as those completed in 1839.

References

1. Henry Bence Jones, *The Royal Institution: Its Founder and Its First Professors*
(London, 1871), 121.

2. Ibid., 258 ff.

3. Warner MSS., Faraday to Abbott, Geneva, 5 September 1814, B.J., *1*,
153.

4. Warner MSS., Abbott to Faraday, London, Sunday 20 November 1814.

5. Ibid.

6. 'Resignation of Professor Brande', *Proc. R.I., 1* (1851–4), 168.

7. Bence Jones, op. cit., 310–11.

8. See 'Davy's laboratory notebook' in manuscript at the Royal Institution.
From the most superficial perusal of this volume it is obvious that Faraday was
carrying on a large-scale business in chemical analysis. In particular, he ran
literally hundreds of analyses of the purity of nitrates, submitted by commercial
interests, and there can be little doubt that both Faraday and the Royal Institution were paid handsomely for this work.

9. Faraday to Dr Lardner, R.I., 6 October 1827, B.J., *1*, 405–6.

10. R.I. MSS., Faraday to John Leighton, Esq., R.I., 1 December 1862.

11. I.E.E., Faraday's Common Place Book, 'Lectures on Oratory by Mr B. H.
Smart', 177 ff.

12. Warner MSS., Faraday to B. Abbott, 1 June 1813. These letters are also
published in B.J., *1*, 65 ff., but since B.J. did not follow the originals exactly,
I have preferred to quote directly from the manuscripts.

13. See below for a more detailed discussion of what is meant in specific educational terms.

14. See, for example, the little red book at the R.I., entitled *Helps and Aids* in which Faraday recounts his successful detection of the source of a bad smell.

15. Warner MSS., Faraday to Abbott, 1 June 1813.

16. Ibid.

17. Ibid.

18. Warner MSS., Faraday to Abbott, 4 June 1813.

19. Ibid.

20. Ibid.

21. Ibid.

22. Warner MSS., Faraday to Abbott, 18 June 1813.

23. Ibid.

24. Ibid.

25. B.J., *1*, 385.

26. R.I., Faraday MSS., 'Friday evenings, Magnetism-Arago, Jan. 26, 1827', 227[A].

I have here taken the liberty of turning Faraday's notes into a continuous paragraph. No violence has been done to the meaning, although the inverted commas are not, strictly speaking, legitimate.

27. This is probably a mistake for John Fuller who was a faithful and generous supporter of the Royal Institution. It was he who endowed the chair in chemistry for Faraday which he occupied from 1833 until his death.

28. Warner MSS., B. Abbott, 'Jottings from Memory in reference to my dear and deceased friend, M. Faraday'. The lecture in question took place on 14 February 1834.

29. For a list of these lectures (as well as the rest of Faraday's works) see Alan E. Jeffreys, *Michael Faraday, a List of his Lectures and Published Writings* (London, 1960).

30. 'Thoughts on Ray-vibrations', in *Exp. Res., 3*, 447.

31. R.I., Faraday MSS., 'An account of Mr Brown's discovery of active molecules existing in solid bodies, either organic or inorganic', 13 February 1829.

32. Arkiv, Akademia Nauki, U.S.S.R., Leningrad, Faraday to Dr Jacobi, R.I., 17 August 1839.

33. Frederick von Raumer, *England in 1835, being a series of Letters written to friends in Germany* (Philadelphia, 1836), 230.

34. [Lady Holland], 'Michael Faraday', *The St. Paul's Magazine, 6* (1870), 293.

Not all Faraday's auditors were so enthusiastic. Alexander Bain in his *Autobiography* (London, 1904), 128, called Faraday's lecture on the magnetic property of oxygen 'confused and unintelligible'.

35. See above, Chapter One.

36. R.I., Faraday MSS., *A Class Book, for the Reception of Mental Exercises Instituted July, 1818*, 'On Imagination and Judgement'.

37. M. Faraday, 'Observations on Mental Education', in *Exp. Res. in Chem. and Phys.*, 463.

38. Ibid., 465.

39. Ibid., 466.

40. Ibid., 469.

41. Ibid., 472.

42. Ibid., 473.

43. L. Pearce Williams, 'Science, Education and the French Revolution', *Isis*, *44* (1953), 311.

44. M. Faraday, 'Observations . . .', 474.

45. Ibid., 485.

46. Ibid.

47. *Proc. R.I.*, *2* (1854-8), 555 ff.

48. *Parl. Pap.*, *21* (1864). Faraday's evidence was given on 18 November 1862, and appears in volume 4 (of volume 21), pt. 2, 375-82.

49. M. Faraday, 'On Wheatstone's Electric Telegraph's relation to Science (being an argument in favour of the full recognition of Science as a branch of Education)', *Proc. R.I.*, *2* (1854-8), 555.

50. Ibid., 559.

51. *Parl. Pap.*, *21* (1864), volume 4, pt. 2, 375.

52. Ibid., 376.

53. Ibid., 377.

54. Ibid., 378.

55. Ibid.

56. The R.I. has most of Faraday's notes for his courses. The course on 'Earth, Air, Fire and Water' began on 8 April 1837; the course on domestic philosophy began in April 1850.

57. When Faraday exhibited the Leyden jar to his audience in 1858, he repeated Musschenbroek's remark that he would not take another shock from it even for the kingdom of France. The Orleans Pretender to the French throne, the Count of Paris, thereupon tapped his neighbour, the Prince of Wales, on the shoulder, clearly indicating that *he* would if it could win him his kingdom. See Sir Frederick Pollock, *Personal Remembrances of Sir Frederick Pollock* (2 vols., London, 1887), *2*, 68.

58. *The Chemical History of a Candle*. Put into Basic English by Phillis Rossiter (London, 1933). See Jeffreys, op. cit., item 464 (1933).

59. For the various English editions, see Jeffreys, op. cit., item 457. I have used the third edition (London, 1861), entitled *Lectures on the Various Forces of Matter*.

60. Ibid., 2.

61. Ibid., 4.

62. Ibid., 49.

63. Ibid., 111.

64. Ibid., 34.

65. For Faraday's rather peculiar views of the nature of force, see below, Chapter Ten.

66. John F. W. Herschel, *Treatise on Sound, Encyclopaedia Metropolitana* cited in Charles Babbage, *Reflections on the Decline of Science in England and some of its causes* (London, 1830), vii.

67. There is a touch of the pathetic in Babbage's life. He began brilliantly as a mathematician and devised a calculating machine that was an ancestor of modern

computers. He never finished constructing it, although he and the Government both poured a fortune into it. In his later years, he spent a good part of his time trying (unsuccessfully) to rid the streets of London of sources of noise which disturbed his concentration. He specifically loathed German bands which seem to have been particularly plentiful in the 1840's and 1850's. His correspondence in the British Museum manuscript collection is filled with drafts of angry letters to various magistrates urging upon them the absolute necessity of abolishing these bands forever. He died a bitter old man who felt that he had not received his just due either from his country or his colleagues. See Charles Babbage, *Passages from the Life of a Philosopher* (London, 1864).

68. Dalton did get a pension from the Government later and this was due, in part, to Babbage's efforts on his behalf.

69. For a more detailed account of Babbage's attack on the Royal Society, see L. Pearce Williams, 'The Royal Society and the Founding of the British Association for the Advancement of Science', *Notes and Records of the Royal Society, 16* (1961), 221.

70. Ibid.

71. *The Quarterly Review, 43* (1830), 305 ff.

72. Faraday to C. Schoenbein, 8 April 1839, in *The Letters of Faraday and Schoenbein, 1836-62*, edited by Georg W. A. Kahlbaum and Francis V. Darbishire (Basle and London, 1899), 62.

73. (London, 1831).

74. Ibid., 4.

75. Ibid., 14. This is a bit unfair. Laplace, after all had worked with Lavoisier on calorimetry, Ampère was more than a narrow mathematician, and Coulomb had certainly not restricted himself to civil engineering.

76. Ibid., 15.

77. See Chapter One, where he had expressed himself so eloquently to Abbott on his post as valet to Davy.

78. Ibid., 21.

79. Faraday to Dr Andrews, 2 February 1843, cited in J. H. Gladstone, *Michael Faraday* (2nd ed., London, 1873), 110. The original is in the Science Museum, S. Kensington.

80. Ibid., 111.

81. An account of the interview (probably slightly fictionalized) was given in *Frazer's Magazine, 12* (1835), 707.

82. The various letters that passed between the parties concerned are printed in B.J., *2*, 57 ff.

83. [D. Brewster], 'Observations on a Pamphlet entitled, "On the Alleged Decline of Science in England, By a Foreigner, London, 1831, Pp. 33", Accompanied by a Preface by M. Faraday, Esq., F.R.S., etc.', *The Edin. J. of Sci., 5* (1831), 343.

84. L. P. Williams, 'The Royal Society . . .', 226 ff.

85. Ibid.

86. Ibid., 228.

87. Minutes of the Council of the Royal Society, 11 November 1830. Cited with the permission of the Royal Society.

88. B.M.Add.MS. 37185, f. 429. George Harvey, F.R.S. to Charles Babbage, Plymouth, 3 January 1831.

89. Printed Minutes of the Council of R.S., 33 and 63.

90. Faraday to C. Matteucci, 18 February 1843, B.J., 2, 176. See also Faraday to W. R. Grove, 21 December 1842, ibid., 175.

91. *The Athenaeum*, 1837, 747.

92. Faraday to Schoenbein, 21 September 1837, in Kahlbaum and Darbishire, op. cit., 33.

93. Ibid.

94. *The Athenaeum*, 1848, 836.

95. Faraday to Schoenbein, R.I., 15 December 1848, Kahlbaum and Darbishire, op. cit., 182.

96. Bib. univ. et pub. de Génève, MS. 2316, 88 A4, f. 65, Faraday to A. de la Rive, R.I., 9 July 1849.

97. Faraday to John Tyndall, R.I., 19 November 1850, B.J., 2, 276.

98. Faraday to Miss Moore, The Green, Hampton Court, 14 August 1861, B.J., 2, 448.

99. R.I. MSS., Faraday to E. Magrath, 23 December 1839.

100. B.M.Add.MS. 37191, f. 484, Faraday to Babbage, 2 November 1840.

101. R.I. MSS., Mrs Faraday to E. Magrath, 14 August 1841, B.J., 2, 153 ff.

102. Faraday to Schoenbein, 16 May 1843, Kahlbaum and Darbishire, op. cit., 109.

CHAPTER NINE

The Correlation of Forces

1. The Theory of the Voltaic Pile

In 1845 Faraday confessed that he had 'long held an opinion, almost amounting to conviction, . . . that the various forms under which the forces of matter are made manifest have one common origin' (2146). His work on the nature of electricity in the 1830's had served to strengthen his conviction for in these researches, especially those dealing with electrochemistry, the conversion of electricity into chemical affinity and vice versa had, Faraday thought, established this principle on firm experimental foundations. That the convertibility of forces included *all* the manifestations of electricity, magnetism, heat, and light was quite explicitly stated by him in 1838 in the Fifteenth Series of the *Experimental Researches* devoted to the 'character and direction of the electric force of the Gymnotus' (1749 ff.). There Faraday suggested that an exhausted electric eel might literally be recharged by passing a current through him in a direction opposite to the one released by the fish.

> We have the analogy [he wrote] in relation to heat and magnetism. Seebeck taught us how to commute heat into electricity; and Peltier has more lately given us the strict converse of this, and shown us how to convert the electricity into heat, including both its relation of hot and cold. Oersted showed how we were to convert electric into magnetic forces, and I had the delight of adding the other member of the full relation, by reacting back again and converting magnetic into electric forces. So perhaps in these organs, where nature has provided the apparatus by means of which the animal can exert and convert nervous into electric force, we may be able, possessing in that point of view a power far beyond that of the fish itself, to reconvert the electric into the nervous force (1790).

From the convertibility of forces it was almost inevitable that Faraday pass to the concept of the inherent unity of force which manifested itself as electricity, magnetism, and so on. This concept, as has been shown, had long guided his researches but it was not a conviction shared by everyone who worked in science. There were many electrochemists, for example, who could perceive no conversion of electricity into chemical affinity and who followed Volta in preferring an electromotive force, quite independent of chemical affinity, created by the contact of heterogeneous conductors. Then, too, there were men of some repute, like Robert Hare of Philadelphia, who found Faraday's ideas so strange as to be incomprehensible.

In the heat of the creative research which occupied Faraday from 1831 to 1839, there was little he could do about persuading his colleagues of the soundness of his views. He was too hot on the track of the unity of electrical phenomena to be drawn off by the false scent of controversy. Yet, if his views were to gain acceptance, these difficulties had to be removed. Having reached his primary goal in 1839 of reducing electrostatics, electrochemistry, and electrodynamics to one, general, concept he could then turn to this problem and give it his attention. Indeed, the failure of his health and the severe effect of overwork upon his mind made it possible for him to do little else. For the time being, the brilliant flashes of insight which had spurred him on unflaggingly were no more. From 1839 until 1845 he added little new to the factual body of science. What he did do was clarify his own thoughts and examine critically those of others. This period is, therefore, by no means barren of interest to the historian. By responding to the proponents of the contact theory of the voltaic pile, he cleared away a good deal of underbrush that had slowed down progress in this field. By answering critics such as Hare, Faraday made his most private thoughts on the nature of matter and force public. One might not agree with him, but at least the foundations of his theory were revealed so that no one could again complain, as Hare had done, of confusion.

The controversy about the origin of the current in the voltaic pile went back to Volta's original announcement of his invention. There was something about a *mouvement perpetuel*, even of an imponderable fluid, which led at least some investigators to question Volta's analysis and to suggest that the current was chemical in origin. It was not until 1828, however, that the contact theory was subjected to an intensive and comprehensive criticism. The attack was launched by Faraday's friend, Auguste de la Rive, and continued in a number of articles published in the *Annales de chimie et de physique,* the *Mémoires de la Société de physique et d'histoire naturelle de Génève* and the *Philosophical Magazine.*[1] These articles had called forth the defenders of the contact theory in Germany and Italy who found it possible to uphold their hypothesis in the face of de la Rive's objections. The reason was simple; de la Rive was passionately convinced of the correctness of his views and adduced many experimental facts in their favour. But, his view of electrochemical action did not rule out the contact theory and it was possible to poke holes in his argument which seriously weakened his case.[2] Thus, in spite of de la Rive's whole-hearted advocacy and not inconsiderable talents, the chemical theory of the pile was still rejected by a number of quite eminent scientists in the 1830's.

The publication of Faraday's Fifth, Seventh and Eighth Series of *Experimental Researches* dramatically altered the relative equality between the two schools of thought on the origin of electricity in the voltaic cell. In these papers, Faraday had not only referred the electrical effects of the pile to chemical combinations, he had shown a direct quantitative connexion between electricity and chemical affinity. The second law of electrochemistry, by revealing the *equivalence* between the quantity of current passed and the chemical affinities associated with the substances deposited upon the electrodes, left no room for the contact theory. Everything was accounted for chemically and there seemed to be no reason to assume a special electromotive force resulting from the contact of dissimilar metals to explain the pile's action. These researches were decisive for Faraday. As he wrote to de la Rive, 'For a long time I had not made up my mind: then the facts of definite electrochemical action made me take part with the supporters of the chemical theory.'[3]

The proponents of the contact theory recognized the challenge to their position and rose to meet it. Marianini[4] specifically directed his fire at Faraday while Gustav Theodor Fechner,[5] one of the first to apply Ohm's law to electric circuits, aimed his arguments at both Faraday and de la Rive. Both Marianini and Fechner attacked the experimental basis of the chemical theory. Instance after instance was cited which seemed incapable of explanation by an appeal to chemical action.

There were, to be sure, many curious facts that appeared to be impossible to explain upon the supposition of chemical action. One may serve here simply to indicate the kind of phenomenon that puzzled people. If one took a simple voltaic cell, composed of an electrolyte and two electrodes made from the *same* metal, there was no current when the circuit was closed. If one of the electrodes, however, were lifted from the cell, dried, and then plunged back into the cell a current was created. How, the proponents of the contact theory demanded, could a chemical reaction explain this? The chemical nature of the two electrodes remained the same so there should not be a current. The explanation provided by the contact theory was hardly a satisfactory one, but it was, at least, an explanation.

According to this view the act of exposing the electrode to the air and then drying it gave it a surface condition different from its mate. From this heterogeneity of surfaces arose the electromotive force which created the electric current.[6]

Since the critics of the chemical theory were concerned entirely with the experiments which this theory seemed incapable of explaining, Faraday's answer was also an experimental one. In introducing his paper, Faraday felt it necessary to warn the reader that he was in for a barrage of facts, not a theoretical discussion.

> I venture to hope [he wrote] that the experimental results and arguments which have been thus gathered may be useful to science. I fear the detail will be tedious, but that is a necessary consequence of the state of the subject. The contact theory has long had possession of men's minds, is sustained by a great weight of authority, and for years had almost undisputed sway in some parts of Europe. If it be an error, it can only be rooted out by a great amount of forcible experimental evidence; a fact sufficiently clear to my mind by the circumstance, that De la Rive's papers have not already convinced the workers upon this subject. Hence the reason why I have thought it needful to add my further testimony to his and that of others, entering into detail and multiplying facts in a proportion far beyond any which would have been required for the proof and promulgation of a new scientific truth. . . . In so doing I may occasionally be only enlarging, yet then I hope strengthening, what others, and especially De la Rive, have done (1799).

But, although it was facts to which Faraday was to appeal, it was theory which convinced him that the contact theory *must* be wrong. In August of 1839, just as he began to collect the mass of experimental data with which he intended to overwhelm his opponents, he noted in his *Diary*:

> By the great argument that no power can ever be evolved without the con-sumption of an equal amount of the same or some other power, there is *no creation of power*; but contact would be such a creation. In all other cases of a constant evolution there is a constant consumption of something, as in
>> Chemical evolution
>> Thermo evolution
>> Magneto evolution
>> Animal evolution
>> Friction evolution [5112].

Such a position came naturally to one who felt that there were, basically, just two forces which manifested themselves in various ways but whose quantity remained forever the same.[7] To have expected the proponents of the contact theory to have surrendered merely because of this metaphysical belief would have been too much, as Faraday knew. And so, point by point, he experimentally demolished all the arguments upon which the contact theory had been based.

There is no necessity of following Faraday closely through the wealth of experimental detail that he now mustered. His purpose was clear and his experimental skill more than sufficient to permit him to obtain clear-cut and unambiguous results. He set out simply to show that in every case in which electricity was generated in a galvanic circuit, there was a chemical action.[8] In the case of the two similar electrodes cited above, Faraday was able to prove that the act of exposing and drying an electrode altered its chemical character. When iron electrodes were used, for example, a thin film of iron oxide formed upon the exposed electrode and thereby altered the chemical situation in the cell. The result was a chemical reaction which generated an electric current in full accord with the chemical theory (1826, 2049). In a similar fashion, Faraday showed that the genera-tion of an electric current was *always* accompanied by a chemical reaction in the galvanic circuit.

The correlation of these two elements might have seemed sufficient to establish the chemical theory. But, as Faraday had pointed out in his introduction, the rooting out of error required far more and intensive argument than the establishment of a new truth. For this reason, he not only defended the chemical theory but attacked the contact theory at its weakest point. This point became evident only when the attempt was made to understand the mysterious electromotive force and discover the laws of its action. Suppose that a circuit of different metals containing no substances that could act chemically upon one another were constructed. According to the contact theory, the contact of the dissimilar metals should give rise to an electromotive force. A simple metallic circuit however, does *not* give rise to a current. Faraday pounced upon this fact and its explanation by the contact theorists.

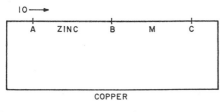

Fig. 1

It is assumed by the supporters of the contact theory [he wrote], that though the metals exert strong electromotive forces at their points of contact with each other, yet these are so balanced in a metallic circuit that no current is ever produced whatever their arrangement may be. So [in the accompanying Figure 1] if the contact force of copper and zinc is 10 →, and a third metal be produced at [M], the effect of its contacts, whatever that metal may be, with the zinc and copper at [B] and [C], will be an amount of force in the opposite direction = 10. Thus, if it were potassium, its contact force at [B] might be 5 →, but then its contact force at [C] would be ← 15 : or if it were gold, its contact force at [B] might be ← 19, but then its contact force at [C] would be 9 → (1809).

There were two aspects of this argument that Faraday attacked. In the first place, it did not seem to him to be sound philosophy to deduce an active and acting force from a situation which, regardless of the metals used (provided there was no chemical action), *always* produced *no* effect. The 'electromotive force' was, in Faraday's eyes, a pure assumption for which there was no evidence at all in this experiment (1809). But, suppose the electromotive force did exist and that this strange and constant balance of electromotive forces were only coincidence. Should it not then follow that such balances could be used to determine quantitatively the relative electromotive forces generated by the contact of dissimilar metals in the same way that today the balance of a Wheatstone bridge may be used to determine relative resistances? Faraday's demolition of the contact theory depended upon this line of argument for he was able to call attention to the protean nature of the electromotive force. It never seemed to act the same way twice. The Sixteenth and Seventeenth Series were liberally sprinkled with allusions to this fact. One such passage must suffice here to illustrate the way in which Faraday underlined the diffi-culties inherent in the contact theory. Having just described, at some length, some of the embarrassments created for the contact theorist by substituting different substances in the galvanic circuit, he vividly con-trasted the two theories. 'The chemical philosopher . . .' he wrote, 'by a simple direct experiment, ascertains whether any of the two given sub-stances in the circuit are active chemically on each other. If they are, he expects and finds the corresponding current; if they are not, he expects and he finds no current, though the circuit be a good conductor and he look carefully for it. . . .'

Again; taking the case of iron, platina, and solution of sulphuret of potassium, there is no current; but for iron substitute zinc, and there is a powerful current. I might for zinc substitute copper, silver, tin, cadmium, bismuth, lead, and other metals; but I take zinc, because its sulphuret dissolves and is carried off by the solution, and so leaves the case in a very simple state; the fact, however, is as strong with any of the other metals. Now if the contact theory be true, and if the iron, platina, and solution of sulphuret of potassium give contacts which are in perfect equilibrium as to their electromotive force, then why does changing the iron for zinc destroy the equilibrium? Changing one metal for another in a metallic circuit causes no alteration of this kind: nor does changing one substance for another among the great number of bodies which, as solid conductors, may be used to form conducting (but chemically inactive) circuits. . . . If the solution of sulphuret of potassium is to be classed with the metals as to its action in the experiments I have quoted, . . . then, how comes it to act quite unlike them, and with a power equal to the *best* of the other class, in the new cases of zinc, copper, silver, etc. . . . ?

This difficulty, as I conceive, must be met, on the part of the contact theorists, by a new assumption, namely, that this fluid sometimes acts as the best of the metals, or first class of conductors, and sometimes as the best of the electrolytes or second class. But surely this would be far too loose a method of philosophizing in an experimental science . . .; and further, it is most unfortunate for such an assumption, that this second condition or relation of it never comes on by itself, so as to give us a pure case of a current from contact alone; it never comes on *without* that chemical action to which the chemist so simply refers all the current which is then produced (1863–5).

The use of *ad hoc* hypotheses by the contact theorists did not stop here, as Faraday willingly pointed out. Having assumed an electromotive force, they could account for observed facts only by piling hypothesis upon hypothesis.

Every case of a current is obliged to be met, on the part of the contact advocates [Faraday insisted], by assuming powers at the points of contact, in *the particular case*, of such proportionate strengths as will consist with the results obtained, and the theory is made to bend about . . . having no general relation for the acids or alkalies, or other electrolytic solution used. The result therefore comes to this: The theory can predict nothing regarding the results; it is accompanied by no case of a voltaic current produced without chemical action, and in those associated with chemical action, it bends about to suit the real results, these contortions being exactly parallel to the variations which the pure chemical force, by experiment, indicates (1874).

The case was now complete. Faraday had removed all the experimental objections of the contact theorists to the chemical theory by showing (in essence) that the contact theorists were poor experimenters. Every case of the generation of a galvanic current *was* accompanied by a chemical reaction, though this had escaped many. The contact theory was shown to involve an embarrassing number of *ad hoc* hypotheses which were altered to suit the circumstances. Furthermore, the contrast between the chemical theory – simple, quantitatively exact, and capable of predicting phenomena – and the contact theory – complex, protean, and incapable of forecasting effects – was depicted in a clear and sharp way. With almost geometrical precision, Faraday laid out his conclusions (in italics).

Chemical action does involve electricity (2030).
Where chemical action has been, but diminishes or ceases, the electric current diminishes or ceases also (2031).
When the chemical action changes the current changes also (2036).
Where no chemical action occurs no current is produced (2038).
But a current will occur the moment chemical action commences (2039).
When the chemical action which either has or could have produced a current in one direction is reversed or undone, the current is reversed (or undone) also (2040).

Such complete and total dependence of the electric current in the galvanic circuit upon chemical action[9] could not in Faraday's view, be anything but the result of a causal connexion. The Sixteenth and Seventeenth Series of the *Experimental Researches* spelled out this connexion in great experimental detail.

The contact theory had been dealt a mortal blow from which it never recovered. By 1850, with the acceptance of the principle of the conservation of energy, the contact theory was recognized as being, *a priori*, impossible and was quietly forgotten. It is interesting, in this context, to reproduce Faraday's conclusion in which he appealed to an argument closely related to that of the conservation of energy. Here, what had served as the conviction stimulating Faraday to his attack upon the contact theory, was now adduced as a basic principle ruling out this theory on theoretical and metaphysical grounds.

The contact theory assumes, in fact, that a force which is able to overcome powerful resistance, as for instance that of the conductors, good or bad, through which the current passes, and that again of the electrolytic action where bodies are decomposed by it, can arise out of nothing; that, without any change in the acting matter or the consumption of any generating force, a current can be produced which shall go on for ever against a constant resistance, or only be stopped, as in the voltaic trough, by the ruins which its exertion has heaped up in its own course. This would indeed be a *creation of power*, and is like no other force in nature. We have many processes by which the form of the power may be so changed that an apparent *conversion* of one into another takes place. So we can change chemical force into the electric current, or the current into chemical force. The beautiful experiments of Seebeck and Peltier show the convertibility of heat and electricity; and others by Oersted and myself show the convertibility of electricity and magnetism. But in no cases, not even those of the Gymnotus and Torpedo ... is there a pure creation of force; a production of power without a corresponding exhaustion of something to supply it (2071).[10]

We are here back to the principle of the conversion of forces and have been led by Faraday, both by experiment and theory, to his most deeply felt belief that power or force could never be created or destroyed.

What was self-evident to Faraday, however, was by no means so clear to his contemporaries. Faraday's concept of 'force', in particular, seemed very fuzzy to many and precisely how 'forces' were converted into chemical affinity, electricity and magnetism, heat and light, was a problem that bothered many who were impressed by Faraday's discoveries. Only by making his own ideas explicit could he hope to dispel this mist. His mind, in the 1840's, was not up to original work,[11] but he could, at least, make his own theoretical assumptions public and thereby hope to convince those who rejected his ideas because they did not understand them.

2. Force and Matter

The publication of the great papers on induction had an astonishingly slight effect when one considers that they challenged the concept of electrical action at a distance and supported this challenge with a large mass of carefully determined experimental facts. William Whewell, in his *History of the Inductive Sciences,* merely mentioned Faraday's idea of induction being the result of the action of contiguous particles. He then went on to point out that the situation was a complicated one and the rejection of Coulomb's theory would seem a bit premature.[12] Faraday's friend, Auguste de la Rive, in his *Traité d'électricité théorique et appliquée,* described Faraday's theory only to reject it.[13] Even W. Snow Harris, whose paper on the elementary laws of electricity in the *Phil. Trans.*[14] provided independent testimony in favour of Faraday's findings, had difficulty in assimilating Faraday's concepts. In 1858, almost twenty years after Faraday had presented his theory, Harris wrote to him to query some of the fundamental ideas presented in the theory.[15]

The most detailed, and certainly the most public, questioning of Faraday's new theory was that of Robert Hare. Hare could not make head or tail of what Faraday was talking about. The fault, as we have already seen, was largely Faraday's, for his reticence on the nature of the basic concepts which guided his thought prevented anyone from grasping exactly what he was getting at. Thus, Hare puzzled over how contiguous particles could be some distance apart, how the inductive force could operate from particle to particle under these circumstances and why individual particles could not have their electric fluid either increased or abstracted to receive a single charge.[16] In short, Hare, a rather conventional atomist and adherent to the fluid theory of electricity, found Faraday's whole theoretical framework foreign and confusing to him. In his answer to Hare, Faraday compounded this difficulty by refusing to remove the causes of the confusion.[17] Instead, as was shown in Chapter Seven, Faraday persisted in concealing his concepts and tried to remove the difficulty by explaining his experiments. Faraday specifically stated, for example, that 'my theory of induction . . . makes no assertion as to the nature of electricity, or at all questions any of the theories respecting that subject.'[18] This was a bit less than frank for by this time he *had* rejected fluids and was quite obviously challenging existing theories. Hare's answer left no doubt that he, at least, felt that Faraday was attempting to alter radically the theories of electrical action then current. Referring to Faraday's remark cited above on the theory of electricity, Hare wrote: 'Owing to this avowed omission to state your opinions of the nature of electricity as preliminary to the statement of your 'theory', and because I was unable to reconcile that theory with those previously accredited, I received the impression that you claimed no aid from any imponderable principle.'[19] This then meant, Hare argued, that induction was merely the creation of what he called an electro-polar state. But why this *state* should be called an *action* escaped him and he confessed himself unable to understand Faraday's definition of induction. Furthermore, he was unable to see how induction and conduction were connected. 'Conduction conveys to my mind the idea of *permeability* to the electric fluid, insulation that of *impermeability*.'[20] Faraday's refusal to eliminate fluids and deal only with forces was clearly the cause of Hare's confusion. The point was, however, of major importance for the very essence of Faraday's theory was the passage of induction into conduction when the particles suffering induction were subjected to forces beyond their capacity to bear.

Hare finally returned to his questioning of what in heaven Faraday could mean by the term, contiguous, when particles could be as much as one-half inch apart. His second letter, therefore, involved essentially these two objections: Faraday's account of induction did not seem at all clear and his theory of matter appeared to Hare to be a rather odd one indeed, in which particles seemed to have varying dimensions for they were always 'contiguous'.[21]

Unfortunately, Hare's second letter was published just as Faraday's mental faculties were at their weakest. In May of 1841 he was able only to acknowledge its receipt in a private letter to Hare and there express an unwillingness to carry on any further controversy on the subject.[22] It was not until 1843 that he discovered that the letter had been published and, as he remarked to the editor of the *Phil. Mag.*, 'as some persons think a letter unanswered is also unanswerable', he felt it necessary to reply. His reply did not answer Hare's objections but merely acknowledged them and reiterated his own faith in his earlier papers.[23]

N

Yet, it would appear that Hare's criticisms bothered Faraday and that he felt it was time, perhaps, to remove the difficulties which Hare had encountered. It certainly seems to be more than coincidence that in 1843 and 1844 Faraday published two papers which specifically addressed themselves to the two points Hare had raised – namely, the mechanism of induction and Faraday's theory of matter and electrical conduction.

In a letter to Richard Phillips, editor of the *Phil. Mag.* dated 4 February 1843, Faraday set out to explain his views 'On Static Electrical Inductive Action'.[24] 'Their value', he insisted, 'consists in their power to give a very precise and decided idea to the mind respecting certain principles of inductive electrical action, which I find are by many accepted with a degree of doubt or obscurity that takes away much of their importance.'[25] It was in this letter that Faraday introduced his famous ice-pail experiment, familiar to every student of elementary physics. Faraday here spoke more explicitly the language of forces, although he still left a small place for fluids. The experiment is a simple one and can best be described in Faraday's words:

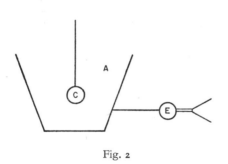

Fig. 2

Let A in the diagram represent an insulated pewter ice-pail ten and a half inches high and seven inches diameter, connected by a wire with a delicate gold-leaf electrometer E, and let C be a round brass ball insulated by a dry thread of white silk, three or four feet in length, so as to remove the influence of the hand holding it from the ice-pail below. Let A be perfectly discharged, then let C be charged at a distance by a machine or Leyden jar, and introduced into A as in the figure. If C be positive, E also will diverge positively; if C be taken away, E will collapse perfectly, the apparatus being in good order. As C enters the vessel A the divergence of E will increase until C is about three inches below the edge of the vessel, and will remain quite steady and unchanged for any greater depression. This shows that at that distance the inductive action of C is entirely exerted upon the interior of A, and not in any degree directly upon external objects. If C be made to touch the bottom of A, *all* its charge is communicated to A; there is no longer any inductive action between C and A, and C, upon being withdrawn and examined, is found perfectly discharged.[26]

From this simple experiment, Faraday drew a number of conclusions. The fact that the diversion of the gold leaves did not change when the ball C was suspended or when it touched the bottom of the ice-pail indicated that 'the electricity *induced* by C and the electricity *in* C are accurately equal in amount and power'.[27] When C was moved about within the ice-pail, sometimes approaching this side, sometimes that, sometimes the bottom, the divergence of the leaves remained constant, 'showing that whether C acts at a considerable distance or at the very smallest distance, the amount of its force is the same'.[28] If a series of ice-pails, separated from one another by layers of shellac, were placed concentrically within one another, still there was no effect upon the gold leaves.

All this indicated to Faraday that 'charging' a body consisted in impressing a certain specific amount of force upon that body. This force, involving the distortion of the particles of which the body was composed, was transmitted through the material particles surrounding the charged body in a direct chain. The total force in these chains was constant, no matter how the position of the body was altered. The process was somewhat confusedly described by Faraday, although he was able to focus attention upon the *force* of the charge and its specific quantity.

> Hence if a body be charged [he wrote], whether it be a particle or a mass, there is nothing about its action which can at all consist with the idea of exaltation or extinction; the amount of force is perfectly definite and unchangeable: or to those who in their minds represent the idea of the electric force by a fluid, there ought to be no notion of the compression or condensation of this fluid within itself, or of its coercibility, as some understand that phrase.[29]

This, in effect, eliminated the fluid theories of electricity, for these theories did depend upon the varying density of the electric fluid(s) within bodies. For Faraday, induction always was the action of a specific force upon the particles of bodies, which action, like that of chemical affinity, was constant.

> The only mode of affecting this force [he insisted] is by connecting it with force of the same kind, either in the same or the contrary direction. If we oppose to it force of the contrary kind, we may *by discharge* neutralize the original force, or we may *without discharge* connect them by the simple laws and principles of static induction; but away from induction, which is *always of the same kind*, there is no other state of the power in a charged body. . . .[30]

Thus Faraday had answered Hare's objections to the connexion of induction and conduction. Induction was the action of a force, presumably by straining the particles of which a charged body and its surroundings were composed; conduction was the result of relieving this strain. There is no record of whether this satisfied Hare although it is extremely doubtful that it did. It does serve to illustrate, however, Faraday's growing willingness to speak *only* in terms of force. There was no mention of the particles of matter, but only of force manifesting itself. It was but a short step from here to the full affirmation of his belief in immaterial point atoms. This step he took in a discourse at the Royal Institution, later amplified and published in the *Phil. Mag.* for 1844 with the title, 'A speculation touching Electric Conduction and the Nature of Matter'.[31] For the first time, Faraday's fundamental ideas on the nature of matter and of electricity were presented to the public.

The discourse was a frontal assault upon the corpuscular theory of matter and an attempt to establish the Boscovichean atomic doctrine. Faraday used two arguments to challenge the Daltonian concept of 'billiard ball' atoms. The first involved the question of the conduction of electricity; the second was derived from purely chemical arguments. It seems perfectly obvious that these were ideas that Faraday had entertained for some years, at least as far back as his early work on induction.[32]

He first summarized the conventional atomic theory held by most scientists of the day. An atom was 'a something material having a certain volume, upon which those powers were impressed at the creation, which have given it, from that time to the present, the capability of constituting, when many atoms are congregated together into groups, the different substances whose effects and properties we observe'.[33] Atoms could not be in contact with one another, but must be separated by space, 'otherwise pressure or cold could not make a body contract into a smaller bulk'.[34] The amount of empty space was considerable, as his current work on the condensation of gases indicated.[35] Now, once this was admitted, the problem of electric insulation and conduction became acutely embarrassing to Daltonian atomists.

> If the view of the constitution of matter already referred to be assumed to be correct, and I may be allowed to speak of the particles of matter and of the space between them (in water, or in the vapour of water for instance) as two different things, then space must be taken as the only continuous part, for the particles are considered as separated by space from each other. Space will permeate all masses of matter in every direction like a net, except that in place of meshes it will form cells, isolating each atom from its neighbours, and itself only being continuous.
>
> Then take the case of a piece of shell-lac, a non-conductor, and it would appear at once from such a view of its atomic constitution that space is an insulator, for if it were a conductor the shell-lac could not insulate, whatever might be the relation as to conducting power of its material atoms; the space would be like a fine metallic web penetrating it in every direction, just as we may imagine a heap of siliceous sand having all its pores filled with water; or as we may consider of a stick of black wax, which, though it contains an infinity of particles of conducting charcoal diffused through every part of it, cannot conduct, because a non-conducting body (a resin) intervenes and separates them one from another, like the supposed space in the lac.

Next take the case of a metal, platinum or potassium, constituted, according to the atomic theory, in the same manner. The metal is a conductor; but how can this be, except space be a conductor? for it is the only continuous part of the metal, and the atoms not only do not touch (by the theory), but as we shall see presently, must be assumed to be a considerable way apart. Space therefore must be a conductor, or else the metals could not conduct, but would be in the situation of the black sealing wax referred to a little while ago.

But if space be a conductor, how then can shell-lac, sulphur, etc., insulate? for space permeates them in every direction. Or if space be an insulator, how can a metal or other similar body conduct?

It would seem, therefore, that in accepting the ordinary atomic theory, space may be proved to be a non-conductor in non-conducting bodies, and a conductor in conducting bodies, but the reasoning ends in this, a subversion of that theory altogether; for if space be an insulator it cannot exist in conducting bodies, and if it be a conductor it cannot exist in insulating bodies. Any ground of reasoning which tends to such conclusions as these must in itself be false.[36]

But, it might be argued, the atoms of metallic conductors may be close enough together so that the electric force could be transmitted by the vibration and impact of these particles. An argument from chemistry was used with great effectiveness to counter this position and lead back to the paradoxical behaviour of space.

Now let us take the case of potassium [Faraday suggested], a compact metallic substance with excellent conducting powers, its oxide or hydrate a non-conductor; it will supply us with some facts having very important bearings on the assumed atomic construction of matter.

When potassium is oxidized an atom of it combines with an atom of oxygen to form an atom of potassa, and an atom of potassa combines with an atom of water, consisting of two atoms of oxygen and hydrogen, to form an atom of hydrate of potassa, so that an atom of hydrate of potassa contains four elementary atoms. The specific gravity of potassium is 0·865, and its atomic weight 40; the specific gravity of cast hydrate of potassa, in such state of purity as I could obtain it, I found to be nearly 2, its atomic weight 57. From these, which may be taken as facts, the following strange conclusions flow. A piece of potassium contains less potassium than an equal piece of the potash formed by it and oxygen. We may cast into potassium oxygen atom for atom, and then again both oxygen and hydrogen in a twofold number of atoms, and yet, with all these additions, the matter shall become less and less, until it is not two-thirds of its original volume. If a given bulk of potassium contains 45 atoms, the same bulk of hydrate of potassa contains 70 atoms nearly *of the metal potassium*, and besides that, 210 atoms more of oxygen and hydrogen. In dealing with assumptions I must assume a little more for the sake of making any kind of statement; let me therefore assume that in the hydrate of potassa the atoms are all of one size and nearly touching each other, and that in a cubic inch of that substance there are 2800 elementary atoms of potassium, oxygen and hydrogen; take away 2100 atoms of oxygen and hydrogen, and the 700 atoms of potassium remaining will swell into more than a cubic inch and a half, and if we diminish the number until only those containable in a cubic inch remain, we shall have 430, or thereabout. So a space which can contain 2800 atoms, and amongst them 700 of potassium itself, is found to be entirely filled by 430 atoms of potassium as they exist in the ordinary state of that metal. Surely then, under the suppositions of the atomic theory, the atoms of potassium must be very far apart in the metal, *i.e.* there must be much more of space than of matter in that body: yet it is an excellent conductor, and so space must be a conductor; but then what becomes of shell-lac, sulphur, and all the insulators? for space must also by the theory exist in them.[37]

The dilemma was now complete. So long as gross matter was assumed to consist of little material particles surrounded by empty space, so long would both the conductivity and non-conductivity of space have to be the conclusions drawn from arguments similar to those used by Faraday. One way out of this dilemma was to eliminate the duality of space and matter by finding some uniform entity that pervaded all space. Boscovichean atoms provided just such a plenum and Faraday now explicitly adopted them.

If we must assume at all, as indeed in a branch of knowledge like the present we can hardly help it, then the safest course appears to be to assume as little as possible, and in that respect the atoms of Boscovich appear to me to have a great advantage over the more usual notion. His atoms, if I understand aright, are mere centres of forces or powers, not particles of matter, in which the powers themselves reside. If, in the ordinary view of atoms, we call the particle of matter away from the powers *a*, and the system of powers or forces in and around it *m*, then in Boscovich's theory *a* disappears, or is a mere mathematical point, whilst in the usual notion it is a little unchangeable, impenetrable piece of matter, and *m* is an atmosphere of force grouped around it.[38]

This idea, Faraday admitted, was a bit difficult to digest, for the mind of the beginner in philosophy will find it strange to conceive a material universe from which matter has been banished. But, as Faraday argued,

all our perception and knowledge of the atom, and even our fancy, is limited to ideas of its powers: what thought remains on which to hang the imagination of an *a* independent of the acknowledged forces? . . . Now the powers we know and recognize in every phenomenon of the creation, the abstract matter in none; why then assume the existence of that of which we are ignorant, which we cannot conceive, and for which there is no philosophical necessity.[39]

This was a sincere and rather desperate attempt on Faraday's part to avoid the charge of 'metaphysics' sure to be hurled at him. What he wished to convince his contemporaries of was that Boscovichean atoms were, actually, *less* metaphysical than those generally accepted. They involved only powers and forces which were, literally, palpable; hence they did not require the mind to soar above experience, but limited the totality of the phenomena of the universe to the basic elements of sensation. It was a noble try, but in an England officially committed to a rather naïve Baconianism, it was doomed to failure. The cry of 'metaphysics' went up and few took Faraday seriously. In the generally favourable review of Faraday's Nineteenth, Twentieth and Twenty-first Series of the *Experimental Researches in Electricity* Dr Henry Holland, Faraday's close friend, wrote in the *Quarterly Review* that this was a metaphysical leap of which he was incapable.[40]

But, metaphysics or not, it did produce a solution to the problem of electrical conduction that Faraday had raised. Matter, instead of being sharply distinguished from space, was continuous with it.

> . . . And in considering a mass of it we have not to suppose a distinction between its atoms and any intervening space. The powers around the centres give these centres the properties of atoms of matter; and these powers again, when many centres by their conjoint forces are grouped into a mass, give to every part of that mass the properties of matter. In such a view all the contradiction resulting from the consideration of electric insulation and conduction disappears.[41]

Matter, thus, filled all space as force and Faraday's theory of induction and conduction was placed in a new perspective. The interpenetration of atoms permitted the kind of tensions upon which Faraday had founded his idea of the inductive line of force. The strains so imparted to the atoms could then represent the electric and magnetic forces. Robert Hare's questionings over the use of the word 'contiguous' also were answered: all atoms were in contact (through their forces) with all others. Faraday's earlier reply that 'by contiguous particles, I mean those which are next'[42] now made perfect sense and the mechanism of electrical action simply involved the transmission of force between contiguous particles.[43]

Electricity and magnetism were imposed forces – that is, they involved a rearrangement of the forces of force-particles by the imposition of other forces. There was one force, however, that served to tie all atoms together throughout the universe. 'The view now stated of the constitution of matter would seem to involve necessarily the conclusion that matter fills all space, or, at least, all space to which gravitation extends (including the sun and its system); for gravitation is a property of matter dependent on a certain force, and it is this force which constitutes the matter.'[44]

Earlier in his essay, Faraday had casually mentioned that Boscovichean atoms were of immense importance in understanding the nature of light[45] and this, together with the idea of the force of gravitation tying the universe together, will justify the violation of strict chronological order and permit us to jump to still another speculation.

It was on Friday, 10 April 1846, that Sir Charles Wheatstone bolted down the stairs of the Royal Institution, leaving Faraday to deliver the discourse. Almost completely unprepared for such an eventuality, Faraday was able to fill up only part of the evening with the announced subject and so, to complete the talk, he revealed his thoughts on the nature of light. These speculations, entitled 'Thoughts on Ray-vibrations' completed his general concept of the unity of force and of the universe.

Specifically, what Faraday set out to do was to eliminate the last of the imponderable fluids. Electricity and magnetism, Faraday was convinced, were powers of matter; heat appeared, as Davy had insisted, to be the motion of the particles of matter; light could be considered as vibratory motion which required the assumption of a luminiferous ether to carry the vibrations. Such a unique substance, alone of all matter devoid of gravity, was suspect to Faraday. Was it really necessary? or could an undulatory theory be devised which eliminated the ether?

What could vibrate? In his 1844 talk he had shown how the particles of matter were all tied together by gravitation. The action of gravity created tensions in lines of particles in each and every direction. From any given point, lines of gravitational force radiated out to the ends of the universe. There were, too, electric and magnetic lines of force extending through space, so there was no lack of 'lines' to pluck and by which the vibrations might be transmitted. Thus Faraday speculated:

> The view which I am so bold as to put forth considers, therefore, radiation as a high species of vibration in the lines of force which are known to connect particles and also masses of matter together. It endeavours to dismiss the ether, but not the vibrations. The kind of vibration which, I believe, can alone account for the wonderful, varied, and beautiful phenomena of polarization, is not the same as that which occurs on the surface of disturbed water, or the waves of sound in gases or liquids, for the vibrations in these cases are direct, or to and from the centre of action, whereas the former are lateral. It seems to me, that the resultant of two or more lines of force is in an apt condition for that action which may be considered as equivalent to a *lateral* vibration; whereas a uniform medium, like the ether, does not appear apt, or more apt than air or water.[46]

Two further aspects of what Faraday called 'the vague impressions of my mind'[47] deserve special attention. The first involved the fact that the transmission of the force of light was a process. Thus,

The occurrence of a change at one end of a line of force easily suggests a consequent change at the other. The propagation of light, and therefore probably of all radiant action, occupies *time*; and, that a vibration of the line of force should account for the phenomena of radiation, it is necessary that such vibration should occupy time also. I am not aware whether there are any data by which it has been, or could be ascertained, whether such a power as gravitation acts without occupying time, or whether lines of force being already in existence, such a lateral disturbance of them at one end as I have suggested above, would require time, or must of necessity be felt instantly at the other end.[48]

This was a subtle, but mortally aimed blow, at the concept of action at a distance. If Faraday were right, and gravity was propagated, then it could *not* be the simple kind of action at a distance so facilely assumed by the mathematical physicist.[49] It was a point to which Faraday was to return in the 1850's and it was to lead him to the composition of a paper on the conservation of force which the casual reader today will find almost unintelligible. The idea, too, that gravitational lines of force were similar to electric and magnetic lines of force led Faraday to suppose that these forces should all be mutually convertible. He was later to attempt the conversion of gravitational force into some other form of force. Here, he was to fail.

The second point in his thoughts on ray-vibrations that should be particularly noted is that the lines of force were all associated with the point atoms. Hence, there were centres of action which, when linked together, formed the line of force. If one focused upon these centres, as Faraday did in the 1840's, then the lines of force were the result of the distortions produced in the particles. The distortion was what Faraday called polarity and the action of force necessarily implied the polarity or strain of the point atoms. His discoveries in diamagnetism were gradually to convince him that such polarity did not necessarily follow from the line of force. The line of force, therefore, was to become increasingly for him the primary datum of all electric and magnetic action and this concept, in the hands of James Clerk Maxwell, was to be the basis of classical field theory.

3. The Discovery of Diamagnetism

During 1844 and the first seven months of 1845, Faraday was occupied with the condensation of gases. This was an activity which placed a minimal strain on his mind for success was largely the result of technique, not new concepts. It permitted him to rest his weary head at the same time that it allowed him to feel that he was still working actively. Nothing was more repugnant to Faraday than the idea of resting on his laurels and it was with great gratification that he was able to report the liquefaction of substances never before condensed. Even in these almost mechanical researches Faraday was able to see the theoretical aspect of greatest importance and devise his experiments around it. In a letter to William Whewell in 1844, he again consulted his friend for a new term to designate that point of temperature and pressure, discovered some years before by Cagniard de la Tour, at which the liquid and gaseous phase appear to merge into one another. This 'critical point',[50] Faraday recognized as fundamental, involving as it did both a critical temperature and a critical pressure for each substance. The critical point gave Faraday the clue he needed for his further work. The planning of his research was briefly recounted in a letter to his friend J.-B. Dumas of the French Academy of Sciences.

> You remember M. Seine's experiments (Ann. de chimie 1843, viii) in the depths of the sea where great pressure was put on certain gases: the results could not be looked at in the compressed state and they were made at common temperatures. You remember also M. Cagniard de la Tour's experiments on ether and in which he shows that at a certain temperature the liquid becomes vapour without increase in bulk. Now if this *disliquefying* point is, as it appears to be, lower with the *more vapourous* and *lighter* bodies existing as gases then there can be little or no hopes of liquefying such substances as hydrogen, oxygen or nitrogen etc. at *any pressure* whilst retained at common temperatures; for their disliquefying points are almost certainly below common or even considerably depressed temperatures. Here therefore you have the key to my course of proceedings – I first sought for a very low temperature and for this purpose used Thilorier's beautiful bath of solid carbonic acid and ether – but then I worked with this bath under the vacuum of the air pump keeping up a continual exhaustion the while, and reduced the temperature so low that the carbonic acid of the bath was not more volatile than water at the temperature of 30°C.; for the barometer of the air pump was 28·2 inches – the external barometer being 29·4 inches. This being done I next succeeded in fitting and adjusting together by caps and stopcocks small brass and *glass* tubes so that I could by means of two successive pumps force in and compress different gases up to a pressure of 40 atmospheres and at the same time submit them to the intense cold in the air pump and look at and examine the effects.[51]

In his paper read in January of 1845 Faraday reported on those substances he had liquefied and solidified.[52]

Throughout the spring and early summer of the same year, with what little energy he had, Faraday continued his researches although there were many weeks when the *Diary* record is blank. Then, suddenly, on

30 August, there was the first entry on another attempt to discover the electrotonic state. This was to begin a period of feverish activity culminating in the discovery of the action of a magnetic field upon light and of diamagnetism.

Why, in the middle of the summer of 1845, did Faraday turn back to experiments he had first performed in 1822? The stimulus for the renewal of old lines of research was the young William Thomson, future Baron Kelvin of Largs. Thomson, only 21 years old in 1845, was one of the few scientists who took Faraday's concept of the line of force seriously. Faraday had met him only a little time before and was greatly impressed with him. In 1845, Amadeo Avogadro sent Faraday a copy of an article on electrical theory which was far too mathematical for him.[53] He turned it over to his young friend asking Thomson his opinion. On 6 August 1845, Thomson wrote Faraday a long letter in which he briefly summarized Avogadro's paper and then went on to tell Faraday of his researches. The letter is worth noting, if only because it is, to my knowledge, the first attempt to treat Faraday's lines of force mathematically. At the end of his letter, Thomson asked Faraday about experiments that Thomson thought ought to be performed, for his theory seemed to predict effects that had not yet been observed.

I have long wished to know [Thomson wrote] whether any experiments have been made relative to the action of electrified bodies on the dielectrics themselves, in attracting them or repelling them, but I have never seen any described. Any attraction which may have been perceived to be exercised upon a nonconductor, such as sulphur, has always been ascribed to a slight degree of conducting power. A mathematical theory based on the analogy of dielectrics to soft iron would indicate attraction, quite independently of any induced charge (such, for instance, as would be found by breaking a dielectric and examining the parts separately). Another important question is whether the air in the neighbourhood of an electrified body, if acted upon by a force of attraction or repulsion, shows any signs of such forces by a change of density, which, however, appears to me highly improbable. A third question which, I think, has never been investigated is relative to the action of a transparent dielectric on polarized light. Thus it is known that a very well defined action, analogous to that of a transparent crystal, is produced upon polarized light when transmitted through glass in any ordinary state of violent constraint. If the constraint, which may be elevated to be on the point of breaking the glass, be produced by electricity, it seems probable that a similar action might be observed.[54]

All three of Thomson's queries are worthy of attention. The first clearly implied that dielectrics (and later, by analogy, diamagnetics) should mutually affect one another when transmitting the electric force – an effect in diamagnetics under magnetic influence that Faraday was to seek for in vain. The second, with magnetic substituted for electric force, was to lead Faraday to broad and general views of terrestrial magnetism and its variations. The third was, of course, the most important. It described an effect that Faraday had long sought for and was never to find. It was discovered by Dr John Kerr in 1875. But, in August 1845, this passage seems to have stimulated Faraday to try once more to detect the strain that, for a quarter of a century, he was convinced *must* exist in bodies through which an electric current was passing. As he wrote to Thomson:

> I have made many experiments on the probable attraction of dielectrics. I did not expect any, nor did I find any, and yet I think that some particular effect (perhaps not attraction or repulsion) ought to come out when the dielectric is not all of the same inductive capacity, but consists of parts having different inductive capacity.
>
> I have also worked much on the state of the dielectric as regards polarized light, and you will find my negative results at paragraphs 951–955 of my Experimental Researches. I purpose resuming this subject hereafter. I also worked hard upon crystalline dielectrics to discover some molecular conditions in them (see par. 1688 etc. etc.) but could get no results except negative. Still I firmly believe that the dielectric is in a peculiar state whilst induction is taking place across it.[55]

It was this firm belief that led Faraday to set up an experiment on 30 August 1845, which was almost identical with one he had first performed on 10 September 1822.[56] 'I have had a glass trough made,' he noted, '24 inches long, 1 inch wide and about $1\frac{1}{2}$ deep – in which to decompose electrolites [*sic*], and whilst under decomposition, along which I could pass a ray of light in different conditions and afterwards examine it' [7434]. As in 1822, there was no detectable effect. Unlike the situation in 1822, there were a number of different modifications that could be made in order to coax forth the desired reaction of the polarized light.

> The Voltaic apparatus used was a Grove's battery of five pair of plates. By the aid of a magnetic breaker and its associated set of 2 coils of covered wire and an iron wire core – either the *continuous current* of the battery – or the *continually intermitting current* of the battery – or the *rapidly recurring series of double currents* obtained by induction from the helices, could be sent at pleasure across the electrolyte in the trough [7439].

Still no effect on the polarized light could be detected [7441–4].

> I made the coming on and going off of the current gradual by interposing in the Electric circuit a glass containing a strong solution of Sulphate of Soda, causing one of the metallic terminations in it to be a metal plate and the other

a fine wire; by dipping this end in and out, *time* was given to the full establishment or rising up of the current – but no sensible effect on the polarized
ray could be perceived [7447].

Arranged certain electrolytes so that platina wires should be the Electrodes,
and the space between (preserved clear for the light to pass by a little wedge of
paper) rendered as small as possible, perhaps the $\frac{1}{8}$ of an inch. The wires were
also so placed that occasionally the course of the ray was along the electric
current and at other times across it.

The different electrolytes were:

Distilled water.

Sul. Soda saturated solution.

Dilute S. [ulphuric] *A.* [cid], 1 vol. oil vitriol + 3 vols. water.

Saturated sol. *Sul. copper.*

The Electric current was applied as a constant current – as a beginning
current – as a ceasing current – as an intermitting current – and also as a
rapidly recurring secondary current.

The light passed through the electrolyte was polarized in a horizontal plane
and occasionally partially depolarized by sul.[phate of] lime – and it was
examd. by a Nicholl's eye piece.

But *no effect* on the electrolytes in any of these cases could be perceived
[7472–9].

There *had* to be an effect! Faraday's whole theory of electrolysis and
induction was based upon the creation of an intermolecular strain in
substances through which an electric current passed. Perhaps the fault lay
with his approach. The 'tension' (i.e. voltage) created by a galvanic
apparatus was small; would not the much higher 'tensions' produced by
static electricity be more effective in throwing the particles of a dielectric
into the electrotonic state? A piece of glass was placed between the terminals of an electrostatic machine and polarized light was passed through
it in various directions [7483 ff.]. Once again no effect was detected. At
the end of a week of intensive experimenting in which every conceivable
change was rung on the experimental arrangements, Faraday summed up
his efforts. 'So all these experiments are *nil* as to any effect produced by
induction or electrolization upon electrolytes or nonconductors which
can be rendered sensible on or by a polarized ray of light' [7497].

The temptation to quit and to disavow the electrotonic state once again
must have been strong. Yet, the hypothesis had served him so well, and
Thomson's independent reasonings supported his own so closely that it
almost seemed impossible that this state did not exist. Writing to his old
friend, Sir John Herschel, he later declared, 'It was only the very strongest
conviction that Light, Mag[netism] and Electricity must be connected
that could have led me to resume the subject and persevere through much
labour before I found the key.'[57]

There was one final experimental path still to be explored. Perhaps even with electrostatic tension, the forces involved were too small to be easily detected. Even a highly charged electrical body could hold only a small weight suspended from it. Compare this to electromagnets which could hold masses of hundreds of pounds in their power. From the patterns shown by iron filings, it was obvious that the magnetic power was exerted in curved lines. In the case of electrostatic induction Faraday had argued that the fact that induction took place along curved lines implied that the transmission of force was from particle to particle. The intermolecular strain thus created was the electrotonic state. Surely the curves of the magnetic lines of force implied equally a 'magneto-tonic' state and, since the magnetic power could be multiplied almost at will by the use of electromagnets, this state might be detectable where the electrotonic state was not.

On 13 September 1845, Faraday began to work with electromagnets. Again his efforts were unavailing. The magnet had no effect on polarized light when passed through flint glass, rock crystal, or calcareous spar [7500–3]. There were, in the laboratory, pieces of the heavy glass that Faraday had made back in 1830 for the Royal Society. This glass had an extraordinarily high refractive index, indicating that it acted powerfully upon light. Given the correlation of forces in which Faraday believed so strongly, should this substance not, perhaps, also be acted upon magnetically in such a way as to affect the plane of polarized light of a ray passing through it. The experiment was easily performed and, finally, the expected result was observed.

> A piece of heavy glass . . . which was 2 inches by 1·8 inches, and 0·5 of an inch thick, being a silico borate of lead, and polished on the two shortest edges, was experimented with. It gave no effects when the *same magnetic poles* or the *contrary* poles were on opposite sides (as respects the course of the polarized ray) – nor when the same poles were on the same side, either with the constant or intermitting current – BUT,* when contrary magnetic poles were on the same side, there *was an effect produced on the polarized ray*, and thus magnetic force and light were proved to have relation to each other. This fact will most likely prove exceedingly fertile and of great value in the investigation of both conditions of natural force [7504].

After this classic bit of English understatement, Faraday threw himself with all his energy into an intensive examination of the new effect. Once again he followed the same course as he had with other new effects. All possible combinations of factors were tried so that a simple law of action

---

*This word is underlined three times in the manuscript.

could be established. The magnetic poles were placed in every conceivable position relative to one another; simple current-carrying helices were substituted for iron-core electromagnets; all the common transparent laboratory substances were substituted for the heavy glass and the effect observed. The thickness of the heavy glass was increased by putting a number of polished pieces together. From these experiments, he was able to draw a number of general laws which he stated in the published paper which made up the Nineteenth Series of the *Experimental Researches in Electricity*.

> I will now proceed [he wrote] to the different circumstances which affect, limit, and define the extent and nature of this new power of action on light.
> In the first place, the rotation appears to be in proportion to the extent of the diamagnetic through which the ray and the magnetic lines pass. I preserved the strength of the magnet and the interval between its poles constant, and then interposed different pieces of the same heavy glass . . . between the poles. The greater the extent of the diamagnetic in the line of the ray, whether in one, two, or three pieces, the greater was the rotation of the ray; and, as far as I could judge by these first experiments, the amount of rotation was exactly proportionate to the extent of diamagnetic through which the ray passed. No addition or diminution of the heavy glass on the *side* of the course of the ray made any difference in the effect of that part through which the ray passed (2162-3).

One factor, therefore, in the extent of the effect of magnetism upon the plane of polarization of a ray of plane polarized light was the distance the ray travelled through what Faraday had christened diamagnetics.[58] Thus, the effect was dependent somehow upon the matter through which the ray passed. This was not, however, the sole cause of the rotation.

'The power of rotating the ray of light *increased* with the intensity of the magnetic lines of force. This general effect is very easily ascertained by the use of electro-magnets; and within such range of power as I have employed, it appears to be directly proportionate to the intensity of the magnetic force' (2164).

This effect was to Faraday the primary one. He entitled the first section of the Nineteenth Series, 'On the magnetization of light and the illumination of magnetic lines of force' and, in the text of the paper stressed this point once again.

> It is time [he remarked] that I should pass to a consideration of this power of magnetism over light as exercised, not only in the silicated borate of lead . . . , but in many other substances; and here we perceive, in the first place, that if all transparent bodies possess the power of exhibiting the action, they have it in very different degrees, and that up to this time there are some that have not shown it at all.

Next, we may observe, that bodies that are exceedingly different to each other in chemical, physical, and mechanical properties, develope this effect; for solids and liquids, acids, alkalies, oils, water, alcohol, aether, all possess the power.

And lastly, we may observe, that in all of them, though the degree of action may differ, still it is always the same in kind, being a rotative power over the ray of light; and further, the direction of the rotation is, in every case, independent of the nature or state of the substance, and dependent upon the direction of the magnetic line of force . . . (2173–5).

Faraday had by no means abandoned his concept of intermolecular strain as the transmitter of magnetic or electrical force. In paragraph (2240) he specifically repeated his views on the dependence of inductive and magnetic action upon the action of contiguous particles. The line of force, however, was becoming ever more real to him, and the particles less so. When the title of this paper was questioned, Faraday replied, revealing once again the hold the lines of force were beginning to exercise over his mind.

I believe that, in the experiments I describe in the paper [he explained], light has been magnetically affected, *i.e.* that that which is magnetic in the forces of matter has been affected, and in turn has affected that which is truly magnetic in the force of light: by the term magnetic I include here either of the peculiar exertions of the power of a magnet, whether it be that which is manifest in the magnetic or the diamagnetic class of bodies. The phrase 'illumination of the lines of magnetic force' has been understood to imply that I had rendered them luminous. This was not within my thought. I intended to express that the line of magnetic force was illuminated as the earth is illuminated by the sun, or the spider's web illuminated by the astronomer's lamp. Employing a ray of light, we can tell, *by the eye*, the direction of the magnetic lines through a body; and by the alteration of the ray and its optical effect on the eye, can see the course of the lines just as we can see the course of a thread of glass, or any other transparent substance, rendered visible by the light: and this is what I meant by *illumination*, as the paper fully explains.[59]

The use of the analogy of a spider's web was particularly revealing of Faraday's vision of the lines of force at this time. The lines of force, like a three-dimensional web, filled the universe and accounted for the unity and harmony of the cosmos. When the strands of the web were plucked, waves of light, magnetism, or electricity passed at incredible speeds throughout space. They were, in short, ray vibrations.

The increasing importance of the line of force in Faraday's mind was not solely the result of theoretical considerations. There was a very peculiar experimental fact that raised the line of force to new eminence.

Although he recounted the experiment in the published paper, it was most clearly explained in the letter to Sir John Herschel already cited (see Figure 3).

> . . . Let [A] represent a square cell filled with oil of turpentine and [B] [C] a ray of light passed through it. Let the circles [D] and [E] represent rotation round the oil of turpentine in the one or other direction and finally suppose that the fluid has naturally *right handed* rotation. Then if the ray be passed

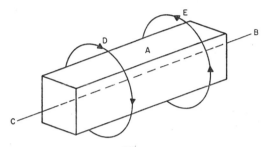

Fig. 3

> from [B] to [C] and observed at [C] the natural rotation will be right handed or according to the circle [D]. If the ray pass from [C] to [B] and be observed at [B] the rotation will still be right handed to the observer at [B] and there-fore according to the circle [E]. Now send an electric current round the fluid in the constant direction of the circle [D]. It will enhance rotation of the ray to the right hand or as the circle [D], the observer being at [C] but *leave the current unchanged* and change the place of the observer from [C] to [B] now the rotation of the ray will be to the observer's *left hand* not as the circle [E] but still as the circle [D] and the same holds good for the rotation by magnetic force.[60]

There was one point that Faraday did not mention, but which had better be made explicit, namely that when the observer changed places, the direction of the ray of light necessarily must be reversed also so that the light will pass from C to B instead of from B to C. Now, what does this experiment prove? It would at least suggest a peculiar property of light. Suppose that the electromagnetic line of force merely threw the particles of the turpentine (or of the heavy glass) into a state of strain, as in Figure 4. No matter which end of the parallelopiped the light passed through first, the rotation would always be to the right. The polarity was in the particles, not the line of force. If a plane polarized ray were passed through this body so that it was reflected from the opposite surface, and returned through the substance, the two effects would cancel each other out and the ray would emerge precisely as it entered.

In Faraday's experiment, this did not happen. When the observer changed position so that all that changed in the experiment was the direction of the ray of light or, if you will, the relative directions of the passage of the lines of force and the ray of light, then the *apparent* rotation of the plane of polarized light changed also. Thus, when the observer was at C

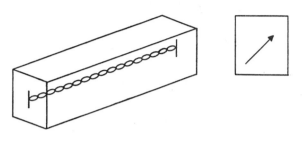

Fig. 4

the ray was rotated to the right; when he observed from B, it was rotated to the left. Since all that had changed was the direction of the light ray, it must somehow be associated with this change. Thus, again, Faraday's attention was drawn away from the condition of the *particles,* and focused upon the direct relations of the line of force and the ray of light.

It is fortunate that a record of the specific concept that now began to occupy him has been preserved. When Sir John Herschel heard of Faraday's discovery, he asked Faraday to perform an experiment for him to confirm some views he had long held on the subject of the interrelationship of light and magnetism.[61] Faraday agreed, but attached a condition to his agreement.

> I must request you [he wrote] to take care of the accompanying paper, not opening it but doing with it as I may hereafter direct. I have certain views and amongst them two which if verified people might say were in some way derived from your suggestions. I do not think it likely your experiment will lead you to them, nevertheless least [*sic*] it should do so I wish to guard my own position by putting on sure record before hand what are my expectations in these respects.[62]

When Faraday reported to Herschel that the experiment had not succeeded, Sir John sent the note back to Faraday who preserved it with the rest of Herschel's letters. It is of great interest for it reveals Faraday's speculative explanation of the experiment with the turpentine. 'I have reason', he had written in the note, 'from experiment to think that a ray is not indifferent as to its line of path but has different properties in its two directions and that by opposing rays end ways new results will be obtained.'[63]

The polarization that really mattered here was not that of the *particles*
but of the *ray of light* and the *line of force*. Thus when the direction of the ray
of light was reversed, the rotation of the plane of polarization[64] was also
reversed when the ray was observed from the opposite end of the parallelopiped. In this case, if the ray were reflected from the opposite surface, it
should return with its rotation *increased,* not cancelled, as would be true in
the case of mere molecular strain.[65] Faraday, therefore, now had two types
of polarity to work with; one was associated with the particles of matter
and followed directly from the theory of point atoms, for when these
atoms were strained, the pattern of forces was changed to give poles to
the particles. The other involved the line of force. At this point, Faraday
did not (nor could he) dissociate the line of force from matter but such a
separation was later to become necessary.[66] The separation was to constitute a fundamental advance in the development of field theory. In 1845
all that he could do was speculate and call attention to the fact that he had
to deal with some new manifestation of the forces of matter. He specifically rejected the idea that the new effect was essentially akin to ordinary
magnetism.

> If the magnetic forces [he wrote] had made these bodies magnets, we could,
> by light, have examined a transparent magnet; and that would have been a
> great help to our investigation of the forces of matter. But it does not make
> them magnets . . ., and therefore the molecular condition of these bodies,
> when in the state described, must be specifically distinct from that of mag
> netized iron, or other such matter, and must be *a new magnetic condition*; and
> as the condition is a state of tension (manifested by its instantaneous return to
> the normal state when the magnetic induction is removed), so the *force*
> which the matter in this state possesses and its mode of action, must be to us
> a *new magnetic force* or *mode of action* of matter (2227).

There were two puzzling things about the new mode of action of
matter. Why, if a state of tension were created by a magnet, did not the
state of tension interact with the magnet to create attractions or repulsions
of the diamagnetic? And why, if the state were analogous to the electrotonic state, were gases unaffected? These were the questions which Faraday now set out to answer, firmly believing that there *must* be interaction
between diamagnetics and magnets, and that gases could not be exempt
from what must be a universal force of nature.

His early efforts again met with failure. On 6 October 1845, he noted in
his *Diary*:

Floated a bar of heavy glass . . . in water, and kept it in the middle of the glass by a wire rising into a tube, etc., and then on the outside of the glass brought the opposite poles of our horse shoe magnet, and left all to ascertain if any effect. Could not discover that the glass paid any respect to the magnet; it kept any position it happened to take up and was not drawn or repelled either into one position or another . . . [7743].

It was not until 4 November that success was achieved. Again Faraday's persistence should be noted in the face of repeated failures. There *had* to be an interaction, for such an interaction was a necessary consequence of his theory. Failure, therefore, only meant that the experimental set-up was not appropriate to detect the effect, and not that the effect did not exist.

The bar of heavy glass . . ., $1\frac{6}{8}$ of inch long and [ ] of an inch square, was suspended by cocoon silk in a glass jar on principle as before . . . and placed between the poles of the last magnet. . . .[67] When it was arranged and had come to rest, I found I *could* affect it by the Magnetic forces and give it position; thus touching dimagnetics [*sic*] by magnetic curves and observing a property quite independent of light, by which also we may probably trace these forces into opaque and other bodies, as the metals, etc. The nature of the affection was this. Let N and S represent the poles and G the bar of heavy glass. It was arranged so as to stand as in the figure [5A]. Then on making N and S active by the Electric current, G traversed not so as to point between N and S but across them, thus [5B], and when the current was stopped the glass returned to its first position. Next arranged the glass when stationary thus [5C], then put on power, and now it moved in the contrary direction to

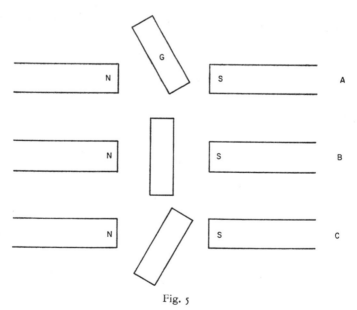

Fig. 5

take up cross position as before; so that the end which before went to the left hand now went to the right, that being the neutral or natural condition [7902].

'How well this shews the new Magnetic property of matter,' Faraday exulted.

'How curiously it contrasts with the results and conclusions of those who say that all bodies are magnetic and point, since the great class of dimagnetics, being nearly all bodies, instead of pointing, tend to stand equatorially' [7908].

Faraday did not know it at the time but he was by no means the first person to observe this effect. Brugmans first observed the repulsion of bismuth by a magnet in 1778. Coulomb appears to have seen a needle of wood set itself *across* a magnetic field; Edmond Becquerel reported the effect on wood in 1827, the same year that le Baillif published a paper on the magnetic repulsion of bismuth and antimony. In 1828 Seebeck reported the same effect with other substances.[68] Faraday's success was not, therefore, the result of exceptional experimental skill. That the discovery of the class of diamagnetics is always associated with Faraday's name is due to the fact that he knew what to do with the discovery whereas the others did not. Commenting on le Baillif's paper on the magnetic repulsion of bismuth and antimony, Faraday remarked, 'It is astonishing that such an experiment has remained so long without further results.'[69] There was, however, nothing really astonishing about it. None of those who observed the effect before Faraday had any room for it in their theories of magnetic action. Magnets either attracted or repelled – they did not set bodies on edge. If they did, it was an anomaly that had to be explained away, not explained. Faraday, however, had already recognized that the new diamagnetic force was a rather odd one. Therefore, although the setting of his glass across the lines of magnetic force was peculiar, it was completely consonant with the peculiarity of diamagnetic action in general.

Faraday, once more, followed his usual experimental procedure. Having found a new effect, he set out to see how general it was. Everything from glass to foolscap paper, from litharge to raw meat was suspended between the poles of his powerful electromagnet. In the Twentieth Series, he listed over fifty substances exhibiting diamagnetic properties.

It is curious to see such a list as this of bodies presenting on a sudden this remarkable property, and it is strange to find a piece of wood, or beef, or apple, obedient to or repelled by a magnet. If a man could be suspended, with sufficient delicacy, after the manner of Dufay, and placed in the magnetic field, he would point equatorially; for all the substances of which he is formed, including the blood, possess this property (2281).

Diamagnetism, Faraday seemed to be saying, was not a rare and exotic thing but connected intimately with the very marrow of our being. It was magnetism which was the exception and diamagnetism that was the rule. Surely such a power, Faraday was convinced, could not help but play a major role in the overall economy of nature. The cosmic implications of Faraday's discovery (as Faraday saw them) we shall discuss in the next section.

4. The Magnetic Properties of Gases and Terrestrial Magnetism

The one area in which neither magnetism nor diamagnetism appeared to intrude was that of the gases. To Faraday, this was impossible. These were basic forces of matter and, even given the exceptional properties of gases which seemed to set them apart from other species of matter, they still must share in its fundamental properties. His work on the condensation of gases, and especially his study of the critical point, had convinced him that there was a basic continuity between the liquid and the gaseous state. If liquids exhibited magnetic and diamagnetic properties, then gases could not be indifferent to the power of the magnet.

In 1845 the action of gases in a magnetic field eluded Faraday. No matter how he tried, he could detect no reaction whatsoever. The gases always occupied the zero position between magnetic and diamagnetic bodies. When they were compressed or when they were rarefied, they still registered 0° when polarized light was passed through them. This strange behaviour led Faraday to remark:

> The magnetic relation of aëriform bodies is exceedingly remarkable. That oxygen or nitrogen gas should stand in a position intermediate between the magnetic and diamagnetic classes; that it should occupy the place which *no* solid or liquid element can take; that it should show no change in its relations by rarefaction to any possible degree, or even when the space it occupies passes into a vacuum; that it should be the same magnetically with any other gas or vapour; that it should not take its place at one end but in the very middle of the great series of bodies; and that all gases or vapours should be alike, from the rarest state of hydrogen to the densest state of carbonic acid, sulphurous acid, or aether vapour, are points so striking, as to persuade one at once that air must have a great and perhaps an active part to play in the physical and terrestrial arrangement of magnetic forces (2432).

There was a possible explanation of the failure of gases to respond to magnetic forces that Faraday suggested. Supposing *all* bodies really were magnetic as Coulomb had suggested. Since these bodies were immersed in an ocean of air, the difference in their reaction to a magnetic field might be caused by the magnetic properties of the air itself.

It is easy to perceive [Faraday wrote] that if all bodies were magnetic in different degrees, forming one great series from end to end, with air in the middle of the series, the effects would take place as they do actually occur. Any body from the middle part of the series would point equatorially in the bodies above it and axially in those beneath it; for the matter which, like bismuth, goes from a strong to a weak point of action, may do so only because that substance, which is already at the place of weak action tends to come to the place where the action is strong; just as in electrical induction the bodies best fitted to carry on the force are drawn into the shortest line of action. And so air in water, or even under mercury is, or appears to be, drawn towards the magnetic pole (2438).

This explanation had the attraction of both accounting for the peculiar action of gases and emphasizing the basic unity of magnetic action. It was an explanation to which Faraday would return some seven years later only to reject it.[70] In 1845 there were seeming insuperable obstacles to its adoption. The gases still preserved their uniqueness by *not* acting upon a polarized ray of light when in a magnetic field. Thus, the continuity assumed by the hypothesis was really illusory since the gases acted here neither like magnetics or diamagnetics, each of which class of substances did act upon a ray of polarized light. A more serious objection was that the rarefaction of gases had no effect whatsoever upon their magnetic action. Thus, by extrapolation, empty space would have magnetic properties and this strained credulity a bit too much. How, after all, could *Nothing* (which was what space was, by definition) have any properties? In 1845 Faraday recognized the difficulty and rejected the hypothesis he, himself, had introduced.

Such a view [he admitted] also would make mere space magnetic, and precisely to the same degree as air and gases. Now though it may very well be, that space, air and gases, have the same general relation to magnetic force, it seems to me a great additional assumption to suppose that they are all absolutely magnetic, and in the midst of a series of bodies, rather than to suppose that they are in a normal or zero state. For the present, therefore, I incline to the former view, and consequently to the opinion that diamagnetics have a specific action antithetically distinct from ordinary magnetic action, and have thus presented us with a magnetic property new to our knowledge (2440).

Perhaps the most revolutionary of Faraday's ideas was to be the assignment of magnetic properties to empty space. In the 1850's he would quietly and without fuss or bother introduce the idea that empty space could transmit magnetic forces and must, therefore, itself be in a state of strain. Upon this idea, modern field theory was to be built.

The main stream of Faraday's thought henceforth was to consist of speculations and concepts dealing with the relationship between magnetic force and the forces of the particles of matter. This will be the subject of the next chapter. A tributary to this main stream was the discovery of the magnetic properties of gases and their relationship to the magnetic qualities of the earth. This aspect of Faraday's work contributed little to the development of his theories of magnetic action, but it did serve to confirm his strongly held belief in the unity of the forces of matter. It also revealed his deep faith in the harmony of the creation brought about by the beneficence of the Creator.

The discovery of the magnetic properties of gases, which had eluded Faraday in 1845 and 1846, was made by Signor Bancalari of Italy in 1847 and reported by his countryman, Professor Zantedeschi.[71] Actually, Bancalari had observed the effect of magnetism upon flame but, as flame may be considered a gas, it took little or no imagination on Faraday's part to realize this was the effect for which he had long been seeking.

Faraday first confirmed Bancalari's findings and devised a number of striking experiments by which the effect could be illustrated. It is interesting to compare the account by Zantedeschi and Faraday. Zantedeschi was interested only in establishing the effect and in indicating the fact that flame had magnetic properties. Faraday, on the other hand, wished to establish the *diamagnetic* character of the flame and to show that the only force acting between the magnetic poles and the flame was one of repulsion. Thus Zantedeschi merely mentioned that when his electromagnet was activated, the flame was repelled, returning to its original position when the electromagnet was turned off. This fact Zantedeschi used only to support the 'universality of magnetism'.[72] Faraday wished to emphasize the extent of the repulsive force in order to call attention to its *difference* from that of magnetism. Hence he was not merely content with showing the repulsion, but wanted to make the repulsive force vividly evident. This he did by using a more powerful magnet than Zantedeschi and showing how the flame not only was repelled but actually could be split in two to avoid the magnet poles. 'When a small flame, only about one-third of an inch high, was placed between the poles, the magnetic force instantly flattened it into an equatorial disc.'[73] Instead of the universality of magnetism, Faraday graphically illustrated the peculiar nature of diamagnetism.

Recognizing that the diamagnetism of flame implied the diamagnetic qualities of ordinary gases, Faraday set out to investigate them individually. The first question was, did the diamagnetic effect depend only upon the elevation of temperature caused by the flame? His reasoning on this question is of some interest for it reveals once again his ideas of the relationship between matter and the magnetic force. He had found that the magnetic effect upon polarized light was increased by the quantity of matter through which the light passed. Hence he wrote,

> It is not, I think, at all probable that the mere effect of expanding the air is the cause of the change in its condition, because one would be led to expect that a certain bulk of expanded air would be less sensible in its diamagnetic effects than an equal bulk of denser air; just as one would anticipate that a vacuum would present no magnetic or diamagnetic effects whatever, but be at the zero point between the two classes of bodies. . . .[74]

There was no doubt that heated gases *were* diamagnetic and Faraday used this fact to detect their diamagnetism. A fine platinum helix was substituted for the taper so that hot gases could be produced without flame. The course of the hot gas could be detected by holding a piece of paper over the poles of the magnet. When the electromagnet was off the gas rose straight up and burned a spot on the paper; when the electromagnet was turned on, the stream of hot gas split in two, repelled by the magnetic intensity between the poles, and produced two burnt spots on the paper on either side of the poles.[75]

The problem that presented itself in determining if unheated gases were diamagnetic or not was how to detect the change in the position of the gas or of its stream of flow. There could be no burned spots used as detectors. Nor could the gases be enclosed in containers because the containers themselves reacted to the magnetic forces and would throw the determination off. If any solid material, such as chalk powder or a dust of any kind were suspended in the gas to indicate its path, all that could be told with real certainty was the effect of the magnetic poles on the dust since there was no guarantee that the dust would not act independently of the gas in which it was suspended. Faraday's solution of this problem was beautifully simple and again reveals that experimental skill which permitted him to study effects with the least possible disturbance from extraneous factors.

> Now arranged an apparatus thus. Three thin glass tubes [A], [B], [C], were tied together by thread and blocks of cork, and placed just over the equatorial line and resting on the edges of the magnetic pole [See Figure 6]; another tube [D] was fixed below, under the magnetic axis and about ⅔ of an inch below the end of [B], to deliver a vertical stream of any required gas; a flexible (vulcan rubber) tube was slipped on to the end of this tube and also on to the short quill of a globular receiver [F]. A coil of bibulous paper was put into the part [I] of the tube [D], and moistened with strong solution of muriatic acid; it thus formed a lining to the delivering tube. Folded pieces of bibulous paper

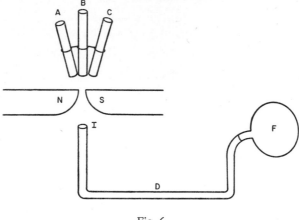

Fig. 6

(about this size) held by copper wire were dipped in strong solution of ammonia and put into the upper part of each of the three tubes [A], [B], [C]. In this case if the globe was filled with any gas lighter than air, the gas remained in the globe when in the position figured, but when the globe was depressed below the level of the tube [D], the gas would go out there between the two poles and ascend up the central tube. The muriatic acid that it would take up at [I], uniting to the ammonia it would find in the tube above, would shew by the formation of mur. amm. cloud, whether and which tube it passed up; and yet whilst passing the magnetic field, the gas would be clear and free from visible fume, so contain no solid or liquid particle to confer any diamagnetic action and thus disturb the result [9121].

With this simple little instrument, Faraday investigated the magnetic properties of a number of different gases. Of all the gases, oxygen was the weakest diamagnetic and Faraday even began to have suspicions that it might be magnetic but he was confused by its weak action in air.[76] His confusion was compounded by the strong feeling that it was not necessary for all bodies to be *either* magnetic *or* diamagnetic. Could there not be a continuity of properties so that magnetism and diamagnetism would shade into one another? Then the observed results would depend upon the relationship between the body being tested and the medium in which the test was carried out. 'The law of all these actions', Faraday wrote, 'is, that if a particle, placed amongst other particles, be more diamagnetic (or less magnetic) tha[n] they, and free to move, it will go from strong to weaker places of magnetic action; also, that particles less diamagnetic will go from weaker to stronger places of action.'[77] The 'zero point' of magnetic action, perhaps associated with a vacuum, was becoming increasingly important. Faraday never found it, but his search led him away from the gases and to other subjects.

In 1850 he returned to the magnetic properties of gases, looking this time for expansive or compressive effects upon the volume of the gas as a whole. This was of crucial importance for his rapidly changing ideas on magnetism, but an account of this work must be deferred to the next chapter. The new experiments, however, led him to realize that oxygen exhibited much stronger magnetic properties than he had realized in 1847. 'The weight of a bubble of oxygen is very small', he noted in his *Diary*. 'What would its weight of iron, in a sphere placed at the same equivalent distance from the axial line, do in comparison of it? Weight for weight, oxygen may be very magnetic' [10941]. The magnetic strength of oxygen could not help but affect the magnetic effects of the earth and Faraday began to explore the connexion between the variations of terrestrial magnetism and the magnetic properties of oxygen. To his obvious delight he discovered that the extraordinarily complex pattern of terrestrial magnetic variation could be explained qualitatively, at least, by three facts; oxygen was magnetic, air was almost neutral, and changes in temperature could so affect the magnetic properties of oxygen that patches of air could act sometimes as strong conductors of magnetic force (i.e. as paramagnetics) and sometimes as poor conductors (i.e. as diamagnetics). From these facts, the mysteries of terrestrial magnetism could be solved.

In the Twenty-sixth Series of the *Experimental Researches,* Faraday undertook to explain the phenomena of terrestrial magnetism by means of his theory. He first showed that nitrogen was magnetically neutral, carbon dioxide was not magnetically affected by heat, and oxygen was both highly magnetic and considerably affected by heat (2854 ff.). These being the component gases of the atmosphere, it was obvious that

> this medium is, by every change in its density, whether of the kind indicated by the barometer, or caused by the presence or absence of the sun, changed in its magnetic relations. Further, every variation of temperature produces apparently its own change of force, in addition to that caused by the mere expansion or contraction in volume, and none of these alterations can happen without affecting the magnetic force emanating from the earth, and causing variations, both in its intensity and direction, at the earth's surface. Whether these changes are in the right direction and sufficient in quantity to supply a cause for the variations of the terrestrial magnetic power, is the point now to be considered . . . (2863).

After first distinguishing between magnetic intensity and quantity (roughly what would today be called permeability and flux density)

(2870), Faraday then proceeded to list the factors in the earth's atmosphere that would affect both. The atmosphere, first of all, 'diminishes in density upwards, and that diminution will affect the transmission of the magnetic force, but as far as it is constant, the effect produced by it will be constant too. The portion of the atmosphere which lies under the heating influence of the sun, as compared to its depth, will more resemble a slice of air wrapped round the earth than a globe' (2879). We, however, are at the bottom of this sea of air where the atmosphere is denser and where temperature effects are probably more intense.

The effect of air temperature could hardly be a general one since it was modified by geographical features such as land masses, oceans, and so on. Fortunately for Faraday's investigation, however, a series of charts of isothermal lines had recently been published in England so that a rough check could be made of the theory.[78]

The variation in the weight distribution of the atmosphere over the earth also would affect magnetic variation.

> There is more air, by weight [Faraday stated], over a given portion of the surface of the earth at latitudes from 24° to 34°, than there is either at higher latitudes or at the equator; and that should cause a difference from the disposition of the lines of force which would exist if there were equality in that respect, or if the atmosphere were away. Again, the temperature of the air is greater at the equatorial parts than in latitudes north or south of it; and as elevation of temperature diminishes the conducting power for magnetism, so the proportion of force passing through these parts ought to be less, and that passing through the colder parts greater, than if the temperature of the air were at the same mean degree over the whole surface of the globe, or than if the air were away. Again, there is a greater difference in range of temperature of the air at the equator as we rise upwards than in other parts, and hence the lower part is not so good a conductor proportionately to the upper part, or to space, as elsewhere, where the difference is not so great . . . (2881).

All these causes of perturbation in magnetic declination and magnetic dip[79] had to be taken into account, although it would seem almost impossible to provide exact quantitative measures of their effects.

These were some of the *possible* variations which might be expected to be irregular and inseparable from one another. There were others that had a distinct regularity and for which, hopefully, a specific cause might be assigned. One of the more obvious was the annual variation and this Faraday felt his theory could explain. As the earth goes around the sun, the two hemispheres are exposed to varying degrees of sunlight through the year. The two hemispheres, therefore,

will become alternately warmer and colder than each other, and then a variation in the magnetic condition may arise. The air of the cooled hemisphere
will conduct magnetic influence more freely than if in the mean state, and the
lines of force passing through it will increase in amount, whilst in the other
hemisphere the warmed air will conduct with less readiness than before, and
the intensity will diminish. In addition to this effect of temperature, there
ought to be another due to the increase of the ponderable portion of the air in
the cooled hemisphere, consequent upon its contraction and the coincident
expansion of the air in the warmer half, both of which circumstances tend to
increase the variation in power of the two hemispheres from the normal
state (2883).

The variation in magnetic power clearly must affect dip; as the northern
hemisphere, say, first becomes a better, then a worse, conductor of the
magnetic forces, the angle of dip will change.

The line of no dip round the globe may therefore be expected to move alternately north and south every year, or some effect equivalent to that take place.
The condition of the two hemispheres under this view may be conceived by
supposing an annual undulation of the force to and fro between them, during
which, though neither the character nor the general disposition of the power
be altered, there is in our winter a concentration and increase of intensity in
the northern parts coincident with a diffused and diminished intensity in the
south, and in summer the reverse (2884).

Such a crowding together and moving apart of the lines of magnetic force
clearly involved variation in the declination as well. Irregularities would
be influenced by local conditions. Since, for example, there is less annual
change of temperature at the equator than elsewhere, the annual variation
will be less. Faraday's theory on the annual variation was supported,
qualitatively, by the observations of Colonel Sabine.[80]

The diurnal variation Faraday related directly to the passage of the sun
in its daily course (2892). Once again he was able to use Sabine's figures
taken from observations at Toronto in the northern hemisphere and
Hobarton in the southern. The correlation of solar motion and diurnal
variation was by no means original with Faraday. What was new was his
explanation in terms of the changing magnetic conductibility of the
atmosphere with temperature variation. The argument is a lovely one,
fitting every figure neatly into place and drawing out the alternation of
cause and effect into a logical chain of considerable strength. There is no
reason to reproduce the argument here for it merely draws upon the
principles already discussed earlier. What is important to notice is the
consonance of theory and fact. Even apparent anomalies disappeared. For
example, at Hobarton there seemed to be an inexplicable weakness in the

conducting power of the atmosphere. Faraday, however, reminds us that according to Dove's temperature charts, the southern hemisphere is generally warmer than the northern; hence, lower conductibility of the atmosphere is predicted by the theory.

The Twenty-sixth and Twenty-seventh Series[81] were impressive papers. For a man who complained that he was finding it increasingly impossible to keep more than two thoughts in his mind at the same time, it was an astonishing performance. Facts were marshalled, hypotheses framed, the theory applied, and the 'fit' between evidence and theory carefully assessed. And, behind it all, in Faraday's mind, was his vision of the earth, wrapped snugly in its lines of magnetic force. To disturb one was to disturb them all just as brushing a spider's web sent a tremor through all the strands. No effect could be isolated; any that touched the line of force here must alter it there. Again, the web reveals his thought; the watch put together by the watchmaker God of the eighteenth-century deist had no function, not even that of telling time. It merely ran. Each thread of the spider's web, however, was part of an overall plan, having a purpose in the total architecture of the universe. Similarly, Faraday could close the Twenty-sixth Series with a query upon the universal Grand Design.

> One can scarcely think upon the subject of atmospheric magnetism without having another great question suggested to the mind. . . . What is the final purpose in nature of this magnetic condition of the atmosphere, and its liability to annual and diurnal variations, and its entire loss by entering into combination either in combustion or respiration? No doubt there is one or more, for nothing is superfluous there. We find no remainders or surplusage of action in physical forces. The smallest provision is as essential as the greatest. None are deficient, none can be spared (2968).

His conviction of the unity of force had led him, through the correlation of forces, to the contemplation of the harmonies of the solar system. His final researches on the ultimate nature of force were to lead him to a view of the cosmos based upon concepts which were to form the foundations of classical field theory.

References

1. The most important of de la Rive's papers are:
   'Analyse des circonstances qui déterminent le *sens* et l'*intensité* du courant électrique dans un élément voltaïque', *Ann. de chim. et de phys.*, 2 Ser., *37* (1828), 225 ff.
   'Recherches sur la cause de l'électricité voltaïque', *Mém. de la Soc. de*

phys. et d'hist. nat. de Gén., Part I, *4* (1828), 285 ff.; Part 2, *6* (1833), 149 ff.; Part 3, *7* (1836), 457 ff.

'Researches into the Cause of Voltaic Electricity', *L. & E. Phil. Mag.*, N.S., *11* (1837), 274 ff.

2. See, for example, Stefano Marianini, 'Sopra la teoria della pila' in *Memorie della Società Italiana delle Scienze residente in Modena*, 20₂ (1833), 347, and the article by the same author, 'Sur la Théorie chimique des électromoteurs voltaïques simples et composés', *Ann. de chim. et de phys.*, 2 Ser., *45* (1830), 28 ff. and 113 ff.

3. Bib. Univ. et pub. de Génève, MS. 2316, 88 A4, f. 54, Faraday to A. de la Rive, R.I., 24 April 1840.

4. Stefano Marianini, 'Sulla teoria degli Elettromotori, Memoria IV. Esame di alcune sperienze addotte dal Sig. Faraday per provare che l'elettricità Voltaica nasce dall'azione chimica dei liquidi sui metalli. Con un'appendice sopra un'anomalia che presentario alcune metalli nella decomposizione dell'Ioduro di Potassio operata dall'Elettricità', *Mem. della Soc. It. delle Sci. residente in Modena*, 21₂ (1837), 205 ff.

5. Gustav Theodor Fechner, 'Justification of the Contact Theory of Galvanism', *L. & E. Phil. Mag.*, *13* (1838), 205 ff. and 367 ff. I have used this translation of Fechner's article because it was the one used by Faraday. The paper was originally published in Poggendorf's *Annalen*, *42* (1837), 481 ff.

6. Marianini, in his 1830 essay, used this example.

7. It is interesting to see here how close Faraday came to the principle of the Conservation of Energy. Yet, it is a miss for one essential element is lacking – Faraday does not have at hand the common measure of work by which the *conversion* of forces could be shown to be quantitatively equal.

8. Fechner had used an electrometer to show that mere contact resulted in difference in charge between the two dissimilar metals after they were separated. Faraday felt that an electrometer was far too untrustworthy an instrument to rely upon to settle a question of such importance as the theory of voltaic action. Hence he dismissed Fechner's views almost out of hand, and concentrated, instead, upon Marianini. See (1808).

9. It should be specifically noted that Faraday was attacking the contact theory *only* as it referred to the voltaic pile. In a letter to C. F. Schoenbein he wrote:

'Dr Poggendorff who was here lately told me of Fechners objections but when he learnt from me that I by no means go the length of De la Rive and that I admit *many other modes of electrical excitement* besides chemical action, I thought he seemed to think that Fechners objections were rather against De la Rive than me.' Kahlbaum and Darbishire, op. cit., 51.

10. For the importance of this statement to Faraday's own views, see Michael Faraday, 'On Dr Hare's Second Letter, and on the Chemical and Contact Theories of the Voltaic Battery', *L. & E. Phil. Mag.*, N.S., *22* (1843), 268. When, in 1844, Faraday collected a number of articles together to form volume 2 of the *Experimental Researches* he added a note recognizing that as early as 1829, Dr P. M. Roget, in his *Treatise on Galvanism* in the Library of Useful Knowledge had explicitly stated the impossibility of a perpetual motion, even of an imponderable fluid. This, then, ruled out Volta's contact theory although few seemed to

be convinced by Roget's argument. Roget's statement was called to Faraday's attention by a letter from Roget to Faraday, 27 March 1840, which is inserted in Faraday's bound copies of his papers at the R.I. at the end of the Seventeenth Series.

11. The Seventeenth Series of the *Experimental Researches*, read on 19 March 1840, was Faraday's second article on the theory of the pile; the Nineteenth Series was read to the Royal Society on 20 November 1845. The Eighteenth Series, read 2 February 1843, was a relatively unimportant paper 'On the electricity evolved by the friction of water and steam against other bodies'. In 1840, an engineer, H. G. Armstrong, wrote to Faraday about the electricity produced by a jet of steam issuing from a boiler. (*L. & E. Phil. Mag.*, N.S., *17* (1840), 370.) Armstrong argued that this phenomenon proved the one-fluid theory of electricity; Faraday's Eighteenth Series was devoted to showing that the electricity produced was the result of friction and no fluids of any kind (except water) were necessary.

12. William Whewell, *History of the Inductive Sciences* (3rd ed., 2 vols., New York, 1894), *2*, 611.

13. A. de la Rive, *Traité d'électricité théorique et appliquée* (3 vols., Paris, 1854–8), *1*, 138 ff.

14. W. Snow Harris, 'Inquiries Concerning the Elementary Laws of Electricity, – Third Series', *Phil. Trans.*, 1839, 215 ff.

15. I.E.E., W. Snow Harris to M. Faraday, Plymouth, 27 March 1858.

16. Robert Hare, 'A Letter to Prof. Faraday, on certain Theoretical Opinions', *Exp. Res.*, *2*, 251 ff. Also, see above, pp. 306 ff.

17. M. Faraday, 'An answer to Dr Hare's Letter on certain Theoretical Opinions', *Exp. Res.*, *2*, 262 ff. Also, see above, pp. 306 ff.

18. Ibid., 262.

19. Hare's second letter was dated 1 January 1841, and appeared in the *L. & E. Phil. Mag.*, N.S., *18* (1841), 465 ff. The quotation is on page 466.

20. Ibid., 467 and 474.

21. A good part of Hare's letter was devoted to expounding his own theory of electrical action. This part does not concern us.

22. This letter is reprinted in *Exp. Res.*, *2*, 275.

23. M. Faraday, 'On Dr Hare's Second Letter, and on the Chemical and Contact Theories of the Voltaic Battery', *Exp. Res.*, *2*, 274 ff.

24. *Exp. Res.*, *2*, 279 ff.

25. Ibid.

26. Ibid., 280.

27. Ibid., 281.

28. Ibid.

29. Ibid., 283.

30. Ibid.

31. *Exp. Res.*, *2*, 284 ff.

32. 'Light and electricity are two great and searching investigators of the molecular structure of bodies, and it was whilst considering the probable nature of conduction and insulation in bodies not decomposable by the electricity to which they were subject, and the relation of electricity to space contemplated as

void of that which by the atomists is called matter, that considerations something like those which follow were presented to my mind.' *Exp. Res.*, *2*, 286.

33. Ibid., 284.

34. Ibid., 285.

35. For this work, done throughout 1844, see M. Faraday, 'On the Liquefaction and Solidification of Bodies generally existing as Gases', in *Exp. Res.
in Chem. and Phys.*, 96 ff.

36. *Exp. Res.*, *2*, 286.

37. Ibid., 288.

38. Ibid., 289.

39. Ibid., 290.

40. *Quar. Rev.*, *79* (1847), 124.

41. *Exp. Res.*, *2*, 291.

42. M. Faraday, 'An Answer to Dr Hare's Letter on certain Theoretical
Opinions', *Exp. Res.*, *2*, 266.

43. Hare remained unconvinced and used Faraday's arguments, instead, to
prove the materiality of the imponderable fluids! See Robert Hare, 'Remarks
made by Dr Hare, at a late meeting of the American Philosophical Society, on a
recent speculation by Faraday on Electric Conduction and the Nature of
Matter', *L. & E. Phil. Mag.*, N.S., *26* (1845), 602 ff.

44. *Exp. Res.*, *2*, 293.

45. Ibid., 290.

46. M. Faraday, 'Thoughts on Ray-vibrations', *Exp. Res. in Chem. and Phys.*,
370.

47. *Exp. Res. in Chem. and Phys.*, 367.

48. Ibid., 371.

49. Laplace, in his *Exposition du Système du monde,* had decided that for all
practical purposes, the propagation of gravity was instantaneous.

50. The term 'critical point' was not used by Faraday. He called it the Cagniard
de la Tour state, a clumsy expression which he quite properly wished to avoid.
The 'critical point' was first used by Dr Thomas Andrews in his Bakerian
Lecture 'On the Continuity of the Gaseous and Liquid States of Matter' (1869).
See *The Scientific Papers of the Late Thomas Andrews, M.D., F.R.S.* (London, 1889),
307.

51. Archives de l'Académie des Sciences, dossier Faraday, Faraday to J.-B.
Dumas, 14 December 1844.

52. 'On the Liquefaction and solidification of Bodies generally existing as
Gases', *Exp. Res. in Chem. and Phys.*, 96.

53. A. Avogadro, 'Saggio di teoria matematica della distribuzione dell'-
elettricità sulla superficie dei corpi conduttori nell'ipotesi dell'azione induttiva
esercitate dalla medesima sui corpi circostanti, per mezzo particelle dell'aria
frapporta', *Mem. della Soc. Ital. delle Scienze residente in Modena*, *23* (1844), 156 ff.

54. William Thomson to M. Faraday, St Peter's College [Cambridge],
6 August 1845. The letter is printed in its entirety in Silvanus P. Thompson,
The Life of William Thomson, Baron Kelvin of Largs (2 vols., London, 1910), *1*,
146 ff.

55. Faraday to William Thomson, 8 August 1845, in ibid., 149.

o

56. Compare *Diary*, *4*, 256 and *Diary*, *1*, 71.

57. R.S., Faraday–Herschel Correspondence, Faraday to Sir John Herschel, Brighton, 13 November 1845.

58. Unlike the terms of electrochemistry, this seems to be Faraday's invention. The model was, of course, dielectric and Faraday's first term was an exact copy – dimagnetic. This was used in the letter to Herschel, cited above. Between the date of this letter and the publication of his paper, Faraday inserted the *a*, as required by proper linguistic usage.

59. *Exp. Res.*, *3*, 1, note 2.

60. Faraday to Herschel, loc. cit.

61. R.S., Faraday–Herschel Correspondence, Sir John Herschel to M. Faraday, Collingwood, 20 December 1845.

62. R.S., Faraday–Herschel Correspondence, Faraday to Sir John Herschel, R.I., 22 December 1845. The experience with Wollaston and electromagnetic rotations had obviously left deep scars!

63. The note is dated R.I., 22 December 1845, and is appended to a letter from Herschel to Faraday, in R.S., Herschel–Faraday Correspondence, dated 22 January 1846.

The second speculation is also worth recording. It shows Faraday's deep faith in the correlation of forces.

'I have already made a certain progress in the endeavour to obtain Electric currents or magnetic force from light by the use of circular polarization natural and constrained and also on other principles which I need not advert to here.'

64. It is difficult to avoid confusion here since the term 'polarization' is being used in two different ways. I wish merely to call attention to the difference. One refers simply to the plane of vibration of a ray of light; the other indicates that the line of force has *poles*, i.e. different ends, so that it makes a difference whether one goes from C to B or from B to C.

65. This was precisely what Faraday did. He was able to increase the angle of rotation by repeated reflections within a glass parallelopiped. M. Faraday, 'On the Magnetic Affection of Light, and on the Distinction between the Ferromagnetic and Diamagnetic Conditions of Matter' (1846), *Exp. Res.*, *3*, 453 ff.

66. See below, Chapter Ten.

67. This was a new, and very powerful, magnet made out of half a link of ship's anchor chain. The link was wound with over 500 feet of wire and was more powerful than any Faraday had ever used before.

68. For these papers see Faraday's reference to them in *Exp. Res.*, *3*, 82.

69. *Exp. Res.*, *3*, 43, note.

70. See below, Chapter Ten.

71. See Professor Zantedeschi, 'On the Motions presented by Flame when under the Electromagnetic Influence', in *Exp. Res.*, *3*, 490, for the circumstances of this discovery.

72. Ibid., 490 and 492.

73. M. Faraday, 'On the Diamagnetic conditions of Flame and Gases', *Exp. Res.*, *3*, 469. For the actual experiments on flame and gases, see [9066 ff.].

74. Ibid., 473.

75. Ibid., 472.

76. Ibid., 480.

77. Ibid., 487.

78. W. H. Dove, *Temperature Tables*, in *Report of the British Association*, 1847 (London, 1848), 373 ff. and 184; and *Report* . . . 1848 (London, 1849), 85 ff.

79. Magnetic declination is the angle, at any given locality, between the line of point of a magnetic compass, and true magnetic north. Dip is the angle, in the vertical plane, between a line parallel to the ground and the line of point of a magnetic compass. This angle is zero at the equator and 90° at magnetic north. It indicates the direction of the terrestrial line of force.

80. Colonel Sabine, 'On the means adopted in the British Colonial Magnetic Observatories for determining the Absolute Values, Secular Change, and Annual Variation of the Magnetic Force', *Phil. Trans.*, 1850, 201 ff.

81. The Twenty-seventh Series added more examples and a laboratory model of atmospheric magnetic action to the Twenty-sixth.

CHAPTER TEN

The Origins of Field Theory

1. The Magnecrystallic Force

The discovery of diamagnetism strongly reinforced Faraday's faith in the convertibility of all forces and clearly influenced his approach to any new phenomenon of this sort. Not only did he attempt to discover the effect in all bodies, but he was now convinced that all processes which brought to light a force of any kind must be reversible. All that had to be done was to discover the proper conditions under which the reverse process could manifest itself, as he had done when he discovered electromagnetic induction. Diamagnetism should certainly be no exception and so, for some years, Faraday strove to reveal the reverse effects of those he had announced in 1845. These investigations were entirely negative and they may be examined only in the laboratory *Diary*, for Faraday did not publish an account of this search.

Over the course of the years, Faraday sought four different effects. Having been convinced by the peculiar nature of the rotation of polarized light in a magnetic field that the ray of light itself had poles, he sought to discover an interaction between light rays which would be completely analogous to the interaction of magnetic poles. Polarized rays of light, passing in opposite directions, should affect one another. Since a light ray was acted upon by a current of electricity in a helix, he also felt strongly that electricity should be produced when light, under the proper conditions, was passed through a helix. Again, his search for a 'photoelectric' effect was to be in vain and even the discovery of such an effect after his death was not under the conditions which he had expected.

An electric current in a helix affected diamagnetic bodies. If diamagnetism were a permanent state, like magnetism in a soft iron bar, then it was to be expected that a diamagnetic would induce a current in a helix under conditions yet to be determined. Finally, the phenomenon of diamagnetism bore some resemblance to that of crystallization for both the diamagnetic force and the crystalline force were capable of acting upon polarized light. Might not crystalline force, magnetic force, and diamagnetic force be related? This line of thought was to lead him (with some outside help) to the discovery of magnecrystallic action.

Faraday was not able to turn to his speculation on the polarity of light rays until January 1846. At that time he devised a series of simple experiments to determine whether two rays of plane polarized light coming from opposite directions would interact. The light from a small lamp was reflected from a thin glass plate set at the angle of polarization so that a ray, polarized horizontally, was sent in one direction. This ray was reflected once again out of its main path to a Nichol prism analyser where its state could be examined. Another, stronger source of light was set up so that rays coming from it could also be polarized horizontally and sent along the path of the first rays, but in the opposite direction. There was no effect observed. Various substances such as oil of turpentine, heavy glass, iron sulphate, and camphine were then placed in the path of the rays, but still no interaction was observed [8646–8663]. Faraday was not convinced by his negative results and noted in his *Diary*, 'Think there ought to be a difference still in the two directions of a ray – and must experiment with light of the Sun or of the stars' [8664].

This was a curious remark. Sunlight, of course, had the great advantage of intensity to recommend it. It could be considered, like Henry's electromagnet in 1831, as a source of intense power which might be necessary to make an effect observable. But starlight certainly had no such quality. Faraday, again, reveals nothing of what he had in mind. Could it be that light from the sun and from the stars, transmitted by lines of force undisturbed by the forces of ponderable matter, was less subject to the perturbations which masked the effect with terrestrial sources of light? We have no answer and Faraday did not pursue the subject further. He remained, nevertheless, persuaded of the polarity of light rays and of the lines of force that transmitted them.[1]

In March 1846, Faraday made his first serious attempt to produce electricity from light. His reasoning was simple. When plane polarized light was passed through a substance surrounded by a helix through which an electric current flowed, the plane of polarization was rotated. It seemed to follow logically (given Faraday's conviction of reversibility) that if a ray of plane polarized light were passed through a substance which naturally rotated the plane of polarization, a current should be induced in a helix surrounding the substance. The experiment was tried, 'But whether the light was on or off or intermitted or reflected – no effect at the galvanometer occurred, i.e. the natural rotation of the Camphine caused no effect' [8688]. Faraday's expectations here were far stronger than those his speculations on the nature of light rays had produced. There was simply too much evidence for the conversion of forces for Faraday to abandon this search after one failure.

In June 1846, sunlight was utilized in 'compressed' form by means of a lens and collimator. His heavy glass was wound with a coil connected to a galvanometer but again no effect was discernible when the light passed through the arrangement [8695–6]. The light was then polarized before passage through the glass; still, no effect [8697]. The polarizer was rotated rapidly about its axis so that the plane of polarization of the light was constantly changing [8698].[2] No current could be detected in the helix.

No further attempt to discover a photoelectric effect was made until September 1847. At that time an intense limelight was used and the ray was intercepted by an opaque screen some 400 times per second. Various media were placed in the helix, but the result was negative once more [9022–7].

There was one possible cause for failure in all these experiments. Faraday was trying to convert light into electricity, yet, in every case there was almost as much light at the end of the experiment as at the beginning. Only a very small amount of light had been absorbed in its passage through the various media and according to Faraday's own ideas on the conservation of force, no effect should have been produced. Somehow the light force had to be 'used up' if it were to appear under the guise of electricity. For transparent substances, therefore, it was necessary to substitute materials in which the light ray would be absorbed and disappear. A dark solution of iron salts, dark quartz and a piece of heavy glass blackened by the presence of reduced particles of lead were all tried but to no avail [9030–2]. The helix still remained passive.

Another possibility now suggested itself to Faraday. Hitherto the ray of light had always gone in the same direction, even when it had been passed through the helix in intermittent flashes. Might not a sudden change of direction create the desired effect? Faraday proceeded to test this idea. Flat, silvered copper was wound around a smooth board in such a way that the strands did not touch one another. The ends were connected to a galvanometer and the board exposed to the sun's rays. Light could be reflected from the wires from any direction merely by turning the board, 'but no trace of any electric current due to the act of reflecting the light could be in any case perceived' [9034]. The silver-coated wire was then blackened with a sulphide solution 'so as to cause absorption of great part of the light – but still no trace of any current produced by the act of absorption could be perceived' [9035]. In spite of this series of disappointing experiments, Faraday wrote: 'Still, I think, there must be some relation between these functions of light and electric forces' [9036]. The effect for which he sought was ever to elude him.[3]

The possibility that diamagnetic bodies might induce an electric current was first examined in August 1846. This problem was of more than passing interest for it involved a tentative hypothesis of diamagnetic action. In November 1845, while Faraday was still trying to fit diamagnetism within the framework of some known theory of magnetic action, he had noted in his *Diary*: 'Is it likely there can be currents formed round the *particles* of air, Glass, bismuth and other bodies than the magnetic metals? If so, they must be currents in the opposite direction, or they would not account for the repulsion in all directions'[4] [8171].

The detection of currents induced by diamagnetics was, therefore doubly important. Such currents would be another piece of evidence for the conversion of forces; if the induced currents flowed in the *opposite* direction to those induced by a magnetic body under identical circumstances, this would show that the electrical currents circulating around the particles of diamagnetics were opposite in direction to those to be found in magnets. It is really extraordinary to see Faraday in 1845 and 1846 still testing Ampère's theory! All his own work pointed away from Ampère's electrodynamic model yet, faced with a new and mysterious action, Faraday refused to ignore even a theory with which he profoundly disagreed.

When a diamagnetic substance was introduced into a helix suspended between the activated poles of an electromagnet, there was no effect [8749–53]. There was no noticeable note of despair in Faraday's conclusion drawn from this experiment. 'Hence,' he wrote, 'I cannot find in diamagnetics any power of producing a current in a helix, like in kind but contrary in direction to that which a piece of iron can produce under the same circumstances'[5] [8754]. His conclusion was in accordance with his feeling that diamagnetism was not merely reversed magnetism but a quite unique force of nature. Ponderable matter was necessary to make the effect evident but it was not at all clear what role the individual particles played.

To produce the expected effect, a cylinder of heavy glass was mounted on an axle upon which was attached a small wheel. A string ran around this wheel to a larger wheel. When the larger wheel made one revolution, the smaller wheel and the heavy glass made twenty-seven. The cylinder also acted as a prism so that a polarized ray sent through it was bent upwards to the analyser (see Figure 1).

When all was arranged in order, so that the polarized beam could be intercepted by the analyser in its way to the eye, then the magnetism was put on and off, and the effect of Magneto rotation was easily brought out in perfection.

Then the glass cylinder was *rotated rapidly*; this caused no disturbance of the image, or of any of the effects when the magnetism was off – nor did it have any more effect when it was *on*; i.e. the rotation of the glass in *either* direction in no way influenced the phenomena, though the parts were travelling with a velocity of about 200 inches in a second [8963–4].

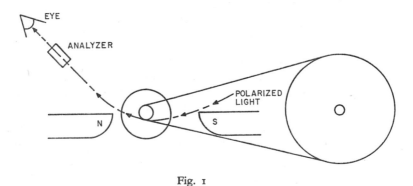

Fig. 1

In 1831 Faraday had rotated a magnet about its own axis and had 'discovered' that the lines of force did not move with it. This had led him to suspect that the lines of force were not the resultant of molecular forces in the magnet. The ability of a diamagnetic to rotate the plane of polarized light even while revolving at a considerable speed appeared, similarly, to rule out the interpretation of diamagnetism as a force inherent in the individual molecules. The rotation of the plane of polarized light seemed, rather, to be dependent upon the intermolecular forces of the diamagnetic. It was the arrangement of the particles in the *mass* of the diamagnetic that influenced the action of the magnetic force upon a light ray. The effect of a magnetic field upon diamagnetics must modify the structure of the diamagnetic material. 'It cannot be doubted', Faraday had written in the paper announcing the effect of magnetism upon light, 'that the magnetic forces act upon and affect the internal constitution of the diamagnetic . . .' (2226). Such an effect was clearly similar to that observed in crystals (2230) so that it was a natural step to take to begin the investigation of the action of magnetism upon crystals themselves.

The step, however, was not taken by Faraday. His full attention was focused on mapping the generality of diamagnetism and in attempting to account for the new force.[6] Furthermore, his health had still not returned completely and he was able to work only sporadically. The peculiar effect of magnetism on crystals was discovered by Julius Plücker of Bonn in Germany. On 3 November 1847, Plücker announced his discovery to Faraday in a private letter.[7]

> I have the honour [Plücker wrote] to send you two small Memoirs containing some new facts which extend your discoveries in magnetism and diamagnetism. I dare to hope that you will find them worthy of your attention. The poles of a magnet are not only the centre of magnetic and diamagnetic force but also of a new force which repels the optic axes of crystals, independently of the magnetic or diamagnetic state of these bodies. This new force diminishes less rapidly with distance than the two other forces.
> In the second memoir I have proven that the same body is magnetic or diamagnetic according to the distance between the [magnetic] poles.
> I am very curious to know what you think of the conclusions that I have drawn from my experiments which I have repeated before many physicists, notably M. Mitscherlich of Berlin who was quite surprised by them.[8]

The articles, unfortunately were of little use to Faraday since he could not read German. He was, furthermore, engaged in other researches during the winter of 1847 and the spring of 1848 and both Plücker's letter and his discovery seem to have been ignored. In the summer of 1848 Plücker visited Great Britain in order to attend the meeting of the British Association at Swansea.[9] He called upon Faraday at the Royal Institution and there described his new discoveries to him. Faraday noted the salient points in his *Diary* and then theorized upon them.

Plücker's results and theory of magneto-optic action were not at all in accord with Faraday's ideas. Where Plücker assumed a passage from the diamagnetic to the magnetic state merely by the motion of the magnetic poles, Faraday saw something quite different. 'It seems to me', he wrote in his *Diary*, 'that the optic axis force is most probably one of position, and not either of attraction or repulsion, and so is different to either the magnetic or the diamagnetic force' [9381]. This strange kind of action whereby a crystal merely aligned itself so that the optic axis was perpendicular to the lines of force of the magnet without any forces of attraction or repulsion followed naturally from Faraday's concept of the lines of force. The optic axis of a crystal is that line in a doubly refracting crystal along which no double refraction occurs. In Faraday's views, it was the direction of no strain in the crystal and hence of no action. Since the line of force was transmitted by a strain, the line of the optic axis was the least able to transmit the strain and so the crystal would turn in that direction which permitted the maximum transmission of force. This would be perpendicular to the optic axis, and neither the particles of the crystal, nor the crystal as a whole would be attracted or repelled, only aligned. The magneto-optic action, according to this view, could be seen simply as a special case of the general action of magnetism upon light.

> Now when heavy glass or other bodies are magnetized and made to rotate light [Faraday wrote in his *Diary*], the plane of no action of light is in the equator, and so corresponds to the optic axis of crystals, which are also lines of no action.
>
> Hence the phenomena are probably one in their general nature, i.e. the magnet *induces* an optic plane, whereas crystals have *naturally* optic axes; but both the optic plane and the optic axis have the same transverse relation to the lines of magnetic force and the same physical relation to the action on a polarized ray of light.
>
> And hence a beautiful relation of the magnetic forces and the forces which act upon a ray of light; or perhaps rather in this respect an approach to identity between them, for the forces which the crystal possesses naturally can be given by magnetism to glass, which is not crystalline, and even to fluids [9385–7].

These musings would appear to have led Faraday to the conclusion that diamagnetic and magneto-optic phenomena were identical. He had already stated that the seeming repulsion of diamagnetics was also an alignment. In this case the law of action was 'that each particle tends to go by the nearest course from *strong* to *weaker* points of magnetic force' (2300). But, Plücker insisted, the two were not alike. As he personally showed Faraday in late August of 1848, the magneto-optic force diminished less rapidly with the distance from the magnetic poles than the diamagnetic force. Thus, if a piece of calcareous spar were placed between the poles of a magnet, a distance between the poles could be found where the magneto-optic and diamagnetic forces just balanced one another. If the poles were moved farther apart, the crystal moved so as to place its optic axis perpendicular to the line joining the poles. When the poles were brought closer together, the crystal, as a whole, attempted to move out of the magnetic field [9419].

These experiments intrigued Faraday and he began to investigate the new force intensively. Immediately his mind leaped to the possibility of detecting the reverse effect of magneto-optic action. On 31 August he argued out his point in the *Diary*. 'The Magneto optic force is not an optic force truly, or not an optic force dependent on the direct action of light, but a physical force existent in the crystal when no light is concerned – and also existent *before* and *without* the induction of the magnet. So differs from the Magnetic and diamagnetic forces, which *are induced* by the

Magnet' [9440]. This followed almost automatically from Faraday's concept of intermolecular forces. Double refraction merely *revealed* but did not *induce* the internal strains that existed in doubly refracting crystals. And yet, as he had earlier stressed, his optical force (i.e. rotation in a magnetic field) must be the same, the difference being only that in his effect, the strain was induced by the magnetic lines of force. This, in turn, Faraday repeated, was what accounted for the optic axis setting perpendicular to the lines of force. For 'then it would follow that both the magneto-optic and the induced optic forces are in their most natural position when in the equatorial plane, for the one which is not induced takes that plane and the other, which is induced, is induced in that plane' [9442]. The natural state of strain in a crystal ought to be detectable in other ways than by the action of light. The exact reverse of his experiment with the action of light on heavy glass in a magnetic field ought to take place. 'The Natural Magneto optic force of a crystal therefore is in a constrained position when the optic axis is out of that plane, and if left to itself goes into it. Therefore if purposely moved out of it, it ought to react upon the Magnet or Electro helix. Hence may perhaps expect that its motion or position ought to induce electrical currents, and hence look for currents induced by the Optic Force' [9443]. Again, the experimental attempt was a failure but Faraday's theoretical considerations were not a total loss. They had, at least, led him to realize that there was not anything specifically *optical* about the magneto-optic force. Light merely detected a condition within the crystal. It was this condition that required investigation. The point is a small, but important one, for it permitted Faraday to work with materials that were crystalline but not transparent. And this, in turn, might permit him, he hoped, to solve a problem that had long puzzled him. 'Many results obtained by subjecting bismuth to the action of the magnet have at times embarrassed me,' Faraday wrote in the Twenty-second Series, 'and I have either been contented with an imperfect explanation, or have left them for a future examination . . .' (2454). What had embarrassed Faraday was that cylinders of bismuth seemed to follow no general law in the magnetic field.

Taking some of these cylinders at random and suspending them horizontally between the poles of the electro-magnet . . ., they presented the following phenomena. The first pointed axially; the second, equatorially; the third, equatorial in one position, and obliquely equatorial if turned round on its axis 50° to 60°; the fourth, equatorially and axially under the same treatment; and all of them, if suspended perpendicularly, pointed well, vibrating about a final fixed position which seemed to have no reference to the form of the cylinders (2456).

Such a situation was painful; it was not that Faraday felt that any law of magnetic action ought to be simple but that he could find no law whatsoever to encompass the strange action of bismuth. Plücker's discovery, perhaps, offered a new avenue of approach and Faraday eagerly exploited it.

In September 1848, he began to investigate the relations between magnetic and crystalline bodies. It was the crystalline forces, not the optic axis, which engaged his attention. One of the first points he had to resolve, therefore, was whether the 'optic axis' took up its equatorial position because of a direct action of the magnetic field upon it, or whether this was a consequence of the action of the magnetic field upon the crystalline forces.

A piece of bismuth weighing about 10 grains, now fixed on a cork and called No. 1, was suspended by a single cocoon thread and placed between the magnetic poles. It vibrated well about a given position which it at last assumed. If the piece were turned horizontally thrgh. 180°, then it came into another position which it equally kept. When this happens, I will speak of the new position as the diameter position, to shorten words. Then a point facing one of the magnetic poles was taken as a new point of suspension, and it again vibrated in position. If now this piece of crystalline matter was subject to a line of force like Plückner's [sic] optical axis, that line should be at this moment in the intersection of the equatorial and the horizontal planes, i.e. an equatorial horizontal line. But on now suspending the piece in the third direction, so that that line should be vertical and so without influence, the piece still vibrated and in either of two diameter position[s], and also pretty strongly. It appears therefore not to have one equatorial axis of setting force. . . .

Is it of necessity that the line of setting force, or the force, must be in the equator? Why may it not be axial, not only here but even in Plückner's results? The condition of one optic axis in the equatorial plane (as in Calc. Spar) is not very conformable to the simplicity of nature's laws [9540–1].

The queries, later in the day, turned into broader questions. 'Both Bismuth and Antimony', Faraday noted, 'appear to have resultants of crystallo-magnetic force in the axial direction as regards the magnetic field. Plückner's resultant seems to be in the equatorial direction, so that the two forces appear to be different' [9558].

After many more experiments, Faraday's views remained inconclusive. Plücker's magneto-optic force and his new crystallo-magnetic force appeared to be different, although there was still hope that the two might ultimately be resolved into a single force of matter [9790–1]. This did not particularly perturb Faraday at this time. He had long suspected the relationship between magnetism and crystal forces for this relationship seemed analogous to that between electricity and chemical affinity.

Having discovered such a relationship, he willingly abandoned the magneto-optic effect and focused upon the magnecrystallic force as he christened it.

The peculiar action of bismuth in a magnetic field could, perhaps, be understood in terms of the alignment, or lack of alignment, of the individual crystals of which the bismuth cylinders were composed. Large pieces of bismuth were broken up by a copper hammer to avoid contamination with iron and individual or regular crystals were selected [9539]. Cleavage planes were clearly visible and these planes served Faraday as guides to the internal structure of the crystal, so that their orientation in the magnetic field revealed the alignment of the individual bismuth particles. When such crystals were suspended in a magnetic field the anomalies that had puzzled Faraday disappeared. Certain planes appeared brighter and smoother than others; these always pointed axially, i.e. along the lines of force joining the poles of the magnet [9546 ff.]. When the lines of magnetic force were distorted, either by placing conical soft iron pieces over the flat magnet poles, or by introducing a piece of soft iron into the space between the poles, the law of magnecrystallic action became evident. In the Twenty-second Series Faraday reported that, '*the line or axis of* MAGNECRYSTALLIC *force* (being the resultant of the action of all the molecules), *tends to place itself parallel, or at a tangent, to the magnetic curve or line of magnetic force, passing through the place where the crystal is situated*' (2479).

This law was simple enough, but it involved a somewhat odd mode of behaviour. The fact that a crystal would align itself along the magnetic lines of force (like iron) implied a polarity in the crystalline particles themselves and in the crystal as a whole. Yet, if a crystal in a magnetic field were turned 180°, it would remain along the magnetic lines of force. The conclusion to be drawn from this was inescapable.

> The directing force, therefore, and the set of the crystal are in the *axial* direction. This force is, doubtless, resident in the particles of the crystal. It is such, that the Crystal can set with equal readiness and permanence in two diametrical positions; and that between these there are two positions of equatorial equilibrium, which are, of course, unstable in their nature. Either end of the mass or of its molecules, is, to all intents and purposes, both in these phaenomena, and in the ordinary results of crystallization, like the other end; and in many cases, therefore, the words *axial* and *axiality* would seem more expressive than the words *polar* and *polarity* (2472).

It would be a strange sort of polarity, indeed, in which the poles were the same but this was what Faraday's experiments indicated. His inability fully to accept this strange conclusion is shown by his substitution of the term *axial* for *polar*. The term merely described the effect, however, and did not explain it. For some thirty years, Faraday had been accustomed to think of molecular action in terms of the polarization of particles and of the masses which they made up. He was not prepared to abandon his concept simply because a rather strange kind of polarity had become manifest. Accepting the indubitable results of his experiments on magnecrystallic action, he conceived of a method for detecting crystalline polarity.

> Hung up Bismuth No. 1. . . . Arranged a helix near it, so that the crystal was in the axis at the mouth of the helix, and then sent the current of 10 pr. of Grove's plates through the helix. Immediately the crystal pointed and could point diametrally. The magnecrystallic axis was in the axis of the helix – and the crystal vibrated well, I think with about half the force it might do at the horse shoe magnet.
>
> So there are hopes that a crystal can induce a current, but the force will be very small. The question is, how is the crystal to be moved. Now, as a magnet, if carried quite through a helix, produces no final result, because the two poles are contrary to each other, here, as they are the same, perhaps the passage of the crystal *quite through* one way may produce one current, and back again, the other [9760–1].

Thus, again, Faraday was attempting to convert an intermolecular strain (even though the strain produced similar poles at opposite ends) into an electric current. As with all his attempts on diamagnetic substances, it was a failure.

The inability to reverse the process in magnecrystallic action and produce electricity and/or magnetism from crystalline forces was reflected in the Twenty-second Series of the *Experimental Researches*. The first part was completely experimental, reporting results and drawing a general law of action from these results. No explanation for this law was offered. In the second part, where Faraday specifically considered the nature of the magnecrystallic force, he could offer no firm hypothesis and had to confess his puzzlement (2586 ff.). His confusion was clearly indicated in a series of queries and notes addressed to himself in the laboratory *Diary*.

> As in Magnecrystallic phenomena the Magnet acts on the crystal, so the crystal also acts on the magnet, and moves it as in the suspended magnet.
>
> Now how does the crystal react? It is not magnetic as iron is, and if in an induced state, what is the kind of action which makes the pole go round it so far?
>
> How are the lines of magnetic force affected backwds. in this action and what are these lines? Are they lines of contiguous acting particles? – or are they like lines of gravitating force or rays of light?

The original state of the crystal is *Magnecrystallic* – but the induced state ought to be distinguished as the *Magneto crystallic* condition.

I do not remember heretofore such a case of force as the present one, i.e. a bringing into position only, without attraction or repulsion.

Extraordinary character of the force – not polar for no attraction or repulsion.

Then what is the mechanical force which turns the crystal or makes it move a magnet?

Is it like the case of the tangential motion in the rotation of the Magnetic pole and wire, in any respect – that, according to Ampère, consists of the two forces of attraction and repulsion?

It is not like a turning helix acted on by the lines of magnetic power, for there there is a current of Electricity required, and the arrangement has poles all the time, and is attracted or repelled.

If we suppose that the axial is the unaffected condition and that it is in the oblique position that the ends of the axial line (M.C.) are polar, giving two attractions pulling the crystal round – then there ought to be attractions at those times, and an obliquely presented crystal ought to attract if nearer one pole than the other – but there appears to be none [9910–19].

There are two points of particular importance in these musings. For the first time since 1833, Faraday suggested a means of the transmission of force that did not involve contiguous particles. Even the thoughts on ray vibrations had, ultimately, depended upon the forces of the mathematical points extending throughout the universe. Now, significantly, there was a distinction drawn between particle-forces and other forces such as gravity and light. Furthermore, gravity and light are non-polar forces;[10] although gravity attracts, it has no opposite, and both 'ends' of a gravitational line of force are similar as are both ends of the magnecrystallic force. During the next eight years, Faraday was to follow up this similarity and modify his ideas on force to a considerable extent.

Of more immediate concern to him was the lack of polarity in magne-crystallic action. Could this really be the case? or was the polarity masked by other forces? If polarity could be detected, then magnecrystallic force could be brought under the general laws of other polar forces. If such polarity did not exist, then magnecrystallic action would cause a radical change in the prevalent theories of force. This point could not have escaped Faraday's attention for other investigators such as Wilhelm Weber, Plücker and Auguste de la Rive presented a number of 'proofs' of the polarity of bismuth where Faraday could detect none. Throughout the late 1840's and early 1850's, Faraday sought to find either a magnecrystallic or a diamagnetic polarity. It was only after these years of fruitless search that Faraday admitted that no such polarity existed. This admission compelled him to reconsider his whole position on the nature of force and the result was to be a hypothesis of extraordinary daring and fertility. It was, in fact, to be the cornerstone of classical field theory.

2. The Search for Polarity

The discovery of diamagnetism attracted more attention from the scientific world than any of Faraday's other discoveries. Electromagnetic induction had been looked for for a decade; the laws of electrochemistry were by no means unexpected and Faraday's theory of electrostatic induction made little impression on the majority of scientists committed to a theory of imponderable fluids acting on one another at a distance. Diamagnetism, however, was something else again. That all matter reacted to a magnet was not to be wondered at, but that diamagnetics behaved so peculiarly in a magnetic field demanded explanation. Between 1845 and 1855 a number of different theories of diamagnetic action were suggested, none of which were perfectly satisfactory. Faraday eagerly explored each new account, subjected its major premises to the acid test of experiment, drew what he could from it, and then abandoned it. Although he was to develop views on diamagnetic action uniquely his own, these theories were by no means negligible in their effects upon his thought. They forced him to come to grips with certain basic problems and, in the process of defining his objections, he clarified his own ideas and developed his own theory.

In 1846 Edmond Becquerel of Paris first begged to differ with Faraday's tentative explanation of diamagnetism and the action of a magnetic field on plane polarized light. There was a slight note of pique in Becquerel's first paper. After all, Becquerel claimed, Coulomb and his own father had reported, at separate times, the very phenomenon which Faraday now had christened diamagnetism. Becquerel had investigated these effects himself in 1845 and was convinced that they were due to small amounts of iron in the various substances examined. All that Faraday's paper did was to persuade Becquerel that bodies other than iron, nickel, and cobalt were magnetic.[11] He was never to deviate from this view, in spite of the rejection of his theory by Faraday and most of his contemporaries.

By insisting upon the essential magnetism of all bodies, Becquerel was able to preserve Ampère's theory of magnetism without change. Ampère's electrodynamic molecule now simply became universally applicable to all matter instead of being restricted to iron, nickel, and cobalt. The reaction of a body to a magnet consisted of the alignment of these molecules or of their electric currents. Thus, from the very start, Becquerel insisted that diamagnetism and the action of bodies in a magnetic field upon light were the results of molecular changes within the bodies.[12] Faraday's conviction on this score, as we have seen, was by no means so strong and he was ultimately to give it up entirely.[13]

It seemed relatively easy to preserve Ampère's theory and reduce diamagnetism to well-known laws. The basic problem to be solved was to account for the repulsion of diamagnetics in a magnetic field. If all bodies were magnetic like iron why were some attracted by a magnet and others repelled? The answer was really quite simple. We need only apply Archimedes' principle of hydrostatics to magnetism. The analogy was perfect. If one asked why some bodies fall and others rise in a liquid or even in the atmosphere when they all presumably have weight and gravitate, the answer is that the heavier bodies displace the lighter and thereby give the illusion of gravitational repulsion or levity. So, with magnetism the more powerfully magnetic bodies displaced the less powerful giving the illusion of magnetic repulsion.[14] A piece of bismuth, for example, was pushed out of the magnetic field by the circumambient atmosphere, not by a repulsive force. This idea, incidentally, led Becquerel to an independent investigation of the magnetic character of gases and especially of the atmosphere which anticipated many of the results reported by Faraday in his Twenty-sixth Series.[15]

With the idea of differential magnetism in which attraction or repulsion depended upon the magnetic relations between the test body and the surrounding medium all difficulties disappeared. Ampère's theory could be preserved and the 'new' diamagnetic state could be seen to be nothing more than the old and familiar magnetism.

There was only one embarrassing part of this theory. As Becquerel himself pointed out, 'How can one account for the fact that in a vacuum all bodies are not attracted by magnets since there are no longer any material particles [of greater magnetic power] surrounding them; substances, such as bismuth, sulphur, phosphorus, etc., are almost as strongly repelled in a void as in the air.'[16] How, in short, could a 'diamagnetic' body be displaced by a stronger magnetic medium when, by definition, there was no medium there? As with so many other problems encountered in the nineteenth century, this one could be solved easily by postulating a new property of the luminiferous ether. 'It is necessary to admit', wrote Becquerel, 'that the ethereal medium by which magnetic action is transmitted is influenced in the same way, although to a different degree, in an empty space as it is in a space containing matter. [It follows] that an empty space acts as a more magnetic medium on the substance which is most strongly repelled, that is, bismuth.'[17]

This solution would appear to be a small price to pay for preserving orthodox magnetic theory. And yet, as was soon realized, it actually subverted the theory. If the ether, *tout seul*, could act as a magnetic body then why bother with ponderable matter? Ampère's electrodynamic molecule thereby becomes superfluous and the idea that magnetic interactions were essentially linked with intermolecular processes no longer seemed necessary. Furthermore, the concept of the magnetism of space meant attributing some rather peculiar properties to the ether. In particular, it implied the existence of circular electrical currents in the ether. Although this idea was later to be taken seriously by James Clerk Maxwell, it was not generally acceptable in the 1840's and 50's. Becquerel's theory, therefore, was rejected.[18]

Becquerel's insistence upon the magnetism of all bodies was most probably the result of his fidelity to the ideas of his father and of Coulomb. Other scientists did not feel any such loyalty to previous concepts and were, therefore, able to accept the fact announced by Faraday that diamagnetism was different in some way from magnetism. Few, however, were willing to accept Faraday's statement that diamagnetism was a basically *new* force of nature. Recognizing that it was not just like magnetism, many physicists nevertheless tried to account for it by utilizing familiar terms and processes. This was the procedure adopted by Hans Christian Oersted in Denmark and Wilhelm Weber in Germany. As with Becquerel, the problem was to explain the repulsion of a diamagnetic in a magnetic field. Oersted's work was strictly experimental and he did little more than report facts. The most important fact was 'that the lower part of a diamagnetic needle, suspended above a [magnetic] pole has the same magnetism as the pole and its upper part has the opposite'.[19] The result was a quadripolar body (see Figure 2) in which the poles opposite the magnetic poles were of the same kind. Hence, the repulsion. Oersted made no attempt to explain why this rather anomalous kind of magnetic induction should occur; he merely reported it.

Weber's work was more impressive. Picking up Faraday's comment that 'theoretically, an explanation of the movements of the diamagnetic bodies, and all the dynamic phaenomena consequent upon the actions of magnets on them, might be offered in the supposition that magnetic induction caused in them a contrary state to that which it produced in magnetic matter' (2429), Weber set to work to see if he could discover such a reverse magnetic induction. The investigation was a difficult one.

Diamagnetic force is much smaller than the magnetic and so the experiments required extreme delicacy of manipulation. Furthermore, how was one to detect the reverse magnetic induction assumed by Faraday? Weber's argument led him to attack the problem in a somewhat indirect fashion.

In 1847 Professor Reich of Freiberg had discovered a curious law of interaction between magnetic and diamagnetic bodies.[20] He found that if a diamagnetic body were suspended between two similar magnetic poles, the repulsive force was not proportional to the sum of the two magnetic powers, but to their difference. Thus, two equal north poles create no repulsion in a piece of bismuth. To Weber, this fact could be explained only in terms of reverse polarity for only in this fashion could the *lack* of effect be accounted for. Faraday's papers had shown that the induced 'pole' of a diamagnetic was always the same as the inducing pole (hence

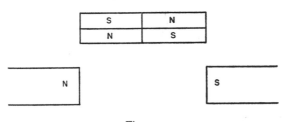

Fig. 2

the repulsion). Reich's work strongly reinforced this interpretation. To prove it irrevocably, all Weber had to do was detect the reverse polarity in a way that would be unassailable. There were essentially two ways to go about this. He could try to find a mutual effect of two diamagnetic bodies upon one another when both were in a strong magnetic field. The diamagnetic forces were so weak, however, that this method appeared unlikely to give the kind of conclusive proof Weber sought.

The second method was the one adopted by Weber. It was based on Faraday's work and was delicate enough to yield conclusive results. By Weber's argument, the molecules of a diamagnetic body in a strong magnetic field were thrown into a polar condition similar to, but opposite in sign, to those of the inducing magnet. The polarity of ordinary magnets could be made manifest by moving the magnet past a conductor in such a way as to generate an electric current. In the same way, an excited diamagnetic should induce an electric current when moved past a conductor. Not only should a current be induced but the *direction* of this current should be *opposite* to the direction of a current induced by a piece of soft iron under the same circumstances. This followed from the assumed reverse polarity of the diamagnetic body.

This chain of argument could easily be tested by experiment. A circular bar of iron about two feet in length and wound with insulated copper wire was used as the source of a strong magnetic field. A hollow wooden cylinder, six inches in length, and wound on the outside with over 300 yards of heavy gauge insulated copper wire, was fastened to the circular end of the electromagnet. The ends of this wire were connected to a commutator and to a very sensitive galvanometer. When the electromagnet was turned on, a bar of bismuth was plunged into and withdrawn from the wooden cylinder. A current, as expected, was induced. When a piece of soft iron was substituted for the bismuth a current in the opposite direction was detected. 'The view advanced by Faraday', Weber exulted, 'appears to be placed beyond all doubt.'[21]

The determination of the diamagnetic polarity of bismuth offered the possibility of reducing diamagnetism to the commonly accepted laws of magnetism – almost. If Ampère's theory of magnetism were still to be considered valid, a few adjustments would have to be made. A magnet could not align the molecules of iron one way and the molecules of bismuth another if magnetism was still to be considered the result of electric currents circulating around the molecules. Weber's way out of this dilemma was ingenious. He recognized that there was a difference between magnetic and diamagnetic bodies. The action of a magnet upon a magnetic body was to align the currents or molecules of this body in such a way that magnetic effects were produced. Looking at the currents surrounding the molecules of the induced magnet, it is easily seen that they will circulate in the *same* direction as those in the inducing magnet (see Figure 3). The molecules of diamagnetics, according to Weber, did not have any electric currents around them. Such currents, however, were induced by a magnet. From the well-known laws of electromagnetic induction it could then be shown that the induced molecular currents would be in the *opposite* direction from the currents in the inducing magnet.[22] Such currents in ordinary bodies, however, were not steady but momentary, existing only while either the magnet or the conductor was in motion. A piece of bismuth did not move away from a magnetic pole only momentarily as the magnet was brought up to it; it moved away and stayed there when there was no motion involved. To get around this, Weber assumed 'that in the single molecules, or around them, closed paths exist in which the said [electrical] fluids can move without resistance'.[23] Of this theory, John Tyndall later wrote, 'This theory, not withstanding its great beauty, is so extremely artificial, that I imagine the general conviction of its truth cannot be very strong.'[24] As with Becquerel, Weber's work stimulated Faraday to pursue the problem of diamagnetic polarity intensively. It was while he was repeating Weber's experiments that he became convinced of the *absence* of such polarity.

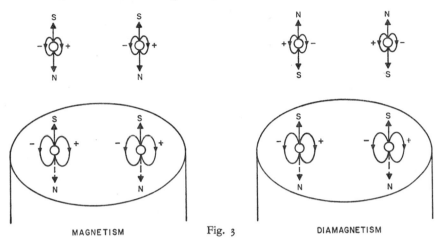

MAGNETISM   Fig. 3   DIAMAGNETISM

There was one final theory of diamagnetism in the 1850's that deserves mention, for it illustrates the lengths to which physicists would go to preserve Ampère's physical model of magnetic action. This theory was enunciated by Auguste de la Rive, Faraday's good friend. De la Rive called attention to a fact that had escaped his co-workers in the area of diamagnetism. Magnetic bodies, he pointed out, generally contain more atoms per unit volume than do diamagnetics.[25] Magnetic bodies, therefore, consisted of atoms placed more closely together than diamagnetic ones. This made it possible for the electric fluids associated with each particle of a magnet to flow from atom to atom as the atoms arrange themselves in a circle. The resultant atomic arrangement (see Figure 4) constituted a *molécule intégrante* of the magnet. It also preserved the electrical currents required by Ampère's theory.[26]

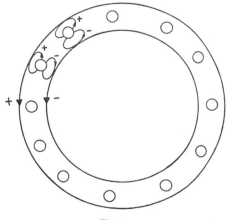

Fig. 4

Diamagnetic atoms, being farther apart, were not able to permit the passage of the electrical fluids from one atom to another. They did, however, link up together to form a *molécule intégrante*. The consequence of this arrangement had best be given in de la Rive's own words.

> What distinguishes diamagnetic bodies from those which are not diamagnetic, is that, their atoms being farther apart, a natural electro-atomic current (*chaine électro-atomique naturelle*) cannot exist; the atoms, therefore, are independent of one another from the electrical point of view and consequently in that state of equilibrium in which their exterior currents neutralize the internal current along the [atomic] axis.[27] If a closed external current [i.e., an electric helix or a permanent magnet] is now brought close to the *molécules intégrantes* composed of a more or less large number of these atoms, this current will be unable to give these molecules a particular alignment since the molecules are not surrounded by an electro-atomic current as magnetic particles are. But, if the current is strong enough, it will arrange the atoms closest to it in a direction such that their axes will be parallel to this external current. Furthermore, their poles will be turned in a sense contrary to those of the polarized particles in the current conductor precisely in an analogous fashion to ordinary electro-dynamic induction. The atoms which are aligned by this powerful influence will, in turn, force the other atoms of the molecule of which they are a part, to turn themselves in order to present opposite poles to one another. This will thus create an electric chain in which the current will necessarily flow in the opposite direction to the external current, since this direction is determined by the first atoms which suffer the direct action of the [external] current. This process will be undergone by the other particles of a diamagnetic body, or at least those influenced by the external current, so that they will each have an electric current around them flowing in a contrary direction to those acting upon them and, thereby, necessarily producing a repulsion.[28]

Tyndall did not find this explanation even worthy of notice. Faraday took note of it, but politely rejected it.[29] It did serve to increase his suspicions of the adequacy of any theory which relied upon imponderable fluids of any kind. As he wrote to William Whewell in 1855:

> I conclude I am right in believing that if diamagnets and diamagnetism had been known to us before we knew any thing at all of paramagnets and paramagnetism, the theory of two magnetic fluids would have applied to it, but could not then have included paramagnetism. It is this idea which makes me earnest in speaking of chambers of little or no action and places of weak magnetic action; for though the old theory of two fluids can account for them, they are not the less important to me who do not believe in that theory. I see in them proofs that the dualities must be related externally to the magnet; and so they come in as necessary consequences of the principles both of paramagnetic and diamagnetic action; but I hope to make all this clearer by degrees; and my hopes are greatly strengthened by the growing admission that the lines of magnetic force represent at present fairly the facts of magnetism.

Into what they may ultimately resolve themselves, or to what they may lead I am sure I cannot say; but if I can only convert the theory of magnetic fluids, and that of electric currents, into two stools, the fall to the ground between them may be more useful than either of them as a seat in a wrong place.[30]

Faraday had been led to this point by his own investigations. His search for diamagnetic polarity had been fruitless and it was this which had forced him to formulate his own hypothesis of diamagnetism.

Almost from the moment of his discovery of the action of a magnet upon light there had been a fundamental tension in Faraday's ideas of the nature of this action. On the one hand, as the sealed note sent to Sir John Herschel indicates,[31] his mind was turning away from molecular action and towards the primacy of the line of force. The fact that the effect was produced instantaneously when a current-carrying helix was substituted for a magnet seemed conclusive proof that no molecular changes occurred in the diamagnetic (2195).[32] Yet in the very same paper, Faraday remarked that

> The theory of static induction which I formerly ventured to set forth (1161, etc.), and which depends upon the action of the contiguous particles of the dielectric intervening between the inductric and the inducteous bodies, led me to expect that the same kind of dependence upon the intervening particles would be found to exist in magnetic action; and I published certain experiments and considerations on this point seven years ago (1709–36). I could not then discover any peculiar condition of the intervening substance or diamagnetic; but now that I have been able to make out such a state, which is not only a state of tension (2227), but dependent entirely upon the magnetic lines which pass through the substance, I am more than ever encouraged to believe that the view then advanced is correct (2240).

The two views of diamagnetic action thus advanced are not really contradictory. The state of tension Faraday felt he had detected could be assumed instantaneously (as the alignment of Ampère's molecules could not). It was really a question of emphasis; was the line of force a line of molecules under tension or did the line of force exist independently of the particles of ponderable matter and merely act upon them? The answer lay in the polarity of these molecules. If the lines of force were nothing but a chain of particles undergoing a linear strain, then the molecules must be deformed. This deformation, in turn, must turn them into polar molecules and such polarity ought to have easily detectable consequences. If the molecules were *not* deformed and simply interacted with the line of force, then no polarity would be expected. That such interaction without polarity could exist was illustrated by ordinary chemical combination.

Here forces interacted to produce chemical compounds but the elements of which these compounds were formed revealed no signs of polarity in their free state.[33]

As early as 18 September 1845, Faraday began to accumulate evidence which later could be interpreted as ruling out molecular polarity. Faraday noted in his *Diary* that 'the *mass* of the *dimagnetic* may be in several pieces and does not require to be continuous...' [7576]. This clearly implied that ordinary intermolecular forces were not involved. One week later, Faraday interposed a piece of the heavy borate of lead glass between the pole of a bar magnet and a magnetometer to discover if there were a specific magneto-inductive capacity analogous to the specific inductive capacity of dielectrics. Obtaining not 'the least signs of any difference' when the glass was present or absent, he concluded that no such capacity existed although, by all analogies and theoretical considerations, it should. The 'magneto-tonic' state was, therefore, somewhat different from the electro-tonic condition and this difference appeared to be attributable to the molecular forces at work in both cases.

It was not until November 1845, that the question of polarity emerged as a real problem to be worked on. The action of bismuth was what began to trouble Faraday then. 'By a single pole', he wrote of the effect of a magnetic field upon a bismuth, 'it would look like mere repulsion – but the law is *from stronger to weaker points of action*' [8127]. This law of action he repeated in the Twentieth Series (2269), but it was merely a description then of what happened. *Why* this was so was another matter. On 12 November 1845, he speculated on this problem.

> With Bismuth the effect . . . appears to be an absolute and permanent repulsion. There is no apparently dual character in the force – is an unique phenomenon as to its kind.
>
> Can there be formation in Bismuth of currents in the *contrary* direction? Such an effect would account for the phenomena. If so, look for and find them.
>
> Then other bodies, as heavy glass, might have a tendency to these counter currents.
>
> There must be something particular in bismuth distinct from copper action.
>
> Would a *Bismuth wire* or rod, carried across the magnetic curves, give a current in the same direction as a wire of copper or a contrary current?
>
> So also of Antimony and Arsenic.
>
> *But* on *the other hand*, is the apparent repulsion an absolute tendency off from the magnetic pole, or only a difference between it and the neighbouring matter, as the air or water?
>
> For the Bismuth goes *from strong* to *weak* points of magnetic action. This

may be because it is deficient in the inductive force or action, and so is displaced by matter having stronger powers, giving way to the latter [8137-44].

Faraday's various ideas (they can hardly be called hypotheses) on the cause of diamagnetic action are here revealed. Diamagnetics may be reversed magnetics as Weber later was to insist. Or, they might simply be magnetic bodies displaced by more strongly magnetic media as Becquerel was to suggest in 1846 and 1849. In either case, they should exhibit molecular polarity and the test of the correctness of these speculations necessarily demanded an investigation of diamagnetic polarity.

We have already examined one of the lines pursued by Faraday in his attempt to discover whether diamagnetics were polar or not. His failure to induce currents in surrounding helices indicated that diamagnetics when *not* in a magnetic field did not appear to have the kind of inducing powers that accompanied the polarity of magnetic substances such as iron. This failure indicated that the currents assumed by Ampère's theory did not exist in diamagnetics when not under magnetic influence. Might they not, however, be *induced* by a magnetic field? And if they were induced, how could they be detected? The obvious way was ruled out. Induced magnetic polarity could be discovered by bringing a magnet near a body; since the *opposite* magnetism was induced if the body were magnetic, the result was attraction and the induced magnet now acted in all respects like a permanent magnet attracting an opposite pole and repelling a similar one. Diamagnetics, however, were repelled by *both* poles of a permanent magnet, presumably because these poles induced similar poles in the diamagnetic body. The polarity of the molecules of a magnetic body could be deduced from the polarity of the mass; no such deduction could be made with diamagnetics since the reaction of a diamagnetic body as a whole did *not* indicate polarity.

Nevertheless, if the assumed polarity did exist, the molecules of a diamagnetic ought to react upon one another as well as to the magnetic force.

A card was placed on the top of the Magnetic core and bismuth in fine powder sprinkled upon it; the card was then tapped lightly to make the particles dance, and they did dance, but nothing particular occurred, the core being *not magnetic*. Then the core was magnetized and the process repeated and now the particles all moved away from a line exactly formed over the circumference of the end of the cylinder, some moving inwards and some outwards but leaving the line clear in the center.

There was no signs of arrangement among the particles inside or outside of the line – no signs of *an attraction* or *repulsion amongst themselves* [8231h, 8231h-i].

On the supposition of molecular polarity this was strange behaviour indeed. Whereas iron filings formed themselves into beautifully specific and clearly defined curves, bismuth particles remained indifferent to one another. They each reacted to the magnetic field but this reaction was confined to the line of force and did not extend to the molecular forces of other, neighbouring particles. This experiment certainly did not strengthen the idea of diamagnetic polarity.

Still working with Ampère's theory of molecular currents, Faraday again attempted to detect molecular polarity. If a magnet induces currents around the molecules of a diamagnetic which circulate in the opposite direction from those in magnetic bodies, then, by analogy, the ordinary currents induced in a diamagnetic conductor ought to pass in a direction opposite to those ordinarily induced in conductors. This was precisely the line of reasoning followed by Weber in 1847. Again, when the experiment was performed the anticipated result did not materialize. The current induced in a bismuth bar was exactly the same as that created in any conductor [8419 ff.].

In 1848, after Plücker had announced the discovery of the magneto-optic effect, Faraday turned again to the polarity of bismuth. By this time, his belief in the existence of any such polarity was weakening steadily. Not only had his most delicate experiments failed to detect any, but the new magneto-optic effect also militated against it. As he was later to state of the magnecrystallic effect, this seemed to be an interaction between the mass of the body and the magnetic lines of force and not an interaction involving the individual molecules. Suspicions of non-polarity were not enough and so Faraday once more sought to discover a polar effect. This time he employed a quite strong magnetic field in which he suspended a bar of bismuth free to swing in the horizontal plane. When another piece of bismuth was brought near the bar, no effect was discerned.

This failure further strengthened his doubts and he was able confidently to challenge Plücker's supposed discovery of bismuth polarity. Plücker had found that when a piece of bismuth suspended near one magnetic pole was approached by another, weaker magnetic pole, the bismuth nearest the moving pole was repelled. This, Plücker felt, showed that the bismuth bar had become polar. Faraday repeated the experiment and remarked that 'all the effects appeared to me easily accounted for by the consequent displacement of the lines of magnetic force [by the moving magnet] – and shewed nothing, as I think, that could not be resolved into the law of motion of a diamagnetic body from strong to weaker places of magnetic action' [9431].[34]

Only six months after what had seemed to be his definitive rejection of reversed polarity, Faraday read of Wilhelm Weber's discovery of precisely the kind of polarity that had eluded him for so long. 'I doubt the evidence as to polarity', he wrote in his *Diary* [10050] but doubts were not enough. He quickly devised an instrument[35] that would intensify the effects reported by Weber and set to work to discover where his German contemporary had erred.

The experiments performed by Faraday in the autumn of 1849 are classic examples of the use of experiment as a critical tool.[36] He first determined that the effects reported by Weber were actually obtained. Having verified this, he began his search for the causes of error. The first was the shaking of his instrument when the various samples were moved into and out of the magnetic field. The 'detector' helix was moved by this, thereby generating a current. Faraday removed the source of error by using separate tables for electromagnet and detector. Still, a current appeared when bismuth moved through a magnetic field.

The experimental set-up must be recalled if Faraday's next step is to be understood. The primary electromagnet created the magnetic field which, according to Weber, induced diamagnetic polarity in the bismuth. When the 'polar' bismuth was now passed through the 'detector' helix, it ought to create a current in the helix. It was the existence of this current that had convinced Weber of the correctness of his views.

Disbelieving in induced diamagnetic polarity, Faraday had to find some other way to explain the undoubted existence of the current that was produced. It was not a difficult task. As the core moved in and out of the 'detector' helix, it cut the lines of force from the electromagnet and, thereby, fulfilled all the conditions necessary for the generation of a current. The currents that could be expected in the bismuth core would be concentric to the axis of the core, thus creating the illusion of diamagnetic polarity.

Substituting a better conductor for bismuth (copper) Faraday then proceeded to test this hypothesis. If the copper were finely divided so that no currents could pass, the effect disappeared [10386] (2658). The same was true of bismuth. As a counter-proof of the effect of the induced currents, Faraday cut the copper into discs which would permit currents to pass concentrically to the discs' axis and the effect was restored [10387] (2659). To drive home his point, Faraday then prepared a helix to use as a core but did not connect the two ends of the wire. No effect was produced when this was used as the test body. When the wires were joined, however, so that a current could flow, the effect was observed (2660). (See Figures 5, 6, 7.)

The fact that iron gave opposite results to that obtained with bismuth,

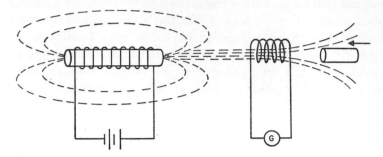

Fig. 5

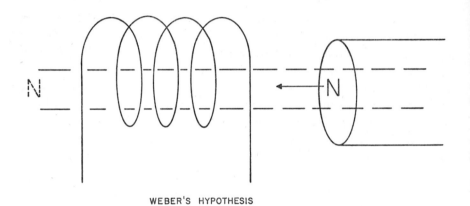

WEBER'S HYPOTHESIS

Fig. 6

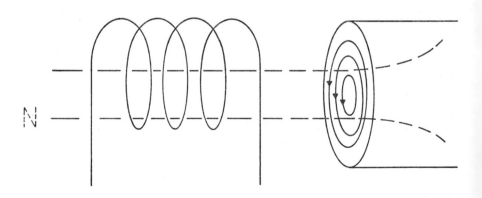

FARADAY'S COUNTER-HYPOTHESIS

Fig. 7

as Weber had predicted would be the case if his hypothesis of reversed polarity were true, was also explained by Faraday. The electromagnet induced a *magnetism* in the iron and it was the magnetism which, in turn, induced a current in the surrounding helix. The resultant current was in the direction to be expected from this double induction and was, indeed, opposite to that produced by a diamagnetic conductor (2666). Weber's strongest argument therefore was shown to be specious. His experiments most emphatically did not prove that diamagnetics possessed molecular currents opposite in direction to those of magnetic bodies.

A specific diamagnetic polarity was not the only conceivable explanation of observed diamagnetic effects. There was, as Becquerel had shown, the possibility that diamagnetics were simply weak magnetic bodies displaced by stronger ones. Acting upon this assumption, two experimental avenues opened up. What would happen if another medium were excluded? Should not the molecules then reveal their basic magnetic polarity? Faraday devised two beautifully simple experiments to discover the effect, if any, of such a condition. 'Supposed it possible that, as a magnet affected a crystal of Bismuth or Antimony, so it might influence their particles when melted and cause the mass to assume a regular crystalline form on cooling' [9646]. When melted bismuth was slowly cooled in a strong magnetic field, no appearance of crystalline regularity could be detected in the solidified piece. 'On breaking it open', he wrote, 'I found it to consist of an innumerable set of crystalline portions in all directions, if any thing even less regularly crystalline than if it had cooled under ordinary circumstances' [9646]. There seemed no room here for a differential effect and, as Faraday put it, 'it appears that the magnet does not influence sensibly the arrangement of the particles in crystallization' [9647].

This was not a conclusive experiment, as Faraday himself later pointed out [9905]. The magnetic power may vanish with high temperature and thereby prevent the appearance of any effect. The influence of temperature could be avoided by working with gases at ordinary room temperature. If a gas were put in an enclosure and then subjected to an intense magnetic field, there should be a change of volume, if any polarity (magnetic *or* diamagnetic) were induced in the gas molecules.

Two blocks of soft iron, each 1 inch thick and 3 inches square, with filed and flattened surfaces, and square frame of copper cut out of a sheet of copper so as to be 3 inches in the side and 0·3 of an inch deep all round, were put together and held firmly by four copper screws, so as to form a very strong iron box having an interior 2·4 inches square and only 1/60 of an inch in depth, for that was the thickness of the copper frame [10714].

Stopcocks were provided. A capillary tube containing a small amount of coloured water was inserted in one of the stopcocks and acted as a very sensitive volume gauge. The slightest change in volume would cause the coloured water to move in the tube. 'Now it was thought', Faraday remarked, 'that if there was any expansion of a diamagnetic gas, or any condensation of a magnetic gas, in the Magnetic field, it would be sensible in this box, where the pole faces formed the interior of the box were only 1/60 of an inch apart, where the field therefore would have great intensity of power and where the gas would be in close proximity to the poles' [10716]. Once again, when the experiment was tried with different gases, no effect could be discerned.[37] Differential action, again, seemed excluded.

Faraday was perfectly aware that in some cases differential action did occur. When a solution of iron salts was suspended (in a thin glass vessel) in a stronger or weaker solution of the same salts, the original solution could be made to act like a magnetic or diamagnetic body, depending upon the relative strengths of the solutions (2363 ff.). The question was, could such differential action account for all diamagnetic phenomena? An important experiment suggested itself. If a body, such as bismuth, was repelled in air, what would happen if the air were withdrawn gradually until a vacuum was obtained? According to the theory of differential action, the bismuth ought slowly to move into the magnetic field as the cause of its displacement was removed. When the experiment was performed, the bismuth remained totally unaffected by the evacuation of the space in which it was suspended (2439). In 1845, when this result was obtained, Faraday refused to draw the logical conclusion that empty space was magnetic (2440).

Hundreds of experiments and five years later, his attitude had become hardened into a flat opposition to the magnetic character of space *as required by the theory of differential magnetic action.*

So then in this view, [he wrote] a body conducting Magnetic force better or worse than a vacuum would have contrary polarities . . . partly according to the views of myself, Weber, Reich and others. But how does this accord with the Ampère polarity . . . or that of a permanent magnet? To do so we must assume, as it appears to me, that all conduction of magnetic force is carried on by circular electric currents round the line of magnetic force in the whole of its course, and in that case that they must exist in a vacuum itself; which is difficult to comprehend according to the Ampère theory, where the circular currents are associated with the particles, or with any other generally acknowl-edge[d], or even any proposed view or even any trial speculation that I am aware of [10834].

That currents of electrical fluids should be associated with the particles of ponderable matter had long ago overstrained Faraday's credulity; to assume that such fluids went around in empty space for no good reason was more than he could accept. But, his own experiments with dia-magnetic bodies *in vacuo* had proved that magnetic force did exist in empty space. In his mind's eye Faraday could see the lines of magnetic force acting where no material cause could be operative. The line of force which had begun as a convenient perceptual aid to represent the forces of matter had, over the years, become more and more physically real to Faraday. The line of force did pass through vacua; this much was certain. Might not the line of force be the key to the unity of force phenomena for which he had so long been seeking? The question was certainly worth asking and as Faraday went about answering it with experiments, ponderable matter gradually declined in importance as the physical reality of the line of force thrust itself increasingly upon him.

3. The Physical Reality of the Lines of Force

Faraday's failure to discover diamagnetic polarity did not upset him. He had, as a matter of fact, long suspected that his search would prove in vain for, as early as 1845, he had been toying with the idea that the real polarity in magnetic phenomena was to be found in the lines of magnetic force and *not* in the particles of magnetic substances. At the same time that he suggested that diamagnetic polarity could account for the repulsion of a diamagnetic substance between the poles of an electromagnet, he also enunciated the general law of this action. 'All the phaenomena', he wrote, 'resolve themselves into this, that a portion of such matter, when under magnetic action, tends to move from stronger to weaker places or points of force. When the substance is surrounded by lines of magnetic force of equal power on all sides, it does not tend to move, as is then in marked contradistinction with a linear current of electricity under the same circumstances' (2418).[38]

The first part of this passage merely states a fact, but it is an interesting fact. It involves the relationship between the magnetic field and the *mass* of the diamagnetic. This, of course, did not rule out the possible polarity of the particles of the diamagnetic body, but it does reveal the way in which Faraday was looking at the phenomenon. This perspective is made even clearer by the second part of the 'law'. There the character of the magnetic action was related to the lines of force; 'lines of magnetic force of equal power' can mean only a uniform *distribution* of the lines of force in space, for there was no way of knowing whether each line represented the same amount of power, nor did Faraday even question this fact. Furthermore, the action of a diamagnetic in a uniform field was rather peculiar if the field induced a polarity of some kind in the particles of the diamagnetic substance. At best, even a condition of reverse polarity should lead to a very delicate metastable condition. The repulsion between the south pole of the magnet and the induced south pole in the diamagnetic could be balanced by the similar repulsion of the induced north pole and the magnetic north pole only when the diamagnetic substance was *exactly* between the two magnetic poles. No such metastable condition, however, was observed. Faraday had stated the facts of the case correctly; in a uniform field, regardless of *where* the diamagnetic substance was placed, it remained. Again, the essential relationship appeared to be between the lines of force and the mass of the diamagnetic body as a whole. This relationship, Faraday realized dimly in 1845, was one of position and not necessarily one of mutual attractions and repulsions.

The discovery of magnecrystallic force in 1848 served to reinforce Faraday's growing suspicion of central forces and their importance. Where Plücker and Weber saw simple attractions or repulsions, Faraday perceived only alignments. The direction in which a crystal set in a magnetic field depended upon two things; the general alignment of the molecules in the crystal and the direction of the lines of force. This alignment, as Faraday had emphasized, in his statement of the law of magnecrystallic action, was *not* due to attraction or repulsion.[39]

In essence, this was the interaction of two 'lines of force'. One was produced by the intermolecular forces which determined crystalline structure in a given body. 'This line', he wrote to Whewell, 'which places itself parallel to the magnetic axis I have called the Magnecrystallic axis to express the *original condition* of the crystal. . . .'[40] The other line was, of course, the magnetic line of force. Both lines, it should be noted, could be considered as strains; they differed, however, in that the magnetic lines were polar, whereas in the crystal, 'I can find no traces of polarity though the setting force be strong.'[41] In 1848 Faraday was still seeking polarity and considered that the inherent crystalline line of force itself must suffer an induced modification in the presence of a magnet which might manifest itself as a polar force.[42] The failure to discover this polarity was to have a curious consequence. In 1848 the interaction of a polar magnetic line of force with the crystalline 'line of force' suggested to Faraday that the crystalline line of force must also be polar. By 1850, however, he was convinced that it was not. Since interaction implied identity, Faraday was to take the daring step then of questioning the polarity of the magnetic line of force.

In 1848, however, the most interesting aspect of magnecrystallic action was that it appeared to be quite fundamentally different from any other kind of magnetic action. Ordinary magnetic substances were attracted by magnets; diamagnetics, except for the unique case of a uniform magnetic field, were repelled. 'The magnecrystallic force appears to be very clearly distinguished from either the magnetic or diamagnetic forces, in that it causes neither approach nor recession; consisting not in attraction or repulsion, but in its giving a certain determinate position to the mass under its influence, so that a given line in relation to the mass is brought by it into a given relation with the direction of the external magnetic power' (2550). This conclusion was distasteful to Faraday. He had already insisted upon the fact that diamagnetism was essentially different from ordinary magnetism. Now magnecrystallic action was, in turn, to be differentiated from both magnetism and diamagnetism. Was it possible that matter reacted in three entirely different ways to the forces produced by a magnet? Even worse, was it possible that the *same* piece of matter could be both diamagnetic and be subject to magnecrystallic forces essentially different in nature?[43] Given Faraday's deep faith in the unity of force, it must have been a source of great concern to him to have discovered magnetic force acting in such a peculiar and contradictory manner. This concern may be seen in the care with which he assured himself that the various magnetic effects did exist and were contradictory.[44] It is also reflected in the fact that it was about this time that he really abandoned hope that all magnetic effects could be traced to induced polarity. To be sure, he continued to look for polarity, if only because Weber and de la Rive were so certain it existed. But, as he saw in 1848, 'what a strange polarity it must be' if magnecrystallic, diamagnetic, and magnetic action were all to be explained by it [9484 ff.].

It is, I think, no coincidence that it was in the Twenty-second Series, devoted to the consideration of magnecrystallic action, that Faraday threw out a speculation that was to lead him eventually to a resolution of the problem of the seeming diversity of magnetic modes of action.

I cannot resist [he wrote there] throwing forth another view of these phenomena which may possibly be the true one. The lines of magnetic force may perhaps be assumed as in some degree resembling the rays of light, heat, etc.; and may find difficulty in passing through bodies, and so be affected by them, as light is affected. They may, for instance, when a crystalline body is interposed, pass more freely, or with less disturbance, through it in the

P

direction of the magnecrystallic axis than in other directions. In that case, the position which the crystal takes in the magnetic field with its magnecrystallic axis parallel to the lines of magnetic force, may be the position of no, or of least resistance; and therefore the position of rest and stable equilibrium (2591).

The possibility that different bodies conducted the magnetic force through them with different degrees of facility was not immediately followed up. For most of the spring and early summer of 1849 very little work was done; in the autumn and winter, Faraday turned to the investigation of Weber's discovery of diamagnetic polarity. It was in this investigation that the first experimental evidence for magnetic conductibility was forthcoming. The currents produced by iron and copper cores moving inside a test helix need not be interpreted as the results of induced currents.[45] They could also be viewed as the results of the differential magnetic conductibility of the core and air [10575 ff.]. Thus, as the iron core moved into the helix, iron, being a better conductor of the magnetic forces than air, caused the lines of force from the main magnet to converge, thereby cutting the surrounding helix and generating a current. When a copper core was substituted for the iron, the copper being a worse magnetic conductor than air caused the lines of force to diverge. This formed a current in the surrounding helix *opposite in direction* to that created when iron was used. Thus, whether one assumed the existence of induced currents and induced magnetism or whether one preferred to account for the final currents in terms of the motion of the lines of force across the test helix, the results were the same. If one chose the latter course this extended the concept of the line of force to still another phenomenon. The emphasis, once again, was removed from matter (i.e. the copper or the iron) and placed upon the lines of force. Another element was added to their reality.

The next conceptual step was not too difficult to take. It involved combining the idea of magnetic conductibility with the law of magnetic and diamagnetic action. The experiments with the iron and copper cores had shown how the magnetic lines of force could be concentrated or dilated by a magnetic or diamagnetic substance. The effect of this concentration or dilation was to intensify or weaken the magnetic field in the neighbourhood of the magnetic or diamagnetic substances. Since magnetic substances tended to move into areas of more intense magnetic strength and diamagnetic substances tended to move towards weaker areas of magnetic strength, this effect might lead to a relatively simple explanation of both magnetic and diamagnetic action.

The hypothesis of magnetic conductibility and the law of magnetic or diamagnetic action could, by 1850, be substituted for the older theories of polar action. Indeed, the new view could predict effects which were rather startling when viewed from the older theory.

Ordinary magnetic action followed directly.

A small sphere of iron placed within a field of equal magnetic power, bounded by the iron poles, has a position of unstable equilibrium, equidistant from the iron surfaces, and at such time a great concentration of force takes place through it, . . . and through the intervening axial spaces. If the sphere be on either side of the middle distance, it flies to the nearest iron surface, and then can determine the greatest amount of magnetic force to or upon the axial lines which pass through it (2810).

This effect can easily be understood by referring to a diagram (Figure 8).

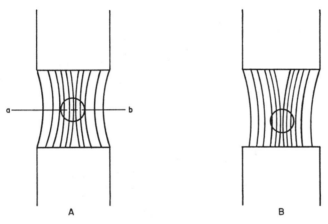

A   B

Fig. 8

In A, the sphere being *exactly* between the magnetic poles creates a concentration of magnetic lines of force within itself and symmetrical about the line ab. In this case the place of greatest magnetic strength is at the centre of the sphere and there is, therefore, no tendency for the sphere to move. If the sphere is displaced the slightest bit, however, the symmetry of A is lost and, as in B, the point of maximum magnetic strength will no longer coincide with the centre of the sphere. The sphere will move towards this point and behave as though it were attracted by the magnetic pole. The interaction, however, is between the lines of force and the sphere, not the magnetic pole and the sphere. The magnet is merely the source of the lines of force.

The repulsion of two iron spheres in a uniform magnetic field could be

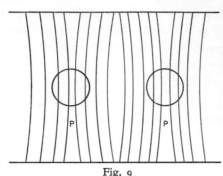

Fig. 9

explained in the same way (see Figure 9). '... the two balls of iron, PP, have weaker lines of force between them than on the outside; and as their tendency is to pass from weaker to stronger places of action, they . . . separate to fulfil the requisite condition of equilibrium of forces' (2831).

If two paramagnetic[46] bodies repel one another it might be assumed (2831) that two diamagnetic bodies would attract one another in a uniform field. Such, however, was not the case. They, too, repelled one another

> for the field is stronger between them ... than on the outsides, as may easily be seen by considering the two spheres DD [in Figure 10]; and therefore this motion is consistent, and is in accordance generally with the opening or set equatorially, either of separate portions or of a continuous mass of such substances . . . in their tendency to go from stronger to weaker places of

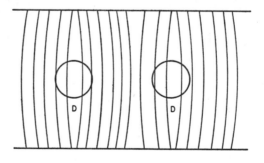

Fig. 10

> action (2831). ... Finally, a paramagnetic and a diamagnetic body attract each other . . .; and they ought to do so, for the diamagnetic body finds a place of weaker action towards the paramagnetic body, and the paramagnetic substance finds a place of stronger action in the vicinity of the diamagnetic body ... (2831). (See Figure 11.)

All these attractions and repulsions, it might be argued, could equally well be explained by appealing to the older, orthodox, theory of induced magnet poles. The two poles of the permanent magnet used as the source of the field will induce opposite poles at the ends of the two paramagnetic spheres. Each sphere, therefore, will have the same polarity as the other and the like poles will then lead to mutual repulsion (see Figure 12). The poles induced in the diamagnetic spheres will be the *same* as the inducing poles, but the spheres again will have similar polarity and the result will be repulsion. The induced polarity of a paramagnetic body will be opposite to that induced in a diamagnetic body, so they will attract one another by ordinary

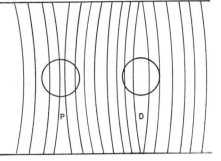

Fig. 11

magnetic action. There was only one difficulty to this approach; there was not, in 1850, any detectable diamagnetic polarity. To Faraday, this was a decisive fact. Moreover, his hypothesis was able to account *both* for the 'attractions' and 'repulsions' *and* for the lack of polarity. Faraday explicitly called this to the reader's attention.

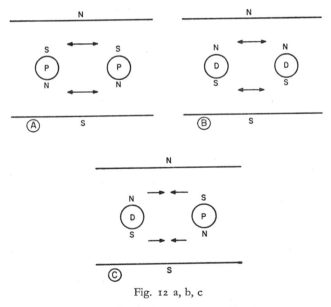

Fig. 12 a, b, c

Let [Figure 13] represent a limited magnetic field with a paramagnetic body P, and a diamagnetic body D, in it, and let N and S represent the two walls of iron associated with the magnet . . . which form its boundary, we shall then be able to obtain a clear idea of the direction of the lines of magnetic force in the field. Now the two bodies, P and D, cannot be represented by supposing merely that they have the same polarities in opposite directions. The 1 polarity of P is importantly unlike the 3 polarity of D; but if D be considered as having the reverse polarities of P, then the one polarity of P should be like the 4 polarity of D, whereas it is more unlike to that than to the 3 polarity of D, or even to its own 2 polarity.

There are therefore two essential differences in the nature of the polarities dependent on conduction, the difference in the direction of the lines of force abutting on the polar surfaces, when the comparison is with a magnet reversed, and the difference of convergence and divergence of these lines, when compared with a magnet not reversed; and hence a diamagnetic body is not in that condition of polarity which may be represented by turning a paramagnetic body end for end, while it retains its magnetic state.

Diamagnetic bodies in media more diamagnetic than themselves, would have the polar condition of paramagnetic bodies . . .; and in like manner paramagnetic conductors in media more paramagnetic than themselves, would have the polarity of diamagnetic bodies (2821–3).

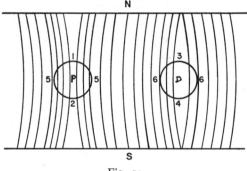

Fig. 13

The speculation so hesitantly put forth in the sealed note left with Sir John Herschel in 1845 was now boldly stated as a fact. Polarity resided in the lines of force, not in the particles of the substance through which the lines passed. This Faraday proved by citing the apparent transformation of a diamagnetic into a paramagnetic body when the magnetic media in which the body was immersed was altered. To the particles of the body, the lines of force remained the same; all that changed was the relative magnetic conductibility of the body and its surrounding medium. Hence the polarity could not be in the particles of the body, but must be sought in the lines of force and in their relationship to one another.

Armed with his theory of the primacy of the lines of force and the manner in which they were conducted through various bodies, Faraday could and did successfully attack the problem of the seeming multiplicity of magnetic actions. Para- and dia-magnetism were seen to differ only in terms of the ease of conduction of the magnetic lines of force. Magne-crystallic action, as Faraday had hinted earlier, was simply a special case of magnetic conduction.

A magnecrystallic substance [he wrote] would then be one which in the crystallized state could conduct onwards, or permit the exertion of the magnetic force with more facility in one direction than another; and that direction would be the magnecrystallic axis. Hence, when in the magnetic field, the magnecrystallic axis would be urged into a position coincident with the magnetic axis, by a force correspondent to that difference, just as if two different bodies were taken, when the one with the greater conducting power displaces that which is weaker (2837).

From this it followed 'that a diamagnetic body like bismuth ought to be less diamagnetic when its magnecrystallic axis is parallel (as nearly as may be) to the magnetic axis, than when it is perpendicular to it' (2839). When the experiment was tried (utilizing Faraday's newly devised and very delicate torsion balance) it was successful.[47] The new hypothesis had again proven its worth by predicting a new effect.

In the Twenty-fifth Series, Faraday maintained the utmost caution with respect to the meaning of magnetic conduction. In the very first paragraph, in which he first made mention of magnetic conducting power, he warned the reader that he was putting forth the concept with the greatest diffidence.

> ... I only state the case hypothetically [he wrote], and use the phrase *conducting power* as a general expression of the capability which bodies may possess of affecting the transmission of magnetic force; implying nothing as to how the process of conduction is carried on. Thus limited in sense, the phrase may be very useful, enabling us to take, for a time, a connected, consistent and general view of a large class of phaenomena; may serve as a standard of meaning amongst them, and yet need not necessarily involve any error, inasmuch as whatever may be the principles and condition of conduction, the phaenomena dependent on it must consist among themselves (2797).

Thus, in pure phenomenalistic language, did Faraday begin the discussion of magnetic conductibility. But it was impossible for him to work with the lines of force without theorizing on their nature. The whole course of his thought for thirty years had been guided by his considerations on the nature of force and the modes in which it acted. It was certainly no time now to cease thinking in this fashion and rest content with mere factual description, no matter how accurate or new. Although his caution was admirable he could not maintain it. As he had written to Schoenbein in 1845: 'You can hardly imagine how I am struggling to exert my poetical ideas just now for the discovery of analogies and remote figures respecting the earth, sun, and all sorts of things – for I think that is the true way (corrected by judgment) to work out a discovery.'[48]

By the time the Twenty-fifth Series was completed, Faraday was more or less convinced of the physical reality of the lines of force even though he did not have the experimental evidence with which to convince others. His own position was revealed by the analogy he drew later in the paper which he had begun by insisting upon the purely hypothetical nature of his speculations. 'There is a striking analogy', he wrote, 'between this conduction of magnetic force and what I formerly called specific inductive capacity (1252, etc.) in relation to static electricity, which I hope will lead to further development of the manner in which lines of power are affected in bodies, and in part transmitted by them' (2846).

One of the great values of analogies in science is that they are forever breaking down. No one thing is ever exactly like some other thing unless they are identical, in which case the analogy turns into identity and its value vanishes. Many phenomena, however, are sufficiently similar to other better-known phenomena to permit us to transfer the laws of action of the one to the other. This immediately illuminates the lesser-known phenomenon and also casts into sharp relief the differences which exist between the two – differences which had before been obscured by the similarities. So it was with the magnetic lines of force. Their similarity to electrostatic lines of force had led Faraday to the discovery of the effect of a magnetic field upon the plane of polarization of light. In the investigations that followed, the idea of the line of force as a line of strain, in approximate analogy with the electrostatic line of force, had served as the guiding thread to the development of his thought. At the same time, however, the analogy was seen to be somewhat less than exact. There were two aspects of the magnetic lines of force in particular which were quite dissimilar to the electrostatic lines of force. The electrostatic lines of force always were polar as the result of the polarization of the 'contiguous particles' by which the electrostatic force was transmitted. To put it another way, electrostatic lines of force always had 'ends'; increasingly after 1848, Faraday began to suspect that magnetic lines of force did not have ends, since it was impossible to separate 'poles' as could be done in electrostatics. Secondly, the failure to discover any diamagnetic polarity ruled out the polarization of 'contiguous particles' as the means by which the magnetic force was carried on. If the magnetic lines of force were strains, it became increasingly more important to discover *what* was being strained, if it was not the contiguous particles which, it will be remembered, filled all space with their forces.

It was not until July of 1851 that Faraday was able to turn his attention fully to the investigation of the intimate nature of lines of force. In part this was due simply to the press of business and the fact that as he grew older he could no longer work as he had done in the 1830's. His mind, although still able to rise to great peaks of originality was, nevertheless, failing. His memory was increasingly bad and he found it ever more difficult to keep the object of his researches before him. There is real pathos in the following passage of a letter to Carlo Matteucci in 1849.

> I have lately been working for full six weeks trying to procure results [he wrote] and have indeed procured them, but they are all negative. But the worst of it is, I find on looking back to my notes, that I ascertained all the same results experimentally eight or nine months ago, and had entirely forgotten them. This in some degree annoys me. I do not mean the labour, but the forgetfulness, for, in fact, the labour without memory is of no use.[49]

The character of his thought also changed at about this time. Before 1850 he had rather carefully hidden his theoretical ideas from the scientific world, using them to guide him from discovery to discovery. By 1850 the long string of discoveries that were to guarantee him immortality in the history of science had come to an end. Never again was he to startle the learned world with some new effect which few, if any, of his colleagues had suspected but which he had deduced from his own hypotheses. The decade of the 1850's, rather, was to be spent in the exposition and defence of his theories. He was not, of course, prepared to abandon experiment but his experiments were now overtly the ammunition with which he supported theoretical positions taken up publicly and in print. His purpose was nothing less than to supply a general view of the modes of action of force.[50] Central to this view was the physical reality of the lines of force.

The basic question to which Faraday turned in the summer of 1851 concerned the interpretation of the pattern made by iron filings sprinkled on a card over a magnet. The filings arranged themselves in lines; were these lines 'real' or were they merely the result of the interaction of the magnet and the iron filings? Faraday had long viewed them as strains of some sort but it was now time to discover their true nature. If strains, to what were they connected so that the strain could be imposed along the line of force? The electrostatic line of force was firmly anchored in electrically excited matter and the strain, transmitted along the curves of the intervening polarized particles, ended in positively and negatively charged surfaces. An electrostatic line of force could start in a charged sphere and leap across a room to the wall. If the sphere were positively charged, the part of the wall where the line of force ended would be negative. The line, and the particles in between were all polar having 'positive' and 'negative' ends. Magnetic lines were peculiar in that they always returned to the body from which they emanated. It was impossible to hold up a sphere 'charged' with north magnetism and trace a line of magnetic force across a room to a south pole on the wall. Wherever a north pole existed, a south was also to be found, nearby, in the same body. The ends of the line of force, then, had to be the poles of the magnet. This was where the strain originated; here must be where the original tension was applied.

When examined critically this explanation made little sense. An iron magnet was, after all, relatively homogeneous. Why, then, should two particular spots, indistinguishable from other places, become poles? Why, to put it another way, should the lines of force terminate at all? From 1845 to 1850 Faraday had gradually convinced himself that the actual particles of magnetic or diamagnetic substances counted for very little in magnetic phenomena. Why, then, call in particles merely to have an anchor for the lines of force? Could not poles be dispensed with altogether?

The first thing that had to be done was to make certain that the lines of force really existed independently of the iron filings that illustrated their forms so beautifully. Since iron itself was magnetic, it was possible that the magnetic curves might be the result of placing iron filings over a magnet and that when the filings were not present, the curves vanished. The use of a compass needle was open to the same objections. If the lines of force were created by the interaction of the needle and the magnet, the needle would still trace them out as if the lines existed independently of the needle. One method alone appeared free from fault. A conducting wire in the presence of a magnet showed no effect; when the wire was moved across the lines of force, a current was generated. The moving wire involved no attraction, repulsion, or other polar effects. The lines of force detected by this method would, therefore, not appear to be created by the presence of the wire. 'So,' Faraday concluded, 'a moving wire may be accepted as a correct philosophical indication of the presence of magnetic force' (3083).

The existence of the lines of force gave no hints about their essential properties. Were they continuous curves, or were they actually attached to points in the magnet called poles? If they were continuous curves, then the lines of force ought to pass through the magnet as well as around it in the external medium. Could these lines be detected *inside* the magnet? Faraday devised a very simple apparatus for this purpose. Two bar magnets were placed side by side with similar poles next to one another. The two magnets were separated by a thin piece of wood, reaching from the middle of the magnets to one end. The two magnets were then placed in a wooden axle so that they could be rotated about their mutual axis. A copper collar was then placed around the magnets at their middle. A loop of wire could now be arranged so as to make contact with the collar at one end and with a galvanometer at the other. Another wire ran from the galvanometer, down the groove left between the two magnets, and then up to the collar. Each element in the apparatus could be rotated separately; the two magnets around their mutual axis, the wire running down the centre on its axis, and the loop of copper wire around an axis more or less coincident with the extension of the magnetic axis [11323]. With this apparatus, Faraday could hope to detect lines of force if they ran *through* the magnet as well as through the medium in which the magnet was immersed. He first repeated the experiments he had done in 1832 with the rotating magnet to be certain that the lines of force did not rotate with the magnet. 'No mere rotation of a bar magnet on its axis, produces any induction effect on circuits exterior to it; . . .' he reported. 'The system of power about the magnet must not be considered as necessarily revolving with the magnet, any more than the rays of light which emanate from the sun are supposed to revolve with the sun' (3090). The conclusion that the lines of force did not move with the magnet reinforced the idea that they were, in a sense, independent of the magnet. This independence must also exist within the magnet. Such independence now could easily be shown. The power of a magnet could be measured precisely in terms of the current generated in a wire cutting the lines of force. Faraday clearly showed that the current (or, better, in modern terms, the electromotive force) was directly proportional to the number of lines cut. When *all* the lines of force were cut, no matter whether the cut was perpendicular or oblique to the lines, the current in the detecting wire was the same (3109–3114). '. . . The quantity of electricity thrown into a current is directly as the amount of curves intersected' (3115).[51] Knowing this, the existence of the lines of force within the magnet could be determined with great precision.

. . . this method of investigation gives much insight into the internal condition of the magnet, and the manner in which the lines of force (which represent truly all that we are acquainted with of the peculiar action of the magnet) either terminate at its exterior, or at any assumed points, to be called poles; or are continued and disposed of within. For this purpose, let us consider the external loop [see Figure 14–A]. . . . When revolving with the magnet no current is produced, because the lines of force which are intersected on the one part, are again intersected in an opposing direction on the other (3110). But if one part of the loop be taken down the axis of the magnet, and the wire then pass out at the equator (3091) [Figure 14–B], still the same absence of effect is produced; and yet it is evident that, external to the magnet, every part of the wire passes through lines of force, which conspire together to produce a current; for all the external lines of force are then intersected by that wire in one revolution (3101). We must therefore look to the part of the wire *within* the magnet, for a power equal to that capable of being exerted externally, and we find it in that small portion which represents a radius at the central and equatorial parts. When, in fact, the axial part of the wire was rotated it produced no effect (3095); when the axial, the inner radial, and the external parts were revolved together, they produced no effect; when the external wire alone was revolved, *directly*, it produced a current (3091); and when the internal radius wire alone (being insulated from the magnet) revolved, *directly*, it also produced a current (3095, 3098) in the contrary direction to the former; and the two were exactly equal in power; for when both portions of the wire moved together *directly*, they perfectly compensated each other (3095). This radius wire may be replaced by the magnet itself (3096, 3118) [Figure 14–C].

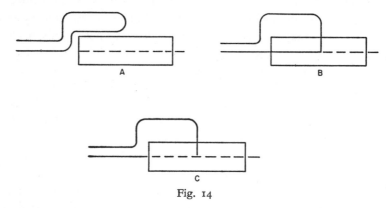

Fig. 14

So, by this test there exists lines of force within the magnet, of the same *nature* as those without. What is more, they are exactly equal in *amount* to those without. They have a relation in *direction* to those without; and in fact are continuations of them, absolutely unchanged in their nature, so far as the experimental test can be applied to them. Every line of force therefore, at whatever distance it may be taken from the magnet, must be considered as a closed circuit, passing in some part of its course through the magnet, and having an equal amount of force in every part of its course (3116–7).

The implications of these two paragraphs were literally revolutionary. If Faraday were correct and the lines of force did actually exist with the properties he attributed to them, then the whole structure of orthodox electric and magnetic science must come tumbling down. The orthodox theories were founded upon central forces acting inversely as the square of the distance; Faraday's new theory rejected central forces. The polarity that was the necessary complement of central forces had been banished. There was no polarity exclusive of the line of force and even this polarity was an odd one.

For my own part, [Faraday pointed out], I should understand the term to mean, the opposite and antithetical actions which are manifested at the opposite ends, or the opposite sides, of a limited (or unlimited) portion of a line of force. . . . The line of dip of the earth, or a part of it, may again be referred to as the natural case; and a free needle above or below the part, or a wire moving across it . . . will give the direction of the polarity (3154).

Thus polarity was the direction of the line of force, and as such, it was a polarity without poles. Since attraction and repulsion must be attraction *to* or a repulsion *from* some point (which then could be considered a *pole*) Faraday explicitly rejected attraction and repulsion as real magnetic phenomena. Not only did his work on magnetic conduction contradict the older forms of attraction and repulsion, but these older ideas were now capable of preventing further progress by blinding men to new approaches. 'To assume that pointing is always the direct effect of attractive and repulsive forces acting in couples (as in the cases in question, or as in bismuth crystals), is to shut out ideas, in relation to magnetism, which are already applied in the theories of the nature of light and electricity; and the shutting out of such ideas *may be* an obstruction to the advancement of truth and a defence of wrong assumptions and error' (3156).

There is no doubt that Faraday knew exactly how unorthodox he was and that his ideas were bound to meet with opposition. He knew, too, from which quarter the opposition would come. Hence his insistence upon the *experimental* aspect of his theory. 'I keep working away at Magnetism,' he wrote to Schoenbein, 'whether well or not I will not say. It is at all events to my own satisfaction. Experiments are beautiful things and I quite revel in the making of them. Besides they give one such confidence and, as I suspect that a good many think me somewhat heretical in magnetics or perhaps rather fantastical, I am very glad to have them to fall back upon.'[52] The mathematical physicist was unlikely to reject the simplicity of the inverse square law for anything so distinctly unmathematical as the lines of force. It was to this point that Faraday addressed himself in what may well be called the credo of the experimentalist. 'As an experimentalist', he wrote, 'I feel bound to let experiment guide me into any train of thought which it may justify; being satisfied that experiment, like analysis, must lead to strict truth if rightly interpreted; and believing also, that it is in its nature far more suggestive of new trains of thought and new conditions of natural power' (3159). Experiment (and his own theories) had led him to the physical reality of the lines of force. It was with considerable hesitancy, however, that he presented his new conclusions on the nature of the lines of force at the end of the Twenty-eighth Series.

> Whilst writing this paper I perceive, that, in the late Series of these Researches, Nos. XXV. XXVI. XXVII., I have sometimes used the term *lines of force* so vaguely, as to leave the reader doubtful whether I intended it as a merely representative idea of the forces, or as the description of the path along which the power was continuously exerted. What I have said in the beginning of this paper . . . will render that matter clear. I have as yet found no reason to wish any part of those papers altered, except these doubtful expressions; but that will be rectified if it be understood, that, wherever the expression *line of force* is taken simply to represent the disposition of the forces, it shall have the fullness of that meaning; but that wherever it may seem to represent the idea of the *physical mode* of transmission of the force, it expresses in that respect the opinion to which I incline at present. The opinion may be erroneous, and yet *all* that relates or refers to the disposition of the force will remain the same (3175).

It was not until 1852 that Faraday insisted upon the reality of the lines of force.[53] In his paper 'On the Physical Character of the Lines of Force', he informed the reader that 'I am now about to leave the strict line of reasoning for a time, and enter upon a few speculations respecting the physical character of the lines of force, and the manner in which they may be supposed to be continued through space' (3243). There can be no doubt that Faraday was firmly convinced that the lines of force were real. The fact that the magnetic force was transmitted along curves, and that these curves were continuous was evidence enough for him. '. . . I cannot conceive curved lines of force without the conditions of a physical existence in that intermediate space, . . .' (3258). The reality of the physical lines of force was thus established. But this reality immediately raised a new question. How was the magnetic force transmitted through the lines of force? The search for an answer to this question led Faraday to the foundations of field theory.

4. The Field and the Transmission of Force

After affirming his faith in the physical reality of the lines of force, Faraday described the way in which the magnetic force was transmitted.

> If they [the lines of force] exist [he wrote], it is not by a succession of particles, as in the case of static electric induction . . ., but by the condition of space free from such material particles. A magnet placed in the middle of the best vacuum we can produce, and whether that vacuum be formed in a space previously occupied by paramagnetic or diamagnetic bodies, acts as well upon a needle as if it were surrounded by air, water or glass; and therefore these lines exist in such a vacuum as well as where there is matter (3258).

This was a statement of fundamental importance for the understanding of Faraday's ideas. It is the first time that he has hinted that he had been forced to modify the views of matter and force that he had propounded and defended in the late 1830's and 1840's. The absence of diamagnetic polarity ruled out transmission of magnetic force by 'contiguous particles'. How, then, was it transmitted?

To solve this problem, Faraday first had recourse to analogy.

> I have elsewhere called the electric current, or the line of electrodynamic force, 'an axis of power having contrary forces exactly equal in amount in contrary directions' (517). The line of magnetic force may be described in *precisely the same terms*; and these two axes of power, considered as right lines, are perpendicular to each other; with this additional condition, which determines their mutual direction, that they are separated by a right line perpendicular to both (3265).

Was the analogy really a deep one, or was it a question of purely superficial resemblance? An electric current, for example, tended, as Faraday put it, 'to elongate itself' (3266), whereas the lines of magnetic force tended to shorten themselves (3266). Electric currents in the same direction attracted one another, but similar 'magnetic axes of power or lines of force repel each other' (3267). But, Faraday insisted, these were not, as they seemed, opposite effects but connected ones.

> . . . they are contrasts which *coincide* when the position of the two axes of power at right angles to each other are considered. . . . The tendency to *elongate* in the electric current, and the tendency to *lateral* separation of the magnetic lines of force which surround that current, are both tendencies in the same direction, though they seem like contrasts, when the two axes are considered out of their relation of mutual position; and this, with other considerations to be immediately referred to, probably points to the intimate physical relation, and it may be, to the oneness of condition of that which is apparently two powers or forms of power, electric and magnetic (3268).

The analogy, so far, was complete and, as Faraday adduced other similarities of action, it appeared that it might be fruitful, indeed, to think of the magnetic lines of force as magnetic currents.

> The magnet, [Faraday noted] . . . may be considered as analogous in its condition to a voltaic battery immersed in water or any other electrolyte; or to a gymnotus . . . or torpedo, at the moment when these creatures, at their own will, fill the surrounding fluid with lines of electric force. I think the analogy with the voltaic battery so placed, is closer than with any case of *static* electric induction, because in the former instance the physical lines of electric force may be traced both through the battery and its surrounding medium, for they form continuous curves like those I have imagined within and without the magnet (3276).

By comparing the magnet to a voltaic pile immersed in an electrolyte, Faraday was able to make perfectly clear an idea which otherwise might have been difficult to understand. Everyone knew (or thought he did) what electrical conduction was and there could be no problem in visualizing the flow of current from one pole of a voltaic cell, through the surrounding medium, to the other pole. Take away the electrolyte and the voltaic cell lost its 'lines of force' and its character as a generator of electricity. Similarly, the surrounding medium was essential if the magnet were to exist as a magnet. Again, Faraday made his point quite explicit. 'I incline to consider this outer medium as *essential* to the magnet; that it is that which relates the external polarities to each other by curved lines of power; and that these must be so related as a matter of necessity. Just as in the case of the battery above, there is no line of force, either in or out of the battery, if this relation be cut off by removing or intercepting the conducting medium . . .' (3277). Without a medium through which the magnetic lines of force could pass, the energy of the magnet would not manifest itself. The magnet would be like a voltaic cell which lacked external connexions from pole to pole. Such a cell, if examined internally, would exhibit none of the electrical energy made possible by the external connexions; it would simply be an interesting mixture of chemicals and metals. In a very real sense, therefore, the electrical energy of the voltaic cell depended upon these connexions. In a similar way, the energy of the magnet could be made manifest *only* when the lines of magnetic force passed through the surrounding medium. The energy of the magnet, then, lay quite literally in the medium through which the lines of force passed, and *not* in the magnet by itself. This was the fundamental concept of classical field theory.[54]

The idea of magnetic currents, although fruitful, contained one major stumbling block to its acceptance. It was not one that Faraday felt it necessary to point out, but it did serve to have him withdraw the analogy in later papers. It also focused attention upon the one aspect of magnetism which his new theory was powerless to explain. The analogy with the voltaic cell can serve to throw this point into prominent relief. The source of voltaic electricity was chemical action; Faraday had been one of the foremost champions of the view that electricity must be the result of a *conversion* of force, and could not arise *de novo* from mere position or contact. To suggest that it could was to deny the principle of the conservation of force and this principle Faraday held to be inviolate. Yet, was not the principle violated by the idea of magnetic currents? From whence did these currents come? What other form of force vanished when magnetic power made its appearance? An iron bar did not change in any way during the time it acted as a magnet. A dynamic effect could not be attributed to a static cause and so magnetic currents were abandoned in favour of static strains. What caused these strains Faraday could not say. The best he could do was describe magnets as 'the habitations of bundles of lines of force' (3295). Why these lines decided to move into magnets was known only to the Deity.[55]

By considering the magnetic lines of force as static strains, Faraday was able to account for the generation of currents in conductors. We must here recall Faraday's idea of a current as the build-up and release of tension.[56] Something similar to this must occur when a conducting wire was moved across the lines of force. The process was carefully described:

> When a copper wire is placed in the neighbourhood of a bar-magnet, it does not, as far as we are aware (by the evidence of a magnetic needle or other means), disturb in the least degree the disposition of the magnetic forces, either in itself or in surrounding space. When it is moved across the lines of force, a current of electricity is developed in it, or tends to be developed; and there is every reason to believe, that if we could employ a perfect conductor, and obtain a perfect result, it would be the full equivalent to the force, electric or magnetic, which is exerted in the place occupied by the conductor. But, as I have elsewhere observed (3172), this current, having its full and equivalent relation to the magnetic force, can hardly be conceived of as having its entire foundation in the mere fact of motion. The motion of an external body, otherwise physically indifferent, and having no relation to the magnet, could not beget a physical relation such as that which the moving wire presents. There must, I think, be a previous state, a state of tension or a static state, as regards the wire, which, when motion is superadded, produces the dynamic state or current of electricity. This state is sufficient to constitute and give a physical existence to the lines of magnetic force, and permit the occurrence of curvature or its equivalent external relation of poles, and also the various other conditions, which I conceive are incompatible with mere action at a distance, and which yet do exist amongst magnetic phaenomena (3270).

It should be noted that Faraday here does not speak of the strain being *in* the wire but only associated with it. If the strain were transmitted solely by the particles of the wire, there would be a detectable polarity in it and such was not the case. The particles, however, existed in space and space, as Faraday had often insisted, could conduct the magnetic lines of force. What appeared to be the case here was the interaction of the forces associated with the wire as a whole and the magnetic lines of force conducted, essentially, by the space in which the wire existed. This brings us no nearer, however, to a solution of the problem of magnetic conduction. How, it may well be asked, are the magnetic lines of force transmitted through the empty space surrounding the wire? Few of Faraday's scientific colleagues would have hesitated for a moment in giving the answer. The ether, that theoretical workhorse of the nineteenth century, could be called in to account for the conduction of the lines of force. This was, after all, to be the orthodox solution after Faraday until Einstein banished the ether from the cosmos in the special theory of relativity. Faraday was not so convinced of the reality of the ether as his contemporaries. He had spent his entire scientific career banishing imponderable fluids from science and it was hardly to be expected that he would take kindly to such an entity as the luminiferous ether. In 1852, however, he was still hesitant. When examining the nature of the lines of force, he asked 'whether they consist in a state of tension (of the aether?) round the electric axis . . .?' In the concluding paragraphs of the same paper, he was even more un-willing to give an explanation of the intimate nature of the lines of force. 'With regard to the great point under consideration,' he wrote, 'it is simply, whether the lines of magnetic force have a *physical existence* or not? Such a point may be investigated, perhaps even satisfactorily, without our being able to go into the further questions of how they account for mag-netic attraction and repulsion, or even by what condition of space, aether or matter, these lines consist' (3297). Except for the intriguing suggestion that space might have a condition, this statement retained the phenomeno-logical garb with which Faraday had clothed the lines of force since he first maintained their reality. As late as 1855, he wrote to John Tyndall, 'You are aware (and I hope others will remember) that I give the lines of force only as *representations* of the magnetic power, and do not profess to say to what physical idea they may hereafter point, or into what they will resolve themselves.'[57]

This was as far as Faraday ever went explicitly on the lines of force. He had presented a considerable amount of experimental evidence in favour of their physical existence. If they did exist physically there was no doubt that they passed through space devoid of ponderable matter. Everyone was then permitted to choose his own hypothesis to explain *how* the lines of force actually did pass across empty space.

Faraday did not cease to ponder the problem and there is evidence to indicate that he carried his speculations farther than the mere statement of facts about the existence of the lines of force. Although these speculations had little or no influence on science in the middle of the nineteenth cen-tury, they are important in a life of Faraday. They reveal, in the first place, the audacity of Faraday's mind. He rejected the ether when almost every-one else felt it to be the very cornerstone of science. His rejection of the ether also led him to a concept of the transmission of force through empty space which, if not understood (as it was not when he wrote it), reduces one of the later papers he wrote, 'On the Conservation of Force', to absolute nonsense. This final aspect of his thought on the lines of force is, therefore, well worth attention.

There is little doubt that Faraday took the idea of the luminiferous ether seriously enough to consider the possibility of utilizing it to account for the transmission of the lines of force in a vacuum. His approach to the ether, however, was quite unlike that of those who had considered it before him. Men such as Young, Fresnel, and Ampère, to mention only a few, were essentially mathematical physicists who sought a model, susceptible to mathematical analysis, which could yield the proper equations for the transmission of force (in this case, light) *in vacuo*. They were not, of course, blind to the purely physical aspects of the ether but these were secondary. If the mathematics came out right, they were more or less willing to gloss over the physical difficulties involved.[58] To Faraday, however, to whom mathematics was a closed book, the physical nature of the ether was primary and when he considered it he looked at it uniquely from the physical point of view.

There is little in his published articles, or even in the published laboratory *Diary* on the ether, beyond some very brief mentions of it. There does exist a manuscript, contained in the eighth folio volume of the manuscript copy of the *Diary*, entitled 'The Hypothetical Ether'.[59] The article is undated, but it would appear to have been written sometime in the early 1850's when Faraday was considering the ether as a possible vehicle for the lines of force. Because of its importance and since it has never before been published, it is worth reproducing here in its entirety.

> The ether – its requirements – should not mathematics prove or shew that a fluid might exist in which lateral vibrations are more facil than direct vibrations.[60]
>
> Can that be the case in a homogeneous fluid?
>
> Yet must not the ether be homogeneous to transmit rays in every direction at all times.
>
> If a stretched spring represent by its lateral vibrations the ether and its vibrations – what is there in the ether that represents the strong cohesion in the line of the string particles on which however the lateral vibration(s) essentially depend.
>
> And if one tries to refer it to a sort of polarity how can that consist with the transmission of rays in every direction at once across a given ether.
>
> If the ether be supposed capable of transmitting direct vibration(s) also – then which is most facilly transmitted.
>
> Which will pass into the ether.

Do the direct vibrations constitute light rays or not.

If so what is the property of this light.

If not what are the results of this direct vibration.

Can not all the light in a ray be polarized by Iceland Spar – and therefore is not all the vibrations lateral – Then there are no direct vibrations.

As rays of heat and actinics[61] can be polarized so their rays or vibrations as lateral as those of light.

Is it possible to conceive a liquid in which there shall be all lateral and no direct vibration.

How do any lateral vibrations in fluids resolve themselves?

The lateral vibrations in pools of water by wind – are soon converted into direct vibrations.

How can the lateral vibrations from a center open out i.e. what becomes of them as to their lateral extent at increased distances – what is the relative magnitude laterally – close to the light center and at 10 or 100 times that distance.

If the same then how do the vibrations open out at the increased distance so as to fill 100 times or 10000 times the same area or how do they superpose close at hand to the center so as to be able to open out to this extent.

Should not a mathematical account be given of the possibility of all these things.

If the ether be uniform in all directions and the transmission of rays shews that – then how is it that a progressive lateral vibration is not very quickly converted by the massy restitution of forces into direct vibrations expanding laterally.

If a tense wire or string in a fluid have a progressive lateral vibration given to it – does any portion of the fluid [illeg.] with it and by it convey lateral vibration – or do they not all quickly become direct vibrations.

The ether, quite obviously, did not enjoy much favour in Faraday's eyes. He simply did not believe that a homogeneous fluid could have the properties required of the ether. In particular, he objected to the idea of an etherial tension. If such existed, where were the forces of cohesion in a fluid whose particles were described as mutually repulsive? And, if it were answered that the tension resulted from the polarization of the individual ether particles, how could this polarity be reconciled with the ability of light rays to cross one another? Finally, although Faraday did not mention it here, a particulate ether transmitting the lines of magnetic force would necessarily become polarized and magnetic polarity had been done away with by his own researches. The ether, therefore, could not serve to conduct the lines of force.

The situation was now a very peculiar one. The lines of force were strains, without anything to be strained. Faraday, however, had mentioned a possible condition of space. Could not space itself be strained? Space, being continuous, would not become polarized by the magnetic stresses; then the lines of force in space could function as the 'tense strings' mentioned in the article on the ether to transmit light. All this is highly conjectural and I can offer only one argument in support of it. Yet this argument appears to me to be conclusive. Having eliminated the ether as the conductor of the lines of force in 'empty' space, only space was left to take on this task. It is this idea of the tension of space which will permit us to understand Faraday 'On the Conservation of Force'.[62]

It must first be stated strongly that in this essay, Faraday was definitely not dealing with the conservation of energy or the conservation of momentum, but with the conservation of force as he understood it. It was failure to realize this that led the anonymous reviewer in *The Athenaeum* to castigate Faraday severely.[63] The reviewer was not really to blame, for Faraday's argument was very obscure. His major point was contained in a passage on gravitational force. It, too, must be cited in its entirety if the analysis that follows is to make any sense.

> I believe I represent the received idea of the gravitating force aright, in saying, that it is a *simple attractive force exerted between any two or all the particles or masses of matter, at every sensible distance, but with a strength varying inversely as the square of the distance.* . . .
> This idea of gravity appears to me to ignore entirely the principle of the conservation of force; and by the terms of its definition, if taken in an absolute sense, '*varying* inversely as the square of the distance,' to be in direct opposition to it; and it becomes my duty, now, to point out where this contradiction occurs, and to use it in illustration of the principle of conservation. Assume two particles of matter, A and B, in free space, and a force in each or in both by which they gravitate towards each other, the force being unalterable for an unchanging distance, but varying inversely as the square of the distance when the latter varies. Then, at the distance of 10, the force may be estimated as 1; whilst at the distance of 1, i.e. one-tenth of the former, the force will be 100: and if we suppose an elastic spring to be introduced between the two as a measure of the attractive force, the power compressing it will be a hundred times as much in the latter case as in the former. But from whence can this enormous increase of the power come? If we say that it is the character of this force, and content ourselves with that as a sufficient answer, then it appears to me we admit a *creation* of power, and that to an enormous amount; yet by a change of condition so small and simple, as to fail in leading the least instructed mind to think that it can be a sufficient cause: – we should admit a result which would equal the highest acts our minds can appreciate of the working of infinite power upon matter; we should let loose the highest law in physical science which our faculties permit us to perceive, namely, the *conservation of force*. Suppose the two particles A and B removed back to the greater distance of 10, then the force of attraction would be only a hundredth part of that they previously possessed; this, according to the statement that the force varies inversely as the square of the distance, would double the

strangeness of the above results; it would be an *annihilation* of force; an effect equal in its infinity and its consequences with *creation*, and only within the power of Him who has created.[64]

The point Faraday wished to make was driven home by another example.

According to the definition [of gravity], the force depends upon both particles, and if the particle A or B were by itself, it could not gravitate, i.e. it could have no attraction, no *force* of gravity. Supposing A to exist in that isolated state and without gravitating force, and then B placed in relation to it, gravitation comes on, as is supposed, on the part of both. Now, without trying to imagine *how* B, which had no gravitating force, can raise up gravitating force in A, and how A, equally without force beforehand, can raise up force in B, still, to imagine it as a fact done, is to admit a creation of force in both particles, and so to bring ourselves within the impossible consequences which have already been referred to.[65]

Upon reading these remarkable passages there is a strong tendency to agree with *The Athenaeum* reviewer that Faraday was simply ignorant of the laws of nature as expressed by mathematicians and should be told respectfully to stick to his last.[66] Faraday, however, was quite willing to admit 'that particles at different distances are urged towards each other with a power varying inversely as the square of the distance'.[67] The basic question was, what was the physical process by which the 'urging' took place.

Faraday's example of the single body, A, provides the necessary clue for understanding what he was driving at. As he understood the action-at-a-distance school, A, all alone in the universe would be simply a body in space, with no gravitational force associated with it. Now, if another body, B, were to appear some miles distant, there would suddenly *and instantaneously* be a gravitational force between them. That this must be instantaneous followed from the fact that the attraction simply o'er-leaped space and involved no process of transmission. This was by no means an original objection to action at a distance. In Newton's own time, men of the stature of Christian Huygens had maintained that Newton was reintroducing occult qualities into physics. Boiled down to its simplest form, the objections to action-at-a-distance in the seventeenth century could be expressed by the question, how does one body know where another body is, so that it can be attracted to it? Attraction is, after all, a psychological attribute and one body is attracted to another because it knows the other is there and is moved by desire towards it.[68] Faraday omitted the psychological dimension, but his criticism followed much the same lines as those of his predecessors. If it takes two to gravitate, what was the *physical* connexion between bodies that brought the gravitational force into operation?

More interesting than recounting Faraday's attack on action-at-a-distance physics is to attempt to reconstruct the ideas Faraday held which led him even to consider the necessity of such an attack. What follows is entirely conjectural and has the sole virtue of shedding some light upon the probable course of the evolution of his theories.

By the 1850's, Faraday was accustomed to think of all forces between bodies as being transmitted by lines of force. Electrostatic lines of force were lines of intermolecular (and polar) strain. Magnetic lines of force were (most probably) strains in space. Gravitation, too, Faraday insisted before 1857, was propagated along lines of force.[69] These lines, like those of magnetic force, clearly passed through space devoid of matter, and were, therefore, most probably also strains in space. A lump of ponderable matter had the peculiar property of imposing a strain upon the space in which it existed and this strain extended throughout space to infinity. Like a magnet, the gravitational force of a given body was quite specific; it was the sum of the gravitational lines of force extending from it or, to put it another way, it was the sum of the strain imposed upon all space. For although the strain was infinite, like an infinite converging series in mathematics, the total amount of 'force' represented by this strain was quite specific. It was, in fact, directly proportional to the mass of the lump of matter. What changed with distance was not the force – this was always constant – but what may be termed the strain density. A mass at distance 10 from the body encountered fewer lines of force than one at distance 1. If the density of the lines of force varied inversely as the square of the distance, then Newton's law of universal attraction followed, *and*, of course, force was conserved.

In a similar fashion, the problem of the introduction of a new body into space disappeared. This body did not react to A (in Faraday's example) but to the strains in space where it, B, appeared. Or, better yet, the strains associated with B interacted with those associated with A to produce 'attraction'. Such action is easily illustrated by floating two needles on water. The strains produced in the surface film of water will cause the needles to come together as though they were attracted by one another. Here, as in the case of gravity, it is the strains, and not the bodies, which actually interact.

If the above analysis is correct, we have traced the line of force to its final formulation by Faraday. It was a strain in space, produced by ponderable matter in one way or another.[70] The laws of nature were the laws of the interaction of various forms of strain. This is what classical field theory was about.

References

1. It should be remembered that Faraday's 'Thoughts on Ray-vibrations' were first presented in April 1846, after these experiments had been performed. He was, therefore, still convinced of the role of the line of force in the propagation of light.

2. This is the equivalent of the rotation of a magnet around its axis as described in Chapter Four. See *Diary* [I–255 ff.].

3. See, for example, the variations of some of the experiments already cited to be found in [9038 ff.] and [9370 ff.].

4. It should be noted that even if the currents did go 'in the opposite directions' (presumably to those in Ampère's molecules) the result would not have been repulsion by both poles, but a simple reversal of polarity.

5. Even here Faraday did not reject the molecular currents entirely. He went on to say, 'They are probably too weak in power to be sensible with this apparatus.' It was not until 1848 that he finally threw out molecular currents [9619].

6. See below, section 2.

7. Plücker's letters to Faraday are preserved in the collection of letters to Faraday at the Institution of Electrical Engineers. Faraday's letters to Plücker are in the possession of the National Research Council of Canada, henceforth identified as N.R.C.C. They have never been published, to my knowledge.

8. I.E.E., Plücker to Faraday, Bonn, 3 November 1847. The original is in French.

The two brief memoirs were: 'Über die Abstossung der optischen Axen der Krystalle durch die Pole der Magnete', and 'Über das Verhältniss Zwischen Magnetismus und Diamagnetismus', *Ann. der Phys. und Chem.* (cited henceforth as Poggendorff's *Annalen*), 72 (1847), 315 and 343. The second of these memoirs appeared as: 'Sur le magnétisme et le diamagnétisme', in the *Ann. de chim. et de phys.*, 3 ser., 29 (1850), 129 ff. Both articles were published in English in the fifth volume of *Scientific Memoirs*, 353 ff. and 376 ff.

9. N.R.C.C., Faraday to Plücker, 16 December 1848.

10. Faraday's hopes that light would have poles had been disappointed and he seems to have quietly abandoned the idea.

11. E. Becquerel, 'Note sur l'action du magnétisme sur tous les corps', *Comptes Rendus hebdomadaires des Séances de l'Académie des Sciences*, 22 (1846), 960. Cited henceforth as *Comptes Rendus*. See also, E. Becquerel, 'Expériences concernant l'action du magnétisme sur tous les corps', *Ann. de chim. et de phys.*, 3 ser., 17 (1846), 437 ff.

12. Ibid., 958.

13. See below, section 3.

14. E. Becquerel, 'Recherches relatives à l'Action du magnétisme sur tous les corps', *Comptes Rendus*, 28 (1849), 624.

15. E. Becquerel, 'De l'action du magnétisme sur tous les corps' (Mémoire lu à l'Académie des Sciences, le 21 mai 1849), *Ann. de chim. et de phys.*, 3 ser., 28 (1850), 283 ff.

At the time of writing his Twenty-sixth Series, Faraday was unaware of this aspect of Becquerel's work but he was able to acknowledge its originality in a footnote to section 33 of this series (2847).

16. E. Becquerel, 'Recherches relatives . . .', *Comptes Rendus, 28* (1849), 624.

17. Ibid.

18. For a discussion of the various theories of diamagnetism, see A. de la Rive, *Traité d'électricité théorique et appliquée, 1* (1854), 456 ff. De la Rive subjected Becquerel's theory to a searching criticism and rejected it. It was not even considered in J. Tyndall's discussion of diamagnetic theories, in John Tyndall, 'The Bakerian Lecture – On the Nature of the Force by which Bodies are repelled from the Poles of a Magnet; to which is prefixed, an Account of some Experiments on Molecular Influences', *Phil. Trans.* (1855), 1 ff. See particularly pp. 38–39.

This paper is reprinted (along with his other papers on diamagnetism) in John Tyndall, *Researches on Diamagnetism and Magne-crystallic Action, including the question of Diamagnetic Polarity* (London, 1870), 89 ff. Further references to Tyndall's work will be made to this volume.

19. H. C. Oersted, 'Précis d'une série d'expériences sur le diamagnetisme', *Ann. de chim. et de phys.*, 3 ser., *24* (1848), 424 ff.

20. Ferdinand Reich, 'Versuche über die abstossende Wirkung eines Magnetpoles auf unmagnetische Körper', Poggendorff's *Annalen, 73* (1848), 60 ff. An English translation appeared in the *L. & E. Phil. Mag.*, N.S., *34* (1849), 127 ff.

21. W. Weber, 'Ueber die Erregung und Wirkung des Diamagnetismus nach den Gesetzen inducirter Ströme', Poggendorff's *Annalen, 73* (1848), 252.

An English translation appeared in Taylor's *Scientific Memoirs, 5* (1852), 477 ff. These memoirs, it should be remembered, appeared in the form of separate journals and the date for the entire volume is for the whole collection. Faraday, on 27 March 1849, noted in his Journal that he had read the translation of Weber's paper [10050].

22. For a detailed account of Weber's theory see W. Weber, 'Elektrodynamische Maassbestimmungen insbesondere über Diamagnetismus', *Abhandlungen der mathematisch-physischen Classe der Königliche Sachsischen Gesellschaft der Wissenschaften, 1* (1852), 483 ff.

Also, W. Weber, 'On the Connexion of Diamagnetism with Magnetism and Electricity', John Tyndall and William Francis, eds., *Scientific Memoirs, Natural Philosophy* (London, 1853), 163 ff.

The account of the development of Weber's theory given in the text is somewhat oversimplified, for Faraday refuted Weber's 'proof' of diamagnetic polarity. Weber, however, felt that he had established it by other means and, in 1852, built his theory around it.

23. Ibid., 166.

24. Tyndall, loc. cit., 137.

25. A. de la Rive, op. cit., 558. This does not mean necessarily that magnetic bodies are *denser* than diamagnetics. Density is a function of atomic weight as well as of the number of atoms per unit volume.

26. Ibid., 570–1.

27. These would appear to be the same currents envisaged by Ampère around his electrodynamic molecule.

28. de la Rive, op. cit., 573.

It is somewhat ironic that de la Rive's model was ultimately to prove applicable (with significant modifications) to the diamagnetism of organic ring structures such as benzene.

29. Bib. Univ. et pub. de Génève, MS. 2316, 88A4, f. 69, Faraday to A. de la Rive, 29 May 1854. For Faraday's public views on the various theories of magnetism see his, 'On some Points of Magnetic Philosophy', *Exp. Res., 3,* 528 ff.

30. Trinity College, Cambridge, Faraday–Whewell Correspondence, Faraday to W. Whewell, 23 February 1855.

31. See above, p. 390.

32. This was the first point of difference between Becquerel and de la Rive on the one side and Faraday on the other. Becquerel and de la Rive were convinced the diamagnetic *must* suffer some kind of molecular rearrangement but neither could answer Faraday's objection of the instantaneous action of the helix satisfactorily.

33. It should be noted that the electrochemical theory devised by J. J. Berzelius *did* assume a basic polarity of the chemical elements. It was the failure to detect such polarity that gave Boscovich's theory a decided superiority over Berzelius' hypothesis.

34. See also [9667 ff.], [9700–2], [10809–10], [10876–84], [12619 ff.], [13189 ff.], [13417–20]. The search for diamagnetic polarity thus occupied Faraday from 1845 until 1854. It was finally abandoned in September 1854 [13481]. Faraday had neglected no lead in spite of his growing firmness of belief that he would never discover a polar effect. It was this belief that spurred him to uncover the sources of Weber's error.

35. There is a diagram and description of this instrument in the Twenty-third Series, *Exp. Res., 3,* 139. It worked on the same principles as Weber's, only with greater precision.

36. For these experiments, see [10330 ff.].

37. There actually was an observed effect, but Faraday easily showed that it was due to the mechanical compression of the sides of the box within the magnetic poles [10726].

38. It should be remarked that this passage occurs in Series XXI, dated 22 December 1845, and shows Faraday's ideas at the very beginning of his search for diamagnetic polarity.

39. See above, section 1.

40. Trinity College, Cambridge, Faraday–Whewell Correspondence, Faraday to Whewell, 7 November 1848.

41. Ibid.

42. Ibid. '. . . as it appears to me that the power by which it [the crystal] points when in the Magnetic field is an *induced* power, I have called it the *Magneto crystallic* force.'

43. In the letter to Whewell cited above, Faraday pointed out that the magne-crystallic force could counteract the ordinary magnetic or diamagnetic

action. 'So strong is the tendency to go into *position* that I can make a dia-magnetic body approach when it would naturally be repelled or a magnetic body recede when it would naturally be attracted by opposing the magne-crystallic condition to the magnetic or diamagnetic condition.'

44. See (2551) ff. and [9599] ff.

45. See above, section 2.

46. The word was coined by Whewell in answer to a plea from Faraday, 1 August 1850. Trinity College, Cambridge, Faraday–Whewell Correspondence. Paramagnetics move into more intense areas of magnetic force.

47. This fits in well with the results obtained by John Tyndall and Herman Knoblauch, 'The Magneto-optic properties of Crystals and the Relation of Magnetism and Diamagnetism to Molecular Arrangement', in Tyndall, op. cit., 1 ff. Tyndall, however, interpreted his results in terms of diamagnetic polarity.

48. Kahlbaum and Darbishire, op. cit., 149.

49. B.J., 2, 250.

50. The published papers after 1850 become much more important in the search for the course of Faraday's ideas and the laboratory *Diary* less so. There were still some speculations confined to the privacy of the *Diary*, but by and large, the *Diary* became the repository of facts from which Faraday could draw evidence for the truth of the theoretical concepts presented in the published papers.

51. It should be noted that this statement of Faraday's law of electromagnetic induction was not directed at electricity at all. Faraday was trying to prove that there was a certain specific amount of 'power' associated with every magnet; the induced currents merely detected this power. Compare with (114) and (213) where Faraday *was* interested in the electrical currents induced. The difference is that in the earlier experiments *each* line of force was assumed to contain the same, specific amount of force while in these experiments Faraday was inter-ested in devising a way of measuring the *total* power of a magnet.

52. Kahlbaum and Darbishire, op. cit., 199.

53. M. Faraday, 'On the Physical Character of the Lines of Magnetic Force', *L. & E. Phil. Mag.*, 4 Ser., 5 (1852), 401 ff. Reprinted in *Exp. Res.*, 3, 407 ff.

In this paper, Faraday continued to number the paragraphs, picking up where the Twenty-ninth Series had left off. I shall continue to use these numbers but the reader who wishes to consult the original paper should look for it in either of the two places cited above, and *not* in the *Phil. Trans.* for 1852.

54. I have here done some violence to history for, although the concept of energy had been introduced into physics as long ago as 1801, Faraday never used it in the same sense in which I have here. By using it, however, it becomes possible to show clearly that Faraday's concept of the magnetic medium did contain the basic axiom of classical field theory.

55. Here, of course, Ampère's theory had the advantage over Faraday's. In (3273) Faraday paid tribute to Ampère but it seems clear that he did not, even here, accept Ampère's theory as Ampère had put it forth. In 1854, in an article 'On Some Points of Magnetic Philosophy', *Exp. Res.*, 3, 528 ff., Faraday quite specifically rejected Ampère's theory.

56. See above, Chapter Five.

57. 'Magnetic Remarks by Professor Faraday, D.C.L., F.R.S., etc.', *L. & E. Phil. Mag.*, 4 Ser., *9* (1855), 253.

58. Ampère is the prime example of this method of attack. It was precisely the number of *ad hoc* physical hypotheses on the nature of the ether that Ampère had made that had led Faraday to reject his theory.

59. This volume is at the Royal Institution. Thomas Martin, in his preface to volume 7 of the published *Diary*, does not mention this paper or give his reasons for not publishing it.

60. By lateral vibrations, Faraday meant transverse vibrations or those in which the particles of the fluid vibrate in a direction perpendicular to the course of the disturbance, thus $\updownarrow\!\circ$. By direct vibrations he meant longitudinal vibrations in which the particle vibrates in a line parallel to the direction of the disturbance, $\leftarrow\!\circ\!\rightarrow$. The first represents a light wave, the second a sound wave.

61. The actinic rays were those which could cause chemical reactions to take place. They were considered, at this time, to be somewhat different from ordinary light rays.

62. *Proc. R.I.*, *2* (1857), 352 ff. Reprinted in *Exp. Res. in Chem. and Phys.*, 443 ff. References will be to the reprint.

63. *The Athenaeum*, 28 March 1857, 397 ff.

64. M. Faraday, loc. cit., 446.

65. Ibid., 448.

66. *The Athenaeum*, loc. cit., 399. See especially the last paragraph.

67. M. Faraday, loc. cit., 463.

68. 'Force' is conserved here by making the moving force one inherent in the body which is moved by desire.

69. See below, Chapter Eleven, section 1.

70. Faraday's concept of gravitation as a strain also subtly changed his picture of the Boscovichean atom. To Boscovich, the forces of his atoms were forces acting at a distance; by denying action at a distance, Faraday reduced Boscovichean atoms to centres of strain. There were, therefore, two kinds of strain possible – polar (associated with the particles of matter) and non-polar (magnetic and gravitational) in which the strain was in space.

CHAPTER ELEVEN

The Last Years

1. Last Researches

During the 1850's when the stream of highly speculative papers on the nature of force and its transmission were appearing in the *Philosophical Magazine* and the *Proceedings of the Royal Institution*, Faraday continued his experimental researches. The pattern of his researches now altered. For twenty-five years one result had led to another and there was an almost steady progression as Faraday tracked down the implications of the results he obtained in the laboratory. The concept of the lines of force and the field now provided him with an overall picture of physical reality. The chain, in a sense, was complete. Only here and there was a link missing, and these Faraday sought to discover. But, by and large, his main effort in these years was to test his own ideas by attacking them. The attempt to discover a connexion between gravity and the other forces of nature was a search for a missing link. His work on the relations of gold to light was an experimental search for the hypothetical ether which he had rejected on theoretical grounds. The investigation of electric discharges through evacuated tubes was stimulated by the apparent existence of electricity independent of matter, something that he had for years considered to be impossible. His last researches reveal Faraday's extraordinary mental honesty and flexibility. For thirty years he had worked within a particular theoretical framework and the value of the theory had been demonstrated time and time again by leading him to new discoveries. Yet, all the evidence amassed in favour of his ideas did not blind him to the possibility of error. Man, he knew, was fallible and so, as his ideas received increasing justification from facts, he redoubled his critical zeal. 'I always tried to be very critical on myself before I gave anybody else the opportunity,' he wrote to Schoenbein in 1855, 'and even now I think I could say much stronger things against my notions than any body else has.'[1] Even the search for the conversion of gravity into some other force was a test of his theories.

That gravity ought to be convertible into some other force of nature followed directly from Faraday's deep faith in the conversion of forces. His faith was considerably reinforced by the solution of the problem of diamagnetic and magnecrystallic action. The realization that the forces involved in these phenomena were not new forces of matter, but simply old ones under a new guise, strengthened his conviction that all force was, basically, the same. In 1849 he sought to bring gravity within the framework of his general theory of force. 'Surely this force', he wrote in his *Diary* on 19 March 1849, 'must be capable of an experimental relation to Electricity, Magnetism and the other forces, so as to bind it up with them in reciprocal action and equivalent effect' [10018].

Given the reality of the lines of force which, in 1849, was already obtruding itself on his thought, his experimental approach was a curious one. One would expect that he would attempt to convert gravitational force into magnetic or electric force, say, by cutting the gravitational lines of force. By analogy with electromagnetic induction, therefore, one looks for a large mass separated from the earth, and the space between cut by a conducting wire attached to a galvanometer. Instead Faraday arranged his gravitating bodies so that they would move along, not across, a gravitational line of force. The reasoning here followed his ideas on the conservation of force and contributed to his final position on this subject. It can, perhaps, best be understood by considering the case of a body attracted (at a distance) by another body. If two bodies, *a*, *b* are separated from one another and both bodies are at rest, body *a* contains only energy of position or potential energy. If we assume that *b* will not move, then *all* the energy of the system is *in a*. Raising *a* from the surface of *b*, therefore, somehow adds energy to *a* but this energy is totally undetectable except by letting *a* fall back to *b*. As *a* falls, the potential energy (a rather mysterious entity) is converted into kinetic energy which is easily measured. To Faraday the conversion of work done into potential energy, by lifting *a* from *b*, and then the conversion of potential energy into kinetic energy was viewed as the gain or loss of force. It should be remembered that the principle of the conservation of energy, with its concomitant concepts of potential and kinetic energy was a very new thing in 1849. The full force of this principle was not to be made manifest until after Faraday's active scientific life was over.

In the raising or lowering of a body, relative to the earth, force somehow appeared and disappeared. A body at a height of several thousand miles would not weigh as much as it did at the surface of the earth. Weight is the most elementary and most obtrusive of the almost intuitive ideas of force that all men have and the decrease or increase of weight simply did not fit into Faraday's concepts of the conservation of force. If weight disappeared as a force, some other force had to become manifest, and vice versa. 'What in Gravity answers to the dual or antithetical nature of the forms of force in Electricity and Magnetism?' he asked himself. 'Perhaps the *to* and *fro*, that is, the ceeding to the force or approach of Gravitating bodies, and the effectual reversion of the force or separation of the bodies, quiescence being the neutral condition' [10019]. Currents ought to be generated, he argued, in the body or in a surrounding helix, as bodies either fell or were raised [10020] and, if this were true, 'then *falling* waters, etc., rising currents of air, smoke, etc., etc., should produce in nature equivalent effects' [10025]. As with electrical and magnetic effects, Faraday's view took in the cosmos and not simply the area of his laboratory.

It also followed, according to Faraday's line of thought, that 'the weight of a body having a current purposely passed round it ought to be affected, i.e. if falling or rising, but not if still' [10029]. And yet, '. . . that a body should have less weight whilst falling and more weight whilst rising than when still or moving only horizontal is a strange conclusion and against the general notion. Still, it may be true, for I do not see as yet that natural conditions contradict it' [10030].

This kind of dialogue with himself was typical of Faraday's approach to research. 'Let the imagination go,' he wrote in 1859, 'guiding it by judgment and principle, but holding it in and directing it by *experiment*' [15809]. There were, indeed, more things in heaven and earth than were dreamed of in his, or anyone else's, philosophy. No harm could come of permitting the mind to soar as high as it could reach provided, always, that the visions were submitted to the acid test of experiment. Even when the chances of success were slim, the experimental approach was usually worth the effort. Commenting on the possibility of the conversion of gravity into other forces, he wrote: 'After all, there is much which renders these expectations or similar ones hopeless: for surely, if founded, there must have been some manifestation of such a condition of the power in nature. On the other hand, what wonderful and manifest conditions of natural power have escaped observation, which have been made known to us in these days' [10032]. Speculation had done its job; it had led him to predict an effect. It was now up to experiment to decide whether the vision were a true one.

More than any other of his investigations, this one seemed to strike at the very heart of the laws of physical existence. 'It was almost with a feeling of awe that I went to work,' he wrote at the beginning of his experimental work on gravitation, 'for if the hope should prove well founded, how great and mighty and sublime in its hitherto unchangeable character is the force I am trying to deal with, and how large may be the new domain of knowledge that may be opened up to the mind of man' [10061]. In this hope, he was to be disappointed.

The experimental apparatus was simple. Various cores of copper, bismuth, iron, etc., were allowed to fall from the top of the lecture room in the Royal Institution to a cushion placed underneath them. The cylinders were surrounded by a helix of copper wire 350 feet long, the ends of which were attached to a sensitive galvanometer (2705). No effect due to the conversion of gravity into some other force was detected. Free fall had no effect on the surrounding helix.

Faraday then varied the conditions for theoretical reasons.

> On further consideration of the original assumption, namely, a relation between the forces, and of the effects that might be looked for consequent upon a condition of tension in and around the particles of the body, which, as we know, are at the same moment the residence of both gravitating and electric forces, and are subject to the gravitation of the earth, it seemed probable that the stopping of the up and down motion . . . in the line of gravity would produce contrary effects to the coming on of the motion, and that, whether the stopping was sudden or gradual; . . . (2711).

In effect, Faraday had changed his viewpoint. Instead of feeling that a continuous change of force (as in free fall) would create a current, he seemed to be returning to the idea of the electrotonic state. The analogy here was with the induction ring experiment of 1831. The particles of a body suspended in a gravitational field must be in a state of tension; they were at the ends of gravitational lines of force. Given the weakness of gravitational forces, it was certainly hopeless to attempt to detect such a state of strain with polarized light. But, the relief or imposition of a state of strain, as the induction ring experiment had clearly revealed, was detectable. If a body (whose particles were in a strained state) were permitted to fall, the strain would be relieved (at least in part) and the relief should become manifest at the galvanometer. Similarly, when the body ceased falling, the strained state should be reimposed and this, too, should cause deflection of the galvanometer needle. Because of inertia, free fall only relieved part of the gravitational strain; if the body were pushed along, all the strain should vanish and the effect should be made larger. This would appear to be the rationale behind Faraday's new experimental tack. The test bodies were vibrated rapidly up and down through a helix and commutators were so arranged that the hoped-for alternating effects coming from the starting and cessation of motion could be combined into a steady effect (2711 ff.). Again the results were negative. Faraday abandoned his investigation with the remark, 'They do not shake my strong feeling of the existence of a relation between gravity and electricity, though they give no proof that such a relation exists' (2717).

It was not until almost ten years later that he returned to the problem. During this period his ideas had developed considerably and, in 1859, he saw the possible effects somewhat differently than he had in 1849. In 1849 he had worked with very small pieces of matter. The cores inserted in the helix were of small dimensions and the effect, if any, would have been too small to detect. In his new experiments, therefore, Faraday intended to work with relatively large masses.

More importantly than this, Faraday had changed his mind on what to look for. Steady currents and momentary 'waves' of force had been eliminated in 1849. Pondering the problem of gravitational force once more in 1859, he perceived dimly that neither was to be expected. The gravitational field was unlike the electrostatic field in that *no* neutral condition ever could be achieved. The mere presence of matter meant the existence of strain; gravitational strain could be eliminated only with the annihilation of matter. There could not be, therefore, a coming on of strain and its relief; all there could be was a strengthening or weakening of a basic condition of tension.[2] Static electrical charge was a similar state of tension around some equilibrium point. Thus, it could be argued, that the ordinary strain associated with a gravitational field was electrically neutral. If this strain were increased it might manifest itself as electrostatic force of one kind, if it were decreased it would manifest itself as electricity of the opposite sign. To put this into the language of more orthodox physics, the energy of position or potential energy would become manifest as electrical charge. Thus, 'if an insulated body, being lifted from the earth, does evolve electricity in proportion to its loss of gravitating force – then it may become charged to a very minute degree either *positive* or negative. When thus charged it may be discharged, and then if allowed to descend insulated, it would become charged in the opposite manner, and so on' [15789].

To test these suppositions, Faraday worked with large masses and the longest vertical distance available to him. A 280-pound weight of lead was successively raised and lowered within the Shot Tower at the Surrey side of the Thames near Waterloo Bridge.[3] The vertical distance through which the lead passed was 165 feet.

Q

'The order of an experiment was to discharge the insulated lead by platinum contacts at the top of the tower, then to lower it, and ascertain if any signs of electricity appeared, when it had arrived at the bottom; – or, to discharge it at the bottom and examine it at the top' (3311).[4] Once again, the results were negative yet, Faraday insisted, 'I cannot accept them as conclusive . . .' (3312). At the end of the paper reporting his failure he suggested that he would like to try again for positive results with more sensitive instruments. He was never to realize this desire.

This was Faraday's last paper submitted for publication. It was dated 16 April 1860 from the Royal Institution and entitled 'Note on the possible relation of Gravity with Electricity or heat'. It continued the numbering of the paragraphs of the *Experimental Researches* and was clearly intended to be a part of these researches. It was sent to the Royal Society for publication in the *Phil. Trans.* and was rejected. The reasons for its rejection throw considerable light upon the relation of Faraday's thoughts to those of his more orthodox colleagues. It was George Stokes (later Sir George) who prevailed upon Faraday to withdraw his paper and his reasons were based upon a rejection of Faraday's whole vision of the unity of force.

I own [Stokes wrote to Faraday] my own opinion is against sending it in for the *Transactions*. It might have done as coming in incidentally, in the body of a paper containing positive results, but it seems to me it would hardly do for an independent communication to the *Transactions*, a communication I mean made at one time, though forming part of a train of experimental enquiry. If such negative results had the effect of correcting a commonly entertained expectation, or if the author's previous labours had led those who had followed them to regard a positive result as probable, or even not unlikely, the case might be different. But to my mind the antecedent probability of a positive result was too slender to justify the publication, in such a solemn manner as in the *Transactions*, of a negative result.[5]

The correlation of forces remained incomplete. Gravity could not be converted into another form of force and today still remains unique among the forces of matter.

Faraday's work on the lines of force and on gravity had led him, as we have seen, to reconsider the question of the ether. In the 'Thoughts on Ray-vibrations', he had explicitly rejected the ether as the means for the transmission of light vibrations. The unpublished paper on 'The Hypothetical Ether' had considered the theoretical difficulties in the way of accepting the ether as an actual physical fluid. The evidence appeared conclusive in favour of the rejection of the ether. Nevertheless, Faraday reopened the question in 1856. Although convinced in his own mind that the ether most probably did not exist, he was still eager to attack the problem experimentally if possible. Since it was light that appeared to require the presence of the ether, it was in the realm of physical optics that the experiments would have to take place. But, it was extremely difficult to devise experiments that could be viewed as interactions between the ether and ponderable matter. The problem was not a new one; it had been attacked in various ways for almost a century, primarily by using crystals or other doubly refracting media. The resultant effects were often extremely complicated and gave no clear-cut evidence of the interaction of the ether and ponderable matter. What Faraday sought was a way in which the minimum amount of ponderable matter could be utilized to achieve a detectable optical effect. Then, hopefully, if there were an ether, its interactions with this matter would become manifest. The object of his quest was clearly described in the early paragraphs of his paper on the 'Experimental Relations of Gold (and other Metals) to Light'.[6]

Light [Faraday wrote at the beginning] has a relation to the matter which it meets with in its course, and is affected by it, being reflected, deflected, transmitted, refracted, absorbed, &c. by particles very minute in their dimensions. The theory supposes the light to consist of undulations, which, though they are in one sense continually progressive, are at the same time, as regards the particles of the ether, to and fro transversely. The number of progressive alternations or waves in an inch is considered as known, being from 37,600 to 59,880, and the number which passes to the eye in a second of time is known also, being from 458 to 727 billions; but the extent of the lateral excursion of the particles of the ether, either separately or conjointly, is not known, though both it and the velocity are probably very small compared to the extent of the wave and the velocity of its propagation.[7] Colour is identified with the number of waves. Whether reflexion, refraction, &c., have any relation to the extent of the lateral vibration, or whether they are dependent in part upon some physical action of the medium unknown to and unsuspected by us, are points which I understand to be as yet undetermined.

Conceiving it very possible that some experimental evidence of value might result from the introduction into a ray of separate particles having great power of action on light, the particles being at the same time very small as compared to the wave-lengths, I sought amongst the metals for such. Gold seemed especially fitted for experiments of this nature, because of its comparative opacity amongst bodies, and yet possession of a real transparency; because of its development of colour both in the reflected and transmitted ray; because of the state of tenuity and division which it permitted with the preservation of its integrity as a metallic body; because of its supposed simplicity of character; and because known phenomena appeared to indicate that a mere variation in the size of its particles gave rise to a variety of resultant colours. Besides, the waves of light are so large compared to the

dimensions of the particles of gold which in various conditions can be subjected to a ray, that it seemed probable the particles might come into effective
relations to the much smaller vibrations of the ether particles; in which
case, if reflexion, refraction, absorption, &c., depended upon such relations,
there was reason to expect that these functions would change sensibly by the
substitution of different sized particles of this metal for each other.[8]

There can be no doubt that Faraday took this investigation seriously.
It occupied him for almost the entire year of 1856. He began to work on
gold on 2 February [14243] and only gave it up on 20 December [15403].
During this period, the *Diary* reveals that this was his sole occupation in
research. The results, however, hardly seemed to justify the time and effort
he had devoted to it. As he wrote to Schoenbein, 'The work has been of
the mountain and mouse fashion. . . .'[9] No effect of the ether was discovered and very little, if any, light was shed upon physical optics. About
the only point of theoretical value that was forthcoming related to the
nature of the gold particles. In February Faraday raised the question, 'If
particles not having continuity can reflect light as a continuous surface,
will it not shew that several separated particles may act at once and therefore at a distance on a ray of light – and then must not the particles be
likened rather to centres of force than to solid atoms?' [14407]. On
16 October he had satisfied himself that the gold films were optically continuous and, therefore, that his conclusion on centres of force must also
follow [15100]. He did not repeat this point in the published paper.

The result of the year's work was the paper which was first delivered
before the Royal Society as the Bakerian Lecture for 1857. It is a curious
paper because so little of it has anything to do with the avowed purpose of
investigating the luminiferous ether. The reprinted paper in the *Experimental Researches in Chemistry and Physics* runs to some fifty-two pages; of
these, thirty have absolutely nothing to do with optics or the ether. They
deal instead with the production and properties of colloidal gold. The use
of the term, 'colloidal', is somewhat of an anachronism for it was not until
1861 that Thomas Graham used the term 'colloid' to describe the kind of
suspensions that Faraday had produced. Faraday was led to them in his
search for small particles of gold which could be used to study their effect
on light. It had long been known that solutions of gold chloride could be
reduced by phosphorus and this simple chemical process appeared to
offer Faraday precisely what he wanted, for the particles of solid gold thus
produced ought to serve his purpose well.

Instead of merely using the suspensions as optical aids, however, Faraday became completely fascinated with them. He lovingly detailed the

various methods of producing them, contrasting the various solvents, insisting upon the necessity of excluding foreign matter, especially that which went with dirty glassware, and describing minutely the differences in the suspensions produced.[10] His discussion of the gold suspensions was more of a natural history than an analysis. Little attempt was made at explanation and by far the greater part simply described methods of producing the various effects reported.

Two points are worthy of our notice; the first because it escaped Faraday's usually acute perception and the second because it was an essential aspect of the colloidal state. After having described the production of colloidal gold, Faraday turned to a relation of the ways in which the colloidal state could be destroyed. Many of the suspensions of gold deteriorated spontaneously, depositing gummy or mucous-like masses on the bottom of the container as time passed.[11] The same effect could be achieved by adding small amounts of other substances. Common salt, hydrochloric acid, the chlorides of calcium, strontium, and manganese, the sulphates of magnesia, manganese, the nitrates of potassium, sodium, barium, magnesia, and manganese, to give only a partial list of the substances cited by Faraday,[12] were all able to bring about coagulation and destroy the colloidal state. 'Ether, alcohol, camphine, sulphide of carbon, gum, sugar and glycerine cause little or no change in the fluids. . . .'[13] And here Faraday dropped the subject. He did not seem to have remarked that the one group of substances was composed of electrolytes and the other group was made up of non-electrolytes. This was, no doubt, the result of his failing memory and his increasing inability to correlate his own thoughts. It may, too, have been caused by the fact that his investigation of colloidal gold was a digression and not, therefore, a subject upon which his entire mental energies were concentrated. In any case, he missed a valuable clue by not perceiving the electrical factor involved. Had he remarked this fact, it might have led him closer to the solution of the problem of the colloidal state. For, the second point worthy of notice is that Faraday recognized that such a problem existed. He did not simply assume that the suspensions were the result of the small particle-size of the gold; some other factor must be involved. There were two phenomena which led him to this realization. When a suspension of gold was boiled, the particles settled out, but they settled out into 'collections looking like little lenses of a deep ruby or violet colour, at the bottom of the flasks containing the fluid. . . .'[14] Thus, the particles of gold could come more closely together than they were in the suspension, but not closely enough to cohere and form macroscopic pieces of gold. This was odd behaviour, indeed, and Faraday only remarked upon it, without pretending to explain it. Nevertheless, he did realize that these gold particles were somehow different from those coagulated by the introduction of salt.

> The particles could fall together within a certain limit, but many weeks did not bring them nearer or into contact; for they remained free to be diffused by agitation. The space they occupied in this lens-like form must have been a hundredfold or even a thousandfold, more than that, which they would have filled as solid gold. Whether the particles be considered as mutually repulsive, or else as molecules of gold with associated envelopes of water, they evidently differ in their physical condition, for the time, from these particles which by the application of salt or other substances are rendered mutually adhesive, and so fall and clot together.[15]

That some repulsive force was necessary appeared also from another fact. In general, suspensions which were blue in colour separated out faster than those which were ruby. By examining the two suspensions optically, it could be shown that the particles in the blue suspension were considerably larger than those that gave the red tint.

> But that the blue particles are always merely larger particles does not seem admissible for a moment, inasmuch as violet or blue fluids may be obtained in which the particles will remain in suspension as long as in the ruby fluids; there is probably some physical change in the condition of the particles, caused by the presence of the salt and such affecting media, which is not a change of the gold as gold, but rather a change of the relation of the surface of the particles to the surrounding medium.[16]

Faraday thus called attention to the fact that those interested in the colloidal state must look for some form of suspending force midway between chemical affinity and simple hydrostatic displacement. It is somewhat ironic that this should turn out to be electrical charge and that Faraday should have completely missed it. Nevertheless, in spite of Faraday's feeling that his mountain of labour had brought forth only a mouse, his investigations were of permanent value. They have since been recognized as fundamental contributions to colloid chemistry, even though they were initiated for a quite different reason.[17]

The third train of research that Faraday followed up in the 1850's was that of the discharge of electricity through gases. It was a subject that had long interested him; in the Thirteenth Series of the *Experimental Researches* he had treated this subject intensively as an illustration of his law of electrostatic induction and conduction (1526 ff.). It was in these investigations that he had noticed the dark space in an evacuated tube near the cathode known ever since as Faraday's dark space. In 1838 this kind of electric discharge had appeared to be easily explained by his theory of electrical action.[18] By 1858 the subject seemed worthy of being looked at again, for new apparatus had made electrical discharge through evacuated tubes a quite spectacular effect.

There were a number of factors behind Faraday's turning to electric discharge in evacuated tubes. To a certain extent, the subject was à la mode in 1857 and 1858. The Ruhmkorff induction coil made it a simple matter to study the phenomenon. It provided a high voltage with very simple apparatus and made it possible to dispense with the large, complicated, and expensive electrostatic generator formerly required.[19] In 1852 W. R. Grove utilized a Ruhmkorff coil for the first time in England for the production of an electric discharge in evacuated tubes.[20] It was not until 1857, however, that the Ruhmkorff coil really caught the attention of British scientists. In one volume of the *Phil. Mag.* of that year four articles appeared on the Ruhmkorff coil and ways of improving it.[21] At this time, too, John P. Gassiot, Vice-President of the Royal Society, received a new and improved Ruhmkorff coil made especially for him and it was with this apparatus and with Gassiot that Faraday pursued his investigations.

Another improvement had been made in the apparatus for exhibiting electric discharge *in vacuo*. Instead of glass tubes, sealed with plugs at either end through which the electrodes protruded into the tube (thus preventing the creation of a high vacuum), Geissler of Bonn had fused platinum electrodes directly into the glass.[22] Gassiot was one of the first in England to obtain these new tubes and experiment with them.

The increased ease of experimentation and the spectacular effects obtained with the Ruhmkorff coil and Geissler tubes were only part of Faraday's reasons for turning his attention to the problem of electric discharge *in vacuo*. In the lectures he delivered before a juvenile auditory (the Christmas Lectures) in 1857-8 on static electricity, he had remarked upon the phenomenon of electrical discharge where it appeared as though something material actually were being transferred across space. 'This transferability', he remarked to his youthful audience, 'is very strange: for it seems to show a sort of independent existence of the power apart from the body yet nothing is more difficult to conceive than properties or force without matter or matter without force.'[23] At the same time, he wrote to Plücker: 'Then again the question of transmission of the discharge across a perfect vacuum or whether a vacuum exists or not? is to me a continual thought and seems to be connected with the hypothesis of the ether. What a pity one cannot get hold of these points by some *experiments* more close and searching than any we have yet devised.'[24] These remarks, it should be noted, were made after he had explicitly rejected the fluid theories of electricity and cast serious doubt upon the existence of the ether. The new phenomena appeared to strike at the very foundations of his thought and so he turned to look at it closely.

Faraday's investigations, with Gassiot, of the appearance and conditions of the passage of electricity through evacuated tubes, or through tubes into which traces of various gases had been introduced, were conducted on two different levels.[25] On the one hand, he was intent on discovering for himself precisely what was going on, so there are relatively long and detailed descriptions which were clearly intended only to provide the necessary raw material upon which his mind could work. The more theoretical parts consist largely in attempts to bring these facts within the scope of his theory of electrical action. It is impossible to tell exactly where Faraday was going in these experiments for he never wrote anything for publication from them. He appears to have been able to reconcile most of his observations with his theory although as we shall see, a few strains, even a few cracks in his theoretical structure, began to show.

Faraday's interest in the new appearances of electrical discharge in tubes filled with rarefied gases dated back to Grove's 1852 paper in the *Phil. Trans.*[26] There was nothing in this paper to alarm him; in fact, the paper was one which strongly supported his theory of electrical action. Grove used Faraday's model of electrolytic decomposition to explain the results of what today would be called cathode ray discharge.[27] This explanation, he felt, was fully in accord with the view of electricity put forth by Faraday in 1838 and advocated by him since 1842. 'These experiments', Grove wrote, 'furnish additional arguments for the view which I have long advocated, which regards electricity as force or motion, and not as matter or a specific fluid.'[28]

In a Friday Evening Discourse on Ruhmkorff's apparatus given on 8 June 1855, Faraday referred to Grove's work and noticed particularly the striations or bands of light and dark that appeared when the electricity passed through an evacuated tube.

'Grove's bands across discharge in rare air . . . phosphorus vapour – lead to thoughts of undulations and interferences – are like stationary undulations. . . .'[29] In 1858, these thoughts also led him to Gassiot's house where he observed the bands in Geissler tubes and singled out those aspects he considered important.

At Mr Gassiot's. Saw his fine experiments on the luminous striae of the Electric discharge, especially with his tubes, and above all with the four horizontal tubes one over the other. Of the phenomena here presented, the following seem to me important: The well developed alternations of light and darkness at intervals of $\frac{3}{4}$ of an inch or more. The displacement of them by the fingers travelling along the outside. The charged condition of the outside giving luminous brushes to the finger or a conductor applied there. The continued recurrence of charge and discharge there, shewn by the continual recurrence of the brushes. The probable intermittence of the charged state corresponding with each recurrence of the luminous state. The probable difference in *charged condition* of the part opposite an obscure space and a luminous space. The capability of applying conducting rings or coatings round the tube at the obscure and the dark spaces and getting indications of the kind of charge by a spark to a little Leyden phial. The capability of moving the luminous spaces by moving these ring coatings. The relation of the coating of a dark place and a luminous place to each other.[30]

The striations appeared, at this point, to be similar to the glow produced when a glass globe was charged with static electricity – the so-called electric light of the early eighteenth century. Faraday carefully determined the static electric charge on the tubes when the dark and light bands occurred and noticed that the bands moved as the hands (and, therefore, the static charge now associated with the bands) passed up and down the tube. At the beginning of his investigation, it appeared that a mapping of the static charge on the tubes might provide all the information necessary for an explanation of the effect.

The analogy with the 'electric light' was not, however, complete. A magnet had no effect on the 'electric light' whereas it did affect the striations. Faraday carefully noted the double effect:

'The influence of the magnet – first in *deflecting* the whole discharge whilst the alternations remain unchanged – next in determining the luminous places; for as the magnet horseshoe moved along the tube, the luminous column with its alternations moved with it – so that large drops or globules of light could be drawn out of the platina wire or sent back into it.'[31] This clearly implied a dynamic, rather than a static, cause but this did not perturb him. He simply shifted attention away from the charged glass tube and considered the contents of the tube.

The light [he wrote in his notes] is not on the surface of the glass tube but in the space – in the medium within.

There must be medium there and this medium acts as a good conductor – as seen in the long thin termination, where it serves for a charging and discharging coating.

The medium there seems to owe its luminosity to its charge and immediately succeeding discharge. Where darkness occurs, probably the discharge more as an uniform than an intermitting effect.

The effect of light perhaps due to a series of charges and discharges at each luminous place.[32]

There was, in a very real sense, a contradiction here in Faraday's approach. Both static and dynamic factors seemed necessary to explain the action of the striae. He was never really able to resolve this difficulty for he was a prisoner of his own theory. Induction and conduction always went together, he had long argued, but together in succession, not together, spatially, at the same time. Was it possible for a body (glass) to be placed in tension (induction) while the tension was constantly being relieved around it, as in the conduction through the glass tube?[33] Faraday was unable to answer this question satisfactorily and, in this sense, his researches here were also a failure. Yet, once again, they are not without interest for Faraday's observational faculties were as acute as ever and he was able, at least, to discover precisely where his theories did not fit.

Early in the experiments, Faraday noticed that the two electrical powers were not exactly equal and opposite. He had already called attention to this fact in 1838[34] and returned to it now. Taking the 'current' in his own sense as something progressive, he was able to determine the direction of the progression. It was, he found, always *from* the negative electrode *to* the positive electrode.[35] This fact was reinforced by the course of his experiments and, at the end of this course of investigation he wrote: '. . . still I feel as if the source of the rays was at the Neg. wire.'[36] It was not for some years that other physicists recognized this fact and gave the name of cathode rays to the phenomenon.[37]

With Gassiot, he separated the two currents in a Geissler tube from one another by use of a magnet.[38] Like Gassiot, however, he did not know what to make of this peculiar behaviour.[39]

For the rest, Faraday was content to record facts and apply his theory to them.[40] Although the possibility that electricity might exist independently of matter had occurred to him, his experiments on electrical discharge through rarefied gases had not forced him to accept this possibility as a fact. And, in spite of the difficulties encountered by his theory in explaining the observed facts, he obviously did not feel that these difficulties were insurmountable. Indeed, his work on Geissler tubes must not have appeared very important to him at all. He neither followed it up, nor published anything on it. I suspect that Faraday felt that he had merely confirmed what he had written twenty years before.

Gravity, ether, electrical discharge *in vacuo* – these were the objects of sustained research after 1855. None of them, however, was Faraday's last investigation. This was performed on 12 March 1862, when he sought for some effect of a magnetic field upon the emission spectra of substances.

> The colourless Gas flame ascended between the poles of the Magnet and the salts of Sodium, Lithium, etc. were used to give colour. A Nicol's polarizer was placed just before the intense magnetic field and an analizer at the other extreme of the apparatus. Then the E. Magnet was made and unmade, but not the slightest trace of effect on or change of the lines in the spectrum were observed in any position of the Polarizer or analyzer.
>
> Two other pierced poles were adjusted at the magnet – the coloured flame established between them, and only that ray taken up by the optic apparatus which came to it along the axis of the poles, i.e. in the magnetic axis or line of magnetic force. Then the Electro magnet was excited and rendered neutral; but not the slightest effect on the polarized or unpolarized ray was observed.[41]

It seems altogether appropriate that Faraday, who had plucked so many of nature's scientific fruits, should leave behind him a seed for the future. Bence Jones reported on Faraday's last experiment[42] and there it lay until 1897. In that year, Zeeman repeated it, feeling that if Faraday had thought the experiment worth doing, it might be worth repeating with better, more sensitive, apparatus. He observed what Faraday had looked for in vain; the spectral line of an element was affected by the magnetic field. It is not denigrating Zeeman's achievement to suggest that the Zeeman effect was Faraday's last discovery.

2. Withdrawal from Practical Affairs

The decade of the 1850's was, in many ways, like that of the 1820's for Faraday. The great flood of ideas which had carried him from discovery to discovery in the 1830's and 1840's had slowed to a trickle and, although the habit of work was still strong, there was little to work on. So, as in the 1820's, Faraday made his talents available to those who could profit from his advice. His last previous work for the Government had been his report on oatmeals for the Admiralty in 1832.[43] In the 1850's, by Government request, he worked at trying to solve the problem of preserving the great paintings of the National Gallery from the effects of the London atmosphere. He also was able to offer some minor advice to the Admiralty during the Crimean War. As in the 1820's, he made himself available to private concerns for consultation on problems which interested him. The most important of these was the problem of the retardation of the signal in telegraphic circuits. It was, too, in the 1850's that his work on lighthouses for Trinity House suddenly accelerated and occupied a good part of his time. All this Faraday eagerly accepted. His memory was too poor for him to attempt any sustained research. His practical activities permitted him to feel that his knowledge was still of some account and that he could still be of some use. It was only when he was incapable of further work that he finally dropped all activities and retired.

By 1850 the problem of the art treasures of the National Gallery was becoming critical. The atmosphere of London was not exactly favourable to the preservation of the original tints of the paintings. In the report drawn up by Faraday, Sir Charles Eastlake, and William S. Russell, the atmospheric environment of the National Gallery was graphically described.

> In considering the position of the National Gallery, our attention was drawn to the vicinity of several large chimneys, particularly that of the Baths and Washhouses, and that connected with the steam-engine by which the fountains in Trafalgar-Square are worked, from which great volumes of smoke are emitted. In the neighbourhood, also, the numerous chimnies of the various club-residences; the proximity likewise of Hungerford-stairs and of that part of the Thames to which there is constant resort of steam-boats, may tend to aggravate this evil; but on the other hand it is to be observed that the very large open space in front and at the back of the building must be likely to establish a greater purity of atmosphere than is often attainable in the centre of crowded cities; . . .[44]

Anyone who has ever experienced a London 'haze' in our era of smokeless zones will appreciate the full body of the atmosphere in 1850.

This, however, was merely the external atmosphere contributed by the industrial revolution. The peculiar hospitality of the National Gallery contributed further ingredients.

> It appears [the Committee continued] that the Gallery is frequently crowded by large masses of people, consisting not merely of those who come for the purpose of seeing the pictures, but also of persons having obviously for their object the use of the rooms for wholly different purposes; either for shelter in case of bad weather, or as a place in which children of all ages may recreate and play and not unfrequently as one where food and refreshments may conveniently be taken.[45]

The daily attendance was estimated at 3,000. In 1849 some 592,470 people had visited the National Gallery so that this was by no means a negligible presence within its walls. The mixture of London atmosphere and human effluvia bathed the paintings in a potent chemical medium.

> This impure mass of animal and ammoniacal vapour [the Committee continued], of which it is difficult and perhaps unnecessary to distinguish and define the component parts, is peculiarly liable to be condensed on the surface of the pictures, and as most of the varnishes used on pictures have a tendency

to chill and become superficially opaque and dull, those impure vapours, by reason of their more easy adhesion to and absorption by the altering surface, probably hasten the dulness by condensation upon it.[46]

At this time, the Commission's main contribution was the analysis of the dangers presented. It was a grim picture, indeed, and it was clear that something had to be done immediately. The recommendation was made and accepted by the Committee that the paintings of the National Gallery be protected by covering them with plate glass. Those who have gone to the National Gallery to appreciate the delicate shadings of a Rembrandt and have had to rest content with their own reflections, have Faraday to thank for the preservation of these quasi-invisible art treasures.

It was to Faraday's and the Committee's credit that this protection was considered to be only temporary and Faraday was specifically requested to look into the possibility of using varnish as a protective covering. This was a possibility that could be explored experimentally and Faraday immediately set to work.[47] A piece of canvas was painted with white lead paint and the whole covered with varnish. One quarter of the canvas was given two coats, one quarter received three coats, and one quarter, four coats. The canvas was then placed in an atmosphere of hydrogen sulphide for several weeks. The results were both encouraging and discouraging. The varnish, it was found, gave perfect protection as long as it remained without flaw. But, after drying for some time the varnish cracked and then the painting was attacked.[48] There seemed to be no escape from this action and the plate glass remained.

Faraday's final undertaking for the Committee was the investigation of possible means of cleaning pictures already seriously corroded by the air of London. This was a straightforward problem; what Faraday sought was a solvent for dirty varnish that would not affect the painting underneath. Turpentine could not serve because it tended to dissolve everything leaving a perfectly clean canvas behind. Ethyl alcohol, it was found, worked well on dirty varnish and left oil paintings unharmed.[49] The only problem was that many so-called oil paintings actually had a varnish base and were, therefore, subject to serious damage when alcohol was applied. Faraday pointed out that it was impossible to tell by visual inspection what the chemical basis of the painting was so that all attempts at cleaning should be made with great caution. Nevertheless, Faraday stressed the fact that it was a chemical problem open to solution by chemists.[50] He, therefore, urged that the Government turn to professional chemists for help, and was confident that someday the cleaning of paintings could be accomplished safely.

Paintings were not the only *objets d'art* which suffered from the chemical soup of the London atmosphere. The great collection of ancient statues at the British Museum, including the Elgin marbles, was gradually being eaten away. Once again, in 1857, Faraday's aid was requested. Faraday inspected the statues and reported gloomily,

> I wish I could write anything satisfactory, in reply to your note about the marbles in the British Museum. . . . The marbles generally were very dirty; some of them appearing as if dirty from a deposit of dust and soot formed upon them, and some of them, as if stained, dingy and brown. The surface of the marbles is in general rough, as if corroded; only a very few specimens present the polish of finished marble: many have a dead surface; many are honey-combed, in a fine degree, more or less; or have shivered broken surfaces, calculated to hold dirt mechanically.[51]

Nor was this merely a superficial layer of grime easily removed by mechanical means.

> I finally used dilute nitric acid [Faraday wrote] and even this failed; for though I could have gone on until I had dissolved away the upper marble, and left a pure surface, even these successive applications, made, of course, with care, but each time producing a sensible and even abundant effervescence, and each time dissolving enough marble to neutralize the applied acid, were not sufficient to reach the bottom of the cells and fissures in which dirt had been deposited, so as to dislodge the whole of that dirt from its place.[52]

The best Faraday could do under these circumstances was to suggest means by which the progressive deterioration of the marbles could, at least, be halted. This simply involved a careful washing with carbonate of soda which, Faraday hoped, would prevent further corrosion.

The preservation of art treasures was not the only subject on which the Government asked Faraday's advice. During the Crimean War, a number of proposals were submitted to the War Office and the Admiralty by private individuals who were convinced that they held the secret to a rapid and decisive victory. One of these was referred to Faraday for his opinion. It consisted of a scheme to take Cronstadt by means of poison gas. Older ships of the fleet were to be laden with sulphur, directed towards the city when the wind was in the right quarter, and set afire. The clouds of sulphur dioxide would then descend upon the population of Cronstadt with frightful results, forcing the Russians to surrender in the Crimea.[53]

Faraday was unable to give an opinion on the matter.

The proposition is correct in theory [he wrote to Sir Byam Martin], i.e., dense smoke will hide objects, and burning sulphur will yield fumes that are intolerable, and able to render men involved in them incapable of action, or even to kill them: but whether the proposition is *practicable* on the scale proposed and required, is a point so little illustrated by any experience, or by any facts that can be made to bear upon it, that for my own part I am unable to form a judgment. I have been on the crater of Vesuvius and to leeward of the mouth; and have seen the vapours (which are very deleterious) pass up over my head and go off down the wind in a long not rapidly expanding stream. I have, by changes in the wind, been involved in the vapours, and have managed with a handkerchief to the mouth and by running, to get out of their way. I should hesitate in concluding that ten or twenty vessels could give a body of smoke, the columns of which, at a mile to leeward, would coincide and form an impervious band to vision a mile broad; but I have no means of judging, for I know of no sufficient facts that can be of use as illustrations of the proposed applications.[54]

This was clearly a problem that was not susceptible to experimental investigation. Faraday was sceptical of the plan and his report could not be interpreted as a favourable one. Justification for his point of view was provided in October when a terrible explosion took place in Newcastle. A warehouse filled with sulphur caught fire and, as *The Times* reported, 'the vapour from the burning sulphur came in dense masses across the river, causing scores of people to fall down insensible. . . .'[55] The death toll from the explosion and the burning sulphur was amazingly small, totalling only some forty persons.[56] Of these, by far the majority were the victims of the explosion, not the sulphur dioxide.

Faraday cited this disaster in favour of his scepticism. 'I have no doubt', he wrote to Sir Byam, 'you have thought of the matter, but I cannot resist referring to the combustion of I think above 2000 tons of sulphur in the middle of a crowded town like Newcastle and *as regards a certain application*, the little comparative evil it has done.'[57]

The Government was not the only body seeking Faraday's advice. His discoveries in electricity and magnetism had provided the theoretical background for a whole host of practical inventions. His well-known experimental ability also qualified him as a trouble-shooter of the first rank and when some electrical apparatus revealed unexpected difficulties of operation, it was natural to call on Faraday for help in resolving them. In 1853 both the cause of pure science and of industry was threatened mildly by a curious phenomenon. Faraday was asked for advice, which he willingly gave, for the explanation he could give corroborated in dramatic fashion the theory of electrical action he had first suggested in 1838.

One of the direct results of the burst of electromagnetic discoveries of the 1820's was the electric telegraph. In 1837 the electric telegraph of Cooke and Wheatstone was put into operation in England and, by 1840, Samuel Morse's telegraph had begun its work in America. In the 1840's there was a rapid expansion of telegraph lines all over Europe and America and a few hardy thinkers even dreamed of an Atlantic cable which would link the Old and the New Worlds together.

The fundamental principle of all telegraphs was the same, depending upon the creation of a magnetic field by an intermittent current. Only the recorders of the magnetic field (by which the messages actually were sent) differed. In the Cooke and Wheatstone telegraph, a magnetized needle was deflected by the passing current; in the Morse telegraph, an iron keeper was deflected by an electromagnet thereby moving a lever which either printed out dots and dashes or produced audible sounds. The telegraphs of The Electric Telegraph Company, directed by Latimer Clark and only incorporated in 1846, used an ink-carrying needle which, when deflected by the magnetism of the electric current, recorded its motion on a moving strip of paper. All three systems relied upon the sharpness of the signal to throw their detectors abruptly into action so that the code, whatever it was, was clearly delineated. Until the early 1850's, there was little or no problem with this aspect of telegraphy. Because the various materials then available for insulating the wires were unsatisfactory, the wires were above ground on telegraph poles and nothing interfered with the transmission of signals. In 1848 Faraday called attention to a new material which had excellent insulating powers and, moreover, was easily adapted to use in telegraphy.[58] Gutta-percha was the product of expanding Empire. It was prepared from the latex found in the stem and leaves of certain trees found in Malaya and, in many ways, resembled rubber. It had, however, certain advantages over rubber in electrical apparatus. It was thermoplastic, and highly resistant to water. It was, therefore, easily worked, unlike rubber which, after vulcanization becomes rather intractable, and was ideal for protecting electrical circuits from moisture. Gutta-percha made it possible to remove telegraph wires from unsightly poles and place them underground. It also enabled telegraph companies to expand overseas. In 1851 the Dover–Calais line was laid linking England to the Continent and, shortly thereafter, submarine cables connected England with Ireland and Holland.

When the new lines were put into operation, a peculiar effect was observed. The signal tended to lose its sharpness. There was a general fuzziness which, while not preventing the successful operation of the telegraph, did serve to create some anxiety in certain quarters. The retardation of the signal obviously was somehow connected with the fact that the wires passed through water or went underground. If there were a relation between the retardation and the length of wire through which the current passed, then the prospects for the success of an Atlantic cable would be considerably dimmed unless the effect could be explained and, somehow, eliminated.

The stimulus for an intensive investigation of the retardation effect appears to have come indirectly from the rather unlikely quarter of the Astronomer Royal, Sir George Biddell Airy. Airy's concern for telegraphs, as such, was minimal but he was intensely interested in the use of the telegraph as a scientific instrument for the more accurate determination of astronomical data. In particular, the rapidity of transmission of the telegraphic signal appeared to make it a perfect means for the determination of terrestrial longitude to a hitherto unattainable degree of accuracy. The telegraph signal could be used to alert observers say, in Greenwich and Paris, so that simultaneous observations could be made and later compared. From these observations, provided they were simultaneous or so nearly so as to be considered such, the longitudes of Greenwich and Paris could be determined with extraordinary precision. And precision was the one thing closest to Airy's heart. When Airy applied to Latimer Clark of The Electric Telegraph Company, he was hopeful both of co-operation and success.[59] Clark was more than willing to assist the Astronomer Royal but he also recognized that the retardation of the signal would seriously affect the accuracy of the results. 'We have lately observed a great and variable retardation of the Electrical current when sent through long lengths of underground wire,' he wrote to the Astronomer Royal, 'which would much interfere with your use of subterranean or Submarine wires for the purpose of determining longitudes, and I think it right therefore to call your attention to it.'[60] Clark was not content merely to report the retardation. He had, obviously, reflected upon the effect and decided to investigate it for the good of The Electric Telegraph Company as well as for the progress of astronomy. Clark had, therefore, invited Faraday to come to the company's gutta-percha works at Lothbury and observe the effect.[61] Faraday accepted eagerly and, on 16 October 1853, he observed the sending and receiving of the telegraph signal first through a 100-mile coil of wire insulated with gutta-percha and submerged in water and then through some 1,500 miles of subterranean wire running between Manchester and London. The fact of retardation was first simply and graphically determined.

Mr Clarke arranged a Bains' printing telegraph with three pens, so that it gave beautiful illustrations and records of facts . . . ; the pens are iron wires, under which a band of paper imbued with ferro-prussiate of potassa passes at a regular rate by clock-work; and thus regular lines of prussian blue are produced whenever a current is transmitted, and the time of the current is recorded. In the case to be described, the three lines were side by side, and about 0·1 of an inch apart. The pen m belonged to a circuit of only a few feet of wire, and a separate battery; it told whenever the contact key was put down by the finger; the pen n was at the earth end of the long air wire, and the pen o at the earth end of the long subterraneous wire; and by arrangement, the key could be made to throw the electricity of the chief battery into either of these wires, simultaneously with the passage of the short circuit current through pen m. When pens m and n were in action, the m record was a regular line of equal thickness, showing by its length the actual time during which the electricity flowed into the wires; and the n record was an equally regular line, parallel to, and of equal length with the former, but the least degree behind it; thus indicating that the long air wire conveyed its electric current almost instantaneously to the further end. But when pens m and o were in action, the o line did not begin until some time after the m line, and it continued after the m line had ceased, i.e. after the o battery was cut off. Furthermore, it was faint at first, grew up to a maximum of intensity, continued at that as long as battery contact was continued, and then gradually diminished to nothing.[62]

A continuous line can convey very little information and the full deleterious effect of the retardation can be appreciated only when the current is intermitted according to some code.

With the pens m and o the conversion of an intermitting into a continuous current could be beautifully shown; the earth wire by the static induction which it permitted, acting in a manner analogous to the fly-wheel of a steam-engine, or the air-spring of a pump. Thus when the contact key was regularly but rapidly depressed and raised, the pen m made a series of short lines separated by intervals of equal length. After four or more of these had passed, then pen o, belonging to the subterraneous wire, began to make its mark, weak at first, then rising to a maximum, but always continuous.[63]

This effect, coupled with the fact that the retardation *did* vary directly with the distance through which the current passed, seriously threatened to halt any move towards the laying of an Atlantic cable. The explanation of the cause of the retardation was at least a first step in the final solution of the problem.

Faraday was delighted with the retardation effect. He cited paragraph 1326 of the Twelfth Series of the *Experimental Researches* to show that, as long ago as 1838, he had anticipated some such effect.[64] The effect, itself, he considered to be dramatic proof of his theory that induction always preceded conduction. The whole process was most clearly explained in a letter he wrote in 1858, in answer to a query on the effect.

When an electric current is sent into a submerged insulated wire the effect may for the moment be considered as two fold, one part *dynamic* dependant on the current, – the other *static*, depending on the momentary charge of the wire. Both may be resolved into one law of action, acting *along* and *across* the wire, but with infinite degrees of difference in the two directions; the difference being as great as that of *insulation* and *conduction*. Your question refers to the *static* part, i.e. the induction of the wire through the gutta percha towards the iron coating or towards the water out- side. Now the true principles of static induction (as I have understood them and endeavoured to promul- gate them for many years past) offer no advantage from the expedient you propose. Suppose the dia- gram [Figure 1] to represent a section of a telegraph cable [A] being the central wire, – [B] gutta percha, – [C] a continuous metallic tube – [D] gutta percha, – and [O] either the outer iron wire or the water. On send- ing a positive current through [A] it, for the moment, induces laterally across [B] [C] and [D] the action terminating at [O] where it raises up the negative state. If you attempt to charge [C] positive at the same time with [A], the charge given to [C] will induce outwards towards [O], not inwards towards [A] – indeed pos. [A] will induce a *negative* state on the inside of [C] and a positive state on its out- side; which, with that given to it purposely, will act with increased force towards [O] rendering its outside equivalently negative.[65]

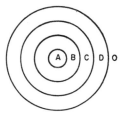

Fig. 1

The purely static action was what prevented the ready discharge of the state of tension, or, in other words, slowed down the current. Static induction also explained the difference between wires in the air and in water. For static induction to take place, the electrostatic line of force had to have an 'anchoring' place. In submarine cables, the water surrounding the insulated wire provided this surface, and the induction could rise to a fairly high level. In air, however, the electrostatic line of force found no such surface and had, therefore, to extend itself to much larger distances before it could discover a firm place upon which it might fasten itself. This greatly weakened the electrostatic effect and, consequently, made the retardation of the current very small.

Faraday merely analysed the effect and suggested nothing as a means of avoiding it in long submarine cables. This was left to the young William Thomson who, building on Faraday's theory, was able to eliminate enough of the retardation to make the Atlantic cable practicable.[66]

The consulting work which probably required the most physical activity on Faraday's part during the late 1850's and early 1860's was that connected with Trinity House. In 1836 he had consented to become scientific adviser to Trinity House, the corporation which had occupied itself since the seventeenth century with the proper lighting of the English coast. From 1836 until the late 1850's there is no record of Faraday's activities in this area. The large box full of manuscripts and reports relating to lighthouses which he left to Trinity House after his death was destroyed during the Second World War by a German bomb. It seems likely that he was not terribly occupied by Trinity House affairs during these years for, as his laboratory *Diary* makes clear in the 1830's, he had little time to spare and in the 1840's his state of health prevented any extensive work. It was not until the late 1850's that there is any public record from which we can catch a glimpse of Faraday at work in this field. In 1860 he summarized the general nature of his duties since his appointment.

> In 1836 [he reported] I was appointed 'Scientific adviser to the Corporation of the Trinity House in experiments on Lights.' Since then a large part of my attention has been given to the lighthouses in respect of their ventilation, their lightning conductors and arrangements, the impurity and cure of water, the provision of domestic water, the examination of optical apparatus, etc., the results of which may be seen in various reports to the Trinity House. A very large part also of my consideration has been given to the numerous propositions of all kinds which have been and are presented continually to the Corporation; few of these present any reasonable prospect of practical and useful application, and I have been obliged to use my judgment, chiefly in checking imperfect and unsafe propositions, rather than in forwarding any which could be advanced to a practical result.[67]

Most of the propositions which were worth considering concerned improvements of the lamps used. With the exception of the Gurney oxyoil lamp, about which Faraday remarked that 'Great exertions were made to perfect this lamp, but its application failed',[68] the other improved lamps or new devices were all proposed in the 1850's. There were a series of reports on the Fitz Maurice limelight (1858), Watson's voltaic light (1854), Prosser's limelight (1860), Way's mercurial electric lamp (1859), and Holmes' magneto-electric light (1857, 1859). Of these, only Prosser's limelight and Holmes' magneto-electric light appeared worth the time involved in trying them out. The reports Faraday wrote on these lights reveal a dimension that is not often associated with Faraday. He had, it will be remembered, voluntarily given up trade and even the lucrative life of a professional consulting chemist. His researches had lifted his mind to the very summit of abstract thought, far removed from the details of ordinary life. In his later years, with his halo of unruly white hair, he looked the very epitome of the kindly, unworldly, absent-minded professor. In his estimation of suggested improvements in lighthouse illumination, however, Faraday showed all the hard-headedness of a Victorian businessman. His first concern, of course, was for the quality of the light, for upon this the safety of many lives depended. But, given a better light, Faraday was not easily convinced that the old tried-and-true system should be abandoned. Prosser's limelight, for example, gave a brilliant light, a good deal better than that provided by the standard oil lamp. The light was produced by the burning of hydrogen in oxygen gas against a ball of lime which gave it its brilliance. Such a process was no doubt quite unexceptionable when used in a theatre, but was it adaptable to lighthouses? Where, for example, were the gases to come from? And, was the process to be utilized, safe, constant, and economical? While Faraday's scientific background made it easier for him to judge the efficiency of the light, it was with the soul of a Certified Public Accountant that he approached its operation.[69] In the case of the Prosser light, the expense of producing the gases, and the unreliability of the apparatus for generating them were considered too great for the light to be generally adopted.[70]

The case was somewhat more complicated with the Holmes magneto-electric light.

> I hope [Faraday reported to the Trinity House] a situation may be selected where the magneto-electric lamp can be safely and effectually tried, for a time and under circumstances during which all the liabilities may be thoroughly eliminated. The light is so intense, so abundant, so concentrated and focal, so free from under shadow (caused in the common lamp by the burner), so free from flickering, that one cannot but desire that it should succeed. But it would require very careful and progressive introduction; men with peculiar knowledge and skill to attend it; and the means of instantly substituting one lamp for another in case of accident. The common lamp is so simple, both in principle and practice, that its liability to failure is very small. There is no doubt that the magneto-electric lamp involves a great many circumstances tending to make its application more refined and delicate, but I would fain hope that none of them will prove a barrier to its introduction. Nevertheless, it must pass into practice only through the ordeal of a full, searching, and prolonged trial.[71]

Experience alone could tell whether the Holmes light was really able to replace the older form. Faraday, in his report, however, explicitly brought out each and every point which would have to be carefully watched, including the cost of running the steam-engine that provided the mechanical energy for the generation of electricity, the higher salaries that must be paid to more highly skilled men, and so on.[72]

In some cases, experiment could count for something and then Faraday threw himself into it. In the autumn of 1860, for example, James T. Chance (later Sir James) of the famous glassmaking firm was encouraged by Faraday and the Trinity House to improve the lenses used in lighthouse illumination. The problem was a tricky one, involving a panel of separate lenses, all built up in a careful fashion to provide the type of focus desired. Faraday was not content simply to wait until James Chance had submitted his finished product and then pass judgement upon it. During the winter of 1860–1, almost every week saw him at the Spon Lane Works in Birmingham, working with Chance and checking each step as they progressed.[73] It was with no small feeling of personal pride that Faraday could report on the results.

> You are aware [he pointed out to the Deputy Master of Trinity House] that, in consequence of certain careful and prolonged experimental inquiries, adjustments altogether new, both as to their amount and their nature, have been determined upon, and put into practice for the first time in this apparatus.
>
> .   .   .   .   .
>
> The apparatus has been put together by Mr James Chance, . . . and being in a proper place I had the focimeter set upon the burner, and a true sea-horizon mark placed in the distance.
> The whole was so true that the ray proceeding to the eye through the middle of each piece of glass passed by the focimeter at the point desired. The greatest departure was but 2mm., and very few of these occurred. Further, the manner in which, as the apparatus revolved or the eye was moved about, the object at the horizon passed laterally from one panel to another, or vertically from one rib to another, showed the perfection of the adjustment of each individual piece by the harmony and consistency of the whole, though there were above 300 pieces of glass associated together.[74]

For this perfection, as the Faraday–Chance correspondence clearly reveals, Faraday could take at least part of the credit.

There was one final aspect of his duties for the Trinity House. After every suggestion had been considered to see if a suggested improvement were scientifically sound; after trial runs had been made on a small scale to illustrate whatever practical principles were involved; after all the questions that could be asked had been asked, there remained the task of determining if the improvement actually was an advance in actual lighthouse operation. This meant that it must be incorporated into actual lighthouse operation and then inspected time and time again. An inspection trip was not always a simple or comfortable affair. Necessarily, these trips had to be made when weather conditions were foul, for it was in precisely this type of weather that the lighthouse *had* to function properly if it were to serve its purpose. In 1861 Faraday was seventy years old and drifting about at sea in fog or snow, noting the visibility of a distant beacon, was not always a pleasure. Sometimes, conditions were such that many a younger man would have waited for better times. In February 1860, Faraday wrote to the Brethren of Trinity House:

> I went to Dover last Monday (the 13th instant); was caught in a snow storm between Ashford and Dover and nearly blocked up in the train; could not go to the lighthouse that night; and finding, next day, that the roads on the downs were snowed up, returned to London. On Friday I again went to Dover and proceeded by a fly that night, hoping to find the roads clear of snow; they were still blocked up towards the lighthouse, but by climbing over hedges, walls, and fields, I succeeded in getting there and making the necessary inquiries and observations.[75]

In spite of Faraday's physical health, this was clearly work for someone younger. He continued, however, to hold his position as Scientific Adviser until 1865, by which time, neither his mind nor his body could stand the strain. In May 1865, he made his last report for the Trinity House and soon thereafter retired, yielding his post to John Tyndall.[76]

3. Retirement and Death

Faraday never really recovered from his illness in 1838–40. The giddiness and general malaise were thrown off by 1845, but the effect on his mind was permanent. In her *Diary* for 30 May 1842, Caroline Fox noted: 'Faraday is better, but greatly annoyed by his change of memory. He remembers distinctly things that happened long ago, but the details of present life, his friends' Christian names, &c., he forgets.'[77] The failure of his memory, never very sturdy, had a direct and important effect upon his work. He did not dare enter areas of scientific research which were being investigated by a number of other people. He simply could not read the literature and retain the various points made by diverse authors. Having once been accused of plagiarism in the Wollaston affair, he had no desire to repeat the experience because, inadvertently, he did not give credit to someone else. 'Want of memory', he wrote later in life, 'made me give up with many lines of research which else I should have worked on and seek for those on which nobody was moving – hence Rotation of light and diamagnetism – hence attempts at reduction of Gravity into the combined chain of forces.'[78] Faraday was by no means unique in his affliction. In a letter from Wöhler to Liebig in 1841, Berzelius was quoted as saying, 'I am now in that period of life where only the memory of previous times remains, but that which happened yesterday or the day before is completely forgotten. For this reason I am only fit for such simple researches as can be completed within a few days, and which do not require me to remember complicated details.'[79] Faraday and Berzelius suffered from what was considered in the nineteenth century to be simply the result of advancing years. There was nothing to be done about it and the true philosopher would accept it calmly and gently. The true effect on the victim has been best described by the German physicist, G. C. Lichtenberg. 'As long as memory lasts', Lichtenberg wrote, 'a crowd of people are working together as a unity: the twenty-year-old, the thirty-year-old and so on. As soon as it fails, one begins increasingly to be alone and the whole generation of selves stands back and mocks the helpless old man.'[80]

The deterioration of Faraday's mental faculties was not steady but intermittent. He would suffer attacks during which he could hardly think at all; a few days or weeks in the country would then clear his head and permit him to pick up the threads of his life again. The attacks became ever more frequent, however, and, after about 1855, he never seemed quite to recover completely. Each attack, therefore, left him with a net loss of mental ability. By the 1860's, moments of lucidity were becoming the exception and general mental confusion the rule. The course of his decline can be followed in his correspondence.

We have already witnessed the effect of his loss of memory on his work in the case of the experiments which he repeated not realizing he had already done them.[81] By 1854 the pursuit of science was increasingly difficult for him.

> Just a few scattered words of kindness, not philosophy [he wrote to Schoenbein], for I have just been trying to think a little philosophy (magnetical) for a week or two, and it has made my head ache, turned me sleepy in the daytime as well as at nights, and, instead of being a pleasure has for the present nauseated me. Now you know that is not natural to me, for I believe nobody has found greater enjoyment in physical science than myself; but it is just weariness, which soon comes on, but I hope will soon go off, by a little rest.[82]

By 1856 his general forgetfulness had extended beyond his science. In the summer of that year he planned a trip to Paris. But, as he admitted to a friend, 'my memory fails so fast that I dare not trust myself alone so I avail myself of the kind aid and care of my brother-in-law Mr George Barnard who accompanies me expressly that he may relieve me in all matters that he can – in fact I am in his hands. He settles when we start and has arranged where we shall go: – he takes all the care of money, passports, hours, routes, Hotels.'[83]

The struggle towards the light was becoming harder and harder, and the fog of his forgetfulness was ever more closely wrapped around him. Occasionally a shaft of sunny memory would break through. 'I seemed to have two or three of your letters unanswered,' he wrote to Plücker, 'and wondered at it but then I remembered that you had been *here* since some of them and we had talked them over.'[84] To try and bend his mind to serious work was an agony, and yet work he must for only in work could he justify his own existence.

> I am in town [he told Rev. John Barlow] and at work more or less every day. My memory wearies me greatly in working; for I cannot remember from day to day the conclusions I come to, and all has to be thought out many times over. To write it down gives no assistance, for what is written down is itself forgotten. It is only by very slow degrees that this state of mental muddiness can be wrought either through or under; nevertheless, I know that to work somewhat is far better than to stand still, even if nothing comes of it. It is better for the mind itself – not being quite sure whether I shall ever end the research, and yet being sure, that if in my former state of memory, I could work it out in a week or two to a successful and affirmative result.[85]

By 1860, attempts at science were very rare, being only sporadic efforts, never carried through to completion. Faraday's entire mental structure was gradually crumbling around him. Where before efforts of the will had permitted him to dispel his mental haze, now he was no longer able to piece together his mental images into a coherent pattern.

> When I want to write to you [he confided to Schoenbein] it seems as if only nonsense would come to mind, and yet it is not nonsense to think of past friendship and dear communions. When I try to write of science, it comes back to me in confusion. I do not remember the order of things, or even the facts themselves. I do not remember what you last told me, though I think I sent it to the Phil. Mag., and had it printed; and if I try to remember up, it becomes too much, the head gets giddy and the mental view only the more confused. I know you do not want me to labour in vain, but I do not like to seem forgetful of what you tell me and the only relief I have at such times is to correct myself and believe that you will know the forgetfulness is *involuntary*. After all, though your science is much to me, we are not friends for science sake only, but for something better in a man, something more important in his nature, affection, kindness, good feeling, moral worth; and so in remembrance of these I now write to place myself in your presence, and in thought shake hands, tongues, and hearts together.[86]

The dimension of memory had almost entirely slipped away. Yet, as the above example clearly shows, Faraday was by no means incoherent or mentally incompetent. He could still carry on almost as well as before so long as he did not have to call upon knowledge of the past. The flow of language remained and, although he worried about his spelling,[87] he was able to write a rather long, chatty, and interesting letter. By 1862, even this talent was deserting him. The present was becoming as confused as the past. His last letter to Schoenbein is a pitiful one. It was probably written in the middle of a particularly bad period of mental difficulty. It cannot be taken to represent his condition all the time, for he was still able to carry out certain practical duties, such as the inspection of lighthouses, but it does show the state to which he was reduced when his mind did not work properly.

> My dear Schoenbein [he wrote]. Again and again I tear up my letters, for I write nonsense. I cannot spell or write a line continuously. Whether I shall recover – this confusion – do not know. I will not write any more. My love to you
>
> ever affectionately yours,
M. Faraday.[88]

Schoenbein realized that his dear friend was disappearing and 'from delicacy of feelings', he wrote to Bence Jones after Faraday's death, 'I did not dare answering that letter; for what could I say or write to our poor friend? and so our correspondence, kept up for a quarter of a century, dropt, not to be taken up again.'[89] So closed one door of Faraday's life.

While his mind gradually faded, Faraday remained, at least through the 1850's, in surprisingly good physical health. In the winter of 1849–50, he suffered from a persistent sore throat which sometimes made it impossible to lecture at the Royal Institution. The cause of this discomfort was apparently his teeth and in the summer of 1850 he had them attended to. The report of his visit to the dentist reveals a good deal about his essential fairness of mind for there are few who, in a similar situation, would be able to see the dentist's point of view so clearly.

> A few words together even on paper (if it cannot be by mouth) are pleasant though I do not find myself good for either just now. Because of much pain in my jaw and the known bad state of my teeth, which I had only hoped to keep through the lectures, I went on Monday morning to the dentist. He pulled out five teeth and a fang. He had much trouble and I much pain in the removal of a deep stump and I think from the feeling then and now he must have broken away part of the jaw bone to get at it, for it is very sore and the head is rather unsteady. On the whole the operation was well and cleverly carried on by the dentist, the fault was in the teeth.[90]

After this, there were few remarks about his health until the 1860's.

The failure of his memory made Faraday realize that his powers were gradually slipping away. In order to conserve his energy for those duties which he considered of the highest importance, he began to withdraw from those which he considered of less importance. In December of 1851 he resigned from the Athenaeum Club of which he had become a member at its first institution.[91] In the same year he also resigned his position as lecturer in chemistry at Woolwich, a post he had held for more than twenty years.[92] In 1857 a deputation from the Royal Society waited upon him to request that he accept the presidency. To his close friend John Tyndall he confided his reason for refusing the highest honour the Royal Society could bestow. 'I must remain plain Michael Faraday to the last; and let me now tell you, that if I accepted the honour which the Royal Society desires to confer upon me, I could not answer for the integrity of my intellect for a single year.'[93]

Throughout the 1850's, Faraday continued to restrict his activities until, as in 1816, they centred almost entirely around the Royal Institution. The affairs of the Royal Society only vaguely interested him; the claims of Government he kept at a minimum; the public role of science which so agitated his contemporaries – Lyell, Huxley, Tyndall – was almost entirely passed by. Only on rare occasions, as with the table-turning fad, did Faraday feel it necessary to speak up. Such another case occurred in 1855 when Faraday took a ride on the Thames. In a letter to *The Times*, he expressed his indignation at what he considered to be a public scandal.

I traversed this day by steamboat the space between London and Hungerford Bridges, between half-past one and two o'clock. It was low water, and I think the tide must have been near the turn. The appearance and smell of the water forced themselves at once on my attention. The whole of the river was an opaque pale brown fluid. In order to test the degree of opacity, I tore up some white cards into pieces, and then moistened them, so as to make them sink easily below the surface, and then dropped some of these pieces into the water at every pier the boat came to. Before they had sunk an inch below the surface they were undistinguishable, though the sun shone brightly at the time, and when the pieces fell edgeways the lower part was hidden from sight before the upper part was under water.

· · · · ·

The smell was very bad, and common to the whole of the water. It was the same as that which now comes up from the gully holes in the streets. The whole river was for the time a real sewer. Having just returned from the country air, I was perhaps more affected by it than others; but I do not think that I could have gone on to Lambeth or Chelsea, and I was glad to enter the streets for an atmosphere which, except near the sink-holes, I found much sweeter than on the river.

· · · · ·

If there be sufficient authority to remove a putrescent pond from the neighbourhood of a few simple dwellings, surely the river which flows for so many miles through London ought not to be allowed to become a fermenting sewer. The condition in which I saw the Thames may perhaps be considered as exceptional, but it ought to be an impossible state; instead of which, I fear it is rapidly becoming the general condition. If we neglect this subject, we cannot expect to do so with impunity; nor ought we to be surprised if, ere many years are over, a season give us sad proof of the folly of our carelessness.[94]

Such concern for the public welfare, publicly expressed, was rare throughout Faraday's entire life and even rarer in his later years. He seems to have felt that the constituted authorities of Government were competent to deal with such problems without benefit of his unsolicited advice. His isolation and insulation from the world protected him from an awareness of the social conditions of the day and, as he grew older, his own failing powers became far more important to him than public issues upon which he felt deeply his incompetence to speak.

The gradual loss of his memory ultimately affected more than his ability to do creative research. It also began to interfere with his duties and responsibilities at the Royal Institution. In 1853 his niece remarked in her *Diary* that 'he has been very anxious about them or rather about his own power. He is much troubled at the failure of his memory.'[95] Faraday's consciousness of his increasing mental difficulties probably stimulated him to the point where his lectures actually were better than those he had delivered before his mind began to fail. Those classics by which he is now remembered throughout the world – *The Chemical History of a Candle* and the *Lectures on the Various Forces of Matter* – were produced in the late 1850's. Nevertheless, there can be no doubt that he was seriously worried by the possibility that his memory might fail him in the middle of a lecture or a discourse to the embarrassment of both him and his audience. In 1858 the discovery of ozone by Schoenbein was scientific news and Faraday wished to report on this new substance to the members of the R.I. In order to give a full and accurate account, he had written to Schoenbein for details, but found himself in serious trouble when he tried to put the facts together.

I think about Ozone, about Antozone, about the experiments you showed Dr Bence Jones, about your peroxide of barium, your antozonized oil of turpentine [he wrote to Schoenbein], and it all ends in a giddiness and confusion of the points that ought to be remembered. I want to tell our audience what your last results are upon this most beautiful investigation, and yet am terrified at the thoughts of trying to do so, from the difficulty of remembering from the reading of one letter to that of another, what the facts in the former were. I have never before felt so seriously the evil of loss of memory and of clearness in the head; and though I expect to fail some day at the lecture table, as I get older, I should not like to fail in ozone, or in anything about you.[96]

By this time, it was becoming clear to Faraday that the great source from which so many of his discourses had flowed was rapidly drying up. Throughout his career as a successful lecturer at the Royal Institution he had reported upon the work of others, but the solid basis of his success had always been his own research. Now this was no more. His visits to the laboratory were sporadic and his pursuit of new truths, by 1858, was an almost hopeless one. Deprived of this resource, he found the duty of lecturing increasingly more difficult to bear. The Juvenile Lectures, in particular, required a logic and continuity which his mind, he felt, could no longer guarantee. Hence, in October 1861, he offered his resignation to the Managers of the Royal Institution in a document full of human interest. Although lengthy, it is worth reproducing here for in it the unique relationship between Faraday and the Royal Institution is delineated in the warmest possible terms.

Gentlemen.
It is with the deepest feeling that I address you.
I entered the Royal Institution in March 1813, nearly forty nine years ago; and, with the exception of a comparatively short period during which I was absent on the continent with Sir Humphry Davy, have been with you ever since.
During that time I have been most happy in your kindness, and in the fostering care which the Royal Institution has bestowed upon me. I am very thankful to you, and your predecessors for the unswerving encouragement and support which you have given me during that period. My life has been a happy one and all I desired. During its progress I have tried to make a fitting return for it to the Royal Institution and through it to Science.
But the progress of years (now amounting in number to three score and ten) having brought forth, first, the period of development, and then that of maturity; have ultimately produced for me that of gentle decay. This has taken place in such a manner as to render the evening of life a blessing: — for whilst increasing physical weakness occurs, a full share of health free from pain is granted with it; and whilst memory and certain other faculties of the mind diminish, my good spirits and cheerfulness do not diminish with them.
Still I am not able to do as I have done. I am not competent to perform as I wish, the delightful duty of teaching in the Theatre of the Royal Institution; and I now ask you (in consideration for me) to accept my resignation of the *Juvenile lectures*. Being unwilling to give up, what has always been so kindly

received and so pleasant to myself, I have tried the faculties essential for their delivery, and I know that I ought to retreat: – for the attempt to realize (in the trials) the necessary points brings with it weariness, giddiness, fear of failure and the full conviction that it is time to retire. I desire therefore to lay down this duty; and I may truly say, that such has been the pleasure of the occupation to me, that my regret must be greater than yours need or can be.

And this reminds me that I ought to place in your hands the *whole* of my occupation. It is, no doubt, true that the Juvenile lectures, not being included in my engagement as Professor, were, when delivered by me, undertaken as an extra duty, and remunerated by an extra payment. The duty of research, superintendance of the house, and other services still remains; – but I may well believe that the natural change which incapacitates me from lecturing, may also make me unfit for some of these. In such respects, however, I will leave you to judge, and to say whether it is your wish that I should still remain as part of the Royal Institution.

> I am Gentlemen, with all my heart;
> Your faithful and devoted Servant
> M. Faraday.[97]

The Managers graciously accepted his resignation as lecturer, but continued his appointment as Superintendent of the house and laboratories of the Royal Institution. He also continued to give Friday Evening Discourses, but his inability to carry on soon became apparent. On 20 June, 1862, he delivered his last such talk. During the course of the evening even his manipulative skill deserted him. He scorched his notes by accident, an event which gave even greater impact to his prepared farewell. At the end of his notes he had written his valedictory.

> Personal explanation – years of happiness here but time of retirement. *Loss of Memory* and *physical endurance of the brain* causes *hesitation* and *uncertainty* of the convictions which the speaker has to urge. II. *Inability to draw* upon the mind for the treasures of knowledge it has previously received. III. *Dimness and forgetfullness* of one's former *self-standard,* in respect of *right, dignity* and *self-respect*. IV. Strong duty of *doing justice to others* yet inability to do so. *Retire*.[98]

The relinquishing of the Juvenile Lectures and the income associated with them, as well as the curtailment of his other outside activities could have caused Faraday serious financial strain. There was no doubt that it did reduce his income so that he had to cut down on expenses for, in 1851, after he had resigned his duties at Woolwich, he cited his diminution of income as a reason for resigning from the Athenaeum.[99] That his circumstances were somewhat straitened can be seen by the following anonymous note appended to a signature of Faraday's now in the possession of the Wellcome Medical Historical Library.

The signature of Prof. Faraday was given me by Sir Wm. Gull, M.D. and the history of it is as follows. Sir William professionally attended Mr Faraday who was in weak health some long time before his death, and withal in not the most prosperous circumstances; he was however too proud-spirited to receive Sir W's services gratis, and one day insisted on having his account sent in: to pacify him, Sir William sent in a bill for £2, and the professor at once wrote a cheque for the amount. This cheque Sir W. did not present for exchange, but laid aside, and only produced it after the lapse of years to tear off this signature, which he gave to me. – An incident which most will consider honorable to both men concerned.

Fortunately for Faraday, there were others beside himself and his wife who were concerned about his health and his situation. Prince Albert had, for many years, served as the Vice-Patron of the Royal Institution and had come to know and esteem Faraday highly. In 1858, at his request, Queen Victoria placed a house on the green near Hampton Court at Faraday's disposal for the rest of his life. Faraday at first hesitated to accept this generous offer for he feared he could not afford the cost of the necessary repairs but when the Queen offered to pay for all renovations, he eagerly accepted. From 1858 until 1862 he was unable to spend much of his time in his house during the busy season at the R.I., for his duties there kept him away. After 1862, however, this became his home and it was here that he was to die.

From 1862 on, Faraday's health steadily declined and his circle of activities grew smaller and smaller. In 1864 he resigned his eldership in the Sandemanian Church, a step dictated only by the greatest necessity, for this was a post he held especially dear. In 1865 he resigned his position as Superintendent of the house and laboratories of the Royal Institution, thus ending his formal duties to the body he loved so well. In the same year he left Trinity House, giving over his duties to Tyndall. From 1865 until 1867 he gradually sank into senility. He now had only occasional and brief moments of clarity – for the most part he merely sat staring into space. Sir Henry Roscoe recounted his last visit to Faraday and his description is a pathetic one, indeed.

In the lecture which I gave at the Royal Institution on the 'Opalescence of the atmosphere' on June 1, 1866 [Roscoe wrote], I explained the action of finely divided matter in absorbing and scattering different rays of light, occasioning red sunsets, and the orange-coloured sun seen through a fog, etc. I wished on this occasion to illustrate my subject by Faraday's researches on the colour of gold films, in which he showed that finely divided gold imparts magnificent purple and green colours, as seen by transmitted light, to the medium, whether liquid or solid through which it is diffused. I found in the laboratory of the Institution the bottles containing the finely divided gold suspended in water, in which, though the vessels had been standing for years, the heavy gold had not been deposited. I did not, however, find in the laboratory any of the gold films which he had prepared with gelatine, and I went up into his rooms at the top of the Institution, to ask him if he would be good enough to lend me some of these which he had preserved in watch-glasses, and put away in a box.

His mind was then failing, and it was quite sad to see that he hardly understood what I was asking for. Mrs Faraday, who stood close by, tried to recall the facts to his mind and said to him: 'Dont you remember those beautiful gold experiments that you made?' To which he replied in a feeble voice: 'Oh, yes, beautiful gold, beautiful gold,' and that was all he would say.[100]

Throughout the spring and early summer of 1867, Faraday's condition remained about the same. His niece, Miss Reid, relieved another niece, Miss Jane Barnard, of her nursing duties for a bit in June and wrote in her *Diary*: 'dear Uncle kept up rather better than sometimes, but Oh! there was always pain in seeing afresh how far the mind had faded away still the sweet unselfish disposition was there winning the love of all around him.'[101] By this time he was unable to move by himself. He said nothing and took no notice of what went on around him. It was as though his soul had already left him to feel ahead for the path which through his entire life he had sought. In 1861 he had written to Auguste de la Rive:

I am, I hope, very thankful that in the withdrawal of the power and things of this life, – the good hope is left with me, which makes the contemplation of death a comfort – not a fear. Such peace is alone in the gift of god, and as it is he who gives it, why shall we be afraid? His unspeakable gift in his beloved son is the ground of no doubtful hope; and *there* is the rest for those who like you and me are drawing near the latter end of our terms here below.[102]

On August 25th, 1867, as he sat quietly in his chair, Michael Faraday died.

His funeral provided the final touch to a life lived in the service of science and his God. There can be no doubt that, had he so desired, he could have been laid to rest in Westminster Abbey to join the ranks of those whom Great Britain wishes to honour through the centuries. There, near Newton, his remains could have been placed to remind generations yet to come of their debt to a blacksmith's son. His real monument, Faraday knew, was his published papers. The electrical power industry and the foundations of field theory were surely reminder enough of what his life had meant and needed neither ornate monument nor marble statue to underline their importance.

In accordance with Faraday's wishes, his funeral was, in Miss Barnard's words, 'strictly private and plain'.[103] He was buried in Highgate cemetery and his grave was marked by a simple headstone on which was engraved:

MICHAEL FARADAY

Born 22 September 1791
Died 25 August 1867

He had remained simple Mr Faraday to the end.

References

1. Kahlbaum and Darbishire, op. cit., 244.

2. Faraday was silent on the relations between the particles of matter which, having centres of force, are essentially polar and the strain of a gravitational field which is rectilinear and polar only in the sense that the lines of gravitational force 'end' on masses of ponderable matter. Whatever this relation, given Faraday's concept of the atom as a centre of force, and given his concept of force (in 1860) as a strain, the resultant state must be one of strain.

3. The Shot Tower was used during the first half of the nineteenth century to mould shot for cannon. The molten lead was poured out in controlled amounts at the top. The lead formed itself into spherical balls as it fell, and was collected in a water bath below.

4. This paper was never published. It exists in manuscript in Folio Volume 8 of the laboratory *Diary* at the Royal Institution. See the preface to volume 7 of the published *Diary*.

5. George Gabriel Stokes to M. Faraday, 8 June 1860, quoted in Joseph Larmor, *Memoir and Scientific Correspondence of the late Sir George Stokes* (2 vols., Cambridge, 1907), *1*, 150. On page 151 is Faraday's answer, withdrawing the paper.

6. *Phil. Trans.*, 1857, 145 ff. The paper was reprinted in *Exp. Res. in Chem. and Phys.*, 391 ff. All references here are to the reprint.

7. By 'lateral excursion' Faraday meant the displacement of the ether particles in a direction perpendicular to the direction of the wave, thus

The 'excursion' is the amplitude of the wave.

8. M. Faraday, loc. cit., 392.

9. Kahlbaum and Darbishire, op. cit., 274.

10. M. Faraday, loc. cit., 405 ff.

11. Ibid., 413 ff.

12. Ibid., 421 ff.

13. Ibid., 422.

14. Ibid., 419.

15. Ibid.

R

16. Ibid., 421.

17. Wolfgang Ostwald in his *Grundriss der Kolloid-Chemie* (Dresden, 1909) refers to Faraday no less than seven times, and cites the paper on gold four times. A more recent text by Neil Kensington Adam, *Physical Chemistry* (Oxford, 1956) states: 'Faraday's studies of colloidal gold are classical' (p. 580) and refers the reader to the paper, 'On the Experimental Relations of Gold (and other Metals) to Light'.

18. See above, Chapter Six, section 3.

19. The Ruhmkorff coil consisted of a primary coil wound around a soft iron core and connected to a battery. A secondary coil of many, many turns was wound around the primary coil. An interrupter was placed in the primary circuit so that as soon as the current flowed there, the circuit was broken and immediately thereafter, the primary circuit was made again. The result was a series of short, rapid bursts in the primary coil. This caused the rapid build-up and break-down of a field of force around the coil (intensified by the soft iron core) and, as this field varied, it generated a very high voltage in the secondary coil.

20. W. R. Grove, 'On the Electro-Chemical Polarity of Gases', *Phil. Trans.*, 1852, 87.

21. C. A. Bentley, 'On the Improved Induction Coil'; E. S. Ritchie, 'On a modified form of Ruhmkorff's Induction Apparatus'; C. A. Bentley, 'On the Improved Induction Coil'; E. S. Ritchie, 'Note on M. Ruhmkorff's Induction Coil'; *L. & E. Phil. Mag.*, 4 Ser., *14* (1857), 160, 239, 319, and 480 respectively.

22. The name, 'Geissler tubes' was given to them by Plücker in his article 'Ueber die Einwirkung des Magneten auf die elektrischen Entladungen in verdünnter Gasen', Poggendorff's *Annalen*, *103* (1858), 88. The paper was reprinted in Fr. Pockels, *Julius Plückers Gesammelte Physikalische Abhandlungen* (Leipzig, 1892), 475 ff. An English translation, 'On the Action of the Magnet upon the Electrical Discharge in Rarefied Gases', appeared in the *L. & E. Phil. Mag.*, 4 Ser., *16* (1858), 119 ff.

23. R.I., Faraday MSS., Faraday's Lecture Notebooks, Six Lectures on Static Electricity (Juv. Aud.), 1857–8, Lecture 2, p. 5.

24. N.R.C.C., Faraday to J. Plücker, R.I., 27 July 1857.

25. Faraday's notes on these researches were bound into Folio Volume 8 of the *Diary* and published by Martin at the end of the seventh volume of the printed *Diary*. The paragraphs were numbered consecutively, starting from 1. References to these pages will be given in the conventional way, i.e. *Diary*, 7, page, paragraph number.

26. Grove, op. cit.

27. It would also be misleading to use the term consistently in this section for it was not yet recognized that there *was* a discharge from the cathode. According to the one-fluid theory, at least, the flow of electricity was from the anode to the cathode (i.e. from + to −, or a flow of excess fluid to a place where electric fluid was deficient). This is why the strange green glow near the anode (caused by the fluorescence of the glass as it was struck by electrons from the cathode) was so difficult to explain in the early years of cathode ray research.

For Grove's explanation of the process of electrical discharge in evacuated tubes, see his 'The Electro-Chemical Polarity of Gases', *Phil. Trans.*, 1852, 95.

28. Ibid., 97.

29. R.I., Faraday MSS., Lecture Notes, Fri. Evg., 8 June 1855 – Rhumkorff [*sic*]. This passage is not repeated in the published account, written by Faraday, 'On Ruhmkorff's Induction Apparatus', *Proc. R.I.*, *2* (1854–8), 139 ff.

30. *Diary*, *7*, 412 [1].

31. Ibid., [2].

32. Ibid., 413 [8–11].

33. The electron theory very nicely removed this difficulty. When electrons moved through the evacuated space, there was a current; when they hit the glass, they gave it a static charge. Faraday's situation was complicated by the fact that the tubes with which he was working contained small amounts of different gases introduced on purpose to see what changes were effected in the colour and nature of the striations. This led to the creation of gas ions, and currents of positive ions passing from the anode to the cathode.

34. See the Thirteenth Series, and above, Chapter Six, section 3.

35. *Diary*, 417 [39].

36. Ibid., 458 [276].

37. Plücker, for example, wrote at the end of 1859 that 'The origin of the current takes place at the positive wire', *Gesam. Phys. Abhand.*, 602.

38. *Diary*, 432 [156].

39. The two currents, presumably, would be that of the electrons *from* the cathode and of positively charged ions going to the cathode. Because of the large difference in mass of the two kinds of particles, the magnet would tend to separate them and give the appearance of two currents.

40. See, for example, *Diary*, *7*, 439 [183 ff.].

41. Ibid. [465].

42. B.J., *2*, 449.

43. See above, Chapter Three.

44. 'Report of the Commission appointed to inquire into the state of the pictures in the National Gallery', in 'Report of the Select Committee appointed to consider the present accommodation afforded by the National Gallery . . . 1850', *Parl. Pap.*, 1850, *5*, 67.

45. Ibid., 68.

46. Ibid.

47. Faraday's experiments on varnish are included in Folio Volume 8 of the *Diary*, Section 21 (not printed by Martin).

48. For Faraday's results, see 'Report of a Select Committee appointed to inquire into the management of the National Gallery, . . . 1853,' *Parl. Pap.*, 1852–3, *35*, 373 ff.

49. Ibid., 375 ff.

50. Ibid., 382.

51. Faraday to Dr Milman, Dean of St Paul's, R.I., 30 April 1857, in 'Report of the National Gallery site commission, together with the minutes, evidence, appendix and index, Presented to both Houses of Parliament by Command', *Parl. Pap.*, 1857, session 2, *24*, 149.

52. Ibid.

53. B.M.Add.MS. 41370 (Martin Papers, vol. 25), f. 328.

54. Ibid., f. 334. It is curious that Faraday did not remark on the moral aspects of this method of warfare.

55. *The Times*, Saturday, 7 October 1854, 7.

56. Ibid., 11 October 1854, 10.

57. B.M.Add.MS. 41370 (Martin Papers, vol. 25) f. 374, Faraday to Sir Byam Martin, 14 October 1854.

58. M. Faraday, 'On the Use of Gutta Percha in Electrical Insulation', *L. & E. Phil. Mag.*, N.S., *32* (1848), 165 ff. Reprinted in *Exp. Res.*, *3*, 494 ff.

59. I have been unable to locate Airy's application to Latimer Clarke. What was contained in it, however, is quite obvious from Clarke's reply, cited in the text.

60. Royal Observatory, Airy MSS., Astrology–Optics, 1853 and 1854, section 12, Latimer Clarke to Professor Airy, London, 13 October 1853.

61. Ibid.

62. M. Faraday, 'On Electric Induction – Associated cases of current and static effects', *Proc. R.I.*, *1* (1852–4), 345. Reprinted in *Exp. Res.*, *3*, 508 ff. References will be to the reprint. The quotation in the text is to be found on page 517.

63. Ibid., 518.

64. Ibid., 513, note 1.

65. Patent Office Library, London, Faraday to C. V. Walker, Brighton, 3 April 1858.

66. William Thomson, 'On the Theory of the Electric Telegraph', in Sir W. Thomson, *Mathematical and Physical Papers*, 2 (1884), 61 ff. For Thomson's role in the laying of the Atlantic cable see Silvanus P. Thompson, op. cit., *2*, 326 ff.

67. 'Report of the Commissioners appointed to inquire into the condition and management of lights, buoys and beacons . . . 1861', *Parl. Pap.*, 1861, *25*. Faraday's evidence, dated 25 February 1860, appears in the appendix to volume 2 of this report, pp. 591–3.

68. Ibid. Faraday submitted a number of reports (now lost) on this lamp in the years 1837–9.

69. 'Reports made to the Trinity House, by Professor Faraday and other persons in the service of that Corporation, relative to the Lime Light of the Universal Lime Light Company, exhibited at the South Foreland High lighthouse', *Parl. Pap.*, 1863, *63*. Faraday's first report, dated 30 September 1861, is on pages 3–5. This is followed by two other reports of little interest here.

70. Ibid.

71. Reports on the electric light to the Royal Commissioners, and made by order of the Trinity Board, *Parl. Pap.*, 1862, *54*, 5.

72. Ibid., 2 ff.

73. The detailed history of this collaboration may be reconstructed from the correspondence that passed between Faraday and James Chance. Through the generosity of Sir Hugh Chance, this correspondence is now at the Royal Institution where it may be consulted by interested parties.

74. 'Report of Professor Faraday on the Smalls Light, Coast of Pembrokeshire, R.I., Jan. 30, 1861,' in 'Report of the Royal Commission appointed to Enquire into the Condition and Management of Lights, Buoys, and Beacons, 1861' (see above, note 67).

75. See above, note 71.

76. B.J., *2*, 470.

77. *Memories of Old Friends, Being extracts from the Journals and Letters of Caroline Fox*, 3rd ed. (2 vols., London, 1882), *1*, 299.

78. Reid, *Diary*, 166. The quotation is in Miss Reid's hand in a section labelled, 'Notes by M.F.'

79. Quoted in Carl Schorlemmer, *The Rise and Development of Organic Chemistry*, rev. ed., London, 1894, 49.

80. Cited in Carl Brinitzer, *A Reasonable Rebel: Georg Christoph Lichtenberg* (London, 1960), 148.

81. See above, p. 445.

82. Kahlbaum and Darbishire, op. cit., 236.

83. Science Museum, S. Kensington, Faraday to Dr Andrews, R.I., 27 July 1856.

84. N.R.C.C., Faraday to Plücker, R.I., 27 July 1857.

85. Faraday to Rev. John Barlow, Highgate, 19 August 1857, B.J., *2*, 380.

86. Kahlbaum and Darbishire, op. cit., 336.

87. In the letter to the Rev. Barlow cited in note 85, he called attention to this new anxiety. 'One result of short memory is coming curiously into play with me. I forget how to spell, I dare say if I were to read this letter again, I should find four or five words of which I am doubtful, "witholds, wearies, successful," &c.; but I cannot stop for them, or look to a dictionary (for I had better cease to write altogether), but I just send them, with all their imperfections, knowing that you will receive them kindly.'

88. Kahlbaum and Darbishire, op. cit., 356.

89. Ibid., 357.

90. R.I., Faraday MSS., Faraday to Mr B. Vincent, Upper Norwood, 25 July 1850.

91. R.I., Faraday MSS., Faraday to E. Magrath, R.I., 6 December 1851.

92. R. I., Faraday MSS., Faraday to Bence Jones, n.p., n.d.

93. John Tyndall, *Faraday as a Discoverer*, 5th ed. (London, 1894), 184.

94. Faraday to the Editor of *The Times*, R.I., 7 July 1855. Cited in B.J., *2*, 363.

95. R.I. MSS., Reid, *Diary*, 12 April 1853.

96. Kahlbaum and Darbishire, op. cit., 314.

97. R.I., Faraday MSS., Faraday to the Managers of the Royal Institution, R.I., 11 October 1861, B.J., *2*, 443.

98. R.I., Faraday MSS., Faraday's Lecture Notes. Gas – Glass furnaces – Siemens, 20 June 1862, B.J. (with some alterations), *2*, 450.

99. See above, note 91.

100. *The Life & Experiences of Sir Henry Enfield Roscoe, by himself* (London, 1906), 136.

101. Reid, *Diary*, 144.

102. Bib. Pub. et Univ. de Génève, MS. 2316, 88 Af, f. 93, Faraday to A. de la Rive, R.I., 19 September 1861.

103. B.J., *2*, 482.

Epilogue

The biography of a man of science can never end with his death. If his contributions to science are important enough to warrant a detailed account of his life, then his effect upon science does not end when he dies. The facts he discovers are rapidly assimilated and become part of the main stream of science. When, as was the case with Faraday, the factual discoveries were the results of a radically new vision of physical reality the process of assimilation is not so rapid. It is a difficult thing to ask one's colleagues to give up the habits of thought of a lifetime and, in most cases, these habits will tend to stifle novelty. One can only hope that a new generation will see the point and justify the new departure. So it was with Faraday, and the purpose of this brief epilogue is to sketch in the metamorphosis of Faraday's ideas from radical speculation to orthodox scientific theory.

Faraday's early career was not particularly controversial. By adopting a very cautious approach in his published papers, he was able to evade dispute and attention was focused on his discoveries of new effects. Thus, through 1838, he kept insisting that his theory of electrical action did not presume to deal with the reality or unreality of electrical imponderable fluids. Most of his scientific contemporaries accepted his facts and fitted them into their own theories of electricity. The only direct challenge that Faraday experienced in these years came from Robert Hare and, as we have seen, Faraday did not meet it directly. He was able, therefore, to talk about and around his theories, dropping hints for those few to whom the hints might make sense, but carefully avoiding a head-on collision with orthodox theory. Even his denial of action at a distance in electrochemistry and electrostatics could be made to fit within action-at-a-distance physics. All that needed to be done was to make the action intermolecular instead of across sensible distances, and Faraday's theory would have been approved by Laplace himself.

In the 1840's and 1850's, Faraday's tactics changed. No longer could he cloak his own investigations with the language of orthodox theory. Action at a distance, whether the distance be macroscopic or microscopic, could not be reconciled with his views of the universe. In fact, action at a distance appeared to him to be hindering the progress of physics and blinding people to the existence of physical processes of fundamental importance to an understanding of the universe. So, the only recourse open to him was to move to the offensive and, utilizing the fruits of experiment, present the most persuasive arguments he could muster. He was never optimistic about the acceptance of his ideas by his contemporaries. He had studied, in himself, the power of prejudice and habit and knew that the most difficult thing in the world was to throw off one method of viewing the universe and adopt another. The concept of the line of force was, he hoped, the physical line across the gulf that separated action-at-a-distance physics from field physics. If only his colleagues would grasp the line of force firmly and follow it to its other end, they could cross this gap and perceive the new world that he saw so clearly. Yet, as his niece noted in her *Diary*, Faraday remarked: 'How few understand the physical lines of force! They will not see them, yet all the researches on the subject tend to confirm the views I put forth many years since. Thompson of Glasgow seems almost the only one who acknowledges them. He is perhaps the nearest to understanding what I meant. I am content to wait convinced as I am of the truth of my views.'[1]

The reaction to the concept of the line of force was not merely one of indifference; it was downright hostile, especially when Faraday tried to extend it to gravitation. As has already been mentioned, *The Athenaeum* suggested that he go back to the R.I. and work up his sixth form mathematics before he ventured again into the deep seas of Laplacian physics. A more reasoned, though no less unfavourable, reaction was forthcoming from the Astronomer Royal, Sir George Biddell Airy. The Rev. John Barlow had written to Airy, calling his attention to Faraday's paper on lines of force, in the hopes of receiving Airy's reaction to Faraday's ideas. Airy was never one to hide his views and responded frankly and forthrightly.

The following [he wrote to Barlow] may be taken as nearly expounding my present views:

1. It seems to me that the question ought to be split into two, namely, (a) Is there any reason for treating the influences of magnetism in any way different from the way of treating the effects of gravitation, &c.? (b) Are these influences to be considered as influences related to space, or related to the bodies sustaining their action?

2. On question (a) I give my opinion without misgiving, as regards the mechanical effects. The effect of a magnet upon another magnet may be represented *perfectly* by supposing that certain parts act just as if they pulled by a string, and that certain other parts act just as if they pushed with a stick. And the representation is not vague, but is a matter of strict numerical calculation; and when this calculation is made on the simple law of the inverse square of distance, it does (numerically) represent the phenomena with precision. I can answer for this, because we are perpetually making this very calculation. I know the difficulty of predicating the effects of evidence on other people's minds, but I declare that I can hardly imagine anyone who practically and numerically knows this agreement, to hesitate an instant in the choice between this simple and precise action, on the one hand, and anything so vague and varying as lines of force, on the other hand.

You know the French mathematicians have calculated the effect of induction accurately on the same laws.

3. On the metaphysical question (b) I have only one remark to make. I do not think Faraday's remark on the bringing a new body into space is pertinent, because no new body is brought into space. We all start with the notion that the quantity of the mysterious ὑπόστασις is never altered. Therefore, when I contemplate gravitation, I contemplate it as a relation between two particles, and not as a relation between one particle (called the attracting particle) and the space in which the other (called the attracted particle) finds itself for the moment. I contemplate it as a relation between two particles, which relation (mechanically considered) has respect to different directions, and has varying magnitude: the said direction and magnitude having very simple relations with the relative direction and magnitude of the two particles. I can easily conceive that there are plenty of bodies about us not subject to this intermutual action, and therefore not subject to the law of gravitation.[2]

I think it fair to suggest that Airy's reaction was typical of those who gave their wholehearted allegiance to the orthodox view of mathematical physics. As such, there are two points in Airy's letter that deserve special attention. Airy's second point illustrates the place of models in Laplacian physics. The model was used to enable one to visualize a physical process and, most importantly, open it to mathematical analysis. What was sought was the law of action, not an explanation of the process. The model, therefore, was expendable and Airy's real point was that Faraday's model was a clumsy one. This was not Faraday's point; clumsy or no, the lines of force were *real* and therefore not subject to the kind of treatment accorded to the purely heuristic models utilized by mathematical physicists to derive equations of action.

Airy's third point was merely a variation of the second. Airy saw gravity as the *relation* between two particles which acted according to the inverse square law of universal attraction. This completely evaded the issue, for what Faraday was after was the *cause* of the relation. 'I do not deny the law of action referred to in all cases,' Faraday wrote to Barlow after seeing Airy's letter, 'nor is there any difference as to the mathematical results . . ., whether he takes the results according to my view or that of the French mathematicians. Why, then, talk about the inverse square of the distance?'[3]

In this exchange of views is to be seen the very heart of the disagreement. Airy's science was founded on the Newtonian dictum, *Hypothesis non fingo*, applied explicitly by Newton to gravity. Faraday could not refrain from framing hypotheses for he realized more clearly than any of his contemporaries that Newton's very refusal had given birth to a theory of action which Faraday now considered to be a deleterious influence on the progress of science.

The wall of opposition that Faraday faced may best be appreciated by an examination of John Tyndall's estimate of Faraday's real scientific stature. Tyndall considered himself one of Faraday's closest friends and in his eulogy of Faraday publicly praised Faraday's 'intuition' of natural processes. In fact, Tyndall tended to dismiss Faraday's deepest ideas with a kind of paternal tolerance.

> It is amusing [he wrote to his dear friend Thomas Hirst] to see how many write to Faraday asking him what the lines of force are. He bewilders even men of eminence, for the very fact of his making these lines of force the medium of his theoretic sight and his having done so much with them convinces the generality of people that they are the final cause of magnetic phenomena. Your remarks on this point I think very correct and very wise. The fact is that an experiment made with reference to the lines of force is virtually made with reference to the principle on which the lines of force themselves depend, and the deeper scientific mind looks through the lines of force after this principle. Faraday's achievements are due to his immense earnestness and great love for his subject and this very mistiness which serves to obscure the verity of matters may have its compensations by rendering the subject attractive and thus wooing a man to work at it with more fervour. I heard Biot once say that he could not understand Faraday, and if you look for exact knowledge in his theories you will be disappointed – flashes of wonderful insight you meet here and there, but he has no exact knowledge himself, and in conversation with him he readily confesses this.[4]

If someone professedly as close to and as sympathetic with Faraday as Tyndall could not understand what he was driving at, what chance did his theories have among his other contemporaries? He was, indeed, fortunate that two men of the stature of William Thomson and James Clerk Maxwell took his views seriously enough to see if they could be turned into a proper mathematical theory.

In 1845 Thomson showed how the lines of electrostatic force could be used to establish a mathematical theory of electrostatic action. 'All the views which Faraday has brought forward', he wrote, 'and illustrated or demonstrated by experiment, lead to this method of establishing the mathematical theory, and, as far as the analysis is concerned, it would, in most *general* propositions, be even more simple, if possible, than that of Coulomb.'[5] Thomson then went on to show how the 'curved lines of inductive action' could be treated mathematically and then proceeded to draw an analogy with magnetic curves. From this analogy he was able to introduce Poisson's mathematical theory of the distribution of magnetism and of magnetic attractions and repulsions. Then, by an intellectual feedback operation he drew the circle closed. 'These laws [referring to Poisson's theory] seem to represent in the most general manner the state of a body polarized by influence, and therefore, without adopting any particular mechanical hypothesis, we may make use of them to form a mathematical theory of electrical influence in dielectrics, the truth of which can only be established by a rigorous comparison of its results with experiment.'[6]

Faraday was, understandably, delighted with Thomson's work for it served to 'affirm the truthfulness and generality of the method of representation'.[7] This, however, was all that Thomson did. He made the lines of force respectable by showing that they could be reconciled with the current mathematical theories of electrostatics and magnetism. He did not, as Faraday had, use them as an instrument of discovery.

It was Maxwell who first came to realize the potency of the lines of force and the field hypothesis in physics. They first seriously engaged his attention in 1855 when he was thinking deeply on the theory of electricity and the difficulties involved in bringing electrostatic and electrodynamic hypotheses into a single theory. This, of course, was what Faraday had done although few people were willing to accept his theory. What Maxwell set out to do was to force Faraday's ideas on those who had hitherto dismissed him because of his non-mathematical presentation. In his paper 'On Faraday's Lines of Force', read before the Cambridge Philosophical Society on 10 December 1855 and 11 February 1856, Maxwell explicitly stated his debt to Faraday.

The methods are generally those suggested by the processes of reasoning which are found in the researches of Faraday, and which, though they have been interpreted mathematically by Prof. Thomson and others, are very generally supposed to be of an indefinite and unmathematical character, when compared with those employed by the professed mathematicians. By the method which I adopt, I hope to render it evident that I am not attempting to establish any physical theory of a science in which I have hardly made a single experiment, and that the limit of my design is to shew how, by a strict application of the ideas and methods of Faraday, the connexion of the very different orders of phenomena which he has discovered may be clearly placed before the mathematical mind.[8]

Maxwell then proceeded to treat Faraday's lines of force using an imaginary fluid with specifically assigned qualities flowing through the 'tubes' of force to represent them. He was able here to do, in greater detail, what Thomson had done in 1845: namely, show how Faraday's ideas could be treated mathematically and how this mathematical treatment did encompass the known experimental facts. Maxwell, unlike Thomson, did not stop there. The lines of force were both a convenient guide to mathematical analysis *and* something physically real. Maxwell, it would seem, was the only person besides Faraday who actually felt that the lines of force did exist and were not just an easy way to represent action at a distance. Maxwell's adherence to this view can be seen most clearly in a letter he wrote to Faraday in November 1857, in answer to Faraday's request of his opinion on the paper on the Conservation of Force. The letter has not, to my knowledge, been published before and because of its considerable interest for the history of field theory, I give it *in extenso* here.

129 Union Street
Aberdeen
9th Nov. 1857

Dear Sir,
    I have to acknowledge receipt of your papers on the Relations of Gold &c. to Light and on the Conservation of Force. Last spring you were so kind as to send me a copy of the latter paper and to ask what I thought of it. That question silenced me at that time, but I have since heard and read various opinions on the subject which render it both easy and right for me to say what I think. And first I pass over some who have never understood the known doctrine of conservation of force and who suppose it to have something to do with the equality of action and reaction. Now first I am sorry that we do not keep our words for distinct things more distinct and speak of the 'Conservation of Work or of Energy' as applied to the relations between the amount of 'vis viva' and of 'tension' in the world; and of the 'Duality of Force' as referring to the equality of action and reaction. Energy is the power a thing has of doing work arising either from its own motion or from the 'tension' subsisting between it and other things.
    Force is the tendency of a body to pass from one place to another and depends upon the amount of change of 'tension' which that passage would produce.[9]

Now as far as I know you are the first person in whom the idea of bodies acting at a distance by throwing the surrounding medium into a state of constraint has arisen, as a principle to be actually believed in. We have had streams of hooks and eyes flying around magnets, and even pictures of them so beset, but nothing is clearer than your descriptions of all sources of force keeping up a state of energy in all that surrounds them, which state by its increase or diminution measures the work done by any change in the system. You seem to see the lines of force curving round obstacles and driving plumb at conductors and swerving towards certain directions in crystals, and carrying with them everywhere the same amount of attractive power spread wider or denser as the lines widen or contract.

You have also seen that the great mystery is not how like bodies repel and unlike attract but how like bodies attract (by gravitation). But if you can get over that difficulty, either by making gravity the residual of the two electricities or by simply admitting it, then your lines of force can 'weave a web across the sky' and lead the stars in their courses without any necessarily immediate connection with the objects of their attraction.

The lines of Force from the Sun spread out from him and when they come near a planet *curve out from it* so that every planet diverts a number depending on its mass from their course and substitutes a system of its own so as to become something like a comet, *if lines of force were visible.*

. . . Now conceive every one of these lines (which never interfere but proceed from sun & planet to infinity) to have a *pushing* force, instead of a *pulling* one and then sun and planet will be pushed together with a force which comes out as it ought proportional to the product of the masses & the inverse square of the distance.

The difference between this case and that of the dipolar forces is, that instead of each body catching the lines of force from the rest all the lines keep as clear of other bodies as they can and go off to the infinite sphere against which I have supposed them to push.

Here then we have conservation of energy (actual & potential) as every student of dynamics learns, and besides this we have conservation of 'lines of force' as to their number and total strength for *every* body always sends out a number proportional to its own mass, and the pushing effect of each is the same.

All that is altered when bodies approach is the *direction* in which these lines push. When the bodies are distant the distribution of lines near each is little disturbed. When they approach, the lines march round from between them, and come to push behind each so that their resultant action is to bring the bodies together with a *resultant* force increasing as they approach.

Now the mode of looking at Nature which belongs to those who can see the lines of force deals very little with 'resultant forces' but with a network of lines of action of which these are the final results. So that I for my part cannot realise your dissatisfaction with the law of gravitation provided you conceive it according to your own principles. It may seem very different when stated by the believers in 'forces at a distance' but there can be only differences in form and conception not in quantity or mechanical effect between them and those who trace force by its lines. But when we face the great questions about gravitation, Does it require time? Is it polar to the 'outside of the universe' or to anything? Has it any reference to electricity? or does it stand on the very foundation of matter – mass or inertia? then we feel the need of tests, whether they be comets or nebulae or laboratory experiments or bold questions as to the truth of received opinions.

I have now merely tried to show you why I do not think gravitation a dangerous subject to apply your method to and that it may be possible to throw light on it also by the *embodiment* of the same ideas which are expressed *mathematically* in the functions of Laplace and of Sir W. R. Hamilton in Planetary Theory.

But these are questions relating to the connexion between magneto-electricity and certain mechanical effects which seem to me opening up quite a new road to the establishment of principles in electricity and a possible confirmation of the physical nature of magnetic lines of force. Professor W. Thomson seems to have some new lights on this subject.

Yours sincerely
James Clerk Maxwell.[10]

Our task is now done. This letter reveals that Maxwell fully understood what Faraday was getting at. He treated the lines of force with respect, and was rather excited by the concept of field theory. The 'new road' was largely to be opened up by Maxwell himself and lead, by the 1870's, to the establishment of field theory as the orthodox treatment of electromagnetism. In this theory, as Maxwell always insisted, the very core were the ideas Faraday had expressed in his life's work.

References

1. R.I., Faraday MSS., Miss Reid, *Diary*, 175. The date of this remark is 7 November 1855.
The 'Thompson' mentioned was William Thomson, the future Lord Kelvin. For his appreciation of the lines of force, see below, p. 510.

2. Airy to Rev. John Barlow, 7 February 1855, B.J., *2*, 352 ff.

3. Faraday to Rev. John Barlow, R.I., 28 February 1855, B.J., *2*, 355.

4. R.I., Tyndall's Journal, 415, John Tyndall to Thomas Hirst, R.I., 5 November 1855.

5. William Thomson, 'On the Mathematical Theory of Electricity in Equilibrium', *L. & E. Phil. Mag.*, 4 Ser., *8* (1854), 53. The paper was first published in the *Cambridge and Dublin Mathematical Journal* for November 1845.

6. Ibid., 55.

7. M. Faraday, 'On some points of Magnetic philosophy', *Exp. Res.*, *3*, 529.

8. James Clerk Maxwell, 'On Faraday's Lines of Force', in *The Scientific Papers of James Clerk Maxwell* (Dover edition, two volumes in one, New York, n.d.), *1*, 157.

9. Faraday disagreed here with Maxwell's definition. 'I perceive that I do not use the word "force" as you define it, "the tendency of a body to pass from one place to another." What I mean by the word is the source or sources of all possible actions of the particles or materials of the universe.' B.J., *2*, 383.

10. I.E.E., J. C. Maxwell to Faraday.

Index

Prepared by Thomas B. Settle

———————————

NOTE: The nature of the technical materials discussed, i.e. subjects in an embryonic state of development, has made precise indexing next to impossible. As far as is practicable, we have organized the scientific topics under the following headings. The reader should also consult the table of contents.

Action
Atomism
Chemical Substances
Chemistry; including organic, physical, photo-, and thermo-
Conservation and correlation
Electricity
Electrochemistry

Electromagnetism
Field Theory
Heat
Light and Physical Optics
Magnetism
Mechanics and Motion
Sound
Wave Theory

Abbott, Benjamin, 8, 12, 21, 22, 26, 27, 29, 35, 39, 40, 43, 48, 80, 81, 87, 95, 321, 323, 330
Academy of Sciences, Paris, 145, 147, 151, 167, 176, 201, 382
Accademia del Cimento, 37
Action:
    Action at a distance, and denial of, 55, 85, 148, 176, 223, 237, 242–4, 250, 253–4, 268–9, 283–4, 287, 291, 293–9, 303, 305–6, 308, 311, 372, 381, 420, 436, 448–9, 453, 457–9, 506–7, 512
    Central forces, 140, 152, 161, 176, 436, 448
    Chemical (*see also* 'Chemistry, Affinities'), 59, 79, 87–88, 220–1, 227–57, 452
    Circular forces, 139–41, 152–6, 161–4
    'Conflicts', 62, 140
    Conservation and correlation of forces, *see separate listing*
    Continuity of forces, 62, 65, 125–6
    'Crystalline force', 408–16
    Diamagnetic action, 381–99, 408 44, 466, 491

Action (*cont.*)
    Dielectric action, 292–4, 297–8, 300–7, 314–15, 383–5, 427, 510
    Distance relation in chemical action, 243–4, 268, 283–5
    Electric action, 20, 35, 53–54, 58–59, 62, 69, 79–80, 85, 137–83, 191, 197, 203, 227–56, 266–9, 275, 286, 299–315, 371, 379, 383–4, 451–3, 466–70, 475–6, 478, 483–7
    Electromotive action, chemical, 145, 149–50, 240–1, 285, 287, 365–72
    Electtomotive action, contact, 364–72
    Electromotive action, inductive, 191, 209–11, 447
    Electrostatic action, 143, 174, 268, 283–315, 365, 372–5, 444, 506, 510–13
    Forces, general, 59, 60–73, 73–80, 123–5, 129–30, 365, 465, 511–13
    Gravitational, 86, 127, 129, 243, 251, 282, 288, 295, 344, 379–81, 419, 421, 457–9, 465–70, 478, 491, 506–13; non-polar, 419
    Identity of 'forces', (unity of), *see* 'Conservation and correlation'

Action (*cont.*)
  Intermolecular forces, 73–80, 88,
    120–3, 127, 128, 165–6, 179, 252,
    268–9, 274–83, 289–96, 299–308,
    412, 415
  Inverse square forces, 73, 232, 243–
    4, 284, 295, 299, 310, 448–9,
    457–8, 508–9, 512
  Laws of action, 143, 167, 387, 416,
    508
  Light action, 59, 415, 418, 419, 437,
    465, 470–1, 472; non-polar, 419
  Lines of force, general (*see also*
    'Field theory'), 161, 163, 194, 200,
    202-11, 290–9, 379–81, 383, 388,
    435, 459, 464–70, 507–13
  lines of force as space strains, 459
  Magnecrystallic action, 408–20, 430,
    436–8, 442–3, 466
  Magnetic action, 53–54, 62–67, 79,
    137–83, 194, 197, 204, 314, 387,
    393–402, 414–59, 466–9, 509–13
  Magneto-optic action, 383–92, 408–
    17, 421, 427, 430
  Non-polar force, 419
  Plenum of forces, 62, 296
  Polar action, 55, 65, 78–79, 88, 305,
    419, 436–9
  Strain, material (molecular-struc-
    tural), 203–5, 308, 388, 391,
    412-13, 436, 459, 468–9
  'Tension', 126–7, 146, 289–94, 299–
    303, 380, 453–7
  Transmission of force, 81, 138,
    175–7, 181, 193, 205, 250, 269,
    282–7, 291, 293, 295–9, 299–301,
    305, 308-13, 386, 388, 400, 413,
    419, 450–9, 465
  Universal attraction, 72–73, 278, 282,
    295
  Voltaic action, 56–57, 275, 364–72
  Waves of force, *see* 'Wave theory'
Adams, George (1750–95), 18
Adams, John Couch (1819–92), 347
Admiralty, 106, 108, 131, 479, 482
Æpinus, Franz Ulrich Theodor (1724–
    1802), 295
Agape, 3, 4–5
Airy, Sir George Biddell, Astronomer
    Royal (1801–92) (*see Plates*), 485,
    507–9

Albert, Prince Consort (*see Plates*),
    335, 499
Alchemists, 71
Amici, Giovanni Battista (1786–1863),
    238
Ampère, André-Marie (1775–1836)
    (*see Plates*), 34, 109, 140–57, 161,
    164–75, 182, 197–8, 204, 208,
    239, 240, 256, 259, 263, 288,
    329, 411, 419, 421–2, 424–5,
    427, 429–30, 434, 455
Ancien Régime, 31
Anderson, Sergeant, 101, 117
Andrews, Dr Thomas (1813–85), 352
Annalen der physik und chemie (Poggen-
    dorff's), 349
Annales de chimie, 43, 230, 349, 382
Annales de chimie et de physique, 46, 201,
    202, 238, 365
Annali di chimica, 58
Annals of Philosophy, 43, 69, 77, 153
Antinori, Vincenzo (1792–1865), 201,
    215
Antologia di Firenze, 201
Apreece, Mrs, *see* 'Davy, Lady'
Arabian Nights, 11
Arago, Dominique François Jean
    (1786–1853) (*see Plates*), 143, 151,
    153, 170–3, 196, 200
Archaeology, 39
Astronomy, 16, 485
Athenaeum, The, 356, 457–8, 507
Athenaeum Club, 15, 324, 495, 498
Atomism:
  Atoms and atomism, 62, 65, 72–73,
    73–80, 87–88, 148, 254–6, 331,
    372, 376–7
  Boscovichean, 73–80, 87–88, 115,
    126–30, 245, 249–50, 279, 294,
    296, 356, 376–80
  Chemical atom, 59, 254, 356
  Contiguous, particulate atom, 250,
    254, 259, 268–9, 286, 291, 295–
    315, 372–9, 388–91, 418–19, 427,
    444, 450–1
  Daltonian, 59, 73, 87–88, 123, 129,
    245, 248, 250, 280–1, 376–8
  Haüyian atom, 88
  Point atoms, 73–80, 87–88, 114–15,
    121–2, 126–30, 148, 245, 248, 250,
    254, 255, 275, 278, 282, 291–2,
    294, 309, 375–9, 381, 391, 472

Atomism (cont.)
Theory: problems, 62, 65, 127, 143, 257
Atwood, George (1740–1807), 18
Aurora Borealis and Australis, 208
Avogadro, Amedeo (1776–1856), 383
Azais, Pierre Hyacinthe (1766–?), 68

Babbage, Charles (1792–1871) (see Plates), 42, 170–3, 182, 196, 251, 350–5, 357, 358
Bacon, Francis (1561–1626), 13, 53, 63, 89, 340, 379
Baconianism, 379
Baillif, Alexandre-Claude-Martin le (1764–1831), 393
Bakerian Lecture (1806), 69, 234, 243
Bakerian Lectures, 69, 119, 210, 211, 472
Balard, Antoine Jérôme (1802–76), 350
Bancalari, Michele Alberto, 396
Banks, Sir Joseph, P.R.S. (1743–1820) (see Plates), 28, 57, 109, 348–9
Barlow, Rev. John, 493, 507, 509
Barlow, Peter (1776–1862) (see Plates), 170
Barnard, Charlotte, 99
Barnard, Edward, 97, 105
Barnard, George, brother-in-law to M. F., 492
Barnard, Jane, niece to M. F., 100, 500
Barnard, Sarah, see 'Faraday, Sarah'
Becher, Johann Joachim (1635–82), 228
Beck, M. van, 150
Becquerel, Antoine César (1788–1878), 151
Becquerel, Alexandre Edmund (1820–91), 393, 420–2, 425, 429, 433
Beddoes, Thomas (1760–1808), 67
Berkeley, Bishop George, 61, 66, 80, 81, 83
Berthollet, Claude-Louis (1748–1822) (see Plates), 24, 150, 230, 250
Berzelius, Jöns Jacob (1779–1848) (see Plates), 46, 142, 254, 258, 350, 491–2
Bibliothèque Brittanique, 43
Bibliothèque Universelle, 43
Biographia Literaria, by S. T. Coleridge, 63, 64

Biot, Jean-Baptiste (1774–1862), 170, 302, 306, 509
Black, Joseph (1728–99), 54, 75
Bolton-le-Sands, 1
Boscovich, Roger Joseph (1711–87), 71, 73-80, 87, 88, 125, 127, 129, 130, 148, 245, 279, 281, 292, 294, 295–6, 356
Botany, 330
Boyle, Robert (1627–91), 60, 294
Brande, William Thomas (1788–1866) (see Plates), 42, 43, 44, 110, 128, 141, 176, 321–2, 328, 329
Brewster, Sir David (1781–1868), 138, 351, 353
Bridell, Mr, 207
British Association for the Advancement of Science, 355–7, 413
British Museum, 482
Brown, Robert (1773–1858), 330-1
Brugmans, Anton (1732–89), 393
Brugnatelli, Luigi Valentino (1761–1818), 58
Brunel, Isambard Kingdom (1806–59), 331
Burney, Miss Fanny, Evelina, 11

Cabinet Cyclopedia, The, 178
Cagniard de La Tour, Charles, see 'La Tour, C. C. de'
Caius College, Cambridge, 260
Cambridge Philosophical Society, 510
Cambridge Philosophical Transactions, 44
Cambridge University, 18, 31, 259–62, 295, 350
Carlisle, Sir Anthony (1769–1840), 57, 227, 228
Carnot, Lazare-Nicolas-Marguerite (1753–1823), 352
Cavendish, Henry (1731–1810), 295
Chance, Sir James T., 490
Chaptal, Jean-Antoine-Claude (1756–1832), 352
Chemical History of a Candle, The, 345, 496
Chemical substances:
Acetic acid, 247
Aetna wines, 44
Alcohol, 127, 280
Alumine (alumina, Al_2O_3), 110–11
Amianthus (asbestos), 235
Aniline dye, 108

Chemical substances (*cont.*)
Antimony, 416
Arsenic, and compounds, 45, 247
Asbestos, 235
Azote: *see* 'Nitrogen'
Barium and compounds, 236–7
Benzene, 107, 108
Benzin: *see* 'Benzene'
Benzoates of:
mercury, 44
iron, 44
zinc, 44
Benzoic acid, 44, 45, 46
Bismuth, 171, 369, 393, 415–17, 419
Borax, 286
Boric acid, 267
Bromine, 350
Cadmium, 369
Camphor, on water, 24, 247, 279
Carbon, 26, 27, 38, 47, 71, 108, 114, 120-3, 128, 153, 171, 277
Carbon dioxide, carbonic acid, 38, 108, 119, 124; dry ice, 382
Carbon disulphide, 29
Carbonic acid, *see* 'Carbon dioxide'
Carbonic oxide, carbon monoxide, 119, 124
Caustic lime, 44
Charcoal, 35, 127
Chloride of nitrogen, 28, 29
Chlorine, 25, 26; as a supporter of combustion, 26, 27; manufacture of, 34, 35, 42; electronegative element, 47, 65, 71, 87, 120–3, 125, 128–30, 150, 222, 239, 260, 267, 325
Cobalt, 150, 172
Copper, refining, 112–13, 114, 170, 227, 368–70
Copper sulphate, 203, 221, 385
Diamond, 37, 38, 71, 78, 87, 114
Ether, 382, 473
Ethyl alcohol, 481
Euchlorine (Cl_2O), 129
Ferro-prussiate of potassa, 486
Fluorine, electronegative element, 47, 65
Gelatine, 243
Glass, optical, 109, 115–20; borate of lead, 286, 386–7
Gold, 27, 112, 118, 125–6, 369, 471–4, 499; gold chloride, 472

Chemical substances (*cont.*)
Graphite, 38, 112, 114
Hydrate of chlorine, 128–9
Hydrochloric acid, *see* 'Muriatic acid'
Hydrocyanic acid, 24
Hydrogen, 26, 27, 38; electropositive element, 47; product of electrolysis, 57–58, 71, 72, 77, 84, 108, 121, 122, 124, 127, 216, 227–34, 236, 239, 250, 253, 254, 267, 274–7, 281–2, 285, 290, 312, 382, 489
Hydrogen sulphide, 481
Hydriodate (HI), 244
Iodide of sulphur, 247
Iodine, first produced by Bernard Courtois, 34, 35, 36, 37; electronegative element, 47, 65, 244, 267, 279
Iron and compounds, 45, 109–15, 117, 118, 119, 150, 164, 170–2, 368–70
Lead, 267, 369
Lead, silicated borate of, 117, 118, 120
Litharge, lead oxide, 116, 117, 119
Lithium, 479
Mercury, 101, 125–6, 279
Muriate of ammonia (NH_4Cl), 35, 274
Muriate of silver (AgCl), 59, 237
Muriate of soda (NaCl), 22, 26, 227, 239, 473
Muriatic acid (HCl), 24, 25, 26, 27, 71, 129, 222, 233, 237, 397, 473
'Murium', the hypothetical substance the oxide of which yielded muriatic acid, 25
Nickel, 45, 113, 150, 172
Nitre, 106, 286
Nitric acid, 35, 482
Nitrogen, 47, 72, 382
Nitrous oxide, 67, 96
Olefiant gas (ethylene: C_2H_2), 122, 124
Orpiment (arsenic trisulphide: As_2S_3), 247
Oxygen, 24, 26, 27; electronegative element, 27; product of electrolysis, 58, 65, 70, 71, 77, 110, 119–21, 217, 227–34, 239, 250, 253, 254, 267, 274–7, 281–2, 285, 287, 290, 312, 382, 489

Chemical substances (*cont.*)
'Oxymuriatic Acid', *see* 'Chlorine'
Ozone, 103, 496–7
Palm wine, 44, 45, 46
Perchloride of carbon (hexachlor-ethane: C_2Cl_6), 122–3
Peroxide of manganese, 26
Phlogiston, 24, 25, 68; = electricity, 229, 238
Phosgene gas, 121
Phosphoric acid, 266
Phosphorus, 29, 45, 46, 47
Platina (Platinum), 35, 110, 113, 116, 117, 118, 119, 152, 221, 222, 244, 274–82, 285, 309, 369, 377, 385
Plumbago, 38
Potash, caustic, 108, 235
Potassium, 25, 70, 71, 101, 369, 377
Potassium oxide and potassium hydrate (KOH), 244, 377–8
Potassium sulphate, 235, 243, 369–70
Protochloride of carbon (tetra-chlorethylene: C_2Cl_4), 123
Realgar (arsenic sulphide), 247
Rhodium, 113
Rubber, 287
Silex (Silica), 17, 110
Silica (Si_2O_5), 116
Silicon, 110
Silver, 112, 113, 125, 126, 127, 171, 221, 369–70
Silver nitrate, 122, 286
Silver sulphate, 237
'Sirium', 45
Soda (Na_2CO_3), 26
Sodium, 25, 26, 70, 71, 479
Steel, 48, 109–15, 124, 145, 153
Sugar, extraction from beetroot, 29, 34, 48
Sulfosalts, 350
Sulphate of indigo, 222
Sulphate of lime ($CaSO_4$), 385
Sulphate of magnesia ($MgSO_4$), 22
Sulphate of soda (Na_2SO_4), 175, 222, 223, 242–3, 384–5
Sulphur, 45, 47, 377–8, 383, 482–3
Sulphur dioxide, 482–3
Sulphuret of potassium (K_2S), 369–70
Sulphuric acid, 26, 34, 113, 122, 175, 203, 219, 228–9, 235–7, 253, 267, 276, 285, 287, 385

Chemical substances (*cont.*)
Tin and compounds, 113, 247, 260, 267, 369
Titanium, 172
Turmeric, 222, 235, 242–3
Turpentine, 481
Volatile alkali (NH_3), 72
Water, 27, 38, 77, 106, 227–32; as an element, 229–31, 236, 239; ice and, 246–7, 248, 274–6, 279–82, 285, 287, 312, 385
Wootz, type of steel, 109–13
Zinc, and compounds, 227, 239, 247, 275, 276, 285, 287, 368–70
Chemistry, including organic, physical, and photo:
Acids, 24, 70–72, 78, 111, 113, 222, 223, 235, 236, 238, 239, 242, 252, 350, 370
Adhesion, 279–80
Aerology (Pneumatic chemistry), 14, 16
Affinities, 47, 55, 59, 62, 69, 78–79, 121, 123, 236–9, 245–57, 267–8, 278–88, 292, 304, 307, 364–72, 375, 416, 474
Alkali, 17, 45, 47, 70, 72, 222, 223, 235, 236, 238, 239, 242, 252, 370
Arbors (Arbor Dianae), 231
Atomic weight, 256
Bonding, ionic and covalent, 247
Boyle's Law, 294, 303
Brownian movement, 330–2
Caloric, *see listing under* 'Heat'
Capillary action, 278
Catalysis, 274–7; effect of heat, 277, 278–83, 291–2, 309
Chemical treatment of heat, 54
chemistry, 9–48, 55, 68, 71, 84, 86–88, 95–96, 106–31, 138, 150, 166, 227–57, 268, 342–3, 351, 377
Cohesion, 47, 70, 246, 251, 278–9, 344, 455–6, 474
Colloids, 472–4; action of various substances on, 473–4
Combination, 20, 69, 76–77, 79, 150, 251, 275, 278–9, 282, 292, 312, 366, 427
Combining proportions, law of, 253–7

Chemistry (*cont.*)
　Combustion, 24, 25, 47, 65, 120–1, 123
　Compound, chemical, 26, 70, 72, 120–1, 246
　Critical point, 382, 394
　Crystals and crystallizations, 72, 75, 79–80, 87, 113–14, 279–80; optical axes, 356, 408–20, 433, 436–7, 471
　Definite proportions, 230
　Destructive distillation, 107
　Diffusion, 278, 282
　Earths, 47, 111, 350
　Ebullition, 278
　Elasticity of gases, 279–82
　Energy, chemical, 151
　Equivalent weights, 254–7
　Etching, 113
　Fractional distillation, 108
　Hygrometric bodies, 279–80, 282
　Ignition temperature, 274–5, 282
　Kinetic theory of gases, 281
　Liquefaction, 127; liquid chlorine, 128–131; of other gases, 130–1, 381–2
　Litmus, 222, 235, 236, 242–3
　Metals, 47
　Molecular polarity, 227–41
　Organic chemistry, 108
　Partial pressures, Law of, 280–1
　Photochemistry, 50; sunlight as a 'reagent', 122
　Regulus, 45
　Ring structure, 108
　Salts, 234–6
　Simple, 35, 70
　Solidification, 127
　Solidification (low temp.), 382
　States of matter, 125, 128–31, 280–1, 381
　Structure, theory of properties, 71–72, 78, 87, 108, 109, 113–14, 115, 148, 150, 412
　Sunlight, as a chemical reagent, 122
　Temperature, 282, 382, 396–7
　Temperature, high, effects of, 125–31
　'Thilorier's bath', 382
　Ultra-violet effects, 59
　Vapour and vapour pressure and limits, 126

Chemistry (*cont.*)
　Variable proportions (in compounds), 230
　Velocity of gases in thin tubes, 123–4
　Volatilization, 125–7, 278
Chemical Manipulation . . . , by M. F., 113
Chesterfield, Lord, 21
Chevreul, Michel Eugène (1786–1889), 35
Children, John George (1777–1852), 181
Chladni, Ernst Florenz Friedrich (1756–1827), 178–9
Christie, Samuel Hunter (1784–1865), 170, 210–11
Christmas Lectures, 344–5, 348, 475
Church of England, 2
City Philosophical Society, 10, 12, 15–20, 30, 46, 47, 48, 85, 87, 89, 95, 130, 322–3, 328
Clapham, Yorkshire, 1
Clapham Wood Hall, 6
Clarendon, Lord, 341
Clark, Latimer (1822–90), 484–6
Clément, Nicolas (1778–1841), 34
Clouds, 24
Cocks, Mr, 48
Coleridge, Samuel Taylor, 62–71, 83
Condorcet, Marquis de (1743–94), 66, 337
Conservation and Correlation:
　Conservation of 'Force', 4, 65, 342, 371, 381, 452, 455, 457–9, 466–7, 511
　Convertibility of action, 408–16, 437, 452, 464–70
　Convertibility of 'fluids', 59
　Convertibility of forces, 62–65
　Creation of power: none, 65, 367, 371
　Diamagnetic and magneto-optic, 414
　Electrical and chemical action, 62, 69, 237–40, 245, 255–7, 268–9, 364–72, 416
　Electrical and magnetic action, 135–83, 193–7, 269, 299, 314–15, 371, 385
　Energy, conservation, 64, 371, 457, 466, 510–13

Conservation (*cont.*)
  Gravity into others, 465–71, 491
  Heat and electricity, 371
  Identity of 'forces' (unity of), 62, 64, 137–9, 156–7, 179, 269, 299, 314, 364–402, 408–9, 435, 437, 470
  Identity of 'substances', 14
  Light and electricity, 385, 408–11
  Light and magnetism, 386, 388
  Magnetism and crystal forces, 415–17
  Momentum, conservation, 457
Consolations in Travel: or, The Last Days of a Philosopher, by H. Davy, 79
Conversations on Chemistry, by Mrs Jane Marcet, 19, 20
Cooke, Sir Thomas William Fothergill (1806–79), 484
Copley Medal, 211
Corps des Ponts et Chaussées, 176
Cosmological evolution, 60
Coulomb, Charles Augustin (1736–1806) (*see Plates*), 55, 142, 143, 170, 284, 288–9, 372, 393, 394, 420, 422, 510
Courtois, Bernard, discoverer of iodine (1777–1838), 34
Crimean War, 479, 482–3
Critique of Pure Reason, by I. Kant, 60
Crosse, Andrew (1784–1855), 356
Cuvier, Georges (1769–1832), 230–1, 352

Dalton, John (1766–1844) (*see Plates*), 59, 72, 73, 87, 123, 129, 251, 254, 256, 280–1, 350
Dance, Mr, Jr, 26, 28
Daniell, John Frederic (1790–1845) (*see Plates*)
Davy, Sir Humphry (1778–1829) (*see Plates*), 19, 20, 25–48, 53, 62–73, 77–80, 84, 85, 86, 95, 104, 107, 110, 114, 120–30, 139, 151–3, 160, 233–40, 243, 252, 254, 268, 320–3, 325, 328, 329, 332, 380, 497
  Laboratory notebooks (*see Plates*)
Davy, Dr John (1790–1868), 66, 128, 212, 216
Davy, Lady, 30, 31, 37, 39–41
Dean, Elizabeth, *see* 'Faraday, Elizabeth (Dean)'

Dean, John, 6
de la Rive, *see* 'Rive'
de la Tour, C. C., *see* 'La Tour'
Descartes, René (1596–1650), 60
Desormes, Charles Bernard (1777–1862), 34
Dictionary of Arts and Sciences, 11
Ding an sich, 61
Döbereiner, Johann Wolfgang (1780–1849), 274–9
Dolland, George, 116, 119
Dove, Heinrich Wilhelm (1803–79), 402
Dove's temperature charts, 402
Dufay, Charles François (1698–1739), 393
Dumas, Jean Baptiste (1800–84) (*see Plates*), 382
Dynamo (*see Plates*), 196, 215

Eastlake, Sir Charles, 480
École polytechnique, 34
Edinburgh Encyclopedia, 138
Edinburgh Journal of Science, 353
Edinburgh Philosophical Journal, 43
Edinburgh Philosophical Transactions, 44
Edinburgh, University of, 2, 4
Eeles Major Henry (1700–81), 17, 18, 27
Einstein, Albert (1879–1955), 206, 454
Élan vital, 63
Electricity:
  Acid, theory of, 58–9
  Animal electricity (*see also* 'electric fish'), 37, 56, 215
  Atomic nature of, 256–7
  Battery, including voltaic, 27, 70, 84, 141, 173, 183, 212–14, 221, 228, 237, 243, 285, 290, 333, 451–2
  Capacitance, 218
  'Cathode ray discharge', 476–8
  Charge, electrical mass, 284, 288–94
  Circuit, electric, 22–23, 56–58, 236, 242, 243, 247, 252, 368, 371
  Conduction, 289, 299, 310–13, 373–9, 452, 474, 478, 486–7
  Conductors, 289–90, 293, 297, 300, 314, 376–7
  'Conflict', 139–40, 152, 154–5
  Contact charge, and contact theory, 56–57, 65, 145, 149, 151, 240–1, 365–72, 452

Electricity (*cont.*)
Coulomb electrometer, 297
Coulomb's law, 298
Coulomb's theories and rejection of by M. F., 283–5, 288–9, 372
Current, *passim*, but *see*, 14, 56–58, 66; theories of bar magnets, 137–83, 194 f., 199 f., 241–57, 311–12, 370–1, 384, 411, 415, 421, 430, 435, 452–3, 467 f.
Curves, electric, *see* 'Field Theory'
De Luc's column, 173
Dielectrics, 292–4, 297–8, 300–7, 314–15, 383–5, 427, 510
Discharges, brush, glow and spark, 300–13; in vacuo, 465, 474–9
Displacement, electrical, 291
Effluvia, 55
Electric fish, eel, torpedo, 37, 212–13, 215–16, 371, 451; gymnotus, 364, 371, 451
Electrical apparatus (*see Plates*), 14
Electricity, 11, 14, 16, 20, 54, 55, 59, 64, 69, 79, 84–86, 89, 125, 138–83, 341, 343, 345, 372, 379, 483
Electricity, 'common' or static, 14–20, 56, 144, 151, 212–23, 241–44, 286–8, 367, 475
Electricity, magneto-, 212–23
Electricity, nature of, 19, 25, 79, 169, 256, 312–15
Electricity, voltaic, 16, 19, 22–23, 25, 27, 56–59, 142, 144, 212–23, 284, 286–8, 364–72
Electrics, 18, 289–90
Electron, 256–7
Electrostatic machines, 11, 14, 144, 213, 216–21, 223, 286, 333, 385
Electrotonic state, 198–200, 205, 285–7, 314, 383–6, 391, 428, 468
Field, Electric, *see* 'Field Theory'
Fluids and fluid theory, 14–15, 17–20, 55–59, 66–70, 84–86, 142–3, 149, 154–6, 165–8, 170, 175, 197, 214, 231, 239, 241, 247, 257, 259, 268, 278, 288–9, 294, 295, 302, 303, 306, 310–12, 365, 372–5, 425, 475, 506
'Forces', *see* 'Action'
Galvanism, 16, 19, 31, 63, 66, 70, 138, 230

Electricity (*cont.*)
Galvanometer, 173–4, 183, 190, 194–5, 199, 206, 207, 217, 218; ballistic galvanometer, 219, 220, 409, 410, 424, 467, 468
Geisler tubes, 475–8
Grove's battery, 384, 418
Gutta-percha, 484–5, 487
Identity of electricities, 37, 56, 144, 202, 211–23, 284, 299–315, 365
Independence of electricity from matter, 240, 474–8
Induction apparatus (*see Plates*)
Induction, electric, 85–86, 173, 217, 283–4, 288–313; in curved lines, 296–8, 372–6, 379, 383–6, 388, 395, 420, 427, 428, 450–1, 474, 478, 486–7, 510
Inductive capacity, specific, 289, 291–6, 303, 314, 384, 428, 444
Insulator, 15, 310, 313–14, 376–8, 487
Intermolecular action, 274–83, 291–300, 304–8
Leyden jar, 14, 150–1, 214, 217, 218, 293, 374, 477
Lines of force, electric, *see* 'Field Theory'
Magneto-electricity, 212, 215; term, 259
Non-electrics, 18
Ohm's law, 210, 220, 366
Permeability, 373
Photo-electricity, 408–11
Pile, galvanic and voltaic, 16, 22–23, 25, 35, 53, 57, 62, 65, 139, 142, 144, 145, 146, 147, 149, 150, 151, 168, 213, 227, 228, 229, 230–2, 240, 247, 255, 275, 277, 285, 305; theories of, 364–72, 385, 452
Poles, and polarity, 23, 55, 146, 168, 173, 222–3, 258, 260, 290, 305–13, 373, 381, 444, 510
'Pressure', 57
Quantity of electricity, measurement, 218–21, 253–6, 311
Resinous electricity, 18, 68
Resistance – Conductance, 209–10, 369
Ruhmkorff coil, 475–6
Shellac, 292–4, 297–8, 374, 376, 377–88

Electricity (*cont.*)
Strain or 'state', 70, 154–5, 168, 180–1, 198–200, 289, 300–1, 313–14, 373–5, 379, 384–5, 453
Tension (voltage), 146, 199, 212, 219, 222, 286, 289–91, 301–9, 379, 385–6, 478, 487
Thermo-electricity, 138–9, 215–16, 364, 371
Torsion electrometer, Coulomb, 293
Vertiginous electricity, 152
Vitreous electricity, 18, 68
Vortices, cartesian, 55
Waves, *see* 'Wave Theory'
Electrochemistry:
Acid theory of electricity, 58–59
Anion, term, 266 f.
Anode, term, 264 ff.
Cathode, term, 264 f.
Cation, term, 266 f.
Combustion, electrochemical theory of, 121
Decomposition, 22–23, 25, 35, 57–58, 69–70, 149, 180, 200, 212, 215–16, 219–23, 227–57, 261, 267, 274–5, 282, 285–8, 296, 300, 311, 384, 476
Electricity in chemical analysis, 35
Electrochemical apparatus (*see Plates*)
Electrochemical equivalent, term, 287 f.
Electrochemistry, 19, 22–23, 58–59, 62, 121, 150, 151, 203, 220–3, 227–69, 274, 282–3, 285, 287, 296, 299, 303–4, 307, 311, 364–72, 506
Electrode, term, 260 f., 275
Electrolysis, 70, 200, 299, 312–13, 371, 385; theory of, 222–3
Electrolysis, laws of (electrochemistry, laws of), 216, 219, 221, 238, 253–6, 274, 366, 420
Electrolyte, term, 260 f., 285–6, 304, 366, 384–5, 452, 473
Electrolytic solution, 176, 200, 219, 286, 312, 370
Independence of action on distance between poles, 242–4, 254
Ion, concepts, theories, 235, 267; term, 266 f.
Lines of force, *see* 'Field Theory'
Poles, existence of in electrolysis, 227–57; term, 258 f., 275–7

Electrochemistry (*cont.*)
Terminology, 257–69
'Volta electrometer', 255–6
Electromagnetism:
Arago's wheel, 170–3, 196–7, 200, 329
Conflict, 155
Disc generator, 195–6
Dynamo, 196, 215
Electromagnet, 169, 182, 215, 386–7, 409, 415
Electromagnet, the R.I.'s great (*see Plates*), 344
Electromagnetic apparatus (*see Plates*)
Electromagnetism, 109, 131, 137–83, 191–223; term, 259, 285, 351
Electromotive force, 209, 257
Fluids and fluid theories, 141
Identity of solenoid and permanent magnet, 164
Induced currents, strength of, 209–10
Induction, electromagnetic, 109, 131, 137–83 (esp. 169–83), 191–211, 268, 282, 408, 420, 424, 426, 466, 468
Fresnel's near discovery of, 145–7
Induction, magneto-electric, 192–211, 212–23
Induction ring (*see Plates*), 468
Poles, 162–4, 166, 181–2, 192
Pulsating currents, 194
Ring experiment, 169, 181–3, narration of, 191–4, 199, 468
Rotations, 151–68, 169; of discs, 170–2, 175, 180, 201, 329
Transverse magnetism, 140–2
Waves of magnetism, *see* 'Wave Theory'
Wollaston's theory, 152–3
Zeeman effect, 479
Elementary Treatise on Chemistry, by A. Lavoisier, 24
Elements of Chemical Philosophy, by H. Davy, 78, 84
Elements of Electricity and Electrochemistry, by G. J. Singer, 85
Elgin marbles, 482
Elizabeth I, 1
Encyclopaedia Britannica, 11, 14, 17
Encyclopaedia Metropolitana, 349

Ericson's air engine, 330
Essay on Heat, Light and the Combinations of Light, An, by H. Davy, 66
Ether:
  Chemical ether – Ampère, 240
  Ether, luminiferous (and dismissal of), 68, 148–51, 168, 174–5, 240, 380, 421–2, 454–7, 470–2, 475–6, 478
Euclidean space, 60 f.
Eulenstein, Mr, 177
Evelina, 11
Experimental apparatus, Faraday, M. (*see Plates*)
Experimental Researches in Chemistry and Physics, by M. F., 44, 472
Experimental Researches in Electricity, by M. F., 141, 181, 196, 197, 200, 202, 206, 211, 213, 259, 263, 275, 283, 285, 287, 288, 299, 300, 301, 304, 305, 307, 308, 315, 359, 364, 366, 369, 371, 379, 384, 387, 393, 402, 415, 417, 418, 421, 428, 437, 443, 450, 470, 486

Faraday family. Here Roman numerals will indicate the generation starting with that of William Faraday, I:
  Faraday, Elizabeth, V, 7
  Faraday, Elizabeth (Dean), III, 6
  Faraday, Elizabeth (Gardner), I, 1
  Faraday, Frances, II, 1
  Faraday, James, IV, father of Michael, 6, 7
  Faraday, Margaret, V, 8, 99
  Faraday, Margaret (Hastwell), IV, mother of Michael, 7, 8, 41
  Faraday, Mary (Hastwell), IV, 7
  Faraday, Michael, V, *see separate listing*
  Faraday, Richard, II, 1
  Faraday, Richard, IV, 6, 7
  Faraday, Robert, III, 2, 6
  Faraday, Robert, V, 7, 100, 107
  Faraday, Sarah (Barnard), V (*see Plates*), 24, 97–102, 104, 106, 153, 358
  Faraday, William I, 1
Faraday, Michael (1791–1867):
  Copley Medal, recipient of, 211
  Diary and notes (*see Plates*)

Faraday, Michael (*cont.*)
  Difficulty with Lady Davy, 39–41
  Electromagnetic priority affair, 200–202
  Experimental apparatus (*see Plates*)
  Failing memory, 43, 102, 358, 445, 491–501
  Formation of the B.A.A.S., 355–7
  Hostility of Davy, 160–1
  Herschel, letter to, 389–91, 442
  Lecture, the Art of, 30, 46, 47, 322–34
  Lecturing (*see Plates*)
  Melbourne affair, 103, 353
  Mind and matter, on, 82–84
  Offer by the University of London, 115–16, 322, 334
  Offered P.R.S., 355
  Photographs (*see Plates*)
  Positions:
    Assistant in the laboratory of the R.I., 29 f.
    Secretary to H. Davy, 31 f.
    Assistant and Superintendent of the Apparatus of the Laboratory and Mineralogical Collection, 42 f.
    Elder in the Sandemanian Church, 104 f., 499
    Lecturer at the Royal Military Academy at Woolwich, 131, 498
    F.R.S., 160
    Director of the Laboratories of the R.I., 329 f.
    Scientific Adviser to Trinity House, 488 f.
  Rebuke by Berzelius, 46
  Reform of the Royal Society, 348–57
  Sandemanian faith, 4, 5, 8, 102–6, 499
  Wollaston affair, 157–61, 491
Fechner, Gustav Theodor (1801–87), 366
Ferguson, James (1710–76), 17
Field theory:
  Boscovichean field, 74–80, 279–81, 292, 294, 296, 311
  Classic field theory, 269, 381, 395, 402, 420, 452, 459, 500, 510–13
  Electric curves, 212, 284, 386
  Electric field, 81, 205, 216, 286, 307, 311, 469

Field theory (*cont.*)
Field, outgrowth of 'electrotonic state', 205
Fields, general, 202–11, 255, 269, 450–9, 464–5, 507–13
Gravitational field, 81, 468–9
Independence of line of force from matter, 204, 391, 412, 427, 438, 444, 447–9, 450–9
Light ray, 380–1, 388–91, 418–19, 437, 456–7, 470–2
Lines of force, electric, 161, 220, 249–50, 290–315; expansion of, 298–9, 381, 386, 388, 444–5, 451–2, 459, 487, 510
Lines of force, in electrochemistry, 231, 249–50
Lines of force, gravitational, 380–1, 419, 459, 466–9
Lines of force, light, 380–1, 408–9, 419
Lines of force, magnetic, 161, 163, 194, 200, 202–11, 220, 250, 314–15, 330–1, 381, 386–93, 402, 412–15, 417–18, 426–7, 430, 434–59
Lines of force, mathematical treatment, 383, 510–13
Magnetic curves, 163, 165, 200, 205–6, 386
Magnetic, 81, 194, 394–5, 416–17, 420–4, 429–59, 479, 510–13
Mapping, 297, 477
Prechtl's sheath of magnetic force, 141–2
Strain, of lines of force, 208–9, 312–15, 380, 444, 445, 459
Fitz Maurice limelight, 488
Forbes, James David (1809–68), 215
Force, *see* 'Action', 'Electricity', 'Electromagnetism' *and* 'Field Theory'
Fox, Caroline, 491
Fox, Robert, F.R.S. (1789–1877), 208, 268
Franklin, Benjamin (1706–90), 14, 17, 18, 55
French Revolution, 7
Fresnel, Augustin Jean (1788–1827), 145–8, 176–7, 179, 455
Friday Evening Discourses, 131, 177, 323, 329–33, 476, 498
Fuller, M. (actually John), 330

Fusinieri, Ambrogio (1773–1854), 277–8
Galileo (1564–1642), 37, 60, 104
Galvani, Luigi Aloysio (1737–98), 56
Galvinism, prize in, 69
Gardner, Elizabeth: *see* 'Faraday, Elizabeth (Gardner)'
Gassiot, John Peter (1797–1877), 27, 475–6, 478
Gay-Lussac, Joseph Louis (1778–1850) (*see Plates*), 70, 72, 202
Gentleman's Magazine, 68
Geissler, Heinrich (1815–79), 475, 478
Geology, 16, 17, 32, 37, 38
Georgia (colony), 3
Gilbert, Davies, P.R.S. (1767–1839) (*see Plates*), 67, 351, 353–4
Gilbert's Annalen, 141
Glas, John, 2, 3, 4
Glasite Church, 2, 3, 4
Gordon, Mr, of the Portable Gas Company, 108
Graham, Thomas (1805–69), 472
Grand Duke of Tuscany, great lens of, 37, 38
Green, Pickslay and Company, steel manufacturers, 114
Grotthus, Freiherr Theodor von (1785–1822), 231–40, 243, 245, 247, 249
Grove, Sir William Robert (1811–96), 27, 475–6
Guest, Mr J. J., iron manufacturer, 111
Gulf Stream, 208
Gull, Sir William, M.D., 499
Gurney Oxyoil lamp, 488

Hachette, Jean Nicolas Pierre (1769–1834) (*see Plates*), 45, 201, 215, 274
Hamilton, Sir William Rowan (1805–65) (*see Plates*), 356, 513
Hansteen, Christian (1784–1873), 99
Hare, Dr Robert (1781–1858), 306–7, 309–11, 365, 372–5, 379, 406
Harris, Sir William Snow (1781–1867), 303, 372
Hartley, David, 63, 66
Hastwell, Margaret: *see* 'Faraday, Margaret (Hastwell)'

Hastwell, Mary: see 'Faraday, Mary (Hastwell)'
Haüy, René Just (1743–1822), 88
Heat:
  Caloric, 54–55, 59, 66–67, 75, 84, 129, 130, 280–1
  Electrically associated, 146–7, 150–1
  General, 14, 20, 23, 53–55, 58, 59, 66, 75, 77, 79, 89, 125–31, 138, 151, 277, 282, 343, 364, 470
  Infra-red radiation, 59
  Latent heat, 54, 75
  Mechanical theory, 53–54, 66, 75, 129–30
  Radiation, 47
  Temperature, 54–55, 126
Helmholtz, Hermann von (1821–94), 256
Helvetius, Claude Adrien (1715–71), 66
Henly's electrometer, 217–18
Henry, Joseph (1797–1878) (see Plates), 169, 409
Herschel, Sir John F. W. (1792–1871) (see Plates), 42, 116, 170–3, 178, 182, 196, 349–52, 354–5, 358, 385, 389–90, 427, 442
Herschel, Sir William (1738–1822) (see Plates), 59
Hirst, Thomas, 509
History and Present State of Electricity, The, by Joseph Priestley, 14
History of the Inductive Sciences, by W. Whewell, 372
Holland, Dr Henry, 379
Holland, Lady, 333
Holmes' magneto-electric light, 488–9
Holy City, 38
'Holy Club', 3
Hooke, Robert (1635–1703), 71
Humboldt, Alexander von (1769–1859), 352
Hume, David, 63, 66
Huxley, Thomas Henry (1825–95), 495
Huygens, Christian (1629–1695), 458
Huxtable, friend of M. F., 28, 130

Ice-pail experiment, 374–5
Imitatio Christi, 5
Improvement of the Mind, The, by Dr Isaac Watts, 12, 13
Ingham, Benjamin, 2, 3

Jacobi, Moritz Hermann von (1801–74), 332
Job, 105
Jones, Henry Bence (1814–73) (see Plates), 7, 320, 322, 479, 494, 496
Joule, James Prescott (1818–89), 65
Journal de Physique, 43
Journal für die chemie und physik (Schweigger's), 349
Journal of the Royal Institution, 177, 181, 261
Juvenile Lectures, 131, 344, 497–8

Kant, Immanuel, 59, 60–69, 125, 137, 148
Kantean Philosophy, 56, 60–73, 228
Kekulé, August (1829–96), 108
Kelvin, Lord, see 'Thomson, William'
Kepler, Johannes (1571–1630), 63
Kerr, Dr John, 384

Laboratory, Royal Institution (see Plates)
Laplace, Pierre Simon de (1749–1827), 298, 352, 353, 506–7
Lardner, Dr Dionysius (1793–1859), 115, 178
Latham, Dr, 358
La Tour, Charles Cagniard de (1777–1859), 382
Lavoisier, Antoine Laurent (1743–94), 24, 25, 26, 54, 58, 65, 70, 123, 131, 230–1, 233
'Lecture on Electricity', Faraday, 1810, 17, 18, 19
Lectures on the Various Forces of Nature, 345–8, 496
Leibnitz, Gottfried Wilhelm von (1646–1716), 81
Lemen, Sir C., Bart, M.P., 268
Leverrier, Urbain Jean Joseph (1811–77), 347
Lewis' Commerce of the Arts, 44
Library, Royal Institution (see Plates)
Lichtenberg, Georg Christoph (1744–99), 492
Liebig, Justus von (1803–73) (see Plates), 334, 491
Light and physical optics:
  Analogy between sound and light, 178–9

Light and physical optics (*cont.*)
  Calcareous spar, 386
  Collimator, 410
  Corpuscular theory, 54, 176
  Double refraction, 413, 415, 471
  Electromagnetic theory of, 331
  Emission spectra, 479
  Infra-red, 59, 84
  Light, 14, 20, 53–55, 58, 59, 66, 79, 89, 138, 151, 176, 364, 382, 386–8, 408–9, 418–19, 449, 455–6
  Nicholl analyser, 385, 409, 412, 479
  Optic axes, properties, 356, 413–16
  Optics, 16, 176, 471–3
  Polarity of, 408–9, 419
  Polarized light, 72, 150, 175–6, 180, 200, 286, 380, 383–91, 394–5, 397, 408–17, 420, 444, 456, 468, 479
  Polarized rotation, 386–91, 394, 408–17, 420, 491
  Radiation, 84
  Ray-vibrations, 380–1, 388, 419, 470
  Refraction, 54
  Refractive index, 386
  Rock crystal, 386
  Silicated borate of lead glass, 386–7
  Spectrum, 59
  Ultra-violet, 59, 84
  Undulatory theory of, *see* 'Wave Theory'
Literary Gazette, 201
Locke, John, 13, 63, 66
Lockean empiricism, 12
Logic, by Dr Isaac Watts, 12
London, University of, 115, 322, 334
London and Edinburgh Philosophical Magazine and Journal of Science, *see* 'Philosophical Magazine'
Longitude, determination of, 485
Love feast, *see* 'Agape'
Lycèe, Le, 201
Lyell, Sir Charles (1797–1875), 261, 332, 358, 495

Magdeburg hemispheres, 292
Magnetism:
  Animal magnetism, 56
  Circuit, magnetic, 193–4
  Conductability, 438–44, 449, 453
  Currents, 451–3
  Curves, magnetic, *see* 'Field Theory'

Magnetism (*cont.*)
  Diamagnetics, 383, 386–94, 394–9, 408–34, 435–44
  Effluvia, 55
  Field, magnetic, *see* 'Field Theory'
  Fluids and fluid theories, 55, 58, 67–68, 143–4, 175, 426–7
  'Forces,' *see* 'Action' *and* 'Electro-magnetism'
  Gases, magnetic properties of, 394–402, 421
  Inductive susceptibility, 171
  'Intensity', 399–400
  Lines of force, *see* 'Field Theory'
  Magnetism, 38, 53, 54, 55, 59, 64, 86, 89, 138–83, 251, 299, 344, 372, 379, 483, 507, 510
  Magneto-inductive capacity, specific, 428
  Magneto-tonic state, 386, 391, 428
  Magnets (in contradistinction to diamagnets), 394–9
  Paramagnetics, 399, 426, 440–2
  Polarity, axial, of bismuth, 356, 417–19
  Polarity, diamagnetic, 381, 419–51
  Polarity, molecular, 172, 318, 427–34
  Poles and polarity, 55, 79, 140–1, 144, 156, 158, 161–8, 172, 182, 195, 204, 314–15, 381, 386–7, 408, 412–17, 420–35, 436–49, 456, 470
  'Quantity', 399–400
  Space, magnetic properties of, 395, 421–2, 434, 450, 454–7
  Strain or 'state', and change of strain, 182, 192–4, 198, 381, 412, 453
  Temperature effects, 433
  'Tension', 391, 423
  Terrestrial, 99, 144–5, 155, 159, 202, 206–8, 384, 394, 396, 399–402
  'Transversal' magnetism, 141–2
  Vacua, magnetic properties of, 395, 397–8, 421–2, 434–5, 450, 455
  Vortices, cartesian, 55
Magnetizing, attempted, 38
Magrath, Edward (*see Plates*), 15, 20, 30, 112, 328
Manchester Memories, 43

Mannin, Mr, 177
Manual of Chemistry, A, by Thomas Brande, 43, 176
Marcet, Mrs Jane (1769–1858), 19, 20, 25
Marianini, Stefano (1790–1866), 366
Mars, Mlle, 333
Martin, Sir Byam, 483
Masquerier, M, 21
Matter:
  Caloric, *see* 'Heat'
  'Continuity' of matter, 125–31
  Gravic fluid, 68
  Imponderable fluids, and denial of, 20, 53–59, 66–70, 84–86, 141, 145, 151, 176, 229, 278, 365, 373, 380, 420, 454, 506
  Nature of, 66, 86, 89
  Ponderable (ordinary), 24, 54–55, 57–59, 70, 75, 149, 205, 411, 422, 427, 435, 459, 471
  Radiant matter, 47, 84
  States of, 86, 120–1, 125–31
  Substance and space, 60–73
Matteucci, Carlo (1811–68) (*see Plates*), 355, 445
Maxwell, James Clark (1831–79) (*see Plates*), 200, 206, 381, 422, 509–13
Mechanical Philosophy, 60
Mechanics and motion:
  Archimedes principle—hydrostatics, 421
  Elasticity, 73–8
  Friction, 23
  Hydrostatics, 14, 16
  Impact, 73–78, 175–6
  Inclined planes, 23
  Inertia, 469
  Inverse square law, 53
  Kinetic theory of gases, 65
  Mechanics, 14, 16, 17, 53–54, 342
  Momentum, 23
  Newtonian science (classical physics), 53–54
  third law, 211, 250, 268, 283, 298, 459
  Skew force, 140
  Velocity, 23
Melbourne, Lord, Prime Minister, 103, 353
Mémoires de la Société de physique et d'histoire naturelle de Génève, 238, 365

Mesmer, Friedrich Anton (1733–1815), 56
Metaphysische Anfangsgründe der Naturwissenschaft, by I. Kant, 62, 67
Meteorites, theory of, 126
Meteorology, 14, 16, 37
Michaelangelo, 220
Michell, John (1724–93), 296
Mitscherlich, Eilhard (1794–1863), German chemist, 108, 413
Moll, Gerrit (1785–1838) (*see Plates*), 169, 181–2, 351–3
Moore, Miss, 358
Morichini, Domenico Pini (1773–1836), 38
Morse, Samuel (1791–1872), 484
Mossotti, Ottaviano Fabrizio (1791–1863), 294–6, 299

Napoleon Bonaparte, 30, 31, 41, 69, 352–3
National Gallery, 479–81
Natural history, 14
Naturphilosoph, 141
Naturphilosophie, 137–8
Neptune, discovery of, 347
Newton, Sir Isaac (1642–1727), 53, 60, 71, 80, 458–9, 500, 509
Nicholl, Dr Whitlock, 260–2, 265
Nicholson, William (1753–1815), 57, 227, 228
Nicholson's Journal, 43, 44, 110
Nobili, Leopoldo (1784–1835), 201, 215

Oersted, Hans Christian (1777–1851) (*see Plates*), 62, 64, 137–44, 151–5, 179, 200, 201, 229, 350, 364, 422
Offset printing, 332
Ohm, Georg Simon (1787–1854) (*see Plates*), 210–11, 366
O'Neill, rebellion of, 1
On the Alleged Decline of Science in England, by a Foreigner, by G. Moll, 351
Oxford University, 2, 3, 31

Pacchiani, Francesco Giuseppe (1777–1835), 233–4
Parabolas, 23

Paris, Dr John Ayrton (1785–1856) (see Plates), 78, 128–9
Parliament, 42
Pavia, University of, 56
Payne, William, 29
Pearson, Dr George, F.R.S. (1751–1828), 109
Peel, Sir Robert, Prime Minister, 196
Pellatt and Green, glassmakers, 116
Peltier, Jean Charles (1785–1845), 364, 371
Perkin, William Henry (1838–1907), 108
Phillips, Sir Richard (1778–1851), 15, 102, 120, 128, 153, 200, 251, 258, 374
Philosophical Magazine, 15, 43, 77, 128, 202, 296, 351, 354, 365, 373, 374, 376, 465, 475, 493
'The Philosophical Miscellany', of M. F., 12
Philosophical Transactions, 43, 59, 77, 128, 201, 202, 212, 315, 331, 355, 372, 470, 476
Pixii, Hypolite, Jr, 215
Planaria, 101, 330
Plücker, Julius, F.R.S. (1801–68), 356, 413–14, 416, 419, 430, 436, 475, 493
Pneumatic Institution, 67
Poisson, Siméon Denis, F.R.S. (1781–1840), 284, 288, 295, 302, 510
Poole, Thomas, friend of Coleridge, 64
Portable Gas Company, 108
Prechtl, Johann Joseph (1778–1854), 140–1
Preliminary Discourse on the Study of Natural Philosophy, by J. Herschel, 178
Priestley, Joseph, F.R.S. (1733–1804), 14, 18, 55, 178, 296
Prince of Wales (see Plates), 345
Principia, 53
Principles of Geology, by Charles Lyell, 261
Proceedings of the Royal Institution, 465
Projectiles, 23
Prosser's limelight, 488–9
Protestant individualism, 3
Proust, Joseph Louis (1754–1826), 255

Quarterly Review, 351, 379
Quarterly Journal of Science, 43, 44, 46, 128, 141, 153, 157, 176–7, 275, 321
Queen Victoria, 499
Queen's College, Oxford, 2, 3

Raffles, Lady, 177
Raumer, Frederick von, 333
Reflections on the Decline of Science in England, by Charles Babbage, 350
Reich, Ferdinand (1799–1882), 423, 434
Reid, Constance, niece to M. F., 100, 101, 500
Reid, Thomas, 66
Relativity, special theory, 454
Remarks on the Architecture of the Middle Ages, by Rev. Robert Willis, 261
Riebau, G., 8, 10, 11, 12, 22, 25, 28
Riffault, Anatole, 157
Ritchie, Rev. William (1790–1837), 211, 213
Ritter, Johann Wilhelm (1776–1810), 59, 62, 228–31
Rive, Auguste de la (1801–73), 151, 238–40, 247, 256, 357, 365–7, 372, 419, 425–6, 437, 500
Rive, Gaspard de la (1770–1834), 125, 166–7
Roget, Dr Peter Mark (1779–1869), Secretary of the Royal Society, 120
Roscoe, Sir Henry (1833–1915), 499
Ross, Sydney, 261
Roux-Bordier, 142
Royal Institution, 19, 25, 26, 29, 30, 42, 44–46, 48, 84, 95, 99, 100, 102, 103, 109, 110, 115, 116, 120, 125, 128, 130, 131, 151–3, 158, 159, 177, 179, 181, 196, 202, 211, 260, 290, 295, 320–5, 341, 343, 344, 353, 358, 359, 374, 380, 413, 418, 470, 494–9
  Library (see Plates), 43
  Laboratory (see Plates)
  Great Electromagnet (see Plates)
Royal Military Academy at Woolwich, 131, 498
Royal Navy, 108–9

Royal Society, 42, 102, 107, 115, 119, 120, 160, 170, 176, 181, 197, 201, 202, 211, 213, 260, 261, 264, 283, 324, 348, 350–1, 353–5, 357, 386, 470, 472, 495
Ruhmkorff, Heinrich Daniel (1803–77) (*see Plates*), 475–6
Rumford, Count (1753–1814), 19, 320, 324
Rumford Medal, 176
Russell, William S., 480

Sabine, Sir Edward P.R.S. (1788–1883), 401
Safety lamp, 44, 45
St Andrew's University, 2
Sandeman, Robert, 2, 4
Sandemanian Church, 2–6, 7, 8, 97, 102–6, 499
Savart, Félix (1791–1841), 178–80
Savary, Félix (1797–1841), 157
Schoenbein, Christian Friedrich (1799–1868), 356, 357, 358, 443, 449, 465, 472, 492–4, 496
Scientific Instruments, *see individual science headings*, 14
Scientific Memoirs, selected . . . of Foreign Academies . . . Societies . . . and Journals, 295
Scott, Dr Helenus, of Bombay, 109
Sects and schisms, 2–6
Seebeck, Thomas Johann (1770–1831), 364, 371
Seine, M., 382
Serullas, Georges Simon (1774–1832), 350
Severn, King and Company, 107
Shakespeare, William, 326
Singer, George John (1786–1817), 85
Sketch of a Tableau of the Progress of the Human Mind, by the Marquis de Condorcet, 337
Smart, B. H., 47
Sorby, Henry (1826–1908), 115
Sound:
　Acoustical figures, experiments, 179–81
　Acoustical induction, 178–81
　Analogy between light and sound, 178–9
　Chladni figures, 177–81

Sound (*cont.*)
　Crispations, 180–1
　Fluid theory of, 68
　Kaleidophone, 177
　Resonance, 177
　Waves of, 380
Stahl, Georg Ernst (1660–1734), 228
Steel, refining, 48, 109–15
Stodart, James, 48, 109, 110-12, 114, 125, 153, 158–9
Stokes, Sir George (1819–1903), 470
Sugar beet, 29, 34
Sugar refining, 48, 107
Sussex, H.R.H. the Duke of, 354–5
System of Chemistry, A, by T. Thomson, 17, 87, 176

Tatum, John, Lectures (*see Plates*), *see also* 'City Philosophical Society', 25
Taylor, Richard, 295
Telegraph, problems of, 479, 483–7
Telescope, 37
Tennant, Smithson (1761–1815), 72
Terminology, invention of electro-chemical, 257–69
Thenard, Louis Jacques (1777–1857), 70, 350
Theoria naturalis philosophiae, by R. J. Boscovich, 73
Thompson, Benjamin, *see* 'Rumford, Count'
Thomson, Thomas (1773–1852) (*see Plates*), 17, 67, 77, 87, 88, 176
Thomson, William (Lord Kelvin) (1824–1907) (*see Plates*), 383–5, 487, 507, 509–13
Tieck, Herr, 333
Tilloch, Alexander (1759–1825), 77
Time, 80–1
Times, The, 351, 354, 483, 495
Tobin, James, 67
Traité d'électricité théorique et appliquée, by Auguste de la Rive, 372
Traité de Physique, by J. B. Biot, 306
Transcendental idealism, *see* 'Kantian philosophy'
Treatise on Sound, by Sir John F. W. Herschel, 349
Trinity College, Cambridge, 18, 259, 261
Trinity House, 479, 488–91, 499

Tyndall, John (1820–93) (*see Plates*), 6, 357, 424, 426, 454, 491, 495, 499, 509
Tytler, James, 14, 15, 17, 27

Vauquelin, Louis-Nicolas (1763–1829), 34
Velocipede, 100
Vest (or West), Dr von, the metal 'Sirium', 45
Vesuvius, 39, 483
Vivian, Mr, copper refiner, 112
Volcanoes, 39
Volta, Alessandro (1745–1827), 25, 56, 57, 59, 65, 144, 145, 147, 233, 240, 365

Watson's voltaic light, 488
Watts, Dr Isaac, 12, 13, 21, 46, 257
Wave theory
    Electric 'waves', 14–15, 17–18, 140, 149, 179–83, 191–4, 199–200, 247–9, 268, 469
    Magnetic waves, 194
    Propagation of wave, 181
    Sound waves, 177–9, 380
    Undulatory theory of light, 145, 148–9, 176–9, 380, 471
    Wave motion of force, 138
    Waves of force, electric and magnetic, 182–3, 191–4, 199–200

Way's mercurial electric lamp, 488
Weber, Wilhelm (1804–91) (*see Plates*), 419, 422–5, 429–34, 436–8
Wellcome Medical Historical Library, 43, 498
Wesley, Charles, 3
Wesley, John, 2, 3
Wheatstone bridge, 369
Wheatstone, Sir Charles (1802–75) (*see Plates*), 27, 177–9, 312, 331, 380, 484
Wheatstone's telegraph, 339, 484
Whewell, William (1794–1866) (*see Plates*), 259, 261, 264–6, 286, 295, 296, 372, 382, 426, 436
Willis, Rev. Robert, 260–2
Wöhler, Friedrich (1800–82), 491
Woolaston, William Hyde (1760–1828) (*see Plates*), 152–3, 156–60, 175, 216, 221, 329, 351, 491
Wrottesley, Lord, 353

Young, Thomas (1773–1829) (*see Plates*), 176, 455

Zantedeschi, Francesco (1797–1873), 396
Zeeman, Pieter (1865–1943), 479
Zodiacal light, 37
Zoology, 330